Advanced Educational Psychology

Ram Nath Sharma
Rajendra Kumar Sharma

PUBLISHERS & DISTRIBUTORS (P) LTD

Published by
ATLANTIC
PUBLISHERS & DISTRIBUTORS (P) LTD
7/22, Ansari Road, Darya Ganj, New Delhi-110002
Phones : +91-11-40775252, 40775214, 23273880, 23275880
Fax: +91-11-23285873
Web: www.atlanticbooks.com
E-mail: orders@atlanticbooks.com

Reprint 2006, 2010, 2019, 2020, 2022, 2023

Printed & bound in India by Atlantic Print Services

Preface

During the course of teaching educational psychology to graduate and post-graduate students, the authors felt the need for a suitable textbook on this subject which may cover the syllabi of Indian Universities and maintain a balanced outlook. The books written by Western authors are set in Western environment and hardly cater to the needs of Indian students. The present book is an attempt to provide a model textbook excluding all unnecessary elaborations and including whatever is required to maintain a good standard. The language of the book is simple and lucid.

In such an attempt as this the authors naturally depend on whatever material has been presented by those who have preceded their efforts. The authors express their deep sense of gratitude to all of them.

Insight in educational psychology depends as much on mutual exchange of ideas among teachers as on personal experience and learning. Any such exchange of views will be most welcome.

THE AUTHORS

Contents

1

Psychology and Education

Even a casual glance at the various aspects of the contemporary process of education will convince any one about the intimate relationship of Education and Psychology. Education is the means to a complete development of man. To achieve a complete development it is essential that the various capacities of the individual be given adequate opportunity of manifesting and developing themselves. And for this a knowledge of psychology is essential. The various stages of the child's development have their own characteristics, tendencies and interests. No teacher can properly assist in the development of a child in complete ignorance of these factors. In this way, education and psychology are fundamentally related.

REVOLUTION IN EDUCATION THROUGH PSYCHOLOGY

The interrelation between education and psychology dates back to very ancient times. Applied psychology in particular has had important relationship with education. The fundamental facts of individual differences and the need for co-ordination of these differences, that form the very basis of applied psychology are no less important from the point of view of education. The successful teacher should pay adequate attention to the individual differences between different students and also attempt a co-ordination between them if he wishes to maintain harmony and order in his class. It is with this fact in view that during their training all teachers are educated in the various branches of psychology. Apart from teaching they come to know enough of general, applied, experimental, genetic, abnormal and the psychology of individual differences.

The extent to which psychology has penetrated into the field of education is so impressive that only the term revolution may adequately describe it. In pointing to the changes in education caused by psychology, Ryan has written, "In many schools of today one finds an atmosphere of friendliness and happy activity. Much of the traditional formality, the forced silence, the tension, the marching is gone. Children's voices are heard in the halls and class-rooms. The younger children come down the stairways, naturally and relatively unrestrained, the older boys and girls through the corridor or outside walks making their way to school rooms, shops, studios, libraries, laboratories and playing fields to tasks that mean something to them, that make demands upon their energies and their imagination, that often involve hard, difficult work, but work that they recognize as creative. Beauty of surroundings is considered a first requirement in their schools—there are flowers about, brightly coloured murals painted by the children, attractive, informal workrooms for the various groups...Art and music have began to play the role that belongs to them as fundamental in education and life."[1]

1. Child-centred education: In early times the teachers were mainly engaged in imparting various kinds of information to the children. In those times children were less the centre of attention, the school claimed more of their energy. Today, it is the child who is the centre of attention in education. Every child is individually considered and treated. Efforts are always made to adapt the curriculum of study to the needs of the child with the result that the brilliant and dull witted children do not study the same subjects. Applied psychology has directed attention to the different abilities and capacities of people. Such an attitude has made it possible for the teacher to gauge the special abilities of his students and to make the best arrangements for the guidance of individual children. The teacher of today should not only be acquainted with teaching but also with students since his profession is now centred about the educand and not about the subject or teacher. The consequence of this change is the reasoning that what matters is not the knowledge or ability of the teacher but the extent to which he succeeds in developing the personality of his students.

2. Emphasis on extra-curricular activities: Previously, education was believed to be a comprehensive process that trained the individual, provided him with a moral character and made him more cultured. In psychology, as it is understood today, the conception of mind has completely changed. Analysis has led to the discovery that many kinds of forces and mental activities take place within the human being so that for the development of the child it is necessary to provide him with different kinds of programmes and subjects so that he may succeed in properly developing all his mental faculties and abilities. At present, variety is believed to be essential in education and it is held to be true that the education of one individual subject includes many different activities and functions, of which the teacher should be aware of. It is only then that he can know the difficulties of the children in understanding the subject. If a child fails to memorize his lesson, it cannot be taken to indicate only a lack of effort, it is equally probable that he has a weak memory, or is not intelligent, or has no interest in the subject or that he is suffering from ill-health. Learning is a complex activity and it is only through a knowledge of its various components that one can diagnose the difficulty of a particular child in memorizing or learning a lesson. The teacher has no alternative but to attend the activity of learning.

3. Reform in the curriculum: Psychology has also managed to bring about important variations and reforms in educational curricula. Now, it is the mental age and not the chronological age of the child that helps to determine

1. Ryan, W.C. *Mental Health Through Education*, New York, Commonwealth Fund, 1938.

the course of study to which he is to be subjected. Intelligence tests reveal the mental age of the child. Different courses are devised for brilliant and deficient children. After the eighth or delta class, the curriculum is subdivided into various parts such as literary, scientific, agricultural or art classes. The educand is given the opportunity of selecting his subject according to his interest and aptitude. Various extra-curricular activities are organised for the emotional development of the educand. These include picnics, dramatic associations etc. Other programmes are organised in order to develop the qualities of leadership, public speaking etc., in the educand. But no course of study or programme is foisted upon him against his inclination. Inspiration is awakened in him according to his interests and his tastes. With the use of audio-visual aids such as television, film projection, etc., education has become more interesting and appealing. Many schools are equipped with radio sets that provide both entertainment and information to the child. The use of analogies is an important method in education. Children who choose to study history are taken to visit historical places. Even a glance at the curriculum of basic education makes clear the extent to which psychology has revolutionized education. Special curricula are also devised to meet the needs of adult education. They suit the psychology of adult individuals.

4. New methods of discipline: Discipline has an important place in education. One of the aims of education is to instil a respect for discipline in the child. But the recent discoveries in psychology have changed the ways and means by which discipline is taught. Previously, physical punishment was one of the chief methods of teaching and imparting discipline among the children. The main motive behind discipline was fear of physical violence and injury. But along with injuring the body of the child it injured his personality as well by making it distorted. Psychologists attracted the attention of the enlightened people to the injurious effect of physical punishment and also suggested alternative means of making children disciplined. A suggestive example is thus: The inmates of a hostel were given to indiscipline during lunch time. They threw morsels of food at each other and wasted much more. The warden made every effort to stop this nuisance and used every means of arousing fear in the children but without success. He never discovered the name of the mischief makers and neither did the boys give up their behaviour. Some time later he was replaced by a new warden who resorted to psychological methods for solving this menace. He made an announcement to the effect that the best behaved table with the most seemly boys would win a flag that would entitle them to twice the normal ration of the most succulent food. The strategy took immediate effect and the indiscipline promptly ceased. The children seated at various tables were now busily engaged in trying to look more disciplined and seemly than all the others so that they now even prevented the more hardened and incorrigible boys among them from mischief. In this way the new warden took advantage of the psychology of children to effortlessly perform a task that had completely foiled all the efforts of the earlier warden with his shock and fear tactics. Now-a-days it has become customary in schools to allow the children to adopt discipline rather than foist it upon them. At the college level it is from among the students that the prefects are chosen to create and maintain discipline among their fellow mates and to help the proctor in maintaining order within the college. Very recently there was a high level debate on the spreading indiscipline among university students in India and almost all speakers put forward psychological solutions because the problem of indiscipline is basically a psychological one. It need hardly be pointed out that the more a teacher knows of the child and adolescent psychology the easier will it be for him to create discipline in the motly group with which he is faced in the class.

5. Education of the total personality: Modern methods of education place great emphasis upon the education of personality. Education is now understood to mean something more than mere reading or writing. It is also understood to involve the development of personality. Many schools have resident psychologists who solve problems related to the personality of the students and give advice to teachers and parents in this regard. At places there are also child guidance clinics that make special efforts towards the correction and normal rehabilitation of problem children or juvenile delinquents. Study of psychology is an essential part of the curriculum of teacher's training. In addition to these individual efforts most states and districts have a bureau of psychology whose functions are to solve the problems of students relating to their personality, to give personal guidance and to give advice to their parents and teachers regarding them. The truth of the matter is that the psychologist has become a link for the child's adjustment between the home and the school since such an adjustment helps to improve his personality. In the role of a specialist his contribution to the school has become indispensable.

6. Psychological teaching methods: In the manner already described, psychology has changed teaching methods lock, stock and barrel. All new research aims at evolving teaching methods that induce the child to learn for himself and thus himself achieve his development. The means of the new teaching methods are radio, picnics, tours of historical places, games, election contests, students' unions etc. It is psychology that has contributed the Kindergarten and Montessori methods of teaching. Special teaching methods have been evolved for the use of blind, dumb, deaf and mentally backward or handicapped children.

7. Improvement in the process of learning: The experiments that psychology has carried on in connection with the process of learning have led to the discovery of many laws that economise on time and yet produce good results in terms of material learned. One example would be Thorndike's laws. The psychologist has stressed the importance of reward and punishment in learning. Research in psychology has aimed at discovering the efficacy and inefficiency of the various methods of learning. The employment of the various methods of learning is improved and made more scientific by a knowledge of their qualities and drawbacks.

8. Emphasis on individual differences: In days gone by, the same curriculum was prescribed for all the students in the class. The development of applied psychology led to the fact that different individuals differ from each other in respect of their interests, intelligence, ability, capabilities etc. This knowledge of individual differences proved a veritable source of revolution for education. Now-a-days the essential pre-requisite to guidance of an educational nature is knowledge of the subject's ability and interests. Choice of his curriculum and other extra-curricular activities is definitely governed by these individual differences.

9. Mental testing and guidance: Mental testing and guidance are important factors in applied psychology. Psychologists have evolved scientific tests to measure intelligence and other abilities. Students can be guided in educational and vocational matters with the help of these tests. Now, education aims both at the complete development of the individual as well as his best possible adjustment to his vocation and of his vocation to his natural abilities. Teachers need the help of psychologists in either of these two matters. Psychologists solve the problems of students through personal guidance and inform them of the job they are best suited to, through vocational guidance. In this way, the co-operation and co-ordination between the teacher and the psychologist in the field of education is on the increase.

10. Reform of the problem children: One of the most notable contributions of psychology to education is the improvement and reform of juvenile delinquents, truents, unsocial and problem children and advise their parents regarding them. To this end the state and district psychological bureau, assist the educational institutions.

Thus, educational psychology provides the teacher with the means to attaining knowledge of the student's nature, capacity, characteristics, needs and motives. This knowledge is the equipment for him to modify his teaching methods sufficiently to attain the goal of education.

PSYCHOLOGY AND THE TEACHER

According to the modern concept of education, the teacher should aim at the complete development of the child. This requires that the teacher should have some definite knowledge of educational psychology. Without this knowledge he is not in a position to understand the child and to help it tide over the initial difficulties in education. The modern teacher is motivated by a desire to make his teaching more facile, attractive and interesting. To attain these ends, he should be able to understand the psychology that informs the teacher of the psychology of students and many other interestingly allied subjects.

In this way, the teachers can solve their teaching problems only with the help of educational psychology. It is clear that psychology, and in particular educational psychology, can help to institute improvements in the modes of teaching. The important facts in this connection are the following:

1. Understanding oneself: Before an individual can successfully achieve something, he should be aware of his ability or incapacity for doing it. In the absence of such an understanding many people choose the wrong occupation and continue to curse their fate for their failures. Hence, if an individual chooses to become a successful teacher, he should first review himself and decide whether he possesses the qualities required of a good teacher. This realization can be gained with the help of educational psychology, since it acquaints the teacher with such diverse facts as the knowledge of his own nature, his mental and intellectual level, ultimate goal, philosophy of life, relations with colleagues and well-wishers, the reactions in society to his behaviour and capabilities, qualities that are either liked or disliked by the students, his own needs, etc. This knowledge helps an individual to become a good teacher. For example, as a general rule, a good and successful teacher is a balanced, sweet voiced, sympathetic and active individual. If the teacher is unaware of the qualities that he lacks within himself, he either scolds his students, thinks black and unwholesome thoughts of society and quarrels with his wife and children. But if he were aware of these shortcomings, such undesirable contingencies would never arise and with the nervous energy conserved thereby he could improve himself and become a good teacher, to the eternal satisfaction of the students and the good luck of society.

2. Understanding the educand: Whatever his field of operation, the individual desiring success should be aware of the people with whom he cannot avoid coming into contact. If the teacher is not aware of the psychology of the children, how and what can he teach them? It is for this reason that John Adams believed that it is more important for the teacher to be aware of the psychology of children than even to be an expert in the subject of his choice. He should be in possession of a wide and diverse knowledge of the main springs of behaviour in the child, its needs, mental level, interests, capacities, personality, etc. The knowledge of the bases or mainsprings of behaviour is most important and essential since the very aim of education is directing and training the conduct of the child. Hence, education and teaching should be based upon the instincts, motives and emotions of the children. The direction of these mainsprings can be changed, but they cannot be removed from the child. Hence, the successful teacher makes efforts to mould them. Whatever the child learns has a close relationship with its needs. Most of the so-called backward and problem children at school are the unfortunate ones whose needs have not been understood and fulfilled in the school. It is because of this that they engage in undesirable activities such as breaking street lights, running away from schools, loitering, besides many other anti-social activities of a comparatively more dangerous kind. Lacking the requisite knowledge of psychology the teacher attempts to correct these faults through punishment but the sensible teacher knows that the roots of these faults and aberrations lie in some one of the child's physical, psychological or social needs. Educational psychology helps the teacher to become aware of the individual differences in the personalities of children and to realize that each child differs from the other in respect of interest, nature, intelligence, upbringing and other factors. Hence, the skilled teacher makes subtle but effective disinclinations between children of different mental levels and varies his modes of teaching according to their individual mental level. In educating children, the teacher has to achieve some synthesis between the needs of the children and those of society. He must evidently be equipped with complete knowledge of the psychology of his wards if he is to be successful at his task.

3. Reform in teaching methods: The science of teaching tells the teacher what he is to teach the children. But the main problem that confronts him is, how is he to teach this? It is in the solution of this problem that educational psychology assists the teacher. It provides knowledge and information concerning the process, modes, important factors, encouraging and hindering conditions etc. in learning. The teacher may help the child in his learning if he has knowledge of these factors. Educational psychology makes a psychological analysis of the methods of teaching and the improvements that can be made in them.

4. Evaluation and testing: The mere fact of having taught does not solve the teacher's problems. It is not the end. He is also concerned with testing and evaluating the knowledge and development of children. Evaluation affords a clue to the actual development of the student. During the process of education both the teacher and the taught are anxious to know the extent to which they have progressed, if at all, and if they have not, to know why they have not done so and what can be done to achieve the desirable extent of success. The solution to such problems as these requires the employment of many kinds of tests and measures besides the evaluation. While the teacher himself examines the student, he also teaches him to develop the ability to make an objective evaluation of his own progress. Since evaluation directly influences motivation, it indirectly influences behaviour. All kinds of testing techniques are based upon psychological facts. Educational psychology not only helps teacher to evaluate the child through the medium of tests but also helps him to judge his own ability as a teacher.

5. Reform in the curriculum: In order that individual and social needs may be fulfilled, it is essential that the planning of the school curriculum should be made keeping in view the individual differences, motives and values, and the principles of teaching should all be based upon the knowledge of psychology. In drawing up the curriculum, the teacher should be aware of the needs of the individual and society, and the methods of learning that can best fulfil these needs. The fact that different methods of learning can be desirable or undesirable in different circumstances and at different levels makes it essential that the teacher should have sufficient knowledge of psychology to achieve correspondence between the level of development and the method of learning to be applied. To put it briefly, to be active and effective; the curriculum must be based upon psychological foundations, this psychological background is provided by educational psychology.

6. Betterment of human relations: Educational psychology has helped the teacher to understand human relations. Teaching and learning afford adequate opportunity for group and individual relations. Modern educational psychology has investigated this phenomenon and helped the teacher to assume the rightful role of a leader in his class. In the teaching process the most important factor is the relation between teacher and the taught. In school the teacher replaces the parents of the child and takes their place in its eyes. The child also forms a picture of an ideal teacher in his mind while on the other hand, the teacher is equally concerned with the notion of what the ideal teacher should be. It is the interaction between these concepts of the ideal teacher that determines the adjustment of the class. Educational psychology assists in improving the relations between teachers and students and in understanding the importance of emotional aspects and relations of learning. The process of education is considerably influenced by the atmosphere that prevails in the classroom. This atmosphere is created both by the relations between the teacher and taught as well as the mutual relations between the students themselves. In this way, each child develops in a group or communal atmosphere and conditions. It is educational psychology that helps the teacher to synthesize the relations between children in the class.

The atmosphere of the school depends, apart from the relations between teachers and the taught, relations among the students themselves, the relations that exist between teachers themselves and their relations with the principal. Psychology renders assistance in achieving the best conditions in this direction.

7. Adjustment and discipline: It is evident from the above exposition upon human relations that the importance of psychology in the adjustment and discipline among students in school is very great. Adjustment implies the success with which an individual negotiates a particular and unusual circumstance. The adjustment is revealing of the relation between the individual and his situation. Its ultimate goal is the achievement of mental health. Educational psychology turns psychological viewpoint upon adjustment, discipline, mental hygiene, in fact, upon everything. Good adjustment applies change and adjustment in both rather than in either of them. To take a simple example, in the changes and adjustments that are necessitated by the relations between teachers and students, it is desirable that the teacher should also change; the student has to adjust himself perforce. The changes that take place in both quarters ensure the avoidance of all damage of any of the personalities involved while they enhance development of healthy individuals. The problems of discipline are also basically problems of motivation and goals. Hence, psychology can be of help in their solution. Sometimes naughtiness is a sign of adjustment process and in such a case the teacher must encourage rather than prevent them. Psychology provides the knowledge that the same behaviour may be due to different motives in different individuals. It is for the teacher to trace the behaviour of the children to the basic mainsprings in motives so that he may be in a position to affect the necessary sublimation and change. And in this task the teacher has to turn towards psychology.

8. Experimentation and research: Educational psychology further assists in experimentation. Whether in theory or in practice, teaching raises many problems for the teacher, the solution of which demands continuous experimentation. Education or teaching itself is based to a large extent upon the trial and error and intelligence of the teacher. In it the teacher cannot invariably depend upon some definite principles. The teacher should experiment to find the solution of the new problems that arise in usual circumstances and to apply the conclusions that he reaches in such work. He has also to turn to experiment and put to the test all new facts or ideas that emerge from the continuous experimentation in the field of psychology. In this way, the daily life in school possesses great research potential in the field of education.

9. Diagnosis and cure of classroom problems: Educational psychology helps the teacher to diagnose and solve the problems that arise in the school room. The following are some important problems of this kind:

(*a*) What can be done for the progress of a backward child?

(*b*) What method can be adopted to improve the mal-adjusted child?

(*c*) How to remove indiscipline in children?

(*d*) How to bring a physically or mentally deformed child to the normal level of study?

(*e*) How can one develop self-motivation in children?

(*f*) How are the problem children to be taught?

(*g*) How are sexual crimes to be prevented among children?

(*h*) How are the delinquent tendencies of the children to be prevented or sublimated?

If the teacher wants to solve these problems, he will have to put an end to the causes that give rise to them. And in order to affect this improvement he should have adequate and comprehensive knowledge of human psychology. Both proper diagnosis and solution of these problems are equally necessary. The first step towards this is for the teacher to analyse his own methods of teaching and process of learning in order to discover their merits and demerits. Then the teacher should discover methods by which he may create in the educand a capacity to adjust himself in unusual circumstances. All these achievements are based upon the psychological knowledge of the teacher.

From the above exposition it is evident that a knowledge of psychology is indispensable for a teacher. Educational psychology is a branch of psychology that specializes in teaching and learning with which it is exclusively concerned. Thus, it is concerned with psychology on one hand and with teaching on the other. In modern democratic societies the object of the teacher is to develop the educand into a conscious, feeling and active being. In this development he achieves adjustment with many conditions in the capacity of an individual. And the decisions and ready intelligence of the teacher play an important role in this adjustment. In this process, the teacher makes use of psychology as a practical science. It is for this reason that the teachers are taught psychology as a part of their training in order that they may be able to bridge the gulf between the lives of educands and the aims of education in modern democratic societies with the resultant adjustment and synthesis.

The teacher has to understand both himself and his students. Psychology offers its assistance in this knowledge and understanding.

EDUCATIONAL PSYCHOLOGY AND GENERAL PSYCHOLOGY

Twentyfive years ago educational psychology had not yet succeeded in claiming individual status for itself and most thinkers were accustomed to think of it as the practical application of psychology in the field of education. In 1922 Gates and others in their book *Psychology for Students of Education* wrote, "In a psychology for students of education most of the laws and principles which constitute general psychology will be utilised." Such a statement regarding educational psychology is now regarded as obsolete and outmoded although no one is inclined to deny that psychology is applied to the field of education. Whereas education is concerned with the ideals of human development, educational psychology tells of the extent to which those ideals can be achieved.

Educational psychology is concerned with the practical aspect of psychology. In its original form, it constituted no more than the application of psychological principles to teaching, but it has now attained to the dignity of an independent science. Modern educational psychology in its present stage of development does not believe in the blind application of psychological principles to teaching but it strives to test their validity by such an application to regular day-to-day teaching. It makes considerable practical tests of psychological ideas before applying them to education. An apt analogy would be the precaution with which a doctor proceeds upon discovering a new medicine a cure for a particular virus. He first tests the medicine upon animals before using it with human beings and then uses it in small quantities upon human beings, which he turns into a regular medicine only when the results of all this experimentation are favourable. In much the same sceptical manner, the modern teacher first tests psychological ideas in practice before applying them liberally and without fear. In this way, its approach to psychology is critical.

Modern educational psychology has its own specific scope, programme problems and methods. In respect of all these factors it comes in to frequent contact with general psychology but it does not depend upon it. In this way, the practical approach of educational psychology differs from the viewpoint of general psychology. While general psychology engages in research in order to test the validity of a general principle, educational psychology busies itself in the search for a practical solution to one or the other problems confronting it. Psychology aims at the presentation and propagation of some general scientific principle, while educational psychology aims at making its own province and task more useful and valuable. In this way, although general psychology and educational psychology have much in common they pursue separate paths. If one enquires of a psychologist as to what use a psychological principle discovered by him can be put to in the field of education, one finds that it may never have occurred to him to consider this aspect of the matter. On the other hand, if an educational psychologist is asked about the relation of his study to the psychology of learning in school conditions he may only express his ignorance. Evidently, then, while general psychology is academic in its approach, educational psychology is professional.

But from this exposition, one should not conclude that educational and general psychology are completely unconnected. Both of them have important relations and many research experts delve into problems that are of interest to both the branches of knowledge. The truth of the matter is that the two psychologies are so intimately related that it is indeed difficult to draw an exact line of demarcation. The principles or facts that the psychologist discovers in the secure but authentic atmosphere of his laboratory are tested for their validity in actual conditions of the school. On the other hand, the teacher is likely to overlook many basic principles in the practical conditions that exist in the school. Consequently if the best results are to be obtained the problem should be considered from both points of view, in this way, general psychology and educational psychology are mutually complementary. Yet, they maintain their distinct status due to distinction in scope, viewpoint, problems, objectives, methods etc.

Many of the postulates of general psychology prove to be of much value to the educational psychologist and he has no qualms about borrowing them. Some of these postulates are the following:

1. Human behaviour is functional and dynamic.
2. At every stage of development the reactions of the individual are influenced by the people, objects, situations, conditions of surroundings, his experiences, needs, shortcoming, and the desire to satisfy his motives.
3. As a general rule the reactions of an individual represent the functioning of a completely synthesized and organised structure of behaviour, but nevertheless, some elements or aspects of behaviour exert an important influence upon his reasoning, activities and sentiments.
4. Any specific viewpoint of study that fails to include other viewpoints also fails to provide facts that are adequately psychological in nature.

QUESTIONS FOR EXERCISE

1. How is psychology related to eduction? Discuss.
2. Discuss the importance of psychology in education.
3. State the main heads under which applications of psychology to education may be described. How far has modern psychology revolutionized the theory and practice of education?
4. Discuss the relationship between psychology and education and explain how psychology has revolutionized educational theory and practice.

2

Educational Psychology and Education

HISTORICAL BACKGROUND

Though one may attribute the origin of educational psychology to Aristotle, the Greek philosopher, but modern educational psychology in Europe is accounted for by contributions of Pestalozzi, Herbert and Froebel. They aimed at making education psychological Educational psychology in its practical form appeared in the twentieth century, to which the researches of Charles H. Judd and E.L. Thorndike have contributed. Among the other psychologists who have helped the development of educational psychology, the names of Stanley Hall, Terman and William Bagley deserve mention. These psychologists applied scientific methods to the study of important problems that beset the process of education. They evolved various methods and laid down new principles for this study.

In the not very far past, many educational psychologists made attempts to apply the principles of psychology and the facts discovered by the various social sciences such as biology, sociology and social anthropology to educational process. In 1940 the Policy and Planning Board of the American Psychological Association set up a committee to examine the achievements and functioning of educational psychology. In 1947, in America, the National Society of College Teachers formed a committee to determine the functions of educational psychology. The latter committee published its report in 1953, which was based on a study extending over five years and in which it laid down the curriculum for the teaching of educational psychology apart from defining the scope of the subject. The field and scope of educational psychology has been continually expanding in the last few years as the educational psychologists are continuing their researches into actual life and problems confronting the process of education.

The preceding brief outline of the history of educational psychology is sufficient to point out the fact that its major development took place in the twentieth century. In spite of its more or less recent origin, educational psychology as developed enough in the last fifty years to be recognised as an independent branch of knowledge.

WHAT IS EDUCATIONAL PSYCHOLOGY?

As is apparent from the term, educational psychology is the psychology that relates to education or to put it differently, it is the science concerned with behaviour pertaining to education. It is also the scientific study of human behaviour in conditions that take their particular form from education. Putting the same differently, educational psychology is the science that applies the principles of psychology concerned with human behaviour and experience to circumstances predominantly educational. In the words of Skinner, "Educational Psychology utilizes those findings that deal specifically with the experiences and behaviour of human beings in educational situations."[1] Apparently, educational psychology is intimately concerned with human personality.

Education is the process of mental development. Hence, educational psychology is concerned with the development of mental processes along with the various social processes. Judd, a famous educational psychologist, wrote, "Educational Psychology may be defined as the science which describes and explains the changes that take place in individuals as they pass through various stages of development from birth to maturity." Educational Psychology, being more than an academic pursuit, besides studying the process of development, also puts forward suggestions for its acceleration.

The process of development is dependent upon and grounded in two factors—maturity and learning. Hence, educational psychology is concerned with the study of both these factors. As Crow and Crow express it, "Educational Psychology describes and explains the learning experiences of an individual from birth through old age."[2] In this way, educational psychology is the psychology of learning, towards which the educational psychologists have contributed by making intensive studies of the factors and conditions determinant of learning.

Briefly, educational psychology makes a psychological study of human development, maturity and learning, and applies the scientific conclusions of this study to actual teaching conditions in order to attain the ends of education. The modern educational psychologist is a specialist in his own right and is deeply engrossed in researches into behaviour significant to education.

NATURE OF EDUCATIONAL PSYCHOLOGY

Educational psychology is a normative science. And like other sciences, it has its objectives of prediction and control of its subject matter. Psychology strives to discover the fundamental principles that govern the interaction between the human being and his environment. In this search psychology employs scientific methods. And such a methodology helps to reach scientific conclusions. Psychology being a normative science, its scope and field of operation have been constantly increasing for the last fifty years, and the use

1. Skinner, C.E., *Educational Psychology*, Prentice Hall Inc., New York (1951), p. 14.
2. Crow, L.D. and Crow, A., *Educational Psychology*, Eurasia Publishing House Pvt. Ltd. (1964), p. 7.

of psychology in different spheres led to the development of various branches of this science. It was the use of psychology in the field of education that led to the development of educational psychology. As it progressed, educational psychologists became alive to the fact that they were not to apply psychological principles to their field without giving them a thought but they were to put these principles to test in the actual and living atmosphere of the school, and thus to test their validity. Consequently, the educational psychologists developed a critical approach and attitude to general psychology. This has in its turn led to educational psychology being regarded as an independent science. The nature of educational psychology is scientific. It employs scientific methods and on the basis of conclusions reached thereby makes tentative predictions about human behaviour in educational situations. It is the research that is being carried on in the field of educational psychology that has made it possible today to make some definitions and reliable forecasts concerning learning and other elements in education. In this manner educational psychology is constantly progressing towards an ever greater objectivity.

ASPECTS OF EDUCATIONAL PSYCHOLOGY

The following are the important aspects of educational psychology:

1. Social aspect: The object of educational psychology is to assist the teacher in his effort to achieve all round development of the educand's personality. The educand is very much influenced by his social circumstances. The process of education entails a constant interaction between the teacher and the taught. The taught receives both an inspiration for study and also its material from his teacher. Working in the role of a social engineer the teacher strives to make the educand an ideal citizen in the context of modern democratic societies. If the student develops obstinacy towards the teacher, he may in time arrive at a condition where he may feel safe in disregarding and refuting the power of society and state. In the social sphere, the student is accompanied by his fellow students apart from the teacher. The social scale of the family is also an important influence. But children who attend the kindergarten bring very little influence of the home with them. Fundamentally, they are not socialized and the teacher has to socialize them by putting them in an adequate and proper social environment. And this socialization is very important for democratic nations. The child acquires his position within the group through constant trial and error and learns to work accordingly.

2. Abnormal aspect: As a general rule, every teacher can confidently expect to find some anti-social and anarchist children in his class. These children, for one reason or the other, have to adapt themselves and adjust to social environment in which they have been placed. To affect any improvement in their mental attitude to their environment, it is essential that the teacher be in a position to understand their mental aberrations. It is here that the teacher gets some very definite assistance from abnormal psychology. In the schools at present many psychologists assist the teacher in curing the abnormalities of many children. At the same time, the teacher and the psychologist co-operate to get rid the child of his feeling of inferiority, excessive day dreaming and general abnormality or unsociability.

3. Individual aspect: Apart from and distinctly more important than either the social or abnormal aspect is the individual aspect of educational psychology. Educational psychology lays great emphasis upon individual differences in education and the science has also devised methods whereby these deviations from the average can be measured and evaluated. In modern educational psychology, three kinds of psychological measures in particular have been developed—(*i*) intelligence, (*ii*) attainment, and (*iii*) personality. The individual abnormalities of different children can be discovered by the use of these measurements and tests so that they can be taught accordingly.

4. Genetic aspect: Merely understanding the social, individual and abnormal aspect of a child's development is insufficient for a complete understanding of the child. For this comprehensive understanding it is necessary to supplement his personal history with his case history. This refers to the genetic aspect of educational psychology. In this practice, a careful record of the child's daily life and his progress is maintained. In this respect it differs from a life history. In clinical psychology the life history of the child is studied with a view to solving some definite problems whereas in the genetic aspect of educational psychology the progress of the child is noted in terms of hours and days. Educational psychologists have conducted many such studies.

SCOPE OF EDUCATIONAL PSYCHOLOGY

Though educational psychology is an independent science, the limits of its field of operation have not yet been determined as the history of its development extends back to only forty or fifty years. Nevertheless, the subject matter of educational psychology can be studied in three different aspects—the educand, the process of learning and the conditions of learning.

1. The educand: The term educand applies to students who individually or collectively participate in the educational programmes. These students taken collectively constitute the class. And in fact the behaviour of the class is none other than the behaviour of these students. Modern psychology gives the teacher an opportunity of improving the behaviour of students whence they can progress in the class. In order to provide proper education the teacher should possess as much knowledge of the educand as is possible for him. For example, the teacher should be aware of the various stages of the educand's maturity since different subjects may be taught more fruitfully than others in different definite stages of maturity. The possession of such extensive knowledge makes it indispensable for the teacher to study the various aspects and stages in the child's development from birth to adulthood. In this way, while he makes a psychological study of the child's progress through childhood, adolescence and adulthood, he also makes a study of the child's progress in physical, mental, emotional, moral and aesthetic aspects, and in the process takes note of the changes that have taken place constantly in this development. The teacher should also be aware of the individual differences of the child. And for the knowledge of his individual differences the teacher must also have some knowledge of the relative influence of heredity and environment upon the developing child. And to gain this essential knowledge of individual quirks and peculiarities the modern educational psychologist makes use of many kinds of measurements and tests. Of the many kinds of tests in use in present day psychology, the main ones are concerned with intelligence, character, personality and vocational abilities. The results of these tests form the basis of the child's education and later on his vocation regarding which he is guided. In using these methods of measurement, the data has to be tabulated, following which informative conclusions are drawn that help in teaching. This is the statistical aspect of educational psychology. Knowledge of the child's intelligence, personality and abilities is essential for the teacher. The measurement of all such factors falls within the scope of educational psychology.

2. Process of learning: The process of learning means the process in evidence at the time when teaching or learning is in progress. The question is, what happens within the child when he is learning? All children learn something either through themselves or through the teacher's teaching. Many of the things that a child learns are often not taught in the class, neither they are comprehended under the curriculum yet the child understands them. The educational psychologist tries to discover exactly what occurs within the child during his learning, why the children grasp the things the teacher teaches them and even more, why or how they learn things that the teacher would prevent them from knowing. This constant effort has led the educational psychologists to the discovery of many principles and concepts that may be of considerable value to the teacher. One of them concerns the complexity of the process of education which leads for removing the difficulty and solving its problems. Hence modern educational psychology is concerned with the psychological problem of learning various subjects, progress in learning them, evaluations of the progress, obstacles that hinder it and ways and means of removing such obstacles.

3. Conditions of learning: This phrase implies the factors or conditions that influence the educand and the process of learning. Some of these factors may concern the classroom, being purely physical such as the quantity and direction of light, normal air and humidity, acoustic conditions, etc. All these apparently minor considerations influence the child's learning but the most important factor among the conditions of learning is the teacher himself. Besides these rather obvious factors, there are many other influential factors that are neither visible nor readily apparent but are nonetheless effective and important for all their invisibility. Of the many such conditions an important one is the attitude of the child's parents toward education and learning in a group. Yet such a condition is not generally apparent. If they do not hold the work of the school and education in very high regard, then this inimical attitude may be harmful for school study. It is even more potent an influence in its effect upon the enthusiasm and interest of the teacher which it may adversely effect. Although this condition does not invade the classroom and as a rule is existing only outside it, yet the teacher has to face and struggle against it within the four walls of the classroom.

Generally speaking, it is the third aspect of educational psychology that is commonly identified with education. Most of the people confuse education with a condition of learning within the classroom and the school in which the teacher is understood to be the creator and manipulator of the conditions of learning. It is true that of the main aspects of educational psychology described above, it is only the third that can be adequately controlled by the teacher and yet it can never be regulated to quite the extent to which people normally believe it to be amenable to control. Nevertheless by confusing education exclusively with this third aspect, people overlook the significance of the other two aspects. Such an attitude tends to make education mechanical and even to oversimplify it. It overlooks and violates the actual dynamic aspect of education in which learning is a conscious process and the educand a progressive and changable being. While educational psychology has helped both the teacher and the taught it has also acquainted the general masses with the real meaning of education so that they may contribute their little mite to the process of education by helping the educator and the educands.

EXPANDING SCOPE OF EDUCATIONAL PSYCHOLOGY

It was only in 1920 that educational psychology attained a definite form. Since then its scope has been changing continually as the discovery of new concepts and new instruments in educational psychology has coincided with the introduction of new objectives of education in democratic societies. The search for possibilities of education in nursery school has led to the opening up of new vistas in educational psychology. Similarly, a view recently voiced by educationists to the effect that children should be taught the democratic mode of life in schools has proved to be revolutionary in educational psychology. In this way, the scope and limits of educational psychology undergo continual change as it is influenced by new discoveries in the fields of psychology and other social sciences on the one hand, and the new concepts and views of educational philosophers on the other. Hence, its limits are indefinite and changeable. This led some authors and teachers to call a meeting to determine the field of educational psychology, but meetings of this nature cannot have any real value. On the other hand, as Gates and others have suggested, meeting that makes suggestions on new needs and problems in the field of educational psychology from time to time can be of more use. When the famous psychologist Cattell, who has done work of considerable value and importance in the field of educational psychology, was asked to define psychology, he enigmatically replied that psychology is what the psychologists do. On similar lines it can reasonably and equally enigmatically be commented that educational psychology is what the educational psychologists do. The researches, experiments, studies and similar activities of educational psychologists determine the scope of the subject. Finally, it must also be kept in mind that educational psychology is a developing science. It concerns itself with new and ever new researches as new problems appear in education and new concepts come to light in the theory of education, with the result that there is no saying what form this science will have in ten years hence and what will its scope be.

WHAT IS EDUCATION?

In ancient times education was interpreted in the sense of imparting information to the student In the opinion of the British philosopher John Locke, the mind of a child is a blank sheet on which anything can be inscribed. Concurring with this notion of the mind, the duty of the teacher was considered to be filling of the mind of a student with information. And to this end, the teachers were engaged in imparting some facts to students who were expected to learn them by rote, failure leading, in some cases even to physical punishment. This conception of education continued to flourish in the middle ages.

One usual question upon being introduced to some one is, how much education have you received, the intention being to find out the academic degree obtained by the person in question. In many cases of employment the employers lay down certain minimum educational qualifications for the applicant. Here, too, education is interpreted as gathering of information. When we usually refer to some commonly understood standard of education we mean that the person in question has spent a definite number of years in education, passed certain examinations or received some particular academic degrees.

But this view of education is erroneous since education is not merely the quantum of information, or the examinations passed or the degrees gained in academic pursuit. Modern educationists understand education to mean the complete process of the development of the individual. The following definitions contribute to a clear understanding of the sense in which education is now understood:

1. According to Painter, "The aim of education is complete human development." The individual is composed of the physical and mental elements, the mental aspect being further sub-divided into its components such as thinking, emotion, sentiment etc. Any education that tends to educate and train only some particular aspect of the individual's total make-up, be it the physical, mental thinking, emotional and sentimental aspect, is not real education. It is a one-sided education. Real education aims at the development of the complete individual, complete in every respect.

2. To quote Pestalozzi, "The main object of education is not to teach but to develop." Accordingly, the real object of the teacher is not to impart something to the child but to effect his complete development.

3. In the words of Froebel, "The task of education is to assist natural development towards its destined end." The human individual enters this

world equipped with some tendencies, impressions and abilities or capacities, and the aim and object of each of these is to attain to its perfection. Education implies the development of these innate faculties and not the foisting of something external upon the child. In the words of Kant, "Education is the development in the individual of all the perfection of which he is capable." Pestalozzi wrote, "Education means a natural, progressive and systematic development of all powers." In the process of education the child resembles a plant, while the teacher fulfils the functions of the gardener whose duty it is to create conditions in which this plant may grow to the fulness of its possibilities. But the real development of the plant depends upon the power and potentiality inherent in its seed. Its absence at the source will make the work of the gardener futile. But the seed, in addition to its own inherent potentiality needs conditions favourable to its growth and development in the absence of which it cannot exhibit its full resources in complete development. The function of the gardener is to get together all such conditions that are suitable to its growth. Once such conditions have been achieved the gardener has to do nothing except to let the plant grow and develop of its own accord. Similarly, the function of the teacher is to create conditions and atmosphere in the school that may suit the development of the child. In the proper conditions, the child will develop his capacities to their full. Once the proper atmosphere and the correct technique of teaching have been arrived at the teacher has only to organise and to supervise.

Education is the process of development

All the hitherto mentioned definitions of education acknowledge the fact that the process of development is in itself education. But one must also be aware of the actual nature of this development. Although in every sphere the ability to learn depends upon development, yet development does not imply learning. Learning requires the maturation of the mind and body as a result of which the child acquires the following qualities:

1. Some knowledge of the environment in which it is placed.
2. Adequate motor control to fulfil his individual needs.
3. Normal linguistic ability to carry on ordinary conversation.
4. Some knowledge of individual and group relationship.

The development of these qualities in the child begins even in the home. The task of the teacher is to continue this development when the child is in his charge.

In fact, this process of development does not cease at any time in life. Accordingly, then education in its liberal interpretation continues throughout the life of the individual. In fact, every successful teacher remains a student throughout his life. While he teaches much to his students, he also learns considerably from them. And many of the successful teachers recognise the fact that the development that their thoughts, personality and abilities undergo in the process of teaching would not have been accessible to them in any other sphere.

Education is both process and result

The word development involves the concept of a process that never ceases. In this way, from the psychological point of view, education is both the process and the result of this process. In its form as a process, it includes all those activities that help the individual to lead a social life and to communicate social traditions, laws, religious belief, language and social institutions from one generation to another. Naturally, then, the process of education in a society continues from generation to generation. The process of education encourages an individual to think, consider, evaluate and eventually to act. In this way, the needs of the individual and society are fulfilled and their welfare achieved. Hence education is an individualizing and a socializing process that furthers personal advancement as well as social living. The results of education comprehend all those results that are the outcome of teaching. The aims of education change when individual abilities, ambitions and cultural needs undergo change. In the same way, the results of education differ in different cultural groups and also in different individuals within one group. But whatever the aim and object, education always helps to improve the personality of the individual and the group.

Formal and informal education

At this juncture it would be better to recognise the distinction between formal and informal education. The education that is carried on in the schools is formal education but it is incomplete as the informal aspect of education is far more important than the formal one. The factors that contribute to informal education are the home, religious institutions, the playground, library, radio and television, the cinema, newspapers, club, theatre, etc. While school teaching according to a set curriculum is an important form of education, the individual develops far more when he is in contact with these informal educational institutions.

Psychology, education and educational psychology

Having understood education to mean the process of development, it is now easy to understand and to comprehend the extent to which educational psychology can be of use to the process of education. The intimate relation between psychology, education and educational psychology is expressed in these words by the educational psychologists Crow and Crow: "Psychology explains the how of human development as related to learning, education attempts to provide the what of learning; educational psychology is concerned with the why and when of learning."[1] Psychology informs us of the levels or stages through which the development of the individual passes in the process of learning. In other words, psychology tells us how development occurs. Education, on the other hand, tells us what we should learn, or what are the aims of education? Educational psychology tells us when and why the child learns. In this way, educational psychology elaborates the why of educand. For example, we know the nature of a student, the limits to which his development

1. *Ibid.*, p. 8.

can reach, the individual and social adjustments that are required in this development and the psychological factors inherent in this development. A knowledge of the various stages in the growth of the child may help the teacher or make a proper assessment and arrangement of the process of his learning. If the teacher is aware of the environmental factors that influence the learning of the child, he may secure a better and more suitable environment for him. Educational psychology analyses and explains the experiences relating to the education of an individual right from his childhood to his adult age. Its subject matter is composed of all the factors that influence learning. And in this connection, new and ever new experiments are being carried on in the field of educational psychology. Educational psychology is a practical science.

In the words of Judd, "Educational psychology may be defined as the science which describes and explains the changes that take place in Individuals as they pass through various states of development from birth to maturity." Educational psychology studies the conditions that retard or accelerate development and suggests to the teacher practical ways of increasing and improving progress. In this way it is a practical science.

Hence, it is evident that to determine the aims of education is not the function of educational psychology. The determination of aims or objects in any sphere falls to the lot of a normative science or philosophy. It is the normative science of ethics that determines the ultimate aim of human life while it is left to logic to determine what is true and untrue in judgements. In the same manner, the ideals of beauty are determined by the normative science of aesthetics. All these normative sciences are nearer to philosophy than to the positive sciences. Determination of aims or objectives does not fall within the scope of science since scientific methods do not reveal objectives. Aims are concerned with values and sciences are not concerned with values. It is philosophy that deals with values because only philosophical methods can reveal them. Hence, the aims of education are determined by educationist philosophers in the field of educational theory. The aims of modern education have been determined by Rousseau, Froebel, Pestalozzi, Aurobindo, Rabindra, Gandhi, Tolstoy and other thinkers of like calibre. It is educational psychology that has contributed its mite by suggesting ways and means of attaining these ends. Hence, the function of educational psychology is not the determination of the ends of education. These it borrows from the science of education. Its real function is to help in their attainment. But on the other hand, "Although psychology cannot formulate the aim of education, a scientific psychology can tell us whether an aim is hopelessly in the clouds, or whether it is possible of achievement." The aims of education can be attained only when they are scientific and psychological, since otherwise they will prove to be hopelessly put of the pale of reality. The reality of the aims of education is put to the test by educational psychology. In this way, even in determining the aims of education the educationists have to turn to educational psychologists for their assistance and advice.

THE OBJECTIVES OF EDUCATIONAL PSYCHOLOGY

In the modern democratic society the aim of education is to socialize the individual in order to encourage him to work for his own welfare and satisfaction and for that of the society with a maximum of effort and inspiration. The conditions of an individual's work are determined and laid down by his desires, ambitions and system of values. In this way, it is only natural that there should be variety and difference between individuals on this score. Yet, in general, society expects of every individual that he will make the maximum utilization of his inherent abilities and potentialities. Complete development of the individual is the aim of education.

In general, the aims of educational psychology correspond with the aims of education. The aims of educational psychology may be sub-divided into two classes:[1]

1. General aims.
2. Specific aims.

The two classes are briefly described in the following lines:

1. General aims: The general aim of education and educational psychology is to affect the development of a complete personality in the child. For this it is essential to develop in the child a capacity for as great self-determination as possible so that he may be active in the continually changing world. In addition to this, the function of educational psychology is to offer requisite assistance to the teacher, the assistance being mainly in two forms. One way would be to improve the actual and personal life of the teacher and the other would be to improve his method of teaching. In this way, while on the one hand educational psychology helps in the achievement of the cultural aims of the teacher, it also, on the other, assists in the achieving and attaining of occupational objectives. Thus, the general aim and object of educational psychology is to search for and discover principles and facts that conduce to the development of a balanced personality in the educand.

2. Specific Aims: The general aims of educational psychology reveal some of its particular objectives. These particular objectives are:

(*i*) To prove the notion that the study of educational psychology helps learning, makes improvement in social behaviour and brings success in the formation or adjustment of personality.

(*ii*) To help determine the aims of education, based on a study of desirable behavioural patterns that have arisen from the process of education.

(*iii*) To contribute towards the development of an unbiased and sympathetic attitude towards the child.

(*iv*) To assist in the complete and proper understanding of the nature and importance of social relationships.

(*v*) To acquaint the teachers with such principles and laws of education that can be utilised by them in solving problems arising in teaching.

1. Skinner, C.E. (Ed.) *Educational Psychology*, Prentice Hall Inc., Englewood Cliffs. N.Y., 1951, p. 29.

(*vi*) To help the teacher in developing an insight into the results of his own teaching and into the habits of others with regard to teaching.

(*vii*) To provide teachers with such factors and methods as may help them to analyse and understand their own behaviour and that of others.

PROBLEMS OF EDUCATIONAL PSYCHOLOGY

Educational psychology is a branch of the applied aspect of psychology, in which capacity it is intimately concerned with facts of human behaviour and experience. Being a branch of applied psychology, it applies these facts to actual conditions of teaching. Hence Skinner is eminently correct when he says, "Educational psychology utilizes those findings that deal specifically with the experiences and behaviour of human beings in educational situations."[1] The educational situation is a state of learning, or one in which the main activity involved is that of learning. Hence, educational psychology is mainly concerned with finding solutions to the problems of how human beings learn. The process of learning helps the individual to develop and this is the aim of all education. Consequently, the most important subject in educational psychology concerns the development of a balanced personality in the child. The reason why so much emphasis is laid on development in the field of educational psychology is that all other problems confronting this science are fundamentally based on different aspects of this single aim. It is for development of the educand's personality that the teacher makes use of facts gleaned from human behaviour and experience in conditions of education, Consideration of the various problems with which educational psychology deals will make these thoughts all the more clear.

Of course, there are so many problems in educational psychology, but the main ones are the following:

1. Development of balanced personality: The main problem that engages the attention of educational psychology is the development of a balanced personality in the educand. A balanced personality is one in whom the intellectual, emotional, ethical and moral aspects are properly blended and synthesized, and function properly. It is a common thing for the child to pick up many quirks and faults of personality in the conditions within and without the home. One of the common experiences of life is that a child develops a faulty and imperfect personality, one in which someone aspect of his being is exaggerated while another equally vital is suppressed, if the co-ordination between his parents is not proper or if he is a spoilt child, spoilt with exaggerated affection and love. There are many thousands of such social and even physical conditions that result in the child's avoiding company of his equals or indulging in excessive day dreaming. Educational psychology studies the characteristics of the child's adjustment, diagnoses the basic causes leading to it and finally searches for ways and means of correcting this error.

2. Provision of motivation: Often enough, the problems that are at the root of various adjustment defects are problems of motivation. Progress is always

1. *Ibid.*, p. 14.

slow in the absence of any motivation. Lack of enthusiasm is a bar to effective progress. A child cannot be developed unless he is given the appropriate and adequate motivation. You may take the horse to the pond but you cannot make it drink water. In the same way, unless some motivation is awakened in the child, the teacher cannot succeed in his work. The problem of creating motivation in the child is a difficult one. It is educational psychology that attempts the solution of this problem. Observation shows that sometimes progress has been accelerated by twenty to thirty per cent by the simple expedients of praise or blame or by creating competition among the children. Problems such as selection of curriculum, choice of various activities within the process of education or learning, etc., are all problems concerned with motivation.

3. Increase in understanding and meaning: Another factor at the root of the motivation problem is sometimes a deficient understanding and an inability to comprehend the implications of the problem existing. It is to this end that the material chosen in teaching now-a-days is such as is drawn from an environment with which the child is reasonably familiar and with which he is conversant enough not to be embarrassed by it. A simple example would be the creation of a model government within the class in order to explain the working of the actual government of the country to the students. In democratic societies the students usually understand the functioning of a democratic system in their student groups.

4. Individual importance of heredity and environment in individual differences: The aim of education is the development of the child. Hence, an important problem facing the educational psychologist is the determination of the relative importance of heredity and environment in the child's development and in causing individual differences among children. Can education change the inherited trait? Can children reach an adequate stage of development on their inherited traits alone if they are placed in a common environment? Is it possible to make a child into anything on the basis of education irrespective of his heredity? The nature of this question is of that type which encourages and inspires the educational psychologist to make a comparative study of hereditary and environmental factors. For example, one important question is the extent to which intelligence can be developed through education regarding which educational psychologists have discovered numerous facts after much investigation.

5. Techniques of maximum progress in learning: Fundamentally, the process of education advances with learning. The most important question that interests the educational psychologist in this regard is what methods of learning facilitate it and achieve the maximum progress? One such question could be, is there any conflict between imitation and creation? Should education pay more attention to the collection of factual details or concentrate on creative activities? Psychology has made considerable experiments with such methods as imitation, conditioned response, trial and error and insight, and has tried to discover the conditions that are best attuned to the application of these methods, the co-ordination between the conditions and methods being productive of the best results.

6. Education of emotions: The proper and adequate development of personality demands the proper and complete development of emotions. An absence of such education of emotions results in many mental diseases such as indiscipline, split personality etc.

7. Measurement and development of intelligence and attainment: Education develops intelligence and attainment. Educational psychologists search for and discover methods and measures whereby one can know how this development can be achieved and once it has been achieved, to know how much development in the child has taken place.

8. Individual differences: Applied psychology is based on the fact of individual differences. Educational psychology, a knowledge that makes practical use of psychology in the field of education, finds out why and in what respects individual beings differ from each other. These differences are so well defined that the skilled teacher cannot function properly unless he can understand them. For example, the mental level of some children is so low that they can be taught even such activities as wearing clothes and eating only with the greatest of difficulty, while some children are so intelligent and quick-minded that the normal teaching and study level of the class is not enough to occupy them so that they soon tire of it. Hence, the educational psychologist attempts to discover the limits, if any, of these individual differences, and even evolves methods for their measurement in exceptional children. The modern teacher discovers these individual differences and then makes efforts to help the children progress individually.

9. Problems relating to learning: Many of the problems of educational psychology are concerned with learning. The main among them are:

(*a*) nature of the process of learning;
(*b*) relation between level of maturity and learning;
(*c*) importance of individual differences in the speed of learning and limits of learning;
(*d*) internal changes taking place within the process of learning;
(*e*) relation between the methods of teaching and the result of learning;
(*f*) modes of evaluating the progress of learning;
(*g*) relative importance of the formal and informal methods of education or learning;
(*h*) psychological effect of social conditions upon the learner.

10. Practical Problems: Educational psychology is no less a practical science than it is a theoretical one. Hence, in it one comes across many problems that arise before the teacher during the process of teaching. Such problems are:

(*a*) knowledge of the nature of every student and the possibilities of their development;

(*b*) individual and social adaptation necessary for adjustment in the modern culture;

(*c*) search for the fundamental psychological causes at the root of the process of learning and teaching.

As educational psychology progresses, it is faced with newer problems. In modern democratic societies, educational psychology is engaged in adapting education to democracy . It has at its disposal the services of psychology on the one hand and of many other social sciences on the other in the solution of problems that it comes across in such an effort. It is on the solution of these problems that the future of democratic societies rests.

QUESTIONS FOR EXERCISE

1. "Educational psychology helps provide a better background for understanding the total job of teaching in all its intricacies."—Skinner. Discuss.
2. What should the prospective teacher seek through the study of educational psychology? Point out those areas of education on which Educational Psychology has a bearing.
3. What is the relation of educational psychology with education and psychology?
4. "Educational psychology utilizes those findings that deal specifically with the experience and behaviour of human being in educational situations." (Skinner)

   Evaluate this statement and discuss the main problems with which Educational Psychology is concerned.
5. Educational psychology is concerned with how people learn. What single topic involved, do you believe, is most important? Why did you select this?
6. Discuss the nature and scope of educational psychology'.
7. Describe the nature of educational psychology and show how it can influence educational practice.
8. Define the scope of educational psychology.
9. Define Educational Psychology. Gates has remarked, "The boundaries of Educational Psychology are uncertain and changing." In the light of the statement, discuss the scope of the subject.
10. What is the use of Educational Psychology to a teacher?
11. What is educational psychology? How does the study of educational psychology help the teacher in his teaching?
12. Which of the following definitions of educational psychology is most acceptable to you and why? Support your answer with examples from your experience during practical teachings:

    (*i*) Educational psychology is a study of classroom problems and their solutions.

    (*ii*) Educational psychology is a science that enables a teacher to understand a student's behaviour.

3

Methods of Psychological Study

Educational psychology is the positive science of behaviour in educational situations. Science is a method. It is distinguished from philosophy on the basis of methodological difference. Science is the study of any object by scientific method. Hence, if educational psychology is to be called a science, it should use scientific methods, *e.g.*, experiment, case history and observation, etc. Experimental method is the most important method in the study of educational psychology. It is this method which has the credit of bringing educational psychology to the level of an exact science Hence, modern educational psychology places greatest emphasis on experimental method.

WHAT IS EXPERIMENTAL METHOD?

According to Garret experiment is a question asked systematically. Thus in experiment, the experimenter has a problem before him. He experiments to find out the answer to this problem. The clarity of the answer depends upon the clarity of the question. The question is based on a hypothesis. Thus hypothesis is proved or disproved by the experiment *e.g.*, suppose that while studying or teaching someone thinks that motivation has its role in study. This is merely a hypothesis. To examine it, it is placed in the form of question—does motivation effect study? To get an answer to this question, it requires psychological experiments. Suppose by the experiments one arrives at the result that motivation is useful in the study: this proves that hypothesis. Now another question might be raised as to how far motivations help in study? This question will lead to further experiments on this line. In this way, various types of enquiries can be made through the method of experiment *e.g.*, experiment regarding the effect of motivation on study. Similarly, the effect of smoking on study, of family environment on the child, the effect of intelligence and practice in learning, etc., may be put in the form of the questions and experiments can be performed to get answers to them. In the experimental method, the observation is held in certain pre-determined conditions. Thus experiment is a controlled observation. It is the observation of the behaviour or activity in fixed circumstances. The characteristic of this observation is that it can be repeated in different places and times without difference in results.

Steps in experiment

There are following steps in a typical experiment:

1. Raising a problem: The first step in an experiment is the raising of the problem *e.g.*, it is said that smoking is harmful to the students. On the other hand some say that it helps in concentration. Those who are neither for nor against smoking, may say that it is not smoking but the personality of the student which is relevant to his result in examinations. This discussion creates a problem about the effect of smoking on physical or mental capacity. This problem may lead to further experiments.

2. Formulation of a hypothesis: The second step in experimental method is the formulation of a hypothesis. In the example of smoking the problem of its effect on physical and mental capacity can be pet in the form of a hypothesis. This hypothesis will be like this "smoking is harmful for physical and mental capacity." Now this hypothesis will be tested by experiments.

3. To distinguish independent variables and dependent variables: The third step in experimental method is the distinction between independent variables and dependent variables. In the examples of smoking the physical and mental capacity will be the dependent variables, since they will be fixed in experiment. Smoking will be an independent variable since the aim of the experiment is to find out the effects of its presence and absence.

4. Controlling the environment or situation: The fourth and the most important step in the experimental method is controlling the environment or situation. There are several difficulties in the above mentioned experiment on smoking. It is just possible that the subject may try to prove that smoking has no effect on physical or mental capacities. But to neutralise possibilities the experimental situation is controlled. In the experiment on smoking, the eyes of the subject were closed by bandage. Two exactly similar holders were used. One of these holders had an electric wire through which the subject might inhale the warm air, while the other holder had a common cigarette. In all the sessions of the experiment all types of sounds, related with smoking were made, *e.g.*, the rubbing of the match etc. At the end of the experiment there were sticks and ashes lying round about, so that the subject think that he really smoked. The subject cannot touch cigarette at any time. The experimenter himself puts and takes away the holder from his mouth. In the sessions, when cigarette was not given to the subject the experimenter himself smoked. To stop the signs received by the smoking sequence of giving and taking away the holders, the sessions of smoking and non-smoking were kept irregular. These special arrangements in the case of experiment of smoking are not necessary in all types of experiments. The arrangements of control differ according to the nature of experiments. In the case of man some special types of controls are necessary so that the subject may not know the principles of the experiment since it is feared that this might make difference in his mental attitude. But in the case of experiments on animals this difficult is not there. So there are different types of controls in the experiments on animals, *e.g.*, Pavlov, in his experiment on conditioned reflex in the dog made special arrangement for the flow of saliva and to gather it outside dog's mouth.

5. Analysis of the result: The fifth important step in the experimental method is analysis of the result. Generally, the subject of the experiment are divided into two groups—one controlled and another experimental. In the experiment on smoking every subject was also his controlled subject. All smoked half times and in the remaining half they inhaled warm air. The experimental group is often called independent variable, since the experimenter can stop it or modify it. In the experiment on smoking, cigarette is an independent variable and the results of its presence have been compared with the results of its absence. For the analysis of the results of the experiment, statistical technique is used.

6. Verification of the hypothesis by the result of the experiment: The sixth step in experiment is the verification of the hypothesis by the result of the experiment. The results of the experiment exhibit whether the hypothesis was right or wrong. In the experiment on smoking, it was found by the comparison of the sessions of smoking, and non-smoking that there was very little difference in the results. Smoking increased heartbeat and the trembling of the hand. This effect was observed more in non-smokers than the smoker subject. No influence was observed on mental capacities known by mental tests. After 18 days of smoking it was concluded that it had very insignificant effect. This result disproved the hypothesis.

In spite of the limitations of the experimental methods, it is undoubtedly the most important and valuable method in psychology. It is by this method that the psychologist arrives at the most exact conclusion about behaviour. But experimental method is limited to only those aspects of human behaviour, where one may hope to arrive at exact conclusions. On the other hand, some aspects of human behaviour are so changeable and complex that one should be satisfied with their observation and arrive at some workable conclusions. The field of experimental method, however, is gradually being widened with the advent of new inventions, regarding tools and instruments. If observation and experimental methods have widened the field of psychology and made it more useful in daily life, it is the experimental method which has secured a respectable place for psychology among the sciences. In the world outside the limits of laboratory, man will always learn by experience and observation, but it is on the experimental method alone that the future of psychology as a science depends.

OBSERVATION METHOD

Observation in child psychology

Every one knows that a bad environment had effect on the child. This, however, cannot be determined by actually placing a child in a bad environment. Which environmental factor effects evil character in the child, cannot be determined by placing him under the influence of the factor. Hence, experimental method cannot work in this case. The child himself cannot be asked about his experience in a certain environment because he cannot analyse his own experiences. Hence, the introspection method is also useless. Thus in cases like this in child psychology, it is only the observation method which can be helpful. The effect of the absence of parents on the child's development can be determined only through the observation of the development of orphans.

Steps in observation method

The above mentioned examples regarding the observation method exhibit some of its particular traits. Roughly speaking, various steps in the method of observation are as follows:

1. Observation of behaviour: The first step in observation method is the observation of behaviour. Observation literally means the examination or perception of some behaviour or processes. In observation everything or phenomenon is directly perceived, *e.g.*, the psychologist perceives the behaviour of animals. If someone has to study the social behaviour of monkeys, he should go where the monkeys are assembled and observe their behaviour.

2. Noting of behaviour: Observation in psychology is a scientific method. Hence, it is not sufficient to perceive a certain behaviour and to remember it. The observation, on the other hand, should be carefully noted down. In the examples of the study of the social behaviour of the monkeys, the observer should carefully note down their various activities.

3. Interpretation and analysis of behaviour: The third step in the method of observation is the interpretation and analysis of behaviour. If the behaviour is noted, it can be analysed at rest and the causes underlying it can be clarified. The movements of hands and legs, the sound, the gestures and other external activities express the internal conditions of the person. In the case of animals their mental conditions are inferred from their external activities. The basis of this interference is not the experience of the psychologist himself, but the behaviour of other animals and his own insight into animal psychology Thus the behaviour is interpreted on the basis of analysis and inference.

4. Generalisation: The fourth step in observation method is generalisation. Scientific principles are based upon generalisations. Psychology is a science, hence its principles are also of the same nature. In observation as a method of psychology, the purpose is to find out general principles. In the example of the social behaviour of monkeys, various psychologists will observe their behaviour, note it, analyse it, interpret it and finally find out general principles through generalisation.

Difficulties in this method

Like other methods of psychology, the observation method has also some defects or difficulties. The main difficulties are as follows:

1. **Influence of personal interest:** In the observation method the psychologist himself observes, hence it is more likely that his personal interest should also influence his observation. In the example of the observation of the social behaviour in monkeys, if a psychologist has an excessive interest in sex behaviour, he will mainly attend to their sex activities and conceive them as more general than they actually are. Along with observation the personal interest also influence his interpretation. An excessively sexual person often interprets non-sexual behaviour of others as sexual. A wicked man finds some wicked purpose even behind the sympathetic action of other. A religious man would interpret even the sexual behaviour of others as pure and religious. Thus the behaviour is interpreted wrongly due to personal interests and attitudes. In the study of child insane and the mentally abnormal person, this difficulty is very much observed because there is much difficulty in the mental activities of these persons and those of the psychologists.

The above-mentioned difficulty in observation method is undoubtedly real, but it can be removed through scientific detachment. The mental conditions of others can be understood through constructive imagination. It is true that few have scientific detachment and constructive imagination, but these can be developed through long practice and training.

2. **The possibilities of bias:** According to the personal views and tendencies of the psychologists, there is a possibility of bias and prejudice in the interpretation of behaviour, *e.g.*, in the countries where prejudices based on colour are largely prevalent, the white psychologists seldom find good or higher traits in the behaviour of black subjects.

Indispensability of the method

But in spite of the above-mentioned limitations and difficulties in the method of observation, it is indispensable in psychology. As has already been pointed out, In many cases other methods are entirely useless and only the observation method works In fact, behaviour requires training and practice to observe correctly and accurately. The observer should first analyse his own tendencies and remove preconceptions, prejudices, attachments and aversions and develop scientific detachment. Many of the things will be left without observation in the beginning or will be wrongly observed, but practice will make observation more accurate. It is experience which makes observation scientific. The expert psychologists can train the newcomers in observation The personal bias, prejudice and errors can be removed by comparison of the notes of several psychologists and through mutual discussions.

GENETIC METHOD

This method is utilised to study human growth and development. This may be done by two types of approaches: 1. Cross sectional or Horizontal, and 2. Longitudinal or Vertical. In the former, different stages of development of several persons of identical age are studied. This helps in comparative study of different individuals and in forming general principles. But for the study of one individual the latter approach is utilised.

STATISTICAL METHOD

As in other sciences so in educational psychology, statistical method is widely utilised. The main steps in statistical method are collection of data, classification, analysis, interpretation, generalization and graphic representation. This method has increased the predictive power of the educational psychologist. It has proved to be particularly valuable in tests of mental abilities and educational attainment.

DEVELOPMENTAL METHOD

Educational psychology not only studies human behaviour at a particular time, but also its development from birth to death. Thus educational psychology traces the mental and behavioural development of the individual from the cradle to the grave. In such a study the educational psychologist has to face many difficult problems which have much importance *e.g.*, the influence of heredity and environment in the development of the person, the favourable and unfavourable conditions of normal development and the phenomena of abnormality. These questions can be satisfactorily decided only when the educational psychologist observes human development in perfectly controlled conditions. If the educational psychologist observes the development of a child in controlled situations, he can be sure about the influence of different factors in it. This, however, is very difficult to put into practice, *e.g.*, in order to know the influence of the unfavourable conditions on the development of the child the educational psychologist cannot put him in an unfavourable condition as that will be very contrary to ethical principles. Thus the educational psychologist will take the help of observation of the development of the child placed in unfavourable circumstances, *e.g.*, orphans, etc. Such an observation obviously, will not give him decisive knowledge as in the case of the experimental method and yet much valuable information will be collected.

Difficulty in developmental method

Another difficulty in the developmental method is caused by the complexity and variety in development. As Prof. R.S. Woodworth beautifully puts it, "The child behaves so much that an observer cannot record more than small samples." Again, mere observation of the child's development will not help the educational psychologist in arriving at any definite conclusion. To get at some definite conclusions, regarding the development, he must have some definite questions and definite hypothesis in his mind. The more the scientist is clear about his question, the more he shall be clear in getting its answer.

A Dynamic approach

Thus, it is clear that the development method is less accurate than experimental method and has more limitations and difficulties, but efforts are being made to make it more and more useful. The developmental method has also been utilised in observing the development of animals and valuable information has been gathered by the comparison of the development of the animals with that of the human beings. The main value of this method is that it keeps a firm eye on the dynamic aspect of behaviour which is often missed in other methods. Human personality is a complex whole which goes on developing from birth through maturity till death. A dynamic approach to psychology requires that particular human behaviour should be studied separately as well as in the light of the entire process.

QUESTIONS FOR EXERCISE

1. "Experiment is observation of concomitant variation and the interpretation of the concomitances as causes and effects." Discuss the nature of experiments in psychology in the light of the above statement.
2. Describe the following methods of study in Educational Psychology:
   (*a*) Genetic.
   (*b*) Evaluation Techniques.
   (*c*) Statistical Method.
   (*d*) Developmental Method.

4

Nature and Nurture

According to John Locke, the British philosopher, at birth the mind of a child is like a slate on which many and varied stimuli make their impression, which take the form of simple and complex thoughts. Modern educational psychologists do not subscribe to this view. Many studies have adequately proved and established that when a child is born he is possessed of many hereditary impressions and that education and environmental factors can change these original impressions to a limited extent only. Modern educational psychologists are of the opinion that human personality and development are the result of interaction between heredity and environment. In this way, the value of innate abilities and impressions that a child receives from his heredity cannot be overestimated in the process of his development. The child is born with physical characteristics, facial features, mental abilities, common tendencies, instincts, etc. A study of them will reveal what the child receives from heredity at the time of his birth.

INNATE POWERS

A child becomes conscious within the uterus, hence he is capable of receiving impressions while still within the womb. Educational psychologists believe the child's mind to have three kinds of innate powers:

1. Mneme: It is the result of collection of impressions received by the child's mind. It functions in the child during pregnancy. Its absence makes education or learning impossible since the impressions that are impressed upon the mind cannot be collected. It is due to this power that the impressions received are also retained, and not dissipated and lost. Impressions leave an indelible mark on the mind in the same manner that a gramophone record is grooved and just as the record reproduces the words contained in it on the touch of a needle in the same manner the mind gives forth its impressions and retentions when they are needed. In this manner, memory is a witness to the fact that impressions are collected within the mind. Such varied factors as good or bad company leave their impression upon the child's mind and it is accordingly that he develops. Good impressions are left on the individual's mind if he comes into contact with good literature, good people and good circumstances, and his development is accordingly all that can be desired. One of the most common experiences of human life is that one recollects things heard many years previously or objects seen long back the moment they are revisited or heard again. In this manner, the impressions and experiences of the various sense organs, the eyes, tongue, nose, ear and skin, are recorded and collected in the human mind, to be reproduced or recollected in the form of memory if and when required. The human mind records every impression after the manner of a camera so that it can be seen later on. But another common experience is that many experiences escape memory. According to the psychoanalysts, this does not mean that they have completely evaded memory and are no longer retained but that they reach the unconscious mind for having been repressed, only to find expression in such various forms as dreams, mental complexes, etc. But it is equally true that everything present in the environment does not necessarily leave an impression upon us since an impression is left if we attend to it. In this way, the relation between attention and impression is a close one, just as the relationship between attention and memory is an intimate one. Attention leads to impression and memory assures us that an impression has in fact been left. But sometimes even the absence of memory and recognition does not bear evidence to the fact that there is no impression in the mind. If re-learning of some subject learned earlier does not lead to any facility only then can it be safely remarked that there is no impression, but otherwise there is nothing to warrant a disbelief in its existence in the mind.

In the process of education it is just as essential to prevent the undesirable impressions from forming on the child's mind as it is to promote formation of good impressions since bad impressions retard and destroy good ones. Hence, it is for the teacher to make as much good impressions upon the child as time and place allow. The effort of making correct impressions upon the child should start while he is in the womb as many of the thinkers believe that a child is susceptible to impressions in that condition. In addition to this the child is impressionable and particularly more so to the influence emanating from the behaviour of his parents. It is for this reason that a pregnant mother is often advised to think and behave in a decorus manner, not that many mothers would do otherwise. Well wishers and teachers can make the child a decent, cultured, serious, ideal citizen by subjecting him to desirable influences and by properly using his powers of mneme.

2. Horme: Another power present in the child, for which he has to thank his ancestry and heredity, is the horme or power of purposive activity. Every thought present in the child's mind has one or the other purpose. And whenever man acts it is with some set purpose. Even the smallest insects have some definite purpose behind every activity that they perform. William Mcdougall believed that every human activity is purposive, and this purpose he explained on the basis of instinct. According to Mcdougall there are 14 instincts in man which lead man into activity in order to fulfil their various purposes. The absence of these instincts would render his entire mental and physical structure useless. According to the educational psychologists, every little human activity is generated by this hormic power. It has much significance for education. The sensible teacher always establishes some connection between some or the other instinct and what he is teaching. In this manner it becomes purposive and the child shows much more enthusiasm in acquiring it. Many psychological studies have proved that when a person is aware of the results of his activity he functions better than when he is unaware of the result because knowledge of it always keeps in his mind an awareness of the purpose being fulfilled by his activity. An activity lacking purpose can never be performed as well as an activity that has a definite and known purpose. The interest and attention of an individual are always fully engaged when his work has some purpose in it, so that learning becomes considerably easier. Modern educational psychologists are of the opinion that education cannot be foisted upon the child. Before a child is taught something he should be acquainted with the purpose to be filled by it. Once this is done half the teacher's battle is won because once the child sees his benefit in the world he will exert himself to his maximum capacity. The children that choose to abscond from school or abstain from study usually find no real purpose in study or they find a stronger purpose in some alternative activity. In this situation nothing is achieved by lecturing to the child or student. The needful can be done only if teaching or learning, from the student's point of view, is made more directly and individually fruitful and purposive. Once this is achieved nothing will deter him from studying, may be not even hunger and thirst, and he will soon be a master of his subject.

3. Cohesion: The third power that a child receives from his heredity is the power of cohesion that lends order, coherence and system to his thoughts and impressions. Systematic thinking is indispensable for solving various problems. The power of cohesion helps to systematize and classify the various impressions received by the human mind. A simple analogy will make the fact clear. All letters and other instruments of postal communication that come in are sorted out at the post-office and classified into the various stations for which they are intended so that they can be easily despatched there. In the same manner every new impression that falls on the mind does not fall haphazardly on the brain but is put in its own class with all its predecessors. This relationship between thoughts can be based on many elements. Thoughts are correlated on the basis of such factors as similarity, nearness, contradiction, etc. Thoughts cannot be systematized if they are not related and unless they are systematic they cannot be properly.used when required as they cannot be reached in time. Just as proper and systematic placing of objects in the house, shop or office makes it possible for them to be reached expeditiously when required., in the same manner thoughts can be systematically categorised regarding their mutual relationship to be available when needed.

The sensible teacher can utilize his knowledge of the power cohesion by making each new thing that he teaches coherent into all that has gone before so that it loses its lack of familiarity. In order that some fact be remembered and recalled at the correct opportunity, it is necessary that it should be correlated with the previously acquired knowledge present in the mind. This relation between ideas is further made possible by the factors in association of ideas. One commonly finds that when a fact is recalled many things related to it are also recalled with the result that often one is confronted by a veritable cavalcade of images running before the mind's eye. Students who are well prepared in their subjects have this experience when they sit in the examination hall. The tendency to create a mutual relation between all thoughts and impressions that make their way into the brain is an innate tendency but its successful utilization lies with the teacher and the student. Any fact that is not in some manner or other related to the existing facts in the mind is soon lost. Hence the systematization of impressions and thoughts is essential both from the teacher's and the learner's viewpoint, and for this the innate power of cohesion can be utilized.

It is evident from the above exposition that the child enters the world equipped with some definite inherited powers. The object of education is to create an atmosphere in which the proper development of his powers can be achieved with a view to the child's proper development. But there is nothing to limit the development of these powers to educational institutions. Taken in the widest sense, the child is always learning something whatever it may be. His environment, be it the school, home, the neighbourhood, always helps in the development of the mental powers that he has inherited. It is, of course, true that in educational institutions the environment is properly controlled so that the influence is always the desirable intended one. Whatever the child turns out to be in later life is the outcome of the action and reaction between his inherited faculties and powers and his environment

HEREDITY

Heredity involves all those physiological and psychological peculiarities which a person inherits from his parents. These peculiarities are transmitted to us through the gene. In this way, the children of white parents are fair while those of dark parents are generally dark. Negro children exhibit all physiological peculiarities of their Negro parents. If one of the parents is fair while the other is dark, the child may be either fair or dark coinplexioned. It is heredity which determines the structure and colour of the skin, the colour of the hair, structure, height, facial features, nasal index, cephalic index, etc.

How does heredity work?

Before there was any scientific investigation, it was believed that the effect of heredity arises from the mixing of the bloods of parents. But nearly one hundred years ago, a priest Mendal proved the fallacy of this theory by his experiments on the seeds of peas. Mendal's experiments and the investigations of other scientists proved that the affect of heredity is transferred from one generation to the next through the gene. By the intercourse between male and female, the sperm cell of the male meets the egg cell of the female and the child is conceived. These cells are made of protoplasms, and they have chromosomes in their nucleus. There are genes inside these chromosomes. The heredity of the child works from these genes determining his physiological and some psychological peculiarities. In human beings every physiological trait has a definite gene corresponding to it. This gene is never found in other because both the parents contribute one gene each. Thus the person gets a pair of gene from his parents for every physiological trait. This is heredity. If these two genes are similar the child inherits that quality, but if the two are dissimilar it is the dominant of the two genes which gives it qualities to the child. Take an example. If both mother and father are not fair, and their genes are of a fair colour, the children too will be, in all probability, fair. If the gene of one of the parents is fair while that of the other is dark, the colour that the child will inherit will come from the more prominent of the two, though it is not inevitable that the child will be fair if the parents are both fair. The real importance is that of the genes. If the child of fair parents is dark, it means that one of the two was carrying dark gene from its previous generations which became dominant at that time. Sometimes one gene lies dormant for generations but flares up or becomes extremely active in one generation. Sometimes there is a change in the power of transmission of the gene. This mutation causes a sudden change in the gene. No one gene can, however, produce some physiological sign by staying away from the other genes. In reality different genes create a condition in which all the physiological traits are determined for the child.

Controversy between heredity and environment

Scholars are not unanimous about the relation between heredity and environment. Some psychologists opine that all physiological and psychological characteristics of the individual find their determinant in heredity. Galton, the eminent author of *Hereditary Genius*, says that genius is an innate quality immune to the environment. On the other, some psychologists think that environment alone is responsible for moulding the character of a person saying that heredity does not in any way effect the individual. Dr. Watson said, "Give me a child and I will make him anything." Thus the supporters of heredity and those of environment theories have been engaged in an extreme controversy.

Relation between heredity and environment

In reality, both heredity and environment share the importance. MacIver and Page have said very correctly, "Every phenomena of life is the product of both. Each determines the character of the individual. Neither can ever be eliminated nor can ever be isolated." Experiments relating to heredity have proved that it is not the sole factor which determines development of the personality of human beings. And similarly, experiments conducted in the field of environment also indicate that it is not the only factor influencing personality. In Altenberg's words, "Each trait requires both heredity and environment for its development."

Heredity and environment are complementary

Actually, heredity and environment are the two aspects of the same element. Davis writes, and very correctly, "Terms like heredity on 'environment' do not refer to anything tangible but to an abstraction." In relation to human development, heredity cannot be imagined apart from environment and neither can environment be imagined apart from heredity. Lysenco has taken an example from nature to explain it. Only wheat will sprout from seed of wheat and the same applies to mustard. But when the farmer decides to sow wheat he has in mind all those things which he needs to make that seed sprout and the extent to which he can lay his hands to them. Obviously, the sprouting of the wheat seed and its development depends on both environment and heredity. David Abrahamson wrote, "What the individual can do is decided by heredity and what he does is determined by the environment." The energies of the individual are in the heredity but it is up to the environment to extract these energies. Lumely has beautifully described this relation between heredity and environment. He wrote, "It is not heredity or environment, but heredity and environment."

Effect of heredity on physiological appearance

To study the effects of heredity on physical appearance, children of many varied races were compared with their parents. From these experiments it was concluded that it is heredity which determines physical appearance. But other scientists pointed out that the effects of food and environment are by no means negligible. Franz Boaz collected examples in which Japanese and Jews residing in U.S.A. had increased in height and the shapes of their heads had also changed.

Effects of heredity on intelligence

Having experimented upon Negroes and White soldiers in connection with their intelligence, Yerkes concluded that due to heredity, there is a difference of intelligence between the two. Clark experimented in New York and Los Angles and contradicted Yerkes in his conclusion that the difference in intelligence between Negroes and the Whites is insubstantial. In an imposing school in New York 10% of the selected 500 students were Negroes, equivalent numerically to the ratio of the Negro population of New York. Besides this, a 9 year old Negro girl registered an intelligence quotient of 200, twice the intelligence of a normal child. Even among the Negroes Klineberg found a disparity between those of the North and those of the South, the former being the more intelligent because of better developed education and environment. Then again, scientists have pointed out that the Negroes are always at a disadvantage in these tests designed specifically for the Whites. Intelligence tests developed for one group do not suit other groups.

J. Mackeen Cattell, in his book *Amerian Men of Science* wrote that if the generations of 885 American Scientists are studied it is seen that 1/5th of them come from the tradespeople, another 1/5th from the agriculturists, notwithstanding the fact that the agriculturists comprise 40% of the population while the handful of tradespeople represent only 3% of the population. From this study, attempts have been made to prove that due to the effects of heredity, some specific groups or classes show a greater propensity or ability for trade than those belonging to other groups. But Cooley, in his essay *Genius, Fame and Comparison of Races* disproved this opinion by recounting the examples of 71 scientists of Europe.

Importance of heredity for personality

It is indisputable that heredity determines the difference of sex and it is on this basis that some scientists contend that heredity determines personality because it is the difference of sex which determines the personality of men and women. People, in general, believe in a fundamental difference in the personality of men and women due to the difference in sex. Thus the qualities of patience and emotion are attributed to a woman and she is called the very picture of love and affection. It is generally believed that their main function is to give birth, to look after their offspring and to work in the house. Every literature holds such typical thoughts that woman is like a creeper which lives entwined about man. Her personality is considerably influenced by man's personality. On the other hand, man by nature is hard, persistent, intelligent, independent and self-supporter. While women take an interest in art and literature, men take an interest in science, mathematics and war and other difficult works.

Effect of sex difference

The popular thought, which attributes difference in the personalities of male and female to the difference in sex is not borne out by facts. One can find among women those who are dangerous criminals, fighters, scientists, mathematicians, politicians. History contains evidence to show that when occasion arose the women did not lag-behind the men in any field. Some famous examples such as Joan of Arc, Madame Curie, Rani Lakshmi Bai, etc. support this view. To some extent it is possible to assert that fundamental difference in the personality of man and woman is not due to the difference in sex. This can be proved by conducting experiments in controlled environments. But most of information collected on this subject comes from the researches of the anthropologists and it has been proved that in varied cultures men and women develop varying personalities and the differences in sex plays very insignificant role. The famous anthropologist, Margaret Mead studied the cultures of Arapesh, Mundugumor and Jhambuli, three native tribes of New Guinea. In the Arapesh tribe no difference in the personality of males and females was discernible, both being equally co-operative and efficient. Men and women in the Mundugumor tribe were equally ruthless and aggressive. In the Jhambuli tribe there was an unmistakable difference between the two. Margaret Mead concluded from this that the development in personality depends upon the culture, not excluding the effect which sex has on the personality of an individual. It is universally accepted that the physiological structure, too, has a significant effect upon personality. The physical energies of man and woman are not the same. When compared to man the average weight and height of a woman is less. Her body is naturally adapted to reproduction and the care of her offspring. Her body is more delicate than that of man and due to the physiological difference caused by the difference in sex, they occupy different places in society and consequently the difference in their personality is quite natural. The extent of difference in the personality of individuals, however, varies with the variation in culture. Thus the extent to which difference in sex affects personality is governed both by heredity and environment. Landis and Landis correctly said, "Heredity explains man the animal environment man the human being."

Temperament

Besides difference in sex, difference in temperament is also an important part of personality. The nature of an individual depends very much on the environment. Temperaments develop according to the environment in which the child grows. Thus the difference in environment affects temperament. Family relations, society, circle of friendship and working conditions all have an effect upon the temperament of an individual. In poverty, temperament becomes hard, irritable, overbearing, etc. Even though it may not be accepted as a rule, no man of experience will deny that the financial status, occupation, nature of life partner and living conditions all have a profound effect on temperament and all these collectively constitute the environment. But the effect of heredity on temperament is more profound than the effect of environment. Temperament depends, to a large extent, upon internal drives which are deeply affected by endocrine glands. In modern times, extensive research has been carried out to find out the effect of endocrine glands on temperament and some scientists have gone to the extent of saying that glands determine personality. People have been classified on the basis of the effect of glands. Scientific discoveries have proved beyond dispute that the effects on temperament once attributed to the environment are actually the effects of glands. The change which occurs in the temperament of boys and girls caused by the increased activity of the sex glands with the coming of youth is inevitable. Besides as the secretion of the thyroid increases, an individual becomes restless and active and if it decreases he becomes slow and lazy. If the parathyroid secretes more a person remains calm but he becomes excited with every fall in the secretion. Research on the effects of the glands located in various parts of the body is m progress. Attempts have been made to bring about artificial increase or decrease in the grandular secretions. Undoubtedly, many ways of improving human personality wall be evolved but to conclude from this, that temperament is determined by glandular secretions or that heredity determines everything in the subject, would be completely one-sided. These secretions have tremendous but unperceived effect. A big change in these secretions is effected by cultural and social environments. For example, the mental disturbance through which adolescents in our civilization pass when they attain youth is absent in many tribes because in those tribes there are no restrictions upon sex relations. Obviously, the change is not exclusively due to the activity of sex glands, but it is also due to social customs. Heredity then does not mould the personality. The above description of the effects of heredity on personality can be beautifully summed up in the words of Biesanz and Biesanz, "Personality is the organization of a person's habits, attitudes and traits and arises from the interplay of biological, social and cultural factors."

The above exposition of the effects of heredity upon physical appearance, intelligence and personality makes it quite obvious that its effects are not similar and equal in all cases. We know from experience that heredity has its most pronounced effect upon physical appearance, somewhat less on intelligence and least of all upon personality. This conclusion is supported by scientific researches.

Effect of environment

Environment has a very significant effect on man. Its effect starts from his birth and continues almost till his very death. The status of the child, youth and old man in the family and society is not the same and as a result of this difference a man's personality, roles, temperaments, ways of thinking, tendencies, inclinations and character is affected. In the same way, the status of the person in places like school, office, occupation, etc., effects his role to a great extent.

Environment can be roughly divided into two parts: Controlled and Uncontrolled environment and Social and Geographical environment. In both the social and geographical environment of man, a part of them is controlled and the other part is not controlled. Both these types of social and geographical environments have a profound effect upon the individual.

The various elements of society like the family, school, occupation, social customs, primitive concepts all affect the individual. In this context one example from family life will suffice. In the opinion of the famous psychoanalyst Sigmund Freud the personality of a person is fashioned in the first seven years, the rest of the life being an expression of those tendencies. Whether all thinkers agree with Freud's opinion or not, all have agreed with regard to the effect of the environment on the family upon the character, nature, mental tendencies, habits, behaviour of the individual, and there are enough existing causes which justify our denial of the full knowledge of the effects of the family upon the individual. This special knowledge can be gained by comparing children brought upon in families and those bread in Government institutions. Havelock Ellis in his *The Problem of Race Regeneration*, says, "The advantages of a mother suckling her baby are more than merely physical, is a stimulus to her affection for her child and a guarantee that the child will receive in other respects the loving care it needs." In childhood parental love affects the stability of the emotions for the child. It is inevitable that excessive love and care spoils the children and lack of affection leaves their feelings undeveloped, which are then unnaturally expressed. The famous psychologist Alfred Adler said that even the birth order of the child in the family effects his personality. This may be expressed or clarified better thus: in the family mother, father, husband, wife, elder brother, sister, younger brother, elder sister, younger sister, beloved child, unwanted offspring all have their respective, dissimilar status which effects their personality.

What is heredity? It is, in a mixture seed form all that a child receives from his parents. The child is born by the combining of two genes of the mother and father. But this seed does not sprout similarly under all conditions. The farmer ploughs the field and sows the seed in it. The seed which lands on the stone does not sprout while the one which lands on the bard land does so with difficulty. The seed away from water sprouts but does not grow because it dries up due to lack of water. If the farmer fails to look after the crops, wild animals and birds would destroy it. The absence of fertilizers would restrict the proper growth of plants. Thus, the mere planting of wheat will not allow one to reap it. It is essential that the crop be given manure, water, etc., at the proper time and it be protected from animals.

The same principle holds true with human beings. Admitted that the child is born with many physiological and mental qualities in a seed form but do these qualities develop similarly under any and all conditions? Two twin children have identical heredity, but W.E. Blatz in his book *Collected Studies on the Dionne Quintuplets* proved very clearly that even identical twins develop differences. Newman, Freeman and Holzinger bred 19 identical twins in dissimilar environments and the studies revealed very slight physiological difference but very marked differences in the peculiarities of personality. Obviously, change in environment changes the effect of heredity. Thus even if the most intelligent child is placed in a bad environment, the growth and development of his genius will become limited and on the other hand, the qualities of average child can be developed to their maximum by placing him in good and helpful environment.

But does this mean that the seed has no importance? Can the mere change in environment make anybody just anything? If a seed of cactus is sown mangoes cannot be had. Environment develops the qualities received from heredity but only to some extent.

In brief, it can be said that heredity is a seed, the environment are conditions for its development. The development of inherited qualities will be according to the environment.

Thus both heredity and environment are important for the education of the child. Both must be improved to realise all round development of personality. While the family provides the heredity the school may provide such environment and may help in maximum utilization of the heredity traits.

QUESTIONS FOR EXERCISE

1. Write a short note on—Influence of Heredity.
2. "An individual at any stage of his development is product of organic and environmental factors working hand in hand." Explain and discuss.
3. "Heredity and environment are co-relative factors." Discuss with special reference to their relative influence in the educational attainment of children.
4. Write short note on Heredity and Environment.

5

Response Mechanism

The knowledge of the nervous system and glands is very much valuable to a teacher. The main points in this connection are as follows:

1. It helps the teacher in the understanding of the diseases of nervous system and glands. Examples of the diseases of the nervous chorea, stammering, stuttaring, hysteria, epilepsy, word deafness and word blindness. These diseases very much hinder the development of the child's personality. Hence efforts must be made to diminish their influence and to curb them. Excess or deficiency in glandular secretions also influences personality.
2. It helps the teacher in the understanding of the physiological basis of the child's development.
3. It helps the teacher in the understanding of the individual differences among children.
4. It helps the teacher in understanding the process of attainment of knowledge and learning, by knowing which he can make desirable changes.
5. It helps the teacher in having correct expectations from the children and in understanding limits of their attainments.
6. It helps the teacher in predicting the course of future development of the children.
7. It helps the teacher in devising suitable teaching methods for particular children.

In fact, the purpose of education cannot be achieved if the nervous system and glands of a child are excessively defective. Thus, a knowledge of these is very much essential for the teacher.

Response Mechanism is that system which helps the organism to adjust itself to the environment and controls its activities. Thus it is due to response mechanism that one finds selection, adjustment, combination, etc , in human behaviour. The response mechanism in animals is divided into the following parts:

1. Receptors: Eye, nose, ear, tongue and skin, etc., are receptors. They receive the sensation. Human behaviour begins through the receptors. It is only after the receptors have received the sensation that the response in the organism begins.

2. Effectors: Effectors include muscles and glands. They make the actual response possible.

3. Nervous system: Nervous system controls the response. It joins the receptors and motor organs.

Human organism is affected by the environment. The sun heat, cold, etc., affect our body. The body responds to external stimuli. This response changes the external environment. When something pinches, the pinched one feels a sensation. The sensation is received by the nervous system through which the receptors and motor organs are connected and the muscles of the hand react immediately so that the pinching object is removed. Thus the receptors receive stimuli from the environment and the motor organs change the environment by response. The human organism has innumerable receptor-cells. In the eye alone there are lakhs of cells. Similarly, the receptor organs *e.g.*, muscles, etc., have innumerable muscle-fibres. The nerves connect the receptors and the muscles and thus make responses possible. These nerves carry the message from the receptors to the muscles. This communication has a speed of 75 Yds. a second. This response takes a very small portion of a second. In times of emergency it becomes even more rapid.

NERVOUS SYSTEM

Nerve is the most important part of response mechanism. It joins the receptors and the effectors. The Nervous sytem is divided into two parts: (1) Central nervous system, and (2) Autonomic nervous system. In the Human organism there is a whole network of nerves and this network presents the structure of the nervous system.

Central nervous system

The Central nervous system is an important part of the response mechanism. The Central nervous system is divided into two parts: (1) The Spinal cord, and (2) The Brain.

The spinal cord is situated in the backbone. It is a white matter having a form as that of a rope. Its upper part is made of white matter while the inner part is that of grey matter. The spinal cord has two types of nerves: (1) Sensory or afferent, and (2) Motor or efferent. These nerves join the receptor and the motor organ. The sensory nerves carry the muscles from the receptor to the centre of the nervous system. The motor nerves carry the message from the nervous system to the muscles. This coming and going of the messages is through the grey matter of the spinal cord. The grey matter forms 50% of the spinal cord and the rest is covered by the white matter. The path-ways of spinal cord are situated just beneath the skin. Its middle part has cell-bodies and the nerve path-ways are in its peripheral portion. In the white matter there are tracts upside and downside. In the grey matter there are associative nerves.

The spinal cord controls the reflex action. In the reflex action the sensory nerves carry the sensation to the brain and from the brain the motor nerves carry the message to the muscles. This reaction is so rapid that it takes almost no time. Besides controlling the reflex action, the spinal cord also joins the external organs with the brain. In it 31 pairs of nerves come from outside. Every pair has a sensory and a motor nerve. These nerves join the spinal cord with the external parts of the body. Thus the external parts *viz.* hands, feet, etc., are governed by the spinal cord. It controls all the learned activities like writing, reading, cycling, typing, walking, running and talking, etc. The brain has not to interfere in all these activities.

Brain

Besides the spinal cord, there is yet another important part of the central nervous system called the brain. The brain is divided into the following three parts:

(1) Cerebrum, (2) Cerebellum, and (3) Mid-brain or Medulla Oblongata or Brain Stem.

1. Cerebrum: The cerebrum is bigger than the cerebellum or brain stem. Hence it is known as cerebrum or big brain. It is extended from the eye-brows up to the centre of the skull. Thus it is the foremost part of the skull. It is also the driest part of the brain. In it the arrangement of the white and the grey matter is opposite to that of the spinal cord. Its upper part is made up of grey matter while the inner is made of white matter. As it has been said earlier, in the spinal cord the upper part is made of white matter while the inner part is made of grey matter. The upper part of grey matter in the cerebrum is known as the cortex. Near it there are groups of nerve cells which form the sensory area and motor area of the brain. The white matter forms the nerve-fibres. The grey matter forms the nerve cells.

In cerebrum there are two hemispheres, separated by a fissure. These hemispheres are called the right hemisphere and the left hemisphere. The right hemisphere is mostly connected with the left part of the body. The left hemisphere is mostly connected with the right part of it. Thus there is a cross relation between the hemispheres of the cerebrum and the parts of the body. On the surface of the cerebrum there are small convolutions or gyres. These convolutions are separated by fissures. These fissures are deep in the matter of the cerebrum. But they do not divide the brain, because under the surface its various parts are linked with each other. There is a fissure in the centre of cerebrum which is known as the central sulcus. It is also called fissure of Rolando. Besides this there is a fissure in the cerebrum vertically. It is called the fissure of Silvius of Lateral Sulcus.

The big parts of the cerebrum are known as lobes. The lobes are interconnected. The cerebrum is divided into four lobes. These lobes are as follows:

1. *Frontal Lobe:* Frontal lobe is extended from the fissure of lateral sulcus to the fissure of central sulcus.

2. *Parietal Lobe:* Parietal lobe is extended from the fissure of central sulcus to the hind part of the head.
3. *Occipital Lobe:* This Lobe is in the hind part of the head.
4. *Temporal Lobe:* Temporal lobe is the portion beneath the brain.

These lobes of the brain are linked by sensory projection fibres. These fibres enter from one lobe to another.

Functional areas: The different lobes of the cerebrum are connected with different types of sensation. The front lobe is concerned with thinking. The complex thinking is mostly in the frontal lobe of the cerebrum. In the central part of cerebrum on one side of the lateral sulcus is the motor area. This is situated somewhat farther than the central sulcus and in the frontal lobe. Besides the fissure of the central sulcus and in the parietal lobe, there is somaesthetic area. This is the area where sensations from skin and muscles are received. In the upper part of the temporal lobe there is auditory area. This is the area where the sensations of hearing are received. In the hind part of the brain is the occipital lobe. Here is the visual area, *i.e.*, the area where the visual sensations are received. Near the lateral sulcus are the areas of taste and smell. A survey of these different areas will also be helpful to understand them fully well.

1. *Motor area:* This is the pre-central gyrus. The pre-central gyrus is a part of the cortex, just in front of the central sulcus. This part is known as motor area, due to the following reasons:

(*a*) A shock to any part of its area results into paralysis of some part of the body.

(*b*) Application of electric current to any part of this area results in the movement in different organs of the body.

Hence, this part can be rightly called motor area. But this part does not govern the motor activities of the body. A cortex which is in front of this area also takes apart in the movements of the different parts of the body. This part is known as pre-motor area. The motor area governs the single movement while the pre-motor area governs the complexes of movements.

2. *Sensory areas of the cortex:* This is concerned with the lower part of those sensory organs which are situated near one another at the upper end of the cerebellum. The nerve-fibres from the eyes, ears and other sense organs meet at this place. The relay fibres also go to meet sense organs from here. It is through this area that the sense organs are related with the cortex.

3. *Somaesthetic area:* This is also called central gyrus. It is just behind the motor area. It is here that here is the main cortical centre for sensation from the skin and muscles. A shock in this region destroys sensitiveness of the skin and muscles.

4. *Auditory area:* The auditory area in the brain is situated in a small part of the temporal lobe. It is here that the sensations from the ears are received. The relay fibres reach the ears from here. A shock in this region results in the destruction of the capacity of hearing.

5. ***Visual area:*** The visual area is situated in a part of the occipital lobe. It is here that the sensory fibres from retina are received. The fibres to the eyes also go from here.

Associative areas: The associative areas are those parts of the cortex which would be included in the motor area. The associative areas appear to be divided into two big parts. One association area is situated in occipital, temporal and parietal lobe between several motor areas. Another association area is situated in the motor area and cerebrum in the front part. The association areas are separated by the association fibres. If these fibres are damaged some sensitive part of the brain is also damaged, *e.g.*, with the destruction of the association fibres of the cortex everything learned is forgotten. With the destruction of the area near the motor cortex, the capacity of speaking and writing is destroyed. With the destruction of the visual area, it becomes impossible to understand language and the man cannot understand words even while seeing them. Some severe damage to the areas of the front part of the brain results in forgetting of something immediately learned, though one can remember something of childhood.

2. **Mid Brain:** The second part of the brain is of the brain stem or medulla oblongata. It is through this part that sensations sent to the spinal cord reach the brain and the responses from the brain reach the lower part of the spinal cord. The work of the spinal cord has already been described earlier.

3. **Cerebellum:** The cerebellum is the third part of the brain. It is situated in the portion behind cerebrum. It is divided in the two lobes. Inside these lobes there are white nerve fibres which are covered by a thin layer of the grey cells. There are some fissures in this part which are deeper than those of the cerebrum. The cerebrum controls the Kinaesthetic movements and co-ordinates the muscular activities.

AUTONOMIC NERVOUS SYSTEM

Autonomic nervous system is an important part of the nervous system in the human organism. It is known as autonomic nervous system, because it is independent of the central nervous system in its action. There is no interference in its activities from the central nervous system. For example, in the emotional state there are many changes in the body which are governed by autonomic nervous system and in which the central nervous system takes no part. But this does not mean that the autonomic nervous system has no relation with the central nervous system. As a matter of fact the spinal cord which is the important part of the central nervous system has also an important role in the autonomic nervous system. Hence, it can be said to be autonomous only in the sense that it controls and governs all those activities in which the brain has nothing to do. The activities of this system cannot be checked even with efforts. It goes on acting independently.

The main function of the autonomic nervous system is the adjustment between the activities of the different parts of the body. Many of its nerves beginning from the brain and the spinal cord reach the stomach and nerves carrying blood. These nerves control the activities of the internal and external muscles. It is the autonomic nervous system which controls the activity of the glands, the stomach and the blood vessels. It is this system which controls the activity of the different parts of the body, *e.g.*, lungs, heart, liver, spleen, rectum, sweat glands, etc. Thus as a matter of fact, this is a motor nervous system. Many of the ganglia of its nerves, cells and also the synapses are situated outside the central nervous system and the central nervous system takes no part in their activities.

The left part of the autonomic nervous system is divided into three parts as follows:

(1) Cranial, (2) Thoraco Lumber, and (3) Sacrel. The Thoraco lumber is the part from the brain stem to Sacrel. The reason to call it thoraco lumber is that the nerves of this part reach the thorax, beginning from the spinal-cord Below thoraco-lumber and in the lower part of the spinal cord, is the sacrel.

The autonomic nerves and the different parts of the body are connected with the spinal cord. Thus the autonomtic nerves are extended up to eyes, salivary glands, mucous membrane, blood vessels, heart, liver, stomach, pancreas, intestines, adrenals, kidneys, bladder, colon, rectum and genital area. Besides these are also extended up to sweat glands and cutaneous vessels. The ganglia and spinal cord are lined by those nerve fibres which reach the ganglia from the spinal cord. In a ganglia there are 22 sympathetic ganglion. The sympathetic ganglion are on the upper surface of the white matter, known as myline. The axon fibres beginning from the ganglia return again to the nerves of the spinal cord.

The autonomic nervous system is divided into two parts: (1) Sympathetic nervous system, and (2) Para-sympathetic nervous system. The activities of both parts are opposite to each other.

1. Sympathetic nervous system: The sympathetic nervous system prepares the body for emergency. It saves the body in the time of emergency. It also works in emotional states. Due to its activity the retina of the eye acts at the time of emergency and the blood vessels of the stomach send more blood to the stomach. As a result of this the digestion stops and so also hunger. The muscles and the brain begin to work rapidly as the intestines stop working and the gastric glands stop giving secretions. The heart beats with a speed since it has to pump blood rapidly. The adrenal glands execrate adrenalin. As a result of adrenalin the blood sugar is increased in the blood resulting into increase of strength in man. Excitement results in the destruction of many cells and the rate of respiration is increased. The water metabolism drops down resulting in dryness in throat and mouth. All these activities can be seen at the time of quarrel or fighting, anger or fear. In the emotional state, the galvanic response capacity also becomes less.

2. Parasympathetic nervous system: Another part of autonomic nerves is para-sympathetic nervous system. It is the link with cranial and sacrel. The main work of para-sympathetic system is anabolism. If includes the concentration of the energy of the body and strengthening of the different parts of the body by this concentration. As the activity of the sympathetic nervous system decreases the speed of the heart beat is lessened and the blood pressure also becomes less. The activity of the salivary glands increases which helps in digestion, resulting in increase in the weight of the body. The pupils of the eyes contract resulting into relaxation of the eyes. The para-sympathetic nervous system controls the activity of the sacrel division. It keeps the bladder, the colon and the rectum healthy and helps in excreting the different kinds of useless and poisonous matter from the body.

The sympathetic and the para-sympathetic nervous system differ from each other as below:

1. In the sympathetic nervous system the ganglion are in the spinal cord near those internal organs of the body, which they excite. But in the para-sympathetic nervous system the gangalion are not in the spinal cord but near bodily organs.
2. In the sympathetic nervous system the whole system works together, but in the para-sympathetic nervous system the different parts are independent.

But this does not mean that the sympathetic and the para-sympathetic nervous systems are absolutely opposite to each other and they are not related. As a matter of fact, they co-operate in spite of these distinctions According to Morgan these systems do not work independent of each other, but co-operate in different proportion according to different situations, *e.g.*, if the organism has to struggle with the environment, the sympathetic system works more and the para-sympathetic system is less active. In the adjustment with environment the para-sympathetic system has to work more while the sympathetic system works less. Thus due to the co-operation of the sympathetic and para-sympathetic systems, there is a balance in the body in both the states of work and rest.

QUESTION FOR EXERCISE

1. How is the knowledge of Response Mechanism useful to the teacher?

6

Instincts and their Transformation

Psychologists do not agree on the subject of instincts. Adam Smith, in his treatise *Sympathetic Basis of Human Activities* has accepted an instinct called sympathy as the basis of all human behaviour The sociologist Trotter, in his exposition *Instinct of the Herd in Peace and War* believes all human behaviour to be based on the instinct of the herd Sigmund Freud, the founder of the school of psychoanalysis, claims the sex urge to be the source of most of the human endeavours. Later on, Freud mentioned the instincts of self-preservation and death. James has enumerated 32 instincts. Thorndike mentioned more than 100 instincts to start with, but then tried to limit them to 40. L.L. Bernard, in his book *A Study in Social Psychology* counted 110 instincts.

McDOUGALS'S THEORY OF INSTINCTS

The most famous and scientific theory about instincts, however, is that of William McDougall. Defining instinct, McDougali calls it "an inherited or innate psycho-physical disposition which determines its possessor to perceive, and to pay attention to, objects of a certain class, to experience an emotional excitement of a particular quality upon perceiving such an object, and to act in regard to it in a particular manner, or at least, to experience an impulse to such an action."[1] As has been pointed out in the above definition, instinctive behaviour tends to concentrate a person's attention on some particular class of objects. There are, therefore, three stages in instinctive action: Cognitive, Affective and Conative. With every instinct a particular emotional excitement is felt. To quote McDougall, "We seem justified in believing that each kind of instinctive behaviour is always attended by some such emotional excitement,

1. Wm. McDougall, *An Outline of Psychology*, p. 110

however faint, which in each case is specific or peculiar to that kind of behaviour."[1] The following are the instincts and the related emotions:

MAJOR INSTINCTS

	Instinct	*Emotion*
1.	Escape	Fear
2.	Repulsion	Disgust
3.	Curiosity	Wonder
4.	Pugnacity	Anger
5.	Self-Assertion	Positive self-feeling
6.	Self-Abasement	Subjection
7.	Parental	Tender Emotion

Besides the above mentioned major instincts, McDougall mentioned some more of them in which the related emotional feeling is not quite as obvious. They are as follows:

MINOR INSTINCTS

8.	Gregariousness	Loneliness
9.	Acquisitiveness	Feeling of Ownership
10.	Constructiveness	Feeling of Creativeness
11.	Food seeking	Appetite
12.	Sex	Lust
13.	Appeal	Distress
14.	Laughter	Amusement

With the exception of laughter, all the above mentioned instincts are found equally in human beings and animals. Among them, the acquired motives such as self-assertion, self-abasement, parental and gregariousness are not universal. Sex, escape, curiosity and laughter etc., are practically universal and innate. Food seeking instinct is found in all animals because all of them seek food. Similarly, the constructive instinct is found in man as well as in animals. To acquisitiveness, the quality of universality cannot be attributed, though it is found in quite a number of living beings. Calling for help in times of danger and seeking help has its own biological importance and is a tendency possessed by most of the animals. As a result of this the members of the society or the family come to the assistance of the victim. The tendency to avoid an undesired and detested object and to have a repulsion for it, is obvious in almost all the animals.

Criticism of McDougall's theory

Although McDougall's theory of instincts was welcomed very enthusiastically, it also gave rise to a lot of severe criticism. J.R. Kantor, a contemporary

1. Wm. McDougall, *An Introduction to Social Psychology*, pp. 25-28.

of McDougall went to the extent of saying that "Nothing worse than McDougall's conception of instincts has ever been conceived in the field of psychology."[1] But the theory of instincts cannot be refuted with such ease. To arrive at any conclusion it is necessary to study the experiments in this field, from McDougall's times to the present day. Psychology being the science of behaviour, the theory of instincts can be accepted only if it helps in some way, to explain the behaviour of living beings meaning thereby that they help to show some specific innate, internal organisation to be the cause of some behaviour. The following are the main objections against McDougall's theory of instincts:

1. McDougall has himself accepted that experience does make very substantial alterations in the instincts. The environment and conditions cause a big change in the behaviour of animals and human beings.

2. McDaugall did, of course, formulate the definition of instinct but he did not point out that at which level the instinct may be seen in its purest and unaltered form in accordance with the definition. Neither he took the trouble of giving a detailed description of the conditions which may arouse an instinct and nor did he make any mention of the related emotions and their physiological and mental signs.

3. McDougall has given a general description of the stimulating conditions for instincts and the corresponding emotions but no such general description can be of help in the understanding of the working of instinct in living beings because the different types of animals differ in respect of their physiological structure and nervous systems. A different description of each class of animals will have to be made if this purpose is to be fulfilled.

4. McDougall maintains that every instinct has a definite neurological basis. He however did not disclose what the neurological basis was, which was precisely the most important and perplexing problem. He failed to supply details of it since experiments on this basis were necessary for every class of animals. They were to be comprehensive experiments.

5. McDougall did relate different emotions to instincts and he also accepted different nervous basis for each of them but there were insufficient experimental data to support his hypothesis.

Sherman in 1927, Pratt in 1930, Irvin in 1932 and Taylor in 1934 all studied the reactions of children under controlled circumstances but they failed to prove anything thereby. Mostly people thought that there was only one central agency or energy which directed all the instincts. Freud's studies in 1925 and Burtt's in 1939 upheld this view. When the distinctions in emotional aspect could not be proved, attention was directed towards the cognitive distinctions in instincts. Every instinct has a specific internal structures which compels its possessor to observe or to play attention to a particular class of objects The same difficulty arose in the recognition of these structures because they became modified by experience or the effect of the circumstances so that it becomes difficult to distinguish between one

1. Kantor, J.R., *Principles of Psychology,* Vol. 3. Alfred A. Knopf Inc., New York, 1924.

and the other. Though McDougall did believe that the instincts had the tendency of adaptation he also gave credence to the idea that their internal patterns may vary. Some experiments revealed that some animals like the hen reacted to some specific stimuli in controlled conditions but they failed to pay attention to objects which they had been taught to pay attention to. This proved the hypothesis that there may be an internal perceptual system. But then, Lashley's experiments proved that many alterations are possible in objects which aroused certain specific excitement. These experiments were carried out in 1938. These made the distinction of instinct difficult. In 1942, in a symposium Burtt came to the conclusion that "Along with lower animals human beings have some inherited tendencies, the more obvious of which are fighting, fear and sex, and perhaps there are others more difficult to ascertain." Even when the instincts were so limited in number, G.W. Allport in a symposium in 1946 refused to accept this declaration.

Thus, though many psychologists believe the existence of instincts in human beings, they give to them an importance far less than the one accredited to acquired motives. In elucidating human behaviour more emphasis is laid on his life history or his family or social conditions than on instincts. Some psychologists seem to believe that McDougall's theory of instincts may be of greater help in understanding the behaviour in animals but it is not very helpful to understand the human behaviour.

Experiments carried out in recent past upon the subject of instincts make it clear that the theory of instincts cannot be dispensed with such consummate ease. In 1951, Tinbergen conducted many experiments in which the unacquired and innate reactions of birds and animals to special kinds of stimuli, were noted. Experiments by other psychologists indicated that there are some innate mechanisms in various animals which are directed specific stimuli. But it is possible that future experiments may show different patterns of specific behaviour in different classes of living beings which may lead to the establishment of some neurological basis. Experiments in connection with learning have thrown light upon this. Some experiments are providing proof for the specific behaviour patterns. To conclude, in its present state, nothing can be said with certainty about the theory of instincts. But one thing is definite, that enough evidence is not available to prove the theory of instincts baseless.

INSTINCTS AND EDUCATION

In modern educational psychology every possible effort is made to base the education of the child on its instincts. Modern education aims at the excitation of one or the other instinct in a child in order to make any and every kind of education, natural and normal. Various instincts in a child are useful in education in the following ways:

1. Escape: In a child one finds the instinct of escape conjoined to the emotion of fear. The intelligent teacher arouses fear and a disgust towards bad things in the child. He also tries to prevent fear and escape from acting in many unnecessary cases. Meaningless fears are thus eliminated.

2. Pugnacity: The instinct of pugnacity or combat is a universal motive. The most important fact that accelerates or excites it is restraint. A child whose means of locomotion are stopped by the simple expedient of being placed under restraint will go red in the face and cry at the top of its voice. Conflict starts the moment one removes a chick from the hen, or makes fun of an irritable individual or prevents an animal from fulfilling and satisfying its instincts. The activity of conflict starts when some motive remains dissatisfied through some external agency.

The object of animal turning pugnacious is to remove the obstacle preventing its progress or to defeat the obstacle. As long as the individual fails to defeat the obstacle or to remove it from his path, his internal, physiological and psychological disturbance continues. The pattern of pugnacity or combat is not the same in all animals or individuals nor are the implements common to all. Animals having long nails or teeth use them in warfare. In most animals it is the male who is pugnacious. He combats the animals of different species, and other males of his own species for supremacy over the females or for food. It is possible that the instinct of pugnacity is somewhat depressed by the female hormones. Human beings and some other animals are known to threaten before actually attacking. Proverbially it is the monkey who is the best showing their teeth, others, by making offensive noises while others show their ungentlemanly instincts by hanging on their chests. Forms of pugnacity are modified by age, intelligence, social and cultural influences and social behaviour. The pugnacious instinct of cultured individual finds expression in more indirect manner. His animosity continues over the years, and his vengeance is achieved in many devious and indirect ways. Litigation is only a form of conflict and it is very common in cultured societies. In fact, it is difficult to believe that pugnacity is only an instinct or an internal motive whose single object is conflict or fight. The instinct to competition may be innate but the pugnacious instinct is activated only when the fulfilment of a motive is obstructed. Anger results in conflict but sometimes anger finds expression in more devious and uncommon ways. An employee who has been severely reproved by his employer is in no position to answer him back in strong language as he goes in fear of losing his job, but as an alternative he lets off his pent up feeling of anger on his wife and children. Sometimes our pugnacious instinct is satisfied when we see others fighting. The tension of conflict is also released and relieved when one plays games or sees others playing or fighting going on the film screen. Within the family the parents prevent many of the child's instinctive actions so that he develops feelings of animosity for them. Children worry the parents so that the latter become angered. Children compete among themselves for the love of their parents. Similarly, some sort of conflict is usually found to exist between the best adjusted pair. In order to protect the household from the painful and often dangerous results of these conflicts, it is essential that harmless means of venting these tensions should be found and applied. Among children, games are the best outlet. Grown ups should be given a chance to get their pent up emotions off their chest once in a while. This is a useful expedient.

3. Repulsion: The intelligent teacher does his best to develop motive of repulsion in the child for unsavoury and undesirable things.

4. Parental instinct: To this instinct is conjoined the emotion of pity. This instinct finds its expression in the older child's love for his younger counterpart and for other living beings:

5. Sex: Sex instinct of a person may be turned into more acceptable outlets such as dancing, music, art etc., by the teacher. And, particularly in the adolescent stage this instinct can be restricted and moulded to provide the desirable development in the adolescent.

6. Curiosity: Curiosity is the most important instinct from the educational viewpoint. It is a fundamental instinct without any definite biological basis. When any living being is confronted with any new or unrecognised object, it is natural for it to desire a complete knowledge or understanding of it. Curiosity in human beings is accompanied by the sense of surprise. Almost all individuals are desirous of knowing new things and new places. When a child is handed something it has not seen before, it will immediately turn it over and explore it to the best of its ability. The child is always ready with an unending list of questions. He never tires of asking questions even if the parent tires of answering them till he is forced to rebuff the child. If the child's curiosity is not suppressed, it continues its exploration and questioning till it finally comes to know its surrounding to its own satisfaction. It is such children who turn into the best investigators and scientists when they maintain their curiosity intact in their adult circumstances.

Teachers who fail to arouse curiosity in their students regarding the subjects of study fail to achieve even a semblance of order and administration in their classes. To curiosity is conjoined the emotion of surprise. An object or thing that surprises the child also arouses curiosity in him. Hence, if a teacher is intelligent he will create surprise in the child regarding the subject he wants to reach with the result that the child will become curious. Once this is achieved more than half the battle is won, since the child starts studying on his own once his curiosity is aroused. Besides arousing the curiosity of the child, the teacher also has to turn it in the required direction. For a child to develop curiosity regarding detective novels or matters of sex may be harmful to him as well as to his normal course of studies. Hence, the teacher must see to it that the child's curiosity takes desirable paths, such as good books and subjects. Being curious about the subject, the child will find interest in its perusal. Thus, he progresses on the path of education without any external instigation. Modern psychologists are thus justified in emphasizing the fact that teachers should arouse curiosity regarding a subject they intend to teach in the class before actually engaging in teaching it.

7. Self-submission: Of course, the instinct of self-submission may prove to be a hindrance in the child's development but the sensible teacher can turn it towards himself and arouse feelings of respect for the teacher and a healthy regard for discipline in the child. Students are prone to accept teacher's mandate without questioning so that success in education becomes possible.

8. Self-assertion: The instinct of self-assertion occupies an important place in the child's character. To it is conjoined the sentiment of self-respect which helps the child steer clear of all undesirable activity and to concentrate only on the desirable one. In order to develop self-respect in the child, the teacher must put before him examples taken from the child's own environment. If instead of punishing a child for his mistake, the teacher tells them that such foolishness is not expected of him or from one of his upbringing then the child will abstain from repeating it. He will also be remorseful. Once the instinct of self-assertion is fully developed, the individual makes his own efforts to progress in life, since he does not want to live the life of insect but wants to hold his head high in society.

9. Gregariousness: A child is gregarious by instinct and he naturally wants to remain with the group of friends. A child does not desire solitude. The teacher can make the best of this instinct and help in the social development of the child. The teacher should keep an eye on the various group tensions that develop within the school and also try to evolve healthy competition, co-operation and team spirit in the children. Blind faith in small groups may be turned to more productive channels when it is turned to love of country and philanthropy. In this way, the child becomes socially mature.

10. Food seeking: The food seeking instinct may be put to much fruitful if indirect use by the teacher as he can instigate the student to greater effort in his study by inspiring him with visions of success in his future livelihood. Young men are seen to work very hard as they are afraid for their bread at a later stage. The instinct of self-assertion also contributes to this process.

11. Acquisitiveness: A child instinctively collects many odds and ends about him and takes great pleasure in doing it. It gives him a feeling of possession and pride. In their tender age children are often seen collecting stamps, match boxes, cigarette boxes and are often seen fighting to the bitter end for them. Within the bounds of the school, this innate tendency of acquisition can be put to constructive use. They can be guided to collect stamps, photographs, old coins and books, etc. But in this process it is essential to see to it that the child does not resort to undesirable methods of augmenting his collection. In the school, the child's acquisitive tendency can be adequately exploited to create a small library or a collection of odd bits, in which the child can retain possession over them and yet allow them to be used by all his colleagues. Children belonging to very rich families, particularly young children, can be inspired to develop their own libraries, laboratories, etc.

12. Constructiveness: It is due to instinct of constructiveness that the child is seen making and breaking many things. The teacher can teach the children to make many small objects of various kinds with clay, colours, wood, stones and small mechanical objects. This has the effect of inspiring children to much greater creative effort when they grow up so that they become scientists and engineers.

13. Laughter: The instinct to laughter is accompanied by the emotion of enjoyment and relief. If the children are made to laugh in class they are more inclined to accept the teacher's suggestions. Hence, the sensible teacher can get the children to perform different tasks by arousing laughter and enjoyment.

TRANSFORMATION OF INSTINCTS

Earlier in this chapter, after instincts have been described, it is mentioned that instincts can be changed or transformed. And from an account of the possibilities implicit in the transformation of instincts it is obvious that the teacher can do much in this direction. Psychologists have established and proved beyond doubt that the instincts with which an individual is born cannot be removed or eliminated out of his system. Hence, it is entirely futile to try to put an end to such instincts as curiosity, sex. constructiveness, etc. in human beings at the same time, it is not expeditious to leave them in their animal and unrefined state to find their own mode of expression and satisfaction. In every society, certain customs and patterns of approved behaviour become obstruction to the fulfilment of the individual's instincts. Hence, transformation and sublimation of instincts becomes something of a necessity, otherwise it is not possible to achieve adjustment between society and individual. Many and varied are the methods that are observed in this connection.

1. Law of hedonic selection: According to the law of hedonic selection human being, by his very nature, selects objects and activeness that are pleasurable, and avoids unpleasant and painful objects and activities. Hence, heeding this natural principle, teachers award the desirable instinct-motivated behaviour of children and punish other instinctive behaviour that is not desirable. But according to educational psychologists, this method being negative, is harmful for the child's development, and it should not be employed as far as possible.

2. Law of inhibition: Believers of this law contend that if the instinct does not get a chance to find expression, it is destroyed. It will gradually cease to exist. The psychologist William James used to believe this law.

MEANS OF TRANSFORMING INSTINCTS

Modern educational psychologists are not inclined to grant complete and unqualified approval to either of the two above laws concerning instincts. Many different studies and experiments have served to create the conviction that no one instinct can be completely destroyed. In the case of people who try to suppress these instincts, they find new outlets and satisfy themselves in various unusual and patently abnormal ways. Hence, the transformation of instincts is attempted through the medium of the process of education. Generally speaking, the following five methods are adopted for the transformation and variation of instincts in human behaviour:

1. Through repression
2. Through inhibition
3. Through contradiction
4. Through redirection
5. Through sublimation.

Detailed consideration upon these various methods of transformation of instincts, and a careful evaluation of their advantages as well as their disadvantages, will make it possible to decide upon the one that can be included in the educational process for achieving this end.

1. Through Repression

As a general rule, no member of any human society has the facility of expression and manifesting his instincts in a completely uninhibited and unchanged form, because such a condition would lead to serious conflict and crisis with the other members of society, the organization of which would immediately be ended Maintenance of reasonable organization within society entails the use of such instruments of social control as customs, traditions, mores, etc., and many of the individuals' activities are obstructed in favour of general social welfare. Hence, it is understandable that the individual may be endowed with many such instincts the unbridled manifestation and satisfaction of which may not be palatable to society. It must be kept in mind, of course, that the society does not regard any individual instincts as bad or undesirable, and neither does it insist upon its exclusion from the body or being. Society only objects to certain specific modes of expression of some instincts for the simple reason that it obstructs and hinders in independence and freedom of other members of society. One example that readily comes to mind, is that of the sex instinct that is not, and in fact cannot be, considered bad or untestable by any society, but every society has its own modes of satisfying this instict that it can consider desirable. If the instinct is allowed to find some other form of expression then society is compelled to hinder and punish the individuals concerned. In Indian society, particularly in the rural background, premarital sexual relations between men and women are not considered very healthy, though there are no restrictions on sex relations between individuals when they are husband and wife. Obviously, it must be essential for the younger generation of the country to keep some semblance of control on their passions as long as they remain unmarried. In much the same manner, it renders control on the specific expression and manifestation of individual instincts.

The most prevalent method of controlling or transforming instincts is that of repression. Normally, if men and women find that some particular instinct is not considered desirable in society, and its satisfaction is not to be sought or is not possible even through devious and mysterious ways, they have recourse to its repression. In other words, they suppress that instinct. As the psychoanalysts have pointed out, when instincts are repressed, they disappear out of the conscious mind, but they are forced into the unconscious mind where they assume such a deceptive form for manifestation that the superego of the conscious mind cannot find any objection to it. It is a common experience that our repressed instincts are manifested in dreams, day dreams, or through the creative medium of art and literature. So far, there is no harm in repressing instincts, but the continued and constant repression of a particular instinct may endanger the mental balance of the individual. Hence, the transformation or control of instincts through repression is a method open to many shortcomings, the major ones being the following:

(*i*) Explosion of repressed desires: As has been pointed out earlier, a person's repressed desires leave the conscious mind and take up their abode in the unconscious from which they emerge in greatly transformed shape and form. There is not much harm in the repression of weak desires, but the repression of a very strong desire can only lead to great increase in tension within the unconscious mind. If even then this repression is carried to its final extreme, tension may increase to such an extent that the repressed desires may explode, as a consequence of which the person may become a mental patient or may even become insane. Even normally, repression has some adverse effect on the individual by disturbing his mental balance.

(*ii*) Destruction of creative energy: Many psychologists have pointed out that the satisfaction of instinctive desires provide the individual with energy for creative purposes. For example, the normal and healthy satisfaction of the sex instinct creates in man tremendous energy for creative work. If, now, these instincts are denied satisfaction and condemned to repression, obviously the individual will be deprived of these creative powers or energy. The energy that could have been utilised towards much constructive and creative expression of the individual is uselessly expended in reducing mental tension caused by repression. In India, because the young boys and girls are not able to form a correct opinion of the expediency of calibacy or continence, they are forced into unnatural repression of the sexual urge with the result that the energy that should have gone into study and development is consumed in self-denial. The main reason behind this is that they are not aware of the proper method of transforming desires that arise from the sex and various other instincts.

(*iii*) Emergence of undesirable characteristics: Extreme repression of instincts prevents the normal development of the person's personality and character, and he manifests many undesirable and harmful mental symptoms For example, it is seen that boys and girls, or grown up people for the matter of that, who are involved in excessive repression of their own sex instinct are prone to view the activities of others with suspicion and that their outlook is condemnably narrow. They show a vain pride in themselves, are very much averse to criticism at the hands of others, and pay unnecessary attention to the character of others. They show a lack of benevolence and natural piety. As a result of all this, their social adjustment is marred. Sometimes even men and women of sterling character are not able to find adjustment and contentment in their practical life. On the other hand, people who do not repress their sexual or other instinct normally exhibit better adjustment. When without good character they have all the best things of life, including respect, they are shocked, and their faith is undermined. In such circumstances, many people develop anti-social tendencies. Hence, it becomes obvious that the formation and development of character requires that the transformation of instincts in the formation of character be affected through more desirable and proper means than repression.

(*iv*) Obstacles to progress: It has been mentioned earlier that the excessive repression of desires originating in instincts leads to the destruction or wastage of much creative energy. Obviously, then, repression can prove to be a very big obstacle in the path of a person's progress. The main cause of this is that repression obviates the normal development of personality, character and mind, makes possible very great harm and denies progress and development.

The above account of the defects involved in repression should not create the impression that repression is absolutely bad. The day-to-day small desires are things that a person is compelled to repress. There is no doubting the fact that if a person does not allow improper desires to arise, and thereby eliminates the necessity of repressing them it is much better but this is not quite possible, even in the case of most sterling characters. The environment in which man lives presents many kinds of enticements and attractions, the only way of avoiding falling for them being repression. Thus repression cannot summarily be abandoned. If its defects are to be avoided one should avoid carrying it to its extreme. Proper habits reduce occasions of repression and forcible control. If bad habits are not formed, the individual finds that opportunities of repression are greatly reduced, hence he should try to avoid situations in which he may be aroused and have to resort to repression. This does not involve an escapist attitude in which the individual seeks to avoid the environment. It is easy to generate good qualities and habits by placing oneself in a good environment, but it is neither easy to live in unfavourable circumstances and continuously fight it, nor particularly desirable. The Christians very temperately beg of their Lord, "lure us not into temptation". To say that we will remain true to our ideals and never lose sight of the path we are required to pursue however hard be the circumstances, is not very psychological. It shows a lack of psychological acumen. Hence, it is best for the teachers to guide their wards into good circumstances and to help them avoid all circumstances that are likely to prove difficult to tolerance.

2. Inhibition

In this process of transforming instincts, it is attempted to place the growing child in circumstances that deny or retard the growth of instincts. For example, in ancient India, Brahmachari or celibate students were forbidden to look upon the face of woman. When they went to the villages to beg, they were ordered to keep their eyes lowered, and even then their visits were infrequent. Dressing elaborately, using hair and other oils or ornamental objects were considered anathema to retaining their celibacy and hence completely denied. The day-to-day routine of this classic celibacy was rather strenuous. It was believed that such measures would either prevent the very origination of the sexual desire in the celibates or kill it as soon as it manifests. Its expediency in this respect is a matter of controversy with modern sex psychology and educational psychology. But this method involves one serious drawback, and this is, that it weakens the instincts. According to many psychologists, inhibition does not kill instincts as they leave the domain of the conscious mind but that they continue to exist in the unconscious world, with the result that while the individual is apparently of a very high moral character, unconsciously he is a potential immoralist. Hence, inhibition as a method is not looked with any favour in the modern age. One very salient illustration of this fact is that many of the members of a recently formed committee, constituted to look into the growing indiscipline among students in Indian Universities, suggested that the colleges and universities should provide greater opportunities for mixing between the sexes in order to solve the problem of indiscipline.

3. Contradiction

Indian educational psychology holds contradiction to be a good method of transforming instincts. For example, in order to be saved from the complexities and intrigues of sex, people are advised to develop brotherly or affectionate feelings for members of the other sex, particularly those who are in no way related to one by ties of blood. If such feelings of commiseration and love developed, the sexual urge will not assert itself, particularly in respect of those individuals for which this feeling is created. In much the same way, the combative instinct can be controlled and reduced considerably if one evolves feelings of universal brotherhood. Such a feeling must be made part of the normal ethos of a group. The basic tenet in advocating the use of contradiction as a method of transforming instinct is that if the contradictory feeling is developed, the one that we want to avoid will not have a chance to create trouble. For example, if sickness is to be avoided, it is best to develop the conviction that one is healthy and this arouses tendencies and conflict.

4. Redirection

One good method of transforming instincts is that of redirection. In this, the mode of manifesting the intinct is completely altered. For example, instead of allowing the combative instinct to waste its energy in unnecessary struggle and destruction, it can be constructively and successfully employed in extricting the oppressed, and guarding the weak. Similarly, the passion or instinct for collection, called acquisitiveness, can be put to good use in the making of libraries and other collections. In redirection, the individual's instinct is turned to benefit the society. It results in the following advantages:

(*i*) In this, like in the case of inhibition, instincts are not weakened; they maintain their strength.

(*ii*) In this, there is no danger of the explosion of instincts as is ever present in the case of repression.

(*iii*) In this, because the person's instincts are turned to good account, his complete development is healthy and desirable.

(*iv*) In this, neither the individual nor society suffers, and both are properly synthesized and adjusted.

(*v*) Through this the emotions can also be desirably altered. For example, the emotion of fear can be turned into fear of God's wrath on evil.

5. Sublimation

One big difficulty in the method of redirection is that fundamentally the function of the instinct cannot be altered. On the other hand, sublimation not only alters the mode of its manifestation but also its fundamental and basic form of nature. According to Freud, "Sublimation is an unconscious deflection of *libido* into other more socially accepted channels." In this manner sublimation can lead to preventing of sex tendencies from expressing themselves in an undesirable manner and transforming them into specially acceptable behavioural patterns. Stressing the importance of changing the basic nature or form of the instinct through sublimation McDougall, in his book *Introduction to Social Psychology*, defines it thus: "Sublimation is a process by which the energies of our instinctive nature are utilized on higher planes of action than the instinctive." In this way, sublimation helps to divert the instinct from its normal and accustomed expression to a superior moral direction, a direction that is better regarded by society. For example, in the sphere of art one can find many poets and artists who originally evinced a very strong hetro-sexual tendency, but which was later turned to the expression of beauty and art. Kalidas and Tulsidas are examples of this fact. According to the psychoanalysts, the god-worship of many great priests and saints, mystics and preachers, evinces a sublimated sexual instinct

Sublimation is universally accepted to be the best of all methods of transforming instincts. It helps to run instincts and emotions to socially accepted and creative uses, while they retain their original natural urge and strength. For example, the sex instinct is sublimated through various kinds of plays, games, literature and art, all of which not as a medium. But in the case of every instinct sublimation can be carried to a certain extent, following which sublimation becomes difficult and can even prove injurious to the individual. Hence, in this respect, too, it is essential that a balanced outlook be maintained.

Education and the transformation of instincts

Education is profoundly influenced by and is interested in the transformation of instincts. A teacher has to transform the instincts of the students in such a manner that they loose none of their natural urgency and that they should be expressed and manifested in a socially accepted and creative manner. It is only natural that the process of transformation, redirection and sublimation should prove to be the teacher's best friends The main burden of transforming his instincts falls mainly on the student himself, but the teacher can assist him in many ways. In this respect the following means of assisting him are important:

(*i*) Creating healthy atmosphere for students: In order to transform instincts it is desirable to have healthy atmosphere in the colleges. The task of maintaining discipline in the college should be entrusted to the students themselves. This will help in maintaining a desirable atmosphere in the institution. In a good atmosphere, the students find a desirable mode of expressing their instincts.

(*ii*) Extra-curricular activities: The instincts of students are sublimated if they are allowed and encouraged to indulge in such extra-curricular programmes as dramatic representation, music, art, discussion, celebration, meetings, picnics, visits to places of historical importance, mutual felicitation, etc.

(*iii*) Catharsis: Catharsis implies providing an opportunity for the instinctive or emotional force in man to find its outlet. Despite reduction and sublimation there remain in an individual certain instinctive urges that have to be manifested in order to ensure his healthy development. It is seen that sometimes scientists and even old teachers try to relieve the atmosphere by cracking indecent jokes, and such practice cannot be condemned. This helps in the catharsis or relieving of repressed tendencies. Colleges should not be very strictly administered, and students should be given adequate freedom and opportunity to meet each other. If they sometimes indulge in tomfoolery of a harmless nature, even in it involves one of the teachers, it should not be frowned down upon with unnecessary severity. Community singing and dancing is another method of achieving catharsis of instincts. When the atmosphere in celebrations and informal meetings is kept free students get an opportunity to express themselves, and the catharsis of these tendencies help to reduce tension.

Briefly, in order to achieve the transformation of his students' instincts the teacher should mix with them, keep an eye on their tendencies and provide them with situations where their instincts can be sublimated or can attain to a certain catharsis.

QUESTIONS FOR EXERCISE

1. Examine critically McDoegall's theory of instincts.
2. What is instinct? Can we speak of human instincts? If so, in what sense?
3. What is meant by instinct? Bring out its relation to Reflex Action. Can it be modified?
4. Point out the use of various instincts in the education of the child.

7

General Tendencies: Suggestion, Imitation and Sympathy

SUGGESTION

The word suggestion does not imply precisely the sense in which it is usually employed in colloquial usage. Suggestion is a mental process in which the thoughts or thought processes of one individual influence and mould those of another. To take a common example, many people will attack any individual if they see a crowd attacking him even if they are not aware of any animosity towards the individual. If two bulls happen to fight in the middle of the road, or If a baton charge is made or even if some people happen to run in some direction without any particular cause they are soon emulated. The main cause at the root of such conduct is suggestion.

DEFINITIONS OF SUGGESTION

It is necessary to turn to some of the definitions of suggestion so that it may be understood more completely and precisely. Some main definitions are the following:

1. McDougall's view: "Suggestion is a process of communication resulting in the acceptance with conviction of the communicated proposition in the absence of logically adequate grounds for its acceptance."[1] In the crowd that is motivated by fear most people are seen running about worriedly and anxiously even when they are not aware of the reason for this anxiety. The reason for this is the suggestion inherent in the mob behaviour. Suggestion is the process of communicating information. The hypnotist employs this power to communicate his desire to others and in this way he manages to induce other people to behave in the manner that he wishes. The utterances of the great leaders and the militarists have the same power of suggestion and the person who hears them finds it beyond his control to resist them.

2. Kimball Young's opinion: "We may define suggestion as a form of symbol, communicated by words, pictures or some similar medium for including acceptance of the symbol without any self-evident or logical ground for its

1. W. McDougall, *An Introduction to Social Psychology*, p. 83.

acceptance."[1] Like McDougall, Young has also placed emphasis on the fact that the suggestion communicated has no logical or self-evident basis.

3. Thouless's view: "The word suggestion is now commonly used for the process by which an attitude towards a system of idea is communicated from one person to another, by a process other than that of rational persuasion."[2]

Characteristics of suggestion

The three foregoing definitions of suggestion point to the following characteristics that are to be found in suggestion:

1. Through the medium of suggestion, some idea is communicated from one individual to another.
2. There is no evidence or logic to support suggestion.
3. Suggestion can be conveyed through any symbolical medium such as language, pictures, etc.
4. Suggestion involves mental images.

In defining suggestion, in view of its fore mentioned characteristics, it can be said that suggestion is a mental process in which an idea, which does not have any evidence or logical basis, is conveyed from one person to another through any symbolical medium such as words, pictures, etc.

Suggestion in education

Many functions are performed in school life because of suggestibility. If we glance at all at the occurrences that take place all around us, we shall visualise the importance of suggestion in education. Suggestion influences not only behaviour with others but also one's own private and individual behaviour. Some students are conversely affected by suggestion, *i.e.*, they act in contradiction to the suggestion that is conveyed to them. Suggestion is sometimes direct sometimes indirect. In the first case the individual is aware of the fact that a suggestion is being made to him while in the second case there is no such awareness. In addition to these, in education one sees the influence of prestige suggestions almost everywhere. The behaviour of the students in a mob situation is an example of collective suggestion. It would be of help to, glance individually at the various forms of suggestion in education, the main among which are the following:

1. Ideo-Motor suggestion
2. Prestige suggestion
3. Auto-suggestion
4. Mass suggestion
5. Negative suggestion
6. Direct suggestion
7. Indirect suggestion
8. Positive suggestion
9. Negative suggestion.

1. Ideo-motor suggestion: As is evident from the name given to it, there is no discrimination here between thoughts and actions, *i.e.*, action takes place almost immediately the thought arises. Hence, in this there is no

1. Young, K., *Handbook of Social Psychology*, p. 10.
2. Thouless, R.H., *General and Social Psychology* (1951), p. 247.

time to think or to discuss. Generally, in suggestions of this kind the mind almost unconsciously accepts and adopts suggestions given to it. The famous psychologist Alfred Binet conducted important experiments in connection with ideo-motor suggestion.

2. Prestige suggestion: The advice of people is accepted in the fields in which they are considered to be specialists. A book of a famous author sells easily even if it is not particularly good. The ideas expressed by the famous scholars and leaders are casually and uncritically accepted by young men. In any political discussion if any person mentions the name of Mahatma Gandhi as supporting the contention that he has put forward, then in all probability his view is accepted by many without further preamble. All these are examples of prestige suggestion. An experiment was conducted by P.A. Sorokin and J. W. Bodyreff in connection with the effect of prestige suggestion. In this experiment 1484 high school students formed the audience for two recorded songs, one of which was said to be the work of a great artist while the singer of the second was said to be a commonplace artist whereas in fact both were sung by good artists. Because of the prestige suggestion inherent in the name 96 per cent students pronounced the first song to be good while the second they unanimously rejected as second rate. After this, the examiner pointed out that there was no difference between the records. Consequent upon this, 51 per cent immediately expressed acceptance, 16 per cent contradicted this view while 21 per cent abstained from expressing any opinion. It should be remembered that only 4 per cent of the students had originally pronounced the records to be the same and these were the only ones to use their intelligence in judging. All the other had been deceived by the suggestion.

3. Auto-suggestion: Much stress has been placed by Indian thinkers upon the importance of auto suggestion in the development of character. The character that an individual develops depends upon his thinking, and the thoughts that he entertains. Thought has power of suggestion. If you are always engrossed in thinking that you are not intelligent and can never score a good division in the examination, then how can you hope to study properly? The doctor always advises the patient to have faith in his cure because the fact of this belief helps to influence the health of the patient and supplements to some extent the medicine that is being administered to him. The famous psychologist Emile Cone cured some patients of mental diseases on the basis of auto-suggestion. By studying the biographies and autobiographies of great individuals one can see that they always placed the highest ideals before themselves to pursue and even in the time of extreme adversity they reassured themselves that in the end they would be victorious and successful. In this way. auto-suggestion has important influence upon the mental and physical condition, behaviour and even success of the individual.

4. Mass suggestion: Why is it that the behaviour of the individual undergoes considerable change when he is in a group situation? The reason why the most balanced and sane individuals who are the very essence of propriety in their private life become almost insane and exhibit animosity and pugnacity in a crowd is that they fall prey to mass suggestion. In one of his studies H.T. Moore has pointed out that students are more susceptible to mass suggestion than prestige suggestion. It is for this reason that one only too often comes across striking students who pay no heed to the utterings of the Vice-Chancellor of the University let alone the poor professor, and victims of mass suggestion that they are, they precipitate the most awful gaffs and do things that cannot be expected of them. By his experiments, C.H. Marple has proved that there is a ratio of 4 : 3 between mass suggestion and prestige suggestion.

5. Contra suggestion: It is often seen that people will indulge in the very activity that they have been warned against. This is particularly true of children who will inevitably touch anything that they have been prevented from touching or that they have been ordered to stay away from, or in other words, the order of abstaining from touching the object gives a contra suggestion.

6. Direct suggestion: Some suggestions are of a direct nature, *i.e.*, the individual who is accepting the suggestion is aware that a suggestion is being made to him. Often the teachers use direct suggestions to improve the work of the educands, and the educands also accept them.

7. Indirect suggestion: But some suggestions are not quite so apparent and bizarre, and the intention of the person suggesting is concealed. He puts forward his suggestions but he does not indicate his intention in doing it. Suggestions of this kind make a greater impression upon the educand.

8. Positive suggestion: The suggestions that are made for the implementation of some order or for accepting some statement are said to be positive suggestions.

9. Negative suggestion: The suggestions that are made for rejecting some order or for abstaining from some particular course of action are said to be negative suggestions.

The degree to which suggestions are important in education is evident by the above description of the various kinds of suggestions, teachers acquainted with psychological facts make use of suggestion to have their ideas and notions accepted by the students and to have the latter behave according to their wishes. Whether we like it or not we are influenced by the suggestions of others at one time or another. And, even otherwise, suggestions can be employed not only to influence others but also for self-development.

IMITATION

When a child attempts to walk impressively like his father, swinging a stick the while, he is imitating. Mead has characterised imitation as the conscious emulation of the behaviour and conduct of others. He writes, "Imitation is self-conscious assumption of another's acts or roles."[1]

1. Mead, C.H., Quoted by K. Young. *A Handbook of Social Psychology*, p. 110.

Process of Imitation

From the psychological viewpoint, the process of imitation is seen to possess the following characteristics:

1. The individual imitating does not indulge in thought or trial and error before he Imitates but immediately becomes involved in the activity of Imitation.
2. The person imitating does not show any previous acquaintance with the activity imitated.
3. In the process of imitation the person imitating performs exactly the same activity as the one being performed before him.

Imitation in education

The activity of imitation possesses much importance for education. In fact, it would be no misnomer to say that a major part of the education of the children is given through imitation. It is by indulging in imitation that the child can make adequate use of the behaviour of others around him. It is imitation which provides him behavioural patterns whereby he conducts himself in the presence of others. It is only through the medium of imitation that customs, traditions, and mores act in society and are maintained intact in their passage from one generation to the next. The human child possesses a great capacity for imitation. Language plays a major part in this imitation and language and pronunciation is acquired by the child only through imitation. In society many forms of behaviour such as dress, etiquette or manners, conversational modes, food, etc, are adopted by imitation. Every educator makes use of the tendency of imitation. The education of social behaviour is based primarily on imitation. It is trenchantly often remarked that one is known by the company he keeps. It is often seen that the students try to imitate and adopt the behaviour, thoughts, ideals and mannerisms of their teachers and because of this a good teacher succeeds in moulding the conduct of the students on the desired lines. It also usually happens that people estimate the behaviour of the children according to the knowledge that they have of their family. It is commonly believed, and in most cases also taken for granted, that the offspring of cultured and well mannered parents will be of a similarly cultured nature while the children of quarrelling parents will be obstinate and quarrelsome At the root of all these notions is the element of imitation. By making adequate use of the tendency to imitation that the human child possesses in great quantity, an able teacher can succeed in moulding the behaviour of his students on cultured lines. It is because of the tendency to imitation that children are so susceptible to the influences of their parents and friends whose behaviour they imitate indiscriminately. It is only because this importance of imitation has been understood that now great emphasis is laid, in every sphere of education, on the concrete presentation of the ideals before the individual that are to be inculcated into him. And particularly, in the various spheres of cultural life such as dancing, music, art, etc., demonstration and its imitation are of great importance.

SYMPATHY

The meaning of sympathy

In the words of Woodwork, sympathy means, "experiencing with another". When one individual shares the pain of other and also shares in their joys then it is said that he is sympathetic towards others. This is common experience that when we meet a person who is smiling we also smile. In a serious atmosphere we have to maintain the serious nature of the atmosphere while we feel almost compelled to feel joyful and happy in a colourful and gay atmosphere. In this way, the play of sympathy can always be seen in day-to-day experience and behaviour.

Sympathy in education

Sympathy plays a very important role in the education of the child. The child learns easily if he is taught sympathetically. While solving the problems concerning the development of the children, their character, personality, learning and discipline etc., the teacher, to be successful, must behave sympathetically. The child should be taught to behave sympathetically with his youngers and equals. This will help in his social and emotional development. Though sympathy is very much innate in the child, it can be also taught by examples. Passive sympathy helps in the study of literature and in aesthetic development. Active sympathy is the foundation stone of moral development. Thus sympathy plays a valuable role in every aspect of the child's development.

QUESTIONS FOR EXERCISE

1. What is suggestion? What are its types? Discuss the role of suggestion in education.
2. Write brief note on— Suggestion.
3. Write short note on— Conditions of suggestibility.
4. What is imitation? What are its kinds? Point out the importance of imitation in child development.
5. Write short note on— Types and laws of imitation.
6. What is sympathy? How does sympathy differ from pity? What is the role of sympathy in the education of a child?

8

Psychological Tendency in Education

One of the major influences upon education in the contemporary world is the impact of the psychological tendency. It had its beginnings with Rousseau, who was a social reformer and educationist rather than a psychologist He is, nevertheless, credited with having once remarked that every child is a book and that all educators should make a study of it and try to understand it. This interest m human psychology was the source of this psychological tendency, for it gave rise to the notion that education should be determined and fashioned by child psychology. The first step in this was to discover the tendencies, interests, abilities and mental activities which can be found in the child. Differences of many kinds are found between one child and another, and hence it is not practical to introduce the same pattern of education for every child. From this standpoint, it can be said that child psychology directs the formation of the syllabus and the teaching method. Both the subject to be taught and the mode of teaching should be appropriate to the psychology of the child and to his mental development. Hence, the importance of applying psychology to the field of education is self-evident. And in fact, this interest in child psychology led to practically a revolution in the sphere of education. Education today has become child centered, because of the impact of psychology. Psychological techniques are adopted to improve the process of learning, and the objective of education is now believed to be the complete development of the human personality . The method of teaching is adopted to and fashioned according to the individual differences found among the educands. The syllabi of many institutions, of education in general, have undergone rapid changes along with discoveries in the field of psychology. Many new psychological methods of administration and inducing discipline have been evolved and tried. To a very great extent, it is true to say that psychology has caused revolutionary changes in the methods of teaching. Even mental testing and guidance are based on psychology. Psychological means are adopted to improve children. Briefly , psychology has helped the educator in understanding himself, his educand, in improving methods of teaching, testing and evaluating, in improving administration and adjustment, in research, in solving classroom problems, etc.

The psychological tendency in education has been assisted by philosophy and science also, because the philosopher and the scientist treat the child's interests, natural abilities, and activeness as important elements in the process of learning. Realists believed that the aim of education was to develop the sense organs. For this a psychological foundation of education is necessary. Hence, whenever the psychologist found anything unpsychological about education, he opposed it and suggested the adoption of psychological elements to replace the unpsychological.

CHARACTERISTICS OF THE PSYCHOLOGICAL TENDENCY

In order to understand the psychological tendency, it is necessary to understand its characteristics, which are the following:

1. **Psychological basis:** According to the psychological tendency, psychology forms the basis or foundation of education, and psychological principles should be applied in every sphere of education.

2. **Child centered education:** The psychological tendency accepts the child as the centre of education, the most important aspect of education, more than which no ether aspect is important. Everything in education, the methods of teaching, the curriculum, etc., should all be adopted to the psychological tendencies of the child.

3. **Study of the child:** In the process of education, there are two poles: the educand and the subject taught while education belongs somewhere between these two. Prof. Adams has said that the task of the educator is not merely to teach Latin, or any other subject but to understand both the educand and the subject. Here, by the understanding of the educand, Prof. Adams implied understanding the psychology of the educand. Hence the educator must try to understand the child and try to adopt his teaching methods and the syllabus according to the child's interests, tendencies and abilities. Only then can education be fruitful.

4. **Importance of psychological opportunity:** According to psychologists, every child has, at one time or the other, psychological opportunity to learn some particular thing, and if this is taught to him at that opportunity, he grasps it without difficulty. On the other hand, learning becomes difficult if the psychological opportunity has passed. Hence, the educator should not try to teach something to the educand at any time, but should wait for the psychological opportunity and exploit it when it arrives. He can even try to create such an opportunity. William James favoured the idea that the educator should take advantage of the child's interest the moment he discovers it, because there is every possibility that in future the child may not evidence interest in it.

5. **Stress on individual differences:** Many types of tests and examinations have now established that many individual differences are found between children. Individual difference refers to any ability or aspect of the complete human personality which is susceptible to measurement. There can be many such qualities such as vacillation, normality, rate of development and learning, the relationship between the various qualities of personality, heredity and the

influence of environment, etc. In this way, one can find remarkable differences between the physical and mental development, nature, rate of learning, ability of learning, specific abilities, interests and personality etc., of children. These individual differences are caused by differences of background, economic status, racial differences, differences of sex, intelligence, specific abilities, mental age, development, etc. Knowledge of these individual differences will help the educator in creating the right attitude to the educand and also help him to devise ways and means of achieving this attitude. He possesses knowledge of the limitations of teaching so that failure does not irritate him, and neither does he hope for the impossible. Once the fact of individual differences came to be stressed, it led to remarkable changes in contemporary education. Numerous methods of individual teaching— such as Dalton plan, Project method, Vinetka method, contract plan, activity programme etc.— were evolved. As a result of knowledge, the size of the class is specified, and different kinds of children are taught differently. All educational and vocational guidance is provided after keeping in mind the individual differences of the student. It is now recognised that the school must have the co-operation of the community and the family to be successful.

6. Improvement in education: Because of the psychological tendency, many significant changes and improvements have been achieved in methods of teaching, methods of administration, etc. Now, it is believed that discipline cannot be taught to the child by thrashing and suppressing him, and that something better can be achieved by turning discipline into self-discipline. As far as possible, efforts are made to make the process of education entertaining and interesting, so that it may achieve the child's physical, mental and moral development. Putting it briefly, education is not something which can be forced from outside, but a process of internal development.

7. Change in the definition of child nature: In education, psychological tendency has led to a changed definition of the child, who is no longer regarded as the young adult but as a child. Hence, the principles of adult psychology are not applied to him because psychological researches have indicated that child psychology differs from adult psychology in respect of perception, conceptualization, imagination, attention, learning, etc. Hence, education is now guided by child psychology, and its definition of the child's nature and personality.

8. Emphasis upon the importance of infancy: The psychological tendency recognises the significance of infancy, and believes it to be the most important stage of man's life. Psychologists have demonstrated that the impressions made upon the child's mind can never be eradicated. For that reason, education is most important during infancy. In the past little attention was paid to the education of children, but now the primary section is considered to be the most important. Almost all modern states are trying to make primary education universal and compulsory.

9. Individual education: Because of the psychological tendency education is becoming more and more individual now-a-days. The aim of education is believed to be the development of the human personality, although social development is also an important aspect of the individual's development. Education is becoming more individual also because increasing emphasis is placed upon individual differences between one individual and another. It is believed to be the duty of the educator that he should pay individual attention to every student in his class, he should understand his difficulties and he should adopt separate methods to teach separate children suiting the method to the child. For this reason, the number of children in one class should be small so that the teacher can pay attention to every student.

10. Importance of guidance: Psychological guidance has become an important and common thing, for it is now believed to be important in child education, in selecting a profession, in solving personal problems. This is due to the impact of the psychological tendency. Educational guidance is provided to the educand to help him choose the subjects of study. Professional or vocational guidance is also provided to help him choose a job while personal guidance is available to help him solve his personal problems.

From the foregoing description of the major characteristics of the psychological tendency it is clear that it has been responsible for revolutionary changes in the pattern of contemporary education. It is also certain that education will continue to change as major changes occur in the field of psychology.

QUESTION FOR EXERCISE

1. Write short note on—Psychological Tendency in Education.

9

Play and Play Way

WHAT IS PLAY?

According to the famous psychologist McDougall, play is a normal innate tendency similar to suggestion and imitation. Though the definition of play varies from psychologist to psychologist, most of them believe that it is an innate tendency. The following definitions of the term will make it possible to understand it better.

1. Valentine's view: According to Valentine, "Play is a kind of amusement in the work." This definition emphasizes an indispensable dement in play, *viz.* amusement. Play is indulged in by people because it yields amusement but such a definition cannot explain all games. It fails to analyse some kinds of play. A simple instance is of the child who plays from morning to evening. In his case, one can hardly be justified in saying that he plays for amusement.

2. Stern's view: "Play is a kind of voluntary, self-constrained activity" This particular definition lays stress on two important elements of play. In the first place, play depends upon the wishes of the individual, and secondly, it is the player participating who himself controls it. If these two conditions are to be found in learning, it too becomes play. This definition gives a good explanation of the play way method in learning. But it fails short in as much as it neglects the element of amusement inherent in play. In addition to being volitional and self-controlled, play invariably included the feeling of pleasure and amusement.

3. Gluek's opinion: "Play is what we do when we are free to do what we will." It is the volitional and independent nature of play that is stressed in this definition. It need hardly be pointed out that the definition is one-sided and incomplete.

4. Thomson's view: "Play is the impulse to carry out cerain instinctive actions." This particular definition of the term lays stress on its instinctive nature. In play the human individual gives expression to those instincts which do not find any manifestation and outlet in his normal life. This particular definition is applicable to the playing of both young children as well as grown ups. But this definition lacks comprehension as it neglects such other characteristics of play as naturality, independence, amusement, etc.

5. Sir T.P. Nunn's view: "Play is a profound manifestation of creative activities." According to this definition play gives expression to the creative and positive tendencies of the individual. This definition of the term is particularly apt for describing the playful activities of children. Putting it briefly, play is volitional, autonomous, instinctive and creative, or an activity that manifests these activities, and which gives amusement and pleasure to the individual.

KINDS OF PLAY

Children are seen indulging in different games as they progress from infancy to adulthood. The games peculiar to the different stage infancy, childhood, adolescence and adulthood, are different. Types of play have been classified in various ways. Karl Gross, for example, has classified games in the following ways:

1. Experimental play: In these games, the children are seen examining and breaking up the objects that are within their reach. It is their method of examining and becoming acquainted with things.

2. Movement play: This classification includes the movements of the hand and feet, running about, jumping, making peculiar sounds etc., that are characteristic of infancy and childhood. It is a natural stage in the development of the child, any interruption in which can have only the worst effect on his development. Till the child attains the important age of two, such games as these form his chief occupation.

3. Constructive play: In playing with objects, the child can either destroy them or construct other things. His earlier efforts are marked by destruction and in his wake he leaves a long trail of smashed things but later on he breaks things only to make others. In fact destructive and constructive activities have close relationship. Children play both kinds of games. They make houses only to break them with all the unconcern of an engineer gone berserk. Constructive games are played both individually and collectively and girls are seen caricaturing the life of their adults in making houses, marrying off their dolls and cooking. The tendency to constructive play is seen in the child from the age of three or four. According to Stern, boys are more blessed with this tendency than girls. Consequently, boys are of an inventive and ingenious turn of mind whereas girls are more imitative in nature.

4. Fighting play: Games of fighting are decided by winning or losing. Their object is gaining ascendency over the opponents. Hockey, cricket and table tennis are examples of individual games. Boxing and wrestling are games of apparent hostility and fighting. Previously, such games were confined to the males but now the females have invaded their province in all games except those in which physical combat is unavoidable.

5. Intellectual play: In modern civilised societies people also play such games as chess and cards that depend mainly on the use of brain. Word building and puzzle solving belong to the same category.

Play at different Age Levels

In addition to the above games, there are some other kinds. There are imitative games in which the participant puts on different disguises and imitates the original. Then, there are inventive games in which the child attempts the invention of different new objects; emotive games such as wishful thinking; volitional games in which the artist tells jokes though the audience is not allowed to laugh, or two people making faces at each other, the one to laugh first being adjudged the loser. After the description of the various kinds of plays or games, we now have the kinds of games that are played in different age groups:

1. Birth to three years: From his birth till he attains the age of three, the infant is seen playing games that involve emotional, perceptive and biological motions. He is interested in playing with gaily coloured objects which he throws around, breaks them and puts them in his mouth. Of all toys, those capable of locomotion are the most attractive to the infant. The very small infant is capable only of throwing his arms and feet about. The infants in this age group also play with coloured charts, paint and brushes, etc. They take keen interest in listening to stories and studying pictures in books. Playing with dolls and making sand edifices is an equally engaging occupation for them. As they continue to grow, they also develop the capacity of continuous concentration and attention. The retention and widening of attention is open to many influences. A child of two can attend to any game from one to seven and a half minutes, a child of three from one to twelve minutes while a child of four can attend to a game from one to fourteen minutes. Basing his statement on his experiments, Van Alystyne has pointed out that the attention in play increases by two minutes with each age level. He found no difference in the games of male and female infants.

2. From 4 to 7 years: In this age group, the number of boys increase along with their variety. The child of four to seven prefers the more active games of driving a baby motor car, riding a tricycle, playing in sand and water, running and jumping, digging and flinging things about. He likes to make different patterns by putting together colourful pictures of wooden blocks. Individual and group games are particularly desired once the child has attained the age of five, a peculiar feature being the desire to play under the supervision of a teacher. The child also takes interest in music, dancing and tales of animals and fairies. Development of mental and creative activities is manifest in the constructive and imitative games indulged in by the growing child. And such games also help in the further mental development of the child. His aesthetic and cultural development progresses further through stories, poetry, acting, music, dancing, painting, etc.

3. From 7 to 10 years: In this age group, the child is primarily inclined to collective games, so that he plays group games much more than individual games. Games such as hockey, cricket and football are played in accordance with some definite rules, and this restriction adds to the child's enjoyment of them. Besides playing these games, the child also takes avoid interest in watching matches between more accomplished artists of this craft. The desire to collect odds and ends is another passion peculiar to this stage in life. Using the check list technique in 1923-26, Lehman and Witty studied the pattern of play among children between the ages of eight and a half years and ten years, finding the following characteristics, peculiar to them:

(*a*) pleasurable physical activities, particularly rhythmic movement;

(*b*) activity of hiding and seeking;

(*c*) activities of imitating and caricaturing the adults;

(*d*) activities of skill;

(*e*) constructive activity;

(*f*) activities providing pleasure through the excitation of sense organs;

(*g*) playing with ropes;

(*h*) plays of music and dancing (particularly among girls).

The participation of the child in group games in this period results in an increase in his social knowledge, in his emotional development and in an increase in mental capacity. Hence, it is all the more desirable that the teacher should organise collective activity as far as possible.

4. 10 to 13 years: Having attained the age of ten the children come to love even more organised and systematic games. They develop team spirit and it is a matter of pleasure for them to play in the team. Some team games involving intellect are also found to interest the youngsters of this age group. Many children in this age develop an astonishing interest in reading stories, and in fact become voracious readers. It is at this stage that definite differentiation between male and female games is apparent. It is the first stage of adolescence. In this age, the female species tends more to constructive and inactive games such as knitting, stitching, painting, etc., rather than to violently active games of running and roaming all over the place. Taking advantage of their desire to be more ladylike in their occupation, the young ladies can be taught all the functions of a housewife. Any knowledgeable teacher can help the child's development by developing in him such characteristics as sociability and discipline, and interest in study and other intellectual pursuits.

5. 13 to 19 years: In this age, the adolescent has grown considerably, and the love of imitative and imaginative games is replaced by an attraction towards more active, collective and courageous games such as hockey, cricket, etc. It is at this stage that the young boy begins to take interest in adventurous tours and journeys. Other more common games teach him discipline, communal spirit, team spirit, etc. His mind and imagination are both fairly well developed. The adolescent tends more to research, constructive games and acting, with the accent on physical exertion of a high order. The girls, on the other hand, drop physically active pursuits and settle down to such domestic activities as knitting, dancing, music, painting, etc. It need hardly be pointed out that this difference in the play interests of young boys and girls is due to the pattern of their respective future roles.

Factors influencing play

Of the many factors that influence play among children, the most important are the following:

1. **Age:** Age is one of the most important factors influencing play. As the child progresses from infancy towards adulthood, his plays gain, in complexity and from haphazard movements become organised games. Growing older, the child comes to appreciate group and collective games in addition to the individual games to which he has been accustomed. Growing much older, passing from adolescence into unmistakable adulthood, the erstwhile child comes to love intellectual games more than physical play. He stops going to the playground and substitutes it in his life by the club where he plays mentally relaxing games.

2. **Sex differences:** Many detailed studies have definitely indicated that the games played by boys and girls in their infancy and childhood are the same. Most of the time they even play together. Nevertheless, despite this fact one does come across some difference in the playing of boys and girls of this age group. Girls are more partial to dolls while the boys are tendencious towards games that call for exertion and a certain degree of toughness. A sharp differentiation between male and female games is apparent only when the age of 8 or 10 is reached, when boys prefer to play with boys and girls with girls. Boys who persist in playing with girls are usually teased by their friends on account of the implied feminity of the boys who do so, and as this trait is not desirable. At the same time, the differences in sex leads to differences in the nature of games played by the two sexes. Boys play with ball, while girls play with dolls. The influence of sex on the form of play is even more pronounced when adolescence is reached. Boys choose to play more courageous, organised and active games, while the young ladies prefer comparatively inactive games involving less strenuous, if any, exercise. Many studies in this direction have indicated that this difference in the games played by boys and girls is not due so much to the physiological differences as to such cultural factors as social tradition and custom, mores and accepted behaviour patterns. In many cultures, both boys and girls play equally challenging games of a physical nature. Even in Indian societies, in families in which the education of boys and girls is not sufficiently differentiated, the girls are equally interested in riding, swimming, tennis, badminton and other physical games. The difference that is attributed to difference in sex is due to the fact that parents do not like girls after a certain age level to play with boys or play the games boys play.

3. **Mental differences:** The researches of Lehman and Witty indicate that normally and generally, differences in mental levels do not exert any significant influence on the kind of play. In other words, the games played by very intelligent, average and feebleminded will not differ widely, if at all. But the fact remains that the games of intelligent boys are more varied and complex than those of their less fortunate brothers; particularly, in the case of games based on intellectual ability, a certain minimum level of intelligence is indispensable. Among students, some take more interest in their studies than

in games, but there is no definite trend regarding this behaviour. Children who spend most of their time with books have little time to devote to collective games.

4. Environmental differences: In addition to the above factors, environment exerts an important influence. This term includes all sort of things such as climate, geographical location, fellow students and friends, traditions and social mores, etc. The form of play is affected if these change. Definite and pronounced differences between the games of children belonging to rural and urban areas, hot and cold climates, plains and mountainous regions, are to be noticed. Boys and girls of urban areas frequent cinema houses while their rural counterparts show greater interest in kabaddi and domestic chores.

THEORIES OF PLAY

Thinkers differ on the psychological basis of play. It has been elucidated by different thinkers in different ways and has thus resulted in many different theories. The psychological elements in play can be understood by a study of these theories. The following are the main theories:

1. Theory of surplus energy: In the opinion of Schiller, a famous German poet, play is the expression or consummation of our surplus energy. The theory finds the support of philosopher Herbert Spencer. It is also called the Schiller-Spencer theory. It is conceived that children do not consume their entire stock of energy in their normal routine of the day, and they play in order to consume the surplus energy created. Among the adult population, individuals engaged in hard and tiring work during the day do not indulge in play as they have no surplus of energy. On the other hand, those who lead a soft life or whose work is confined to less tiring pursuits, feel the need of physical exertion in play. Reasoning in this vein, the theory further suggests that play is a kind of safety valve for people through which the excessive energy is exhausted. If this surplus was not to be consumed through the medium of play, the further development of the body could possibly be hindered and obstructed.

This particular theory of play fails to analyse and explain some definite kinds of play. It does succeed in explaining certain aimless activities of the child such as flinging its arms and feet about, but it fails to provide satisfactory answers to many questions, some of which are:

(*a*) Why do people continue to play even when they are tired?

(*b*) Why does play always have a definite pattern?

(*c*) Why do the games of different animals differ?

(*d*) How does play help in the development of the child while the surplus steam that is exhausted from a system engine is completely wasted?

2. Recreation theory: According to the German Lazares and the English Lord Kames, an individual regains the energy in play that he has lost or consumed elsewhere. This explanation of play has been supported by G.T.W Patrick. It is opined that people indulge in play as it affords amusement and amusement refreshes the individual whereby he repossesses the lost energy, it is for this reason that one sees among the individual playing even those who have been exhausted during their vocational pursuits. They find amusement in play.

This principle succeeds in elucidating the role of amusement in play and is applicable almost exclusively to the exertions of grown up people. It fails to explain how or why children play as there can be no question of their being so exhausted as to need recuperation through amusement. Then, again, there are some old people who spend to entire day in playing chess and Chicheckers. Does this pattern of behaviour conform to the view that people play in order to regain energy consumed? In fact this continued indulgence in play leads more to exhaustion than to freshness or energetic condition.

3. Anticipatory theory: Melbranche was the first to propound this theory, but it was elucidated at length by Carl Gross. Having made a minute study of the play of many different living beings Gross came to the conclusion that in play living beings practise the activities that will be required of them in their adulthood. Pups fight because when they become dogs they will have to fight for their life. A kitten runs after a ball and rips it apart in the manner cats are seen doing with mice. Similarly, the babies of reindeer are seen moving with long and swift strides. The same phenomenon is observed in the case of human children. Female children rehearse their later married life in their childhood games of playing with dolls, making houses and marrying off their dolls. On the other hand, the male child usually rehearses his future life in playing at being a professor, engineer, shopkeeper or the like. According to Carl Gross, the more developed the life of a species, the greater will be the variety of games their offspring are seen playing. In the same proportion the playing period in life will continue to a later stage. Being the most developed living being, man suffers his issue to continue in the playing stage for a longer time than other animals. On the other hand, among the undeveloped animals and insects such as bees and lizards, the baby engages in its business of life immediately it comes into possession of a fully developed body. But one sees play in the comparatively developed animals such as cats, dogs, monkeys, reindeer, etc. In man, almost one-third of his entire life span is spent in playing, and among the more civilized of his race the games played are so varied that one would require a veritable volume to describe all of them in detail. The games played in civilized societies are more numerous than in comparatively uncivilized tribes. Similarly, children belonging to a higher social circle play more games and play them for a longer period than do children who belong to a lower strata of society. The variety of games increases with developments in the nervous system. Accepting the anticipatory theory of play as superior to the theory of surplus energy, Sir T.P. Nunn has remarked astutely, "Nature invented play not merely as a means of disposing harmlessly of the young animal's superfluous energy, but as a device for using that energy to prepare him for serious business of life."

It cannot be doubted that the principle propounded by Carl Gross does succeed in explaining many kinds of play, bodies bringing to light, by implication, the reasons why play is adopted as a method of teaching. It also elucidates the psychological basis of play yet one can object that all play is not rehearsal or anticipation of the serious business of life. In particular it can be objected that the theory fails to offer any explanation of adult play. Then again, in what sense is playing cards a preparation for future life and there can be no denying that children do in fact play cards?

4. Recapitulatory theory: Stanley Hall, a famous American scientist put forward the Recapitulatory theory of play in refuting the anticipatory theory. According to Stanley Hall, "Anticipatory theory is very partial, superficial and perverse since it ignores the past where lies the key to all play activities."

In the opinion of Stanley Hall, the reasons for the child's play should be looked for in his past, rather than in his future. "The heart of youth goes out into play as into nothing else, as if in it men remembered a lost paradise."[1] It is the view of Stanley Hall that every tribe or race passes through many varied stages in its development and evolution, the impressions of which are to be found in its children at their birth. The stages through which the human race has passed in its development over a period of some thousand years are present in children in the form of minute and significant impressions, and these are the impressions that are recalled by them in their playing. This recollection is the essence of Nature. For example, the embryo within the mother's womb passes through all the prominent stages of evolution of all animals before it enters the specifically human stage. In this way, the child relives the uncivilized and aboriginal stage of the human race in its play. Hunting and playing, hide and seek are not the anticipations of any future life. In the words of Ross, "Hide and-seek, chasing, hunting and fishing, stone throwing, the building of houses and shelters, especially in trees, the fascination of caves, all remind us strongly of the youth of the race."[2] In this way, most of our play patterns are a recollection or reproduction of the activities of man in his uncivilized stages.

Stanley Hall's theory does explain some particular kinds of play, such as hunting, climbing mountains, roaming etc., but it cannot claim to explain all kinds of play. Studies conducted by Lahmen and Witty have contributed to reduce the impact of this theory as they show that the various forms of play are not reminiscent of the various stages of the being's development as these forms are subject to variations caused by seasons, place and sex. Secondly, modern scientists do not subscribe to the view that the qualities acquired by the human race are present in children in the form of impressions.

5. Cathartic theory: Aristotle used the word catharsis to explain or elucidate the effect of tragedy in drama. It means purification or purgation. Just as some medicines purge the body of its undesirable poisons, the tragic drama also

1. Stanley Hall, *Adolescence*, p. 21.

2. Ross, E.A., *Groundwork of Educational Psychology*, p. 104.

purges the human soul of its suppressed desires and pent up emotions. The principle of catharsis also influences the causes of those of human games that are reminiscent of the aboriginal or tribal man. Hunting, war, wandering or travelling all over the globe, are expressions of those suppressed tendencies in man that have been present in him since his undeveloped and uncivilised state. These tendencies do not find expression in the normal social progress, in civilized society. In this way, play is a cathartic process. A somewhat similar explanation of the phenomenon has been offered by Freud and other psychoanalysts. In the words of Sir T.P. Nunn, "Men cannot shed altogether the ancient tendencies to cruelty and vice but play is at once a means by which the mischief may be taken out of them and a means by which they may be transformed into impulse of ethical value."

Despite its wide application, the principle of catharsis does not explain the causes of all kinds of play. Nevertheless, it is an important theory. Its reality and rationality has been acceded to by Sir T.P. Nunn.

Concerning the above theories of play, one can safely concur with Sir T.P. Nunn that they are mutually complementary rather than contradictor. The various theories succeed in explaining some particular form of play but they all prove inadequate if they are required to explain all the various forms. While some kinds of play are an anticipation or rehearsal of the future life, other forms give the impression of being recollections of man's activity in his tribal and uncivilized state. Some games are an outlet for the individual's excess energy that he cannot put to better use, but there are some forms of play which yield him pleasure and amusement. And almost all forms of play are cathartic in one respect or the other. Apart from this, there are some kinds of play that are a mixture or compound of the amusing, recollecting and cathartic games. In this manner, the psychological basis of play is a composite of consumption of surplus energy, amusement rehearsal or anticipation of future life, recollection of the functions of man in his primal state, and the catharsis through manifestation of many tendencies that cannot be expressed in the normal daily routine of an individual's social life.

IMPORTANCE OF PLAY

Plays contribute considerably to the development of children. They help in the child's physical, mental, emotional, aesthetic and character development. They not only afford it pleasure, but also provide a means of expression for many instincts. Play is one of the media through which the child can easily give expression to his general and common tendencies. In this sphere he is completely free of restriction, and he turns to many kinds of play through internal inspiration. Although the guidance of the teacher can be of much advantage even in the sphere of play, yet it is desirable that there should be no unnecessary interference on his part. However systematised and regularized the game may be, it must never be allowed to lose its natural spirit. It should never be permitted to become as serious as a vocation usually is.

The importance of play can be guaged when it is studied from the following points of view:

1. Physical or biological importance: As has been pointed out, and is itself fairly evident, play helps in the physical development of the child. And in infancy there are many games that are in fact indicative of the child's biological growth. Games give sturdiness to the limbs of the child. Many waste products of the body are released when the blood circulation is accelerated and when the child breaths rapidly or deeply. The heart and the lungs benefit by the exercise involved in playing games. Without this physical exertion these parts of the body will not develop properly. The body is further benefited by the enjoyment that the child and even the grown ups derive from games. After play people are seen embued with a new energy and freshness. Many forms of play prepare the child physically for the battles of life ahead of him. In this way, most of the outdoor games are beneficial to the physical development and well being of the child and the psychological well being of his parents.

2. Mental importance: The physical importance of games is itself indicative of their importance from the mental viewpoint also. Physical well being is always conducive to the proper mental development and health of an individual. Different games provide opportunities for the exercise of different powers and capabilities present in the child. Some games may compel him to enjoy his imagination while others may require making decisions by the child yet another may call for memory excellence while in a different game he may have to call upon his patience and concentration. These opportunities help in the development of the various mental capacities called into play. In games the individual has to confront and win over different and ever changing circumstances and eventualities with the result that he develops resource and courage. It also leads to his mental maturity. Play also assists in the child's attaining some mental balance.

3. Emotional significance: Play helps in the revelation and expression of many repressed emotions so that the individual is purgated of them. In the process of playing he learns to express control and sublimate or transfer his emotions. Games help the individual get rid of destructive emotions such as feeling of futility irritability, the tendency to quarrel without any reason, fear and anxiety. The more desirable emotions are developed to take their place. Emotional stability is attained through games and the individual develops the tendency to realistic thinking rather than day dreaming.

4. Social importance: It is through games that the individual develops such qualities as discipline, co-operation, sympathy, benevolence, law-abiding and leadership. When children belonging to different social levels come together in the playground, the main distinguishing and dividing features and barriers present between them are lost and they come much closer to each other, than they can in other social and economic spheres. In this way, play is one of the important means of removing the sense of social discrimination and distinction between classes. In the collective or group games, the child is motivated by the interest of the entire group rather than by any individual motive. Such a realization of the community of interests leads to the development of sacrifice and team-spirit. Collective games help in the development of social and community consciousness.

5. Educational importance: The above elucidation of the importance of games is not intended to convey the impression that the teacher has no role to play in the process. This is not anywhere near the truth. The truth of the matter is that if the phenomenon of play is to yield all its physiological, emotional and social benefits, it is indispensable that the teacher should come forward with constructive suggestions from time to time. Further, he should be present at game time in order to direct and guide the children. Modern primary education techniques make use of play in teaching children of a very tender age. In these techniques, games combine with teaching to develop the child. It is not only in the stages of infancy and childhood that games can be utilised to develop the child, but they be employed even in the education of adolescents and adults who can be made into well developed and ideal citizens of the nation through the simple expedient of being allowed to play the games that they desire. Men and women should play games that harmonize with the tasks and vocations that they have chosen for their future lives. And these games will vary from adolescence to adulthood. It is fallacious to think that girls have less need of playing than boys, but it is very essential in their case that the games they play are such that help them in the preparation for their lives.

Cure through play

Now-a-days plays are also utilized to get rid of many mental problems and character difficulties of children. The reason behind this is cathartic power of play. The emotions that the child is unable to express, due to the necessity of social life and general conformity and is forced to repress, cause many abnormalities in his personality and behaviour. Many methods based on play have been evolved to free the mind of the child of these abnormalities. The most significant gain in the use of play as a cure is that the child is not aware that he is undergoing treatment with the result that the treatment becomes natural and efficacious. Secondly, in cases of these abnormalities and maladies, according to Meleniklein, children express their problems symbolically in their play. The analysis of these symbols of abnormalities can help in their cure. It is for this reason that Meleniklein has supported the cure of mental disorders through the medium of play. Play therapy methods are based on different kinds of play, but the basic principle common to all of them is that the child is to be placed in an environment in which he can facilely and freely give expression to his internal feelings and conditions. In plays oriented to this end, social circumstances and conditions are created in which many of repressed tendencies of the child's behaviour can find ready expression. Among therapeutic methods and games the important ones are recreation therapy, finger painting, psycho-drama etc.

1. Recreation therapy: Recreation therapy is the most natural method of psychological treatment. One important cause of juvenile delinquency is that the creative faculties and tendencies of the child are not afforded any opportunity of natural expression. The result is that they burst out in a destructive torrent and the adolescent becomes a criminal and delinquent. Recreation therapy provides the child with adequate means and opportunity for developing his creative faculty. He is allowed to make houses, castles, etc. The main object behind these games is not the imparting of any knowledge to them, but of providing children the chance to manifest their mental tendencies and predilections. This satisfies the children and they avoid the danger of becoming abnormal. One major advantage of play is that it develops social qualities in children. The children come to possess feelings of brotherhood and co-operation, which preclude the development of anti-social feelings. Recreation therapy makes use of both individual as well as collective games.

2. Finger painting: The second important method of psychological cure through play is that of finger painting. In this method, the child draws by his fingers. He is provided with many colours and a sheet of white paper. The child is directed to draw any figure that he pleases with his fingers in any colour that takes his fancy from among the colours provided to him. Of course, the real object behind this is not to have the child draw some figure with skill but to give him the chance to get rid of his emotional tension, the figure acting as a medium or excuse. The child often spreads much colour on the paper, and even spreads on some parts of his own body and clothing. In this manner whereas he is given the chance to do as he wishes, much of his emotional tension is destroyed, and he again becomes a healthy child.

3. Psycho-drama: Another method of mental therapy through play is that of psycho-drama. It was invented by the psychologist Moreno. In this method the child is invited to take part in an imaginary drama. This acting is psychological. The purpose of this acting is not to teach him the art of acting but to pursuade him to give expression to his feelings. Even the role to be acted is chosen by the child himself, and it is through his own desire that he chooses to express feelings of anger, pleasure, hatred and conflict. The child becomes so engrossed and lost in his acting that he has no compunction in expressing any emotion. Evidently, through his acting he manifests his repressed emotions and attains a peace of mind. In this manner, psychological acting leads to emotional catharsis and a balanced frame of mind. Psychological acting is indulged in both individually as well as within a group. Group acting is so conducted that the individual child has his choice of roles and he selects the one he finds suitable. Most often in this connection the role chosen involves winning castle or overcoming a giant. Through the medium of role, the child gives expression to and gains relief from his aggressive and destructive tendencies.

PLAY AND WORK

Some people say that play should be treated as work and work as play. What they mean is that one should play with the same interest with which one works and work should be made to yield the same pleasure that play does. Play as you work, and work as you play, certainly, but do not forget that the two are distinct. Such proverbs are characteristically misleading as they seem to suggest that work and play are the same. Such a notion is psychologically wrong and indefensible. Work and play differ mainly in the following respects.

1. Difference of objectives: When you see a child playing, you may be inclined to enquire of him as to what he is doing and why, and normally the answer would be that he is playing, and that he is playing for the sake of play. In this way, play is a normal and common tendency, an objective and aim in itself. Play is indulged in of its own accord, rather than from any external motivation. Usually it is seen as the contradiction of work, with the result that all children more interested in games are considered lazy. Many young students run away from school and spend their entire time in playing and roaming about. If one enquires the reason of things from a card player, the almost inevitable response is that one may play and see for oneself. The pleasure resulting from it constitutes the reason why it is played. Now to take up the cudgels on behalf of work, one immediately perceives that no work is done without any motive and definite objective. All the hundreds and thousands of vocations peculiar to the human animal, including study and labour, are pursued with some objective in view. The actual aim may be accumulation of wealth or the achievement of fame, or any other conceivable aim, but no work can be aimless. Work is not its own objective; one does not work for the sake of working. It is the thought of fruit to come in the future that infuses courage and enthusiasm in the worker labouring in the present. But while playing a game, every moment brings its own fresh pleasures and amusements, there are no future fruits to be considered. Its pleasure is in the moment. Of course, one may astutely object that one ever present motive in play is the desire to defeat and overcome the opponent. Then how can objective or aim be used to distinguish between games and work? But if in answer to this question, one were to ask what the winner gains in defeating his adversary and what the latter loses in being defeated, then it would have to be admitted that there is nothing concrete involved. In fact, as Drever has pointed out, the objectives and aims of play belong to the world of imagination while the aim in working belongs to the essential reality and concreteness of the world and everyday life. One often finds that work carries with it the letters of compulsion while no such feeling accompanies play.

2. The meaning of play is within the act of playing while that of work lies outside: According to Drever, 'In play the value and significance of the activity is found in the activity itself, whereas in work the value and significance of activity is found in an end beyond the activity." In this way, every moment spent in play brings its own rewards in terms of pleasure and amusement, whereas work is accompanied by no such pleasure. Usually it is the opposite, as work is attended by pain and effort. It attains fruition long time after it itself has been completed.

3. Play gives immediate and work remote pleasure: Man is by nature an epicurean who turns towards things that bring him pleasure and instinctively turns from objects that bring him pain and misery. Hence, in both work and play the aim and object of the child is obtaining pleasure but while play yields its pleasures immediately and in the present, the pleasures to be had of work are slower in coming. It sometimes never comes at all even in the future, and sometimes even brings pain and suffering.

4. Play creates energy while work consumes it: All work and no play makes the proverbial Jack a dull boy. Play is a kind of recreation. It takes away the individual's fatigue and brings him balmy rest. It is for this reason that young and old, none are averse to playing. But this does not mean that play does not result in physical exhaustion. But the fatigue that results out of playing differs in nature from the fatigue that originates in hard work. The fatigue of play is health giving. Of course, excessive practice in competitive games may harm physical acts as a tonic both for the body and the mind, provided games are not played in excess of the body's energy. Such a condition can be easily recognised if one observes the physical condition after play. The individual should be refreshed and enthusiastic about the work before him, and should have the energy to perform it. In physical games the blood circulates rapidly through the body so that many undesirable elements present in the body are eliminated and the individual feels lighter and more energetic. After the day's tiring routine most people feel the need for some form of recreation and enjoyment. Play is one form of it. On the other hand, work reduces the efficiency of the individual. Hence games and work should be rationally synthesized.

5. Difference in mental attitudes: Play and work differ in respect of their accompanying mental attitudes. Play is independently indulged in without any hint of compulsion whereas work is associated with the feeling of necessity and inevitability. The necessity may be due to some external compulsion such as the order of a superior or it may be imposed on the self from within. Man naturally engages in and concentrates upon play, but where work is concerned, concentration is a matter of conscious effort rather than one of effortless ease. The feeling of responsibility is conspicuously absent when one is playing, he is not answerable to anyone and he has nothing much to lose if he makes a mistake as nothing valuable is at stake. But on the other hand, in work the individual is conscious of a certain burden, and he is answerable to certain other individuals if he fails to perform his functions efficiently. He is responsible for the work he is allotted, and he is very likely to become a prey to boredom easily. It is for these reasons that the child, in his infancy and childhood, is allotted little work and more play. Even the things that he is taught are presented in such a manner that he treats them as child's play. But when he attains adolescence and adulthood, he is entrusted with work involving greater and greater responsibility. He even comes to perform such responsible functions avidly and enthusiastically.

Despite the above superficial points of difference between work and play, there is little if any fundamental dissimilarity between them. There can be a sharp and precise dividing line that demarcates the two and divides them into watertight compartments. The child learns both from play and work, in both he finds material that helps to develop his character, and both are essential and beneficial to him. Then, every individual can obtain some pleasure from the work he is engaged in by orientation and conscious effort. And in the case of very efficient and capable individuals, it is said that work is child's play for them. The ease and comfort with which famous authors compose voluminous works appears play to them. In fact, the ability with which an individual introduces the pleasure of play into his work depends upon the efficiency with which he can perform that work. To quote Sir T.P. Nunn, "An agent thinks of his activity as play if he can take it up or lay it down at choice or vary at will the condition of its exercise, he thinks of it as work if it is imposed on him by unavoidable necessity, or if he is held to it by a sense of duty or vocation." The person who approaches his work with the idea of duty or vocation soon tires of it, and achieves very little. The person who looks upon it as play and accepts it willingly and freely excels in it both quantitatively and qualitatively. To take a simple example, the gardener engaged in the gardening can choose to look upon his job as play or as a vocation. In the first instance, the work will afford him much pleasure whereas if he chooses to treat it as a vocation he will be depriving himself of considerable pleasure.

PLAY WAY OF EDUCATION

It is the intimate relation between play and work that has led to the useful employment of play in the field of education. Modern educational psychologists are inclined to lay stress on the play way method in the education of infants and children. Caldwell Cook is credited with introducing play way education of children. Cook observed that children play truants and run away from schools, show a lack of interest in studying and invent all sorts of causes to play uninterruptedly. He conceived the idea that if some sort of amusement is created in education, then the children would take as much interest in school as they take in the playground. Accordingly then, the intention of the play way method is to make education natural, free, amusing and interesting. It was Sir T.P. Nunn who pointed out that play also achieves the objectives of education in as much as both play and education lead to the individual and personal development of the child. "It is hardly extravagant to say that in the understanding of play lies the key to most of the practical problems of education." The adoption of this conception led to the development, perfection and adaptation of many play way methods and techniques. A somewhat cursory study of these play way methods will lead to an insight into the importance of play in the process of education. The main methods of this kind are the following:

1. Kindergarten: The kindergarten method of infants was evolved by the German educationist Froebel. The word kindergarten implies the garden of children. At its root is the principle that just as flowers and plants flourish in the free and unrestricted atmosphere of the garden while the gardener only looks after them, in a similar manner children should be allowed free and independent development in schools while the teachers only occasionally interfere to look after them and to ensure that desirable conditions are maintained. And the fundamental activity for independent development is play because a child naturally indulges in playful activity. Such qualities as independence, dynamicity and effort, can be imbued in the child through play and these qualities can be made the foundation of his character. Hence Froebel emphasized the imparting of such subjects as gardening, natural science, mathematics, language, religion, and physical training through the play way. And for the play way, Froebel also evolved many instruments and objects. These objects of play can also be called gifts. He created gifts pertaining to many categories or levels. The first category contains six balls of different colours, the second has material figures in the shapes of cubes, cones and circles. The fourth, fifth and sixth categories contain gift of tabloid, stick and ring, respectively. These gifts impart knowledge of colour, lines and points, surface, forms, etc., to the child. In the kindergarten method, the children play various games with these gifts, the games being occupations. The education of the children takes place through these occupations.

2. Montessory method: This method of play way education was evolved by Doctor Maria Montessory of Italy, and it has gained fame in her own name. It is based on principles similar to the kindergarten method of child education. In this method, too, it is play that is the basis of education but it differs from it in respect of the fewer number of things and apparatus for education. It is the personal independence and self-dependence of the child that is more stressed in this method. In it, the responsibility of education is thrown on the children themselves in order that they may develop spontaneously. The mental bases of child development are freedom, self-education, discipline or training of sense organs and the practice and training of useful practical activities. Various games and toys are used to acquaint the child with the forms and sizes of objects, and to develop his sense organs. The Montessory method of education has no provision for any control and administration, so that the question of any physical punishment does not arise. Predetermined curricula and a fixed time table are not insisted upon in this method of education.

3. Project method[1]: Another method of play way education that has been evolved in America is called the project method. It is a fairly recent innovation. In this method, the children are given different projects to perform and complete, such as cooking, stiching, knitting, making chairs and tables, setting up shops, and organising markets, etc. It must of course be remembered that all the projects that they are required to perform have some connection with their needs. Education thus becomes purposeful. All the work to be performed in these projects is left to the children, the teacher's only function being guidance and general superintendence. These activities

1. Kilpatrick, W.H., *Foundation of Educational Method*, The Macmillan Co., New York, 1925.

of the children are savour of naturalness, independence, freedom and activity. They are part and parcel of play.

4. Dalton method[1]: This method of play way education was developed by Mrs. Parkhurst. This method has three distinct parts—independence, sociality and individual performance. It is characterised by a lack of any systematic time table. The classrooms are called laboratories. And the laboratory for each subject is separate. In these laboratories the children work according to their own inclinations and inform the teacher to look after them and to assist them. Education takes on the appearance of play and becomes more palatable.

5. Heuristic method: The originator of this education method was Armstrong. In this method the children are, from the very start, induced to do research and invention. Knowledge imparted to them is through the inductive method, in the forms of questions and answers. Direction and assistance of the children is the teacher's function.

6. Scouting: Sir Baden Povell is responsible for this method of play way education for children. Scouting helps in the social, emotional and character development of the child, but more often it is not reckoned to be a complete method of education, being employed as a complement to some other method of teaching in a school. Secondary importance is more usually attached to it.

Students take part in it very enthusiastically and in the camp and community life learn such qualities as self-dependence, co-operation, socialization, administration, leadership, etc., which fit him for ideal citizenship. Such is the importance of the institution and the children are invited to do works of social welfare in crowds and organized meetings. Social development of the child is thus of a high order. Scouts often go out on long tours with the result that their knowledge of natural things is extensive. As a method of education scouting has proved most useful in the case of adolescents rather than infants. Now-a-days, in Europe and even in India, youth organisations similar to scouting are being organised for male and female adults.

7. Dramatic method and appreciation lesson: It is the dramatic method that is in vogue for the teaching of languages, of history and geography in schools. In a way, this method, too, is a play way method of education. Children appreciate and enjoy the literature, art and music that they are studying. Its efficacy lies in the expression of the child's own sentiments and feelings, as well as in the development of his aesthetic sense. In this manner, the dramatic method and appreciation lesson help in making a course of study as interesting and engrossing as play.

From the foregoing cursory survey of the modern educational methods, it is evident that modern educational psychology lays much stress on education being imparted through the media of play. The plays utilised in education are both group plays and individual ones. The use of the play way

1. Parkhurst, H., *Education on the Dalton Plan*, E.P. Dutton and Co., New York, 1922.

method in education has proved useful in the infant and childhood states, but not so much when adolescence is attained. An adolescent is inclined to look upon himself as an adult, with the commensurate realization of responsibility, and secondly by this time it is essential that he be acquainted with the grim realities and problems of life besides being fitted to solve them.

QUESTIONS FOR EXERCISE

1. Discuss briefly any two theories of play and their bearing on education.
2. Distinguish between work and play. Discuss the importance of play way in modern education.
3. How will you distinguish between play and work? How will you use play impulse in educating children?
4. What do you understand by play way of education? Discuss any two such play way methods which provide freedom in education.
5. How is play spirit being introduced in modern method of education. Give examples.
6. Describe games played at different ages and point out their educational and other importance.
7. Describe factors which influence play. How is play used in the reform of children?

10

Main Stages and Aspects of Development

Educational psychology studies human development, the study starting not with the infant's birth but before it while it is in embryonic form within its mother's womb. The child's development within the womb is a very important phase of his entire development. Hence, there have been detailed studies of the human embryonic state. The human being originates in the form of a fertilised ovum. Gradually and continually, this fertilised ovum shows signs of structural and functional development. In the structural development, the ovum cells multiply in number and increase in size. These cells are of two kinds, the germ cells and the somatic cells. The germ cells help the germ plasm to develop from one stage to the next higher level. The somatic cells are concerned with the development of various physiological parts such as bones, muscles, nerves, etc. Besides changes in structure, the functions of the embryo also take on variety and complexity. Functional development occurs with the addition of new activities. While the human being is in the embryo, the structural and functional developments take place in the nature of two mutually supplementary aspects of total development.

Psychologists have divided the embryonic development of the being into several states. These states and a brief mention of them are given below:

1. Germinal period: The period beginning with conception of the child and lasting for a period of two weeks is called the germinal period of the being's development. During this period the being exists in the form of a fertilised ovum, not being given any external nutrition and continuing in an independent and unmixed state. Lacking nutrition it does not develop. The form of the fertilised ovum is that of an egg, and its cells are equally divided.

2. Embryonic period: The period from the third to the eighteenth week of pregnancy is called the embryonic period, during which the embryo gets nutrition from its parent. As a result, its form undergoes rapid change. In this change there is a hive related to the ovum and it is situated between the cells that lie in between the Omniotic sac and the Yolk sac. In this hive, the cells lying next to the yolk sac are called the endoderm cells while those lying next to the omniotic sac are called the ectoderm cells The cells of the first kind prove of help in the development of the digestive and the respiratory systems, while the latter or second kind of cells lead to the development of the nervous system and the skin or epidermis. The mixing of the two kinds of cells leads to the development of a new layer called the mesoderm. Development of the two kinds of cells leads to the creation of muscles and bones. Cellular structure which is originally flat and convex, gradually spreads out. Every cell has its own peculiar position, and if it is changed, its characteristic features will also undergo some change. For example, if it would originally have developed into skin, it will develop into the muscles of the eye on changing the cells. Certain chemical substances are also of importance in the separate and individual development of the cells. These chemicals are called organisers. Besides these, the development of the embryo is influenced by the use of light, electrical field, X-rays, and other chemical rays.

3. Fetal Period: In the development of the being this state begins with the eighth week, and in it a number of cells increase, following which their size improves. Change in this stage is very rapid.

As has been pointed out above, the child's development during pregnancy is characterised by two types of development, the structural and the functional. The following two laws are accepted in respect of structural development:

(a) Law of cephalocaudal development: According to this law, in the development of the embryo, the development starts with the cephalic portion or the head and gradually proceeds to the tail portion. In this way, this law of development shows the direction of the bodily development. This law applies to growth as well as differentiation.

(b) Law of proximo development: According to this law, the progress in development is more rapid in peripheral parts than in the parts situated in the centre.

In structural development, the structure of the nervous system is a very important one. In this development, the first layer of the ectoderm cells turns inwards to form the neural tube, the major portion of which, the spinal cord and the upper part develops into the brain. In the fifth week of development, the medulla, cerebellum and the mid brain become distinctly visible. The nervous system develops very rapidly during the fetal period. Muscles begin to be formed even before the nerves and sensory organs. Almost all the sensory parts develop in the being before delivery or actual birth. The development of vision starts with the second week, and continues even after pregnancy. Receptors concerned with olfactory sensation reach maturity in pregnancy in the case of some children. Taste cells develop in the third month, that is, during the fetal period. Besides this, during pregnancy, the being attains the power of feeling sensations of pressure on the skin.

Functional development during pregnancy is divided into two parts, those of motor development and sensory development. Their description follows:

1. Motor development: During pregnancy, the embryo, shows constant activity that can be discovered with the help of the stethoscope 14 to 16 week before birth. During this period, this movement is also felt by the pregnant woman carry ing the child. At the age of three months the heart starts beating, and after 18 weeks this heart beating becomes audible. In this period, some motion is also evident in the chest. In the seventh month, the organs of digestion evince some movement while there is sometimes some tension of the urinary bladder. Children born in the sixth month of pregnancy produce certain sounds. Research experts have made study of the embryonic movement in rats, cats and pigs, etc., and compared it with the movement in human animals. This research has shown that till a certain stage of development is achieved, the embryo does not show any reaction to any stimuli. In the beginning the tail section does not show any reaction, but it is evident when maturity of this part sets in. The movement starts with the leg, continues to the knee and can then be seen successively in the foot and the ankle. Minkowski and Hooker have conducted important research in connection with motor development. The two laws concerning structural development are also applicable to motor development. According to Toghill's principle, in functional development there is a movement from the general to the particular.

Putting it more explicitly, it can be said that first general activities appear, and then through gradual development these general activities are divided into particular activities that become distinct.

2. Sensory development: The second important aspect of motor development is that of sensory development In the eighth week, the embryo becomes susceptible to epidermic sensations. Later on, it reacts to pressure and temperature sensations. According to the law of cephalocaudal development, in sensory development epidermic reaction is the first to appear, while sensibility of the rest of the body are also in evidence, but the sensation of pain does not develop during pregnancy, while the ability to recognise and react to direct smell and taste is engendered during pregnancy. Some experiments have shown that the child can react to strong sensations one month before it is born.

The diagram given on next page represents the various states of motor development, personal, social behaviour, language, adaptive behaviour, at varying levels of maturity in the child from the time based upon the book *Development Diagnosis, Normal and Abnormal Child Development* by Gesell and Amatruda.

As has been shown in the figure, mentioned above, the bodily parts develop gradually in the child during its pregnancy. After birth during the 4th, 16th, 28th and 40th weeks, the eyes, hand, back and fingers attain expertise respectively. In the ninth month movements of the legs and feet are evident.

At the age of one year and half, babbling sounds are produced, which are the rudiments of speech. At two the intestines and the bladder are brought under control. At the age of three years, he develops the capacity for thought and reasoning. And when attains five, he shows the tendency to socialization.

MAJOR STEPS IN DEVELOPMENT

Man is a being who is constantly developing in its life time. This development of his passes through various stages. Having passed through these steps, an immature and erring child develops into the properly developed and matured adult. Although there is some difference of opinion among thinkers regarding the various steps in development, yet generally human development has been divided into the following four stages:

1. Infancy
2. Childhood
3. Adolescence
4. Adulthood.

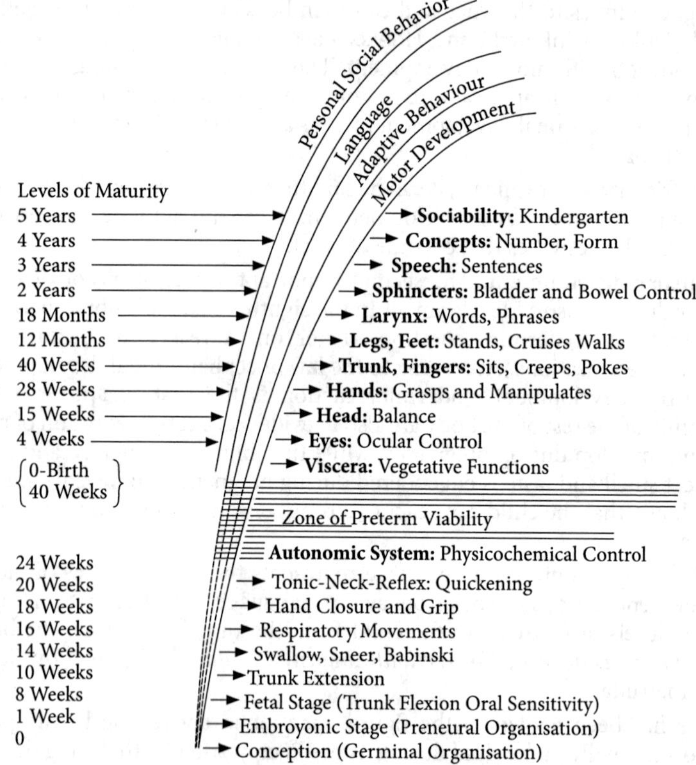

Fig. 1. Maturation of human behaviour

These above mentioned four stages in the development of the human child were determined by Rousseau, the French philosopher. Establishing the age levels that correspond to this division, the educational psychologists have pointed out that infancy lasts from birth till six years, childhood from six to twelve, adolescence from twelve to eighteen while adulthood should be accepted to extend from eighteen till the individual ceases to develop. It is the common belief among modern educational psychologists that by the age of twenty the individual usually completes all kinds of development. According to Dr. Jones, before adolescence or by the age of twelve the child attains to a kind of pseudo-maturity. Following this infancy and childhood are reflected in adolescence and adulthood. According to modern psychologists, the most rapid development in the child takes place in two stages, the first time when the infant is about two, and the second time when he is between ten and twelve years of age. It will be necessary to reflect upon these above steps in development from the standpoint of physiological development. It should be remembered that though all children pass through these various stages of development, yet all do not go through them at the same age. The female child, for example, generally reaches each one of these stages some two years ahead of the male sex. Nevertheless, generally speaking, the physiological development that takes in the different stages can be seen in all children.

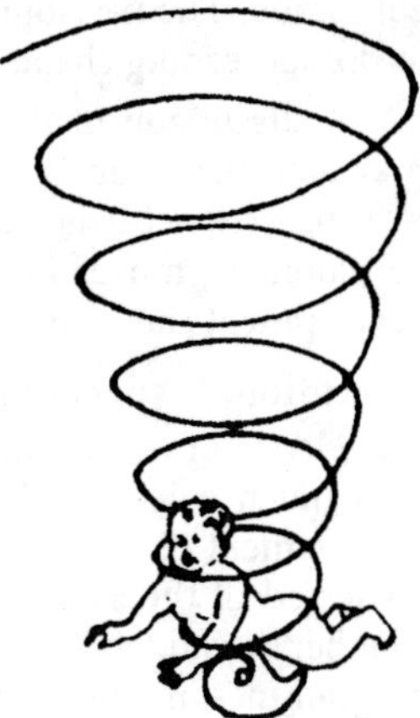

Fig. 2. Spiral development of the child

Major aspects of development

As a general rule, the development of the individual in each step can be divided Into the following aspects: (1) Physical development; (2) Mental development; (3) Emotional development; (4) Ethical and Aesthetic development; (5) Social development.

The physical development of the individual includes the development of his various physical parts, his height, weight, nervous system, internal organs, lungs, heart, sex organs, etc. His mental development includes the progress of his Intelligence, special abilities, capabilities, tendencies, imagination, reasoning, and other mental elements. In emotional development, the evolution of different instincts and emotions leads to the formation of sentiments and the progress of sentiments to character. Moral development includes the evolution of the moral character, and aesthetic development the evolution of aesthetic sense and artistic tendencies. In his social development, the individual learns to move and live according to the rules of his family, group and society, and to adjust to it. Educational psychology studies all these aspects of the development of infancy, childhood, adolescence and adulthood. The development of these aspects will be the subject of reflection in the succeeding chapters.

A discussion of the various stages and aspects of development makes it evident that human development is not linear, but spiral. In other words, in progressing further it turns back and then moves forward again. This development moves both horizontally as well as vertically. This nature of development can be understood from the figure given in Fig. 2 on p. 97.

Educational aspect of development

Knowledge of the various stages and aspects of the educand's development is of much value for the teacher. The object of education is the complete development of the educand. Hence, it is evident that the teacher should be possessed of the aspects of development so that he may be able to discern whether the student is lagging behind in any aspect. The curriculum and other programmes in school should be designed to expedite the overall progress of the educand. Where the curriculum does not seem likely to succeed, recourse should be had to extra-curricular programmes in order to ensure progress. In examining the student, it should be kept in mind that all his various aspects are being evaluated.

Modern education is based on the psychology of the educand. And the educand's psychology conforms to the stage of his development. Hence, by knowing the stage of development through which an individual student is passing the teacher can know his psychology, can base hopes of his development and progress in various departments accordingly, and can mould his method of teaching accordingly. Having a knowledge of the various aspects and steps of development, the teacher can form a dynamic attitude towards education and the educand.

QUESTIONS FOR EXERCISE

1. Write note on: Periods in prenatal development.
2. Sketch the growth of behaviour during prenatal development.
3. State the different periods in prenatal development.
4. Discuss the factors that influence prenatal development.
5. Explain the meaning of development of growth.
6. Distinguish between growth and development. Discuss general principles of growth and development.
7. "Rate of growth and development varies between individual, and between different development areas within the same individual." Explain the principle of rate of growth and development and say how it affected your teaching.

11

Physical Development

FOUR STAGES OF PHYSICAL DEVELOPMENT

Although there is some slight difference of opinion regarding the various stages of physical development, die majority of thinkers are in favour of dividing it into the following four stages:

1. Infancy
2. Childhood
3. Adolescence
4. Adulthood

INFANCY

Infancy is divided into two stages of development, the first lasting from birth to three years, thereafter the second stage lasts till the child is six years of age.

The child develops very rapidly in the infant stage. At birth, the child is bodily unattractive because the skin is lined, the face puffed up and red, the size of the head approximately one-fourth of the body and the rest of the body unbalanced. When born the child is about twenty inches in height, but grows another 10 inches before its first year is completed. Generally, the child is between seven and seven and a half pounds in weight, the male child being taller and heavier than the female. In the first year, both weight and size increase at a very rapid pace. Height increases about 50 per cent in this period while the weight doubles in six months and trebles in another six. The proportion of the head to the body also changes, being one-fourth at the time of birth, the head becomes one-eighth of it as it develops. In the process of development, the head becomes one-eighth of the body, the length of arms and legs also increases as the child comes to require them more and more in his adaptation to life outside the womb.

Weight of the brain increases rapidly during pregnancy and immediately after birth. By the time the child reaches the age of four his brain gains 80 per cent of its final weight, another 10 per cent being added by the time he is eight. The final 10 per cent is acquired by his twentieth year. It is between the ages of 4 and 6 that the main part of the brain develops in weight. Sex organs develop in thc opposite manner, as during the first 14 years of development they develop only to 20 per cent while the remaining 80 per cent is completed in the next six years.

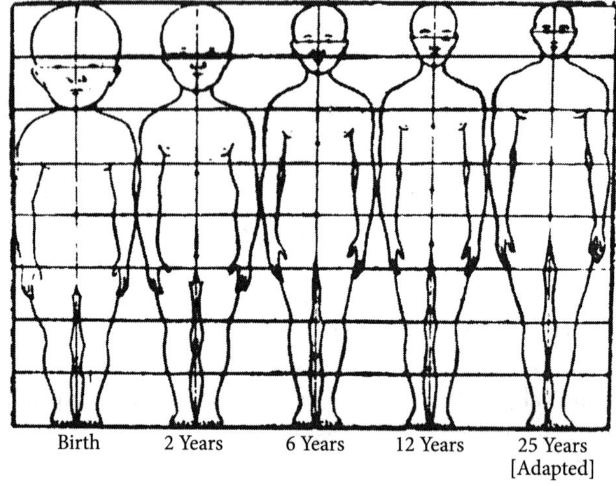

Fig. 3. Proportion of physical parts since birth upto twentyfive years of age

Normally, the height of the child at birth indicates the height he will attain in adulthod, but there are about 20 per cent exceptions to this rule. Although there is never any very rapid physical development yet one can see individual differences in the speed and time of it. Normally, one sees an inclination towards the average in the increase in height. Those who grow fast, slow up as they reach the average, but those who increase in height relatively slowly, develop rapidly as they attain to the average.

Describing infancy in respect of height and weight, Thorpe has written[1] that according to a recent survey the average weight of a child at birth is 7-13 pounds, irrespective of sex and race. In this connection, the weight of boys was, on the average, 0.2 pounds more than the weight of newborn infant girls. The weight of white newborn babies was 0.25 pounds more than the offspring of negroes, but the weight of the child at birth is not influenced by social and economic status. Another survey, older than the one mentioned above, indicated that the weight of 85 per cent children at birth is between 6 and 9 pounds, and the height between 17 and 22 inches. The rapidity of the development of infants can be gauged from the fact that, on an average, male children increase upto 7 and 1/8 inches in 9 months, while female children increase 6 and 3/4 inches during the same period. Increase in the weight of children is even more significant and well marked, as the average child doubles its weight in six months. The weight of a male baby whose height is 24 and 1/8 inches is 19 and 11/16 lbs. while the weight of a female child of the same height is normally 19 and 5/16 pounds. Similar researches have

1. Thorpe, L.P., *Child Psychology and Development*, The Lowell Press Co. (1955), p. 102.

thrown additional light on the development of the child. Research carried out at Harvard University over a period of 12 years has indicated that the child's development during the first two years of his life is very rapid. Then, the rate of development decreases. Generally, the development curves of both sexes were similar. Besides Harvard, other American universities such as Yale, Michigan, Iowa and California, have also carried out detailed research into the development of children. Studies conducted by Preyer, Stanley Hall and Carl Murchison as well as Arnold Gessell, have yielded important data. It must, of course, be remembered that there are wide differences in the development of height and weight in individual children, the causes of the differences being attributable both to environment and heredity. Height and weight of a child in development are a testimony to his good health which influence his mental and emotional development also.

Another area in which change continually takes place is the proportion between the various parts of the developing child's body. The head becomes smaller and reduces in proportion to the body, while the hands and feet gain in size proportion.

Development of internal organs

Teeth are absent at birth, but within a year the child begins cutting teeth that are called milk teeth. In his infancy, the internal organs of the child's body undergo constant development. The most prominent ones to develop are the digestive organs, lungs, muscles, nervous system, nerves, sex organs and glands. This development achieves balance between the various internal organs.

When the child is born, he has a nervous system adequately developed to deal with his environment, to react to its external stimuli and to adapt and adjust to it. Muscles normally do not develop during the child's infancy. There is no evidence to indicate that the child breathes inside the womb, but as soon as he is born he begins breathing and blood circulation continues. While inside the womb the heart beat is very low, but immediately following birth, the heart beat gains considerably and becomes rapid. As the size of the heart increases, it becomes stronger, the heart beat and the speed of blood circulation in the arterial system both slow down to become steady. According to physiologists, during the first month of infancy , the child's heart beats upto 140 times a minute, but in the first six months it slows down to about 100 times a minute. While the child is still in his infancy, he develops the means of excreting all water waste from the body and combating all attacks of virus and other disease germs. On the contrary, the development of sex organs in infancy is exceedingly slow.

Important facts about the infant's development

The child's weight decreases in his first two weeks of his life because much of the water in him evaporates. But this decrease is soon made up. Some precautions are required on the part of the parents if the child's physical development during infancy is to be maintained. The following are these important facts:

1. **Food:** Food is one of the most important considerations in child care. The speed of growth being very rapid, it is essential that the child's diet be both balanced and administered at the proper time. In this connection, Laird and his associates conducted an experiment in which some children were kept on an exclusively milk diet, others on a diet of milk and other nutritive foods, and still other children on normal food. After some weeks it was noticed that the children on a milk diet had progressed some 8 per cent more than the children on a normal diet. Similarly, children kept on milk and other nutritive foods had progressed some 16 per cent more than those on the normal diet. Generally speaking, all doctors and scientists believe that milk is the best food during the period of infancy, as in this period the bones develop and strengthen at a rapid pace, and milk is essential for this development. As long as the child retains his so-called milk teeth, his best and most nutritive diet is milk, and among the varieties of milk the very best is the variety that is the easiest to digest. Mahatma Gandhi believed that goat's milk was the most digestible but scientific opinion dares to contradict this view in favour of cow's milk. The latter is beneficial for mental development besides, its more obvious advantages for bodily development and improvement. Tinned milk, if it be not too old, can also be administered without any ill-effects. In some cases, tinned milk does not prove efficacious and leads to serious ailments of the stomach which can become complicated and even fatal. Concerning baby food, Spiller has opined that the child should not be given any solid food, but should be given only milk and fruit. The child's milk teeth cannot bite and masticate hard food, nor can his intestines digest it.

2. **Clothes and cleanliness:** In infancy, the child's bones are very weak and tender Consequently, it is necessary that much care must be exercised in cleaning and washing him. The use of good oils for delicate massage is good for the child, but the massage must be very tenderly conducted. Lack of attention to the child's cleanliness can result in his contracting many diseases. In the Indian type of climate the child should be bathed at least once daily, and his bed cleaned with the same periodicity. It can be kept free of urine and other waste matter excreted by the child by the use of bedsheets made of rubber. More generally speaking, it is desirable that the child's bed and clothes should never exude any bad smell. Bad smell creates bad effect on the child's health. Of course, the best thing that can be done is that the children should be trained to excrete by the clock, that is, at set times. Tight fitting clothes interfere with the free circulation of blood with bad effect on his delicate health. Clothes should thus be reasonably loose, but not necessarily of the toga variety. Of course, it is reasonable that the child should be protected from the cold by warm clothing, but it is better if he is not suffocated in them. He should not be smothered in his clothes, the pores of his skin should be given as much chance to breathe as his lungs. It is best that the child should be loaded with the least clothes to protect him, since the habit of counteracting the heat and cold that

he acquires at this stage usually lasts him his whole life. The sun's rays, so long as they are not strong enough to burn the skin, are always beneficial to the skin, but if one would be convinced of their real utility, one should enquire of the infant, for it is the infant who derives the greatest benefit from them. How surprising it is, that while people in the Western hemisphere, where the climate is much colder, try to keep their children in as few clothes as possible, in a hot country like India people literally load them with clothes. In winter, it does the child's tender bones much good to be massaged with oil and then laid out in the sun to be strengthened. The body gains by massage and sun bathing because the child gets vitamin D from the sun's rays, which helps in his cutting teeth at the right time.

3. Sleep and up-bringing: It is in his infancy that the child requires much sleep and can normally get it. He should be allowed to sleep like a sapling, not a log, as long as he feels like it, since the proper amount of sleep helps in adequate and proper development of the body. Normally, at this age, the child awakens only when he feels hungry and goes to sleep immediately his stomach is filled. He spends the larger span of his time in sleeping. In the first month the child wakens only when he is hungry, but sometimes it is also because he has tasted milk, so that it is not a good practice to feed him milk whenever he cries. Such intemperate feeding spoils his digestive system and has the worst effect on his health, besides leaving him susceptible to many dangerous diseases. It is scientifically more desirable to feed the child by the clock, and to allay his crying by presenting him with toys or by any other means available, such as crooning to him, if that can possibly put a stop to his crooning. Children are normally very much attracted by brightly coloured objects and if they manage to get their hands on them they begin to suck them. On the bed the child flings his arms and legs about, much to his own good as it exercises his limbs though in a somewhat unconventional manner.

Havelock Ellis, the famous thinker, emphasised that the importance of mother's milk for the child exceeds its purely nutritive value. Besides nourishing the baby, the act of feeding symbolises the mother's love for the child. From this point of view, it is desirable that the child's care and nourishment should be in the hands of his mother. It is never good to leave this function to a servant or a nurse. It has particular ill effects on the child's emotional development as the love that he bears his mother he cannot give to any other person, and in the absence of adequate reciprocation from the mother, his emotional development is adversely effected. An individual concerned with the child's nourishment and general care has to keep in mind all the needs of the ward as at this stage the child is himself unable to communicate his needs being unskilled in the use of his tongue. Hence, many of the diseases that the child contracts at an early age are the effect of his parent's or guardian's carelessness. If the child cries, it is best to make some effort to divine the cause of his discomfort. It may be that his ear or may be stomach paining, and for this it is better to use the medicine a doctor prescribes than to give him more milk and try to put him to sleep.

Love and affection are always very potent influences in the child's life but these should not outstrip the limits of propriety and spoil the child. From the physiological point of view, it is not desirable to carry the child in one's lap for long times. As far as possible, the child should be allowed to rest in a recumbent position and he should be diverted by the use of toys if he cries. Some people make it a practice to put a rubber nipple in the child's mouth whenever he cries. This too, is not a very commendable habit as it is possible for the child to contract many diseases if the nipple is unclean or unhygienic. What is even more important is that once a child becomes habituated to its use, it is difficult to wean him of it. But even then if it must be used, then all care must be taken to keep it clean. In this stage of his life, the child is a delicate sapling, and he must be handled with the greatest care, the least strain proving harmful. One should never be rough with the child's body. Even overexhaustion is harmful for the developing child. The child is fully capable of keeping his body requisitely exercised as he is guided by an inner instinct to run and move about as much as his frail body requires. Hence, it is never a very good idea to try to keep the child exercised. Just as a young plant fares well if it is well tended and provided with requisite amounts of sun, water and manure, the child develops well and without difficulty if it is properly looked after, given the correct food and the necessary sleep and the exercise that he requires. Some parents betray unnecessary anxiety regarding the physical development and growth of their children. Although, normally, every child should attain a certain level of height and weight by the time he reaches a particular age, yet there are always exceptions. Some children have a tendency to learn bodily structure while others are more liberally supplied with fat at their birth and they tend to collect it more and more. Hence it is not sensible to feed the child excessively in trying to make him fat or strong, but is in fact a kind of torture for the child. In this connection, and in connection with all physical development, it is always preferable to adopt the golden mean, since almost all kinds of excess is harmful for the body. And in the child's infancy, his physical development depends upon the intelligence and rationality of his guardians.

Infancy prior to childhood

Following the first three years of his life, the second stage in the child's development is the time between three and six years of age. This period is considered by some to be the precursor of childhood, or the last stages of infancy, as it falls after infancy but before actual childhood. It comprehends the development that takes place between the ages of three and six. While the first three years of the infant's life can be called the period of agglomeration, the period under consideration can be called the stage of maturity. In other words, all that the child acquires in the first three years is strengthened and made stable in the next three. Evidently, no fresh bodily development takes place in this period, only the old development is capitalised upon and made permanent. Children appear to be very naughty and irrepressible in the first three years, but they acquire a medicum of reserve in the next three, and appear comparatively serious. In the first stage, it is easy and desirable to guide him in as many ways as possible, but in this latter period it is best not to interfere in his development and maturity. This stage, too, requires that all possible attention be bestowed on him in respect of his physical as well as his mental comfort.

CHILDHOOD

Physical and other development in the child that takes place between the ages of six and twelve is in the childhood period. In other words, the period from seven to nine years of age is the period of acquisition or agglomeration in which development takes place, while the time between the ages of ten and twelve is the period when maturity of this growth takes place.

(*a*) ***Period of growth:*** The child is as restless in the growth period of childhood as he was in the same period of his infancy. At this stage, his interest in the objects of his environment is continually on the increase. This time is the best to start his education. His education at this stage should be so designed as to make the most profitable use of his instincts. From the bodily point of view, development is not very rapid, as such rapid development is visible either at the age of two or of twelve. Games are particularly important for the physical development of the child. Every effort should be made to interest the child in games by which he can profit both in respect of body as well as of mind. This age is particularly important in respect of possibilities of ingraining good habits and high ideals in his mind. He should be taught to lead a disciplined and regular life, and his various physical and mental needs should be quickly attended to. His physical comfort must not be neglected. In fact, bodily development does not imply the child's becoming large and broad, but rather the possession of such qualities as energy, ethusiasm, freshness, the capacity to labour, etc. It is only when the child possesses these qualities in abundance that he can properly be called healthy. Elementary physical training and light drill at school at this stage is desirable.

(*b*) ***Period of maturity:*** In the maturity period, the child specially develops a social consciousness. He should be encouraged to meet others and co-operate w ith them, but at the same time a sense of proportion is always to be admired. The child should never be allowed to become a vagabond or truant. Such healthy habits as collecting stamps, post cards, etc., can be inculcated.

ADOLESCENCE

The second stage when the child develops very rapidly is the period of adolescence, after the first stage in his infancy. The same pattern of three years of growth and three following years of maturation can be assumed to exist in this period of the individual's life also. Maximum physical development takes place in the first three years. Normally, adolescence appears at the age of 11 and 12 in girls and at 12 and 13 in boys. Commonly, boys are taller and heavier than girls, but in adolescence between 12 and 14 it is the female who is both taller and heavier as she develops earlier than the male child. It is for the same reason that in these years girls consider boys of same age as younger and prefer to be with boys a couple of years older than themselves. Another characteristic is the desire for mixing between toys and girls. In adolescence, boys and girls attain 90 per cent of the height that they are going to have in later years. In other words, by the time a young boy is 14 he has developed to 90 per cent of his ultimate or final stature. But it takes him another six years to cover the remaining 10 per cent. On the other hand, the weight of the adolescent is only two-third of what is going to be. Even after the adolescent has stopped growing upwards his weight continues to increase at a rapid pace. Compared to boys, girls gain in both height and weight faster but the development in these directions also stops earlier. Consequently, the adolescent girl looks more developed than her male counterpart of equal age. Muscles, in particular, develop mainly only after adolescence is over. In this age, physical education is most important and very meaningful. Sex education is equally important as it is in this age that boys and girls develop the characteristic features of their respective sexes. Girls develop lady-like features. Of the many changes in the girl, the most perceptible is the roundness of the breasts and hips while among the boys their faces become adorned with beard and mostaches. While the girl's voice becomes sweet, the boy's sound takes on a deeper and more thrilling note. Within a year or two of adolescence, both male and female attain the capability of procreation.

Notable facts concerning adolescence

Physical exercise and games are important for physical development in adolescence. The well balanced body shows apt proportion between length and weight. Much of this proportionate development depends upon the exercise taken. But neither height nor weight are in fact indicative of the healthy taste of an individual's body. Physical health finds adequate expression and recognition in the enthusiasm, energy, swiftness and interest with which he performs his functions. Although it is always desirable for youth to be active and vibrant in adolescence, yet one should guard against excessive exercise that completely tires the body, as such exhaustion has adverse effects on the body's development. Nutritive food is as important for getting rid of exhaustion as rest is. Exercise, too, should be balanced. It should be remembered that the physical development of a player's body is sometimes impaired by his playing a particular game in which only some of the bodily organs are exercised and strained. Excessive indulgence in such a game can have only the least desirable effect. But even if regular practice of the game benefits these parts, the other organs of the body are not benefited. Hence, generally speaking, it would be more efficacious to induce adolescents to take interest in physical education rather than spending long and weary hours in the pursuit of perfection in the various competitive games. Schools should divert their expenditure on coaching schemes to the physical education of their students. This measure will help to improve the level of health among adolescents. Proper exercise steps up blood circulation with the result that many waste materials are thrown out of the body, while other parts of the body such as lungs also develop better and faster. Physical capacities are also developed beside the progress of the body itself. Ignoring the exceptions, one could draw up a chart of the various physical capacities as correlated to the various stages in physical development. From adolescence to adulthood, the grip of the hand, the length and strength of the feet, neck and the middle portion of the body, all develop equally. The golden formula for proper physical development at this period of life is proper food and adequate exercise, without excess in either of the two. Of course, there can be no common level of food and exercise for every one. The amount of food, rest, sleep and exercise that an individual requires can be found out from experience or from his friends or teachers. Provision of sex education can help the young boys and girls to form the proper attitude towards bodily development concerning sex. Suppression of any feeling on account of fear will only have adverse effects on them. Their clothing should be such as not to restrict the growth of their bodies. Just as at any other stage in life, it is not advisable to wear very tight clothes, as they will harm the body even if they do appear temporarily attractive and smart. And, particularly among the young girls, it is essential for the development of the breasts and the hips that they wear slightly lose and comfortable clothes. Any female child who aspires after beauty can begin practising her wiles from this age. Hence, in this respect some intelligence is the adolescent's best companion.

ADULTHOOD

This period of life begins where adolescence ends. By this time the individual usually attains the age of 20 and completes his development in respect of height, weight, nervous system, bone structure, etc. It is equally important at this stage also that adequate attention be paid to food, sleep, rest, regular pattern of life, exercise, etc. Similar principles also hold true, that is, there should be no excess in any one direction. It is perfectly correct to indulge in slightly more exercise than previously since it helps in the development of muscles, and the attainment of due proportion between the various parts of the body.

QUESTIONS FOR EXERCISE

1. Describe the stages of physical development. What care should be taken to help physical development during infancy?
2. Describe the physical development during adolescence. Suggest important care to be taken during this period.

12

Motor Development

STAGES OF MOTOR DEVELOPMENT

Development of the motor ability is an important part of a child's physical development. In motor development, changes in activity can be observed through the physical progress. For example, before acquiring the ability of walking, the child passes through a number of stages. Although individual differences are visible in motor activity, even to the extent of individual styles of walking being very distinctive, the approximate time of the development and appearance of certain motor activities in physical development can be established. In motor activities, the motor control starts with the head, in other words, the child first starts by holding his head erect and focusing on various objects with his eyes. Following this, the child learns to grip objects and then to crawl and walk on his knees. This is represented in the figure given on next page. In the child's motor development over the first two periods the following stages are evident:

Age in months	Motor Activity
1.	chin high
2.	raising the chest
3.	gripping and releasing object
4.	sitting with some assistance
5.	lap-sitting and holding objects
6.	sitting on high chair
7.	playing with object
8	standing with some help
9.	standing while holding on to furniture
10.	moving on knees
11.	raising oneself while holding on to furniture
12.	walking while holding someone
13.	climbing stairs
14.	standing without assistance
15.	walking alone.

Fig. 4. Motor development at different ages in the child

For motor development it is essential that the child be given adequate freedom. If the child is always carried and is not allowed to move around, its motor development is likely to be retarded. The child should have adequate space to play in. If it is left to its own devices on the floor, it will be seen moving its legs and feel.

Patterns of crawling and creeping

The beginning of a child's motor development is with the activities of creeping and crawling. Different children exhibit different patterns of these activities. In the following Fig. are illustrated the various physical positions that are adopted by the child in developing from the crawling and creeping to the walking stage. These physical positions have been illustrated in the following order—(1) Motion of new born's crawling. (2) Less motion in the hind part while it tries to raise the head. (3) Control on the movements of head and shoulders improves. (4) There is considerable development in the upper part, while the hip remains on the floor. (5) Contradiction between the motion of the head and shoulder, and the hips, with the result that raising of hips leads to lowering of head and shoulders. (6) Motions of rocking in which the hip bone is kept above the ground. (7) Complementary movements of creeping. In starting movement some children creep on the stomach, others move on all fours while still others propel themselves by swinging their hips along the surface. Different children start creeping and crawling in different ages. Generally, the child who begins his crawling early also walks erect in shorter time. Although motor activity develops along with general progress of the child, but in encouraging the child to walk wooden or other scooters or rollers can be used. This can induce him to learning walking earlier.

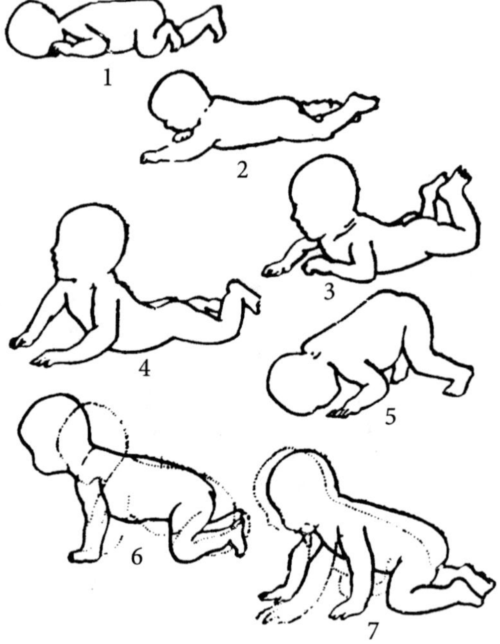

Fig. 5. Patterns of crawling and creeping

MOTOR DEVELOPMENT AND EDUCATION

Motor development is an important prerequisite for man's motor learning. Along with other development, motor development continues during childhood and adolescence. And in this, much importance is attached to various physical movements and exercises. It is for this reason that in modern colleges, academic teaching and training is accompanied by various physical exercises, games and many activities that require motor activity. It helps to develop in child many handicrafts that assist him in his adopting some particular career. Some such handicrafts are stitching and sewing, wood work, typewriting, cooking, etc. Motor control is essential in all handicrafts. Motor development is an important part of overall comprehensive development.

Important factors in motor development

Many factors cast a very profound influence upon the child's motor development. The object of motor learning is the acquisition of skill in some particular physical movement or employment. And to gain skill in any work that requires handling it is essential to start with the fundamental movements, and to progress gradually to the more complex motions. It is only because the child learns motor control in his childhood that he can, at a later stage, learn the handling and control of motor cars, cycles, etc. The motor activity patterns formed in infancy are helpful in the learning of different handicrafts and games. Where these patterns are of help in certain cases, they also hinder the learning of other crafts. The motor patterns that are advantageous to the pursuit of a particular game can prove to be harmful in the playing of another.

Important factors in the teaching of motor activity[1]

Physical education proves very valuable in the learning of physical skill. In addition to this, in modern colleges, the teachers help the students to acquire various kinds of skill and knowledge in handicrafts. The following points should be kept in mind in rendering this assistance:

1. Knowledge of effective methods: Before turning to the teaching of motor skill, it is necessary for the teacher himself to be aware of the most effective ways and means of achieving that skill. It helps him to impart his information more successfully as well as win the admiration and confidence of his students. Once the confidence is developed, it is only natural that they should pay attention to his teaching, and to do their best to emulate the movements made and described by him, thereby making his task easier.

2. Encouraging the students in the use of effective techniques: Having gained confidence in the teacher, the student acquires the right mental set for acquiring motor skill. Now, the teacher has to encourage him in the use of methods that have proved successful in the attainment of that motor skill. In the beginning he is not able to perform these actions perfectly because before the skilled and refined actions can be done there are the unrefined and unskilled actions to be mastered. The student fails repeatedly in acquiring the skill he requires by the use of these unskilled and unrefined movements, with the result that he becomes discouraged, and may even become so despondent as to throw up the training. It is for the teacher to foresee this contingency and to prevent it, by tendering encouragement and sympathy. Certain people entertain a groundless fear of water and hence of swimming with the result that when they try to learn it, they are apt to give it up after the first or second ducking. In a situation of this kind, it is for instructor to encourage constantly so that enthusiasm may not flag. As in the case of all other learning, the motor learning is also susceptible to the inevitable plateau of learning in its curve. The intelligent instructor can discover the reasons whereby this plateau is arrived at, and contrive to remove it. As a result, the student progresses further, and continues to do so. Hence, in order to develop motor skill, the developed and progressive methods of learning should be employed so that hindrances and obstacles in learning be reduced to a minimum and progress be the most satisfactory and regular The method of teaching should conform to the needs of education, and should change as the subject to be taught changes.

1. Crow and Crow, *Educational Psychology*, p. 286.

3. Minimum possible destructive criticism: Just as the student is susceptible to constant encouragement and good words from the teacher, he is influenced by strong critical comment from the same source. He is so affected that he may become despondent and discouraged. Hence, even if he makes mistakes, the student should be corrected and advised sympathetically, and criticism reduced and kept to the minimum. It should he indulged in only if it becomes inevitable, and even then it should be only as much as is absolutely necessary.

4. Stress on the right activities: The main cause of failure in motor skill is the following of wrong activities or actions by student. On the other hand, it is essential to make a habit of the right actions. It is desirable for the teacher to take each action involved in any motor activity separately and demonstrate it to the students, following it up with continuous practice of it in his own presence.

5. Stress on speed and exactness for skilful working: Generally some people hold the view that any work done rapidly is not successful. This is quite true of any work at its outset, when one is learning it. In the beginning it is desirable to make a habit of working slowly but avoiding all mistakes and faults. In learning motor skill it is particularly important to note that no wrong habits are formed, even if progress is thereby quite slow and retarded. The speed or work should be improved gradually. Sometimes accuracy and skill improves by working rapidly at the outset. In learning cycling, one learns the proper balancing and control only if one immediately takes to riding fast, without any fear of the falls one is going to suffer. On the other if he begins by cycling slowly and pays attention to his faults, he is sure to sustain many falls and learn only with great difficulty. But this fact is not true of many motor skills and activities.

Once a very strong habit of some motor action has been formed, it becomes quite automatic and does not require constant attention to be performed. If a person has learnt his cycling well, he can travel through a crowded market without any apparent attention to his movement. He can in fact allow his thoughts and attention to wander, to some extent, to other things while he continues forward without endangering his own safety or that of others. Having attained motor skill in some department, in addition to the automatic control on the physical movements involved in it, the individual is also in a position to control the mental state involved in that motor skill. An expert cyclist need not ponder over every individual situation to decide when he is to be break to a hault or when to pick up speed. His unconscious does this for him.

6. Proper and adequate practice: Constant repetition of some movements is not sufficient in order to generate motor skill in them. It is essential that adequate and proper practice of the activity should be indulged in, in a state of complete mental consciousness of it. The practice must be mentally attended too. Many such factors as the nature of skill, the age and interests of the educand, the conditions of learning, the time taken in learning and practising period of rest, the desired level of skill, etc., influence the result of practice, and changes in these factors are reflected in variations in the final achievement. In practising it should be remembered that the practice should conform to the method required in actual practice. For example, if a child is required to write with a fountain pen at a later stage, he should be made to practise with a fountain pen and not a quill pen. Similarly, the proper tools of expert use should be employed in training individuals in wood work, carpentry, leather working, etc., and as far as possible the things made during practice should be the same as are required to be made once the training is completed.

7. Practice with an aim: While practising for the gaining of motor skill, the educand should be aware of the objective, and should be constantly mindful of it. The teacher should measure his progress by examining him in terms of this objective. If the student is aware of his aim, he progresses faster and more satisfactorily, and his interest also is maintained. Knowing his aim, he is aware of the skill that he must attain. In this, the teacher can also put some example before him. In the absence of such an example, the student may stop working after he has learnt only a very little, in the impression that he has in fact become skilled in his pursuit.

By keeping in mind these factors that influence the teaching of motor skills, the teacher in college can make very skilled workers of the students. In this, he will have to pay individual attention to each student, because the problems, capabilities and abilities of individual students differ. Some of them can learn one piece of work in a very short time, while others may take much longer to master the same. As it is bad to hinder and obstruct the fast workers by holding them up in their progress, it is also wrong and impolitic to force the slower workers to go faster. Similarly, it is not very fruitful to hope for all students that they will attain the same level of competence and skill in any motor activity for which they are being trained. All people cannot be equally successful in one particular skill, irrespective of the quality of implements and equipment used as well as the time taken in training them. Practice should be made to conform to age and capability. Small children should be forced to practice for shorter periods of time, while older people can benefit by longer sessions of work. And the period of rest between the periods of practice should be longer in the case of young children with less skill than in the case of older people with greater skill in the work. Practice should avoid fatiguing the individual as much as possible, but the time of practice should also not be so short that the workers may not even warm up. In this connection it is best to maintain a balanced and cautious outlook.

QUESTION FOR EXERCISE

1. Describe the major steps of motor development.

13

Emotional Development

A child is born possessing some innate emotions, though there is no unanimity of expert opinion concerning the number of such emotions. According to William McDougall there are 14 emotions attached with 14 instincts. The sentiment of self-regard is the basis of an individual's character. Besides, the character is also comprised of such desirable emotions as pity, wonder etc. Their development leads to elevation of character. Other emotions that are part and parcel of character, but, are not desirable, are fear, anger, hatred etc. The development of such emotions only deprives the individual of his energy as it is consumed in destructive effort resulting in inadequate adaptation to society. Emotions influence an individual's adjustment with other individuals in society and determine his conduct towards them. Although man is a rational animal, much of his conduct is determined by emotions and instincts. Hence, human development is considerably influenced by the emotions. Various emotions arise due to different stimuli conditions. Besides the presence of stimuli, another factor that sometimes hampers the adjustment of an individual is the excess of some one emotion. This is evident in both mental as well as physical adjustment. Emotions change in form as the child grows into the adult individual. Many detailed studies have revealed that emotions constantly develop and undergo considerable transformation. Emotional development, too, is studied in relation to the individual's situations and conditions. The normal states of the development of a human being are infancy, childhood, adolescence and adulthood. The present study proposes to adopt this division and study emotional development in this context.

EMOTIONAL DEVELOPMENT IN INFANTS

The emotional element is present in the child from his birth as is evident from his crying and vigorous movement of body parts. These movements bear adequate evidence to the presence of emotion at birth in the child, but it is difficult to determine the emotion that is related to a particular form or pattern of the child's conduct. Generally, before any emotional activity can be indulged in, the child should be able to interpret the stimulus. Hindrance in the fulfilment of some desire in a child leads to emotional excitation. In infancy, the child is unable to transfer his emotional reactions from one's situation to another. The studies that Bridges conducted concerning infant emotional states revealed that the child's emotions increase with experience, but they are very changeable and unstable. Anger and fear in infancy are indicative of general obstruction or pain. As the child develops and passes to a higher stage of life, his emotional pattern can be determined with increasing precision and accuracy. In order to study the child's emotions during this age some scientists took photographs of many children depicting such emotions as pain, anger and fear, under normal conditions. In one cinematic study, in which a movie camera was employed, it was revealed that the individual child's conduct during the first few days after his birth does not show any determinate emotions, but within a year, emotions of his nature become more specific and definite. Most observers of a photograph of a ten month old child could determine the emotions with such accuracy and similitude that the concurrence could not be attributed to coincidence.

By the time a child reaches his first six months, his facial expressions and other bodily positions are specific enough to make it possible to distinguish between such emotions as anger and fear. There is continuous variation in the manifestation of emotions during infancy. For some time after birth, the infant smiles when it sees a human face and later on it also laughs audibly. In studying children of four weeks, Gesell distinguished between expression of hunger, anger and pain. Even though it differs from child to child, yet the expression of these emotions is so specific that the mother can always determine the cause of her child's crying while another's child's crying may not convey any meaning to her. Similar expressions of fear, pleasure and affection can be seen in the child's first year of life.

In the process of this emotional development, the child gradually evolves definite patterns of reaction to stimuli that cause emotional reaction. In the beginning, the child's activity, on becoming angry, is not definite and neither is there any solution of the situation that gives rise to anger. As the child grows older, he exhibits a more patterned effort in solving the problem that arouses anger in him. Nevertheless, some inconsistent activities are always to be seen in an individual's emotional behaviour. Besides emotional expression, the intensity of emotion can also be used as a criterion of distinguishing between emotional states. Emotional expression is intense at times, while at others it is comparatively calm and weak. The child who literally becomes mad when deprived of his feeding bottle, at the age of seven months, shows much more composure and less violence when he has occasion to be angry at seven years. In this manner, the gradual development of emotional states is accompanied by variations in emotional intensity as well, although even in adult life some people behave with almost lunatic violence when emotionally disturbed. As the infant approaches childhood, his crying and yelling becomes considerably less than during earlier infancy. This condition is more particularly noticeable in the child's behaviour outside the house. The change is the result of many factors. By the time he enters childhood, the infant is in a position to express his feelings through language. He can substitute abusive language for crying when incensed at something. He also realizes that it may not be desirable or proper for him to show his anger at all times. Even if he has cause to be angry with someone older than himself, he can indiscreetly express his displeasure as he is likely to be beaten for his trouble. Another reason is that his friends tease him if he cries, and this injures his self respect, with the result that he chooses other alternatives for expressing his feelings of resentment. In the later stages of infancy, the child moreover reacts less violently to emotionally disturbing situations. Nevertheless, novel situations that he comes across provide him with emotional experiences, but the result that any situation will have upon him depends on his learning and maturity. In the first six or seven months, a child runs shy of a strange face and runs from it, because by then it achieves enough maturity to distinguish between familiar and strange faces. It is very essential that in one's dealings with children one should understand their emotion. In this connection parents and teachers must exercise proper restraint and caution, since this is the age in which the child can be moulded as desired, and emotional development is an important aspect of his development. The child's emotionality is completely bound up to his hopes, desires and ambitions. An important element in the child's emotional development is the affection that others give him as well as the affection that he himself harbours for others. Any loss of his affection can lead to very strong feelings of jealousy, resulting in serious adjustment problems in the family. As the child starts taking interest in new things that come within his sphere, the occasions that bring him pleasure and satisfaction also change. He finds much pleasure in learning and finding occasion for exercising the knowledge of climbing stairs, riding cycles, etc. The scope of a child's activities widens along with the increase and development in his abilities, a corollary of which is an increase in opportunities for greater and more diversified emotional experience. In this manner, a child's emotional development moves parallel to his physical and mental development. One also sees emotional reactions in children to some imaginary situations because in his infancy the child is very sensitively imaginative. Experience of emotions and feelings from novel things increase as his objectives, purposes, desires and plans increase. Watson believed that a new born infant has three fundamental emotions—fear, anger and love. Sherman and Bridges have criticised Watson's contention on the basis of considerable experimentation. Nevertheless, most other psychologists, also accept Watson's enumeration of three emotions in the infant, and that he develops his other emotions by the mixture of these basic emotions. Hatred, for example, is the result of a mixture of anger, fear and indifference. As the age of the infant increases, the feelings and expressions of these emotions also change. Experiments have indicated that while a two years old child is not afraid of a snake, one of four years is. One important element in these changes is the imitation of the elders behaviour.

EMOTIONAL EDUCATION IN INFANCY

The parents and teachers should be careful that no particular emotion in the child reaches a stage of excessive or extreme intensity as this sometimes leads to serious physical damage or impoverishment. Extreme fear can even lead to death. Most of the things of which a child is afraid create fear in him only because he has learned to fear them. Parents and other near relatives are capable of making a child a hero, a coward, an angry or placid individual, irritable or forbearing. Concrete behavioural examples are more effective and influential than lectures. If the parents set the child good example, he is more likely to learn to control his emotional expression. Along similar lines various circumstances can be stimulated in the family whereby the development of undesirable emotions in the child is obviated, while the expression of desirable ones is encouraged. For example, if the parents meet out fair and equal love to all the children there is no jealousy among them on this account. Secondly, if the parents are intimate with the children, many emotional tensions are avoided. Emotional development of a child is further open to such influences as the behaviour of other children in the neighbourhood because when the child is two or three he goes out to play with children of his own age, and takes part in all kinds of activities. The parents should also try to keep an eye on the child's companions and game programmes as bad company is almost certain to have undesirable effect on his emotional development. It is said that many of the world's bravest people become brave because they heard their parents talking of the bravery of bygone heroes. Hence, emotional development depends in the main upon the education given by parents and teachers.

EMOTIONAL DEVELOPMENT DURING CHILDHOOD

Emotional development during childhood is more susceptible to the influence of friend circle than that of the family. The friends can either belong to the neighbourhood or to the school. It is in this age that the child first goes to school. Hence, his emotional development is now also open to such influences as the teacher's behaviour and the atmosphere within the school and classroom. The proper emotions can be wilfully created in the child by the teachers setting the appropriate examples, the same measure also being effective negatively in blocking and preventing the development of undesirable emotions. Creating a proper atmosphere for the child is equally important. He must be encouraged to take interest while at the same time the child should have a sense of belonging and should not feel a stranger in school. These are the methods by means of which ideal character can be developed in the child. In childhood, the manifestation of emotions becomes more specific and precise but the child is devoid of the impetuosity of infancy. At the same time, the child shows no reaction to many things that in infancy led him to react violently. He does not show anger at being bathed or dressed, neither does he show any fear of strangers. In this age, the child is almost invariably the member of someone or the other group, in the activities of which he participates actively. Sometimes, undesirable and harmful tensions and hatred develop among different groups, in which case it is necessary for the teachers and well wishers to intervene and remove the tension generated, as such tensions can lead to the development of undesirable emotions and complexes. Fear is engendered in the child if physical punishment is used to teach him, the outcome being his desire to escape from study. Gentle behaviour on the part of the teacher pays dividends in the form of proper emotional development and adjustment. It is for this reason that more women than men are employed to teach small children. The atmosphere in both school and home should be as free as possible since only then the child can freely manifest emotions. If free expression of emotions is hindered because of the presence of excessive control and strict discipline, the child develops all kinds of mental complexes which are very harmful as regards his mental health and development. Presence of good ideals in healthy school and domestic atmosphere is itself a sufficient condition for the natural development of laudable emotions. Similarly, if the ideals present in the school and at home are low and detestable, then even the greatest amount of precaution and care cannot avoid the development of improper emotions. Repression only leads to the suppression or control of the expression of emotions, but not their destruction, and this repression is often more dangerous than if the emotions were expressed.

Emotional development in adolescence

Adolescence is the period of life when the individual shows signs of development in every respect. Hence, it is only natural that the expression of emotion should undergo similar modification. For example, the adolescent is very sensitive to any injury to his prestige. A physical deformity is so magnified in its evil effects that it even enters his dreaming state and modifies it. Many of his emotions he suppresses externally but they find expression in the form of day dreams. The high intensity of the sexual instinct is one reason why the adolescent is more prone to react to love than to any other emotion. This emotion finds expression in the form of excessive and almost obsessional attraction to the individuals of the other sex. As the adolescent's field of knowledge widens, the situations that give rise to emotions in him also change. He becomes angry if his country is attacked by another nation, he can even show displeasure at any instance of injustice that comes to his notice, and he can even rebel against society. He develops hatred for authority if administration is strict.

EMOTIONAL MATURITY IN ADULTHOOD

Emotional development reaches its maturity in adulthood. In these stages, the various emotions such as fear, anger, hatred, discrimination, pleasure, etc., can be distinctly seen in an individual, and generally their patterns of expression can also be recognised. Emotional reactions in this age are influenced by such complex factors as values, desires, ideals, viewpoints and common ethos of the society. Manifestation of emotions also is relatively refined, the adult being normally possessing the discretion to hide his emotions when the occasion so requires. Even when angry, he does not immediately give it expression but stores it in his mind to manifest it sometime days later when the opportunity presents itself. In this age, the various problems that face the individual concern vocation, marriage, family and new responsibilities, being problems that exert considerable influence on his emotional development.

If these problems are properly solved, then his emotional development proceeds along desirable paths. On the other hand, such problems as failure to secure the desired profession, continued unemployment, undesirable marriage, increase in the number of children, unsound economic position, absence of domestic calm and bliss can only help to create such emotions as anger, fear, hatred, jealousy, insecurity, etc.

EMOTION, SENTIMENT AND CHARACTER

Emotion is the intense disturbance of an individual. It is mental activity which comprehends feeling and motor set, an experience and activity that is directed by the individual's internal structure. It is temporary, though it disturbs the individual while it lasts. On the other hand, sentiment is a permanent structure. It is a mental creation that exists even when the occasion for its manifestation has passed. This difference lies in the mental facts and mental activities, of the structure of nervous combinations or the extension of mental combinations on the one hand, and the experiences and activities organised by that structure on the other. In the words of William McDougall, "The emotion is a mode of experience, a way of functioning and a way of activity. The sentiment is a fact of structure, an organised system of disposition which endures, in a more or less quiescent condition, between the occasions upon which it is brought into activity."

Sentiment determines the form of emotions. In this manner, sentiment is the cause of emotions, and emotions are the result of sentiment. But on the other hand, emotions are also the causes of sentiments, and sentiments their results, as sentiments are formed out of emotions. The kind or nature of emotions that we have regarding a person or an object will determine the sentiment that will be formed regarding it.

Development of sentiment

Some emotions are present innately in the human being. These are called simple emotions, examples of which are fear, surprise, anger, sorrow, etc. Besides these, some other emotions are also developed such as jealousy, love, hate, etc. As the social circumstances of an individual undergo change, these emotions are inspired by various objects. For example, one person may give him cause to fear while another may encourage him to love and affection. When many emotions concerning the same object or individual combine to form a permanent structure, then a sentiment regarding that individual or object is formed that conforms to the original emotions which it had aroused. A child loves the mother, and her presence gives him pleasure, as she satisfies his emotions of possession, sexuality, pleasure, love, etc. Hence, the child develops a sentiment regarding the mother, that is a composite of these emotions.

Sentiment and character

Character is the system or organisation of sentiments. And in this system one master sentiment rules over all the other sentiments. As long as the individual's sentiments are scattered and lack system, he has no character. Thus any individual who exhibits signs of being led by one sentiment at one time and by another at another time is called characterless if the term is interpreted in the psychological sense. It is in this sense that it has been remarked that women have no character. In the character formation the individual's sentiment of self-regard directs his emotions of love, friendship, hatred etc. From the moral viewpoint, a character is high if the master sentiment is high and valuable, but if it is not so the character is said to be low. In this way, it is one thing for a character to be organised and stable, and another to be high or low. One is a psychological concept while the other is a moral concept.

Moral character and character

Here, it is essential to keep it in mind that fundamentally, character does not imply moral character. It was the German philosopher Immanual Kant who chose to interpret the term character in the sense of moral character. In ancient Greece, the term character referred to the moulds used for making coins. In order to prevent the minting of false coins, each mould was so formed as to be difficult of imitation. The same sense continued even into modern English. It is for this reason that some people qualify the term and use the expression ethical character if they want to distinguish between good and bad character. In the words of Skinner, "One's character, defined by the history of the word is all that makes him or her unique, different from everyone else." In this manner, character includes all those special features of an individual's personality that serve to make him distinctive individual. Yet character is more commonly interpreted to be a system or organisation of sentiments.

Sentiment and culture

The intimate relation between character and sentiment is further evinced by the evolution of different kinds of character in different cultures. Sentiment is closely related to culture, since in every culture attempts are made to develop certain definite sentiments in an individual so that his social adaptation is facilitated. Concerning the importance of sentiment in society, William McDougall has written, "The growth of sentiments is of utmost importance for the character and conduct of individuals and of societies, it is the organisation of the affective and conative life. In the absence of sentiments our emotional life would be a mere chaos without order, consistency, or continuity of any kind and all our social relations and conduct, being based on the emotions and their impulses, would be correspondingly chaotic, unpredictable and unstable " An individual's social conduct is guided by some values, values that are related to his sentiments. Hence, sentiments have a special significance for the individual's character. For example, individuals who attach much value to sacrifice, service or benevolence usually possess sentiments of patriotism, linguistic attachment or philanthropy. It need hardly be pointed out that in the absence of these sentiments no such values could possibly survive.

Process of character formation

The process of character formation originates in childhood, to which the child's life in the home and school, and social and cultural life in his surroundings contribute. Character is formed of the organization of sentiments. Sentiments are formed of the organisation of emotions. Some emotions are innate while others are acquired. Both the acquired as well as the innate emotions contribute to the formation of sentiments. In social situations different emotions become bound up with different objects due to the simple and natural process of mental association. For example, the child delights in his mother's approach and he manifests the emotion of love towards her. If he comes to harm through the agency of some animal or situation, he learns to fear it. When fear is strengthened by indifference and anger, hatred is generated. Gradually, these various sentiments combine into a complex that is called character. An individual's character is known through the ruling or prominent sentiment which directs all the other sentiments. In the character of a patriot, for example, the sentiment of love of country becomes the sentiment of self-regard. and all other sentiments are directed by it.

1. Character and culture: Character formation is also influenced to a considerable extent by culture, since different values and different sentiments develop in different cultures. In the words of Kimball Young, "Sentiments are products of cultural conditioning, they may be closely allied to our fundamental values, or they may be relatively fleeting in their strength and importance." In this way, individuals develop differing sentiments in dissimilar cultural situations. For example, on the one hand at one place the sentiment of world brotherhood is developed, while on the other the sentiment of racism leads the white to hate the black. The sentiments that people of a nation have for their national flag, national anthem, etc., are not to be seen among the nomadic tribes. The presence of the sentiment regarding an object completely changes its value from its material worth. Love letters and engagement rings carry far more value than their material worth for the possessor. But their value depends upon the worth of engagement of marriage that a particular culture allows or considers feasible. If marriage is considered less valuable, all things attached to it will naturally have less value. Consequently, the sentiments concerning all these objects will be less strong. In this way, the individual's moral, aesthetic, social and religious sentiments are determined by his cultural environment. They change if the environment changes. Sentiments help the individual in his adjustment to culture, so that any change in culture is reflected in changes in this adaptation. Yet, some sentiments may also be caused by the individual's peculiar and unique nature. If they are not consistent with the cultural environment, these sentiments are given the stigma of abnormality and efforts are made to cure the individual. Conforming to the cultural environment they come to be treated as desirable, even though in a different culture they may be regarded with aversion.

2. Character and habits: Habits are important element in the individual's behaviour. Much of his day-to-day conduct is determined by his habits. Thus, character is expressed in habits though it cannot be said that character is the sum total of habits.

3. Character and volition: Volition is a very important element in character It is will power that develops the character. People of strong wills stick to their principles without flinching while the weak willed people show a lack of this spirit and are easily diverted from their paths by the least obstruction. Hence, the intelligent teacher tries to develop volition in his students. For this it is essential that every student should be given the maximum possible opportunity for performing some task on his own initiative. This helps to maintain their active tendency, and their volition also improves. The child should be encouraged to complete the day-to-day tasks that are set to him, and when he successfully completes his work, he should be praised. Failure to do this, discourages the child, and he develops the sense of lack of confidence. It should also be kept in mind that the student should not be loaded with so many tasks that it becomes impossible for him to perform any, since this too reduces his ability to determine the course for himself.

4. Character and imitation: Imitation is an important element in the psychological development of character. It is a matter of common sense that children imitate the conduct of teachers and all family members who are senior to them in respect of age. Teachers and parents represent ideals to the child, whom he imitates both consciously and unconsciously. Hence, it is desirable that the examples set to the child by the teachers and parents should be of brave and high characters. Before the teachers and parents can hope to improve children, they will have to improve themselves.

5. Character and suggestion: Formation and development of character is also duly influenced by suggestion. These suggestions to the child can be conveyed through good stories, tales and high ideals. From the psychological viewpoint, it is the positive rather than the negative mandate that gives the more adequate and effective suggestion to the child. If the children are to be prevented from plucking flowers, it is much better to direct them to protect flowers than directing them not to pluck flowers. Similar sensible and psychological methods should be applied in guiding the child in other matters.

6. Effect of reward and punishment on character: Punishment and reward also occupy an important place in the development of character. In the ancient system of education, punishment was an important element. One English proverb prevalent at the time was 'Spare the rod and spoil the child.' But the application of psychology to the field of education has led to continuous decline in the importance of punishment in education. According to Mumford, if punishment can at all be effective, the most it can do is to prevent doing of some wrong. In this way, the main function of punishment is negative, as it can only prevent the performing of some apparently harmful activity by the child. But it cannot help the development of the child's character as such development requires, the presence of high and valuable sentiments in him. But this need not be interpreted to mean that punishment should never be applied. Even modern psychologists are not averse to the occasional and judicious use of the rod, but they sanction it only if all other practices fail to yield any positive results. According to Dumville, we cannot completely deprive the educational system of punishment. Sometimes punishment appears to be the only tool that can prevent some wanton misconduct. But punishment is a measure that is to be brought into force when all other tools have failed. In fact, as Pestalozzi has pointed out punishment can be meted out even when the school is instituted as the house of love, since it helps in the development of character. But it is best to avoid its use as far as possible. What is most essential in this respect is that the individual being punished should harbour no doubts in his mind as to the purpose of punishment. He should be completely aware of the fact that the punishment is intended for his own improvement and not inspired by a feeling of retribution, because the child's loss of faith in his teachers and parents can have only the worst effect upon him. It is equally incorrect to give extreme punishment since it either causes a loss of confidence in the child or strengthens hatred and disgust. This can only hinder the progress and development of his character.

7. **Character and emotion:** A child's character development is improved by developing high sentiments in the child. Sentiments are created by emotions. The development of proper and high sentiments in a child demands psychologically effective behaviour on the part of his parents and teachers. From the psychological viewpoint, the conduct of parents and teachers regarding children should be loving and sympathetic, but, of course, this hardly means that the child be spoiled with excessive affection and tolerance, even in the matter of bad habits. If a proper character is to be evolved in a child, it is essential that he be prevented from acquiring bad habits, and this is a task which needs the co-operation of both parents. What more often happens is that while one parent is scolding the child, the other takes his side in the argument, which can only have a bad effect upon the child. Nevertheless, as long as possible the only weapon to be used with a child is the rod of love, wielded with understanding and insight, since the absence of love and affection leaves the child's emotional aspect undeveloped and he does not attain to the full maturity which is desired.

8. **Character and knowledge:** Finally, increase in knowledge is also important for the development of character. Herbart has stressed the importance of knowledge in character development. A person who is not knowledgeable is not in a position to make the distinction between good and bad, with the result that complete development of character does not occur. It is for this reason that education is an important tool of character development, although this is no reason to suppose that the uneducated or illiterate person is devoid of character. In fact, education brings within reach all the means of developing character. And, as long as the individual himself does not use these means to the best advantage, his character is not likely to develop to any extent. In the process, the teachers and parents can only help.

CONTROL OF EMOTIONS

A child's behaviour is more guided by his emotions than by his intellect or reason. His behaviour distinctly manifests the influence of emotions such as fear, love, anger, hatred, etc. Some emotions guide him to extremely desirable and likeable forms of conduct but when in the grip of other emotions, he descends to the level of beasts and behaves in the most detestable manner that can only lead to ensure from his elders. Thus, the necessity of controlling emotions becomes evident. Experience and behaviour show the extent to which emotional imbalance is harmful both to the body and the mind, as it results in kinds of nervous and mental diseases. But the control of emotions through their repression is no less harmful. Psychoanalysts have made a detailed analysis of the various neurosis that result from such repressions. The best method of controlling emotions, in fact, is to prevent the occasion and opportunities that excite emotions, Auto-suggestion is another means of controlling emotions. If one makes it a practice to avoid using emotion they will weaken through disuse. When the stimulus of one particular emotion is wilfully conjoined to another emotion, the undesirable emotion will disappear. If the emotions can also be expressed through some harmless and innocent channel, then the excitation that accompanies emotions is destroyed, thus facilitating the control of that emotion.

QUESTIONS FOR EXERCISE

1. Trace the development of emotions in childhood. How can emotions be trained? Illustrate your answer with suitable examples.
2. Trace the emotional development in children up to the adolescent stage.
3. What is the inter-relation of emotion and sentiment? How are sentiments formed? What is their value in character formation?
4. Explain the formation of character from the psychological point of view.
5. Write a short note on Sublimation.
6. (*a*) Discuss the process of emotional and social development during adolescence.

   (*b*)What is emotional maturity? Discuss its characteristics.
7. What is an Emotion? What are its characteristics? Trace the development of emotion from infancy to adolescence.

14

Intellectual and Mental Development

The mental development comprehends the development of intellect, mental capabilities, imagination, thinking, emotion, volition and other mental processes. The teacher's duty is to assist the child in the development of his abilities. This development is education. Education that does not result in development is not worth the name. Functions of the human brain are three *viz.*, to know, experience and to reach decisions. It is the teacher's function to see to it that each of these three activities of the child are developed as completely as possible. Mental education is concerned with knowing, experiencing and reaching a decision. The process of knowing comprehends perception and cognitive knowledge. The individual makes use of an object in its absence through employing his imagination and memory. Knowledge also includes reasoning and deciding. It is for the teacher to help the young child in perceiving, imagining, reasoning and reaching decisions. It is equally the duty of the teacher to understand the child's problems and look at them from the child's viewpoint.

INFLUENCE OF ENVIRONMENT ON MENTAL DEVELOPMENT

The social environment is pregnant with influences that affect the mental development of a child. Having grasped this simple tact, the sensible teacher searches the environment for an explanation of the difficulties that arise in the mental development of children. It is of course, not implied that heredity is any the less influential in the mental development of children. Generally speaking, it is from heredity that the child acquires a particular mental level and specific mental abilities. These abilities can be developed further to the best advantage under certain propitious social circumstances. But the objective of improving the environment in order to study the influence that environment has on the child's mental development, that education professes, is very important. Environmental influences can be divided into the following classes:

1. **Influence of family:** The child's education begins in the home. It is within the family that the development of his mental abilities starts. Hence, if the family possesses a favourable intellectual atmosphere, the mental development of the child is speeded. Possession of radio and television help in increasing

the child's fund of general knowledge, and he tends to be better informed. In rich families, the child has available many other resources besides these that help to add to his knowledge. Imitating his parents and brothers and sisters, the little infant learns a lot. If their mental development is good, the child is more apt to progress fast than if such is not the case. An atmosphere of autonomy in the family makes a child self-sufficient and self-reliant, and his mental faculties develop properly. Parents should make their best effort to satisfy each inquisitive query proceeding from the child, and to persuade the young child to think for himself. Maternal influence, in particular, is well known on the mental development of the world's greatest saints, scientists, leaders and thinkers. The child's mental development is susceptible to such diverse influences as the relations between his parents, the number of brothers and sisters, presence of other relatives in the family, the relations existing between the child himself and his parents, the social, economic and cultural level of his family, general administration or discipline within the family, peace and comfort, etc.

2. Neighbourhood influences: Once the child becomes mobile by learning to move about, he moves outside the sphere of household, and becomes intimate with other elements in the neighbourhood. As he grows, he even becomes member of the group of children who are knitted into a team because of their contiguity. These friends and colleagues exert an important influence on his mental development. Guardians should pay attention to the activities of this group and to their best do guard against the children acquiring bad habits.

3. Influence of social environment: After the house and the neighbourhood, the next potent influence to which the child is exposed is the school. Normally, a child enters school at the age of three or four, and is thenceforth, susceptible to such influence as the conduct of his teachers, the curriculum, method of teaching, environment of the school, the character and behaviour of his colleagues. In this connection the following facts are worth noting:

(a) Teacher's behaviour: Parents in the family and the teacher in the school take the place of the child's ideals. If the teacher himself has a wide mental horizon and treats his young students with love and affection, the children will be able to develop their minds in a free atmosphere. On the other hand, a staunch disciplinarian for the teacher may harm the students by deforming their mental development.

(b) Method of teaching: Modern educational psychology places much stress on research in the field of teaching methods. Research already conducted in this sphere indicates that different teaching methods influence the developing mind in different manners. A proper method of teaching will help to develop a healthy and comprehensive outlook, whereas other methods may make the child narrow minded and hinder his mental development. Whatever the teaching method, the teacher should aim at making the student think and understand for himself rather than force him to learn by rote. And the children should make the best effort to prepare their own notes from books, instead of having them dictated to them by the teacher. Private tuition also helps to make the student narrow minded and dependent upon the work of others. His mental powers are not developed. Secondly, students should be dissuaded from the use of brief and inferior help books made with a view merely to pass the examination. Many students prefer to learn answer to questions by rote and thus get through the examinations. But this method is not conducive to proper mental development. The truth of the matter is that there is no short-cut to mental development, it being the outcome of considerable labour, persistent and consistent effort. Children should be encouraged by their teachers to study as much as they possibly can. The extent to which a child can study continuously depends upon his age and individual ability and this factor should be kept in view when advising a student to study.

(*c*) ***Curriculum:*** Mental development in children is also influenced by the curriculum adopted in the various schools in which they study. A study of mental development in children has revealed roughly the various subjects that a child should be required to study at various age levels. Putting too great a strain on him in the form of exercise books can only hinder and obstruct his mental development. Secondly, if the curriculum is such that the subjects taught are dry, arid and mechanical the whole process becomes a burden. Fear of failure in the examination compels him to learn enough material to ensure his success, but his mind does not approach even the least towards the goal of complete development.

(*d*) ***Extra-curricular activities:*** According to modern educational psychologists, complete mental development of the child cannot be achieved only through study, since formal education alone does not provide occasions for the practice of all mental skills and abilities. Thus, most modern schools provide opportunities as debates, picnics, travels, tour of historic and important places, gardening, scouting, N.C.C., dancing, music, painting, acting and formal student unions. Such programmes help in the improvement of both mental abilities as well as the various aspects of child's personality.

(*e*) ***Administration and discipline:*** For the proper mental development of children, it is essential that the schools in which they study should be properly administered, but teachers should be advised to maintain discipline through love, affection and sympathy rather than through physical punishment. In modern educational institutions, the discipline of the school is entrusted to a few chosen students themselves. Similarly, the organisation of the various programmes organised within the school, such as picnics, games, competitions, etc., is also put in the hands of students. This method has the effect of removing any consciousness of a burden, as they learn to discipline themselves. Being self-imposed, discipline loses the element of burden. A hostel warden had recourse to a brilliant psychological device for putting an end to organised indiscipline among his students. He announced that the dining table which showed the least disturbance during dinner would be awarded with a flag, which would entitle occupants of that table to twice the normal rations of the choice morsels of food. This system worked wonder with the disciple of the children, and the students strove to maintain discipline among themselves. Even if one of them felt inclined to be naughty he was speedily dissuaded by his table inmates. In this manner, the use of psychological ingenuity solved the warden's problems without any undesirable strife. Generally speaking, it is likely to prove profitable if the care of furniture and other classroom equipment is made over to the students themselves. If this is done, the students themselves will deter those among them who are of a more ambitious but perverted turn of mind. Nevertheless, there is no way of completely avoiding some system of awards and punishment in schools. There is little to worry about awards, as there is little chance of their being injudicious in nature or time of presentation, but care must be taken to convince the punished child that he is being punished for his own good. Normally, one should avoid severe physical punishment of children because this adversely affects their personality.

4. Influence of cultural environment: The child is open to the cultural environment whether he be in school, in his neighbourhood or at home. The cultural environment is made up of ideals, objectives and values. Mental development is healthy and comprehensive if these elements are themselves valuable. But if these factors lack real value, mental development is likely to be hindered or if may take turns that are not desirable.

Mental development implies living being's adjustment of his conduct with the conditions and circumstances of his environment, with the object to attain certain ends. The correlation between physical and mental development can be seen right from infancy. Consequently, while the two year old is apparently more developed physically than a one year old child, it is equally perceptible that he is mentally developed and superior to his juniors in all. But there is inevitability in that a child of five must also be mentally superior to a child who is of four because individuals differ in respect of the speed with which they develop mentally. Nevertheless, mental development in most children progress at approximately the same rate which is consequently the average. Educational psychology tries to locate this average. The cells of a child's mind develop continuously, and in this manner the various parts of his brain gain in complexity. Hence, his mental development takes the form of vertical development.

MENTAL DEVELOPMENT DURING INFANCY

The infant shows very few signs of rational behaviour. His main functions are eating, sleeping and fulfilling various other physical needs. In this manner, he is primarily concerned with his own comfort but experiments have proved that the child can react to visual and tactual stimuli although these stimuli and the consequent reactions show lack of order and system. In the first three years the infant begins to give evidence of mental qualities that are to be his capital for the years of life to come. Roughly speaking, in the first six years of life, till he attains the age of seven, the following characteristics are to be seen in his mental development.

1. Choice of alternative methods in the satisfaction of needs: The infant is fully conscious of such physical conditions and needs as hunger, thirst, sleep, regulation of temperature, etc. As he progresses, these needs settle into a definite pattern, and the methods of satisfying them also become definite. In this process, the infant is often seen displaying his selective capacity. In general, the infant makes efforts to avoid all unpleasant and painful circumstances. At the same time, much of his behaviour is motivated by the desire to distinguish between one person and another. He has desire to attracting attention and winning praise from others. In the first year, he learns to walk and to talk. In the next two years there is rapid progress in his ability of walking, talking and detecting various objects within his environment through the use of his sense organs. At this age, the infant slowly but inevitably becomes aquainted with the objects and living beings that form part of his environment. He comes to know them by their names, and also to reckon their spatial distinctions and relations.

2. Lack of temporal knowledge: For the infant, the conventional divisions of time such as today, tomorrow, the day after or the week and year are meaningless as he cannot distinguish between them.

3. Questioning in such terms as why, what and who: As has been pointed out, and can be observed without much difficultly a growing infant evinces a continuous and unflagging curiosity and interest in the objects and living beings in his environment. Hence, he constantly asks questions from his parents and teachers. Questions such as why is this?, why does that not happen?, what is this? who is this? are characteristics of the child. His queries are virtually ceaseless, and the questions come so rapidly that the infant does not even bother to wait for an answer to one before going on to another. When he is very much surprised, he often even forgets the very question he has just asked. These questions are not motivated so much by his quest for knowledge and information as they are an expression of his developing mental capacities.

4. The world of make belief: In this age, the infant tends to live in a world of make belief, of which he himself is the creator. By donning his father's clothes he impersonates his papa to his own delight, and the acquisition of a stick effects an immediate transition to the schoolmaster. He makes a horse cut of a long stick while some fruit suggest dolls to him. On seeing different animals, he assimilates them into his world of imagination. It is equally easy for him to roar like a lion, to growl like a dog, to make the sounds of a goal or to impersonate a cock in sound, His imagination also transforms him into objects and machines. One often comes across children playing as trains and aeroplanes. Young boys and girls live the life of their parents in an imaginary world in which they marry off their dolls and make brides and bridegrooms, and houses of sand which are as unstable as their imaginings. Such behaviour is as indicative of imitation as it is of a colourful and active imagination.

5. Variety of imagination: Often enough, the infant himself is the hero of his imaginary world, and away from the real world, he lives delightedly in his own sphere. Evidently, imaginings of a child display astonishing variety.

6. Tendency towards self-assertion: According to Alfred Adler, the famous psychologist, the most prominent and strong tendency in the infant is the tendency towards self-assertion. He normally yearns to exhibit his physical and mental abilities and win acclaim of the elders.

7. Distinction between self and others: The infant is normally very conscious of his self, being primarily an individualist. He sometimes gives the impression of being selfish, and he does not show to advantage at such moment. He often sticks to his demand and obstinately tries to have his way. And if one infant succeeds in getting something, another who has seen him at it is even more obstinate in his demand for it, even though he may have nothing, to gain from it. But if he chooses to decline something, it needs much patience to make him yield the point. In fact, the ego develops gradually in this age.

8. Surrender and enthusiasm: Even though his ego develops continuously in this period of his life, the infant also exhibits, in certain special circumstances, qualities of surrender and enthusiasm. They are not normally evident.

9. Intellectual development: The infant's intellect starts developing in infancy, differences between intellect of various children being readily evident. As the infant develops intellectually, his understanding and his knowledge of the various objects around him increases.

10. Solution of simple problems: As the infant gains in intellectual maturity, he learns to solve simple problems. At the very beginning, these problems normally relate to the activities and actions of the hand and feet. Having studied infants between the age of 19 and 44 months Alpert came to the conclusion that infants in this age also manifest evidence of existing insight. Intellectual development is evident from the ability by which the infant solves various problems as they arise. According to Herter an infant of five is able enough to solve problems through the use of concrete material as well as linguistic symbols.

11. Development of memory: The infant has great ability in learning by rote as is evident from the success with which they have heard many times. Despite the fact that they hear the same songs and folklore many times, they evince the same rapt interest every time. And as far as stories or poems are concerned, they remember them so well that they can correct the person reciting to them, if he should happen to make a mistake.

12. Development of mental abilities: Infants manifest the development of such mental qualities as observation, comparison decision, etc. As the body develops, their sense organs become more and more sensitive and acute with the result that they can perceive objects better. Simultaneously, linguistic ability also shows signs of improving. Gradually, the infant learns to distinguish linguistic symbols. Starting with small individual words, he progresses to the understanding of simple sentences, and in a short time learns to speak with considerable fluency and authority. These mental capacities of children can be seen in their play. He also develops constructive and aesthetic imagination. Coloured pictures are also intriguing for infant. He takes great interest in collecting things and in the construction of things with whatever material that comes to his hand.

13. Desire to assist his parents: Infants are as usually very much interested in assisting their parents, and when given the opportunity they become very enthusiastic and delegated. They show preference for cooking with the mother and helping the father to carry small weights about the house. In this the infant not only wins praise from his parents, but also gets an opportunity to give expression to his individuality.

14. Development of mental abilities: The infant's mental abilities reach the stage of complete development by the time he is six. These are the one that can help him to conduct himself like an individual in any group of human beings. On the one hand the infant manifests the desire to co-operate with others, while on the other hand he expresses difference from others in respect of attitudes and behaviour.

15. Development of sex tendencies: Generally, the development of sex organs during infancy and childhood is rather slow, but psychologists as Freud have irrefutably proved that the child has present in him the sex tendency and that it constantly develops. According to Freud infancy is the stale of self-love, as the child finds pleasure in exploring the various parts of his own body. On this theory, sucking of the thumb is expressive of the sexual tendency. In this state, the infant loves himself, but very soon the infants develop love for their parents. In this love, Freud has also detected the presence of hetrosexual love. According to him, one can see the Oedipus complex present in male children while the male infant loves the mother and the female the father.

16. Instinctive behaviour: Much of the infant's behaviour in the infant and pre-school period is generated by instincts. Although the infant also develops intellectually, yet he prefers to have his instincts satisfied without delay. He starts crying at least delay in preparation of his food. At the smallest and most trifle things he throws herself upon the ground and becomes adament. He does whatever pleases him, but avoids anything that promises him pain. It is evident that in this one period of his life, he is not aware of moral and ethical considerations and compunctions in his behaviour.

17. Dependence upon others: As in the first three years of infancy, in the next three years also is the infant dependent upon other persons such as parents, brothers and sisters, relatives and servants. He needs the assistance of others even in the fulfilment of such elementary needs as taking food, bathing and putting on clothes. As yet he does not possess self-confidence and self-reliance. He even fears going out of the house alone, and prefers to take someone with him for protection and companionship. He depends upon others to such an extent that even the activities that he is capable of performing by himself he requires of others to perform it. If he falls, he tries to attract attention but does not get off the ground without the help of others, preferably the parents.

18. Imitation: Much of what an infant learns of behaviour is acquired through the imitation of other individuals in the family. He is continually influenced by the behaviour of the parents among themselves and other infants in the family. Hence, a majority of the habits that an infant has can be traced to someone or the other individual member of his family because he imitates them without going into propriety of the habit he is thus forming. He shouts if he sees others making a noise, but if he finds them quiet and peaceful, he does not disturb them but chooses to be equally quiet. Such habits as lying or stealing things are formed in like manner.

19. Curiosity: An infant's curiosity is almost always at a fever pitch, and there is no end to the questions he can devise concerning the most mundane and uninteresting object that comes in his way. Answers do not interest him as much as asking questions. He revels in roaming around outside as he comes to see many novel things. This innate curiosity of the infant can be skilfully exploited to the child's advantage by his parents and teachers who can tell him many things and turn his thoughts into desirable and profitable channels.

20. Influence of love and affection: An infant is apt to react very violently to the least criticism and disrespect or disgrace. The arrival of a new baby in the family interests the infant but if he comes to be disregarded by his parents his attraction turns into hatred, jealousy and distaste, which can sometimes take a very serious turn. He requires loving and sympathetic treatment from his parents which, if it is not forthcoming, can hinder his mental development. He hates any correction or reproof. Strong discipline does not win his sympathy and he tries to rebel against it. In this age, the father should pay more attention to the male infant since its absence can lead to the development of hatred in the children. This consideration finds its theoretical support in the Freudian theory of Oedipus and Electra complexes.

21. Creative impulse: In this age, one of the most manifest tendencies in the infant is the creative impulse. He busies himself in making or collecting things, as the activity gives him the satisfaction that he too, can do what all others do. Much of what he does is motivated by the desire to do all that he sees his elders doing, and it affords him much pleasure if he is given the opportunity of doing it. According to Western educational psychologists, in this period of the infant's life, it is desirable that the parents should spend some time with the children as it affords them the best education that there can possibly be. The same function can be performed if the infant is sent either to the Kindergarten or the Montessory school but only in case these schools are really excellent, as otherwise it would be futile to entrust the children's education to them. It is in childhood that the foundation of good and bad habits as well as character are laid so that it is essential that the child be properly looked after.

THE INFANT'S EDUCATION

It is evident from the foregoing consideration of infant's mental characteristics that the teacher must pay the utmost attention to his development in the process of education. It is for the teacher to arouse the curiosity of the infant in any subject that he wishes to teach. Once this is achieved the teacher can confidently leave it to the infant's enthusiasm to understand the lesson properly. Whatever the nature and irrelevance of the questions that an infant asks, he should never be irritably reproved. A teacher must do all in his power to answer each and every question that an infant puts.

1. Use of instincts in teaching: The infant's education should be based on his instincts. If the infant's self-respect is injured, his tendency to self-assertion is seriously impaired. Sympathetic and loving behaviour can induce the infant to surrender to the teacher and honour his discipline. An infant's enthusiasm should never be suppressed as it may lead to the formation of mental complexes.

2. Teaching through actual objects: As the infant normally tends towards imaginative wanderings, the teacher should employ concrete objects in training and teaching him. Although it is essential that the infant's imagination, and particularly aesthetic imagination be activated through dance, music, painting, etc., his formal education should be conducted through the use of concrete things such as wooden blocks etc.

3. Importance of sympathetic and loving behaviour towards the child: Modern psychologists unanimously opine that the behaviour of a teacher towards the infant should be one of sympathetic understanding and love. If the infant works to his satisfaction, it should be encouraged further by kindly words of praise.

4. Need for making the child self-reliant: Understanding of infant's mental development makes it evident that the teacher should do his best to provoke self-reliance among his students. In fact, in modern democratic societies, the very aim of education is to make the child self-reliant and independent individual. For this it is essential that he be given small minor tasks to perform on his own initiative. He can be assisted in the process of learning but this assistance should take the form of guidance and should never be so excessive as to render the infant utterly dependent upon the adviser. Actually, the duty of the teacher lies in looking after him as he develops himself, not to develop the infant, whose intelligence, mental abilities, and memory and other capacities develop of their own accord as he grows older. It is upto the teacher to satisfy the needs of the infant that arise during this process of development. And for this it is essential to develop the right kind of atmosphere in the school since once this main task is achieved successfully, the teacher's function is reduced to one of intelligent participation and supervision. The atmosphere depends upon the presence of games and toys, attractive and interesting curriculum, healthy schoolrooms and the right adjustment in the mutual relations between the teachers and students, and the students themselves.

Keeping in view all that has been said above, modern schools are seen employing the latest methods of education and experimenting with them. Western countries are making increasing use of radio and television in the education of infants. The programme is varied when infants are taken to view educationally important films. The infant's stock of knowledge is increased by taking him to new gardens, exhibitions, historic and other interesting places. Communal qualities are generated in the child by encouraging participation in collective programmes that are organised in the school. In this manner, the modern teacher who is at all knowledgeable, keeps in mind the mental development of the infant and tries to set the educative process to conform to the infant's mental mould.

MENTAL DEVELOPMENT DURING CHILDHOOD

The period of childhood extends from a person's sixth to eleventh or twelveth year. The following are the major characteristics of his mental development in this period of child's life:

1. **Stability:** The most characteristic mental feature of childhood is stability. In other words, this age has been called the state of pseudo maturity because in this period the child gives false impressions of maturation. In his childhood, the little chap becomes fairly well acquainted with his environment, and loses the wide-eyed innocence that marks his infancy.

2. **Maturation of gregarious instinct:** The gregariousness that the child evinces in his infancy reaches its maturity in childhood. Now he prefers more to be with children of his own age and shows no interest in staying alone. Coming of new people in the family gives him pleasure. He develops interest in fairs or games and becomes a regular member of the group of neighbourhood children.

3. **Curiosity:** The curiosity of which the infant gives evidence in the infancy increases when he reaches childhood. No longer content with the more passive method of asking questions and waiting for an answer, he longs to make actual and personal acquaintances with his surrounding environment. But he continues to ask his questions. His curiosity can be put to good use by exciting it in respect of many desirable habits.

4. **Moral norms:** As a member of a group, the child learns to obey certain moral norms. He is so much led away with the idea of group membership that he does not shrink from telling untruths to his parents and teachers if it is required of him by his group. From this age, the child can be made to think in terms of good and bad, and foundations for his moral character are laid.

5. **Extorversion:** In this period of his life, the child appears to be preeminently an extrovert. He takes less interest in his own self than he does in his surroundings, being more attracted towards concrete objects than the flickerings of an imagination. He has developed practical interests and yearns to achieve something of real worth.

6. **Play:** While in his infancy, the child invents imaginatively the modes of play to entertain himself, but in his childhood he turns to the forms of play prevalent in the concrete world. Even his imaginings now take a more mundane turn, as they are closely connected with the real world. He is motivated by the desire to achieve something useful. Hence he can be taught many things even as he plays.

7. Acquisitive tendencies: Having reached childhood, the child is often observed manifesting sense of possession and right. He likes to collect various kinds of things and by encouraging him to collect useful things like stamps, old coins, toys, etc., a very good habit can be inculcated.

8. Latent sexual tendencies: According to Dr. Jones, the child in this age does not manifest any self-love, Oedipus or Electra complexes because in childhood his sexual tendencies are latent.

9. Imitation: In childhood, too, as in his infancy, the child possesses a strong tendency towards imitations of others. Observing others in doing various functions and making things, he is inspired to do something of the same kind. Sometimes he imitates others in private, in order to obviate the chance of other people laughing at him.

10. Creative tendencies: The child manifests an instinctive creative tendency. He is positively inclined towards making new friends and making objects out of mud and sand. He can be encouraged to play with wooden blocks in this age.

11. Influence of praise and blame: In this period, as in most other periods of life, the child is happy when praised but pained when reproved. He is encouraged when praise falls to his lot, while he feels discouraged when he is criticised. Consequently, it is his constant endeavour to do only those acts that bring him the praise and acclaim of everyone involved, it being a different matter if he falls foul of his parents or teachers and wins the reproof in trying to do something that his friend's circle thinks praise-worthy.

12. Extension in the field of interest and thinking: In childhood, the child's field of interest and thinking widens considerably. He finds much delight in seeing pictures of and reading about human beings and animals to be found in the various parts of the world. He cannot restrain his curiosity if something mysterious falls in his ear.

13. Revolting against strict discipline: In this age the child resents any strict discipline, be it in the home or in the school, and fosters feelings of revolt against it. If strong discipline is exercised upon the child, outwardly he seems to succumb to it, but inwardly he seeths with revolt and pent up anger which sometimes leads him to run away not only from school but even from the home.

14. Solving problems: In this age, the child takes special delight in solving puzzles and various kinds of problems, so that the power of abstract thought also develops in him.

EDUCATION IN CHILDHOOD

Knowing the various mental characteristics of childhood, a teacher can do much in the way of making education natural and easy. The following points are important in this respect:

1. The child can be taught such things in communal situation as telling the truth, honesty, obedience, discipline etc. The teacher can induce

many desirable traits in the children by setting a good example and ideal.

2. Making good use of the gregarious instinct, the child can be indulged to take part in scouting and other team games. These activities can help in the development of qualities like co-operation, humility, leadership, organisation, justice, patriotism, social service etc., in the children so that they may be ideal citizens when they attained their adulthood.
3. His extrovert nature can be put to good use in sending him on extensive tours of the country so that his knowledge increases. The child's personality develops through participation in extra-curricular activities.
4. Collection of useful things is a good habit and it can be ingrained in the child by teaching him to collect such things as stamps, photographs, rare coins, books etc.
5. His curiosity can be aroused regarding novel thing and he can then be left to learn many new things.
6. His imitative methods can be put to the most advantageous use by performing useful activities in his presence so that he may learn to emulate them.
7. The foundations of a good moral character can be laid by praising good things in his presence and condemning all bad things, also in his presence.
8. New subjects can be introduced in the form of puzzles and problems to the child that he may be attracted to solve them. Education is simplified in this way.
9. Creation of an atmosphere of love and affection both at home and in the school, besides creating opportunities for the teachers and students and parents and children to work and play together, can help in his mental development and in the development of his personality.

It is evident from the above description that a knowledge of the progress of mental development in childhood makes possible better education of children.

MENTAL DEVELOPMENT IN ADOLESCENCE

The English word adolescence is a derivative of the Latin 'adolescere' which means to grow to maturity. This age begins from twelve and continues till the age of twenty. In the words of Jersild, "Adolescence is the period through which a growing person makes transition from childhood to maturity." Adolescence, in the opinion of most educational psychologists, begins between the age of 12 to 14 years. Compared to boys, girls enter the period of adolescence a couple of years earlier. According to Dr. Jones, adolescence is the recollection of infancy. It parallels the states of infancy and childhood in being patterned into two conditions, the first of growth and the second of maturation.

(*a*) *State of growth:* In this state, the adolescent is seen to be very active and unstable as well as disturbed. He gives the impression of being somewhat lost, and is subject to rapidly varying moods of dejection and elation, enthusiasm and deep lethargy, etc. The main thing concerning this period in life is that the adolescent is no longer a child but an adult, though the society in which he lives continues to treat him as a child. Secondly, he climbs down from the dizzy heights of imagination that he reached in his infancy and childhood and steps firmly into the real world. Both these factors engender in him a constant fear of reproof and criticism at the hands of others. He often becomes helpless and pitiable, shy and repressed. This does not indicate that he runs away from the real world, but that he tries to modify it according to his own notions. In efforts of this kind, elation and dejection is often seen wearing a look of anxiety.

(*b*) *State of maturation:* By the time he enters this stage, he has calmed down a bit and shown signs of stability. He carves a niche for himself in his society, and gradually, his tendencies, habits and activities become stable and regular.

Mental characteristics of adolescence

In adolescence the individual is so transformed that he wears a new and unrecognised look. Mental changes in this period of life find their best expression in the work of poets as they depict the mental states of young men and women. Adolescence exhibits the following mental characteristics generally:

1. Development of mental abilities: In adolescence the individual's nervous system becomes more strong with the result that his mental activities show greater tenacity and system. Ability to think, to solve problems, to differentiate and evaluate are some of the more prominent characteristics and abilities that he exhibits.

2. Sexual development: From the psychological viewpoint, the most significant characteristic of the period of adolescence is sexual development. According to Dr. Jones, the repressed sexual force of infancy, that continued latent through the period of childhood, once again awakens as the individual passes through various stages of sexual development. The truth of the matter is that even if it is not the only tendency, sexual tendency is undoubtedly the most prominent and stable tendency to be found in adolescence. Hence, to disregard it is to make a fatal mistake as it is the most harmful form of negligence conceivable. The development in this sphere is so rapid that his entire personality appears to be coloured by it. Sexual development in adolescence finds its expression in attraction towards strangers, rather than towards parents as in the case of infancy. It announces its presence even in such small activities as the young boy's anxiety and nervousness, biting of fingernails, putting a pencil in one's mouth, tying knots in handkerchiefs, etc. Both physical and mental teaching in this age can use the sexual tendency as an important force. Normally, the development of the sexual tendency passes through the following three stages:

(*i*) *Auto-eroticism:* In the beginning of adolescence, sexual tendency manifests itself in self-love, but this self-love differs from the infant's self- love. In infancy, the child finds physical pleasure in exploring and touching various parts of his own body. But in the adolescent self-love, the individual dresses himself well and meticulously, observes his face continuously in the mirror, and does his very best to make himself as presentable as possible. Many young men and women passing through this stage can be seen humming as they look at themselves in the mirror. They are content to be with themselves and love only themselves. As yet they have no time to observe and appreciate others. Freud calls this the state of narssicism. The term has a long story behind it from which the term originated. Narcissus was a Greek prince of almost unparalleled beauty, who could not find anyone more handsome than himself, he loved himself, probably justifiably. A flower is called narcissus, and it grows by the side of lake in such a manner that its image is visible in the water. Young men and women in their teens behave in a similar manner as they love to look upon themselves and beautify themselves. One of the most prominent and common malpractices in which the adolescents indulge is masturbation. The American psychologist Kinsey, in his famous report, has mentioned the various ways in which young men and women derive pleasure from their sexual experiences. Sometimes the feelings of guilt that arise as a result of indulgence in these activities lead to the formation of complexes that are very harmful to the mental development of individuals. The one and only means of escaping such consequences is proper sex education. In order to impart the right attitude towards the sexual tendency to young people, it is essential that teachers and parents tell them everything frankly so that they may adopt this healthy attitude.

(*ii*) *Homosexuality:* Progressing from the stage of self-love, young boys and girls are attracted to members of their own sex, either older or younger than themselves. Homosexual love of this age is accompanied by great anxiety and deep affection but later on it turns into heterosexual love. Persons of this age can often be seen caressing each other, roaming together, preferring only each other's company, sleeping together, praising each other and finding other modes of expressing their mutual attraction. Some girls also develop the habit of exciting each others sexual organs. Similar aberration is present in boys in the form of sodomy, which leads to feelings of guilt and crime if the person is reproved for these activities. Such bad habits can be got rid of only through the medium of sensible guidance and sex education of the children by the parents and teachers. It is always desirable that adolescence passing through this phase should be controlled sensibly but it is equally essential that all control exercised over them should be in the form of loving advice rather than punishment.

(*iii*) *Heterosexuality:* The state of homosexuality in adolescents is succeeded by sexual maturity, a state of moral heterosexual relations between men and women. Young men and women who have attained this age can often be seen being attracted to members of the other sex, meeting each other, talking inessentially for hours on end, putting their best feet forward to attract the other and hold such attention adopting the latest fashions to appear the more attractive, going for walks together, visiting picture houses together, caressing each other and sometimes even going to the extent of actual sexual intercourse, though this often has disastrous results as the girls become mothers even before they are married. The strength of this sexual tendency can neither be curbed nor can any strict control upon it prove efficacious even if it is considered desirable. Excessive restrictions on meetings between boys and girls in colleges and universities only leads to greater indiscipline and misconduct. Hence, many educational psychologists have advised that instead of restricting communication between them, relations should be encouraged. On the other hand, the traditions that have continued in our culture stress the complete segregation of the sexes during this period. In the modern context any effort at emulating these traditions can only prove foolhardy in the future, and in any case such efforts are not likely to prove efficacious. Uncontrolled and impassioned contacts can only lead to such ostensible and detestable consequences as suicides, unmarried mothers, social corruption etc. Hence it is essential that the youth of today be provided with proper sex education and encouraged to develop a healthy attitude towards sex. This will have the desirable effect of preparing them for responsible parenthood when they ultimately get married.

Another method of solving problems of the sexual impulse, besides sex education, is inspiring young men and women to develop interest in various kinds of games and sports, dances, singing, art, painting, etc. It is a matter of universal regret, particularly among the enlightened population of the nation, that nearly 99% of teachers and guardians find it embarrassing to discuss any sexual matter with their young charges. The consequences are undesirable as the young inexperienced adolescent learns the same things from bad and uncouth companions who convey to him all the aberrant forms of sexual information. Such a situation is true of many civilized societies, and all the more of India. When the adolescent observes that his teachers and guardians prefer to keep all sex information secret and concealed from him, he forms a guilt complex regarding sex. Due to the normal stage of development he can do nothing to abate the force or strength of the urge, and he is helpless as no assistance from his teacher is forthcoming. Thus, he either indulges all his energies in trying to control the instinct, losing all interest in studies in which he cannot concentrate or forms obnoxious and deforming habits, or as an alternative contracts serious mental diseases through excessive repression. Hence, teachers and parents should assist adolescent males and females to organise, control and sublimate the sexual impulse through adequate sex education.

3. Hero worship: Generally speaking, adolescents evince a strong tendency towards hero worship, though the criterion of heroism is not the same in all children. Possession of any quality that attracts an individual child the most is sufficient qualification for a man or woman to become its ideals. While one child may regard a wrestler as a hero, another may profess allegiance to a scientist, yet another may be devoted to a film personality or a political leader. In schools some teachers impress their students considerably with the result that they come to be tenderly and affectionately regarded by them, also being imitated by the tender children. Sometimes this hero worship turns in love. It is not till considerably later that the young man turns his thoughts to his own heroic qualities, when he begins praising them. The tendency to hero worship can be turned to good account by inculcating a proper character and personality in the child's mind. For this it is essential that the teacher himself should represent the highest ideals, as he is the best example that the child can facilely imitate.

4. Religious feelings: Many adolescents become positively and deeply religious in this period of their lives. One can often observe them loving God in some one image, talking to Him, sacrificing themselves to Him and praying to Him. India is particularly productive of such specimens since, for one, the religious tendency is deeply ingrained in the people's mind, and for another, in Indian society young boys and girls meet great leaders and famous personalities on very rare occasions. While religious tendency protects the young inexperienced child from many bad habits, it sometimes helps in making him somewhat impractical. Teachers can help to create a healthy attitude towards religion.

5. Gregariousness: Adolescents are always acutely desirous of being among their friends, of praising them and of improving their relations with them. Often, they form definite groups in which each adolescent has his specific status and a role to suit it. This status and role plays an important part in determining his status and role in adult life.

6. Extroversion: In this period, the child once again regains his extrovert flamboyancy, taking deep interest in his surroundings and other individuals, their activities and conflicts. In school, too, he likes to take part in all kinds of activities. And it is a matter of joy with him if he can spend the larger part of his time in the company of his friends. Various individuals become engaged in programmes of social service and welfare. In this manner does the adolescent announce the interest that he takes in the real world. This interest can be usefully exploited to ingrain in him such useful qualities as self-dependence, self-determination, co-operation, discipline, honesty and the quality of maintaining good relations with others or develop the social instinct. This is the age in which the foundations of good citizenship can be deeply laid.

7. Lack of stability and adjustment: It has been pointed out earlier, too, that in his adolescence the growing individual is at the threshold of his life although he is rarely if ever considered an adult by his seniors. From the psychological point of view, he takes himself seriously enough not to consider himself a child, and likes to be treated as an adult. Evidently, he shows considerable instability and lack of adjustment. His adaptation to his environment is upset by such small considerations as the growth of pimples on his face or the presence of other small physical deformities In fact, it is a stage in which he learns to lead adult life in every sphere and direction. Hence, the presence and continual development of problems is only natural. And these problems are susceptible to ready solutions if the seniors are prepared to extend their sympathetic co-operation and guidance.

8. Excessive sentimentality: The adolescent is very sentimental and emotionally unstable, although at this age his mind is fairly well developed. Of the many feelings that drive him, the strongest are the desire to win praise and self respect, any injury to or repression of them leading to serious malformations and even open rebellion. Sentimentality can be turned to good use in developing cultural traits in the adolescent. Participation in programmes of dancing, acting, music, painting, etc., makes the emotional life more stable.

9. Excessive imagination: Although the adolescent is as much in this world as any other living, yet he is prone to much imaginary flights into the world of fancy. The smallest thing can persuade him to temporarily abandon the world of reality and turn to the imaginary world. Such excessive imagination manifests itself in the strong tendency towards day-dreaming, but some gifted children express their creative and aesthetic imagination through literature, music and painting, besides other arts.

10. Particular interests: In adolescence, as the individual develops both in mind and body, his interests vary. Progressively the boys and girls develop the interests of their adult counterparts. Girls show this development in such interests as the use of various cosmetics, efforts at appearing beautiful, reading or taking interest in romantic novels, love stories, dramas or poems, participating in music, art and acting programmes etc. Boys manifest their approaching adulthood in the form of various active games, running around, doing acts of valour, developing a vocation that they are to pursue in their adult life. Both boys and girls take constant interest in developing friendship with members of the other sex and maturing it to fruition through conversation, intimacy, letters and romance.

11. Development of the mind: In adolescence, the mind develops rapidly. The cells of the nervous system increase rapidly, and the chemical composition of the nerves also undergoes a change. In this way, the mind and the nervous system rapidly matures. In this period along with physical and mental development, practice helps to develop mental abilities. Linguistic ability also registers improvement during this period. In his adolescence the child develops the vocabulary that he possesses. His vocabulary reveals general intelligence. Mental development, too, reaches its apex in adolescence. Despite the inevitable individual differences that are invariably present, mental maturity achieves its completion normally by the age of twenty. Practice or experience contributes considerably to this maturation. Normally, the individual's intelligence continues on the same level, or, in other words, even in different ages the intelligence quotient of an individual remains more or less the same. Many detailed studies have revealed that during the first five years of life, the mental development is greater than that achieved during the following five. In this manner, the mental development during the ages of 10 and 15 is greater than that during 15 and 20, in respect of rapidity. At the age of ten, the mental development of a child is at its fastest. Following this, as the child approaches the stage of adolescence the speed of mental development slows down. In his infancy, the child only acknowledges and indicates the feeling of sensations, while at the age of three he is in a position to distinguish between objects, animals and human beings. At six, he is capable of describing a picture that he has seen, but in his adolescence he rises above description to the level of interpretation of the pictures that he sees, in this manner, one can see constant development and improvement in the mind's reactions to stimuli. Generally, an individual's memory is tested by the number of digits he can remember after they have once been announced to him. In adolescence, the ability to remember digits improves with age, and reaches its highest peak at the age of twenty.

Education of adolescents

The sensible teacher can make his teaching psychological if he has knowledge of an adolescence's mental development. The intensity and proper use of imagination can help to make an individual a poet, painter, sculptor or a psychologist. Intelligence, observation, reasoning and thinking having reached the required state of development in adolescence, the school and college curriculum can be fairly diversified and made comprehensive. The truth of the matter is that actual education begins only in adolescence since at this stage the young boys and girls treat themselves as adults and they come to entertain a serious and responsible attitude to their education. What is needed is that the teacher should inspire them to work hard in their studies through self-inspiration.

1. Physical development is rapid during adolescence. The bodily structure develops at a rapid pace. This age is the time of revolutionary physical development as in this age young boys and girls attain to their maximum heights and specific bodily developments, conforming to their respective sexes. Hence, they should be trained in games and beneficial exercises In educational institutions, they should be specially trained in health and bodily development since, if they do not pay attention at this stage they are not likely to appear handsome later on in life.
2. The extreme sentimentality of adolescence can be used to induce the girls and boys to learn literature, music, art and science. This age is propitious for the teaching of all subjects. Transfer of learning during this period is considerable.
3. Good conduct, proper interests and good habits of living can be developed in boys and girls by making adequate use of the strong sexual tendency that is a strong motivating force. In adolescence, the sexual organs of the boys and girls undergo rapid development. In girl, the menstural cycle starts while the boys are subject to nightly emissions.

The sexual organs are covered by hair. Persistent development in the girl's breasts sometimes leads to pain. Lacking knowledge of the basis and cause of all these physiological changes, boys and girls are often subjected to much perplexity. Many of the girls are not even aware that the blood emitted during the menstrual cycle does not happen to them alone but to every other girls passing the same stage of development. This leads to much anxiety and sometimes even results in the creation of guilty feelings. Not knowing the manner in which they should dress hygienically during the menstrual cycle they are sometimes put in very embarrassing situations that are very painful to them. They are even rendered ridiculous. It is a matter of no little sorrow and pain that much changes are inevitable in the lives of every young men and women, but almost all of them have to get over them through trial and error. The parents, who have themselves been through these conditions, are content to leave the helpless children on their own resources and wit. This is not a desirable practice. In this connection it is for the parents to inform the children of all necessary details and methods, without making secret of anything. It is never a good practice to hate or scold or deliver moral lectures if one sees an adolescent developing bad habits. It is a matter of physiology and psychology, and it should be treated accordingly. It is for the teacher to inform the growing boy and girl of the complete facts about the male and female body, and to train them adequately in all forms of hygiene.

4. Hero worship and idealisation are two very useful tendencies with which the adolescent is endowed. This stage in his development is particularly efficacious for laying the foundations for a good character. He should be given the lives of great men to read and to draw what lesson he can from them. High ideals stand revealed to him, and he can think in terms of greater characters as opposed to the imaginative pictures of heroes that he has been sketching to himself. The adolescent should be persuaded to read extensively. It is never desirable to prevent him from reading stories and novels. All that is needed is that he should be intelligently guided in forming his taste by being taught to read interesting works of great novelists and psychologists so that his knowledge of human nature increases and his sexual tendency reduces its hold upon him.
5. The adolescent is by nature a rebel against the traditions and customs prevailing in his society. His rebellious instinct can be chanelled to good use by the teacher who can help to develop a generation which hates all the bad traditions and rids society of them. Adolescents can easily be induced to think of social development and improvement. They can be taught to rise above their narrow interests and comprehend the spirit of nationality, internationality and universal love.
6. It is no less important to impart ethical, moral and religious education to the child. Although all educational psychologist fail to see eye to eye

on this subject, moral and religious education can benefit the recipient only if it is psychological and simple.

7. In adolescence, the individual should be given vocational guidance after his mental capacities, inclinations and interests have been examined. His education should conform to the vocation that he is going to pursue in the future so that he may not be a misfit in any occupation but should rather be able to earn a comfortable living, establish a household and contribute actively to national development.

MENTAL DEVELOPMENT IN ADULT AGE

The individual steps into his adulthood at the age of 18, having passed through his adolescence. Consequently, in most countries the individual is considered an adult when he attains 18 years of age, and is vested with the rights of responsibility for his own actions, independent judgement, marriage, pursuit of a vocation, establishing a household and inheriting property, besides other sundry rights. Before this all these rights are denied to him, transferred mostly to his parents and guardians. It is evident that it is justifiable to treat a person of 18 as fully responsible. His interests are now concerned with the objects and individuals that form part of his environment. Reality replaces the world of imagination. An adult is faced with the necessity of finding solutions of the practical problems with which he is confronted in his day-to-day life. Among the various functions that he chooses to perform are the necessities of finding a vocation, earning wealth, marrying and finding his place and status in society. Similarly, the erstwhile girl passes through the roles of young women, wife and mother while the boy passes through the stages of young man, husband and father. Both the man and the woman accept the burden of citizenship of the nation.

From the physiological point of view, the individual is completely developed in this period of his life. By the time an individual attains his twentieth year, all his mental faculties are fully developed and he is fully equipped to use them in practical life for performing the greatest of works. In the opinion of some people, an individual's mental capacities start receding or deteriorating after he passes the age of 20, or at least that there is no further development of them. But many researches only serve to disprove this contention. On the basis of research and study it can be said that man's mental power and capabilities reach their ultimate peak at the age of 35 and 40. This peak is followed by a general decline in mental powers, through the deterioration of the physiological machine or the reduction of energy characteristic of old age. Similarly, in attaining the ages of 35 or 40, the individual reaches the very peak of his learning. At this stage it is also relevant to keep in mind the importance of practice. Although it can be confidently asserted that after the age of forty the nervous system and sense organs of man are susceptible to such changes as reduce his mental power, but it is evident in the case of many scientists and scholars that they have produced their real masterpieces only after they have passed 40. It is said of Sheikh Sadi, the famous Persian poet that he began the study of Persian after he had crossed 40. Yet, it can generally be said that man's mental powers are at their peak between the ages of 20 and 40, and it is in this period that he is likely to achieve the greatest mental feats. If practice, experience and maturity continues, mental powers are found virtually intact even when the individual descends to old age.

At this stage, the individual is possessed of the quality of self-direction since his knowledge and power of reasoning are acute and developed. An adult should do his best to maintain his good habits. Constantly awake and alert individual always learns something even from the most mundane and apparently insipid situations in life. Ambition is another important factor in this stage of life. It is the motive force that constantly propels the individual towards further progress, but one should not be blinded by it to the realities of life. Much research and study has succeeded in establishing the fact that the guidance and advice of old people is always desirable in marriage, vocation, etc., and no adult should, ignore it. Moral and religious education assumes special significance in this state. As a matter of fact, it is only now that the individual is fully aware of good and bad, and is in a position to mould his future as he desires. This does not mean that the influence of family and society is in any way lessened, but rather that the individual can create his own environment. Sentiments of self-respect and benevolence are the basis of an adult's moral education. Briefly, adults can make a success of their lives by taking advantage of their education, the experience of their parents and other older people and by self-education.

QUESTIONS FOR EXERCISE

1. What is the influence of environment on the mental development of the child? Explain with examples.
2. Point out the main characteristics of mental development in childhood.
3. Mention the psychological characteristics of children of 6 and 11 years of age. Discuss the suitability of the activity method of education during this period of child life.
4. Write short note on—psychology of adolescence.
5. Describe mental and moral characteristics of adolescence.

15

Development of Speech and Language

If a child's birth has been normal, then he gradually gains command over language after passing through the different stages of linguistic development. This development is a process and its different stages cannot be distinguished from each other. Neither is it necessary that each one of these stages should be distinctly apparent in the linguistic development of every child. Language ability does not develop and improve at the same rate in all children, and neither does it take the same time.

According to psychologists, a child speaks his first word when he is 13 or 14 months old. Language development therefore should be considered from this point. The period preceding this can be said to be a kind of preparation for the evolution of linguistic ability because during this period the child indicates his experiments to other by making various audible sounds. These sounds and signs that he makes play an important part in the development of his language ability.

PRE-LINGUAL COMMUNICATION

A child needs some means of communication by which he can communicate with the other people around him. Even during his infancy the child develops some signs and indications which help to transmit his needs to other people. Psychologists differ in their opinion about the first crying sound of the child at the moment of birth. Some consider it a desire to communicate while others think it is a reflex action. Nevertheless, all psychologists agree that the child develops some kind of sign language to communicate his needs. Even when the child is three weeks old he uses different sounds and physical movements to indicate such physical conditions as hunger, cold, pain, wetness etc. In this manner one observes the following three kinds of signs in a child while it is preparing language development:

1. Crying: This is the child's first sound and it does not have to be learnt for it is automatically produced by the vocal organs. Crying is uncontrolled and irregular. According to Leibnitz and Stuart, the child cries during the first two weeks without any particular cause. Crying does not bring forth any tears but the breathing becomes irregular, pulse rate increases, the fist are clenched and the body becomes red. Despite the fact that this crying is not motivated the child normally quietens down if it is picked up by the mother. After the third week this variety of crying grows less. Normally, crying in the first seven weeks indicates an excess of hunger, noise and light. According to Watson the child cries because of hunger, exhaustion and fear. Buhler has indicated numerous causes of a child's crying—birth, light, high pitched sound, physical discomfort, interruption of sleep, exhaustion, hunger, difficulty in movement caused by tight clothes, the taking away of toys, fear, etc. Many children are found to cry immediately before they are fed and before they go to sleep. When a child is of three months he cries when he wants to attract the attention of grown up people, A four month child cries when he is not allowed to play. A nine month child cries when he observes his mother going towards another child. Studies of the clying sound of children have indicated that they utter the first sounds of vowels. If the parents pay too much attention when the child cries, then the child develops a habit of crying whenever he needs anything. It is better to attend to the child immediately he cries so that he should not have to cry for a long time in order to be attended to. Crying for long periods has a bad effect on the child's digestion, besides which it also causes nervous tension and loss of sleep. This creates a feeling of insecurity in the child, for he feels that he is being ignored by his parents. All these things have the effect of making future social adjustment difficult. Physical development also suffers.

2. Babbling: The stage of babbling begins in the third month and continues upto the eighth month. During this period the child's vocal organs develop. A child makes those sounds which give him pleasure, and he repeats them because they add to his pleasure. If his parents indicate their delight at the sounds he is making then the child feels encouraged to go on repeating them. Most of these sounds are meaningless and should be treated as such. Older people, on the other hand, try to read some meaning into them and they say that the child is trying to say something. The child has to make an effort to produce such sounds. According to Jersild, these sounds later on die out and the child does not make them. In the beginning these sounds have some vocal quality, although the child learns to pronounce consonants only when he sports his front teeth. Some sounds become more definite than others because of repetition. Hurlock believes that the child continues to babble upto the age of twelve months. But it would be more accurate to say that the period of babbling depends upon the development of the child's speech organs and the encouragement he receives to speak. Babbling gives pleasure to the child and he is often seen babbling to himself. He grins and laughs when he hears the sounds proceeding from his own mouth. Compared to the normal child a deaf one does not babble so much because he cannot hear the sound that he is himself making. It is in the process of babbling that the child learns gradually to control his vocal chords.

3. Gestures: The child uses different types of gestures and signs to express his meaning to others. He uses several parts of the body to make gestures. If he does not succeed in conveying his meaning through gestures he begins to weep. In infancy several types of gestures are spontaneously visible, as for example, moving the head from side to side smiling, stretching arms, weeping, throwing legs etc. The parents follow the meanings conveyed by the child through these gestures. As the child learns to speak, the use of gestures becomes less and less, because they are not needed any more. But gestures are used even now due to imitation and sometime to emphasize certain words.

After passing through different stages of language development the child gradually begins to understand different words and their uses. At the age of 18 months he can use ten to twelve simple words on an average. Some children can use as many as one hundred words at this age. In next three or four months, the child's vocabulary increases very fast. At the age of 3 years his vocabulary may include words in four figures and this goes on increasing till the age of 12 years when it reaches the limit of 10,000 words or more.

LANGUAGE DEVELOPMENT IN DIFFERENT AGES

Some psychologists have described language development in different, ages. This can be divided into the following three periods:

1. From two to three years of age: During this period the child begins to use words to form sentences. He uses pronouns though he cannot use 'I' and 'me' properly. At the end of this period he begins to use plural and past tense. A child of three years can make complex and compound sentences.

2. Four to five years of age: At the age of four the child's ability to form a sentence is considerably improved and he begins to make use of the rules of grammar. He is very talkative at this age. He is interested in almost everything and asks questions without waiting for the answers. It appears that curiosity is not the only cause behind these questions, a reason is the exercise of the growing vocabulary. At the kindergarten age the child achieves sufficient control over words, though he cannot understand their subtle meanings.

3. After five years: At this age most of the children go to school. They use language intelligently in talking to other persons. The school and the home play a very important role in language development at this stage. The child also learns to pronounce correctly.

STAGES IN LANGUAGE DEVELOPMENT

The following are the four important stages in a child's language development from the point of various elements of language:

1. Comprehension: Comprehension means the ability to understand the meanings of the words uttered by others. According to the psychologists the child's power of comprehension develops even before he begins to use words. The child can comprehend more words than he can speak. The ability of comprehension plays a more important role in learning any language than the ability to speak. Though it is not definite as to what part gestures and words play in comprehension, it can be said that they play a very important part in it. If gestures are used along with words in teaching the child, his learning is facilitated. According to Hurlock when gestures are used with a child of 18 months, he understands the meaning more properly as compared with mere use of words. The psychologists Gessel, Termann, Merrill, Cattel, Garrison and Mcarthy have investigated into the child's ability of comprehension during different periods of age. It has been found that an infant of four months moves his head while hearing human sounds, and smiles at her mother. At the age of 6 to 8 months he hears the words attentively and also tries to pronounce them. At the age of 12 months the child can understand simple commands and instructions and also follow them. At the age of 5 to 6 years the vocabulary of the child is so much developed that he can understand the talks of unknown persons. He can comprehend the meanings of stories told to him. He can understand similarity and distinction between words. It has been found by experiments that the child's power of comprehension can be immensely increased by means of radio and television.

2. Building a vocabulary: The vocabulary of a child increases by hearing of other's using different words. One can find general and particular words in a child's vocabulary. The general words are those which can be used in many situations, *e.g.*, sleeping, walking, good, bad, man, woman, etc. The particular words are those which are used in different situations at different ages. As a general rule the former type of vocabulary is more developed than the latter kind.

In the development of general vocabulary the child first learns nouns and uses them in language. In these also he first learns words which are useful for him and which are easy to understand. On the other hand, he seldom uses words which are difficult to pronounce and finds it difficult to learn them. Thus, the child learns pronouns in due course. He learns nouns at the stage of babbling, *e.g.*, daddy, grand-father, uncle, etc. The verbs are used after learning nouns. In the beginning simple verbs such as come, go, get-up, sit down, etc. are used. At the age of 18 months, the child begins to use adjectives, such as cold, warm, good, bad, etc. and adverbs such as here, there, where, etc. According to Jersild in learning pronouns several types of 'I' are used and 'you' is used less often because the child is generally self-centred. According to the experiments of Young, Mcarthy and Garrison, the uses of pronouns and adverbs are very much found after the first two years of age. At the nursery school, the child is found to use more pronouns, verbs and adjectives than nouns.

The growth of vocabulary is intimately connected with intelligence and motivation. These factors are not only conducive to the learning of the new words but also in finding new meanings of words already learnt. In the first two years the child's vocabulary grows slowly. It increases very fast after he enters the school, because there teachers teach new words and their uses. Vocabulary increases by contact with new things, persons and places, hearing a radio, watching television, and reading story books. The psychologists have found out that the range of words in the vocabulary of the school-going children is from 20 to 24 thousand in the first class, 50,000 in the VI standard and 88,000 in the High School. Some psychologists including Smith, Mcarthy and Jersild have supported the conclusion of Crow and Crow that at the age of 12, the average vocabulary of a child is 10,000 words, while in exceptional cases it may go upto 30,000 words or more. The increase of vocabulary helps the child's talking as well as his writing. The progress of a child in education can be estimated by the range of his vocabulary because he knows the world around him through words. In modern times the wide use of radio, television and films in the school for the purposes of education has very much helped the increase of vocabulary. In the words of Garrison, "In an age of radio, television, films, rapid transportations and world relationship, the child needs to know many words and to be able to use them. Failure tends to result in impaired social adjustment."

The above discussion concerns with the development of general vocabulary. At the age of 3 the child begins to develop particular vocabulary. This includes words of different types, such as, words showing respect, etiquette etc. As the child learns to behave with the elders, he learns such words. Secondly, as the child sees things of different colours, he knows the names of different colours. Again, at the age of 2 years the child learns numbers. At the age of 5 and 6 years, the child learns to distinguish between different seasons, days, months, etc. At the age of 4 or 5 years he can distinguish between different coins. Just before adolescence, the children are seen talking in secret language, which is formed by different techniques.

3. Formation of sentences: Upto the age of one year, the infant generally uses only one word. He begins to construct incomplete sentences involving two or more words at the age of 2 years. At the age of 4 and 5 years he uses compound sentences. This ability of the sentence construction increases upto the age of 9 to 10 years, when the child can construct several types of sentences. The ability of constructing sentences increases with the cultural level of the child. According to Gessel. Garrison. Mcarthy and Jersild, a child of two and a half years uses complete sentences. The girls are generally more advanced than boys in sentence construction, because the speed of their intellectual development is more than that of boys.

4. Correct pronunciation: According to Hurlock the child learns to pronounce by imitation of others. If the others are pronouncing wrongly the child also learns to pronounce wrongly. Hence, pronunciation can be improved by demonstrating correct pronunciation to the child. 'In adolescence the pronunciations are more or less established and cannot be easily changed. The child's pronunciation improves after the age of 18 months and it is sufficiently improved at the age of 3. Besides age, one finds individual differences in pronunciation. While some children pronounce very correctly at an early age, others fail to do so, even at the advanced age. The main cause behind this distinction is the differences in the development of vocal organs, occasions of training and the amount of motivation. In the beginning the child's pitch of speaking is high, but upto the age of 3 years he learns to adjust it. The child should not be bluntly snubbed for speaking in the high pitch because this adversely affects the development of his vocal organs.

FACTORS IN LANGUAGE DEVELOPMENT

1. Physical health: If the child remains very ill during the first two years of life, it very adversely affects the language development in him, because firstly he does not get contact of other children, secondly he has no motivation to speak because his needs are fulfilled even without asking and thirdly he is often asked to keep silent. According to Gassel and Garrison, the deaf children leant to speak very late and their pronunciation is mostly incorrect. In comparison with other children their vocabulary is very much limited, because they cannot learn by imitation.

2. Intelligence: Almost all the psychologists admit that the level of intelligence is closely related with the ability of speech. The language development goes along with the increase in the level of intelligence. The children who are mentally undeveloped seldom develop average vocabulary. A mentally deficient child of five years of age has generally a vocabulary of an infant of 1½ years. On the other hand, the superior child has a vocabulary more than the average. He begins to speak at least four months earlier than the average child. The mentally deficient child, on the other hand, sometimes lags behind the average child for three years. But all the children are not same in this respect. About one-third of the mentally deficient children begin to speak at the proper age. The superior children not only learn to speak early but adopt the developed pattern of speech at an early age. They cannot, however, think with the elders. Sometimes some children who are very much advanced in language development in the beginning gradually lag behind even the average. Similarly, some children who appear to be very intelligent in the primary classes lag behind others in higher classes.

3. Socio-economic status: The psychologists generally believe, that in comparison with the children coming from lower socio-economic status, the children from higher socio-economic status have a wider vocabulary and more linguistic ability. Some psychologists have admitted a distinction of eight months period in the language development according to socio-economic status. Among the new comer children in the schools the children coming from families of higher socio-economic status generally depict developed vocabulary as compared with that of the children coming from poor families. This, however, does not mean that socio-economic status is the sole determinant of linguistic ability. In fact, the influence of socio-economic status makes distinction in the circumstances of children. Generally, the parents occupying a higher socio-economic status are more intelligent and more educated as compared with others. Thus, it is natural that their children should be more intelligent than those who belong to a lower socio-economic status. Secondly, better means of learning such as radio, television, magazines etc., are available in the family of higher socio-economic status and these in their turn favourably influence the intellectual development of the children. Thirdly, the children learn words by imitation of their parents. It is therefore natural that the modes of speech and the vocabulary of the children coming from families of higher socio-economic status should be more refined than of those children who come from poor families. Again, in the families of higher socio-economic status, the parents pay more attention to the intellectual development of their children. All these factors at the higher socio-economic status favourably influence the linguistic development of the child.

4. Sex differences: A comparative study of the linguistic development of boys and girls has revealed that in comparison with the boys the girls begin to speak earlier and they can use longer sentences at an early age. The language development, length of sentence, purity of construction, uses of words, power of comprehension and ability of pronunciation of the girls is much more than that of boys. On an average their vocabulary is bigger that of the boy of the same age and they develop a wider vocabulary at an early age. This superiority of the fair sex over the male is maintained upto a considerably higher age, so much so that at the stage of complete language development the girls are generally much more advanced than the boys. This distinction in linguistic abilities according to sex differences has been explained in terms of differences in family situations according to Mcarthy. In infancy the girls generally identify with the mother and the boys with the father. But while the girls get sufficient company of the mother, the boys do not get as much company of the father because he is generally absent from the house. It is due to this lack of contact with the parent that the linguistic development of the boy suffers. The explanation given by Mcarthy has not been admitted by other psychologists. In fact, the superiority of the girls in linguistic ability can be accounted by the fact that their general development is two years earlier as compared with the boys and they reach adulthood two years earlier. It is hence that their linguistic ability is much more as compared with boys of the same age.

5. Family relationships: The studies conducted by Mcarthy, Thomson and others among the children brought up in orphanages have shown that the language development of orphans lags behind the children brought up in average families. The orphan infants weep more and babble less. They begin to speak at a late age and use few sounds. An important cause of this deficiency is the absence of opportunities of the imitation of the parents. The psychologists have also found difference in language development according to birth order in the family. The real reason behind the distinctions, however, is not birth order itself but the difference which it makes in the child's contact with the parents. According to Davis and Mcarthy the language of the elder child is much more improved than that of the younger children because he gets more contact of the adults in the family. But if the youngest child also gets sufficient contact of the parents, his linguistic development not lag behind because of his birth order. Other studies have revealed that the linguistic development of the twins lags behind the development of children born alone because the twins are generally weaker.

6. Bilingualism: An important factor in the language development of the child is the fact whether he has to learn one or two languages in the house in his early age. In some modern Indian families, the child is so much confused by hearing a mixed language that he cannot pronounce correctly either his mother tongue or English and cannot improve vocabulary in any. From this point of view it is better if the child is encouraged to speak his mother tongue and the same is spoken to him. If the child is taught two languages right from the beginning the burden is likely to hamper his language development and more particularly his thinking because he often fails to decide as to which word should be used at a particular occasion. In order to learn two languages he has to memorise double words every where, with the result that his vocabulary in any one language does not improve appreciably. It is more so because often the grammar of two languages is also different. Thus the Indian parents who try to speak in English with their children right from the beginning and encourage them to do so, stunt the mental development of their children and unnecessarily load their mind with a foreign language. The psychologists have unanimously agreed that the child should be taught through his mother tongue and the same should be spoken to him A foreign language can be taught to him only after he masters his own mother tongue.

7. General Growth: The general growth of the child very much influences his language development. If the general growth is better the language development will also be better. The child in this case will begin to speak earlier and his vocabulary may be wider. On the other hand, if the general growth is deficient, the child will be lagging behind others in language development as well.

SPEECH DEFECTS

Sometimes some speech defects are observed among children in small classes and these must be cured before any appreciable development in education takes place. While on the one hand these defects create difficulty for the child while speaking, on the other hand, the social adjustment is also affected, because other children laugh at his defect. If the defect is not removed at an early date, the child develops inferiority complex. He either keeps silent before others or tries to escape from society. He cannot achieve high marks in the class nor can he lead his fellows. He develops a sense of insecurity. Thus, it is necessary to make all efforts to remove speech defects in the children. The main speech defects are as follows:

1. Lisping: This speech defect involves change of sound of letters and words. Its main cause is the continuity of the infantile mode of speech. The infant cannot pronounce words correctly. He changes their sound but gradually this defect is automatically eliminated. If the child continues to speak like an infant till late age, the defect requires to be cured.

2. Slurring: An important speech defect is slurring by which the child is unable to pronounce correctly. Sometimes this is due to too much haste on the part of the child, because he wants to express everything in no time. This defect is sometimes found among children who are used to be among strangers, so that when such a situation arises they become tongue tied or whatever they speak cannot be understood. Sometimes slurring is due to emotional tension because of excessive fear or some other emotion. These defects causing slurring can be removed easily, but if slurring is due to some inherent defect in the vocal organs, it cannot be completely removal unless these organic defects are removed.

3. Stuttering and Stammering: Stuttering and stammering, though closely related, are separate activities. In stuttering the child pronounces the same letter repeatedly before pronouncing a word. In stammering, on the other hand, he fails to produce any sound for some time, which results in embarrassing types of gestures and facial expressions. These again create emotional tension and difficulty in social adjustment. The tendency of stuttering is generally observed among children of 2 to 3 years of age, but it is gradually removed with the advance of age. Some exceptional children, however, stutter even at a late age. The defect of stammering, on the other hand, is continued till late age. Studies conducted regarding the causes of stuttering and stammering have revealed several important facts. According to Russell and Dunlop stuttering and stammering is due to learning faulty ways of speech by imitation of others. Other studies have revealed stammering to be hereditary. According to some psychologists stammering is the result of change of handedness which creates emotional tension. According to Johnson, Soloman and others stammering is mainly due to emotional tension as observed in excessive fear. It is, however, observed even in the absence of emotional tension, the causes in such a situation being sense of insecurity and maladjustment. According to some psychologists, stammering is because of lack of balance among the two hemispheres of the brain. According to others, a main cause of stammering is auditory amnesia. Sometimes stammering is because of physical deficiency or certain inorganic phosphates, proteins and potassium.

From the perusal of the above-mentioned causes of stammering and stuttering, it can be easily understood that while some of these can be removed, others cannot be removed. The presence of speech defects in childhood is sometimes due to lack of sufficient training and maturity. As these factors are provided, the speech defects disappear. The guardians and teachers should therefore encourage children to pronounce correctly. If they make haste in speaking, they should be taught to speak slowly. But if speech defects are continued till late age, efficient physicians must be consulted for their cure. Some defects can be removed by means of surgery. It requires much patience on the part of the guardian, teacher and the physician, as well as the defective child to remove various defects of speech.

QUESTIONS FOR EXERCISE

1. Trace the stages in the development of language in children. What are the major environmental factors that contribute to this development?
2. What are the main stages of speech development in children? Give a short account of each.
3. Describe the sequence of speech development in children.

16

Sexual Development

Being related to the sex glands, sex is organic need. It is a means of giving birth and sustaining the species. It is known by the seasonal menstrual changes in the female mammal. Its manifestation has become very complex, in view of the restrictions placed by the society, though its importance cannot be denied. Sigmund Freud, the founder of the school of psychoanalysis, believed the sex motive to be the most important and comprehensive of all.

The inception of the sex motive is due to the excretion of a gland. In the male it is caused by the excretion of the sex glands, while in the female due to the ovaries. The circulation of the blood carries it to the brain, the resulting behaviour being of a type not normally observed. The normal activity due to this motive is an interest in the members of the opposite sex, and a particular type of behaviour towards them, the goal being the mating of the male and the female. In the lower species, the sex activity is related to the seasons, being the highest in spring when the daylight is of a longer duration. The light has an effect on the brain via the eyes, and it excites the sex instinct.

A distinction between sex drive and lust, similar to the one made in the case of hunger and appetite, must be made. While the drive for sex is based upon the sex organs; lust is kindled by either the beauty or femininity of the female or the masculinity and strength of the male which act as stimuli besides the organs. The proximity of a member of the other sex may also create lust. In human society cinema, colourful clothes, make-up etc. are elements which excite lust.

Sex activity in human beings is very complex. Hence, in order to ascertain its natural or real form, it has been studied among animals. Rats were experimented upon in this connection. A rotating drum was attached to the rat trap. There is a board in the drum which records its rotation in any direction. The rotation of the drum is a measure of the distance travelled by the mice.

Experiments with this instrument proved that male rats show less activity without any particular pattern of change. The female rat runs a mile in the first three or four days, but on the fourth and fifth day her activity is very much increased. When extremely active she covers a distance of 15 miles in a day. The effect of the ovaries should be investigated because the absence of the sex organs does not alter this behaviour. It seems that this behaviour is due to the excretion of the ovaries. The level of sex activity is reduced by castration but not completely stopped. An injection of testosteron steps up this activity. Thus, the effect of the glandular excretion is unmistakable. Besides the sex glands, other glands such as the pituitary and the adrenal, also affect the sex activity. Though the individual analysis of the effect of the three glands has not been made, it is definitely established that they do play a part in sex behaviour.

Seasons do not affect the sex activity in humans as much as they do in animals. The excretions of the sex glands have a specific effect. With the extraction of the ovaries a development of the signs of femininity in a girl is stunted. But the removal of the sex glands does not substantially affect the sex activity in developed people. Quite possibly, this is the result of the habits formed in the presence of the glands. The sex activity can be restored by an injection of glandular extracts, at a late age, if it is impaired in any way.

The sex motive is not equally intense in every man and woman. The intensity of the motive and the means of its fulfilment vary from individual to individual. Quite a few people are abnormally sexual either due to excessive glandular excretion or social stimulation. The famous Kinsey report has thrown adequate light on the vast differences in human sexual behaviour. Excessive repression leads to the reduction of lust in a normal person. Abnormal sexual practices start in childhood because the child tries to satisfy his sexual motive in some way. These result in many perversions concerning sexual behaviour in adults. These perversions are far more numerous in human beings than in animals due to the social restrictions imposed on the sex motive in human society.

But is there some mating instinct, in humans and animals? As has been mentioned earlier, there is undoubtedly a mating instinct in animals like rats belonging to the lower species. The experiments on rats have shown that two months old rat reared separately from the female shows an abundance of activity indicative of the sex instinct, and if released with a female ready to mate, he very soon mates like a normal rat. Even in the absence of previous experience, the rats exhibit a definite pattern of sex behaviour and mating activity when they attain adulthood. Apparently, mating is instinctive in rats because they do not have to learn it. In the higher species the pattern is not so well established. Experiments on chimpanzees, carried out at the Yale University show that these animals learnt sexual behaviour by trial and error over a long period of time and that the pattern is different in each. Though experiments have not been carried out on human beings, it is obvious that the patterns of sexual behaviour are mostly acquired and learnt by seeing, trial and error or other methods. Therefore, it is difficult to say that there is a mating instinct in men similar to the sex instinct.

CYCLES OF SEXUAL MOTIVATION

Sexual behaviour runs in cycle; *i.e.*, it becomes intense and it disappears. These cycles are of three main types:

1. Life Cycle: In this cycle sexual behaviour is seen more clearly in a major period in the life of the organism. For example, youth is such a period.

2. Seasonal Cycle: In this cycle intensity of sexual behaviour in males and females is high in some special seasons.

3. Estrous Cycle: This cycle depends upon the secretion of endocrine glands. For example in mammalian females changes in intensity of sexual behaviour is seen in different phases of menstrual cycles. There is a low beginning period, a peak period and again a low end period of sexual activity in the cycle. In the human beings and other mammals extensive studies have been made on the above three phases of sexual behaviour. It has been found that many endocrine secretions affect the sexual behaviour of the organism. These are Estrogens, Prolactin and hormones from the anterior pituitary. Useful information about sexual behaviour has also been gathered by many studies of pregnancy. For example, it has been seen from the studies on rats that once pregnancy occurs, there is no sexual drive in the female rat till she gives birth to the babies. But a few hours after the birth of the babies sexual drive again becomes intense in the female.

Influence of environmental factors

Besides the endocrine secretions, influence of environmental stimulation on sexual behaviour can be seen on almost all animals. Learning and experience of the organism has also a great influence on it. No generalization can be made about the influence of environment for all the species. But the influence of light is seen in almost all animals. Greater length of the day in winter and spring is an important cause of greater intensity of sexual behaviour in fish, birds and mammals. Light also affects Estrous cycles. This is supported by the experiments on rats. Besides light, the effect of temperature on sexual behaviour has also been established. Influence of olfactory stimulation is also well known.

Influence of physiological factors

Influence of various harmones like androgens and estrogens on sexual behaviour has been established. Giving these harmones to many animals makes them sexually active before the age of maturity. Similarly sexual behaviour can be induced off season by injecting these harmones. It has been observed that sexual potency declines in old age in man and other animals. In lower animals like rats, injection of harmones in old age brings back sexual potency. This has not been successful in the case of man. Physiological factors, besides old age are more important in human beings than in lower animals.

It is clear from the above discussion that sexual behaviour of the organism is affected by sex harmones on the one hand and experience and learning on the other. These two influences work through the nervous system. As is clear from the figure given below, beside the harmonal factor sexual behaviour of the organism is also controlled by the neural factors like spinal cord and other brain structures. Sensory stimulation has a special importance in arousing sexual behaviour. Androgens influence the sexual behaviour of male whereas

Estrogens influence female behaviour. Spinal cord integrates genital reflexes of males and females. Hypothalamus acts as an integrative centre and organizes the patterns of sexual activity.

Influence of sensory factors

As has been said earlier, sensory factors have important role in arousing sexual behaviour. One or more senses may contribute in sexual arousal. Substances having characteristic smells secrete from the genital tract of the female rat or dog; specific type of sounds are given by the cat; skin of the sex organs of monkeys becomes red; and many signs are seen in the birds. Besides these, tactual and kinaesthetic cues have important contribution in the total sexual behaviour. In the absence of these stimulations, change in sexual behaviour may occur. Even if the sensory contributions of other organs are not essential, smell, hearing or vision have important influence in sexual behaviour. But it cannot be said that sexual behaviour of the organism depends totally on the sex organs. Female rats showed normal mating behaviour after removal of the uterus and vagina. This finding was also confirmed by the studies on cats. Thus taken together, it can be said that sexual behaviour is not aroused by any particular kind of stimulation but on the total amount of relevant sensory stimulation. In some instances it has been seen that hormones have a special contribution in sexual arousal. Besides this, the influence of various structures of the brain is also important. The most important neural structure is cerebral context. Hypothalamus is another important structure which acts as an integrative centre. Spinal cord mediates in the control of genital reflexes. These findings have been confirmed by the experiments on rats and cats.

It is clear from the above discussion of physiological aspects of sexual behaviour that stimulation from various senses, harmones and neural structures like hypothalamus and cerebral cortex have important influences in the sexual behaviour of the organism.

THEORY OF PSYCHO-SEXUAL GENESIS

In the opinion of Freud the sexual instinct in man has biological as well as psychological influence, and he believes that most tendencies that result in mental illness have a psycho-sexual aggressivity genesis According to Freud, the sexual instinct becomes evident in man in infancy and for this reason frustrations of human life have their origin in infant life. Freud also put forward the contention that from the psychological viewpoint there is no distinction between normal and abnormal individuals and that their behaviour should be elaborated on similar principles and theories. The development of mentally ill people does not differ from those of normal people in kind, and this contention of Freud has been borne out by the observation of normal and ill children. Just as sex problems are evident in adults along with other frustrations or abnormalities, the children also evince them. A fact that is generally recognised by abnormal psychology today is that every mental disease has its psychological as well as physiological aspect.

Sexual tendency in children

Freudian theory of the presence of sexual instinct in children was intensely objectionable, and was severely chastised, but modern sexologists and psychologists as well as physicians recognise this fact. For attaining adulthood in sex it is essential that infantile sexuality be repressed. The sexual instinct passes through a latent period from about 7 to 14 years of age, after the infantile stage has been passed and before adolescence is attained. During this period the sexual instinct is latent, but later on in youth it is again revived. Freud has always seen the human personality as a being that is involved in interaction with the environmental forces. Through the process of this interaction the individual has to suffer many frustrations and repressions that reap a considerable change in the personality.

Stages in development of sex instinct

Freud has described the following stages in the development of the sex instinct:

1. Oral stage: In this much of the actual activity is confined to oral biting and oral sucking.

2. Anal stage: In this two tendencies are prominent—the anal expulsive tendency and the anal retentive tendency. In this stage the child is imparted toilet training and this has considerable influence upon his personality. If too much frustration is effected his personality develops all kinds of abnormalities.

3. Phallic stage: In this condition most of the frustrations are concerned with infantile masturbation.

4. Period of latency: In this the experiences of sexuality are latent, not apparent.

5. Genital stage: In this sexuality is again apparent, and following this stage sexuality is manifested in normal adult relationships.

Importance of sex development

A normal development of human personality requires essentially that the person's sexual development also be quite normal, since its abnormal development can be the cause of many mental diseases and illnesses. Sexual adjustment in adolescence is a very important factor, and, for this, sex education is desirable. In the five stages of sexual development mentioned in the last section there are present four kinds of frustration, such as oral, anal, phallic and genital frustrations. The form of these frustrations changes nominally in differing cultures. And the extent to which a normal personality can develop in some particular culture depends upon the extent to which normal expression to human tendencies is permitted in its environment.

QUESTION FOR EXERCISE

1. Critically examine the various levels of psycho-sexual development of the child.

17

Moral and Aesthetic Development

MORAL DEVELOPMENT

Moral development within the family

A child's moral development, no less than his mental, emotional and social development, passes through various succeeding stages, being a gradual process. The child's first initiation into the mysteries of good and bad is through his parent's acceptance and rejection of his various actions Any action that meets with his parent's disapproval and invites their criticism is categorised by the child as bad or wrong. On the other hand, all actions sanctioned and welcomed by the parents are accepted as good and correct. A contributory factor to this opinion is the presence of punishment or reward. Here, the child's moral development is dependent upon his emotional development. An action that automatically results in reward brings him pleasure, so he considers it good and right. Where punishment is the result of an action, the child's reaction is the feeling that it is bad, conjoined to the realization that it is wrong. In this way, the child forms his concepts of good and bad, although, evidently, many of such conceptions may be incorrect. For example, in families in which the parents think it incorrect for children of different sexes to play together, the children also consider it undesirable. On the contrary, families that impose no similar restriction help their children to think well of the practice. These notions of good and bad that the child adopts in his infancy continue into a fairly large part of his childhood also. The truth of the matter is that the foundations of a child's moral development are laid in his infancy.

Moral development in school and neighbourhood

While the child quits the boundaries of the house and wanders out into the neighbourhood in search of suitable companions for his play, he becomes influenced by the notions of the good and bad that prevail among his chosen companions. He adopts the ethos of the group of which he has become a member. He learns to think in concurrence with the group and think well of things that have its sanction while he castigates anything that his group chooses to look down upon. It sometimes occurs that he is so profoundly influenced by this new ethos, that he rejects all that he has learned at his mother's knee. It is natural that the child's moral conduct in this age and in childhood should exhibit signs of inconsistency. For example, he thinks ill of lying, stealing, deception under certain circumstances but is prepared to condone such conduct when the circumstances are different. The propriety of his moral behaviour depends to a great extent on his learning. It is further influenced by his reactions, daily life, desires and prejudices. Children accept many things as acceptable and beyond censure when they see their seniors doing them in the school and at home, and having done so they adopt it as a part of their own pattern of conduct. It becomes assimilated in their natural behavioural pattern. Hence, the responsibility of parents and teachers in the child's moral development is very great.

Generally speaking, an individual's moral notions and concepts are determined by laws, traditions, religious ideals, customs, etc. in an individual's development, but there are many instances of exceptions to it. Neither does an individual invariably accept the general concept of propriety in a particular case, nor does he invariably proceed upon the actions he himself thinks correct and proper. Hence, moral development is a complex process in which the action and interaction of an individual and other people surrounding him is of great importance. Even in his infancy, the child does not exclusively depend upon another's notions of propriety, but chooses to form his own criterion, however rudimentary it may be. Many studies have shown that sometimes these conceptions are so strongly entrenched in the child's mind that it becomes difficult to change or modify them.

Moral development during adolescence

An adolescent's moral development, during the most crucial stage in an individual's development, is peculiarly susceptible to the effects of his mental and social development. Detailed study and analysis has revealed that in this age, the sexual urge of both male and female adolescents is particularly intense. Hence, it is only natural for the notions of good and bad to become associated with sexual behaviour. Since the laws pertaining to sexual behaviour differ considerably in various cultures, the moral concepts and conduct of adolescents do not exhibit any universal conformity but differ according to their culture. Sex education has the best and most profitable influence upon the adolescent's moral development at this stage. Actually, in this age, it is best to utilize the technique of sublimation and modification of manifestation rather than that of suppression. Many educational psychologists also advocate moral and ethical teaching in schools. But it is commonly and generally accepted that moral education is best imparted through practical representation of best ideals and values rather than through academic teaching and preaching of them. It is equally important for both teachers and parents to do their best to set the best example to their wards. Another factor that is equally important in respect of its influence upon the moral development of the child is the atmosphere prevailing in the school.

Influence of society and culture

Besides the school and family, the general social atmosphere also affects the moral development of individuals. It is for this reason that moral behaviour and conduct of individuals belonging to cultured and uncivilised societies show such marked differences that they appear almost incompatible. It is in society that an individual's axiological concepts are formed. Although the contemplative among society's members do not blindly conform to the social morality, the greater majority of them do follow, more or less unthinkingly, the general morality prevailing in society. Hence all individuals who set examples to the multitude, individuals such as leaders, great personalities, saints, scientists, literatures, actors, etc., influence the moral development of the individual. In addition to this, more indirect matters such as employment or unemployment, inability to secure the desired profession, economic status of the family, practical adjustment, peace in the family, intellectual and educational status, moral level of friends and intimates, presence of immoral institutions such as prostitution etc., in society, also cast a serious influence upon the moral development of the individual.

Moral development normally exhibits individual variations within very wide limits. There can be no saying what the actual moral implications of a particular instance will be for an individual, though generally speaking, good situations normally have a desirable influence.

AESTHETIC DEVELOPMENT

Development of the aesthetic sense in family

The tendency of creativity and aesthetic appreciation is evident in the child from the very beginning. It is this tendency that is the basis of his aesthetic sense. Emotions also help in this. Young children find much pleasure in drawing all kinds of figures with colours and pencils. The artistic compositions and productions of children are their natural self-expression, although elders may find it difficult to find anything artistic in them. This self-expression can be further refined through guidance and direction from teachers. If children are encouraged to examine artistic creations, their ability to appreciate and to create art increases gradually. But it should be remembered that it is not possible to develop this aesthetic ability in all children. Similarly, the aesthetic sense, too can also be developed only to a definite extent in children. This development includes many hereditary qualities and environmental factors. Fundamentally, family tendencies are very important. Children of parents who themselves possess aesthetic sense and a creative approach can be expected to progress fairly, rapidly in this direction. It is only natural to expect a child to praise his parents if he observes them drawing pictures, and to try to imitate them. He is also encouraged by the criticisms and comments that are forthcoming from admiring parents. Sometimes, such behaviour is found to be so effective that all the children in a family do their very best to win the admiration and praise of the parents. Evidence of the effect of family atmosphere upon aesthetic sense and artistic tendency is implicit in the number of artists and aesthetes that are present within succeeding generations of a family when once a great artist is born in it. Here, both heredity and environment are effective.

Development of the aesthetic sense in school

The aesthetic sense of the child next develops in the school. Schools that encourage artistic expression, painting and acting normally develop child's artistic sense better than other schools that take such subjects as a matter of course. In the beginning, the child does not care to attend to other's remarks on his artistic expression, and neither is he bothered how closely his painting approximates to the model. In the first and second classes a child does his drawing without any model. But by the time he reaches the third class he makes all possible effort to draw to a model. And in this stage, he is more amenable to comments from his teachers. Extreme criticism has adverse effect because it discourages the child, hence even his blunders should be pointed out with the greatest of tact and discretion. If so handled, the child will normally make his own effort to improve his work.

Method of expression

Expression of the aesthetic sense takes place through the medium of making clay toys, decorating flower vases, stitching, knitting, music, dance and other arts. Individuals differ in the manner in which they give expression to their artistic cravings. Some children prefer clay modelling to other forms of art while other children find it more diverting to draw pictures with pencil or paint. Aesthetic sense finds better expression if the children are provided with the objects that they desire to have. In schools the decoration of school rooms and verandahs can profitably be left to the children. Development of the aesthetic sense is more influenced by informal educational methods than by formal ones.

Aesthetic development in adolescence

Informal education is more influential and consequential in the adolescent stage since in this age, young boys and girls go to colleges to learn various forms of art. Artistic expression and manifestation of the aesthetic sense in this period of life is influenced by the individual's family background, interest, abilities, means of artistic expression, attitude of the parents and teachers, etc. Besides teaching children the intellectual appreciation of beauty, efforts should be made to inculcate in them a sense of beauty. Such training can be made facile by seeing good films, natural scenic beauty, art galleries, beautiful buildings etc. This has the effect of encouraging the students to appreciate beauty.

Many factors cast important influence upon the child's aesthetic development, the more prominent ones among them being the following:

1. **Age:** As the child grows older, his aesthetic sense in respect of his clothing, mode of life, interests and tendencies, etc. also gradually develops. Although it is not possible to distinctly define the various stages of aesthetic development according to the child's age, in the same child one can observe progress in the

aesthetic sense as he grows older. It is also true that the aesthetic sense that some children possess is so acute as to be unusual even in adults. In his infancy, the child's artistic tendencies find their natural and unmodified expression. Gradually, the artistic sense comes under the influence of his experience as well as his mental physiological capabilities. Important results and conclusions were obtained from experiments concerning the development, with age, of the child's aesthetic sense. In this experiment, the ability of children to keep time to music was put to the test. The maximum possible score being 400, children of two scored 84, of three scored 109, of four scored 153 while those of five obtained 192 points. Evidently, then development of aesthetic sense improves with age.

2. Intellectual development: The main reason why increase in age influences the development of aesthetic sense is that intellect increases with age. Generally speaking, each art requires many kinds of abilities, such as sensory acuity, motor activity, perceptual acuity, power of imagination, aesthetic determination, etc. It need hardly be pointed out that as these capacities gradually develop, the child's aesthetic sense will also develop. It is another matter if a child develops so rapidly as to equal or improve upon the general level evident in adults.

3. Physical development: Certain art forms such as dancing require balance, rhythm and unity. And for this, it is essential that the child attain to a certain minimum level of physical development. If the children who are taught dancing are too small, they will not benefit by the training as much as they would if they had attained to a higher level of physical development.

4. Experience: Experience is an important component of aesthetic sense. As the experience of a child in some particular art form increases one comes to expect better performances from him. Even otherwise, adult artists place much emphasis upon experience and practice.

5. Means: Means are an important factor in experience. Different art forms need different means and tools as painting requires colours, brushes, plates and paper, etc. If these means are not available, a child is not in a position to paint even if he feels so inclined.

6. Training: Many detailed studies and examinations have indicated that it is in the organised training and atmosphere in school that the child develops and improves his aesthetic sense. Not only are the various art forms taught in the classroom, even such activities as stitching, knitting, decoration etc. need training for proficiency to be achieved. This training in so many spheres benefits not only the children but also the elders. Nevertheless, in training them, the teacher has perforce to note students' maturity, age, experience, etc.

As long as the child does not manage to attain a certain specific level of mental maturity it is not desirable to instil art into him through the apparently mechanical tool of training. The knowledgeable teacher collects all proper means for child's artistic expression only after he has taken due note of his maturity. Using these available means, the children themselves develop their aesthetic sense, For instance, a child of three or less is not in possession of enough maturity to be able to use colours, pencils and other apparatus for drawing. Children, do of course, draw things but even they themselves would be hard put to it to explain their creations if they were asked. They give their creations the most bizarre titles, which they also promptly forget.

7. Atmosphere: Atmosphere is another element that exerts considerable influence upon the development of aesthetic sense. As has been pointed out earlier, atmosphere both in the house as well as in the school is important in this respect. Design of the school room, furniture, the children's dresses, decoration and window glasses can be so arranged as to help in the child's aesthetic development. Further aesthetic development of the child can be effected in the work room where he can be induced to make dining tables and other such items besides taking part in decorating the school, decorously darning clothes and doing numerous other small things. The child's aesthetic sense is further stimulated by the criticisms levelled at him by his friends and colleagues. Importance of social influences on an individual's aesthetic choice is evident. In fact, the school and home influence the child in their role of parts of a wide and comprehensive social organism. In society, one often sees very wide and overwhelming changes in songs, musical instruments, furniture, general architecture, poetic forms, literature, hair styles, and different fashions, etc., as time moves on the change helping in the aesthetic development of the individual. It can be made more effective through the use of radio and cinema as media of mass communication.

8. Individual differences: But, ultimately, any aesthetic experience is an individual and personal experience. It can originate in many individual factors. For example, an individual can find an ideal adjustment through the constant study of literature or music. But as he gradually attains to perfection in these arts, he again comes to accept praise and admiration. In trying to develop and improve the aesthetic sense of the children, the teacher should keep in mind their intelligence, abilities, physical and mental development, attitudes, domestic atmosphere, quality and defects of personality, social and emotional development, etc., as individual differences in these respects have the greatest consequences. Generally speaking, the tools used in different arts should differ with the age of the child playing them. The differences in the aesthetic ability of a child of 4, a child of 12, and an adolescent are evident, and their training should conform to their age level, for which it must be suitably modified. On the other hand, the artistic activities of different children within the same age level will show startling differences. At one end are the really proficient while at the other are children almost completely devoid of all artistic sense, but the majority of them are somewhere between these two extremes. It is only natural for children to have differing aesthetic development. The child's internal emotional life is another normally incalculable factor that seriously influences his or her artistic expressions.

Briefly, then, the following are the important points in a child's aesthetic development:

1. Aesthetic development is a part of the complete development and develops corresponding to it.

2. The associations in which an individual develops create an atmosphere important in determining the nature and direction of his aesthetic development.
3. The individual's aesthetic values evolve from his surrounding and his reactions. In this development the fundamental causes of the development of his internal life can be found.

It is evident from the above delineation that an individual's aesthetic development is a complex process and despite the influence of many important factors, the most essential elements are the individual's personal abilities and personality traits.

QUESTIONS FOR EXERCISE

1. Trace the development of moral concepts in children. Give illustrative examples.
2. Give a brief account of the development of moral values in children.
3. Explain the effect of family on the moral development of the child.
4. Write short note on—Moral Sentiment.
5. Describe the various stages of moral development in children.
6. Write short note on—Development of Morality.

18

Social Development

A big controversy has developed among thinkers on the question of the mutual relation between individual and society, but all are agreed that this relation is an intimate and close one. Actually, the society precedes the individual because society is not an exclusive characteristic of human beings but is also found in animals. Its life is longer than that of the individual and while the latter may come and go, it goes on continually. But, on the other hand, society has no existence in the absence of individuals, of which it is formed. Individuals constitute society. Individuals influence the society. It is society that makes individuals cultured. The child's personality depends to a large extent upon his social environment. Almost everything that he learns is acquired from society. Only the capacity of learning is his own. It is in society that his self or ego develops whereby he is called a human being. Every society has its individual organisation. Each exercises control over the individual and group which appear to be two independent units. But nevertheless, the existence and development of both depends on each other.

SOCIALIZATION: ITS AGENCIES

Socialization is the process whereby an individual learns to behave in accordance with social traditions and mores. The human child possesses a tendency towards imitation. The child develops according to that environment in which he lives. The individual tries to win the praise of the group in which he lives. Man is a social being. He, of his own nature, tries to adopt the culture of society. Man becomes what he is by socialization and it is by virtue of this that he is believed to be superior to animals. Socialization brings balance to his personality because the social aspect of personality also is very important. Through socialization the individual learns to control himself in the interest of society and realizes his responsibility towards others. Socialization develops in him the community feelings and he learns to co-operate with others.

Individuals influence each other by means of imitation, suggestion and sympathy. In addition to these, social institutions and associations also carry out the individual's socialization. The individual is influenced by many processes in society, praise and blame, co-operation and conflict, submission and ascendency. These help to form his personality and individuality. Education is the most prominent means to socialization.

Socialization in the family

The family plays perhaps the most dominant role in the individual's socialization. The child finds much to learn in the behaviour of his family members, parents, relatives and friends. He imitates them in their mannerisms, behaviour, cliches, etc. He tries to avoid such activities which result in punishment or which are considered bad in the family. It is the family environment which forms his good habits and it is in the family that he acquires criminal tendencies. In the book *New Light on Delinquency and its Treatment* Healy and Bronner have written that juvenile delinquents mostly hail from families which at one time or another, have suffered some hindrance in the fulfilment of social relations. Psychoanalysts, prominent among them are Freud and Adler, have proved that a man behaves in society according to whatever he has become in the family. Termann, the author of *Psychological Factors in Marital Happiness*, has said that only those individuals can make marriage a success whose parents were contented. The preface writer of *Women of the Street*, a searching book on London prostitutes, has stated that the problem of prostitution is the problem of the parent-child relationships. Boys and girls are spoiled when family contentment and peace are lacking. Many similar circumstances give birth to many thieves, murderers and prostitutes.

Other influences in socialization

But it is incorrect to believe socialization to be dependent exclusively on the family. Other institutions and associations outside the family also wield influence on the development of man. When the child has grown a bit, he leaves the sanctity and protection of his home to go out and plan, at such a time he is very susceptible to the influence of his playmates. The child in the school, is in addition to the effect of education, vulnerable to the influences exerted by the personalities of his teacher and friends. In much the same way, young men and women learn to conduct themselves and to give expression to their views, such a process being an outcome of education and constant association with teachers, the unique environment, fellow collegiates, etc. Following college education, the individual's occupations and marriage are important factors of socialization. Both men and women are strongly influenced by the personality of their life partner, and their future depends upon this to a large extent. In this way, the child in the family becomes successively the protector, husband and father. These new responsibilities and rights teach him very much. In brief, socialization is a process which begins at birth and continues unceasingly until the death of the individual. Like education it too is an incessant process.

In the Fig. given on the next page the proportionate breadth of arrows shows the comparative influence and interaction of different individuals and groups on the child. Thus family exerts maximum influence, then come the play groups, school, religious group, children club, community and larger cultural patterns. Interaction is maximum with pals, then with friends and casual acquaintances.

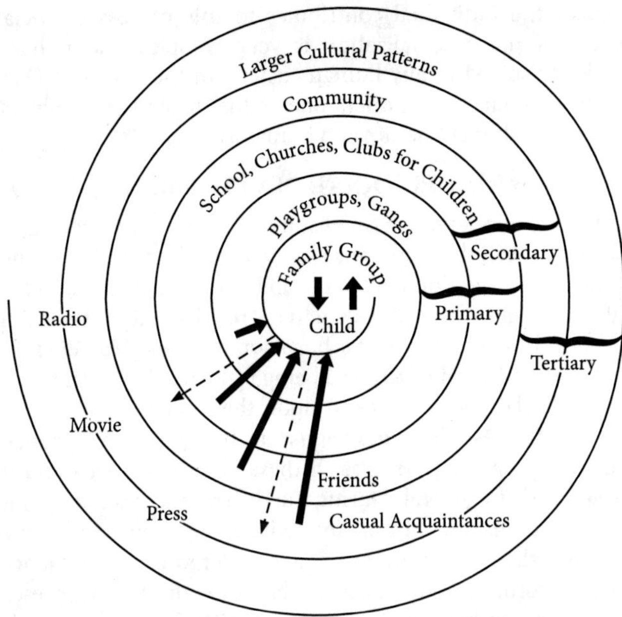

Fig. 6. The expansion of the horizon of child's experience and the resulting interaction. From P.J. Brown, *The Sociology of Childhood*, p. 45.

NEED FOR SOCIALIZATION

The question why is socialization necessary for the development of the individual is best answered by the examples of human beings who were for some reason, nurtured outside society. Human beings of this kind are described by Gesell in his work *Wolf's Children* and *Human Child* and by Davis in his essays. In 1920, in India, two children were found in a wolf's den, of which one of eight years old and the other couple of years younger. The second died after the lapse of only a few months while the first continued to live for six years. She was named Kamla. The girl was completely innocent of the modes and ways of human behaviour. She walked on all fours, growled like a wolf and could not speak. She became nervous at the sight of human beings as undomesticated animals tend to do. In this way, due to the absence of socialization, she possessed none of the characteristics of human being save for her bodily structure. She was taught to speak, wear clothes and eat. In this way, she could learn some human behaviour due to the influence of socialization after a period of some years.

Socialization is not the exclusive but a prominent source of individual's development, because heredity also has its importance. The development of the individual, with the spread of culture through socialization, is impossible. The 'self' of the individual develops only due to socialization. Every social relationship of the individual contributes to this process of socialization. The problem of man's socialization is very complex and it has not yet been completely solved in any human society. In the words of Davis. "The improvement of socialization offers one of the greatest possibilities for the future alteration of human nature and human society."

WHAT IS SOCIAL DEVELOPMENT

In defining social development, Sorenson has written, "By social growth and development we mean the increasing ability to get along well with oneself and others."[1] Thus social development is the ability or skill by means of which an individual maintains order and system in his relation with other beings in his neighbourhood, besides adapting his behaviour to them. Man is a social being influencing the conduct of others and being influenced by their behaviour, in his turn. Social relationships depend upon the mutual adjustment between such behaviour. Interests, attitudes habits, etc. bear much importance for this mutual behaviour. Development of all these elements is part and parcel of social development in general. During the different stages that an individual passes, social circumstances in his immediate neighbourhood, his relations with others and their expectations of him undergo constant change. Social development accords an individual the ability to adjust to his present social circumstances and to behave in accordance with the wishes and desires of other people. If adult men or women were to be seen playing with dolls, it would be considered socially undesirable and improper whereas it is perfectly reasonable for a child to indulge in this sort of entertainment. Due to social development, the individual's conduct conforms to the requirements of his age, his social status and social functions. In the words of Powers, "Social development can be defined as the progressive improvement, through directed activity, of the individual in the comprehension of the heritage and the formation of flexible conduct patterns of reasonable conformity with this heritage."[2] In this manner, stress is laid upon unceasing progress and development. The individual's social circumstances are constantly undergoing change, and the individual must perforce change with these circumstances. This is the process of his actual social development.

Characteristics of socially matured individual

Having understood the behavioural patterns of a person mature from the social standpoint, it will become easier to comprehend the implications of social development. An individual, mature from the social standpoint, is one who co-operates with all those with whom he comes into contact, and contradicts them only when such a course of action becomes inevitable. He is never ill-mannered, choosing instead to appear very well mannered, considerate and friendly to all and sundry. Consequently he has a large circle of friends.

1. Sorenson, H., *Psychology in Education*, Mc-Graw Hill Book Co, New York, 1954, p 209.
2. Powers, F. F., *Educational Psychology*, Prentice Hall Inc. (1945), pp. 102-3.

An adult, who has attained that stage, as required by the social standpoint, evinces great interest in art, study, games, etc. He studies the works of the greatest authors, and takes interest in games and forms of recreation suitable to his statge in life. His activities and conduct are scrupulously in conformity with his age and sex. He mixes with people easily, yet occasionally prefers some solitude. He has the power of independent decision and judgement. He gives every evidence of being well balanced and adjusted within himself and in his behaviour towards other individuals.

Socially undeveloped individual

On the contrary, an individual who is undeveloped or immature as looked at from the social standpoint, is one who hesitates in society and shows signs of being embarrassed. He experiences nervousness when in the presence of others. He depends to a large extent upon the decisions of his mother and is attached to her, having a very small circle of friends and acquaintances. He finds it difficult to carry on with others.

It is evident from the above description that social development comprehends physiological and mental status, qualities of personality and emotional development.

Having understood the meaning of the phrase social development, one is now in a position to study and understand the child's social development in infancy.

SOCIAL DEVELOPMENT IN INFANCY

The child's social development takes place gradually as he advances in age. The newborn baby performs very few social functions, being both consciously and unconsciously concerned with the fulfilment of his physical needs. But before long, he exhibits signs of reacting to individuals who help him fulfil these needs. The only thing that his early activities show is that he has started understanding the objects and individuals in his environment. By the time he completes his first year he forms specific patterns of behaviour regarding the adults with whom he comes into contact. He is also influenced by their interests and other things.

Similarly, as the child grows older, the patterns of his play also evince many significant changes. When he is two months old, the only thing he is capable of is holding the wooden block proferred to him. But when he is two years old, he plays with his toys without the need of any external intervention, besides which he tries to dispossess other children of their toys and to take all toys for himself. Gradually, the feelings of 'I' and 'mine' develop and strengthen, but at the same time he also learns what 'you' and 'yours' mean. In the third year, he also recognises the right of other individuals over his toys, thereby learning to share his possessions with others. It is only after this period that the child shows any desire to co-operate in group games.

Moving from the egocentric behaviour of the first three year to the pre-school period, the child's conduct begins to appear socialized. In infancy, the child is almost completely 'egocentric and selfish, not being inclined to give any of his possessions to any one else. As his social development progresses towards ultimate maturity, he learns to divide and share his own with others and to co-operate with them. Even then, the intelligent children maintain some independence and individuality. Most of the child's games in the pre-school period are egocentric. On entering school he enters the first stage of his socialization and immediately becomes a member of the group of his own sex. Boys group with boys, and girls with girls. In school, the child is particularly sensitive and susceptible to other's behaviour towards him, particularly the conduct of his seniors. Till four or five years of age boys and girls play together. As the child gets greater opportunity to meet boys of his own age, his socialization accelerates. In the words of L.B. Murphy, "He becomes a member of a small world of children, all near his own age, although differences in age may vary with the arrangement in different groups. This world of children furnishes, from this time on, a major part of his social diet. He is constantly assimilating this, by direct imitation of patterns of other children, by spontaneous reaction to things which they do or to situations which they create, by resistance to this pressure, by repeated experience of tensions aroused by their mere presence."[1] In the kindergarten and montessori education systems, the child's social development is further facilitated by the opportunity that children get to play together. It has been pointed out before, too, that in this age group one can find groups of children formed on the basis of sex differences. But it is equally usual for two children of opposite sexes to become quite friendly and intimate due to reasons of proximity or convenience or the absence of other children. The truth of the matter is that the presence of sex distinction among children's play is the result of criticism or interference from seniors. In this age, friendship normally lasts for no more than a couple of days. Some children of course find it easier than others to make friends.

Living in the group, the child gradually evolves the communal sentiment. As he grows, he also acquires notions of propriety and impropriety, although children are seen differing in their individual opinions on this point. These concepts are primarily influenced by the attitudes of parents and teachers. The child himself, in his play, shows little or no consciousness of sex difference, a state of mind that is normally found to exist in the childhood that immediately precedes the period of adolescence.

Although development of social behaviour in the child exhibits considerable individual differences, yet Buhler saw from his investigations that more than 60% children show similar patterns in social development. This can be seen from the following table constructed by Buhler.

1. Murphy, L.B., *Social Behaviour in Child Personality*, Columbia University Press (1927), p. 49.

Responses of infants to adults, observed in 60% or more of the cases[1]

	Age in months
Returns glances of adults with smiling	1 to 2
Is quieted by touching	2 to 2
Cries when adult who is attending him leaves	2 to 3
Smiles back at adult	2 to 3
Disturbed when approached	2 to 3
Returns approaching glance with 'lalling'	3 to 4
Displeasure when loses glance of adult	3 to 4
Quieted by caressing	4 to 5
Disturbed by the sight of people	4 to 5
Striving for attention by 'lalling'	7 to 8
Stretches out hands towards adults	7 to 8
Cries when adult stops talking	7 to 8
Strives for attention by movements	8 to 9
Pulls on the clothes of adults	9 to 10
Offers adult an object	9 to 10
Imitates movements of adults with a plaything	9 to 10
Organises play activity	10 to 11

In studying the ages in which specific forms of social behaviour in children were first manifested, Gassel and Thomson found that although some specific activity could be expected of a child at some specific time period, yet a considerable difference is also in evidence regarding the behaviour of individual children. While Buhler has studied the social development of the child's behavior towards adults, he has also studied its development in respect of other children. This is to be seen from the following table:

Responses of infants to other infants observed 60% or more of the cases

Observes other child	4 to 5
Smiles at other child	4 to 5
Cries if other child receives attention	8 to 9
Offers toy to other child	8 to 9
"Lalls" to other child	8 to 9
Imitates movements of another child	9 to 10
Opposes toy being taken away	9 to 10
Organises play activity	10 to 11
Strives for attention by means of "lalling"	10 to 11
Ill-humour if another child moves away	10 to 11
Setting aside toy and turning towards another child	11 to 12

1. Buhler, C., *The First Year of Life*, John Dev. Co. (1930), pp. 56-57.

SOCIAL DEVELOPMENT IN CHILDHOOD

Most children go to school when they attain to childhood. Hence the social development of this period is particularly influenced by the atmosphere in school and playground. It is a part of the teacher's job to provide by creating such an atmosphere in the classroom, school and playground in which healthy social development of the child may take place. Games have a special significance for the child's social development during this period of his life. Teachers should organise such games that provide satisfaction of the child's social needs, and the needs of his social development. And, in this, it is desirable if individual differences between children are also kept in mind. As a general rule, the child's social behaviour is not fixed or properly patterned by the age of six, it being influenced by such factors as his social consciousness, the ability to mould himself according to the rules in force in school, physical experience and mental development, etc. The moment a child enters the portals of his school, he is faced with new problems of social adjustment.

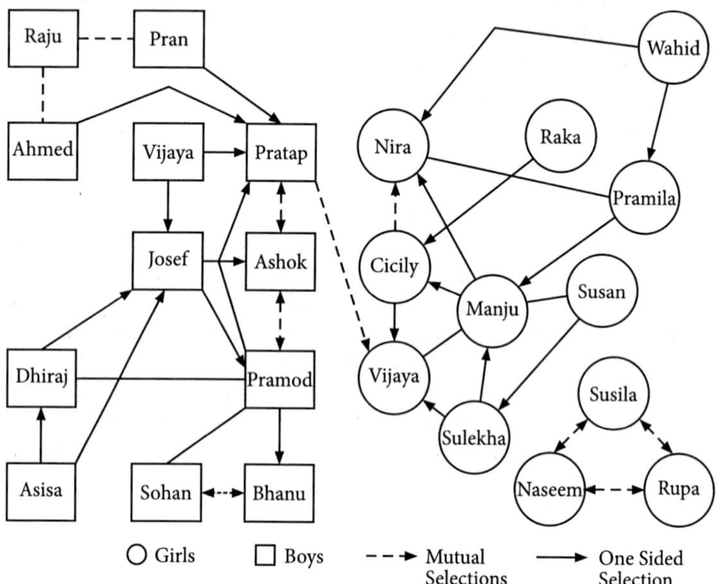

Fig. 7. Based on Ruth Cunningham's *How to construct a Sociogram*

Between the age of 6 and 12, the child begins adjusting rapidly to his changing and varying social world. Now he is usually a member of one or the other group, which exhibits a code language, places of meeting a leader, special purpose of various activities, etc. The members of the group evince a definite loyalty to the group, do not hesitate to obey the orders of the leader and to emulate him and experience considerable freedom and independence. These same groups later on, in adult life, manifest themselves in the form of committees and societies. In this age, boys and girls form their groups among members of their own sexes, because of a definite and clear differentiation between their habits, interests, desires, etc. This fact is further clarified by the following sociogram which is based on a testing of the mutual selection of boys and girls, and of the one-sided selection. In this, only two children have made a mutual selection, Pratap and Vijaya, while all other boys have chosen boy friends, and girls have selected girl friends. Sushila, Nasima, Rupa are girl friends by mutual selection. Manju is liked by four girls. Susan, Pramila, Sulekha and Vijaya. Waheeda and Susan are not selected by any one though each of them has selected two friends. Similarly, proceeding on the same lines, find out who is the most popular boy in his group.

In this period of his life, the child is away from home for a considerable part of the day, yet the affection of parents and teachers is in no way reduced. While he aspires to the social values of his own group on the one hand, he is equally anxious to win the love and esteem of his parents as well as of his teachers, although it can sometimes happen that out of loyalty to the group he may feel compelled to neglect his parents and teachers and their entreaties. For, he is particularly anxious to win esteem in the group. Sometimes, in the group he indulges in activities that are considered specifically anti-social. In the case of children who indulge in such activities, fundamentally a great responsibility lies in the environment within the home and family. In families where the parents have no hesitation in giving praise and affection to their children, it will be seen that the young individuals indulge in proper and desirable activity. On the other hand, neglected and consequently rebellious children are apt to indulge in detestable actions, and later on turn into juvenile delinquents. It is necessary that the teachers keep an eye on the development and active manifestation of such tendencies within the child groups within his domain. Groups provide opportunities for the development of the qualities of leadership, so that in their adult and more responsible years, the boys and girls can turn to leading the nation. It should be kept in mind that all children do not evince the same liking for the group. Some children tend to avoid groups and prefer to stay with one or two children of their choice. There may be occasions of conflict between these individualistic boys and the bigger groups. And, there is no essential rule that members of the group are intelligent while those boys and girls who tend to shun the group are slow-witted. It is perfectly possible for the opposite to be true. Secondly, there may be some personal reasons which may actuate the individual to stay away from the group, but generally it is best to live in the group, as it benefits the individual's social development.

The child's social development is influenced in an important manner, by the mutual interaction between childhood groups, competition, conflict and co-operation.

According to Bridges, the following table can help to reveal the extent to which a child's social development has taken place, if at all. Positive answers indicate development, while negative ones indicate the opposite:[1]

1. Bridges, K.M.B., *Social and Emotional Development of the Pre-school Child*, Kegan Paul, 1931.

1. Played with another child.
2. Spoken to another child.
3. Occasionally made social contact by touching or pushing a child.
4. Imitated other children's actions.
5. Imitated children's words.
6. Imitated children's laughter.
7. Often spoke to other children.
8. Originated new play activity with other child.
9. Joined group of children in play.
10. Sought another child's approval.
11. Asked another child for help .
12. Always given up toys at fair request.
13. Usually waited turn.
14. Tried to defend own right to materials or place.
15. Pointed to others' errors.
16. Tried to help others.
17. Stopped work to aid another child.
18. Comforted another child.

Further indication of desirable adjustment can be measured in terms of the extent to which a child *has not* rather has—

19. Turned away to avoid another child's friendly advances.
20. Usually stayed out of group marching or games.
21. Claimed others' toys.
22. Interfered with others' work.
23. Destroyed others' work.
24. Created disorder in group or led others into mischief.
25. Frequently pulled or pushed others.
26. Frequently complained of other adult for own gain.
27. Harassed new child by scoffing or shunning.
28. Hit or pinched others for fun several times.
29. Bitten or spit at other for fun several times.
30. Teased in other ways, causing irritation or discomfort.

SOCIAL DEVELOPMENT IN ADOLESCENCE

When the child attains the age of 13-14, he undergoes radical and startling changes of a mental as well as physical nature. It is natural that his social development should also undergo some change, the phenomenon under consideration being influenced by many various factors. It is effected by interests, needs, feelings of insecurity, values, attitudes, responsibility, viewpoint, etc.

In adolescence, the child becomes exquisitely conscious of his sex. Because young girls grow up two years earlier than their male counterparts they prefer to associate with boys a couple of years their seniors. But on the other hand, the social distance between boys and girls also widens, with the result that boys associate with girls or criticise them, but in either condition they are fully conscious of the other sex. Similarly, the girls who are seen continuously blaming and criticising boys pay considerable attention to the boy's criticism and behaviour, besides which they attend to the activities of the male sex in one or the other respect. But immediately the child enters the adolescent stage, he rarely professes extreme heterosexual tendency of a very intense nature. Generally, in this age, the boys and girls are more keen on seeing each other and being seen by the others. They try to attract and hold the attention of each other through such tactics as wearing extraordinary clothes, dressing their hair in the latest fashions, peculiar conduct, etc. They want to make their presence felt and known, so that they are even conspicuous by their absence, if such an occurrence becomes unavoidable. In this manner, relations between heterosexual individuals are not very well defined during the early stages of adolescence. One of the main reasons why they are so disturbed and ill at ease in the presence of each other is that they are conscious of a strange attraction that is new to them, and they cannot divine the reasons for it. Consequently, while they like to be with each other, they feel embarrassed and reticent of each other. In social conditions created within the school, girls and boys can adopt the proper patterns of behaviour between the sexes under sympathetic guidance of the teachers. It is essential that teachers as well as parents should be very careful when acting in this connection. In order that they may be able to adjust properly in their roles of husband and wife, it is essential that during adolescence each develops the right attitude towards the other sex. One very important factor that contributes to this attitude is the atmosphere in which the child lives at home. In this age, the groups are not as well organised and systematic as the groups of childhood, and their purpose is mostly social. Important social activities of young men and women are dances, singing sessions, picnics, mountain climbing etc. In western countries, in all such outings the number of individuals from either sex is almost equal, so that every one has his companion. Some boys and girls do not participate in such a big group, but choose to develop relations with an individual of the other sex. But people who choose to live in big groups do not entertain a good opinion of such solitude lovers. One finds considerable loyalty in conflict and even physical violence. Members of a particular group have the same conversational style, dress, modes of conduct, etc., and they mostly prefer to be together. Adolescents talk incessantly of their school and college, but they also show considerable interest in philosophical issues, national and international matters, professions, games and other subjects of universal significance. But their greatest pleasure is derived from their conversation on the other sex. It is another matter that some individuals pretend to be revolted not only to talking of such matters, but even upon hearing them mentioned in their presence for some or the other reason. In adolescence, young men and women take considerable interest in their appearance, behaviour and presentability, because they have great zest for living and enthusiasm for every project that is put to them. In matters of appearance and dress, they imitate others, particularly adult men and women, whom they try to emulate in every respect. Leaders of adolescent groups are chosen on the basis of health and energy, loyalty, enthusiasm, sportsman spirit, organisational skill, originality, sympathy and many other qualities of personality. Common interest and traits lead to the formation of very strong, staunch and intimate friendships in this age; such friendships sometimes last a life time. Such profound friendship between individuals of different sexes even results in matrimonial ties.

In the domestic sphere, young boys and girls of this age are often found contradicting their parents and thus causing conflicts. On the other hand, the parents contribute their little mite to this general communion by constantly interrupting and correcting the youngsters on some ground. Both sides are equally anxious and desirous of foisting their respective views upon the other, and each side is dissatisfied with the views of the other, although they unanimously resent any external interference in their differences of opinions. Besides these more or less common problems, the individual may have his own problems of adjustment that result in his disappointment, anxiety and dejection. In this age, every individual wants that he or she should develop fully and beautifully into a man or woman, and is disgusted and worried if he does not. Not only does physical development satisfy him; he also wants mental and intellectual development so that he may appear intelligent and able to his friends. Thus, different individuals make their best effort to gain proficiency in many different spheres such as studies, dance, music, various kinds of games and arts, etc. Some of them gain their specific place in society through sympathetic, co-operative and benevolent behaviour. While on the one hand, it is eminently undesirable to be completely indifferent to public opinion, it is equally futile and dangerous to be completely infatuated with the idea of winning public acclaim and being in the good books of every person. People of this kind make every effort to become leaders through reasonable and unreasonable means.

Occupational interests of the individual are also significant for his social development. In different societies, some specific professions are more respected and regarded than others, so that most of the adolescents prefer to adopt these professions. Success and failure in such schemes has important influence upon their social development.

From the above description of social development during adolescence, it is apparent that in this age individuals are in particular need of guidance and direction. Factors such as sexual desires, occupation, family, adjustment in school or college and others pose such problems for the young immature person that he is incapable of solving, and in which the interference and advice of his elders, both parents and teachers, is very desirable.

Social development and education

In every stage of social development of the child, education contributes much, but this education is not the literacy thrust upon the child through books and lectures. The real and incalculable factors that exert this influence are the extra-curricular programmes, the school's atmosphere, rules of conduct in schools, radio, cinema, newspapers and magazines, etc. Group camp almost invariably have a healthy influence upon the individual's social development or socialization. It helps to form his character and develop social qualities. He acquires good habits and develops the qualities of leadership, he also gets many opportunities for developing many kinds of skill. In the informal atmosphere of the camp, individuals can meet and mix with greater freedom and informality so that their social education is set in motion. In this manner, teachers and parents can co-operate to give adequate facilities and opportunities for the healthy social development of infants, children and adolescents.

SOCIAL DEVELOPMENT IN ADULTHOOD

Social development continues into adult age. In this period of his life, the person's social development is affected by such tangible and strong influences as the peace and calm of married life, permanent and suitable occupation, good social and economic position etc. From the social standpoint, signs of a developed adult are—friendship, control over emotions, power of leadership, desire and ability to co-operate with others, economic independence, family independence, good tastes in respect of entertainment, social and moral level of a high order, cultured and pleasant mannerisms, and good heterosexual relationships. Possession of these qualities, helps the individual to adjust properly in society, their absence depriving him of this essential capacity. Even his physical and mental development have important repercussions on his social development. In addition to these rather personal qualities, other broader and more social factors that influence his social development are atmosphere in family and occupation, the general and cultural atmosphere of society. It is essential for the individual's happiness and peace that he possesses social maturity. It would be no exaggeration to state that the lack of social maturity might make his life well nigh impossible. Here it should be remembered that normally the individual develops completely, that is proper physical, mental and emotional development makes it imperative that his social development also be excellent. It is equally true that incomplete development in any of these aspects leads to incomplete social development. Education is an attempt at just this complete development of the individual, and it necessitates the co-operation of the teachers as well as the parents.

FAMILY AND SOCIAL DEVELOPMENT

Human personality develops in a social environment. In the childhood the personality of an individual is very susceptible to change and variation. He can be turned in practically any desired direction. The famous psychoanalyst Freud has contended that the personality of man is formed in his childhood and the period after that marks only its development. In view of the fact that the experiences, habits, etc., acquired in childhood are so extremely important, the family situation also becomes important because the childhood of the individual is spent within the precincts of the home. The family situation can be regarded as comprehending three factors—(1) relation of parents to child, (2) order of the child's birth, and (3) presence of brothers and sisters and other members in the family. The important role played by the family in the formation of the child's personality can be clearly realized after these three aspects have been studied.

Relation between child and his parents

Having affected a psychological analysis of the importance of the parent-child relationship the psychoanalysts have tried to show why the child is influenced to such a great extent by his parents and the relation in which he stands with them. According to Freud the parents are particularly present before the child as ideals. They are more powerful and strong and can perform all activities efficiently. The child effects an identification with his father unconsciously. He wants to become as his father. It is often seen that the young child dons the clothes of his father and imitates his manner of walking and talking. The child behaves precisely as do his mother and father. Besides identification, the second element in this is that of imitation. The child learns much by imitation. There are many activities that the child learns to perform merely by observing and imitating the older members of the family. For the child, the parents are as examples and it will be very difficult to prevent children from indulging in activity in which the parents themselves indulge particularly when they do so in front of the child. This difficulty arises because he feels that what the parents are doing should be done. In this both identification and imitation are included. The child also receives suggestions from his mother and father. The activities in which the mother and father indulge automatically suggest themselves to the child. In this way, the process of identification is not the only process that is activated in the relationship between the child and the parents but is supplemented by the process of imitation, suggestion and sympathy. According to Freud, the viewpoints of the male and female child towards their parents are not identical. Freud believes that the sex instinct is innately given in the individual and is present at birth. In this opinion, the child does not suck his mother's breast merely because he is hungry but also because it gives him pleasure. His mother is not exclusively the source of his nourishment but also the basis of his feelings of pleasure. Freud has further postulated the instinct for heterosexuality in children. Accordingly the male child loves his mother more while the female child shows greater attachments to the male parent. The mother is the boy's beloved. Hence, naturally the father becomes his opponent and sometimes he sees that he is deprived of his mother's love only because of his father's presence. Often his mother leaves him and goes to his father when the latter comes. Consequently, the boy regards his father as a rival. On the one hand, he respects the father because he is the ideal, on the other, the child also hates him in his capacity of opponent.

Criminal tendency and the parent-child relationship

The misbehaviour of the parents or their neglect of the children are important factors due to which children often become juvenile delinquents. According to the report of *Women of the Street*, an important research on the prostitutes of London, the problem of prostitution has its origin in the relationship between the child and the parents. Often, when the child is deprived of parental love and is sternly punished frequently he is filled with the desire to revolt and disgust so much so that he runs away from the home when he gets the opportunity to do so. Once away from the home he falls into criminal ways. If neglected by his parents the child feels helpless and alone as a result of which he develops many kinds of complexes. The child becomes a delinquent also when the parents try to conceal too much from him. For example the children are very apt to ask their parents as to where they came from or where the younger child came from and they are often misled. When they come to know of their true source from servants or from their friends they develop a sense of insecurity because they are deeply hurt when they come to know that their parents do many things that they would not have the children know. This sense of insecurity often lures children into sex crimes.

Need for balance

In this way, both excessive neglect and excessive love and affection are not to be desired in the relationship between the child and parents. Both are the origin of difficulties concerning the personality and all kinds of problems take root in the mind of the child. Similarly it is harmful both to place absolute control on the child as well as to leave him to his own mechanisms almost entirely. If the child is given too much freedom he does not develop any respect for authority and cannot be governed. If he is placed under excessive control, his personality is not allowed to develop and he is obsessed with a sense of inferiority and sometimes even turns to crime. The truth of the matter is that if the child is to be disciplined and educated a bitter pill must be swallowed. It is very difficult to bring up a child. In this connection it is necessary that there be much balance and understanding. Then there can be no one universal rule that can apply to all children. Some children are amenable to greater control while others, respond to a lighter degree of authority. On the other hand all children are not similarly influenced by authority just as all children do not react in the same manner to parental love or neglect. All that has been said before is true in a general way but it is also open to exceptions.

Influence of discrimination

Sometimes parents discriminate between their children in behaving towards them. They have unlimited love and affection for one while another receives only scolding and punishment. Sometimes it is the beautiful child that is loved while the ugly one is neglected and disregarded. Whatever the reasons at the root of this discriminatory behaviour it is bad because it arouses feelings of hatred for each other among the children. When the child observes that his brother or sister is being loved more than he is, he becomes anxious to revenge this injustice. Sometimes he is even seen possessed of aggressive tendencies. He also tries to harm the other children in one way or the other. He is seen to be disappointed, insecure, fearful, etc. But it is also possible that the child may try to win the admiration and love of others in society and at school by appearing to be better than others in order to make reparation for the deficiency in family love that has been accorded to it. Whatever the outcome, it is completely undesirable and psychologically unjustified to indulge in this kind of discrimination between the children.

Effect of the character of parents

The personality of the child is also appreciably influenced by the moral thoughts and conduct of the parents because usually the child looks upon his parents as ideals on which to mould his life. In order to inculcate morality in the children the parents should place an example before them in the form of their own exemplary behaviour. There are very few children who can mould their behaviour according, to social values and conceptions even when they have seen their parents indulge in theft, sexual immorality, falsehood, deception and other forms of misconduct. In Miss Eliott's study the parents in 67 per cent broken homes and 44 per cent unbroken homes, were indulging in immoral behaviour. If the mother indulges in prostitution her daughters have no inhibition against it and they would have no difficulty in imitating and proceeding towards immorality and corruption.

Effects of the mutual relation of parents

The personality of the child is further open to an`other important influence *viz.*, the 'mutual relation between husband and wife. If the husband misbehaves, towards the wife then the child, particularly the male child, takes exception to it and this increases his hatred for the father. This can, under certain circumstance lead to terrible consequences. Similarly, if the wife misbehaves with husband, the female child in particular is likely to dislike it and hence she hates her mother. Constant conflict and quarrelling between husband and wife leads to the creation of an atmosphere of insecurity in the home which is not at all conducive to the development of the child's personality. If the relations between husband and wife are good the children have a good and encouraging ideal in front of themselves which they can imitate to good effect. They then try to be good themselves. It is only natural for the child to develop some personality defects if the relation between his parents is not good.

Effect of the broken family

When the relationship between the husband and wife deteriorate, the family is reduced to a broken family. This is because the relations between no two members retain their original charm and goodness. A broken family is one in which the family relation have been severed. Family does not mean the living together of some individuals but rather the intimate and profound relation that exist between them. In the absence of this intimacy the family is disbanded and in the broken family juvenile delinquents are reared and, brought up. In the broken family the children are not looked after or cared for.

According to some specialists, the broken family tends to create the criminal tendency in the female children more than it does in the male child. In 1947 in Bombay there were 386 boys and 169 girls under the child care society. Of these two boys and two girls had their parents in jail serving sentence for some or the other crime while 2 boys and 5 girls were victims of harsh behaviour and 5 boys and 6 girls were victimized by immoral insecurity. In the broken family the relation between the husband-wife, parents-child and brother-sister do not remain healthy. Hence, it is natural for boys and girls to tread the path of mistakes, crime and degradation.

The personality of the child is susceptible to the influence not only of the relationship between itself and its parents but also by the personality of his brothers and sisters. This influence seems to be more pronounced in the case of girls because they are not quite as exposed to external influences as the boys are. If the older children in the family indulge in criminal activity the younger are very likely to follow suit or at least to be profoundly influenced. If the sister is a criminal or indulges in immoral acts, the younger sister will also imitate her or at least she is likely to do so. The individual is socialized in the family. If the child finds other children in the family who are not much older or younger than it then the child finds a good atmosphere in the family. If there is only one child in the family then it does not find this social atmosphere which is so conducive to its development and its development is to some extent adversely affected. But this deficiency can be compensated if the parents play with the children.

Effect of the financial status

The financial condition of the family also influences the development of the child's personality. If the financial condition is good and the parents can adequately satisfy the needs of the children then the children are generally not possessed with the sense of inferiority and want and they do not turn to crime. But if the financial condition of the family is extremely bad then the personality of the child suffers. Merrill has written that if the income of the family is low the children also have to work and their education is thus left incomplete. The child's personality does not react very appreciably to the conditions of work. Many of the desires of the poor children are left unfulfilled in order to satisfy which they turn to criminal activity. Poverty induces feelings of dissatisfaction and inferiority. But this does not warrant the conclusion that the poverty of the family will inevitably have a harmful effect upon the child's personality. Sometimes the children, both male and female, become delinquent even though, and sometimes because, the financial condition of the family is very good. On the other hand the children of the poor learn the lesson of self-reliance from the very start.

From the foregoing description of the parent-child relationship and the effect of various family conditions on the personality of the child it is evident that they are very important. In fact, it is these elements that are responsible for the development of the main characteristic of the individual's personality.

Family has a nuclear situation

Family is the first institution in the history of man. In the ancient age men lived in small families, which lacked any kind of organisation or permanence. But they served to fulfil simple biological and psychological needs. Generally, the family consisted of husband and wife and their offspring. The powerful men possessed many wives and thus they lived in big families with their wives and children. When man became oriented in agriculture, many families formed a group and stayed permanently at some place for farming. When these people started partaking of each other's pain and happiness as neighbourly gestures, social relations increased and in this way many families formed a community and the next step was the creation of nation. In this way family is that primary group which slowly evolved into human nations.

Family is a fundamental unit of human society. Its foundations rest upon man's biological and psychological needs. In the modern age, many functions of the family have shifted to other institutions but nevertheless, there are many biological and psychological needs which man cannot satiate without a family. Havelock Ellis in his penetrative essays, has shown that the importance of mother's milk for the child cannot be obtained in any other manner. Psychologists have proved that the absence of family affection has a serious impact upon the child's development. Sexual passions can be satisfied even outside the family but it can never be the source of emotional fulfilment. That 'man is a social animal' implies that man cannot live without a family. Thus family is a fundamental unit of society.

The family has a nuclear situation in human society. In primitive societies the entire organisation is based on family units while the division of labour m society is also based on the family. In the complex structure which is society today, the family has lost some of its importance, but even today the activities of most members are for the family or contiguous to it. It is seen that people work and labour more for the comfort of their wives, children and other members of family than even for personal comforts. Thus even now the family is the nucleus of a major part of man's activities.

Society depends upon family

Proper social organisation depends upon proper organisation of families. If the families disintegrate in some society, then the society will never be safe. One major cause of social disorganisation is family disorganisation. Families develop the characters of the members of society. Freud and other psychologists have proved that a child, when a man, exhibits the same character and mental tendencies which he acquires in the family. In the opinion of Adler, a man's role in the family determines his role in society.

Family socializes individual

In this way, a person is socialized in the family. Defining family, Merrill writes, "Family is an enduring association of parent and offspring whose primary functions are the socialization of the child and the satisfaction of the members." According to Dewey and Tufts the family is a social agency for the education and protection of the race. It is in the family that the child acquires such important qualities as sincerity, sympathy, self-submission and realising responsibility etc. It is the character developed in the family which helps the child in becoming an important and responsible member of society. Wright was quite correct in stating that in every family, the child gets an opportunity for free expression of thoughts and developing his entire personality Psychologists have incontestably proved that the proper development of the child is impossible, without a good environment in the family. The tendencies and habits which he acquires in the family, he finds impossible to shed later on. According to Freud, the viewpoint of a child towards the senior in the family determines his attitude and viewpoint towards the elders in society. The child's first school is his home and family. According to Prof. Collingwood, the child's education should be in the hands of the parents in family. The parents should participate in all the child's activities. A child learns much by imitating his superiors. Mahatma Gandhi and such thinkers paid personal attention to the development of their children. It is the family which imparts practical education to the child concerning the customs in society, conduct, other important elements of culture, preservation of health, love, sympathy, co-operation etc.

It is evident from the above account that family is the primary and fundamental unit. Confucious remarked quite correctly that if you want to improve society improve its families. Society will improve automatically when the families improve.

Family is the conveyor of traditions

The family moulds the character and personality of the individual. It is through the family that society imparts its culture to the individual. Thus, the family is very important in the form of socializing agency. In the essay, *The Family Conveyance of Tradition*, Paul Schreker wrote that a particular function of the family is to sanction children, like marriage, the institution of family is constituted by different elements of culture. It is due to this reason that it has religious, judicial, political, art and linguistic aspects. Whenever a new thought impresses itself on an age the family takes a new form in order that the upbringing and mental tendencies may be harmonious to that thought. Politics and law were dominant in Rome, so the family organisation there was such as to ensure the upbringing of children in harmony with the culture. Today, the economic order is predominating. So the family has changed its form, it makes the mental tendencies concur with the new culture, in this way, the family makes individual harmonious with the culture of society. In the family, the child acquires knowledge about the current customs, mores, traditions etc.

Social control through the family

A social life is a web of relationships. In order to maintain these relations properly a system of rights and duties is organised which will avoid any conflict between the members of society and allow them to develop as complements to each other. In order to avoid any breach of this harmony between the individuals in society, the society applies numerous kinds of control on the individual. They are taught to obey the elders, have sympathy for the young and for others. A strict control over sex relationships is necessary for maintaining the social order, otherwise disintegration will spread over the complex social life of today. Relationships between men and women will lose their solidarity. Illegitimate children will be born with no one to look after them. Although the anthropologists Mead and Malinowski have discovered societies where control over sex relations is inordinately lax without disturbing the social order but such an order is completely contradictory to the thinking of today's cultured person. It is the family which does this work of controlling sex passions for society. In all cultures, the families exercise some degree of control over the unmarried members till they attain the matrimonial state. In the same way, the family acts as a preventive to individual in keeping him from bad habits and crimes like drinking, theft etc. Not many parents could like their children to embark on careers of crime. Even the worst person tries to prevent his children from adopting similar habits and consequently any objectionable behaviour on the part of children is punished and laudable effort suitably rewarded. They thus drop bad habits and learn good things. In this way the making of a good citizen in society depends upon the parents.

In every society some values and ideals are regarded as high and signs of culture. Whichever person exhibits these in greater measure is respected in society. For example, Indian society treats religious and spiritual qualities as supreme and a person who is possessed of them is appropriately respected everywhere. Besides, in India, pre-marital and extra-marital sexual relations are controlled as a necessary measure. The responsibility of creating these values in the individual, which are treated highly in society, lies with the family. It is true that the character of every person is different from any other by nature but the family environment also has a big hand in forming them. Most of the famous religious persons of the world like Gandhi were deeply influenced by someone religious person in their respective families. In the making of great men the mothers have always had a major part to play. The differences in the ideals of people related to different cultures are born in their families.

Mother tongue in the family

In every society the culture, conduct and values are very strongly related to the language spoken. Literature is the mirror of culture in society and literature is based on language which plays by no means a mean part in man's socialization. The credit for the complex order of human society must go to man's linguistic superiority over other animals and the language one picks up in the family. Human children brought up by animals in the forest are seen completely ignorant in matters of language. They communicate their wishes by signs in animal language, walk on all fours, eat raw meat and exhibit the least signs of humanity. A child brought up in an animal family grows like an animal as a child brought up in a human family grows into a human being. To go even further, a child developing in a cultured family is cultured while one brought up in baser circumstances is coarse. The child is first taught language in the family. This is his mother tongue through the medium of which he exchanges thoughts. If some Indian child is brought up in some English family, English will become his mother tongue. Thus, the major element in the child's socialization in the form of language comes to him in his mother's lap.

Besides the above mentioned elements, an individual receives a number of other things from his family. Not unusually, even the person's occupation in society is decided by his family. Even in the modern age many people carry on the paternal business and occupation for which they are trained in the family from the start. It is in no uncommon occurrence that a jeweller's child shows interest in the same business from his infancy and becomes able very soon.

Thus, in brief, the family educates the individual in culture, conduct, behaviour, customs, tradition, religion, laws of thinking, ideals, values, occupations, obedience of duties and proper use of authority, etc. It would be no exaggeration to say that the family is the most important institution in man's moral development.

SCHOOL AND SOCIAL DEVELOPMENT

A child's personality is influenced by his school, where he comes into contact with his teachers and his colleagues. At home the child's ideals are his parents and in school he forms his ideals around his teachers. A child hates a teacher who is cruel and uses the stick. He tries to revenge himself on such a teacher, but if the teacher is kind and considerate the child loves and worships him. Both the personality of the teacher and his behaviour toward the child influence the child's personality. A teacher is bigger than the child in size as well as in mental stature and he can make many demands upon the child. For this reason the child likes the idea of developing to the same size as the teacher. At home the child identifies himself with his parents while in school he identifies himself with his teacher but only when the teacher has a magnetic personality. If the teacher's own personality is not very strong he does not have much influence upon the child. On the other hand the teacher's way of thinking and moral conduct influence the child's thinking and behaviour. The teacher's standard of living, modes of behaviour, conduct, etc., all affect the student. Putting it briefly, every quality, good or bad, of the teacher that is manifest in his behaviour towards the child, leaves some influence upon the child's mind.

Influence of playmates and classfellows

Normally, the child's classfellows in school are his playmates and friends, though, sometimes, the child makes friends with children belonging to other classes. A child studying in a higher class normally behaves in a highhanded manner towards the child of a lower class. The same thing happens when two children of different age levels come into contact. An older child's behaviour towards his junior may be either loving or cruel, for in any case the younger child treats the older with fear and respect. Another factor is the competition in matters of study that occurs between children, for it can, on the one hand, induce the child to develop emotions of jealousy, hatred and disgust, while on the other it may inspire him to greater effort and independence.

Influence of group on the child

Individual influences do count but the most important influence upon the child in school is the influence of the group of his colleagues in the playground. Children tend to form groups with those boys and girls either with whom they play or the ones with whom they indulge in mischief. These groups compete with each other, while within the group there are always wrangles for leadership. Within each group, each particular child occupies a definite place and plays a distinct role. Each group has a complement of recognised members and an entourage of those who attach themselves to the group. There is a leader within the group whose intimate friends form the inner circle of the group. It is the function of the leader to look after the functioning of the gang, to do the thinking for the gang and to be its mainstay and its moral support. In certain groups the brain is provided by one child and the action by another. It is for the brain to draw up the plans and for the dare devil to carry them out. Another common feature of such groups is the comedian or jester whose sole function is to play the fool and to keep his group amused. It is possible for such groups to have one child playing the role of the scape-goat. Functions within the group are allocated according to the ability or the capacity of each individual child. In fighting gangs the strongest boy automatically assumes the mantle of leadership while in mischievous groups the most intelligent boy becomes the leader. A child's function in any such group coincides with his personality, while the performing of this function influences his personality.

Growth of community sentiment

Modern psychology does not credit the existence of any group mind distinct from the mind of the individual, but in group situations the laws of group behaviour are freely employed. A college is a psychological group Qualities such as discipline and co-operation can be evolved in the students only after some community feeling has been injected into them. William Mcdougall has pointed out several conditions that are necessary for the development of a group mind. They can be put to good use in developing community sentiment in colleges. They are:

1. **Permanence of the group:** A college, in its role as a group, should possess certain degree of permanence or physical stability. Naturally, some students join the college every year while others leave it, and some change is always going on in the shape of additional buildings, staff members changing their colleges, etc. But despite this change there is some permanence for the average student who spends two to four years in one college while in exceptional cases this period even extends from ten to twelve years. If the teachers in a school are not unnecessarily changed at a rapid rate and some of the college rules are maintained, the students derive a sense of permanence and the realisation that

the college has a distinct nature. This can help them to develop a community feeling, which is part of their greater community feeling comprehending their society as a whole.

2. Study of the form of the group by members and the member's understanding of its duties and functions: Each student is a member of the college group. He can have community feeling for it only if he learns to regard it as a group, realises the duties that he has to perform as a student, and has knowledge of the college's rules and methods of working. For this reason it is desirable for the teachers to introduce their new students every year to the institution as it is, what it stands for, how things are run in it and what is expected of the newcomers. It is only in these circumstances that each student will be able to play his role in achieving the ideals of the college.

3. Contact with other groups: Community feeling does not develop only by taking part in the functions of one's own group. It is necessary that members of different groups should intermingle. Occasions for such contact can be developed by organising debates, discussions, dramatic performances, games and sports. But on all such occasions it is necessary that the feeling of the contestants for each other should be those of friendliness and respect. Should these feelings be lacking, the healthy development of any community feeling is not easy. In all such programmes students come to regard themselves as representatives of a particular college, with which they identify themselves. It is for the honour of this institution that they have to fight. Community feelings will inevitably result.

4. Development of community tradition: In a college, as in every other group, the members keep on changing every year but the community life of the group can be maintained for years at a time if a community tradition is developed. Old students who keep up their contact with their old college play an important role. Old Boys Associations can perform a useful function by renewing contact with the newer generation of students and by holding meetings and thus keeping alive the traditions of the colleges. Many colleges and universities are famous for some particular tradition. Some colleges can boast of a fine tradition of discipline while another college may be producing the best students. If the old students and teachers are successful in keeping up these traditions every year the newcomers are encouraged to do their best. In this manner the communal life of the college runs smoothly.

5. Division of labour among members: In every group different individuals are entrusted with the performance of different duties. Without this division of labour the life of the group cannot run smoothly. In a school or college, in particular, it is desirable that individual students should be entrusted with the task of looking after the discipline, the gardens and lawns, the classrooms, the library and the reading room, etc., and of organising cultural programmes. If the student is compelled to perform such functions he learns to shoulder responsibility and to take decisions on his own. Besides, he feels some personal interest in the functioning of the college and this gives vitality to his understanding of the community spirit.

In addition to the above factors pointed out by McDougall, certain other means can be adopted for the development of a group mind in students. If meetings of the entire college are held from time to time, the students develop a sense of identity. If the students' parents are invited to cultural programmes healthy atmosphere is generated in the college. Teachers of literature, music and art can contribute to the life of the college by making their teaching more colourful. Another way of improving community life is to have community prayer in the morning before teaching work begins and parades in the evening. When students are encouraged to participate in the celebration of a national day, prize distributions and the selection of different committees, they feel part of the college. The tone of the college has very great influence in this respect. And a good tone can be developed only when the life of the college is disciplined, marked by cooperation, law and order, high moral level and an advanced level of mutual relations. This happens only when the teachers themselves set high standards and do not hold themselves aloof from their students. Teachers are the leaders of students and for that reason the responsibility of presenting the students with desirable ideals devolves upon them.

SOCIAL ISOLATES

Because of some physiological or psychological shortcomings some children find it impossible to mix with other children of their own age or to make friends with them. Hence, in their social life, such children tend to be isolated, and this isolation has the worst effect upon their mental, social and moral development. They tend to exaggerate their feelings of inferiority and to dress their sense of self-respect and self-confidence. The development of their character suffers in the process.

There can be many causes of social isolation. Physical handicap can be one cause. Defects of hand, foot, eye or of speaking can hinder the child. Feeble children also tend to avoid other children. Abnormality, physiological or mental, obstructs the socialization of the child and prevents him from mixing in the group.

A social isolate is the child who cannot make his own friends in society. For this he has to depend upon his parents or teachers. And such help should be forthcoming. He should be introduced to other children who can accept him into their group, but even then care should be taken that these children should not indulge in any activity which should make the isolate wish to run away. Such children are extremely emotional and even the slightest misbehaviour disturbs them considerably. If the child suffers from no physiological or mental abnormality but is still an isolate then his isolation arises from emotional causes, the majority of which have their origin in the family environment. The family environment may be made unbearable if the parents are extremely excitable, destructive, vicious or corrupt. A healthy family environment is the first requirement for the healthy social development of the child.

SOCIAL STRATIFICATION AND EQUAL DEVELOPMENT

Social stratification is a common feature in every social group, for different individuals occupy different social groups. In some societies these groups are based on social prestige, as is the case in India, where there are caste groups. In other societies they may be based on the economic status in which case there will be the low income, middle income and high income brackets. Generally speaking, the child is not conscious of the group to which he belongs, and it is seen that if children from different groups are allowed to mix informally they do not give any indications about their groups. However, in almost every case one finds the influence of the parent's group on the child. Parents themselves constantly tell their children about the groups and the relation in which they stand to each one of them. People belonging to the poor group tell their children to stay away from the children not belonging to their income brackets. In India individuals belonging to the higher castes do not allow their children to mix with the children of the lower castes, or the so-called untouchables. It is, putting it briefly, the parents who are responsible for developing class consciousness in their children, and later on this has a very profound influence upon the socialization of the children. In America it has been found that while many white children do not feel the least inhibition in playing with negro children, their parents instil into them various kinds of fear associated with the negroes. Thus a deep-rooted prejudice against the negroes is created in the children's minds. Similar tendency can be seen among the Hindu and Muslim communities in the country. It is now apparent that children are influenced by social stratification only because of their parent's teaching.

ROLE OF COMPETITION

Competition is an important factor among the various stimuli that encourage the child to work. This stimuli does not function for children less than two years of age. By the age of six the workings of this stimulus can be seen clearly. In this manner, the child's earliest behaviour pattern shows objectivity but later on he develops the tendencies of competition and co-operation. In the early stages this competition is limited to winning the love and attention of the parents. It can occur when the child wants toys and other things to play with. Before the age of three this tendency does not play an important role in fashioning the child's pattern of behaviour. During this period the child is kept occupied with his toys and has little patience with what other children are doing. Gradually, he develops a feeling of competition. This occurs in most cultures, but in certain cultures where this tendency in children is looked down upon, the child does not develop it to any great extent. Obviously, the tendency to competition is the result of social and cultural environments. Besides, even in one culture the same child may show a spirit of competition on one occasion but not on another. Or, one child may have a deep desire to compete while another may be indifferent. There can be many factors responsible for this variation, among them the child's order of birth in family, the behaviour towards him of his parents and other relatives, result in any competitive activity.

The spirit of competition plays an important role in the child's development. In individual competition the child exerts all his energies in getting ahead of the other child and this improves the rate of his development. When the child is a member of a group competing with another, his energies are directed at securing victory for his own group. This improves his community spirit. It has been observed in a series of experiments that wherever there is scope for comparison with another's performance the child improves his own performance owing to competition. If the spirit of competition can be intelligently employed, it will yield positive results. But this can be done if the difference between the competitors is not very large, because if one is far more powerful and accomplished than the other, then inferior competitor is likely to lose his self-confidence in the process of competing. It is this factor which controls the independent child's choice of competitors. Left to himself the child will move among children of his age and capacity so that he can compete with them. It is essential for the parents and teachers to remember that healthy competition can take place only within a group with a small range of individual differences.

Competition must necessarily be healthy. In healthy competition the child is inspired to work more than he is accustomed to and to do better than the others in his group. For this he has no need to employ dishonest means, so long as the competitor is not much better than he is. Healthy competition does not contradict co-operation: in fact it encourages co-operative enterprise. It is, then, best to encourage healthy competition rather than to stop or to increase it. Parents and teachers can create circumstances in which the child can compete. Care must be taken to ensure that competition does not rise to a level where the child is forced to adopt improper means.

ROLE OF DISCIPLINE, REWARD AND PUNISHMENT

There can be no two opinions about the importance of discipline in an organisation but the definition of the term discipline itself has raised some problems. Educationists differ in their opinion of it. It becomes important, therefore, to be sure of what discipline means. An unscientific definition of discipline would normally include such activities as obeying the rules of the college, respecting the teachers, arriving in the class on time, abstaining from conversation during lectures, not damaging college property, doing all work required by the teacher, not quarrelling with one's juniors, avoiding the use of unfair means during an examination, non-stealing, etc. And in fact, each of the above activities is directly concerned with maintaining the organisation of the college in its normal condition.

Difference between discipline and order

There is subtle but distinct difference between discipline and order because no discipline can exist without an order. Discipline on the other hand, comprehends much more than order. In the words of T.P. Nunn, "Discipline is not an external thing like order but something that touches the inmost springs of conduct. It consists in the submission of one's impulses and powers to a regulation which imposes form upon the chaos, and brings efficiency and economy where there would otherwise be ineffectiveness and waste." Real or actual discipline, is therefore, seen to rest on character. Training in order is the training of character. Outlining the difference between discipline and order Rusk, the educationist, has pointed out that while order denotes the child's behaviour at home or in school, discipline is taken to mean the training of character, which is far more comprehensive than order.

Object of discipline

In the words of Welton, "The aim of all true discipline is the training of conscience which consists in cultivation of the good will and development of moral insight." Training in discipline is given to develop a man's moral insight. And training of insight implies the development of a good will in the child. Disciplined children accept good work and avoid bad. If the insight develops the child's moral insight also develops and he learns to judge what he should do and what he should not. A disciplined child does not have to be told to do this and not to do that, whether he is at home, in the school, in society or anywhere. He can judge for himself and he does what is right and avoids that which is bad. Discipline aims at underlining the importance of morality in education. Herbert, another educationist, has remarked that the objective of education is morality, meaning that education aims at making the child moral. And this aim can be achieved only when the child develops a sense of morality.

Discipline in the classroom

Some people think that the teacher who has the quietest class maintains discipline most effectively. There is no doubt that a disciplined class in not noisy but the mere fact of absence of noise does not make a class disciplined. Discipline is not merely staying quiet, for it comprehends many other things. Some teachers have recourse to suppression to maintain quiet in the class. There may be quiet in the class but it cannot be said to be discipline. The following methods can be adopted to maintain discipline in the class:

1. **Interesting method of teaching:** It is desirable for the teacher to teach even the most arid subject in such a manner as to make it interesting for the students. If this does not happen, the students soon get tied up, they yawn in the class and if possible make a lot of noise. If the mode of teaching is effective, the students take a natural interest in the subject and discipline is automatically maintained.

2. **Alertness:** Discipline also depends upon the degree to which the teacher is alert. If the teacher is himself inclined to sleep or yawn in the class, there is little possibility of his maintaining interest and discipline among the students. When he is himself wide awake the students tend to behave because they are conscious of his eyes upon them and they realise that he will object to any

undesirable activity on their part. If there is real discipline the students behave not because they are afraid of being punished but because they want to co-operate with the teacher.

3. Definite rules of behaviour in the class: If discipline is to be maintained, there must be definite rules of behaviour in the class of which the students should be made cognizant on the first possible opportunity. It sometimes happens that the student does things he should not, only because he is not conscious of these rules. If for example, the teacher has pointed out that students should raise their hands and attract his attention if there is any difficulty the students will do so and there will be no disturbance during his teaching. Neither will the students feel that their difficulty has not been explained to them. After he has framed the rules the teacher should see whether the rules are being obeyed. If he finds any students disregarding the rules he should advise the students to change their mode of behaviour. This forces the students to realise that there are some rules of behaviour in the classroom and that decorum must be maintained.

4. Creating a sense of responsibility in the students: Self discipline is based on the sense of responsibility. Hence in order to maintain discipline in the class the students should be encouraged to be responsible. It should be made clear to them that keeping peace in the class, following the rule, keeping the furniture in order, etc, are all their responsibility. The task of keeping order and peace in the classroom should be left to the students so that they can create discipline themselves.

5. Impartial behaviour: Some teachers are partial to some students in the obedience to rules, and where they would punish some students they let others go scot free. This partiality is very dangerous because there can be no discipline if the teacher behaves inconsistently. Both the students, who is discriminated against and the one who is discriminated in favour, tend to get out of hand because in either of them the attitude towards the teacher takes an undesirable turn.

6. Training in discipline: Finally students should be told about the advantages of discipline and order in the class. It helps to maintain discipline. The students should also be told how orders or laws should be obeyed. It is at times desirable to ask the students to make their suggestions about improving discipline in the class. This will make them feel that establishing discipline is their own task and they will be encouraged to co-operate with their teacher.

Methods of discipline

Norman Macmunn has analysed the different ways of maintaining discipline in the class in his work *The Child's Path of Freedom*. The main methods are the following:

1. Repression: In the past, repression was used to create discipline in schools the world over. Gradually, psychologists raised their voices against this treatment with the result that this method is looked down upon everywhere.

2. Impression: In this method of establishing discipline the teacher makes use of his personal impression instead of punishment. He treats the children with love, in return for which he gets their affection and respect. Children behave themselves with such a teacher.

3. Emancipation: Another method which differs from the methods of repression and impression, is that of emancipation. In this method the child is left to himself and is allowed to see for himself which actions are desirable and which are not. If this is done he will naturally learn to distinguish between right and wrong, and will avoid undesirable activity. Proponents of this method have hinted at the mode of teaching discipline through nature. If the child puts his hand in the fire it is immediately burnt by the fire. Nature punishes without warning.

ROLE OF REWARDS

Meaning of reward

Reward literally means that which is given to an individual in return for what he has done. Under this definition even punishment would become a negative reward. But more usually reward is not interpreted in such a liberal manner and is taken to mean only positive award. Reward, therefore, is the good and proper consequence of good and desirable actions. It can take the form of some concrete physical prize or even merely psychological satisfaction at having done a thing well.

Kinds of rewards

Reward can take almost any form, but the more common ones are the following:

1. Oral reward: Oral rewards are given in the form of praise. The praise may even take the form of a certificate, a medal or a shield. It can also be praise, done individually or in public.

2. Physical reward: Schools and colleges have a tradition of giving things as reward. Such useful objects as books, sports equipments, clothes, are normally given.

Each of the two above forms of reward have their own significance. Oral reward or recognition has the effect of satisfying the self-respect of the child and of encouraging him to repeat such activity in future. Its drawback is that words of kindness are forgotten, sooner or later. On the other hand if the words of praise are rendered concrete in the form of a cup or shield or some other form of reward, they will continue to encourage the child in his future life. In this connection books have their own significance because they not only impart knowledge to the child but can be retained by him for long periods. Sports equipment is the next best choice because it is liked by almost all children and also helps to enhance his prestige in the eyes of his friends. He can also derive pleasure by using this equipment and can also thereby improve his health. Equipment meant for outdoor games is better than that for indoor games. In fact, anything that has utility can serve as a reward, but that which has durability also is better than another which can be used up quickly.

Aim of reward

The aim of giving a reward can be judged from the significance that such an act has. These aims are:

1. Encouraging correct, and proper activity: Education aims at directing the child's activity towards a desirable end and preventing it from turning towards the undesirable. Prevention is affected through the medium of punishment and encouragement for good activity through the medium of reward. Rewards delight the child for the moment, but they also serve as an incentive for repeating the activity which brought about the reward. Rewards help to instill the right habits in a child and to improve his character.

2. Recognition of desirable activity: It is only natural for a child to be recognised as the author of some desirable action after he has done it. He desires such recognition from the teacher or parent. Rewards are the token of this recognition, and once recognition is granted the child can hardly wait to do it again. Recognition is directly linked with self-expression. A child desires to express himself and also to have this self-expression recognised by his teachers.

3. Setting good examples to other students: As a normal rule, rewards and awards in colleges are presented in a big gathering in which all students are present. Sometimes the parents of the students are also invited to join in the celebration. When the child goes forward to receive his cup, shield or certificate while his friends, parents and well-wishers look on, he feels delighted and very pleased with himself. At the same time the other students are also spurred on to do something which will put them in a similar position.

4. Encouraging healthy competition: Healthy competition is an important factor in communal life. Students try to do better than their neighbours, and they do better than they would otherwise if the concrete result of this compensation is present before them. It is often seen that the bright students in a class compete hard for the first position because of the prize that goes with this position. They also exert themselves in the sports field because they are aware that the winner will receive a prize and a lot of cheers. Awards have played an important role in encouraging healthy competition in studies and in game. Besides, awards can be given not only for mental and physical excellence but also for moral excellence, for if a tradition for giving an award for the best behaved student is established in the college it will encourage the students to make a good job of it. Awards can help the child's development of character by encouraging him to excel in all walks of life.

5. Encouraging hard work: If a child wants to win some award it is necessary for him to put in a lot of hard work. Hence, when there is some reward, the child tends to work hard in every sphere, the mental, physical and the ethical or moral.

Principles for giving Awards

If benefit is to be derived from the giving away of prizes it is desirable that some system should be followed. It is essential to take care of the following aspects:

1. **Reward based on ability:** In the first place, the reward should be directly proportionate to the student's ability and the student should realise that he unquestionably deserves the reward being given.

2. **Limited number of awards:** If almost every student in the school or college can win one prize or the other the entire system of prizes loses its value, for it then fails to stimulate competition. Prizes therefore should not exceed five in number.

3. **Prizes subsequent upon effort:** It is never proper to give a prize for some quality acquired by birth. Prizes should be given for things which involve effort and hard work, and the prize should be given for the maximum effort shown. It should also be realised that winning a prize entails effort as well as talent.

4. **Three or four prize distributions in a year:** If primary and secondary schools have three or four prize distributions in a year it will help to maintain the enthusiasm of the students at a high pitch during the entire year. They will continue to compete with each other and their effort will not flag due to lack of encouragement. This will help the teaching and the maintenance of standard.

5. **Prizes for least interesting work:** If prizes are allocated to activities in which every one naturally takes interest nothing useful is achieved for the incentive is already there. It is desirable to keep prizes for subjects which are important in their own right but which normally do not arouse interest in the student.

6. **Prizes should not have high exchange value:** It is not desirable to have a prize which is itself worth a lot of money. A student should not desire to obtain the prize merely because it is valuable in terms of money. But at the same time the prize should not be so cheap as to arouse no enthusiasm in the student.

7. **Encouraging healthy competition:** In making arrangements for prizes the teachers should take care that this should not lead to jealousy, hatred, formation of rival groups and other undesirable associations. The aim of having awards is to create a spirit of healthy not unhealthy competition.

8. **Prizes should be announced well in advance:** Before the competition begins students should have sufficient notice of the fact that there is a prize. This will provide them with sufficient time to work and will also keep them organised and hard at work for a longer period.

9. **Impartiality in awarding a prize:** It is absolutely essential that the person or persons entrusted with awarding the prize are completely impartial. If

some partiality or discrimination takes place it not only robs the prize of its importance but creates ill-feeling among the students.

10. Prizes should coincide with individual and communal feeling: Prizes should be such as to arouse the individual and communal interest of the student. It is for this reason that some awards are set aside not for individual performance but for the performance of a team as a whole, whether it is a sports team or a class inter-school and inter-college competitions help to develop a healthy community spirit.

ROLE OF PUNISHMENT

Punishment means the pain and suffering caused to students with a view to improving administration and curing ills. Punishment can also take two forms—physical and mental. Physical punishment is given through the medium of causing pain to the body. This pain may be mild or severe. Milder forms of physical punishment are asking the student to stand on his seat or in a corner, forcing him to run around a field twice and similar punishments which do not cause too much suffering. Severe physical punishments can take almost any form, but among the better known are pulling the ears, beating with a stick, slapping, pinching, punching, or even giving a severe thrashing in the presence of the entire school. Mental punishment can be given by admonishing, criticising, demeaning, or a variety of other methods. At times, this mental or physical punishment is further supplemented by economic punishment in the form of fines.

Objectives of punishment

As a general rule punishment can have three main objectives—taking revenge, curing a fault or improving, or setting an example for other people so that they may not do such a thing. Punishment meted out in the college may have any one or even more of these three motives behind it. At times the students who disturb the discipline of the college are punished in front of a assembly of all students so that other students may be discouraged from following their footsteps. Punishments of this kind are often severe for they have far-reaching consequences, and without severity they lose their meaning. At the school level it is quite common for the headmaster to call a meeting of the entire school and then to proceed to thrash the recalcitrant students severely. The very sight of this is often enough to deter most of the other students from such activity. In the present day, however, almost all punishment aims at improving the student and curing him of his bad habits. Mental punishment in any case has no other objectives, because it can neither serve as an example to others nor can it be used for revenge. Many teachers inflict mental or physical punishment upon their students when they feel that they have been insulted. Such activity is absolutely improper and an individual capable of it has no right to be a teacher. There can be no doubt, that students have been known to injure the dignity of the teacher, and it is only natural for the teacher to feel infuriated. But although he may desire to get a little of his own back by pushing the student, such a desire can hardly be said to be proper. Punishment should be meted out only when the student can be improved by it, or when such punishment will set an example before the other students and guide them along the right path.

Excessive use of punishment

During the middle ages punishment was a common thing while in India even today excessive punishment is not unknown. In rural areas in particular it is common. If a student fails to turn up at school three or four boys are sent to bring him there, and they do so by dragging or beating him. When he finally does arrive he is then set upon by the teacher who literally makes a pulp out of him. He is then forced to stand in the corner in a bent position with a brick balanced on his back. Many schools follow a standard procedure for convincing the students that punctuality is the king of virtues. The headmaster closes all approaches to the school and takes up his position at the gate with a thick rod in his hand. All students arriving late are welcomed at the gate by the headmaster, given a sound thrashing and then allowed to proceed to the class, with a hefty kick to speed them on their way. After this few students would dare to be late again, and if he is there is every chance of his playing truant from school rather than risking the punishment This tradition of inconsiderate punishment is not restricted only to primary and secondary schools but even to high schools and intermediate colleges. Besides, the tradition is not peculiar to India, because worse examples of excess in this direction can be found in the history of education in many Western nations. Prof. Cubberley has written of a schoolmaster named Haubberley who appears to have had a Teutonic taste for a variety of things. This master has recorded that in his 51 years and seven months of teaching life he administered 9,11,527 strokes with the cane, 1,24,010 strokes with a stick, 20,989 strokes with a ruler or a piece of rope, 1,36,715 strokes with the hand, 10,235 strokes on the face, 7,905 ear boxings, and 11,15,800 slaps on the head. In addition to this he had a vocabulary of 2000 abusive terms some two-thirds of which were taken from the German language while the rest had been invented by the teacher himself. This example proves the extent to which mental and physical punishment was inflicted upon the students. Excessive punishment is normally inflicted when there is a desire to suppress the individual punished. It is taken for granted that the individual is, by nature, a cheat and bounder and that if he can be prevented from doing his dark deeds it is only through the fear of punishment.

Consequences of excessive punishment

There can be many consequences of excessive punishment, almost the only desirable one being that it may frighten the individual into submission. It may result in permanent injury or even, in some extreme cases, in death. There can be no doubt that when other children see punishment of this order being given, they are inspired to stick to the straight and narrow path of virtue. Mental punishment is no less harmful than physical punishment. It has been seen that students commit suicide after they have been criticised and ridiculed beyond edurance by their teachers. And, on the other hand, it has also been observed that if the teacher limits himself to criticism and ridicule, the students imagine that he is either a fool or incapable of administering physical punishment. In such cases they become even more unmanageable.

Propriety of excessive punishment

Generally speaking, it may be said that excessive punishment can never be justified, particularly if it is physical punishment. It should, therefore, never be used to excess. Among its consequences are impaired hearing, loss of limbs and even death. Further, it can only succeed in creating feelings of hatred and revenge against the teacher in the student's mind. There have been cases where a student has been compelled to revenge himself upon the teacher and to bring about the latter's death. Such reactions can have no value and they reflect upon the system of education as a whole. Even the students who are deterred from anti-social activity when they see another student being punished, do not have any feelings of love or respect for the teacher. They are inspired only by fear and disgust.

Similar consideration applies to the subject of excessive mental punishment. If the student commits a mistake he should not be ridiculed or criticised so severely that he may be compelled to seek revenge or that he may develop a permanent inferiority complex. This can only have a bad effect upon his character. And all such influences only serve to encourage indiscipline, not to discourage it.

These considerations should not create the feeling that punishment should be given up. Adequate punishment is desirable and at times even necessary. There are some students who, if they are not thrashed, grow impudent and feel that nothing can happen to them, whatever they may do. This confidence leads them to do things which are completely undesirable. Such students must necessarily be taught that there is a divinity that shapes our end, even if the divinity takes the form of a ruler or cane. If students who disturb the discipline of the college go unpunished the rules and regulations of the college lose their meaning for such students. If the importance of the rules is to be brought home to the erring students it is necessary that there should be provision for punishment. What is important is that this punishment should then be administered without discrimination.

Principles underlying punishment

Punishment should be administered only on principle, so that it may not lose its meaning. The following things should be kept in mind—

1. Punishment should be such as to improve the erring student.
2. Punishment should be example to other students so that they may be deterred from following the same path.
3. Punishment should never be excessive.
4. Punishment should be in direct proportion to the magnitude of the misdemeanour.

5. Physical punishment should be administered by the headmaster, but this individual should not display any anger. Punishment should be an act of justice.
6. Punishment should not take the form of ridiculing or insulting a student.
7. Punishment meted out to the student should be recorded in his report book and sent to the parent.
8. There should be no discrimination while punishing a student.
9. For all violations of discipline there should be fixed punishment. In all such violations the punishment must be inflicted upon the culprit. When the punishment is fixed the student either accepts the inevitable or decides to behave himself.

Finally, it can be said that if the above points are kept in mind framing punishment in the college the students will definitely improve. Good examples will be set to the other students. The success of all punishment depends to a great degree upon the psychological insight and intelligence of the teacher.

QUESTIONS FOR EXERCISE

1. What do you understand by discipline? Why is it needed? When is punishment the most effective method of disciplining the child?
2. How will you define discipline? Discuss the role of reward and punishment in inculcating discipline among children.
3. Discuss in brief the elements of good discipline. What are the effective rewards for children?
4. Discuss in brief the good educational practice in discipline. What cautions should be observed in educating for discipline?

19

Group Dynamics, Leadership and Social Factors in Education

According to Oxford Concise Dictionary peer means equal. Thus peer group is the group of equals. Such is a social group. A social group is that aggregate of persons which is like a unit and whose members have some common aims, interests, stimulations and emotions together with mutual social relations and social interactions. Through the medium of all these, members of a social group influence each other and are tied to each other. According to Bogardus, "A social group may be thought of as a number of persons two or more, who have some common objects of attention, who are stimulating to each other, who have common loyalty and participate in similar activities."[1]

CHIEF CHARACTERISTICS OF GROUP-LIFE

Just as to classify the groups is a difficult task, similarly to point out the characteristics of group-life is also a difficult problem. Even then some characteristics of group-life can be described. They are as follows:

1. The members of a group are related to each other: Simply a gathering of persons cannot be called a group. The members of the group should be inter-related. In fact, this social relation is called a group. Cuber has written, "A group is any number of human beings in reciprocal communication."[2] Maclver and some other sociologists have also admitted the social relations to be the fundamentals of the group-life.

2. Group implies a feeling of unity: A feeling of unity is essential for every group. By virtue of such feeling, members of a group treat each other as their own and a sense of sympathy between them develops.

3. Members of a group have a sense of we-feeling: By a sense of we-feeling, the members of a group help each other in performing their duties; and they defend collectively against the harmful powers. They treat others as the outsiders and try to make their group prosperous and self-sufficient.

1. Bogardus, E.S., *Society*, p. 5.
2. Cuber, J.F., *Sociology*, p. 303.

4. The interests of the group members are common: A group includes those persons who are related to each other in such a way that they should be treated as one. For it, the interests of the persons of a group should tend to be common because, this similarity promotes unity.

5. There is similarity of behaviour in a group: As the interests, ideals and values of the persons of a group are common similarly the behaviour of the persons also tends to be similar. A social group is not merely a group of persons, but it is a continuation of their behaviour.

6. Control of group over the actions of the members: The main reason behind the similarity of behaviour in group-life is that actions of the members are controlled by the group. In each group there are some customs, norms and procedures which are acceptable to everyone and the dissenting members of the group given punishment. Even if the group fails to punish a person disobeying these, he shall be severely criticised by public. In this way, every one has to obey the social norms. In fact, without some norms, the existence of group life is practically impossible.

7. The members of a group are affected by its characteristics: Each group possesses some social characteristics which separate it from the similar and dissimilar groups. These characteristics affect the members constituting the group. The effect may be of different nature for different persons, but still all the members are affected by the group.

8. Common values: Each caste has its own specific common values as help to distinguish it from other castes and also tie its members in the thread of unity. In this way, the social values of the Brahmins and the Shudras, the Kshatriyas and the Vaishyas, can be seen differing considerably. The caste panchayats are very vigilant in enforcing the obedience to these social values and people who deviate from them or transgress their bounds are exterminated from the caste. They are subjected to social isolation and ostracism. They cannot again marry into the group. In a similar vein the example of family can also be considered. The social values of the members of a family are common and are traditionally respected and communicated to the succeeding generations. They are clearly expressed in the mutual behaviour of the members. Thus Members of the social group are bound together in the tie of common values.

9. Mutual obligations: The relationship between the members of a social group is further strengthened through their mutual obligations, beside their common social values. The family is a fine example of this. In the family, all the members have complementary obligations to each other. Children obey the orders of parents and try to conform to their desires. Husband and wife love each other. The husband fulfils the needs of the wife, while the wife obeys the orders of the husband besides co-operating with him in all activities. In this way, the members of the family are bound to each other by the ties of mutual obligation.

10. Mutual expectations: In a social group, the members are entitled to expect love, sympathy and co-operation from others. In the family the husband expects his wife to love him while his wife expects reciprocation of this affection. When this desire is turned into despair, the family relationship is destroyed and divorce is imminent. In the same way, the parents expect their offspring to accede to their wishes while the children expect from their parents love and sympathy coupled with help to rise in future. The disintegration of the family sets in when these desires are not fulfilled. While the family is a much close knit social unit, even the neighbourhood is related to each member through mutual expectation. In all social groups that human beings form members have expectations of each other. If the people of one's own clan were not to share in one another's joys and sorrows, then what is the use of any clan. All individuals hope that in times of joy and sorrow the people belonging to their clan will participate and render the occasion befitting of a social being. And so long as this mutual expectation is being fulfilled, the organisation of the group is maintained intact. If in any school, the student were to refuse to show obedience to his teacher and the latter were to abstain from helping the student in his pursuit of knowledge, how long can such a school last? Thus, a social group retains its existence only as long as its constituent members fulfil their responsibility by satisfying the mutual desires among them.

The example of the family as a social group can serve to illustrate the fore-mentioned characteristics of group-life. Among the members of the family there are relationships such as husband-wife, father-son, brother-sister etc., and all of them work for the interests of the family in a mood of mutual co-operation. Each member treats every other member as his own, and despite all the differences that there may be between their attitudes and tendencies, they share some common ideals and values. It is because of the common interests that the family works as a well knit unit. Family control is exercised on each member. Disobedience of the laws of the family leads to serious altercations between the head of the family and the children while even the senior members do not escape censure. Each member bears the indelible stamp of his family characteristics. This characteristic is so prominent that the study of an individual's behaviour affords some clue as to the type of family in which he must have been bred. These characteristics of the group life are to be found in other groups in greater or lesser degree.

Social organisation is the organisation of social groups. And social groups are the units of social organisation. Hence, the organisation and the disintegration of social organisation is dependent upon the integration or disintegration of the social groups. The social group, as is evident from the term applied to it, is a group the basis of which is social relationships. The family, for example, is a social group.

The above discussion of group life may be useful in understanding how to create group life in school. Social consciousness can be created by arranging social programmes. Guardians may also be invited to participate in several such functions. Group songs and group parade is also useful. Celebration of national festivals in school affects the tone of social life. This tone is improved by means of discipline, co-operation, moral level and mutual relationships. The teachers should present good examples and improve their relations with the students.

LEADERSHIP AND EDUCATION

Qualities of leadership

In the analysis of leadership, the greatest importance from the practical viewpoint, is that of the qualities of leadership. While this knowledge of the qualities of a leader on the one hand reveals the kind of person the leader is, it also on the other hand, shows the qualities that an individual should possess if he wants to become a leader. Once again, different scholars have attributed different qualities to leaders. Some of the important views will be described here.

Constituents of leadership

In connection with leadership, Pigors regards the following as indispensable:

1. Common Cause, 2. Leader, 3. Follower, 4. Present situation.

Qualities of leadership according to allport: Allport has included the following in the qualities of leadership:

1. Trait of ascendence, 2. Physical power, 3. High mobility, 4. Erect, aggressive carriage, 5. Tonus, 6. Tenacity, 7. Face to face mode of address, 8. Reinforcement of energy, 9. Restraint, 10. Inscrutability, 11. Expansiveness in the field of action, 12. High intelligence 13. Understanding, 14. Keenly susceptible to social stimulation, 15. Tact, 16. Zeal, 17. Social participation, 18. Character, 19. Drive.

Coffin's classification: Charles Bird has recounted no less than 79 qualities in a leader, but in this long list of qualities, many of the qualities have been repeated. Coffin has tried to place these qualities in some limited classes. According to Coffin, the qualities of a leader can be included in the following classes:

1. *Intelligence:* sharp intellect, insight, intellectual, far-sightedness, skill and acuity.

2. *Moral Sensitivity:* honesty, just, proper decision, benevolent viewpoint, moral outlook, selfless and idealistic, love of truth.

3. *Imagination:* originality, imagination, foresight, curiosity, comprehensive interests and mental flexibility.

4. *Restraint:* restraint, self-control and profundity.

5. *Drive and determination:* inspiration, enthusiasm, mobile or dynamic personality, candidness, aggression, desiring name and fame, bravery, determination, patience, concentration, the tendency to pursue to an end.

6. *Responsibility:* respected, candid, charactered, believable, organised, aware of duties, lover of work, concentrated.

7. *Self-reliance:* awareness of purpose and direction, self-reliance, confidence, the ability to take decision, enthusiasm and unvarying decision.

8. *Dynamic physical characteristics:* physical power, shape, ability, tonus, straight body, etc.

9. *Imperturbability:* balance, optimism, benevolence, patience, decisive, energetic, and positive nature.

10. *Social responsiveness:* adaptability of social motivation, taking part in social activities, friendliness, affection, sociability, extrovert tendency and influence on other.

11. *Easy maintenance of good relations with others:* acuity, sympathy, co-operation, humanity and a knowledge of human nature.

Coffin has further done the job of making these 11 classes even more brief by dividing all the qualities into 3 classes:

(1) *Planning*—1. The ability to know problems. 2. The ability to evolve plans for solving these problems.

(2) *Organisation*—3. The ability to organise the necessary objects and individuals to ensure the success of the plans. 4. The ability to organise the entire system and have it function as one unit. 5. The ability to introduce sudden changes.

(3) *Persuasion*—6. The ability of distributing responsibility among different individuals for the implementation of the plan. 7. The ability of successfully examining the entire plan. 8. The ability of keeping his own control on the entire system of organisation.

All qualities, physical and mental, are needed for leadership

From the various opinions on the different qualities which a leader should necessarily possess that have been described above it is evident that it is not sufficient for the leader to be the master of only physical qualities. Here it must be remembered that in the animal world the most powerful animal is the leader but in human society physical power alone is not sufficient. Yet the importance of the qualities of physical power and an attractive personality is not inconsiderable. One can often see intellectual ability and attractive physical personality going together in the human leader. By his experiments, Partridge has proved that all the individuals who scored the highest in the Army Alpha tests were tall, attractive and of an independent nature. This view, held by Partridge is one-sided, because one often finds a complete lack of physical charm in intellectual giants and leaders. One only need be reminded of Socrates and Chanakya. On the other hand, it would be equally incorrect and baseless to state that in the modern world, only intellectual achievements are enough to bring leadership to an individual. Actually, in order to become leader, an individual should be possessed of many qualities of the personality and in particular skill in behaving, in addition to physical and intellectual qualities.

Education for leadership

But the mere fact of the existence of these qualities in an individual is not sufficient an insurance of successful leadership. It is true that the leader possesses in innate form the qualities of leadership, but as Plato observed correctly they also require to be educated. In a democracy, leaders can be discovered and created through the medium of education and public programmes. For this responsible tasks should he entrusted to the men and women of the younger generation. They should be given the opportunity of coming forward and expressing themselves. Youth festivals should be organised in order that the youngsters may be able to display their qualities. In this way, when there will always be new leaders to replace the older and retiring leaders, the society and the nation will be able to progress constantly and at a fast pace.

QUESTIONS FOR EXERCISE

1. Write short note on—Group Dynamics.
2. Write short note on—Education for Leadership.

20

Intelligence: Theories and Tests

The word intelligence forms part of our ordinary stock of words which we use everyday. In the field of psychology too, the word intelligence finds fairly comprehensive use but it has been defined in a number of ways by the scientists. Some of these definitions are given as follows:

1. Intelligence is the ability of adjusting to new situation: According to Wells, "Intelligence is the property of recombining our behaviour pattern so as to act better in a novel situation." In William Stern's opinion, "Intelligence is the ability to adjust oneself to a new situation."

These definitions are faulty in the following respects—

(*a*) They fail to clarify the full scope of intelligence.

(*b*) Intelligence and adjustability are not the same. Intelligence is innate but adjustability is mostly learnt.

2. Intelligence is the ability to avail of past experience: Both Ebbinghaus[1] and Thorndike[2] define intelligence as the ability to make profitable use of past experience. In other words intelligence is the ability of learning.

The definition has the following defects —

(*a*) Learning and intelligence are not identical because learning depends on many factors besides the latter.

(*b*) This definition too does not describe the full scope of intelligence

3. Intelligence is the ability of abstract thinking: According to Garrett, one may define "Intelligence as including the abilities demanded in the solution of problems which requires the comprehension and use of symbols."[3] In Terman's opinion "Intelligence is the ability to think abstractly."[4]

This definition suffers from the following defects—

(*a*) Abstract thinking is not intelligence, it is only a part of intelligence.

(*b*) This definition fails to describe the complete scope of intelligence.

---

1. Ebbinghaus, H. *Memory*, Trans. by H.A. Ruger and C.B. Bussenius, New York, Teachers' College, Columbia University.
2. Thorndike, E.L. *Animal Intelligence*, New York, Macmillan Co., 1911.
3. Garrett, H.E., *Statistics in Psychology and Education*, 3rd ed., N.Y. Longmans Green, 1947.
4. Terman, L.M. Merril, M.A. *Measuring Intelligence*, Boston, Houghton Mifflin, 1937.

4. Intelligence is the conglomeration of many powers: In Wechsler's opinion, "Intelligence is the aggregate or global capacity of an individual to act purposefully, to think rationally and to deal effectively with his environment."[1] Computing the different powers of intelligence, Husband said, "An intelligent person uses past experience effectively, is able to concentrate and keep his attention focused for longer periods of time, adjusts himself to a new and unaccustomed situation rapidly with less confusion and with fewer false moves, shows variability of response is able to see distant relationships, can carry on abstract thinking, has a greater capacity of inhibition or delay and is capable of exercising self-criticism." Actually Husband has given a very good description of an intelligent person but intelligence cannot be accepted to be the sum total of all these qualities. The psychologists however, differ in considering intelligence as a single ability or a collection of many abilities. A description of the different theories concerning the nature of intelligence will help to understand the various interpretations of the form of intelligence.

NATURE OF INTELLIGENCE

The following are the main theories concerning the nature of intelligence:

1. Monarchic theory: This theory holds that intelligence is a single ability which affects all the activities of the individual. According to Victoria Hazlitt, intelligence is a general ability which determines the various specific or particular abilities. This theory has not been proved to be correct. It has been observed that sometimes otherwise intelligent people show less than average ability in many acitivities. For example, Darwin had a very bad handwriting.

2. Oligarchic theory: This theory postulates that intelligence is an average of mutually independent abilities. Binet believed this theory. Experiments disproved this theory showing that mental abilities are independent.

3. Mutlifactor or anarchic theory: Thorndike[2] is the most prominent among those who believed this theory. This theory holds that intelligence is the mean of undetermined independent rudimentary abilities. Spearman has criticised this theory.

4. The two-factor theory: This theory was conceived by Spearman[3] who held that intelligence has two factors—(1) General intelligence or G, and (2) Specific intelligence or S. General intelligence affects every activity but the effects of the specific intelligence are confined to specific activities. General intelligence whether in lesser or greater degree is constant. Specific intelligence is of various types, the several types being independent of each other. They differ from individual to individual. This intelligence of a person is normally correlated with his general intelligence.

---

1. Wechsler, D., *The Measurement of Adult Intelligence*, 3rd ed. Baltimore, Williams and Wilkins, 1944.
2. Thorndike, EL. and others, *The Measurement of Intelligence*. N.Y. Teacher's College, Columbia University, 1928.
3. Spearman, C.E., *The Abilities of Man*, Macmillan, 1927.

Staffens and Brown have upheld Spearmen's theory on an experimental foundation. But others assert that adequate experimental data, in its favour, is not available. Hence even Spearman's theory cannot be said to be universally acceptable.

In fact many experiments are still needed to formulate an all embracing definition of intelligence. In this connection, a universally acceptable theory has yet to be worked out.

THEORIES OF INTELLIGENCE

C.E. Spearman's theory

Spearman presented his famous two-factor theory of intelligence in the work entitled *The Two-Factor Theory of Intelligence*, published in two volumes. In this work he has concerned with describing the nature of intelligence and how far it may be tested. According to him a current approach to intelligence will be federative. This approach sees unity in difference. According to Spearman federative theory is, "an eclectic approach" which is better than other approaches. He calls it two factor theory having general intelligence or 'G' and specific abilities or 'S'. Later on, he developed a three factor theory in which specific types of abilities were called S1, S2, S3, S4 and so on. He found that Binet studied individual differences of native endowment. In it S factors were found correlative. According to Spearman each S is different from others. Memory testing indicates another type of specific intelligence than learning. We find that in addition to 'G' there are too many S'found in a person. Viewed from the point of practical performance an individual is guided by both 'G' and 'S'. A radio mechanic is displaying a specific ability and so is a speaker but it would not achieve practical results attained by G. The mass of S is unlimited. Theoretically each individual demonstrates endless type of S. On the other hand, G is fixed and permanent. All actions are determined by both, 'G' and 'S'. 'G' varies from individual to individual but it is fixed in each person. We cannot change 'G' but we can improve 'S'. This point has been used by critics against Spearman since it underrates the possibility of education.

'G' is the monarch though S are independent. Spearman sums up different problems involved in intelligence in his theory. His view was to judge intelligence by performance. He explained his theory with reference to analogies from politics. In politics one finds anarchic, oligarchic and monarchic approaches. These three approaches applied to intelligence give us the view that none of them explains behaviour. Spearman followed a path in between monarchic and anarchic theory. In his theory 'G' is universal and 'S' is individual, Later on, he accepted group factors. This modified view was popularised by Cyril Burt. Thus, in the ultimate analysis there are three factors: 'G' and 'S' and Group Factor.

Thurstone, L.L.: Factorial theory

According to Thurstone the present stage of intelligence theory is a continuation of the early factor analytic approach. This phase is third in progress and Thurstone is one of the most important contributors. Thurstone believes that different mental faculties make up the complex concept of intelligence. These faculties are sorted out by factor analysis. Among these the most important are verbal, numerical, perpetual, memory and visual, special and many other factors. Initially Thurstone believes that these primary factors put together form the notion of intelligence. Afterwards it was accepted that intelligence is a second order factor correlated with these primary factors. Thurstone's theory was further extended by J.P. Guilford.

Thurstone's first major application of his centroid factor method improved upon Spearman's theory. He said, "We have not found the general factor of Spearman and we cannot report any general common factor in the battery of 56 tests." Spearman reworked Thurstone's data and charged that this rotational process had submerged the general factor. American factorists, however, found Thurstone convincing. They were attracted by his description of abilities in terms of 7 primaries. These primaries were more amenable to specific definition. Thurstone was able to replicate his findings on samples from two other populations. Thus he gave credence to his method and results. However, in a couple of events some turbulence in his 7 dimension atmosphere was noted. The first of these was a minor study by one of his own students. Thurstone, however, renamed it maturational level. He found that the primaries were themselves inter-related. He admitted that a general factor was needed to explain the inter-relatedness of the primaries. This led to the idea of oblique axes which were regarded as representing the primaries as first order factors. The general factor prevailing the primaries was dubbed as a second order factor.

As against the five tendencies specified by Spearman, Thurstone specified 7 fundamental tendencies in the human beings. These mental abilities were not clearly specified by the then prevalent tests. Psychometric factor, however, helped in their identification. As has been already pointed out, these were called primary mental abilities. According to psychometric scale intelligence is a composite of related mental abilities some of which are more closely associated with learning and consequently on their basis the prediction of scholastic attainments is more easily possible. The same factors are found at each age level though the test material was radically changed. According to P.E. Vernon, the latest authority in this field, it is profitable to study different mental faculties adopting the factorial model of Thurstone when we are dealing with a homogeneous or highly selected population. But with more heterogeneous population in which there are ethnic groups or sub-groups, the 'G' factor tends to dominate and therefore Thurstone's model is not very useful.

J.P. Guilford's theory of intelligence

Guilford's theory of intelligence starts with an analysis of motivation for creative thinking. Thus he first of all analysed intellectual drives. Tracing the history of development in this area he concluded that the creative thinker derives secondary satisfactions from the fact that others approve his activity.

He experiences satisfaction by knowing that what he does is beneficial to humanity. However, in some cases there are creative producers who derive sadistic satisfaction through their inventions. Interests are motivational traits. They represent tendencies to be attracted to certain kinds of activities. According to Guilford, "A number of dimensions of interest in different kinds of thinking, including interest in reflective thinking, logical thinking, artistic *versus* realistic thinking, convergent thinking, divergent thinking, and a factor of tolerance of ambiguity, have been demonstrated." The scores for these interest variables and motivational traits have been found to correlate significantly. Associational fluency tests correlate with need for adventure and with tolerance for ambiguity. Expressional fluency tests correlate with liking for rejecting thinking. Originality tests correlate with liking for divergent thinking. Taking together these facts demonstrate the great complexity of motivation for problem thinking, creative thinking and problem solving. According to Guilford there is always a need for a supply of information for successful creative work. The genius is not only more creative but also has a bigger wealth of information. There is, however, some difference of opinion about the role of this information. It is generally believed that most recall it replicative. According to the informational view there is considerable transform reform.

Thus after analysing problem solving and creative production J.P. Guilford admits the role of the following factors in it:

1. **Information:** This has already been discussed above.

2. **Systems:** This is one of the most important products of information. The system may be vague in form and outline but it is needed to unify thinker's efforts. Guilford surveys various studies in this field and concluded that some sort of system is a must for any creative work.

3. **Incubation:** Incubation is a period during which there is often no apparent activity but definite progress towards a solution. This period may be few hours or few years. The progress during incubation is due to persistent desire to solve the problem. It has been found by experiments that periods of incubation occur after an individual drops an idea for some time and returns to it later. The benefits of incubation have been admitted by so many creative persons themselves. According to Poincare (1913), during incubation there is unconscious problem solving. Guilford rejects the hypothesis as telling us nothing. He points out that the fatigue hypothesis also fails to account for benefits derived from delays of time intervals longer than required to recover from fatigue. He also rejects the hypothesis advanced by Woodworth in 1938 that incubation provides an opportunity for a new start on the problem.

According to Guilford the best hypothesis is transformation hypothesis Our best prospect of learning in this area lies in the direction of discovering the principle governing the occurrence of transformation, conscious or unconscious.

4. **Insight or Intuition:** According to Guilford we are still much dependent upon anecdotes about the role of inspiration in creative production. Most

of the anecdotes mention emotional accompaniments of inspiration. It can be said that the amount of emotion depends on the strength of motivation, the amount of frustration, the size of the intuitive leap and the value of the result. There can be no doubt about the fact of sudden insights and intuitions in problem solving. Intuitive ideas come with various degrees of clarity and completeness and with no apparent effort. It is a key idea by working out of which the whole can be developed. Psychologists have described characteristics of insight in their studies. From anecdotes it is gathered that intuition comes after controlled thinking is abandoned and free association is working. However, there is frequent mention of hard work preceding incubation and intuition, relaxation is a favourable condition for recall of information. According to Guilford, "The creative product is, after all, a result of selective recall."

5. Environment conditions: About the role of environmental condition in creativity and problem solving, Guilford writes, "There is a greater agreement that lack of distractions and freedom from interruptions, even from threats of interruptions, are important conditions. Some idiosyncratic conditions are also reported."

6. Personality differences: Some studies show that the occurrence of intuition is connected with personality differences. According to Guilford, however, it is not easy to find out and establish causal relationships in this connection.

7. Previous experience: According to Guilford insight involves not only previous experience but also new elements. By surveying different studies in this field he concludes that previous experience is definitely useful in creative activity but the latter is not a direct result of the former. There is little Information regarding degree of motivation as a condition of insight. According to Guilford one finds strong effort followed by relaxation being favourable for inspiration. It cannot be easily decided as to how the specific nature of the motivation may effect the shaping of solution.

8. Flexibility: According to Guilford, "There are three different kinds of flexibility in thinking, each with its distinct place in the structure of intellect model. One is flexibility with respect of classes, the readiness to shift from class to class; a second has to do with transformations in divergent production activities; and the third type pertains to redefinitions or transformations in connection with convergent production." He maintains that flexibility with respect to classification is an important asset for the creative thinking. He also examines the relationship of flexibility and divergent production of transformations.

9. Redefinition and functional fixedness: These are vital in conversant production. Guilford mentions three abilities in this connection. Failure to discriminate between systems of failure to affect transformations interfere with redefinition. Implications and evaluation play important role in the creative process. Evaluation occurs at the end of the total creative process. Another important factor useful here is suspended judgement. This is, however, not always useful. A number of studies point out that constructive or destructive reactions to criticism is also an important factor in the creative process.

10. Reactions to criticism: According to Torrance the number of high quality ideas produced by the constructive reading group exceeds those produced by the critical reading group. Other studies highlight the fact that the kind of preparation has a bearing upon the score made in examination with different kinds of items. It was found that those who made evaluation, gained. There is more to learn by making self and other evaluations. What is learnt is probably in terms of ways of applying standards and criteria of judgement. One should be cautious in drawing blanket conclusions in the area of evaluation. Other studies have found interaction effects by evaluation among children. It is better to have it, than not to have evaluation at all. However, in some cases unevaluated practice produced more originality than evaluated practice.

Intelligence theory of A.R. Jensen

According to Jenson conceptional learning is the high water-mark of intelligence. He tested this hypothesis upon students. His studies analysed IDs (Individual Differences) in learning. This was an attempt to develop a science of learning. Understanding of IDs is necessary in order to know the causes of achievements. Intelligence is a complex phenomena which is made still more complex by IDs. The effect of an experimental variable on the performance of individual can often be on a group of individuals. The fact of IDs is against the 'Hollow Organism' approach research on learning. Knowledge of IDs provides both a source of hypothesis about the nature of learning processes and a means of testing certain deductions from theoretical formulations. It is through the manipulations of independent variables that we can discover and further investigate IDs in dependent variable.

1. The taxonomy of conceptual learning: According to Jensen it is necessary to analyse the structure of conceptual learning before any attempt to study IDs. He distinguishes between concept formation and that concept learning task can be analysed and classified in many other ways in terms of the degree of control over the various independent variables involved in the learning situation.

2. Categories of individual differences: Jensen distinguishes between intrinsic and extrinsic sources of IDs in learning. The extrinsic sources include age, sex, intelligence, motivation and personality. Intrinsic sources exist in the processes of learning. Most of the variance in learning cannot be measured by psychometric tests. Therefore we need to study IDs in the intrinsic processes of learning. Conceptual learning is highly complex and presents considerable difficulties concerning conditions of transfer, etc. Even under the best conditions half the true ID variance is due to extrinsic attainment. According to Jensen the factors in short term memory tasks account for some of the IDs variance in concept attainment tasks.

3. The need of a theory of individual differences: A theory of individual differences is necessary since an enormous number of independent variables interact with subject variables in concept learning, According to Jensen the variety of IDs in different types of learning has a limited number of Genotypic sources. He intended to measure basic factors and to devise means of their measurement. For this purpose the factor analysed simple learning tasks. He identified three different kinds of interfering factors, "One involving principally retroactive inhibition, one involving proactive inhibition and one involving interference due to response competition." On the basis of his studies he concluded, "There are a number of features of concept learning, however, such as strategies, which are not stared to any appreciable degree by simpler types of learning. These independent variables which seem more or less peculiar to concept learning also probably interact with subjects and will have to be investigated in their own right on the level of concept learning."

4. The current state of knowledge: According to Jenson the interaction of IDs with concept learning can be found out by highly analytical experimental approach. Most of our knowledge about IDs in conceptual behaviour is based upon clinical literature. Most of these findings are not sufficiently analytical. The scientific value of the clinical tests is practically nil.

5. Intelligence and concept learning: According to Jensen knowledge of everyday concept is highly correlated with measured intelligence. Most of the studies in this connection were too simple to explain the complex process of concept attainment. According to Jensen IDs in psychometric tests can be understood in terms of processes disorder in the learning laboratory rather than *vice-versa*.

6. Manifest anxiety and concept learning: The relationship of an anxiety and concept learning has been studied and conclusions have been drawn that there is a positive correlation between the two. Some other studies, however, showed negative correlation. According to Jensen, "Concept attainment seems to be facilitated by high drive or anxiety when the relevant dimensions for the attainment of the concept are high in the subject's hierarchy of hypotheses or mediators. When the relevant dimensions are low in the subject's hierarchy of mediating responses, anxiety or high drive hinder concept attainment."

7. IDs in spontaneous verbal mediation: Jensen has drawn attention to the tendency for non-social, non-verbal stimulus situations to elicit verbal mediational behaviour subjects, in the studies of IDs in conceptual behaviour. The tendency for concept learning to be verbally mediated increased with age. But there is spontaneous tendency to mediate verbally in learning and problem solving situations. Most of the concepts are learned as well as they are capable of being evoked by stimuli. Studies have shown that age, intelligence and social class are correlated to verbalisation of concepts.

Intelligence theory of Jean Piaget

The most important work on Piaget's theory' of intelligence as published in 1950 under the title. *The Psychology of Intelligence*, by Routledge and Kegan Paul, London. His theory of intelligence may also be found in another work. *The Origins of Intelligence in Children* published by International Universities Press, New York.

Piaget demonstrated that the young child develops concepts and aids as a result of manipulations and experiments which are not arranged by those who would educate the child. This is incidental learning. It occurs throughout the development of the child. It is not a product of acculturation. To the extent all persons in a society are exposed to comparable conditions for learning, individual differences are not the product of acculturation. They are rather directly related to individual differences in the physiological structure which support intellectual functioning. Influences which effect the structure occur largely independent of accumulation. Similarly, the influences of heredity and maturation are also independent. Thus, to the extent that measured intellectual abilities involved primarily aids and concepts which are products of incidental learning, the abilities will have been formed under a unitary set of influences.

About the role of motivation as a determinant of intelligence Piaget maintained that there would be shortage of the anticipatory schemata which are built upon previously existing classifications and other learnt relations. Piaget's observations and his theories provide a basis for a critical revaluation and assessment of various theoretical beliefs. J. McV. Hunt has in this connection compare Piaget's view with those of Gessel. In his theory of causal basis of the epigenetic changes in behaviours and thought Piaget emphasized accommodation, assimilation and the lack of equilibrium between aspect of the infants behavioural repertoire and the encountered circumstances. According to him organisms make adoptive changes in their encounters with environment circumstances. He defines accommodation as modification in a sensory motor schema. Assimilation is internalization of the accommodative change. It occurs when the child employs the newly modified sensory motor or conceptual schemata in a novel situation. Equilibrium means the stability of a behavioural organization. When the infant or child encounters circumstances beyond the limits of his sensory motor systems the equilibrium is upset. This leads to accommodative modifications. If the circumstances are not too far beyond the limits of sensory motor systems, these systems become modified in the attempt to accommodate the circumstances. In the intellectual domain ready-made systems of information processing become extended with means. The preconceptual images are transformed into accommodative modifications which Piaget calls intuitive regulations. These regulations are further transformed into the concrete intellectual operations. These intellectual operations acquire an equilibrium but they are inadequate to provide a basis for the examination of those operations. Piaget and his collaborators found the appearance of formal operations of thought during adolescence. At this stage the direct perceptions in investigations and the imaginal standards of what life and society might be, supply the standards that motivate the adolescence towards reforming the world that exists. According to Piaget, "Logic is the mirror of thought." Man may yet invent new modes of thought in the process of copying with the new instruments of his own inventions. Piaget has presented a picture of behavioural and of thought, that come with the infant's and child's interaction with the circumstances. Piaget is an interactionist, neither hereditorial nor environmentalist.

Piaget's observations are highly dissonant with extreme environmental reason. He finds a very limited number of quite highly organized behavioural system in human neonate. These include: (*a*) Sucking, (*b*) Looking, (*c*) Listening, (*d*) Vocalising, (*e*) Grasping, (*f*) The various motor activities of the trunk and limbs. He emphasizes that each of these is a ready-made sensory motor organisation at birth. He was not concerned with how these organizations came into being before birth. He showed an impressive correspondence between sensory motor organisations and those systems in traditional neurology. His observations attest to the effect of encounters with circumstances but the infant organism is not a blank page.

Piaget's observations and his theorising provide evidence and conceptions dissonant with the conceptions prevalent among S-R behaviour theorists that organisms tend to be passive and inactive until driven into action by impelling stimulations. His observations provide evidence of ontogenetic origins of actions. He found the human neonate with various ready-made systems which have been already referred. His observations imply a redefinition of stimulus. He observed that his children exhibited, "New behaviour relating to the objects which have disappeared." These new efforts brought on by the escape of objects from conceptual contract occur only after the child has had repeated perceptual contact with those objects. The recognitive familiarity in a young infant is the basis of, "Spectacles of interest". He cited examples of, "secondary circular reactions". His observations provide a foundation for expectations and intentions consonant with a mechanistic view of living beings. His observations are highly relevant to the S-R conception of learning. They imply a variety of kinds of learning. His conceptions of accommodation, assimilation and equilibrium are useful in the explanation of learning.

Piaget's observations strongly suggest that the modifications in behaviour come at the point in time that the learner encounters circumstances that will not permit him to proceed as he anticipated. These are circumstances that upset the child's equilibrium and enforce him into accommodative modifications. Piaget views the child as highly active, with an end in view, from the physiological stand-point the child can be expected to anticipate what is coming and to have intentional ends in view. Reinforcement would consist in achieving the child's anticipating the goals.

Piaget accepted organized wholeness of sensory motor, perceptual and conceptual structure of schemata. Thus he agrees with Gestalt psychology. According to Gestalt theory the laws of organization are principles of concept attainment, which are two forms of concept learning. In this connection three distinctions must be remembered:

1. There is concept learning on the basis of primary stimulus generalisation.
2. Concept learning depends largely upon discrimination learning.
3. Concept learning involves transfer of learning on the basis of symbolic mediating responses.

The first two types of concept learning are those based upon primary stimulus generalization and those based on discrimination. The third category includes only those tasks in which the concept could not be attained except by means of symbolically mediating learning. This type of concept learning introduces a host of sources, of ID variants that are not apt to play a prominent role in similar types of learning. According to Jensen, "'Mediated concept learning will be affected to a large extent by transfer of learning from the subject's past experience. The subject's verbal repertoire, the structure of his verbal associative network, the strength of the subject's tendency to make verbal responses to non-verbal stimuli and other such processes which are a mixture of nature and nature will figure among the main determinants of IDs in concept learning of the mediated variety." Finally, distinction must be made between tasks that involve only concept identification, without any learning whatever being tapped by the task and tasks that involve learning parameters. It is generally easier to measure IDs in status. However, Jensen was concerned with IDs in processes. He maintained equilibrium. Piaget maintains the dilemma of either organised wholes or the atomism of isolated sensations or reflexes as quite unnecessary. He presents a third alternative view in these words, "A perception may be a synthesis of elements, or else it may constitute a single whole, or it may be a system of relations (each relation being itself a whole, but the complete whole becoming analysable and not relying at all on atomism). This being the case, there is no reason why complex structure should not be regarded as the product of a progressive construction which arises, not from 'syntheses' (of atomistic elements), but from adaptive differentiations and combined assimilations, nor is there any reason why this construction should not be related to an intelligence, capable of genuine activity as opposed to an interplay of pre-established structures." Piaget made sensory motor adaptations in the psychological development of his own three children. He explained the successive co-ordinations as providing the basic thought, the hierarchical nature of intelligence and intellectual concepts. Following the six stages of sensory motor development the sensory motor systems of the infant become internalised as imitative imagery combines with imitated vocal signs of early languages. These are gradually modified in the accommodations demanded by communications into intuitive regulations. At each stage after the first sensory motor stage, the child's anticipation of the end or goal of his action or thought serves to unify the system. Thus while Piaget readily accepts the Gestalt principles of organisation, he shows maximum dissonant with the notion that the laws of organization are constant in the course of human development. According to him the systems of behaviour and of thought are seen to develop into more complex hierarchical organizations in the course of the child's sensory motor and informational interaction with his environmental circumstances.

INTELLIGENCE TESTS

Intelligence tests are classified according to the activities prescribed in them. These are as follows:

1. Verbal Tests.
2. Non-Verbal Tests.

As the name itself suggests, Verbal tests make use of language while the Non-verbal tests include such activities which do not necessitate the use of language. Both these types are suitable for individual as well as group tests. Consequently, Verbal and Non-verbal tests are capable of further sub-division into two classes—individual and group. Thus, finally there are four types of intelligence tests:

1. Verbal Individual Intelligence Tests.
2. Non-verbal Individual Intelligence Tests.
3. Verbal Group Intelligence Tests.
4. Non-verbal Group Intelligence Tests.

1. Verbal individual intelligence tests

The very name verbal individual intelligence tests, suggests that these are intelligence tests given to individuals, or in other words they are meant to test the intelligence of individuals. Language finds adequate use in them. Binet Simon tests and the various revisions are all included in this classification.

2. Non-verbal individual intelligence tests

It is quite apparent from the above example that in verbal tests, the child's knowledge of language is more in demand and therefore the use of these tests is limited to students or literate persons. But these verbal tests cannot be used in the case of illiterate individuals as these tests involve an extensive use of language which fails as a medium to measure the individual differences between the illiterates. Consequently, illiterate individuals are tested with the help of Non-verbal Individual Intelligence Tests. The name itself indicates the nature of these tests. These tests involve the least possible uses of the linguistic ability and are similarly almost unaffected by knowledge derived from books. One example of these non-verbal tests is the Performance Intelligence Tests.

It would be in keeping with the context of our discussion to understand in detail the Performance Intelligence tests as an example of the non-verbal individual intelligence test. According to Munn, "The word performance is usually applied to tests which require a minimum use of understanding and language." Thus, these tests make use of items requiring responses and not language and these tests can be applied to children, illiterates, feeble-minded individuals as well as foreigners.

Difficulties in individual tests

Some difficulties are felt in the operation of both the verbal and non-verbal types of individual intelligence tests. They are roughly as following:

(*a*) *The difficulty of time:* The individual intelligence test takes an hour usually and only one person can be tested at one time. Obviously, at this rate it would be essential to have a very big number of trained examiners and in spite of that it would be difficult to test all the people.

(*b*) *Need for experienced examiners:* The second obstacle, in the individual intelligence tests, is the need for experienced examiners because the correct result cannot be arrived at if the examiners are inexperienced. At the same time the availability of such a large number of trained personnel is a near impossibility.

Notwithstanding these difficulties, in some circumstances the individual intelligence tests become unavoidable. This is because the level of accuracy reached by the individual intelligence test in the assessment of a person's intelligence, is outside the reach of the group intelligence tests.

3. Verbal group intelligence tests

The group intelligence tests own their origin and evolution to the difficulties from which the individual tests suffer. As the name suggests those are designed to test the intelligence of a group and not of an individual. All the people in the group are given the same directions and have to perform the same activities. Even the score of the result of group intelligence tests is calculated by machines thus not depending upon the necessity of skilled examiners, accompanied by an economy of time.

An excellent example of group intelligence tests is afforded by the Army alpha and beta tests, which were evolved during the World War I in order to test the American soldiers. For example, it revealed separately the feebleminded, men capable of becoming skilled specialists, men capable of becoming officers, men needing some training, etc.

Difficulties in verbal group tests

Even after taking all the precautions, some difficulties are discernible in the verbal group intelligence tests which can be eliminated only by reverting to the individual intelligence tests. It is due to these difficulties that the individual intelligence tests are considered more realistic than the group intelligence tests. The difficulties of the verbal group intelligence test are fundamentally as follows:

1. *Difficulties relating to co-operation in test:* In these tests it is difficult to judge whether the examinee is extending his full co-operation or not.

2. *Difficulty related to the balance of the subject:* In these tests it is difficult to determine whether the physical and emotional balance of subject is even or disturbed.

3. *Difficulty related to the ease of the subject:* In the verbal group intelligence tests it is difficult to ascertain if the subject is feeling at ease and free or restrained.

4. *Possibility of cheating by the subject:* Another difficulty in these tests is that no one can testify whether the person has written the answer himself or copied it from his neighbour.

In spite of the difficulties which arise in the verbal group intelligence tests, they have their own advantages due to which they are used comprehensively. As has been said before, the advantages are the same as the difficulties of the individual intelligence tests.

4. Non-verbal group intelligence tests

As has been mentioned before, the verbal intelligence tests are meant only for the literates because of the requirement of a linguistic ability. It is for this reason that the non-verbal group intelligence tests have been created, the subjects making a minimum use of language but performing, instead, many activities. One example of the non-verbal intelligence tests is Cattell's Culture free tests and the N.I.I.P. test.

In these non-verbal group intelligence tests the examiners have to explain to the examinees even the simplest directions which are also demonstrated as far as possible. All this is done to make the least possible use of language. There are some performance tests in three group intelligence tests, in which the examinee draws some lines according to his abilities, fills in some empty spaces, draws some simple figures, or performs some simple activities. Some psychologists do not give credence to these non-verbal tests in their role of measuring intelligence of the subjects while on the other hand some psychologists consider them to be better than verbal tests. For example, in Alexander's opinion, "A complete performance battery will be a better measure than a complete verbal battery."

The truth is that even if non-verbal group intelligence tests are not more important than verbal tests, they are certainly not less important than these tests Some of their peculiarities are as follows:

1. **Comparison of various human groups:** The first obstacle in the comparison of human groups of various languages and culture is the difference in their language. This obstacle can be overcome by the non-verbal group intelligence tests and a comparison between different human groups is rendered possible.
2. **The testing of illiterate soldiers:** The verbal group intelligence tests are manifestly inapplicable to illiterate soldiers for the testing of their intelligence. Consequently, the abilities of illiterate soldier are assessed by employing the non-verbal group intelligence tests and the possibilities of their learning are known.
3. **Intelligence testing in children:** The linguistic ability is very low in the case of children and consequently the verbal group intelligence tests cannot be given to them. Apparently, intelligence testing of children will have to be done by the non-verbal group intelligence tests.
4. **Advice to some specific classes:** The above exposition on the non-verbal group intelligence tests has made it obvious that these tests have proved the most successful with some specific classes of people. Thus, the result of these tests render great assistance in advising people of this group.

INTELLIGENCE QUOTIENT

The idea of I.Q. was utilized first of all in 1916 in the Stanford Binet test. I.Q. is the ratio between mental age (MA) and chronological age (CA). The chronological age is determined from the date of birth and the mental age by tests. For example, if the average score of children of 13 years in age turns out to be 75 in some test then any child whose test reveals an average of 75, will be said to have a mental age of 13, whatever be his chronological age. After 14 years of chronological age, mental age does not increase. Even children of the same mental age differ. Mental age does not increase with the chronological age. Having understood properly the mental age, if is easy to understand I.Q. The equation of the calculation of I.Q. is as follows:

$$\text{I.Q.} = \frac{\text{MA}}{\text{CA}} \times 100$$

As is evident from the above equation, to calculate I.Q. (Intelligence Quotient) the mental age is divided by the chronological age and then multiplied by 100. To take an example, suppose a four years old child has a mental age of the three years. His I.Q. will be calculated with the help of the following equation:

$$\frac{3}{4} \times 100 = 75$$

Actually the I.Q, reveals the mental ability of the individual on the basis of which he can be directed about his future. It is essential to keep in sight the limitations of the idea of I.Q. in order to understand it well enough. Its main limitations are as follows:

1. I.Q. is not the quantity of a person's intelligence.
2. All the tests do not yield an identical I.Q. Consequently, none of the I.Qs. indicated by any one test is completely reliable.
3. No person is devoid of intelligence so that I.Q. does not start from zero.
4. I.Q. changes at least every three years.
5. Even when a person is examined by the same test a number of times, the I.Q. shows a change. This difference differs from test to test. For example, in Wechsler Bellevue Test, the difference is up to 5 points whereas in the Stanford Binet Test, the difference is up to 4 points.
6. The I.Q. of every child does not remain constant. In some it registers.
7. I.Q. is the result both of heredity and environment. Thus a change in environment may change the I.Q. According to Garrett the good or bad environment may show a difference of 10 points.

In his book, *Great Experiments in Psychology* Garrett has classified people according to their I.Q. and shown their percentage in the population, as in the following table:

IQ	Classification	Percentage
140 or above	Very Superior	1.5
120 to 139	Superior	11.0
110 to 119	Bright	18.0
90 to 109	Average or Normal	48.0
80 to 89	Dull, Normal or Backward	14.0
70 to 79	Very dull	5.0
0 to 69	Feeble-minded	2.5

In this context, some other important things known from experiments are:

1. There is a possibility of increase in I.Q. along with a rise in the social and economic status and a possibility of decrease in I.Q. with degradation.
2. The I.Q. generally remains constant from 5 years to 14 years of age.
3. The mental level develops gradually.

Many scientific researches have made it clear that there is no invariable relation between I.Q. and success in school work. But in children with a higher I.Q. there is a possibility of success in school work.

QUESTIONS FOR EXERCISE

1. What is Intelligence? Examine the Spearman's Principle of Intelligence.
2. Write short note on—Thurstone's Factorial Theory of Intelligence.
3. Discuss J.P. Guilford's Theory of Intelligence.
4. Describe Intelligence Theory of A.R. Jensen.
5. Describe Intelligence Theory of Jean Piaget.
6. Explain the characteristics of intelligence tests and give a brief account of various types of intelligence tests.
7. Write a short note on—Intelligence Quotient.

21

Learning and Conditioning

WHAT IS LEARNING?

The following are some definitions of learning which should make it clear:

1. Learning is change in behaviour: In J.P. Guilford's opinion "We may define the term very broadly by saying that learning is any change in behaviour, resulting from behaviour."[1] In this definition a distinction between change in behaviour due to maturity and change in behaviour due to learning is not clear though both these activities occur simultaneously. In the words of Woodworth, "Typically at least learning consists in doing something new, provided this something new is retained by the individual and reappears in his later activities."[2]

2. Learning is an organisation of behaviour: According to Garrett, "Learning is that activity by virtue of which we organise our response with new habits."[3] Thus the element of organisation in learning is very much important. Guilford too, maintains that learning involves organisation of behaviour. Thus in learning to ride a cycle we have to organise the activities of turning the pedal, balancing the handle, etc. in order to be reasonably safe with the vehicle. It is another matter that a person does not learn this organisation at the outset and that he may take much longer time to learn to balance the handle than the time he may take to learn to turn the pedal. But his learning of the activity of cycling will be complete only when he accomplishes this organisation.

3. Learning is the reinforcement of a new activity: R.S. Woodworth maintained that the learning of a new act is an addition to the person's store of experiences. Clarifying the statement further, Woodworth says that reinforcement, too, is an indispensable element in the act of learning because it helps forming only successful responses and weeding out the unsuccessful ones. To quote Woodworth "An activity may be called learning in so far as it

---

1. Guilford, J.P., *General Psychology* (1956), p. 343.
2. Woodworth, R.S. and Marquis, D.G., *Psychology*, Methuen and Co. Ltd., London, 1949, p. 491.
3. Garrett, H.E., *Great Experiments in Psychology* (Rev. Ed.), New York: Appleton Century, 1941.

develops the individual in any way, good or bad and makes his environment and experiences different from what it would otherwise have been."[1]

The psychologists who stress external behaviour consider learning to be a change of behaviour while those who lay emphasis on internal changes are convinced that learning is change in the perception of the individual. Combining these two views, Murphy writes, "From this point of view it would be legitimate to regard learning as a modification both of behaviour and of the way of perceiving."[2] The following definition of learning given by Hilgard is an essence of all the foregoing definitions offered by other psychologists, "Learning is the process by which an activity originates or is changed through reacting to an encountered situation, provided that the characteristics of the change in activity cannot be explained on the basis of native response tendencies, maturity or temporary status of the organism."[3]

LEARNING AND MATURATION

Learning changes behaviour and so does maturation. Thus sometimes it becomes difficult to say definitely as to which of the subject's activities are the result of learning and which are the consequences of maturation. Automatic activity, random acts, reflexes and instincts and sudden expression of emotion can be accepted as unlearned actions and the result of maturation, but in most of the activities of human beings it is difficult to decide whether these activities result from maturation or learning. In fact, these activities develop both due to learning and maturation. Take the example of learning language. It is true, of course, that a child is manifestly incapable of learning language until he reaches a certain stage or age in maturation, but it is also equally true that he does not learn the language just because he attains that stage. The language is taught to him.

An experiment on co-twins indicates the extent of the changes in behaviour caused by maturation and the extent to which changes may be affected by learning.[4] The purpose of the experiment was to measure the extent of advantage of learning in such activities as climbing the stairs. Two twins were chosen for the experiment because due to the similarity in heredity, the speed of maturation is the same and any changes which may occur may be attributed to climb the stairs from her fortysixth week. On examination this twin 'T' failed to climb at all at the age of 46 weeks and had to be aided up all the 5 stairs. In the space of four weeks she climbed all the stairs in 26 seconds.

When 'S' was placed on the stairs at the age of 53 weeks she climbed all the five stairs unaided but it took her some 45 seconds. After two weeks of practice 'S', at the age of 55 weeks, traversed the distance in 10 seconds. In this way, at this age 'S' was ahead of 'T' who, at a younger age had practised three

1. Ibid., p. 532.
2. Murphy, G., *An Introduction to Psychology*, 1951, p. 248.
3. Hilgard, E.R.. *Theories of Learning*, Methuen. 1958, p. 13.
4. Extracted from a treatise, 'Maturation of Behaviour' by M.B. McGraw, published in Carmichael's book *A Manual of Child Psychology*.

times as much. 'S' was three weeks older than 'T'. Thus in spite of all kinds of learning, T was left behind due to a lack of maturity.

This experiment proves that learning plays an insignificant part in reflex and other physiological activities peculiar to one's species. Those activities which appear in all human beings at a certain age, are due to maturity. Those activities which do not inevitably appear in every person are affected by maturation to the extent that they can be learnt with ease at the age of maturity. Some examples of this type of activities are swimming, horse riding climbing trees etc. The learning of these activities is made more facile by motor, sensory and neural maturation.

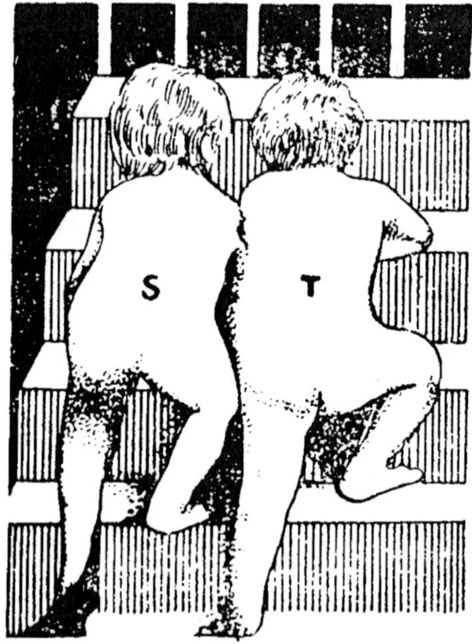

Fig. 8

The above exposition on the relation of learning and maturation provides some very practical suggestions for learning and training. It is not useful to make an attempt to teach a child forcibly before he matures. Many parents try to precipitate their children into higher classes with the help of coaching, at a young age. This coaching cannot have a lasting or permanent effect and the children become weak in senior classes. The teaching of the proper job at a specific age depends on many factors, two of which are the child's mental and physiological development. But a general age for the beginning of the teaching of various subjects can be established. For example, it is comparatively easier to study algebra at 15 or 16 than it is at 11 or 12. This relation between maturation and gaining justifies the suggestion for the fixing of a minimum age limit for admission in universities.

THORNDIKE'S LAWS

One of the most accredited among all the current theories on the laws of learning is the one presented by Thorndike in America. About its importance Tolman writes, "The psychology of animal learning not to mention that of child learning—has been and still is primarily a matter of agreeing or disagreeing with Thorndike or trying in minor ways to improve upon him. Gestalt psychologists, conditioned reflex psychologists, sign gestalt psychologists all of us here in America seem to have taken Throndike, overtly or covertly, as our starting point."[1]

Thorndike first presented his theory in his book *Animal Learning* published in 1898. The clearest form of his theory is seen in his three volume treatise *Educational Psychology*. His theory may be understood in a systematic way with the help of three major laws which are as follows:

1. Law of Readiness.
2. Law of Exercise.
3. Law of Effect.

Writing on the subject of the importance of these laws in the activity of learning Thorndike points out, "Both theory and practice need emphatic and frequent reminders that man's learning is fundamentally the action of the laws of readiness, exercise and effect."[2] Thus in Thorndike's opinion man's learning takes place according to these laws.

He drew learning curves for men and animals and concluded from them that usually, the methods employed are similar in both classes. Until 1930 Thorndike laid particular emphasis on these three laws.

Law of readiness

The law of readiness describes those situations in which the person who learns either invites the object of his learning or rejects it. Readiness includes all those preparatory adjustments which immediately precede the activity. Reminding the learner of his past experiences, mental preparation for the understanding of new things, diverting his attention towards the subject to be learned changing the environment to suit the learning are all included in readiness. These induce a man to be naturally ready for learning. This readiness creates a mental set for learning and turns the learner's mental attitude towards the subject to be learned.

In Thorndike's view the law of readiness is active in three following conditions:

1. When a conduction unit is prepared to go into action, its work is quite satisfactory because nothing is done to alter its working.
2. The inactivity of a conduction unit and any reaction may arise in connection with that deficiency.

1. Tolman, 'The determiners of behaviour at a choice point,' *Psychol. Bull.*, 1937. 16. 1-41.
2. Thorndike, E., *The Psychology of Learning*, New York: Teacher's College, Columbia University 1913, p. 23.

3. When a conduction unit is forced to act while it is not prepared to do so its behaviour is of a nature calculated to excite anger.[1]

It is quite obvious from the above description that the readiness for learning is known by the tendency for learning in the learner. The tendency for learning results in self-contentment on learning. If the learning is obstructed, even in the event of the presence of the tendency to learn then deep discontentment may result. Thus while on the one hand, the tendency towards learning is an assistance in learning, it may, on the other, be a source of discontentment in case the learning is impeded or completely absent. For an experiment arouse the curiosity of a child in some object and then desist from giving it to him and it will be seen that his discontentment increases which is abated when he is in possession of the object and has understood it. Similarly, teach a caged monkey the method of securing fruit from outside the cage but do not give him the opportunity of experimenting with his skill. It will consequently, be extremely agitated and it will be satisfied and peaceful only when you let it experiment with its method and obtain fruit with effort.

In this way the law of readiness is related to mental preparation. In reality, Thorndike's conduction units do not mean anything physiological, but rather the tendency to an action. Thus readiness means a mental preparation for action. The law of readiness was not one of increase but of preparatory adjustments and it is incorrect to interpret it with physiological development or physiological growth.

In his books, *The Fundamentals of Learning* published in 1932 and *The Psychology of Wants, Interests and Attitudes* published in 1935, Thorndike practically separated the law of readiness from the other laws of learning. Now, he considered the wants, interests and attitudes to be contributory in learning, in place of readiness. We progress in learning by the motivation furnished by our wants, interests and attitudes. A person cannot learn an activity with ease towards which he is unfavourably disposed. Thus, with this modification or correction, they do not mean the same thing. Thorndike described the law of learning in words more appropriate than the ones he had previously used.

Law of exercise

The second important law in human and animal learning is the law of exercise, which is based on the laws of use and disuse. The repeated application of an activity fixes it firmly in the mind while on the other hand the relation is weakened through continuous disuse. Whenever there is an appropriate situation, the activity which is firmly entrenched, might take place. This law taking a cue from this universal experience, emphasizes repetition in the activity of learning. Repetitive application of the activity results in the formation of a habit in the muscles and the nerve fibres of the brain so that there is a facility in its execution in case of need.

The element of understanding in repetition was not adequately stressed in Thorndike's law of readiness. For example, it is a rule that if repetition, in

1. Thorndike, E.L., *The Original of Man*, p. 128.

the memorising of a poem, is complemented by an attempt to understand and mutually relate the different stanzas, the learning may be affected with ease. Not so with Thorndike, who considered the mechanical repetition in learning individually sufficient. This type of memorising becomes rote learning, a highly undesirable thing and the forgetting of one line results in the forgetting of the rest while the recollection of the important line is of no use because the order is lost. The scientific method makes a clear understanding of the subject matter and constant renewal quite as important as constant repetition. Thus, Thorndike's mechanical repetition came in for a lot of criticism and he reacted by affecting modifications.

At a later stage, Thorndike laid emphasis on controlled practice in exercise, which was comprehensive enough to include an association of ideas, clarity of meaning, maximum effort in learning and the use of the ease of learning in the activity, besides repetition, on which he had laid stress previously.

Law of effect

The meaning of the law of effect is the effect of learning. The answer to the question regarding the success or failure of learning has very significant bearing on the law now under study. Success brings with it satisfaction and along with it a strengthening of the relation of the experiences. Failure increases dissatisfaction and the absence of the relation among the experiences weakens them. Thus, we may compare success to a reward or failure to a punishment and the desire to repeat success or avoid failure as the inevitable antecedents.

In 1932, Thorndike propounded a new theory on the basis of his experiments about the law of effect, and this he entitled 'Spread of Effect'. This novel theory postulates that the activity of learning does not confine its effects to itself because correlations and the strength of adjustments are not left uneffected. For example the son of a shopkeeper is ahead of his class in arithmetic because he has already learnt some accountancy in connection with sales in the shop. Thus the spread of effect, by implication, means the spread of success, reward etc.

Two objections have been raised against Thorndike's law of effect. The behaviourists contend that the two words satisfaction and dissatisfaction, being subjective are incapable of describing animal behaviour. Thorndike used them in an operational form and did not use them as indicators or symptoms of internal experience. As he writes, "By a satisfying state of affairs is meant one which the animal does nothing to avoid often doing things which maintain or renew it. By an annoying state of affairs is meant one which the animal does nothing to preserve often doing things which put an end to it."[1] The conditions of satisfaction and dissatisfaction are recognised by their effect on the adjustment which is what the law of effect indicates. Thus, Thorndike's law of effect cannot legitimately be called subjective. The second objection raised against this law is that because the effect is existing while its causes

1. Thorndike, E.L., *The Psychology of Learning*, New York, Teacher's College, Columbia University, 1913, p. 1.

have disappeared, it is incorrect to credit the effect of the present situation to past effects. The effect is either present or will be known in the future. But this objection, too, is groundless. The effect tells of the possibilities of the reaction taking place in the future. The accuracy of the forecast or prophecy is a matter to be examined at a later stage and it is not correct to say anything about it in advance. The real cause for this objection against Thorndike's law was the emphasis placed on the backward influence left by the neurons, by Thorndike himself. In simple language the law of effect means that activity is encouraged by reward or success and is impeded by punishment or failure. As Thorndike said, this law of effect is direct and does not need the assistance of thought. In the saying of this, Thorndike indicates the principle of reinforcement which is accepted in the theories of conditioned response.

In 1935, Thorndike made some modifications in the law of effect, based on experimental findings. He now said that the influence of reward or punishment is not equivalent and neither is it paradoxical. The effect of reward is far more influential than that of punishment. The strengthening of associations due to reward is not paralleled by the demoralisation caused by dissatisfaction. Thus the person who is learning should be as much satisfied as possible in order that he may learn with success. Encourage the child when he does something and congratulate him besides rewarding him with the object of desires in order to bring the desirable spirit in his learning.

These major laws enunciated by Thorndike are of great practical importance. Very few of us fully realise the effect that reward, encouragement, praise etc. have on learning. These theories are of importance not only in the teaching of others but also in personal learning. An interest in the activity to be learned should be created in the learner be it oneself or some other, because this will greatly expedite learning. And, the meaningful practice of the learnt activity will help its retention in no small measure.

Subordinate laws

Other five subordinate laws were also mentioned by Thorndike in relation to the three major ones studied above. His later expositions however, sometimes contain their description while at other occasions they are lacking in it. He does not consider these subordinate laws to be of equal importance with the three major ones mentioned above. These five subordinate laws are:

1. Multiple Response: The first subordinate law is called multiple response. A person seeks to solve a novel problem placed in front of him in accordance with his instinctive and learned behaviour because his search is conditioned by these two. There are multiple responses in the behaviour which guide a person in achieving success and make learning possible. The learner reaches the solution by the variation in the response.

If the activities are multiple the person would never get the correct solution. The theory of learning by trial and error is founded on multiple responses and diversified reactions. If a person adopts a particular method of approach but does not change it in case of failure and gives up his attempts if nothing new suggests itself, that person will never learn anything. The person who is learning should constantly change his steps until he achieves complete success.

2. Set and attitude: This is the second law of learning. Learning is conditioned by the attitude and set of the learner. The response of a person in a specific situation is dependant upon his adjustment in a particular culture. On seeing an idol a Hindu child may bow his head but a Muslim will not pay any respect. Both these responses are affected simultaneously by current tendencies. In an extraordinary situation, the worshipper may even throw the idol. The set or attitude decides not only the response of the individual but also the object from which he will derive satisfaction or dissatisfaction. A first class student cries on scoring 50 per cent marks while a third class student feels delighted with the same score. The reaction of a student on scoring a certain number of marks depends upon the set attitude and the tendency present in him at the time.

3. Prepotency of elements: The third subordinate law of learning is the prepotency of elements. Every problem has some fundamental prepotent elements. The learner gets greater success if he bases his response on these elements though this depends on the insight and capability of the learner. This kind of capacity is of great help in thorough learning. The insight into a mathematical problem of a student of this particular subject cannot be equalled by that of a student of languages because the student of mathematics will grasp its fundamentals with ease.

4. Response by analogy: This is the fourth law of learning and is called the law of assimilation. A person will respond in a manner similar to the one in which he has behaved previously if he finds some similarity between the previous situation and the new one. Even if the elements of similarity between the old and new situations are none too numerous, the response will be similar to that in the past.

5. Associative shifting: This is the fifth and last law of learning. The title quite obviously indicates that the response of the learner shifts. This shifting is done in respect of the basic stimulus or some related associative stimulus. To take an example, a dog starts salivating, when it sees food, and approaches the bearer with its tail wagging. The result of constant repetition of this phenomenon is that the dog wags his tail on the mere perception of the man and the dish. Thus the response, originally directed to the food, is now aimed at the man and the dish because both these objects are associates of the main stimulus, the food. Thus an associative shifting in the response is observable.

All the laws, subsidiary and main, presented by Thorndike are important in learning, both for the teacher and the student. They are applied comprehensively in education though all the psychologists are not agreed upon the truth and usefulness usually attributed to them.

The above described laws of learning are not intended to convey the impression that Thorndike's attention was confined only to the laws. Actually, Thorndike paid even greater attention to the practical aspect of education and made attempt to absolve the difficulties of the teachers and taught alike. Thus, Thorndike attended to the specific aspects of learning and did not rest content with a general description of the activity. He has mentioned many factors which may assist in learning, but which are not implied in and cannot be derived from his laws of learning. For example, he has stressed the following five factors which assist in the progress of learning:

(*i*) Interest in the work.

(*ii*) Interest in improvement.

(*iii*) Significance.

(*iv*) Problem Attitude.

(*v*) Attentiveness.

To these five, Thorndike added another two which, in his opinion, are not indisputable. These are absence of irrelevant emotion and absence of worry. Thus, he encouraged practical experiments and measurements. He himself conducted experiments throughout his life and made continuous progress in his theory. He is fundamentally a behaviourist, notwithstanding his acceptance of the effect of introspection on human beings and his frequent use of the subjective terms. He encouraged the psychological revolution in the field of education.

PRINCIPAL FORMS AND METHODS OF LEARNING

The principal forms or methods of learning are, learning through imitation, learning through conditioned response, learning through trial and error and learning through insight All these four forms are equally utilised by animals as well as human beings.

Imitation

Learning through imitation is one of the most important forms of learning. The human child learns mostly through imitation. It is a common place observation that children imitate the behaviour, habits, manners and ways of adults. In imitation the learner exactly copies the behaviour of another person without understanding or thinking. Whenever this copying is observed, it is said that one has learned through imitation.

The main characteristics of learning through imitation are as follows:

1. The imitator never does it before imitation, but performs the activity only after seeing it in another.
2. In imitation the learner exactly copies the activity performed before him.

Among the living beings man is the best imitator. In human learning, especially that of the human child, imitation has an important place. In an experiment, 42 children of 1st Standard were selected.[1] Two boxes were placed on two chairs in a room as shown in the Fig. 9 given below. There was a bit of

1. Miller, N. and Dollard, J., *Social Learning and Imitation*, New Haven; Yale University Press, 1949, p. 124.

candy in one of the boxes. A place was fixed to start with. The leader of the boys was told which box was to be opened. As he opened the box, he found a piece of candy. Then another boy was asked to open either of the boxes. If this boy imitated the leader, he got the piece of candy. If he did not imitate he got no reward. In every experiment both boys were made to stand on the start.

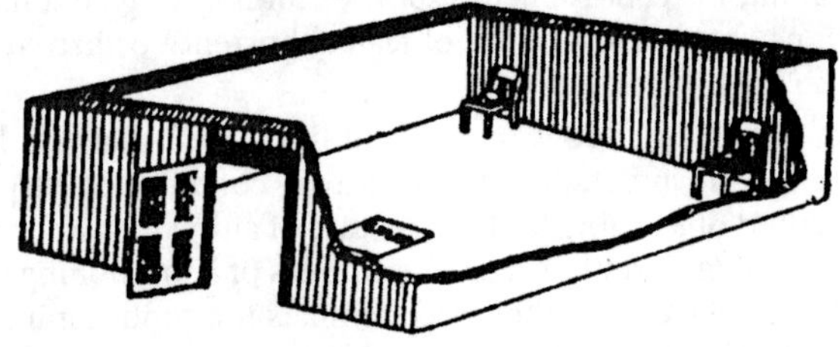

Fig. 9

In the first experiment both boys were told that "Here are two boxes here and there. There is a piece of candy in a box. You have to find the piece of candy. He will get first chance, then you will get chance. If you could not get in the first chance, you will get another chance." The leader was always given first chance. The piece of candy was not always kept in the same box, 22% of the boys imitated in the first chance. The rest 80% boys did not imitate. These boys might have reasoned that because the leader has already taken out the piece of candy from the box, so it could not be there. On an average, in one out of 3 experiments every second boy imitated the first boy. When the situation was changed and four boxes were placed on the four corners of an imagined square, 75% of the children imitated. This shows that the tendency of imitation learned in the first situation was generalised or transferred into an individual direction. In other experiments the children were rewarded for not imitating the leader. This tendency of not imitating the leader was cent-per-cent transferred to new situation. It is important to note in this experiment that the children were asked to imitate an activity, which they could easily do, *e.g.*, all of them could reach the box, open it and take out things from it. In the complex activities this point is even more important.

The process of imitation is very important in learning. The teachers make a wide use of this fact. Education becomes easier and more perfect by demonstration. In the teaching of dance, music, etc., demonstration is very important since imitation has an important role in them. The efficient teachers generally demonstrate whenever it is possible and encourage the students often to imitate the manners, ways, methods and habits etc , of the teachers. Thus by presenting good ideals himself, the teacher can easily create the same among the students.

Conditioned response

As a general rule the higher the species of the animal, the more easily conditioning of response is achieved. Thus conditioning should be easiest in the case of human beings. But man is a complex animal and hence the factors which distract his attention are larger in number than in the case of other animals. However, in spite of these distracting elements in conditioning of responses it certainly remains one of the most important methods of learning, especially in the case of children. In childhood many of the responses of the child are conditioned to particular objects and even when the individual becomes an adult, his conditioned response continues *e.g.*, if a man behaves wrongly with us, we develop a kind of fear, abhorrence or hatred with every person resembling him.

Modern psychology does not admit the view that all learning is conditioning, but no psychologist denies that conditioned response is an important method of learning both in the case of animals as well as of human beings. A person can find hundreds of examples of conditioning of response in his daily life. In the case of the tamed animals the conditioning of process is very much used to teach so many activities. The conditioning of response as it is established can also be extinguished. In the establishment of the conditioning the stimuli has to be repeated while in its extinction the stimuli is not repeated. Thus in the example of Pavlov's dog, if the dog's response has been conditioned by the ringing of the bell, it will be de-conditioned if food is not served in spite of the ringing of the bell or food is served without ringing the bell. Similar examples of de-conditioning process can be found in the case of human beings. Suppose a person is used to get out for a walk to a bridge with a certain friend, he will always remember his friend when he is absent. The sight of the bridge will make him recall his friend, because he always used to come with him to bridge. Thus the bridge and the presence of his friend have been linked. Now if the friend is absent and returns after a long time and the man has to go alone for a walk, he will forget his friend gradually and the sight of the bridge will no more awake the memory of him. In this example one finds de-conditioning of a certain response to a particular stimulus. Just as a response can be de-conditioned, it is also re-conditioned. Conditioning, de-conditioning and re-conditioning of the response are governed by the same fundamental principles.

TRIAL AND ERROR

The method of trial and error is used in the following circumstances:

1. This method is used when the learner is completely motivated and can see the goal clearly. If the cat is not hungry she will not try to come out of the cage or leave to attempt after trying it without success for some time. The cat tries to come out of the cage simply because she is hungry and knows that there is food outside the cage. In the absence of the food outside the cage the cat will not try to come out of it. Thus it is clear that motivation as well as the presence of the goal is necessary for awakening the response in learning through trial and error.

2. The method of trial and error is used when perception alone or learned activities are not sufficient. If the cat could come out of the cage by merely moving in some direction, there was hardly any need of several trials and errors.

3. The method of trial and error is used when the learner fails to find the solution of the problem. In Thorndike's experiment the cat used trial and error method simply because she did not know how to come out of the cage. In the case of human beings in such situations, if the subject knows the solution of the problem, there is hardly any question of trial and error. It is only when he fails to find out the solution of the problem that he proceeds blindly, tries in various directions, commits errors, eliminates them and finally arrives at the successful response.

Thus the method of trial and error is widely used both by animals as well as by human beings. In the case of human beings however, this process is somewhat different, because man has better powers of perception, understanding, intelligence and language etc. Man uses the method of trial and error, but he also takes the help of language and other instruments in the process of learning.

INSIGHT

Insight is an important constituent in the solution of problems, and is found in the higher class of animals and human beings. It is the best method among the methods of learning.

According to the gestalt psychologists, a person can deduce the solution by insight if he preceives the situation as a whole. A German gestaltist, Kohler, prepared some simple problems for experiments with dogs, hens, monkeys, and chimpanzees. In an experiment a hungry animal was released from the house while some food was placed behind the fence adjoining the wall. Both the dog and the hen trotted around in the vicinity of the wall but as soon as they found the way out they made their exit and reached the food. This perception of the change in the meaning of the wall is insight. Before the insight the wall was an insuperable obstacle, but after insight it was no longer an obstacle but an object necessitating circumvention The result of insight is the understanding of new relations, the discovery of new patterns and the formation of new organisations.

The most famous experiments conducted by Kohler, in relation to insight were those that were carried out on chimpanzees. Some bananas were placed outside the cage of a chimp called Sultan, who was then given two sticks so constructed that they could be fitted together. Sultan tried to pull the bananas with the sticks, an effort which he kept up for an hour, but he got tired of the attempt and gave it up for playing. While playing he brought the two ends together and suddenly he got an idea which resulted in his fitting the smaller stick in the hole of the bigger one. He then used the two together to draw the banana inward. The two sticks disintegrated but he fitted them together again. He then pulled in everything within reach as if he were trying out his discovery. The next day he took far less time to fit the two together. It is a peculiarity of insight that once the solution is learnt, it is not forgotten though its memory may become hazy with the passage of time.

The above experiments make it quite obvious that learning by insight has certain characteristics of its own. They are briefly as follows:

1. Insight is sudden.
2. Insight alters perception.
3. Old objects appear in new patterns and organisation by virtue of insight.
4. Insight is relative to the intellectual level. The higher species of animals including human beings have more insight than the members of lower species.
5. In insight understanding is more useful than dexterity of hands.
6. In Woodworth's opinion, insight is sometimes hindsight and at others it is foresight. To quote him, "Foresight is seeing the way to the goal before taking it or perceiving the uselessness of a certain lead without trying it and hindsight is observing that a lead is good or bad after trying it. When the whole situation is clear and above board, there is a good chance for foresight, but when important characteristics of the situation have to be discovered by exploration and manipulation, hindsight is the best we can except.[1]
7. Previous experience is of assistance in insight, though the excess of previous experience does not necessarily increase insight because organised perception too is an essential factor in learning.
8. Maturity also effects insight as evidenced by the smoother working of insight in older age than in adolescence.
9. If the pieces essential for the solution of the puzzle are present together when perceived, insight comes about earlier.
10. Some psychologists say that learning by insight is associative learning. Insight appears suddenly after the manipulation of thoughts or objects for a small though significant length of time.
11. The insight gained in particular circumstances is of assistance in other circumstances. A verbal formula is generally extracted by people learning by insight and this formula is capable of facile application to other circumstances.

The above mentioned characteristics of learning through insight apply both to the human and animal learning. The solitary difference is the fact that a human being by virtue of his superior capacities of experiencing and understanding, observes relation between various objects quickly and sees the patterns concealed in them with alacrity. He is assisted in this by language. As a matter of fact insight occurs only when the learner perceives the related link hidden in the activity. The learning curve is altered suddenly due to insight Insight is impossible in an extremely unfamiliar problem, because familiarity is very necessary for insight. A student of literature will have no insight in any scientific problem because he does not know even the a b c of science. When the subject of study becomes a part of life, insight becomes easier. History

1. Woodworth, R.S., and Marquis, D.G., *Psychology,* Methuen and Co. Ltd., London, 1959, p. 507.

can be made alive by exhibitions, Geography by travelling, and Arithmetic by shop accounts. Familiarity is also important besides the theoretical study.

One example of human learning by insight will suffice. A student of Arithmetic tries hard to solve a difficult problem of Arithmetic. He tries many methods but fails to secure a solution. He gives up and lays it aside or goes to sleep. After some time suddenly or when he is awakened the solution suggests itself and he notes it down in his note-book. When he is confronted with similar problems in the future, he will have no difficulty in solving them.

The insight method is superior to imitation or conditioned response because both the latter methods take more time.

Trial and error emphasizes the acquisition of motor skill but in insight mental effort is stressed upon.

While insight depends upon perception, trial and error depends upon sensory motor co-ordination.

The person keeps an eye on the goal, in trial and error and all activity is goal-directed but insight is in the unconscious mind which exerts the most while the conscious activities are either very few or aimless.

Every new problem has to be tackled from the very beginning if the trial and error method is used. On the other hand, both generalisation and differentiation are present in insight, which adds to the possibilities of transfer of learning and the use of old insight in the solution of novel problems.

Students will be permanently helped by the use of the insight method of learning in place of the trial and error method in their study and other daily activities. They will also be able to conserve their energy. Suppose that a person has to arrange furniture in a room. An average person will determine the position of the table by using the trial and error method and shifting the table from place to place. An intelligent person will take up a position from where the whole room is visible, and imagine all the possible positions of the pieces of furniture in an imagined framework of the room and then place the respective pieces accordingly. But this does not mean that trial and error method is not meant for the intelligent. By no means is this so. In many novel situations progress is not possible without it. An intelligent person should use both these methods according to the needs of the situation.

CONDITIONS FAVOURABLE FOR LEARNING

Psychologists have experimented widely on different subjects of learning and prescribed the different factors favourable to each of them individually. Different conditions are ideal for different subjects of learning in the presence of which learning is quicker, more efficient and permanent and it is desirable to pay close attention to these conditions.

Generally speaking learning may be accepted to be of three types:

1. Cognitive, Perceptual and Conceptual.
2. Motor.
3. Affective-Conative.

It will be advantageous to describe the ideal conditions for the three types of learning individually.

Conditions favourable to cognitive learning

The cognitive, perceptual and conceptual types of learning is made more effective by the following conditions:

1. Beginning the work with enthusiasm: The absence of enthusiasm is a detrimental factor because while it prevails no perceptual or conceptual learning can be carried into effect. Learning is an active process and one which demands effort, the more enthusiastic a start, the more success is likely to attend the learning. Mere perception is inadéquate for the understanding of a perceptual subject while personal application gives better results and this is the reason for the importance given to experiments in the study of psychology. The slow speed in learning is largely not due to lack of intelligence but due to the absence of enthusiasm.

2. Distribution of the time of study: It is better to learn a subject by introducing intervals in the time of study than to study uninterrupted for any length of time. The study of any subject should always be conducted on the interval pattern of time distribution. Spaced learning is better than unspaced learning.

3. Presence of assisting factors: The presence of assisting factors is of advantage in both perceptual and conceptual types of learning. The assistant factors in conceptual learning are—dictionary, tables and graphs, preparing an outline, writing a precis, taking notes etc. For perceptual learning, the use of laboratory instruments in perception is desirable.

4. Whole or part learning according to the material to be learnt: The approach to learning whether as a whole or part, depends upon the capacity of the learner and the quantity of the subject to be learnt. The whole method is good for intelligent learners and in shorter subjects while the part method is used with advantage by the intellectually weaker learners in large subjects. Suppose we have to memorise a poem. Now, if we read the whole poem at once, the relation between the various lines will become clear and assist in the learning of it. If, on the other hand, the poem is difficult and lengthy, it would be better to divide it into parts than to study it as a whole. A student used to the part method of study finds the whole method inflexible and cumbersome. As a matter of fact, as far as the matter of studying book is concerned, it is better if the student first reads the whole book and then studies the chapters individually.

5. Assistant habits: These too are of some importance in learning. To succeed, the student should form the habits of consulting the dictionary, making a fixed time-table for study, not working when exhausted, using sketches, illustrations and briefs, studying alone in the morning and evening, repeating the lesson, preparing according to plan and with regularity, minimising lip movement and reading silently and concentrating the mind etc.

6. Other assisting conditions: Besides the conditions mentioned above the following conditions also assist in study—absence of fatigue and boredom, presence of average brain, mental capacities, and active attention to nervous or emotional tension, absence of economic worries, absence of worry about personal and family problems.

Conditions favourable to motor learning

The above mentioned conditions are also applicable to motor learning as much as they are applicable to cognitive learning. Practice is of great importance in motor learning, because it is the only way of obtaining skill. Reward is preferable to punishment but in some cases punishment may prove efficacious. Healthy rivalry also effects progress in motor as well as other learning but it should not be allowed to assume harmful proportions. The knowledge of result favours motor learning and it is an important condition because motor learning is not possible without it. In an experiment, ten students were made aware of the results while they were being trained. After some time, the light was switched off so that they no longer received any knowledge of the results. Consequently their learning curve steadily declined. The students were aware, upto the 200th time, of the results, but on subsequent occasions the light was switched off and they lost the results of their work. The knowledge of results create a tendency to repeat the successful work. While there is improvement in effort the enthusiasm is magnified or boosted. Similarly, it is better to vary the work or to provide rest intermittently than to work uninterrupted for too long a time.

Conditions favourable to affective-conative learning

Those conditions which assist mental learning also assist, to no small degree, the conative-affective learning. This type of learning can also make considerable use of practice. The learning of emotion is also significant in these kinds of learning. In affective-conative learning, as in all others, punishment is of consequence in the cessation of mistakes while the making permanent of a response or the encouragement of efforts is helped by reward. The elimination of the various types of tensions is also useful because they interrupt learning.

LEARNING CURVE

Learning is not always a continuous process. Sometimes there is a steady progress in learning while at other times there is hardly any progress at all. Sometimes one notices even retrogression in the process of learning. Thus when progress of learning in the case of a student of telegraphy is shown on a graph paper, one finds a learning curve rather than a straight line. In the learning curve given in the Fig. 10, the upper curve shows the speed of the words sent per minute. The rise of the curve shows the progress in sending or receiving of the words. At one end of the curve, one notices a plateau of learning.

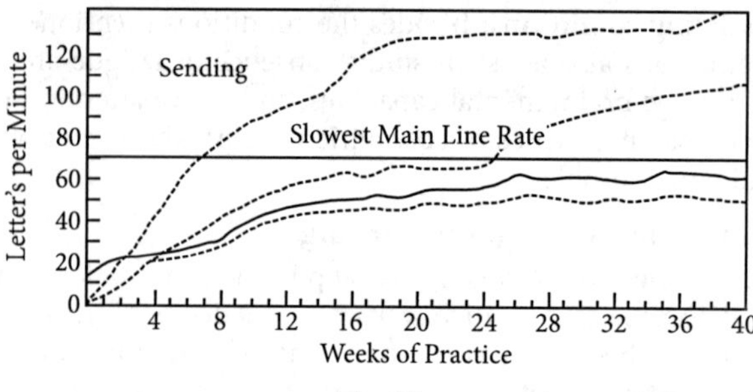

Fig. 10

Two facts are clear from the above figure of learning curve—initial spurt and plateau. The initial spurt can be seen in the curve of all types of learning. In the learning process there is a progress in the beginning and the speed increases with the increase of practice. In the subjects where insight is possible it increases learning very much. But in other types of learning the learner sometimes reaches a stage when the curves instead of going upwards seem to be horizontal and no progress is recorded for a certain distance. The flattened surface is called *plateau of learning*. In the Fig. 10 given above one finds the recieving curve rising gradually till it arrives at the physiological limit after which a flattened surface is noticed. The curve again rises after the plateau of learning. The reason for this rise is the co-ordination of the simpler habits with the complex ones. In the Fig. 10 given above there is no plateau in the sending curve.

Causes of Plateau in Learning

There can be several reasons for the plateau of learning, of which the most important are the following:

1. **Absence of the proper motive:** The most important cause of plateau is the absence of proper and sufficient motive. In the case of factory labourers it has been observed that their speed increases after getting sufficient bonus.

2. **Insufficient co-ordination of the simpler habits with the more complex ones:** As it has been said earlier, learning requires co-ordination of the simpler habits with the complex ones. When this co-ordination is achieved, progress is noticed. Hence insufficient co-ordination between simple and complex habits is one of the causes of plateau in the learning curve. This can be seen in the habits of sending the letters and words in telegraphy.

3. **The conflict of old habits with the new ones:** Learning requires new habits. Hence there is conflict of the old habits with the new ones *e.g.*, a man used to a particular method of learning will find it difficult to leave it and to adopt a new though more profitable method.

But when learning by a particular method reaches the physiological limit, further progress becomes difficult. In the case of the curve of time when a man reaches point after which he cannot progress it shows his physiological limit. As, for example, every sportsman has a physiological limit, beyond which he cannot break his records. If one finds no progress even when a certain task is done with the right process, one should suppose the existence of physiological limit. But it is very difficult to determine the right method. The daily amount of work put in by the labourer should not be taken as his physiological limit, because in the presence of new motives he shows more progress. Often one wonders as to how much more work he can put in due to some new motives. It has been seen that a young man who did not like to work for long hours, could work for 12 or 14 hours due to motivation from his beloved or wife etc. As a matter of fact man is the most dynamic and adjusting animal and this physiological limit is not the same with all men of the same age. On the same age level some men can always work more than others. Again, in the same person also, physiological limit is changing and flexible. It is a common place experience that a man can work more while young in comparison to his old age. Again, the physiological limit in different types of learning is also different with the same learner. Hence the physiological limit for a particular man in a particular type of learning at a particular stage can be determined only by experiment. But no one can deny that such a limit does exist and that the learner cannot improve upon it appreciably.

FACTORS IN HUMAN LEARNING

Many factors assist the process of learning. The main factors can be divided into the following classes:

(*a*) Psychological factors

(*b*) Physiological factors

(*c*) Physical factors

(*d*) Social factors.

(*a*) Psychological factors in learning

The most important factors in the process of learning are the psychological factors because ultimately learning is a psychological process. The following are these factors:

1. Generalization: Whenever an individual goes through many similar and comparable experiences he discerns the common element among them and on its basis formulates a general rule that has considerable influence on his future conduct.

2. Facilitation: Facilitation is an important factor in learning, because it is human nature that man finds it easy and convenient to learn activities that are simple and interesting.

3. Differentiation: Where the human individual generalizes on the basis of common experiences and objects he also distinguishes between dissimilar objects, or compares them in such manner as to bring out the dissimilarity.

4. Inhibition: Inhibition is an obstructive psychological element or factor in learning. As is evident from the name, in this some psychological element prevents or inhibits the process of learning of some special kind or obstructs it.

5. Integration: Whatever the individual learns he also integrates. This integration helps to improve one's insight into the subjects learnt. For example, it is essential to integrate the various activities learnt in cycling.

6. Expectancy: Expectancy is another important psychological factor in learning. Whatever we learn, the mental state immediately preceding it is called expectancy in which the individual is prepared and anxious to face the results of learning. Anticipatory reactions prevent the individual from many attractions.

(*b*) Physiological factors in learning

Learning is more a psycho-physiological process than a purely psychological one, or in other words, it also causes changes in physical activity. Important physiological factors in learning are the following:

1. Fatigue: In a state of fatigue the individual's capacity to learn is considerably reduced, and all that is learnt is also easily forgotten.

2. Drugs and intoxicants: Intoxication has the worst kind of effect on learning, and intoxicants are obstacles in learning. Some drugs help the process of learning because they improve the individual's capacity to learn.

3. Diseases: Disease, be it physical or mental, obstructs learning as it reduces the capacity to grasp and learn. On the other hand, health positively influences learning.

4. Excited physical condition: An. excited bodily state, arising out of emotion or some other cause, hinders learning.

5. Sex differences: Learning is not much influenced by sex differences, nevertheless men and women have facility in learning different works and activities because of their special physiological characteristics.

6. Difference of age and maturity: Before any particular activity can be acquired, it is necessary to attain to a particular level of maturity that can only come at a particular age level. Hence, age and maturity are important factors in learning.

(*c*) Physical factors in learning

Man lives and learns in a physical environment. Hence, many physical factors also assume some importance for the learning process. For example, purity or impurity of air, high or low temperature, quantity, direction and nature of light, noise, amount or percentage of humidity, arrangement of sunlight and other atmospheric conditions influence learning.

(*d*) Social factors in learning

Man is a social animal, all his activities being influenced by his social conditions. The main social factors that have an influence upon learning are the following:

(1) Imitation, (2) Suggestion, (3) Sympathy, (4) Praise and Blame, (5) Competition, (6) Co-operation. These social factors in learning have been described at various points in this book, hence the lack of any necessity to elaborate upon them at the present place.

COGNITIVE LEARNING

Cognitive psychology is the branch of psychology that includes the study of processes involved in sensing, perceiving, remembering and thinking. The cognitive point of view in psychology stresses the importance of purpose, knowing, understanding and reasoning in behaviour. It was first emphasized by the Gastalt psychologists in their investigation of perception, learning and thinking, particularly as they opposed traditional associationistic theories and methods of research involving these processes. For decades beginning in the 1930s and 1940s E.C. Tolman attempted to make the cognitive point of view compatible with behaviouristic methods in the study of animal learning. He used the maze as a model. He argued that the animal learns by developing a cognitive map of the apparatus. More recently cognitive psychology has come to be identified with the point of view that the organism is an information processing system analogous to electronic detection, storage and retrieval system.

Any theory of learning that postulates intervening variables of a cognitive nature in order to explain learning may be called cognitive theory. In contrast stimulus response theory emphasizes reinforced responses and avoids the use of central cognitive constructs as explanatory concept. An example of stimulus response theory is the theory of contiguous conditioning by Guthrie.

OPERANT CONDITIONING

Classical conditioning is the theory of conditioning propounded by Pavlov. Conditioning approaches have been classified as classical conditioning known by the name of Pavlov. Operant conditioning is known by the work of Skinner. Skinner's system of operant conditioning is a descriptive behaviourism which seems to establish the laws of behaviour through the study of operant learning. An operant is an emitted response, in contrast to respondents, a class of behaviour studied by the technique of classical conditioning utilized by Pavlov. B.F. Skinner, the American psychologist, pointed out in contrast to the classical conditioning by Pavlov that operants may be studied independently of the stimulus conditions that give rise to them. Indeed, in the usual case the stimulus may be unknown. The experimental arrangement for studying operant behaviour in the laboratory consists of what has come to be known as Skinner box. The Skinner box is an enclosure in which the animal is maintained free from distracting stimuli and in which he can receive a reinforcement upon emitting the proper operant. In the case of the rat, the operant is a bar press, and the reinforcement is a pallet of food. As many times as the rat presses the bar, a magazine will deliver a pallet and conditioning will proceed at a rapid rate. More recently the pigeon has come into extensive use in the Skinner box. In this case the operant is pecking at a dot, and the reinforcement is a measured bout of grain.

The fundamental law of operant conditioning is that if the occurrence of an operant is followed by a reinforcing stimulus, it will increase the rate of responding. The rate of responding is typically measured during a run to extinction, since the time consuming process of eating during the reinforcing series obscures the rate of responding. These reinforcers may be both positive and negative. Positive reinforcers are the stimuli such as food, water or sexual contact. These directly increase the probability of a response. On the other hand, negative reinforcers strengthen the probability of a response only when they are removed from the situation. Examples of negative reinforcers are electric shocks, bright lights, loud noises, etc.

The most important variable associated with reinforcement is the time schedule on which the reinforcing stimulus is delivered. Continuous reinforcement is the regular presentation of the reinforcement with each operant response. Intermittent reinforcement is irregular reinforcement delivered according to a predetermined time schedule. There are two important types of intermittent reinforcement, interval and fixed ratio. In interval reinforcement the reinforcement is given at certain fixed intervals of time such as every two minutes, regardless of how frequently the animal responds. Under such conditions the periodic reinforcement and the shorter intervals yield the highest rates of responding. On the other hand, in ratio reinforcement, the animal is given reinforcement after a certain number of responses. For example, the pigeon might get a portion of grain only after pecking ten times. In ratio reinforcement very high rates of responding can be maintained with high ratios, provided these are approached gradually. Reinforcement schedules may also be arranged as variable intervals or variable ratios under special research conditions. Secondary reinforcement occurs when a stimulus not originally a reinforcer becomes reinforcing through association with a reinforcing stimulus. For example, if a weak light is flashed each time the reinforcement is delivered upon the pressing of the bar by the animal the light will come to have reinforcing qualities. It can be used to maintain bar.

Factors of conditioning

What are the factors which are responsible for conditioning? Which elements are essential for its establishment? Factors controlling conditioning are given below in brief:

1. Effect of motives: For conditioning the stimulus must have the capacity to produce the response. In Pavlov's experiment, the dog was hungry. Therefore, it associated the bell with the food not food with the bell. Thus, the motive has an influence on the learning of conditioned response.

2. The time relations of the two stimuli: The time relations of the two stimuli are very important in conditioned response learning. It is essential that the new stimulus (cs) is given before the response ends. The natural order is that first new stimulus (cs) is given and then the old stimulus (ucs). In Pavlov's experiment the bell is rung before the food and food is given before the response to the bell ends.

3. Repetition of the stimuli: Food is given to the dog after the bell for many such relations. If the dog gets the food always with the bell then it begins to salivate to the ringing of the bell only. But once the response is conditioned, the two stimuli need not be repeated together continuously. In Watson's experiment when fear to a hare is developed in the child, producing a loud sound suddenly in the presence of hare once a while was enough for the child to remain afraid of the hare.

4. Absence of the distracting stimuli: Conditioning becomes difficult if some other stimulus is present with the two stimuli (cs and ucs). The lesser the distracting external stimuli are, quicker is the learning of conditioned response. In Pavlov's experiment, a sound-proof room was for this purpose.

Application of conditioning

In general the conditioning becomes easier, the higher the species of the organism is. Thus learning by this method should become easier in the case of human beings. But man is so complex an organism that stimuli which distract him and interfere in his learning are numerous. In spite of this, conditioning has a great importance in the learning of a child. Many of our responses are conditioned to particular things in childhood and these remain fixed even in the adulthood.

Stimulus generalisation or induction can be studied by a process of having the reinforcer delivered upon presentation of a positive stimulus and not delivered upon presentation, of a neutral or negative stimulus. For example, a tone of 256 Hz may be followed by a delivery of food, while a tone of 100 Hz will be followed by a delivery of food. The animal will learn to press the bar only in response to the positive tone. The limits of discrimination may be studied by gradually reducing the separation between the stimuli.

The learning of complex skills can be studied by a process called shaping. In shaping, a series of acts is gradually brought under control of the reinforcement by reinforcing each separate act in turn. Thus through shaping a seal can be taught to play "My country Tis of the"on a calliop by first reinforcing the animal for approaching the instrument, and then for pressing the first correct key and so forth until the complete performance can be runoff for a final single reinforcement.

Skinner's basic techniques of operant conditioning have been extended into the use of human teaching machines that operate on the principle of self-reinforcing learning. The use of reinforcement shows that human symbolic behaviour can be learnt according to the same principles that apply to more elementary forms of learning. Skinner and his associates have attempted to extend their method of operant conditioning into the field of behaviour therapy. In all his studies upon animals Skinner used a box like structure in which the correct operant of mechanism brings the animal a reward. This was known as Skinner box. In some boxes elaborate controls are maintained upon temperature, humidity, external sound, lights and orders. With small animals the operation in the Skinner box requires the pressing of a bar. With bird it requires the pecking of a spot.

CLASSICAL CONDITIONING

Experiment by pavlov

Many experiments have been done on animals in connection with conditioned response learning. First experiment was done by a famous Russian physiologist Pavlo, on dog around 1900. Pavlov made an opening in the dog's cheeks by operation so that drops of saliva from the salivary glands were collected in a test tube and the amount of saliva could be measured.

In this arrangement food is delivered to the dog through the window. A bell rings simultaneously or just before the food saliva begins to come out from the dog's mouth on the ringing of the bell. Saliva from the dog's mouth is collected in calibrated glass tube. This activates recording mechanism through a lever and the experimenter is able to know the number of drops of saliva fallen and whether the salivation was regular or not.

Pavlov wanted to prove that all learning is conditioning. Modern psychology does not accept this view. But no psychologist can deny the fact that conditioned response is a very important technique used in teaching many things to pet animals. For example, if a bear is to be taught dancing to the sound of the drum, it is made to stand on a hot plate and the drum is sounded as the animal lifts its feet. After some time it begins to lift its feet at the sound of the drum only. Many examples of the application of this method can be given in daily life. At the time when the husband normally returns home, the wife expects her husband coming at each sound of the bell on the road. Your hand always goes to the right pocket for the purse though it is in the left pocket, because the purse has been taken out from the right pocket so many times that the activities of taking out purse and pulling hand in the right pocket are associated with each other.

Another form of conditioning is negative adaptation, meaning learning not to make a response. This is, in fact, a form of conditioning. It is very useful in the change of habit. In negative adaptation a particular response is inhibited when a second response takes place. For example, if an adult male rat is given an electric shock as it reaches the female rats, it will gradually learn to turn away from the female rats. If a drug is mixed in the drink of alcoholics so that they begin to vomit, then they will tend to avoid the alcohol.

Extinction, discrimination and generalization

In the study of learning process a physiological psychologist aims to find out its physiological basis. What change takes place in the body or brain of the animal when after many trials in a puzzle box it learns to get out of the puzzle box? In other words, the aim is to find out the extent to which learning of the organism depends on his body and brain. In this connection physiological psychologists are specially interested in conditioned response learning out of the various methods of learning. Pavlov did important experiments on the dogs and found out what changes took place in brain structure during conditioning. Similarly, experiments have been conducted upon rats, cats and dugs on Avoidance conditioning. Instrumental learning and Discriminative learning. Physiological psychologists have attempted to find out the role of brain, receptors and muscles in these types of learning.

Experiments on conditioning

Most important experiments in connection with learning have been done on conditioning. Following three types of experiments fall in this area:

1. **Classical conditioning:** In classical conditioning experiments typically, a signal is presented to the animal (dog and cat). This is followed by an electric shock to some region of the animal body. For this procedure to be called classical conditioning, shock must always follow the signal.

2. **Conditioned emotional response:** Conditioned fear or any other conditioned emotional response may be observed during conditioning. For example, a rat is placed in a Skinner box and first given classical conditioning trials. A click is given and then follows the electric shock. After three minutes of this practice, one or two intense shocks are given. The emotional reaction which occurs to these shocks is well-established for a long period.

3. **Avoidance Conditioning:** Three different techniques are commonly used in this group: (*a*) Paw flexure, (*b*) Jumping response, and (*c*) Shuttle response. In paw flexure technique the animal learns to avoid the shock by raising its paw. This technique is also used to establish differential conditioning. In jumping response technique the animal learns to avoid the shock by jumping. In the third technique of avoidance conditioning, the animal (rat, cat, dog or monkey) is placed in a box having two compartments. The compartments are separated by a hurdle. The animal gets the shock while crossing the hurdle. The animal learns to avoid the shock by shutting over the hurdle.

DISCRIMINATION LEARNING

Intensive experiments have been done in physiological psychology on discriminative learning. In these experiments the animal learns to discriminate between two or more stimuli, conditioning methods are many times used in such learning. An attempt is made in these experiments to find out the neural mechanism of discriminative learning. The animal is trained to discriminate between specific stimuli. Then a test is made to see whether the animal remembers the discrimination learnt after a particular part of the brain has been removed. Though this process appears simple, it has many difficulties in practice. First of all, we must distinguish between the sensory capacity and learning capacity of the animal. Secondly, the method of learning is very important. Besides this, some other influences on the animal are also important. For example, the influence of habit is one of these. Again, it is not always possible to find out as to which structure of the brain is essential in learning. Influence of the following four factors has become clear from the experiments on discrimination learning:

1. Separate effect of brain lesions on sensory capacity and on learning capacity is observed.
2. Influence of specific method of learning is observed.

3. Different effects of a lesion on retention and relearning ability are seen depending on time after the operation.
4. Effects of the injury of various specific brain structures are different.

Intensive experiments on different animals have been done in the field of discriminative learning with respect to various sensory capacities involved. In somaesthetic sense, experiments have been done on Thermal discrimination, Roughness discrimination and Form discrimination. It has been inferred from these experiments that posterior parietal area of the cortex has a special role in somaesthetic discrimination learning. When this area is removed other parts of the brain may take over its function to a limited extent only.

In auditory discrimination, experiments have been conducted in connection with the intensity of sound, frequency of sound, tonal pattern and auditory localization in space. From all these experiments important facts have been found about auditory discrimination. Similar experiments have been conducted about visual sense. It has been attempted to find out as to which parts of the brain are responsible for the memory loss. In order to find out the functions of different regions of the brain, each separate part has been partially or totally removed and its effect on learning and retention has been observed. Important facts have been found out from these experiments.

VERBAL LEARNING

Verbal learning is cognitive, perceptual and conceptual type. It is made more effective by the following conditions:

1. Beginning the work with enthusiasm: The absence of enthusiasm is a detrimental factor because while it prevails no perpetual or conceptual learning can be carried into effect. Learning is an acting process and one which demands effort; the more enthusiastic a start the more success is likely to attend the learning. Mere perception is inadequate for the understanding of a perceptual subject while personal application gives better results and this is the reason for the importance given to experiments in the study of psychology. The slow speed in learning is due largely not to lack of intelligence but to the absence of enthusiasm.

2. Distribution of the time of study: It is better to learn a subject by introducing intervals in the time of study than to study uninterrupted for any length of time. The study of any subject should always be conducted on the interval pattern of time distribution. Speed learning is better than unspaced learning.

3. Presence of assisting factors: The presence of assisting factors is of advantage in both perceptual and conceptual types of learning. The assistant factors in conceptual learning are dictionary, tables and graphs, preparing an outline, writing a precis, taking notes, etc. For perceptual learning the use of laboratory instruments in perception is desirable.

4. Whole or part learning according to the material to be learnt: The approach to learning whether as a whole or part, depends upon the capacity of the learner and the quantity of the subject to be learnt. The whole method is good for intelligent learners and in shorter subjects while the part method is used with advantage by the intellectually weaker learners and in large subjects. Suppose we have to memorise a poem. Now, if we read the whole poem at once, the relation between the various lines will become clear and assist in the learning of it. If, on the other hand, the poem is difficult and lengthy, it would be better to divide it into parts than to study it as a whole. A student used to the part method of study finds the whole method inflexible and cumbersome. As a matter of fact, as far as the matter of studying books is concerned, it is better if the student first reads the whole book and then studies the chapters individually.

5. Assistant habits: These too are of some importance in learning. To succeed, the student should form the habits of consulting the dictionary, making a fixed time table for study, not working when exhausted, using sketches, illustrations and briefs.

PROBABILITY LEARNING AND PROGRAMMED LEARNING

According to the theory known as probabilistic functionalism, the psychological behaviour is best understood in terms of the probability of success in dealing with goal. Thus probability learning maintains that learning is determined by probability of response. Probability of response means the frequency of occurrences of a response relative to the theoretical maximum frequency of occurrences of that response, or class of responses under a given set of conditions. The table giving the frequency with which a variability is likely to occur under certain specified condition is known as probability table. Probability theory is based on certain assumptions concerning the uniformity of nature, laws of change, equality of opportunity of occurrence of certain events and complementary errors cancelling each other out if sufficient observations occur. Thus probability learning theory depends on trial and error.

As against the probability theory the programmed learning means learning according to programming by the psychologist. Programming includes the preparation of tapes, cards or other devices to be fed into a computing machine. Typically, programming consists of supplying information relative to the kind of operation wanted, the actual data to be completed, and the sequence of operations, if the latter are complex. For many of the more frequently used programmed operations, prepared tapes are available to instruct the machine. Contemporary psychologists are using programmed learning for various purposes.

SIGN GESTALT THEORY

Tolman has advocated this theory in explaining learning. The main features of this theory are given below:

1. Behaviourism: Tolman is a behaviourist and is against the introspection method. Here he agrees with the ideas of Watson.

2. Molar theory: Tolman's theory is molar, whereas Watson's theory is molecular. According to it, although group behaviour is made of individual behaviour, yet in defining behaviour, group should be emphasized and not the individual.

3. Goal directed behaviour: This group behaviour is taken by Tolman to be goal directed. According to it, every behaviour has some aim, and the form of it is established by the means of reaching the goal, obstacles, etc.

4. Changing behaviour: The group behaviour of an organism is not stable and fixed, but it is changing because it seeks to employ the least energy in behaving.

5. Definition of behaviour through intervening variables: Tolman has defined behaviour on the basis of intervening variables. These intervening variables are of two kinds—ircumstantial and individual. Intervening variables mean the events or conditions which are presented in stimulus and response. The intervening variables can be imagined on the basis of mutual relation between stimulus and response. Tolman calls stimulus a free intervening variable, and calls response a development intervening variable, because response depends on the stimulus. Although the relation between stimulus and response is subjective, yet it can still be measured in objective form. Intervening variables are not only physiological and physical, but are also psychological. There is place in them also for cognitive and purposive processes. Demand and expectations are two main intervening variables. On the basis of these, Tolman, like Gestalt psychologists, is called centralist. Here his ideas are quite different from the ideas of Watson who is a behaviourist. While Watson's viewpoint is physiological, the viewpoint of Tolman is psychological. While Watson regards behaviour to be only mechanical, for Tolman, it is goal directed.

Basic principles in sign gestalt theory

Osgood divides the theory of Tolman into the following four parts:

1. Motivational principles: Before the theory of Tolman was presented, most of the psychologists were of the opinion that an organism repeated only those actions which satisfy its motivations. Hull is of the opinion that organism performs some actions to remove the tension which is produced on presentation of some need. It decreased its tension. In this way, these psychologists regard reinforcement as something necessary in learning. On the other hand, according to Tolman, while reinforcement is necessary for activity, it is not needed in learning. To prove his idea, Tolman made a learning experiment. In this experiment, some rats had to learn a puzzle. Experiments on three groups of rats were made. The rats of the first group were fed after they were taken out of the puzzle-box. The rats of the second group were not fed after they were taken out of the box. The rats of the third group were not fed in some of the first attempts but they were fed in some of the last attempts. It was seen as the result of these experiments that the rats of the first group in comparison to the other groups, learnt to come out of the puzzle-box in the shortest time. The rats of the second group could come out of the puzzle-box only after making many efforts. The rats of third group began to show progress in learning as soon as the feeding began and started coming out of the box very soon. Through this experiment, the fact was clear that, although the rats learnt to come out of puzzle-box even in the absence of a reward, yet the reward helped them in learning to come out of the box. Here Tolman, laying great stress on the learning of the rats of the second group, has said that they could learn to come out of the puzzle-box even in the absence of a reward or motivation. It is clear that motivation is not unavoidable for learning. On the other hand, Tolman acknowledges the effect of motivation in learning. It can be seen, in connection with the rats of the third group, that although they had learnt to come out of the puzzle-box, they were yet not expressing it in the absence of motivation.

The experiments made by Reynold, Spence and Lippit have raised a doubt in the truth of the conclusions reached by Tolman in his experiments given above. Spence and Lippit also made experiments on the rats through the medium of a special kind of puzzle. The rats in the puzzle were constantly allowed the facility of reaching food and water. Through many experiments, the rats were taught that in the puzzle-box there was food to their left and water to their right. After teaching this, the rats were kept thirsty for some time and then were let loose in the puzzle-box. As soon as they were free, they at once ran towards the route to water. Next time they were kept hungry for some time therefore when they were allowed to enter the puzzle-box, this time again they ran towards water. In explaining this behaviour of the rats, Spence and Lippit stressed the fact, that in the first instance, the rats had taken the route to water, and therefore on the second occasion too, although they were hungry, yet they ran towards water because a necessary cognitive structure to take the route to food could not be formed in them. This disproved the idea that an organism learns with the help of demand and expectation.

Through the above experiment, the learning theory of Tolman appears doubtful. Enough experimentation to reach a definite conclusion could not yet be made.

2. Associative principle: According to Watson, an organism learns to respond to a specified stimulus. An organism learns the signs to achieve some specified goal. Its behaviour cannot be explained by regarding it a mere chain of responses. When a rat is put into such a puzzle-box in which there is food in the centre, it learns the different signs to reach the food. By learning in this way, a cognitive picture of the situation is formed in its brain. To prove the validity of the sign gestalt theory, Tolman has referred to many experiments on place, learning and reward, expectation, etc. It was proved through experiments on place learning, made by Tolman and his companions, that a rat recognises the various signs on its route to reach a goal. In one experiment, there were three loutes of different distances to reach the food. Now, when the rat was let loose, it learnt to reach the food by the shortest route. When the route was closed, it learnt to reach the food by a big route. This experiment shows that a rat also follows the minimum effort theory in learning. It aims at discovering the shortest way to reach the goal.

As has been said before, Tolman, to prove the validity of his theory, refers to the reward experiment. A psychologist, named Tiklepaugh, in one of his famous experiments, showed some monkeys two pots, one containing a banana and the other containing nothing. Both the pots were covered. Now, when a monkey was given an opportunity, he always recognised the pot containing banana and opened it. Later the banana was removed from the pot and some beat root leaves were placed in it instead, which a monkey does not like. When the monkey opened the banana pot and found the leaves in it, he did not make some specified response, but only response to specified signs.

3. Reinforcement principle: Thorndike and Pavlov lay special stress on the effect of reinforcement in learning. According to Tolman, learning is high when the sign significant expectation is strong. If expectation of an organism is confirmed, through some special signs, the sign gets fixed in its brain. On the other hand, if the expectation, through some sign, is non-confirmed, the sign becomes weak. In this way, an organism recognizes the importance of some specified sign through confirmation and non-confirmation Tolman, while explaining this fact, has said that the strength of field expectancy depends on various intervening variables such as immediate action, motivation and repetition, etc.

Osgood has raised the following two objections against the reinforcement principle of Tolman:

(*a*) How can a cognitive relation be established among expectations?

(*b*) Expectation for an organism comes after an action, how, therefore, can it be weakened or strengthened by its former attainment? Tolman has given no satisfactory answer to these objections raised by Osgood.

4. Action principle: This is Tolman's fourth theory in learning. According to it, there should be an adequate demand on the part of an organism to learn some action. Along with his demand, the experience of an organism also helps in discovering an adequate response. Due to its experience, an organism has some expectation from its specified response. If this expectation is confirmed by this response, the organism learns this response. In this way, according to Tolman learning depends on demand and expectation.

Evaluation of Tolman's theory

Through an argumentative analysis of the different theories of learning, Tolman noted that every theory was based on the study of a special problem and no attention is paid to any other problem. Therefore, in order to save his theory from being one-sided, Tolman acknowledges different standards of learning. Among these, learning through a connecting response belongs to be lowest standard, because it only establishes a relation between some stimulus and response. Trial and error theory of a higher standard than this, because in this theory, one of the many presented alternatives has to be chosen. Learning through insight is the learning of the highest standard. According to Tolman, all these standards of learning can be explained through the Sign Gestalt theory. In this connection, Tolman advocates the following three theories to explain learning.

1. Capacity Law.
2. Law relation to the nature of material.
3. Law relating to the manner of presentation.

Tolman has mentioned many sub-laws to the above laws. According to him, learning depends on the learning capacity of an organism and the complexity of learning. Individual differences are found in the ways of learning due to the difference in learning capacity of different organisms. In other words, organisms with different kinds of learning capacity acquire different standards of learning.

REINFORCEMENT THEORY

Clark H. Hull presented the reinforcement theory to explain learning. This theory therefore is also called the Hull theory. Hull gave no importance to consciousness in learning. He has presented Behaviourist and Instrumentalist explanation of learning. Practice is of special significance in instrumental learning. Hull has explained complex learning on the basis of simple learning as the other behaviourists have been doing. But, on the other hand, Hull has an opinion different from that of other behaviourists like Watson, etc., in many things. For example, Watson, in the law of results by Thorndike, does not accept purpose and insight, etc., in learning; whereas Hull accepts their importance in learning. Contrary to the Tolman's view, Hull does not accept the view that a sign or significance is learnt in learning. According to him, in learning an organism learns to respond to a stimulus. An organism collects learning gradually on the strength of practice. According to Hull, the process of organism, affecting collection, depends on its practice. In this way, his theory is called goal gradient or reinforcement gradient. It can said to be a refined form of the law of effect of Thorndike.

Like Watson, Hull also gives a molecular explanation of the behaviour in learning. Here his opinion is against the opinion of Tolman, but Hull has regarded the molar and molecular viewpoints as objective and not subjective.

According to Hull, the importance of motivation in the process of learning is very great. Motivation does the work of a drive in organism. An organism cannot learn anything in the absence of motivation. It is motivation on account of which it performs some specified action. This motivation, on the one hand, forms a habit resulting from practice and, on the other hand, it is a source of practice in performance. When an organism lies inactive, it does lack practice, but there is an absence of motivation. This motivation may be about food, freedom from some painful condition or about any other thing. As soon as motivation arises, the organism becomes active. In the presence of motivation, the actions of an organism are goal directed. When it gets a reward in acting in a particular way, it repeats the same action and, in this way, the specified response is confirmed by the reward in the form of motivation.

On the other hand, the tendency of repeating the responses, which are not rewarded, is weakened. In this way, reward strengthens the relation between stimulus and response in an organism. It is this reward which is called reinforcement. Hull has accepted reinforcement of two kinds—primary and secondary. Primary reinforcement means those stimuli which affect some motivation in a direct form. For example, for motivation of hunger, food does the work of reinforcement, and the action, which brings food to the organism, is repeated in the organism. The other kind of reinforcement is secondary, an example of which is watering of the mouth on seeing food.

Goal-gradient or reinforcement-gradient is the central point of Hull's theory. His theory is therefore called reinforcement theory. The attainment of goal brings stability to the relation between stimulus and response. It reduces the tension of the organism which helps it in learning the specified response. For example, when a hungry rat is let loose in a puzzle-box, it learns to take the shortest route to food, because it brings a ready reward.

As has been said before, Hull, like Thorndike, accepts the importance of practice in learning. When an organism repeats the specified response to some stimulus again and again, a close relation is established between them. According to Hull, along with practice, reinforcement is also necessary here. In the absence of reinforcement, a mechanical practice alone is of no use. Needless to say that Hull's opinion here is different from Throndike's mechanical theory of learning. Hull also agrees with other behaviourists that learnings of all kinds can be explained on the basis of connecting response. Hull has presented 16 laws to explain the different aspects of learning, among which the laws of motivation and reinforcement the chief laws and the other laws are derived by these two laws. Hull has expressed his theory with the help of the following formula:

$$SER = f\ (H \text{ and } D)$$

In this formula, capacity of response has been shown by the letter S, to determine practice by H and motivation by D. Middle reinforcement have special importance in the process of learning, Hull has accepted physiological and physical reinforcements in learning. He does not accept reinforcements of other kind.

According to Hull, there are two main aspects of the transfer of learning, one of which is limited by stimulus and the other by response. The transfer limited by stimulus has been explained through generalisation, and the transfer limited by response is explained through habit family hierarchy. When an organism fails in some situation due to some specified response, it tries some other response which previously brought success to it.

Similarity in the theories of hull and tolman

As is clear from the aforesaid explanation of Hull's theory, there is no concept, specially new, in it except the concept of reinforcement. So far as the question of the importance of reinforcement is concerned, the psychologists do not deny it. But Hull could not prove his theory through experiments.

A psychologist, named Finan, through his experiments has supported the Hull's theory of reinforcement in learning. But, in opposition to Hull, Tolman does not consider reinforcement as necessary for learning. The main objection raised against reinforcement theory was that if a response of an organism in learning is established by reinforcement, how does it learn in the condition of pain. Secondly, Hull's theory, however, true it may appear about the learning for rats, cannot be taken to be true about the learning for a man. Hull has not been able to give a correct answer to these objections. The importance of his theory lies in the fact that he encouraged various new experiments to be made about learning.

Hull and Tolman, both try to tell about the rats as why they make a choice on presentation of alternatives at the time of discovering a route to the puzzle-box and what they learn in doing so. In this way, their theories are the attempts to explain 'why' and 'what'. In the process of learning, there is a response to some stimulus. Various intervening variables work in the establishment of a relation between stimulus and response. Hull and Tolman. both accept the importance of these intervening variables and try to explain them. Both these psychologists consider learning different from performance.

Difference between the theories of Hull and Tolman

In spite of the above similarities, there are the following differences between the theories of Hull and Tolman:

1. Hull has explained the process of learning on the basis of reinforcement. According to him, the organism picks up a practice of repeating a specified action on account of reinforcement The organism learns a proper response to the goal of reinforcement. On the other hand, according to Tolman, the organism learns, not the response, but the sign or significance of a stimulus. In other words, it learns the kind of response which should be made on presentation of a particular kind of sign. In this way, it learns a cognitive pattern. This very cognitive pattern directs it to its future response.
2. According to Hull, learning can be explained by defining Thorndike's law of effect. On the other hand, Tolman's law of effect is the law of performance and learning cannot be explained through it.
3. Hull has regarded incentives necessary for learning. On the other hand, although Tolman accepts the importance of incentive in learning, yet he does not consider it necessary for it.
4. According to Hull, reinforcement theory works at the root of all kinds of learning. According to Tolman, there are various ways of learning, all kinds of learning cannot be explained through any one theory.
5. Hull and Tolman, both accept the different forms of intervening variables. According to Hull, all intervening variables have one and the same form, because learning also has only one form. On the other hand, because Tolman accepts many forms of learning he accepts variables also to possess many forms. While Hull has accepted only

the physiological and physical variables, Tolman, besides these, accepts also the psychological variables.

It is clear from the aforesaid theories of Hull and Tolman that while Hull has given special importance to stimulus, Tolman has given importance to response. Otherwise, in other things, both these psychologists have been supporting one and the same fact in two ways. Whereas Hull's attempt to explain the laws of learning through mathematics provides a scientific basis of the theory of learning; Tolman has, by accepting various forms of learning reduced the controversy among different theories.

QUESTIONS FOR EXERCISE

1. Define learning and show its relationship with maturation.
2. Describe Thorndike's laws of learning.
3. Explain principal forms of learning.
4. Write a short note on Cognitive Learning.
5. Explain operant conditioning and discuss its application.
6. Explain classical conditioning and describe important experiments on it.
7. Write a short note on Discrimination Learning.
8. Write a short note on Verbal Learning.
9. Write a short note on Probability Learning and Programmed Learning.
10. Explain modern theories of learning profounded by Tolman and Hull.

22

Transfer of Training

WHAT IS TRANSFER OF TRAINING?

It is a matter of common observation that learning to do one thing makes it easier to perform some other action. The son of a trader is sometimes good at arithmetic in class because he is required to look after the accounts of his Father's establishment. When learning from one purpose is also utilised in another situation not originally envisaged in a training, it is called transfer of training. In this manner, knowledge of mathematics helps in the study of physics and chemistry. In the figure given below, the difference between the learning curves of two groups as a result of transfer of training is illustrated. One of the groups has had pencil paper training for an overall twentyfour times while the other has had none.

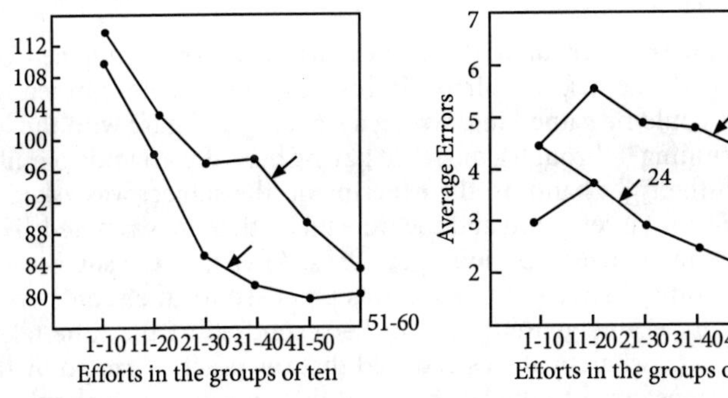

Fig. 10

Kinds of transfer

Transfer of training is normally of the following two kinds:

1. Positive transfer of training: In this transfer, training of one kind has positive or beneficial influence upon learning of another kind and learning is assisted thereby. For example, in an experiment, one group was taught Latin while another group was not, members of either group having common interests and similar level of intelligence. Now both the groups were put in the same class and taught by one single teacher who endeavoured to teach them

English. It was found that the group knowing Latin picked up the language and acquired proficiency in it much earlier than did the other group that was ignorant of Latin. The reason for this was that the training in Latin was positively transferred to the learning of English.

2. Negative transfer of training: In this the training acquired in one kind of learning has a negative influence upon learning in some other connection, or in other words, it obstructs this learning. For example, individuals interested in wrestling are often found to be weak in academic pursuits because wrestling deprives them of much of their energy and they have little left for any intellectual labour. In this way, wrestling proves to be obstructive to academic learning.

In certain cases, training or learning has no influence or effect at all, just as the learning of a Hindi poem has not the least effect on memorising facts of geography. In such contexts there is no transfer of training. In this way, transfer of training should involve at least some obvious influence or effect. If that effect is favourable then it is positive but if it is disadvantageous it is negative.

EXPERIMENTS PERTAINING TO TRANSFER

In the recent past, psychologists have made extensive tests and experiments concerned with the transfer of training and education, these efforts throwing considerable light on the subject under review. The major experiments in this connection have been conducted on sensory motor transfer, transfer concerning memory, reasoning and ideation, subjects in school, problem solving etc.

1. Sensory motor transfer: Starch[1] made experiments concerning sensory motor transfer with the help of mirror. In his experiment he examined the expediency that could be gained in drawing a star shaped figure with the left hand while examining it through a mirror, it having been drawn under similar conditions with the right hand. In the experiment, the subject was asked to draw the figure with his left hand and the time taken therein was noted. This practice was continued over a period of ten days. After this, the subject was asked to use the other hand, and this too was practised for the same period of time. In this it became aparent that in the second effort the time taken was appreciably less, whereby it was deduced that the practice gained by the right hand was transferred to the left hand. In this connection, it should be mentioned that experiments conducted by Evert[2], Munn[3] and Bray[4] have elaborated this transference in a different sense. They came to the conclusion that progress in the above experiment is not the outcome of any transference of training from the right to the left hand, but rather that this influence is

1. Starch, D., in *Psychological Bulletin*.
2. Evert, P.H., *Pedagogical Memory*.
3. Munn, N.L., in *Journal of Educational Psychology*.
4. Bray, E.L., in *Journal of Experimental Psychology*.

the outcome of increase in the subject's self-confidence, improvement in his understanding of the problem, improvement of method, etc.

Webb[1] experimented with the paths of a hide and seek and came to the conclusion that the practice of one sensory motor activity can be transferred to another sensory motor activity although the extent of this transference depends upon similar elements in the two activities as well as upon their essential points of difference. In this experiment Webb tried to transfer the practice of one particular maze to the tackling of five other mazes. To begin with, the man or animal was trained in tackling one particular maze and was then led to four other mazes and the effect of previous training observed in the skill transferred to the latest tackling. After this round of activity had been completed the subject was allowed to practise upon one maze and the influence of practices on other mazes on this one maze activity was observed. It was observed that in either condition learning in one maze definitely helped in the learning of other mazes. In this experiment Webb found the extent of transference of learning varying from 20 to 77% among various individuals.

2. Transference concerning memory: Among the experiments concerning transference in memory those of W. G. Sleght are important. In his experiments he adopted the controlled group method, a group of female students being divided into four small groups. The first controlled group was not imparted any training. Another group learnt a poem for twelve days for a period of one half hour every day. The third group worked for a similar period for an equal number of hours but instead concentrated upon population and import-export tabulated figures. The fourth group of women spent the same period of time for twelve days in trying to learn historical, scientific and literary prose tracts read out to them. It was a kind of oral learning for them. These four groups were examined before and after the following elements being examined in the process:

1. Learning names and dates verbally.
2. Remembering non-sensical words verbally.
3. Remembering poetic pieces both read out by the teacher as well as read out individually.
4. Remembering prose tracts both read out by the teacher as well as read out individually to one self.
5. Remembering the fundamental idea of a poetic piece verbally introduced.
6. Remembering the order of nine numerals seen once.

The above experiments concerning the transference of memory yielded the following facts:

1. Every group showed progress only in the matter practised upon.
2. Learning of one kind had sometimes a favourable and sometimes an adverse influence upon learning of another kind.

1. Webb, L.W., *Psychological Source*, N.Y., 1917.

3. Learning poetry had beneficial influence upon the learning of tables, meaningless words and prose whereas it had adverse influence upon the learning of the idea of a poetry piece or words.

Sleight came to the following conclusions:

1. Practice does not lead to any appreciable improvement in the general memory, and neither is there any evidence of working of a general memory.
2. Related and unrelated complex memory functioning came to light in very large numbers.

Although some other experimenters have discovered greater advantageous transfer of memory than Sleight has found, yet these tests do not prove that practice can help in the development of memory. The truth of the matter is that the functioning of memory is a complex process and the outcome of transfer depends upon the specific activity practised.

Memory transference was experimented upon by William James even before Sleight. James learnt by heart some 158 lines from Victor Hugo's poem *Satyr* and noted the time taken in the effort. Then for 38 days, for a period of twenty minutes a day, he tried to commit to memory the first book of Milton's *Paradise Lost*, which contains almost 800 lines. After this effort he learnt another 158 lines from *Satyr*, and in this case he found that the time taken in obtaining the same skill as in the first case he took more time than had taken in memorising the first 158 lines, before he had turned to Milton. Following this, James made memory experiments upon four other individuals. Three of them showed economy of time in memorising information after they had learnt one specific piece for a long time, but the fourth individual showed no appreciable progress as it took him the same time as it had taken him before the practice. James's experiments in this direction, prove, or at least indicate that the act of memorising cannot be improved upon through practice, although it has been observed that Jame's experimentation made no provision for the use of a scientific method of observation.

3. Transference of perception: In an experiment conducted by Thorndike and Woodworth in 1901, it was observed that in estimating the area between 10 and 100 square centimetres educated or trained individuals showed an improvement of 1/3 over the estimate of an area between 150 and 300 square centimetres. But another individual was given to practise upon estimating lines between half and one half inches long, and it was found that he showed no skill had been obtained when he was asked to estimate lengths between six and twelve inches.

4. Transfer concerning reasoning: Educational psychologists have also made important experiments concerning transfer. W.H. Winch[1] made a study

1. Winch, W.H., Transfer or Improvement in Reasoning in School Children, *British Journal of Psychology*.

of the transfer of school children's skill in solving arithmetical problems to the solution of other problems of reasoning. In this experiment, one definite group of students was put to practising the solution of arithmetical problems for ten weeks while another group of equal strength was allowed to work according to the regular curriculum with the exception of arithmetical learning. Of the two groups, the one with training in mathematics or arithmetic showed 30 per cent results. On the basis of this and other similar experiments it is believed that training in mathematics is transferred to other reasoning problems, and that much training helps in the solutions of rational problems.

5. Transference concerning ideation or ideals: Using some of Aesop's fables as the basis of his tests Barrel examined the extent to which they help in the development of ideals. In this test two experimental and controlled groups of children and adults were selected. Between the first and second tests, lessons were read out to the experimental groups for periods varying between 12 and 20 minutes and the group was trained in analysis, imagination and generalization. Following examination it was observed that the experimental group made better progress than the controlled group.

6. Transfer concerning problem solving: Educational psychologists have also studied the question of transfer in the field of problem solving, although no distinct conclusions have been reached. In this connection S. T. Gray[1] made an experiment upon the transfer of code substitution. In this experiment the code substitution of two comparative groups was made the basis of tests. Following this, one of the two groups was taught a new code in which the logical connections were emphasised. The results of the test indicated that the group trained to observe rational relationships in its code performed its work some 20 per cent better than the other group.

Judd's[2] experiment is one of the famous ones among the many concerned with the solution of problems. In this it was required to strike a target in water For this two groups of children were selected from the fifth and sixth grades. For the experiment one of the two groups was made aware of the occurrence of refraction in water of light rays, while the other group was allowed to proceed in ignorance of this fact. To begin with, both groups were asked to aim at and strike a target 12 inches below the surface of water. It was found that neither group showed any appreciable superiority or efficiency over the other in this practice. Now the target was raised to a height of four inches above the surface of water and again the students were required to aim at it. Now the trained group did better in their performance than did the untrained group. Judd came to the conclusion that the trained group had been able to establish a correlation between their first practice and the second, and had drawn upon their initial training as a result of which they had performed better than their

1. Gray, S.T., A comparison of two types of learning by means of a substitution tests, *Journal of Educational Psychology*.
2. Judd, C.H., in *Educational Psychology*.

untrained friends. Judd's conclusions have been supported by experiments of others such as Ruedigear[1], Mendrickson, Schroeder[2] and Gates etc.

7. Transfer between educational subjects: As a general rule it is believed that some subjects, as compared with others, help in disciplining the mind, and their study helps in the study of other subjects. Educational psychologists have made many experiments to measure this transference value of different subjects. Thorndike[3] conducted an experiment upon 8000 students in 1922-23, in which the subject examined was the influence of one year's study in a high school upon intellectual activity. Tests made before the study and after it in this experiment showed that in the tests following the study 23 extra points were gained over the score made before the study. In this experiment it was also observed that some 50 per cent of the progress made is due to the student's experience of examinations and the other 50 per cent the outcome of one year's study of the curriculum. In this study, too, some students showed better progress than others. The best student who constituted one per cent of the entire group improved to the extent of 20 and one half points, while one per cent of the least progressive children showed improvement only to the extent of one and half points. From this it was concluded that the intelligence of children also influences their progress in the study of different subjects.

Many of the educationists believe that a study of grammar is very important for mental discipline. For an examination of this belief, in one experiment, children on common level of intelligence who belonged to the seventh grade were divided into two groups. Now the children in both groups were examined through several measuring scales. Following this one of the two groups was taught grammar for a period of three months, while the other group was taught to compare words and language. After the period was over, the groups were again rigorously examined, it being revealed thereby that the group that was taught grammar progressed in the faculty of distinguishing similarity and dissimilarity while its progress in other faculties and abilities was in no way better than that achieved by the other group.

W.H. Winch[4] conducted experiments in order to find out the extent to which a practice of adding and subtracting or problem solving in arithmetic lead to the development of a sense of logic in the subject. In the experiment, boys aged 10 and possessing similar ability in the solution of logical problems concerning arithmetic were taken, and divided into two groups. One of the two groups was taught the solution of arithmetical problems for ten days, for a period of thirty minutes a day. The other group was given practice in drawing.

---

1. Reudigear, W.C., The indirect effect of mental function through education, *Educational Review*, 36, 1908.
2. Mendrickson and Schroeder, Transfer of training in learning to hit a submerged target, *Journal of Educational Psychology*, 32, pp. 205-213, 1951.
3. Thorndike, E.L., Mental discipline in high school studies, *Journal of Educational Psychology*.
4. Winch, W. H., Further work in numerical accuracy in school children.

Following the ten days, the two groups were examined in a manner intended to reveal reasoning ability in arithmetic, the examination yielding similar results for both groups. These results led to the conclusion that no distinct and precise relationship between the logic in arithmetic and addition-substruction or problem solving can be established. In another experiment concerning the study of mathematics as a source of mental development it was seen that the studying of descriptive geometry led to a 32 per cent improvement in the understanding of geometry but only a 7 per cent improvement in the understanding of other subjects.[1]

In 1921—24, H.D Rugg[2] conducted experiments to study the influence of Latin learning on the further learning of English. It became obvious from this study that children knowing Latin showed a progress in learning English of some ten per cent over other children who were ignorant of Latin. It was concluded thereby that the knowledge of Latin helps in the speaking or learning of English. Children who had learnt Latin for one year showed that they were better in learning English than other children who had not studied Latin. The former secured better marks in the subject. This was found to be particularly true in the speaking of English. It was also found that this was true not only of English but also of Spanish and French, composition in which is facilitated by a knowledge of Latin. But this difference in the progress of those who know Latin and those who do not was not apparent over a long period of time. Experiments of Clifford Woody showed that even the knowledge of French can help in the learning of English, although French does not help in improving English sentence structure or selection of words. It was consequently concluded that the knowledge of some languages may prove to be efficacious in the learning of other languages.

Thorndike made most extensive experiments in studying the transferability of school subjects. In one of his experiments he took some 13,500 students of the tenth, eleventh and twelveth classes. In this experiment the object was to determine the influence upon the reasoning power of the study of different subjects. The following influence of a one year study of ten subjects upon success or achievement in examination was evident from the experiment.

The following conclusions are to be drawn from the table given on p. 267 :

1. There is very little difference in the transference of the power of general reasoning between such administrative subjects as Latin, arithmetic, etc., and such practical subjects as physical education, cooking, drawing etc.
2. The importance of all subjects on the power of reasoning or logical thinking is in fact equal, and there is no subject better or worse than any other.

1. Ref. *Journal of Educational Psychology*, Vol. II, No. 5, 1911.
2. Rugg., H.D., Educational Determination of Mental Discipline in School Studies, *Educational Psychology Monographs.*

S. No.	Subject group	Influence of achievement in examination
1.	Algebra, geometry, trignometry	+2.99
2.	Civics, economics, psychology, sociology	+2.89
3.	Chemistry, physics, general science	+2.71
4.	Arithmetic, accounting	+2.60
5.	Physical training	+0.83
6.	Latin, French	+0.79
7.	English, history, business, art	+0.00
8.	Shorthand, cooking, sculpture	–0.14
9.	Zoology, agriculture	–0.48
10.	Business	–0.48

The following summary, made by Pedro T. Oreta, is based on the various conclusions of tests concerning the transference of school subjects between 1890 and 1935:

1. 22% tests showed very distinct and special transferability.
2. 48% tests showed appreciable transferability.
3. 9% tests showed very little transference.
4. 3.9% tests showed no transference.
5. 7.2% tests showed transference along with obstacles.
6. 3.9% tests showed transference in spite of obstacles.

It is evident from the above summary that it is not possible to call the study of any one subject definite or administrative in the learning of other school subjects. While some tests have revealed some degree of transference, other tests have shown negative transference or even complete absence of it. It was only in a very small minority of tests that a transference of 92.9 per cent was recorded. And in 5.4 per cent of cases, the degree of transference that was recorded was accounted for by the difference in circumstances under which the tests were held. Hence, the following are the present conclusions regarding the transference of school subjects:

1. Some branches of learning are positively influenced by practice in some other subjects.
2. Study of some subjects does not help the study of other subjects in the least.
3. Study of some subjets proves to be an obstacle in the learning of some other subjects.
4. Of all the principles put forward concerning the phenomenon of transference not one has proved to have any universal validity.
5. Rote learning of any subject does not lead to its transference in any other subject.

THEORIES CONCERNING THE TRANSFER OF TRAINING

Ancient theory

The principle of transfer of training took birth with the formal education system. According to this system, there are some subjects the study of which strengthens the faculties of the mind and which in turn help the study of other subjects. It was believed, for instance, that the study of Sanskrit, Latin and Mathematics disciplined the mind which then found it easier to grasp other subjects communicated to it. These notions of the formal education system were based upon faculty psychology which conceived of the mind as a conglomerate of various powers of faculties such as observation, memory, reasoning, decision, etc. Hence, it was essential that subjects should be chosen with a view to strengthening these faculties. The faculty of reasoning, for example, was believed to be strengthened by the study of mathematics, and that has helped the consequent study of law, philosophy and all such subjects that required the constant application of logical thinking.

Modern theories

Modern psychology does not give any credence to the faculty psychology. Hence, modern psychologists abandoned the above elucidation of the principle of transfer of training, and replaced it with a multiplicity of explanations and principles. The following four theories are among the more important of them:

1. Thorndike's theory of identical elements: According to Thorndike's opinion, identical elements are transferred from one situation to another situation, as for example, a knowledge of psychology helps in solving labour trouble and unrest.

2. Judd's theory of generalization: According to this view the recipient of one kind of training generalizes the experience, knowledge and habits attained in it, and utilizes this product in the new conditions created in the learning of another form of training. And, this transference is possible only if the recipient observes some similarity of elements between the two kinds of conditions.

3. Sandiford's theory: According to Sandiford, there is no essential difference between the theories of Thorndike and Judd, as both have said the same thing, *viz.*, that due to the similarity or identity of elements, training in one circumstance leads to its transfer in the other. According to Sandiford, this transfer depends upon the individual's intelligence as only the perceptive individual can observe an identity of elements in two circumstances and make generalisations. It is his view that the power of generalization is indicative of the individual's intelligence. He conducted tests to substantiate this view that the intelligent student can assimilate facts that he has gleaned from the perusal of newspapers in his paper on the languages whereas the unintelligent or backward student cannot utilise newspaper information in his language papers. Similarly, negative transfer of training will be equally powerful in the intelligent person's case. An intelligent person adept in English will have difficulty in learning the Hindi idiom because of his practice in the other language.

4. Skinner's view: According to Skinner, purely oral information cannot be utilized in transfer of learning so long as the person is incapable of using that in practical circumstances, and that the person's knowledge about using facts is not commensurate with or in proportion to his knowledge of the facts themselves. Secondly, if the individual carries a prejudicial attitude towards any learned fact, then this knowledge will not be of help in the gaining of other knowledge. Thirdly, a scientific interest helps us in the accumulation of knowledge, but it does not render any assistance in the transfer of knowledge. It becomes evident from these three points advanced by Skinner that only knowledge or scientific interest alone are not enough for transfer, it must also be used in practical conditions.

Important elements in transfer of training

It is evident from the above description that contemporary psychologists are desirous of discovering the conditions that help in the transfer of training. Many experiments have also been performed concerning this phenomenon. The more important facts gleaned from this extensive experimentation are the following:

1. Subjects of learning differ in respect of their transference value: Experiments upon the transference of subjects that are taught in school seem to indicate that these subjects have differing transfer values. As has been pointed out before, modern psychology does not believe that any one subject can serve to discipline the mind, yet there is no denying it that the transfer value of mathematics and science is very high Then come the languages and social sciences. History and English have no transfer value. Cooking, stitching and dancing have a negative transfer value by which is meant that knowledge of them makes it difficult to learn other difficult subjects.

2. Transfer is particular, not general: From the facts used in the preceding illustrations it should not be concluded that the knowledge of language or science helps in the learning of every subject. It has further been pointed out that transfer takes place only if there is identity of circumstances or elements. Sanskrit may be of help in learning either Hindi or Bengali, as Sanskrit words are numerously used in these languages but a knowledge of Sanskrit can be of no conceivable use in learning Urdu or Persian. It is more probable that pronunciation may be adversely influenced by such knowledge.

3. Transfer depends much on the learner's intelligence and innate ability: It has been clearly stated earlier that transfer is considerably influenced by the learner's intelligence. Experiments indicated that the ability of the best one per cent students of high school as far as transference is concerned, is something like twenty per cent more than that of the worst one per cent students. Similarly, an individual can make use of his knowledge only through innate ability, and transfer is possible only if there is utilization of knowledge.

4. For achieving transference it is essential to study subjects that admit of transfer: Accordingly, if training in Sanskrit is to be transferred, then Hindi or Bengali should be taught, while proficiency in Latin can be utilized in the teaching of English.

5. Transfer depends upon the use of information: It has been mentioned more than once at previous stages that no knowledge of subject that has been grasped can be transferred unless it is first utilized in practice. Moral teaching in school can only be transferred to social education if the student makes use of it in his day-to-day life.

6. Transfer is due to similarity of material and methodology: It, too, has been frequently pointed out earlier that the transfer of training can only be achieved in the learning of that subject which has some affinity with the first in respect of matter as well as methodology. Arithmetic can be transferred to book-keeping.

From this description of transfer of training it is apparent that it depends upon the learner's intelligence, innate ability, knowledge, practical ability, and use of acquired information in practice. Transfer takes place in particular subjects that have similar materia! and similar methodology, and in the teaching of such subjects Transfer takes place in different quantities in differing subjects. There is no transfer in some while it is negative or obstructive in others.

QUESTIONS FOR EXERCISE

1. What is transfer of training? Describe its kinds and rules.
2. Discuss important theories concerning transfer of training.

23

Thinking and Reasoning

WHAT IS THINKING?

Thinking which is a complex mental activity, cannot be easily separated from learning, memorising etc. As Warren puts it, "Thinking is an activity concerning ideas. It is symbolic in character, initiated by a problem or task which the individual is facing, involving some trial and error but under the directing influence of that problem and ultimately leading to a conclusion or solution of the problem." Thus, the activity of thinking originates from some problem and involves the response of the individual to this problem. The solution of the problem takes place internally and not in the form of external activities. Thinking continues till the person becomes fatigued by this effort. There cannot be any thinking in the absence of some problem. Problems in human life come in an incessant stream and they have to be solved by thinking. No general rule can be laid down regarding the circumstances which create problems. The reactions of the same individual to different situation are not identical or even similar. One situation may appear problematic to one person while a number of other persons may find nothing of the nature of a problem in it. The problems of different persons like philosophers, scientists and religious minded persons are dissimilar. The problems of a logician appear meaningless to the uninitiated but the logician is immersed day and night, in a search for their solutions. Some problems are theoretical while others are practical. The problems of study in B.A. are practical but the problems of the logician are theoretical. The solution of practical problems assists day-to-day life while the solution of the theoretical problems leads to the satisfaction of curiosity.

Nature of thinking

Thinking, the mental solution of problems, requires the use of the symbols instead of the objects. Thinking involves the solution of problems by employing the trial and error method. There is a kind of flow in the activity of thinking, one problem leading to the thinking of another by reminding the person of that other problem. Thus many things come to the thinker's mind when he is thinking. The instruments of thinking, images, imagination signs, indications and such like are also internal. Thinking continues to be an internal activity unless and until it takes the form of verbal thinking.

Thinking is symbolic behaviour

The aim of purposeful thinking may be discovery, either a solution to it is found or, instead some new idea is found. This process involves both analysis and synthesis. There is foresight in thinking because the remotest possibilities of the future are thought of in advance. Hindsight is also an element of thinking because it involves use of material collected from past experiences. Thinking is done with the help of abstract signs of real objects, which adds to thinking the element of abstraction.

INSTRUMENTS OF THINKING

Thinking calls for the assistance of percepts, images, concepts, signs and formulae, of which it makes abundant use. These are the essential instruments of thinking.

1. Perception: Percepts are important factors in thinking, affording material to it. They also stimulate thinking. Suppose we have seen our friend stealing something. This perception will set us thinking in order to discover ways and means of preventing out friend from this bad act. Many other percepts will assist in this thinking. We will, with the help of memory, try to recall the perceptions of the past behaviour of our friend in order to see the causes which may have set him on this wrong path of life in the hope of discovering ways and means which may be expected to cure him.

2. Image: Image, too, is a kind of symbol which includes the faint recollection of perceptions. Past experiences of an individual move around in his mind in the form of images. Images may be recalled through a conscious effort but they also flash on the mind involuntarily. Many experiments have indicated that images are not quite as essential to thinking as they were previously considered to be. The use of images in thinking depends in no small measure on the method of thinking which the individual employs. Some people use other symbols in their thinking, instead of images. It is not essential that a singer must have auditory images in order to be good. Thinking in philosophy and political science makes better use of words than images. Similarly subjects like arithmetic make very infrequent use of images. Sometimes a person experiences difficulty in making the other person comprehend his thoughts just because they differ in their ways of thinking.

3. Concept: Concepts are the abstract forms of past experiences. Humanity is the quality of the human species, found equally in all human beings. A concept is a general idea and, as the example makes clear, it is founded upon perception. The concept of humanity cannot be formed without the perception of human beings, because humanity is the common element in the perception of human beings. An abstraction of humanity from human beings is necessary in order to proceed from perception to concept. Concept, formed with the help of abstraction, is mental. Concepts extend the limits of thinking to include both the past and the future. Reasoning cannot be done without concept, which are not abstract and general. These are the indispensable elements of thinking. Classification of objects is done on the basis of concepts. While it differentiates between different classes of objects and creatures, it also shows the similarity between individuals of the same class. Conceptual thinking takes place by a few concepts. Thus one concept is the symbol of many objects. But all concepts are not equally extensive. For example, creature is more comprehensive than human beings which in its turn, is more comprehensive than Indians. Indians are included in human beings who are included in creatures.

4. Symbols: Concepts are made use of in thinking mainly with the help of symbols, which are representatives of general thoughts. Whenever our thoughts turn to human beings, the human figure which occupies our mind is a general figure, not that of any specific person. The image of a dog is a symbol of dogs in general. One or its numeral equivalents are symbols of unity while two or 2 symbolizes dualism. The sound of a whistle may be the symbol of a policeman or a watchman. The noise of the fire engine is the symbol of fire. Thus, the use of symbols in thinking saves time and energy.

5. Signs: Symbols and signs are intimately related. Symbols change to signs. In daily behaviour symbols are used extensively in the form of signs. The whistle of the watchman is a sign of his presence, and the green flag is a sign of the departure of the train. Arithmetic makes extensive use of signs *e.g.*, + indicates addition, – subtraction, × multiplication. Similarly a^2 means $a \times a$. The use of symbols as signs simplifies thinking even further. There is some difficulty in establishing the symbol of the concept and the sign for the symbols, in the beginning but once this difficulty is overcome the activity of thinking proceeds at a greater speed. Once we get used to them, we make use of these symbols without any conscious thought about their meaning or representation. The learning of a language presents an initial difficulty in the recognition of letters, but their subsequent use in understanding of signs in algebra takes some time, problems can easily be solved afterwards. The facility in use of language in thinking is due to the use of symbols. The letters are symbols in language, but in other languages pictures serve the same purpose. Some languages replace symbols by signs.

6. Formulae: Besides the symbols and signs, the use of formulae also results in the economy of time and energy. One small formula contains a world of meaning Comprehensive use of formulae is made in arithmetic and science. In Geometry for example, the formula πr^2 represents the relation between the radius and the circumference. The compound water is represented by H_2O which means that two atoms of hydrogen and one of oxygen combine to form water.

Thus, thinking makes very extensive use of percepts, images, concepts symbols and formulae. Among them, concepts, symbols and formulae indicate the importance of language in thinking.

FAVOURABLE CONDITIONS IN THINKING

Thinking which can stand as proof, is faultless and logical thinking which requires the elimination of faulty method. Many conditions favour conclusive thinking. The major favourable conditions are as follows:

1. Interest and attention: Both interest and attention favour thinking. Conclusive or authoritative thinking is extremely difficult if not impossible when the subject is such as does not interest us. Attention too, is difficult in the absence of any interest. On the contrary, both attention and thinking are natural in a subject which does interest us. If, for example, we find arithmetical problems interesting, we enjoy thinking about them and we find no difficulty either in attending to them or doing some deep thinking.

2. Strong motivation: Strong motivation is needed in valid thinking, the latter being impossible in the absence of motivation. Organized and controlled thinking need strong motivation. Thinking involves the solution of problems. The effort of the mind in thinking corresponds to the strength of motivation for the solutions of problems. Motivation maintains enthusiasm and postpones fatigue. Necessary mobilization of energy for thinking is made easier by motivation, in keeping with the saying that where there is a will, there is a way. The extent of desire conditions the amount of thinking in the search for the solution and an individual will not rest content until solution is found.

3. Alertness and flexibility: Alertness and flexibility also favour valid thinking, because they serve to keep external faults from contaminating thinking. Alertness checks mistakes and fallacies from creeping into thinking. Flexibility keeps thinking free from conservatism and blind belief. An alert person keeps new methods, ways and views and makes use of them in thinking whenever necessary. In this way he immediately understands the meanings of assisting symbols, signs and formulae in thinking and makes use of them. Thinking aims at the solution of problems, and it is necessary, therefore, that there should be no mistakes and no omission of details, the latter requiring alertness. If one solution or possibility in thinking does not serve the purpose it has to be discarded and another one should be taken in its place. This needs flexibility. Thus, both alertness and flexibility serve useful purpose in thinking and, at the same time, make themselves essential.

4. Time Limit should not be rigid: When a solution to some problem is being sought, the time limit provided should not be too rigid because if it is so, then normal thinking is hampered and our mental faculties become invalid. Very inflexible and short time limit cannot admit of valid thinking. Time limit for any interesting problem is superfluous because as it is, every person exerts himself to the maximum. But if the subject is uninteresting, a time limit which is not rigid may be imposed upon.

5. Wide range of wisdom: The wide range of wisdom is also a favourable factor in thinking. Thinking needs insight, which is constituted of hindsight and foresight. A proper development of the faculties of the mind is essential for these activities. If a solution is to be evolved it is essential to keep an eye on the various aspects of the problem and their mutual relationships and this too, needs a developed and mature range of wisdom.

6. Incubation: Another factor which favours thinking is incubation. If the solution of some problem proves elusive despite strenuous and persistent effort, it is advisable to lay aside the problem and to involve oneself in some other activity. While one is engaged in this other work, the mind ponders over the earlier evolved through pondering in this manner. Nothing definite has come to knowledge about the process of incubation, but it is common experience that if the problem is left in this way, the solution often comes suddenly or at least, its solution is facilitated when it is taken up again. But incubation proves advantageous only when the problem is set aside after it has been fully thought over, with all energy. Incubation does not imply running away from the problem or from collecting adequate material for the problem, because in that case incubation is useless.

ELEMENTS WHICH OBSTRUCT THINKING

Thinking is a mental process which needs alertness, flexibility and motivation besides a wide range of wisdom. There should be voluntary or independent reasoning in this process. If these factors are absent or if the opposite conditions are present, thinking will be adversely effected or hindered. The following are the prominent factors which hinder thinking:

1. Emotion: Emotions hinder thinking because strong emotion disturbs the mental equilibrium and thereby obstructs thinking. Even if thinking is pursued in an emotional state, it will be extremely one-sided and biased. It is no uncommon experience that people cannot think when they are excited by emotions like anger, sex, fear, hatred, love, etc. If the emotion is very faint, the speed of thinking will be augmented instead of being hindered. But, for correct thinking it is better to have control over the emotions.

2. Suggestion: Suggestion also obstructs thinking, because it makes it one-sided. Thinking moves along the path suggested. If, for example, someone is told that he will not live for any length of time, his thinking will be very badly effected, making him a pessimist. But it is not essential that suggestions are invariably harmful to thinking because healthy suggestions assist thinking. Self-control strengthens self-confidence and assists in thinking out the solutions of problems, the absence of suggestion is, however, considered desirable in pure thinking.

3. Prejudice: Prejudice, like the two aforesaid factors, has a detrimental effect on thinking, the only point of distinction being the extent of damage, which is more in this case than in the two cases discussed earlier. The word 'prejudice' suggests the meaning namely some preconceived idea. If we are going to start thinking on some problem with an inclination in a particular direction, all our thinking will be coloured by our bias and will not be impartial. If we have already accepted some particular person as our benefactor, any harm that he may inflict upon us will be attributed to some other person without casting any doubt on this person. The same applies to prejudice which we may have about some occupations because even if they are suitable we don't spare a thought for them when we are confronted with the choice of one of those professions because we shall ignore their advantages and commonly disadvantages. It is obvious from these examples that when prejudiced, thinking becomes partial and incorrect. Pure thinking requires the elimination of all prejudices in thinking.

Besides the hindering factors detailed above, there may be many other allied factors, such as ignorance about the laws of logical thinking and defects in personality. If a person has to think correctly and conclusively he must have some other qualities of the mind besides the absence of these hindering elements.

WHAT IS REASONING?

Man's life is an endless stream of problems, for which the individual has no ready-made formula or solution. Being unequipped with the proper solution, he requires to think and reason before he can solve the problem. Reasoning is the highest form of thinking that needs a well organized brain. The process of reasoning requires two conditions—first, that the person's mind should have completely formed concepts, and second, that he should be endowed with the power of reaching decisions. It is because the children lack these two faculties that they are not able to reason. In the process of reasoning, the individual reasons from the past known circumstances to the present or future unknown conditions on the basis of past experience. In this manner, reasoning helps to reach certain conclusions concerning the future without anything having been achieved in actual practice. Evidently, such an application needs some imagination as an essential part. To see an object lying on the table is to perceive it, when we think of it we are thinking, but if we try to know how that particular object came to be on the table at all, we fall into the process of reasoning.

Evolution of reasoning power

In different individuals, the extent of reasoning ability is different Consequently, some individuals find it easier to solve difficult problems than others. Generally, the person who is a specialist in a particular sphere has greater facility in reasoning about problems relating to that sphere than one who is a novice to it. The power of reasoning gradually develops in human beings. Children embark on reasoning out solutions of their problems even before they begin going to school As they develop, then ability to reason grows and becomes stronger. Knowledge of a particular subject also makes it easier to reason out problems relating to it.

Steps of reasoning

John Dewey described reasoning as speculative thinking and analyzed it. describing the following steps in it:

1. **A felt difficulty:** An individual stalls reasoning only when he is confronted by some specific problem. Hence, it is essential that he should experience the presence of some particular difficulty that requires solution. It may be a theoretical or a practical problem.

2. **Locate and define difficulty:** The second step in reasoning, after the presence of a difficulty has been established, is the location and defining of it. For this one is required to analyse the problem or difficulty and to track it down to a specific position, besides defining or elaborating it. Experience and ability of a student are called into play in this effort.

3. **Locate, evaluate and organize information:** Before the individual embarks on reasoning upon a problem, it is only natural for him to require all possible information concerning it, and for this he must collect such data. It is not an uncommon occurrence for well reasoned solutions to prove wrong because they were formulated on insufficient data. It is for this reason that in solving problems in many spheres, the reasoning of specialists is accepted without question by others who accept their results. Before looking for the solution of a problem, it is necessary to see whether one is in a position to gather all relevant data. Once information has been gathered, it is essential that it be evaluated because some pieces of information are more valuable than others. For example in the investigation of a crime, one piece of information may help to clear the whole picture for an individual if he reasons with it. Hence, the evaluation of all available information is an important part of solving the problems. After information has been evaluated it should be organized and classified. The classes into which specific information is to be divided depend upon the insight of the examiner.

4. **Evaluation of hypothesis:** Classification of concepts helps to bring to light the patterns concealed in the information, on the basis of which an individual can evaluate any hypothesis that he has formed in solving the problem. In solving problems an individual proceeds by first forming some hypothesis, and as new information continues to pour in, his first hypothesis is strengthened or is contradicted, in which case it has to be discarded in favour of a more appropriate hypothesis. After the pattern of concepts is precisely known, one's preconceptions of hypothesis can be evaluated, and the correct one decided upon.

5. **Apply the solution:** The next step is the application of solution or inference to solving the problem since only then can the validity of the inference be actually known. In the foregoing example, concerning the juvenile delinquent, the teacher utilizes the conclusions he has reached in trying to cure the child by basing his cure on them and if the results are satisfactory, the conclusions have been borne out.

TRAINING RATIONAL THINKING

The steps in the process of reasoning that Dewey has pointed out can be utilized in the solution of problems concerning education. For this, it is needed that the thinker possess a scientific attitude, self-confidence and patience. The teacher himself must be capable of scientific and unbiased reasoning, as he cannot otherwise teach his students to reason with clarity. In training the children to think rationally in school, it is necessary to keep following things in mind:

1. Acquaintance with problems of daily life: In order to acquaint the child with the problem, the subject that he is taught should be related to real life. It is only when the illustrative examples in study are taken from day-to-day life that the child can think of the problems with any facility.

2. Development of necessary qualities: Rational thinking requires experience, intellect, firm determination and other qualities such as persistence and application. And of these, with the exception of intelligence, all the others can be developed through efforts. Hence, efforts should be made to develop these in the child.

3. Solution of problems of practical utility: Children should be asked to solve problems of practical utility. One such problem could be the following: Draw nine spots in such a manner as to create three lines, each of which contains three spots, and, without lifting the pencil from the chart draw lines that connect all the spots. Ability to solve such problems can be developed. In addition to this, children should be made cognisant of the problems that occur in daily life, and inspired to solve them.

4. Knowledge of special subjects: Solution of specific kinds of problems inevitably requires skill in the appropriate subjects. Hence, the teacher should pose problems before the students only after they have gained adequate knowledge of such subjects.

5. Acquaintance with environment: Problems on which the student is required to cogitate should bear relation to his life. And for this it is essential that he be acquainted with his environment. Knowledge of the individual, associations, institutions and processes that occur around him will make it possible for him to comprehend their problems, and he will himself be inclined to reason out a solution of them. And the mistakes that they makes in such reasoning should be corrected by their teacher. Students devise all kinds of arguments, when concerned in a debate to prove their point. The sensible teacher can, after the debate is over, individually or collectively, bring to the notice of the students the fallacy in their reasoning.

6. Knowledge of logic: A study of the general principles of logic will be especially beneficial to a training in reasoning. The teacher himself should be acquainted with the general rules of logic, and he should impart them to the student. Lacking knowledge of these principles, even some really well educated persons are seen reasoning incorrectly and illogically.

Briefly, then, there are two main elements in training in reasoning—knowledge of the subject concerned with the problem, and knowledge of the rules of logic or reasoning. In addition to this when the students get adequate opportunities of reasoning and arguing, they develop good reasoning ability that starts them in good stead in life.

QUESTIONS FOR EXERCISE

1. State and explain the fundamentals of the process of thinking.
2. Thinking is the mental solution of problems. Discuss.
3. Describe favourable and unfavourable elements in thinking.
4. Write a short note on—Reasoning and education.

24

Concept Formation

WHAT IS CONCEPT?

Concepts are the abstract forms of past experiences. They are general thoughts. The development of concepts in the human mind is gradual. The formation of concepts starts with the inception of the activity of thinking in the child because thinking is not possible without concepts. As the child comes into contact with new objects, new concepts take form in his mind and develop. At the outset of this origin and development of concepts, the child adds the concepts of natural things which he had perceived, to the concepts of living creatures. He thinks about the stars and the moon in the same manner in which he thinks about human beings.

CONCEPT FORMATION

Many mental activities take part in the formation of concepts, some of the important ones being as follows:

1. Perception: The formation of concepts or conception, starts with perception. The concept of human beings cannot be conceived if human beings are not perceived or if only one human being is observed. The observation of many human beings is essential to the concept formation. Thus comprehensive perception is the first step towards the formation of concepts.

2. Analysis: Analysis of the traits of the concepts is second step towards concept formation. It is not possible to identify a man as a human being and as distinct from other living creatures unless its traits are analysed. Thus the analysis of human beings is essential to the concept of human beings.

3. Comparison: It is the third step towards concept formation. In the previous example, comparison of the analysed qualities of various persons is also necessary. This comparison supplies us with the knowledge of the similarity or identity and dissimilarity or diversity of human beings. Analysis of traits alone is not enough to form concepts. The comparison of these traits is also essential.

4. Synthesis: The next step, after analysis, is the synthesis of similar traits for concept formation. This synthesis of similar traits is arrived at with the help of abstraction, rather than the addition of traits. Dissimilar traits are disregarded in synthesis. Discrimination is needed for the separation of similar and dissimilar traits; after which the generalization of the similar ones is effected though this would leave the process of synthesis incomplete unless assimilation were also effected. Some psychologists separate these activities from synthesis.

5. Naming: Naming is the final step in concept formation and as even concept has a name, naming of every concept is essential. Consequently, after synthesis each concept gets a name. For example, the name human will be given to it after the peculiarities of human beings have been synthesized and then the concept of human will be ready.

New concepts originate in the mind with the increase and extension of knowledge, but the individual does not make any conscious effort towards their formation which goes on automatically. If someone asks us for our idea of a human being, the answer may not suggest itself all of a sudden. All we would possibly say is that a human being is one who has humanity. The definition of humanity would be, even more difficult. But we make frequent use of the word 'human' in our daily lives and find no difficulty in if. In reality, the above steps in the development of concept have been discovered by analysis.

CHILD'S CONCEPTS

According to Warren, "Thinking is an ideational activity, symbolic in character, initiated by a problem or task the individual is facing, involving some trial and error but under directing influence of the problem set and ultimately leading to a conclusion or solution of the problem." Thus thinking starts from some problem and it culminates in the solution of it. The children have to exercise thinking in order to solve their own problems. The child's thinking, however, can be distinguished from that of adults by the following characteristics:

1. From gross to subtle concepts: The process of the development of the concepts in the child proceeds from gross to subtle. The child's concepts are generally more gross than that of the adults.

2. Ambiguity of concepts: The child's concepts are more ambiguous and indistinct as compared with the adult's concepts. With the child's mental development, the clarity of the concepts increases.

3. Indefiniteness of the concepts: As compared with the concepts of the adults, the child's concepts are more indefinite. They become definite as he advances in mental development.

4. Simplicity of the concepts: As compared with the concepts of the adults the child's concepts are more simple. He begins to understand the concept of human being at the age of 27 months and knows that both male and female are human beings. At the age of 42 months he has the concept of fruit including mango, banana and other fruits. The child knows that brinjals, carrots, etc , are all vegetables. Thus as he becomes more and more mature the concepts in the child's mind become more and more complex.

5. Concept of the whole: As the child perceives the whole thing and does not attend to parts, he first forms the concept of the whole and later on that of the parts. In thinking he first understands the general meaning and then arrives at the particular meaning.

6. Wrong concepts: In comparison with the adults many of the concepts of the child are wrong. He develops right concepts by means of education. The false concepts lead to maladjustment and therefore they must be replaced by right type of concepts through education. There are several reasons of child's forming wrong concepts. In the first the child is given much false information regarding many things. The adults do not care to tell him the truth. Secondly, the child's experiences are very much limited and therefore lead to the formation of wrong concepts. Several superstitions prevalent in the family of the child also lead to false concepts. Besides some wrong habits, false expectations and defects of the sense organs also result in the formation of wrong concepts.

The concepts of the child can be improved by means of education at home and in the school. This is necessary for the development of child's thinking.

DEVELOPMENT OF CHILDREN'S CONCEPTS

Concept means a general symbol representing some particular experience. Thus the child develops different concepts at different stages of development. The concepts multiply with the increase of experience. In the beginning they are simple because the nervous system and sense organs of the child are undeveloped. In the beginning many of the child's concepts are illusory and wrong. It is difficult for the child to form right concepts unless he has attained sufficient experience. The development of concepts in the child depends on the following factors:

1. Interest and attention: Up to the age of 3 years, the child cannot concentrate for more than 6 seconds. At the age of 5 years this limit is increased up to 13 seconds. It is after this age that the child can attend to a thing for some time. He can now attend to complex problems, the duration and span of his attention increase. These are intimately related to his interest. Besides, the motives also affect attention.

2. Physical adjustment: As the child manipulates different things in his environment his physical adjustment increases. This adjustment leads to such experiences which cannot be attained by means of sense organs only. For example, he learns to distinguish between different qualities concerning the sensation of touch.

3. Questions of the children: The child tries to understand his environment by asking questions to his adults. This trend starts at the age of 3 years and continues up to the age of 6 years. The answers which he gets to his questions lead to the formation of various concepts. It is, therefore, necessary that the child should be given correct answers to his questions, otherwise he will form wrong concepts about different things. Most of the questions of the child are concerning what and where. After the age of 4 years the child asks about why, how and when. The answers to the child's questions must be simple so that he can understand them. He should be given answers in terms of his own experience, because if anything has not been experienced by the child he will not understand it. In the beginning the child's questions are mostly concerning the immediate incidence and concrete things. Gradually he asks questions about abstract relationships and far off things. As he begins to read he searches answers to his questions in the books.

4. Defects of the sense organs: The child attains experience by means of his sense organs. The Defects of the sense organs therefore influence his concepts. For example, the deaf children do not develop the concept of sound while the blind children have no concept of colour.

5. Intellectual ability: The intellectual ability plays an important role in the development of child's concept. The conceptual knowledge of the child increases in proportion to his intellectual ability. This in its turn leads to the formation of new concepts.

6. Opportunities of learning: The concepts in the child's mind develop in proportion to the opportunities of learning which he gets. Thus as the child learns more and more he forms new concepts of different things.

7. Experience: Both direct and indirect experience helps in the formation of concepts. It is hence that the child's concepts are less accurate in comparison with the concepts of the adults. The experience increases with age. It also increases through education, particularly through the extra-curricular activities. It is hence that the child's mental development is influenced by his socio-economic status.

8. Influence of class: The conceptual development of the child develops with the rise in socio-economic class. It is because in the higher socio-economic status the child comes into contact of more things and gets more varied type of experiences.

DEVELOPMENT OF SOME IMPORTANT CONCEPTS

An analysis of the development of some important concepts in the child's mind will give an idea about his conceptual development.

1. The concept of self: The infant develops some type of concept of self at the early age of 6 months, though he cannot put it in language. He plays with his own physical organs and smiles at his reflection in the mirror. After gradual learning he distinguishes between different sense organs and physical parts of the body. At the age of 2½ years he can recognize different parts of the doll's body. According to Termann, a child of three years of age, can tell his name and knows about his sex. Between 3 and 4 years of age, the child pays very much attention to himself. The young girl tries to make up imitating her mother and admires herself as an individual distinct for other children. On the one hand, the child forms concepts regarding his body, form and complexion, while on the other hand, he forms concepts concerning his internal feelings, attitudes and ideas All these are concerned with his inner life. Sometimes the child fails to distinguish between these two aspects of his self.

It is only after gradual development that the child becomes a social being in which both these aspects of self are synthesized.

2. Concept of space: The concept of space plays an important role in perception and conception. Even a small infant can distinguish between here and there. He gradually learns to distinguish between right and left, forward and backward and different directions. A child who passes most of his time at home finds it difficult to move outside. But as soon as he succeeds in finding out his way he does not like to be led by others. He finds that outside his house and in the neighbourhood there are many places of interest. This is more so when the child gets opportunity to visit far off places with his parents. By these experiences he forms a concept of large distance. The distance is inferred by means of experience. By his experience the child knows that there are many wards in the city and each ward consists of several streets and lanes. In every street he finds many houses and locates his own house. In the beginning he recognizes distance by demonstrations from others, it is only after going to school that he knows about yard, feet and inch. At the High School stage the child does not really understand a mile's distance though he may know the number of yards in a mile.

3. Concept of time: The child lives in the present. Before the age of 3 years, tomorrow has no meaning for him. It is only after it that he begins to distinguish between now and then. He gradually distinguishes between yesterday and tomorrow. Before going to school he learns the names of different days in the week. Though he has no knowledge of months in a year it is at the age of 8 years that he can accurately tell days and months. The child has to learn to see the watch and tell the time. Before the age of 12 years he cannot understand the relation between different times and units of long duration.

4. Concepts of form and colour: A child below the age of 3 years can recognize form and colours. From 3 to 6 years of age he can combine colour. At the age of 6 years he can combine different forms. In the beginning the child cannot distinguish his parents from other males and females, but he very soon begins to recognize them. At the kindergarten stage the child is influenced by the different types of colours and forms. This also helps in the formation of the concept of space. Playing with the toys helps in the formation of the concepts of forms and colour.

5. Concept of number: A child can recite numbers between 2 to 3 years of age. According to Tarmann and Merrill, a child of 4 years can count two things, while a child of 5 years can count four and that of 6 years can count 12 things. A child of 6 years can count numbers upon 100. At the age of 7 years, he can add and subtract numbers and solve simple questions of multiplication and division. At the age of 9 years, the child develops numeral concepts up to 1000.

6. Concept of weight: In the beginning the child connects weight with size and thinks bigger things to have more weight. Gradually he learns to distinguish between size and weight and knows that the weight of a thing cannot be determined unless it is taken up by hand.

7. Concept of currency: The concept of currency develops only when the child starts using it. He now learns to distinguish between different coins and they become meaningful for him. Even before going to school some children collect coins given to them. After going to school they learn to spend them. At the age of 6 years the child can recognize different coins separately. A child of 5 years of age does not know the relationship between coins and cost. Within 2 years he understands that he can secure many things and services in exchange of coins.

8. Concept of causation: At a very early age the child knows that he has to behave differently with different persons. At the age of 2 to 4 years he knows what type of behaviour is expected of him towards different persons. He knows which cause leads to a particular result. By using different things, clothes, etc., and experiencing the consequences the child forms the concept of causation. These concepts, however, are concrete. The child cannot think of abstract causation.

BRUNER'S MODEL OF CONCEPT LEARNING

J.S. Bruner suggested a model of concept attainment and structure in teaching. He proposed that economy in thinking and responding requires that we categorise phenomenon according to their common attributes. An attribute is a property or characteristic of an object which differentiates it from the other. Colour, texture, form, size, number of parts position and sound are examples of attributes. We categorise objects having common characteristics into one group. For example, we categorise certain animals having four legs, a tail and a barking voice as dogs. Similarly, we can also categorise more abstract concepts such as enemy or friend, artisan or professional, etc. For teaching about a concept the teachers must identify such attributes of that concept which differentiate it from others. For example, dog and cat have four legs and a tail, but cat has a different voice than the dog.

Bruner studied the strategies people use in acquiring a concept. He used a set of cards, some cards having borders, others without. All the cards have centre figures varying in shape (square, circle or cross), in colour (red, green or black) and in number (single, double or triple). Each card thus combines four attributes: figure shape, figure number, figure colour and presence or absence of borders. Each attribute has three values (variations) as listed above. The subject is told that the experimenter has a concept in mind, say red circles, and the subject was to identify that concept. The subject is asked to select a card and then told by the experimenter whether or not the card was an instance of the concept. With these data in mind, the subject would select another card to determine further the attributes of the concepts and would continue doing so till he finds the answer *i.e.*, the card with red circles.

Burner identified four strategies in concept attainment: (1) simultaneous scanning strategy, (2) successive scanning strategy, (3) conservative-focusing strategy, and (4) focus-gambling strategy.

1. Simultaneous scanning: In this type of strategy, the subject uses each positive instance (each correctly identified card), to deduce which combinations of attributes and values are no longer valid. The subject must keep in mind simultaneously all the rejected combinations in order to narrow down the range of subsequent alternatives. This technique is not very efficient since it places a great deal of strain on the subject's memory.

2. Successive scanning: In this technique the subject makes an overall estimate of each correct characteristic of the concept and tests each one by one. This is called successive scanning since the subject tests individual hypothesis about the correct characteristics one at a time in succession. The technique is also inefficient as the subject may choose redundant cards which give no new information.

3. Conservative focusing: In this technique, each attribute is tested by selecting a card that is different from a focus card in only one attribute. If the new card is still a positive stance, then the subject knows that the varied attribute is not part of the concept. If, however, the changed attribute yields a negative instance, then the attribute is a part of concept. For example, the concept to be attained is 'red circle'. Assume that the subject encounters a positive card with three red circles and two borders. This card becomes the focus card and each variable is examined by selecting additional cards. The selection sequence is given below. A plus sign in the parentheses means that the card is a positive instance of the concept, a minus sign in the parentheses means that the card is a negative instance.

Four cards: 3 red circles, 2 borders (+) 2 red circles, 2 borders + First decision; eliminate 'three figures' as a relevant variable.

3 green circle, 2 borders (–) second decision: retain red as relevant attribute value.

3 green crosses, 2 borders (–) third decision: retain red circle as relevant attribute value.

3 red circles, 1 border (–) fourth decision eliminate 'two borders' as relevant attribute value

Conclusion: The concept is 'red circle'.

This technique is more efficient since the subject uses a correct instance as a point of reference and selects additional cards to test each attribute value individually.

4. Focus gambling: In this strategy the subject focuses on a correct card, but varies more than one attribute at a time. This technique can give early result if cards chosen yield a positive instance. If, however, the subject encounters a negative instance, he cannot tell which attribute was essential. In that case he has to revert to simultaneous scanning technique to test hypotheses. This strategy is called gambling since the subject takes a chance varying two attributes at a time.

Bruner's strategies of concept learning can be applied in science teaching. The use of discovery and inquiry techniques in teaching science provides the pupils with experiences quite similar to the card, tasks used by Bruner. For example, if we want the pupils to invent their own system of classification of plants and animals, they can do it by identifying the attributes and putting the plants or animals with common attributes in one group.

JEAN PIAGET (1896-1980)

Piaget was a Swiss educator. He was a naturalist and a biologist by training. At an early age of 22, he obtained his doctoral degree in Zoology on 'Mollusks of Valias'. He neither undertook any formal study nor passed any examination in psychology. However, he is regarded as one of the pioneers in psychological investigation. He read philosophy, psychology, sociology, etc., very deeply. He pursued clinical research at the Alfred Binet Laboratory at Paris. By observing, dissecting and experimenting with children, he developed his education theory regarding learning by children. His work as a professor of child psychology at the University of Geneva made him famous throughout the world.

Piaget began his study of child development with the careful observation of his own three children. From this beginning his investigations were gradually extended to other children. These investigations resulted in the publication of a large number of papers and books.

Publications

1. *The Language of Thought of the Child* (1923)
2. *Judgement and Reasoning in the Child* (1924)
3. *The Child's Conception of the Physical World* (1926)
4. *The Moral Judgement of the Child* (1926)
5. *The Origin of Intelligence in the Child* (1932)
6. *The Child's Conception of Number* (1941)
7. *The Child's Construction of Physical Quantities* (1942)
8. *Play, Dreams and Imitations in Childhood* (1945)
9. *The Child's Conception of Time* (1946)
10. *The Child's Conception of Movement and Speed* (1946)
11. *The Construction of Reality in the Child* (1937)
12. *The Child's Conception of Space* (1948)
13. *The Psychology of Intelligence* (1950)
14. *Logic and Psychology* (1953)
15. *The Construction of Reality in Child* (1954)
16. *The Strategy of Genes* (1957)
17. *The Growth of Logical Thinking from Childhood to Adolescence* (1958)
18. *The Child's Conception of Geometry*
19. *The Early Growth of Logic in the Child* (1964)
20. *Mental Imagery in the Child* (1969)

21. *The Mechanism of Perception* (1969)
22. *The Psychology of the Child* (1969)
23. *Science of Education and the Psychology of the Child* (1969)
24. *The Origin of the Idea of Chance in Children* (1975)
25. *The Grasp of Consciousness.*

Aims of education

Piaget stressed the following two aims of education:

1. **Creativity:** The principal goal of education is to create men who are capable of doing new things, not simply repeating what other generations have done. Education should create men who are creators, inventors and discoverers.
2. **Critical evaluation:** The second aim of education is to form minds which can be critical, can verify and do not accept everything they are offered.

Learning

Piaget revolutionized thinking and understanding about the intellectual growth of young children. According to his theory a child goes through a series of development stages which are as under:

1. **Development stages:**
   (*i*) Sensorimotor (birth to two years)
   (*ii*) Preconceptual (two to four years)
   (*iii*) Initiative (four to seven years)
   (*iv*) Concrete operations (seven to eleven years)
   (*v*) Formal operations (eleven years and onwards).
2. **Meaning of learning:** Learning includes a wide range of activities. Rigid distinction like classroom for instruction, laboratory for practicals, recess for amusement, mathematics for developing computational ability, athletics for strengthening the body muscles, etc., are unnecessary. Piaget's approach helps to tie together what have been treated as separate subjects.
3. **Role of learner's actions:** Action stresses the role of active exploration. A child is active when he stares at objects. A child is active when he stares at an organism. A child is active when he studies his body parts. A child is active when he lifts something. A child is active when he carries things. A child is active when he arranges things. Children are usually active for most of their time. There is no doubt that some of these activities may be rather aimless or unnecessary. However, most of these activities are purposeful.
4. **Role of practice:** An important part of Piagetian model is repetition of an act by a child. The role of practice varies with the development. Concepts are the products of a long history of action. A child may take three or more days to complete a puzzle. Each day he appears to go through the same sequence Child's actions upon the environment are repeated again and again with slight modifications each time. Piaget depicts the child as somewhat slower and methodical and systematic in acquisition of new ideas.

5. Motivation: According to Piaget, a learner desires to reduce his internal conflicts by keeping his thoughts harmonious and in equilibrium. It is only through playing, imitating, exploring and questioning that a child gradually comes to distinguish the achievable from non-achievable and logical, from illogical. To Piaget, the progress towards this end is an inherent property of cognitive style as are eating, drinking and breathing in the physiological field.

6. Memory: Memory is a symbolic representation of how the child has schematized what he saw. Experiments conducted by Piaget reveal that after six months, 61 per cent of the children from 4-8 years of age regressed in their memory ability if tested by recall or evocation.

A reconstruction test involving the child with some material showed regression in 4-5 years old but 48 per cent progression among 6-7 years old. Piaget holds that recognition is perceptual and reconstruction is internalized imitation. Each experiment and regression (gradual loss of memory) is determined by initial conceptual understanding and is altered by new understandings.

7. Interest: According to Piaget, the interest of the child at any given movement depends upon the system of ideas he has acquired plus his affective inclination. A child tends to fulfil his interests in the direction of greater equilibrium. Equilibrium, according to Piaget, is development and the ability to think in a logical and rational manner.

Implications of Piaget's views:

1. A child's development is retarded if he is not allowed a fairly wide sensory and motor experience in his early years.
2. Real events and concrete objects play an important role in learning.
3. In science and mathematics, learning from physical environment is more important than what is learnt from people, books or television.
4. A teacher should arouse curiosity of the child through planned activities.
5. Children should be treated as children.
6. Children should be made active.
7. Children like to find out themselves by their own activity.
8. Children learn speedily if we provide concrete material to them.

Theory of cognitive development

Piaget asserts that learning is a function of development. Cognitive development, intellectual development and development of intelligence are more or less synonymous.

1. Intelligence: Intelligence is a way of behaving. Behaving is reflected in an individual's 'adaption' to the environment. Adaption takes place through the interaction of'assimilation' and 'accommodation'. An intelligent behaviour requires a balance between assimilation and accommodation. This balance is called 'equilibrium'.

2. Assimilation: Assimilation implies incorporation of something from the environment. New ideas, concepts and stimuli are taken in and incorporated into one's existing set of scheme. A scheme is the organized pattern of behaviour which the child develops when he is engaged in any activity . For example, when a child is engaged in sucking, there is a certain pattern of movements of the cheeks, lips and hands. When a child is confronted with a new object, he will try to understand the new object by applying his old scheme to it. He adapts himself to a new object by assimilating it. His old scheme does not change in the process.

3. Accommodation: Accommodation involves modification or change in some elements of an old scheme or learning a new scheme which is more appropriate for the new object. A baby who has already got a scheme of sucking mother's breast accommodates to the object placed in the mouth-finger, nipple, pencil, a toy—depending on its shape, form and the size. The baby develops a new scheme or a modified scheme. This is called accommodation.

Thus a baby assimilates when he understands and perceives the new in the light of his old perceptions. A baby forms a new scheme when he modifies or changes his old perception to suit the new. This implies adjusting or accommodating. In this way a baby forms new structures or schemes and consequently develops cognitive capacity. A reference has already been made to the four periods of cognitive development.

Educational implications:

1. It provides a broad developmental perspective to the educator for building a curriculum for the pre-school children.
2. The description of developmental stages and qualitative aspects of intellectual growth is very useful in providing a suitable educational practice.
3. The cognitive theory states that the child is to be actively involved in the teaching-learning process for his intellectual growth.
4. Piaget-based curriculum requires that children should not skip any stage.
5. The pre-school child is at the pre-operational level. The educational programme at this stage should provide concrete operations.
6. The pre-school programme should enable the child to integrate the information
7. A child should be helped to develop internal consistency of the system.
8. Most of the activities of the Piaget type require simple equipment and material
9. Drilling in skills is to be avoided.
10. Teaching-learning situation should be geared to a point where the child is neither too familiar nor too unfamiliar with the objects and ideas.

11. A variety of cognitive activities like story telling, rhymes, singing, etc., are included in the programme in a systematic manner. There is a deliberate attempt to develop cognitive growth.

Suggested play activities on Piaget's model

Dr. (Miss) T. Saraswathi, Reader, M.S. University, Baroda has suggested the following:

Play activity no. 1

Skills Aimed at: Developing one-to-one correspondence, observing shapes of objects, noticing similarities and differences, matching.

Materials required

(*a*) Two 12" × 18" pieces of tagboard and cardboard.

(*b*) Coloured pencils to colour the outline.

(*c*) Small objects: Block, key, combs, scissors, books, buttons, rubber bands, toys, paper clips, corks, coca-cola lids (any object available).

(*d*) Containers for the objects if tagboard, cardboard and coloured pencils are not available, the outlines of the objects could be drawn on the floor with the help of chalk.

Activity: The child takes out one object at a time from the containers and names it. He then tries to place the object on its outline only in one trial. Children who are very confident may like the challenge of attempting to reproduce the arrangement on the answer board.

Getting started

The teacher might discuss the activity as follows: Can you find what shape this key has on the answer board? Why do you choose this one? Good, try it and see, Good, Find where all the others go?

Ideas for follow-up discussion

1. What did you do with the objects? How did you know where they would go on answer board.
2. Point out to an object which is round. How many objects are green? How many are not white, not red, show me.
3. Show me something used to hold things together.
4. Point to an object that unlocks a lock.

Play activity no. 2

Skills aimed at: Learning about the natural environment of various animals, classifying animals according to their habitate, making comparisons, drawing conclusions.

Materials required

9" × 12" sheets of tagboard, cardboard and paper. Picture showing 'in water', 'on land' and 'in the air'. Pictures of animals that live mostly in water, in air and on the land.

Activity: The child sorts out the pictures under appropriate category placing together the animals which live in water, in air, on the land.

Getting started: The teacher might say, showing the picture 'if this animal mostly lives on land where will this picture go'. If he mostly lives in the air where will this picture go? Put the pictures where you think the animals mostly live.

Ideas for follow-up discussion

1. Name all the animals that live in water, in air, on land.
2. Name one animal which is very small and lives on land.
3. Name one large animal. Do you know the name of the largest bird? The tallest bird?
4. Show me some pictures of animals whose names you do not know and I will tell you their names.

QUESTIONS FOR EXERCISE

1. What is a concept? Describe experiments to illustrate the process of forming a concept.
2. Distinguish between the concepts of children and adult.
3. What are the factors influencing development of children's concepts?
4. Trace the development of some important concepts in child's mind.
5. Explain Bruner's Model of Concept Learning.
6. Explain Piaget's views on concept formation.

25

Memory and Forgetting

The conscious level of the human mind is not the solitary level of mental activity. The impressions of various experiences become permanent at the subconscious stage and they come to the conscious level whenever they are needed or whenever there is that relevant context. Experiences are not obliterated from the mind with the passage of time, but rather, they remain in the mind permanently, in the form of memory and can be recalled with effort and recognised. But, it is common experience that people do not remember their experiences completely and a major part is not even remembered. Thus remembering and forgetting are matters of everyday experience. Memory is a general word which includes several mental activities like recall, recognition and retention. A person experiences ease in relearning an activity which he had learnt previously but had forgotten. This proves very obviously that the previous learning had not been wiped of completely but had left an impression on the mind or a change in the nerves which facilitated relearning. People do not completely forget the story of any movie they have seen but recount it with ease when they are requested to do so. If someone else takes on the tedious task of telling the story of the same film, they affirm it because they are reminded of it, and if they hear any song from the film played anywhere they are easily reminded of that too. Thus, there is retention, recall and recognition in the memory of an experience, which make it a complex activity.

PSYCHOPHYSICAL ACTIVITY

Bentley[1] and his followers maintained that experience acquired by a person leaves impressions or marks on the brain in the form of memory traces. These form the basis of memory as a functional tendency, because retention ends when these traces are wiped of. These psychologists have established that retention is a physiological process. But Bartlett[2], Piron, Gibson[3] and some other psychologists have attempted to show that memory is a mental activity independent of memory traces. They have proved by examples of stories, pictures, etc., that memory depends more on mental states like interests,

1. Bentley, M., *The New Field of Physiology*, New York. D. Appletone Century, 1934.
2. Bartlett, F.C., *Remembering*. N.Y., Macmillan, 1932.
3. Gibson. J.J., *The Reproduction of Usually Perceived Forms*, J. Exp. Psychology, 1929 12, 1-39.

motivation, bias etc., than on repetition of experiences. This makes memory a mental activity. But just as every mental activity has a physiological basis, so is the case of memory. Briefly, memory is a psycho-physiological activity.

PROCESSES IN MEMORY

Memory is preceded by learning and therefore, memory involves four processes or activities in general. These are as follows:

1. Learning
2. Retention
3. Recall
4. Recognition.

Two of these four activities namely learning and retention are essential in memory. Recall succeeds learning but there may be no recognition. Sometimes retention is followed by recognition without any recall. Besides learning and retention both recall and recognition are necessary for complete memory. Sometimes it is recall which takes place first to be followed by recognition but equally often the order of the two activities is reversed.

Favourable conditions in memory

To study the favourable conditions in memory, it is necessary to study the favourable conditions in learning, recall and recognition. The favourable conditions in learning have been already discussed in the chapter on learning hence it is unnecessary to mention it here. Therefore we shall only discuss the favourable conditions in retention, recall and recognition.

Favourable conditions in retention

Many experiments have been carried out on the subject of retention and many psychological and physical conditions have proved useful. Some of the main conditions which are favourable in retention are:

1. Nature of material: The following characteristics in the material to be retained help in its retention:

(*i*) *Intensity:* The intensity of the stimulus assists in the retention of a subject. Weak or indistinct stimuli do not stick in the mind for any length of time. Clear photographs can be remembered with ease.

(*ii*) *Distinctness:* Distinct stimuli like strong light, striking beauty or ugliness and such like can be retained for a long time. We forget an ordinary person easily but we remember one for a long time if he be extra-ordinary in any way.

(*iii*) *Recency:* Recent experiences are retained for a longer time and a diminution in their retention occurs with the passage of time.

(*iv*) *Meaning:* Meaningless experiences do not linger long in the mind while meaningful ones can be retained for long with little effort.

2. Duration: A stimulus which continues for a long time, can be retained for a longer time in the mind. A stimulus of a shorter duration will be. correspondingly, retained for a shorter duration.

3. Amount of material: If the subject being persued is long it will be retained for a longer time while a shorter subject will take less time before it is forgotten. The amount of material to be learnt has a suitable effect on its retention, there being two reasons for the phenomenon—(*a*) A man has to make less exertion in order to learn a shorter subject, while a longer subject demands more effort and therefore, the retention is more lasting, (*b*) In the longer subject as compared to the shorter, the person finds more meaning and relates the various parts of the subject together. All this helps in retention.

4. Amount of learning: The extent of retention is directly proportional to the amount of learning, that is to say that retention will be more if the amount of learning is large. A subject studied more stays longer in the mind while one studied less will remain in the mind for a shorter period. Overlearning has a favourable effect on retention.

But this does not mean that retention will go on increasing with the learning because after a certain limit disinterest, fatigue and monotony may have a derogatory effect on retention. Therefore, increasing and strengthening effects of overlearning confine themselves to a certain limit.

5. Methods of learning: The methods of learning, too, do not fail to impress the retention of a subject. Learning by the whole method instead of the part method, the spaced method instead of the unspaced method and the active method instead of the passive method result in better and longer retention.

6. Speed of learning: The faster the learning the better is the retention. Thus the people learning faster seem to retain the subject learnt for longer periods as compared to the slow learners. For example, a child grasped mathematics later than his contemporaries, but when it came to language, making no pretentions he was far quicker at it. His retention of language was far more than that of mathematics. Actually, the speed of learning indicates the inclination and interest towards a subject and hence learning is faster and retaining longer.

7. Feeling: Freud and other psychologists assert that we retain pleasant experiences for a longer time than painful ones. Thus feeling attached with a certain experience has an important role to play on its retention.

8. Attention: If greater attention is paid while studying a subject the retention will be better. On the contrary, the retention will be weakened by lack of attention.

9. Sleep: Some time elapses after study, before the subject is assimilated in the mind and if this time of assimilation is used for sleep, the memory traces get a good opportunity to settle down in the memory. Psychologists however, differ in regard to the cause of the effect which sleep has on retention.

10. Mental review: If some experience is incessantly contemplated upon, its retention is better than one about which the mind does not trouble itself. Really speaking, by mental review a repetition of the subject is caused which strengthens retention.

11. Mental set: A person retains those things for a longer period which coincide with his mental set. A religious person remembers phenomena relating to religion for a long time and a sensuous man remembers incidents of sexual interest.

12. Apperception: Apperception means the assimilation of learned subject with the knowledge already present. The retention of a newly learned subject is greatly facilitated if it is assimilated with the present store of knowledge to start with. And on the other hand, a longer time is needed for retention if this assimilation is not effected.

13. Intention: This, too, is important for retention. If a subject is learned with the express intention of being retained, the aim will be fulfilled. But if there is no such intention, the subject is wiped off from the memory of the person after some time. Learning gathered with a view to appearing in the examinations is remembered better and things picked up here and there, in the ordinary course, are easily forgotten.

But it cannot be concluded from this that any learning carried out for retention will be necessarily retained. It only implies that retention is better if there is intention to retain the subject than when there is no such intention.

14. Massive experience: The retention will be more if the experience is massive. A person who has loved never forgets it because it effects his whole personality. A person retains that experience longer which is of greater value to him than other experiences. When the value attached to the experience is lost, the experience too, slips out of the mind.

Favourable conditions in recall

Generally the factors which favour retention also have a good effect on recall. In other words, it means that recall is better if the retention is good. But this is not always so. There are some factors which favour the recall of experience over and above the factors favourable to retention. The major ones are as follows:

1. Favourable mental and physical condition: Recall is comparatively easy when both the mind and the body are healthy and fresh. An adverse and indifferent physical and mental condition hinders recall.

2. Perfection of clues: Recall is done with the help of clues which are stimulators of recall. To take an example if we learn a poem, we cannot recall it without the help of the title, the first line or the clue to some part of it, and clues are necessary for the recall of anything in the mind. The completeness of the recall depends upon the completeness of these clues.

3. Mental set: The mental set of the individual, too, affects recall. A religious minded person remembers religious subjects easily while a sensuous person finds it easy to remember things associated with sex or social life.

4. Context: Context too helps recall. When writing an essay, or talking, things pertinent to the context keep on flowing to the focus of attention. The recall due to the context does not stop with only one thing. It leads to another and this reminds of a third thus forming a chain of linked thoughts and experiences which often take a person so far that he forgets the context in which conversation started.

5. Motives: When the person is under the influence of a motive, he has such clear recall of related incidents that he sometimes has hallucinations.

6. Feeling: Recall is affected by feelings of pleasure and pain. Incidents and experiences attached with the feelings of pain and pleasure are recalled easily than those attached with indifferent feelings. Pleasurable experiences are comparatively easily recalled.

7. Effort: This has a very significant effect on recall. Unless the extreme limit of effort has been passed, recall generally increases with the effort. When this limit has been exceeded recall becomes difficult. In fact it is the wrong type of effort which hinders recall and it can take a variety of forms like the effort which creates an emotional state, the one which exhausts, or the effort made in the absence of or against the clues. But, if on the other hand, the effort is made with confidence, keeping in view the clues, recall will be affected favourably.

8. Absence of inhibition: Recall is better in the absence of any inhibition, because inhibition obstructs it. Inhibition may be caused by the conflict of the simultaneous arising of two activities or by repression and again by fear or other emotions. A student forgets everything in the examination because he is nervous. A doctor cannot remember the name of the patient in whose treatment he was completely unsuccessful. These three examples respectively illustrate the effects of emotions, repression and conflict on recall. The only solution is the elimination of inhibition, if recall is to be improved. These obstacles in recall are called Reproductive Inhibitions.

Favourable conditions in recognition

As a general rule, the conditions found favourable for retention and recall are equally favourable to recognition, and in view of this fact, only two conditions will be mentioned here.

1. Mental set: Recognition is assisted by the mental set, in the manner in which other factors assist memory. Recognition is correct when the mental set is favourable and it is incorrect when the mental set is unfavourable. For example, we recognize the same voice if this element of expectancy is absent. But on the other hand, mental set may cause faulty recognition because you may take every knock at the door to be the one made by the person whom you are waiting for.

2. Confidence: This, too, is an indispensable element in recognition. In its absence even correct recognition becomes infested with doubt and mistake occurs. In fact, only trial and error can regulate the amount of self-confidence which one may have in a particular situation.

LAWS OF ASSOCIATION

Roughly speaking, there are two types of Laws of Association—Primary and Secondary .

There are three Primary laws of associations—

1. Law of Similarity
2. Law of Contiguity
3. Law of Contrast.

The secondary laws are of four types—

1. Law of Primacy
2. Law of Recency
3. Law of Vividness
4. Law of Frequency.

The primary laws of association

1. Law of similarity: Upon perceiving one thing, people remember things resembling the object of their perception. Past experiences are recalled if a similar experience is undergone in the present. A person will be reminded of his dead beloved if he sees the least bit of similarity in the personality of any person he sees now. When describing beauty, people are often heard remarking that his nose is like some body else's while his eyes resemble those of a third person The two persons, the one who is seen and the one who is thereby remembered, are never seen together and the association is therefore not due to proximity. There is association but it is not complete enough to cause the perceiver to mistake one for the other. In this case the association may be with any small part of the individual like the face, gait, way of talking, degree, education, wealth, name, etc.

2. Law of contiguity: Association results between two experiences which take place together. A person's friend habitually wears a cap and if he puts off his cap he will be curious to know the reason for this departure from his common practice. The friend reminds him of the cap, because the constant vision of the two together associates the memory traces of the cap to those of the friend himself. This is an example of spatial contiguity, but besides this there is temporal contiguity in association. The flowers on the mango tree remind one of mangoes because the flowers precede the mangoes. In this way, the experiences which occur in a particular order in respect of time are also associated and the perception of one reminds us of the other.

The relation of the First and second lines of a poem is not the same as that of the first and third. Of course, the relation of the second to the third may be similar. Thus the first reminds of the second, and second of the third, but First line does not remind us of the third line of that poem.

3. Law of contrast: Two mutually contradictory things, activities, persons voices, etc., have a tendency to be associated with each other. One perception is reminiscent of that with which it is contrasted while one thought directs attention to the one in contrast. Extremely hot weather makes people think of cold or rainy weather. A dark skinned person reminds one of a fair complexion person who in his turn does the same for the dark person. Pleasure-pain, heat-cold, dark-fair, long-short, good-bad, upright-inverted, and other contrasts go together and the memory or perception of one leads to memory or perception of the corresponding one which stands in contrast but all psychologists do not accept this law of contrast to be a primary association.

These primary laws of association are closely related to each other. The law of contrast is based on the laws of similarity and contiguity. The collection of mutually contrasted experiences or the thoughts of the primary laws of association lead to the formation of a relation of association between them. All religions discuss such ideas as virtue-vice, hell-heaven, good-bad at the same time. Youth reminds of old age and old age of youth, not just because they belong to the same species. Good and bad are qualities of work and virtue and vice are the results of the same. Hell and heaven are two forms of after life while youth and old age are two conditions of this life. Similarly, heat and cold are two forms of temperature just as pleasure and pain are of feeling. Thus vice reminds of virtue and not of heat while pleasure reminds of pain and not of cold. In reality these three laws are so closely related that it is difficult to separate them. Sometimes, the law of similarity comes under the law of contiguity and sometimes the law of contiguity under that of similarity. The continuity of interest and attention relates all the memory traces in the mind. From the point of view of experiences of life, law of contiguity comes first, the law of similarity is second while the law of contrast is of the least important among the laws of association.

The secondary laws of association are—

1. Law of primacy: If all the other facts remain undisturbed, the first impressions of learning or experience stay firm for a longer time. For example, the first lines of a memorized poem or a song heard are remembered for a long time while the rest is forgotten.

2. Law of recency: Other things being equal, the most recent impressions can be remembered with ease and alacrity. The concluding part of a story can be repeated with ease because these impressions are the most recent.

3. Law of vividness: The recollection will be easier and more lasting if the experience is vivid.

4. Law of frequency: If an experience is repeated very often in the mind, its recollection will be easy and it will stay for a longer time.

The secondary laws of association resemble those of retention and recall and are therefore different from the primary ones, which explain why association comes about. Associationists have tried to explain all mental activities of memory on the basis of association. But the laws of association work with the help of the interests and mental tendencies of the individual, in the absence of which the former are rendered ineffective. All things observed together are not associated in the mind due to contiguous perception. Thus the laws of association cannot take the place of the assisting factors in retention and recollection though they help to explain particular mental behaviour.

ECONOMICAL METHODS OF MEMORISING

Many experiments were conducted in psychology, with a view to effecting economy in memorising. In the experiments attempts were made, after experimenting with different methods of memorisation, to find that method by which the maximum material may be memorised in the shortest possible time. The economy of the following methods has been brought to light:

1. **Recitation:** The mental repetition of something is called recitation. Recitation makes the subject firmer than if it were read over and over again or repeated. Mental repetition is an active way of study. This saves time, at the same time assuring the longer retention of the subject.

2. **Spaced and unspaced methods:** As the name suggests, the spaced method of memorisation is one in which there are time intervals in the memorisation and the subject is connected to memory after various sittings. On the contrary, the memorisation in the unspaced method is done at one sitting, without any intervals being introduced.

Many experiments were performed in order to assess the economy effected by these two methods. In Ebbinghau's opinion, the spaced method is more economical in the memorisation of meaningless material. Belborn and Vilian opined that the spaced method is better in the memorisation of poetry and prose. Lashley considered the spaced method to be better while Cook approved of the unspaced method.

The economy in the use of either the spaced or the unspaced method depends upon the abilities of the individual and the nature and extent of the material. A short poem of 8 to 10 lines should be memorised at one sitting On the other hand, it is generally difficult to memorise a poem comprising 200 lines at one sitting because the possibilities of fatigue in attempting to learn so long a poem without rest are very great. Actually, the spaced method has many advantages over the unspaced method. Not only is the fatigue eliminated in the interval, but there is an opportunity to contemplate on the subject learnt. This helps to remove the monotony caused by long periods of study and it enables a person to keep his attention focused on learning. The interval also eliminates any wrong activities and prevents their repetition. There is no general rule about the interval between two sittings and it depends on the individual and the subject though it can be said that the interval should be long enough to remove the fatigue of the last sitting and strengthen the memory traces.

3. **Part and whole methods:** To study something by the part method is to divide it into parts before studying or memorising it. On the other hand, a subject is read according to the whole method when it is read from start to finish, as a whole. The experiments carried out to measure the superiority of these methods over each other have not yielded consistent results. Sometimes the part method showed better results while on other occasions it was the whole method which excelled. Lotti Steffens concluded from his experiments on children and grown-ups who were required to study meaningless material,

that the whole method saved 12 per cent of time as compared to the part method. Contrary to this Pechstein in an experiment, instructed 6 persons to learn 32 times employing the whole method, at the same time instructing 6 others to do the same by using the part method. When the results were compared the people using part method in their memorising had taken less time than the other six. Pechstein concluded that the part method is more advantageous than the whole method.

Actually the two methods part and whole are not contradictory. The application of one or the other method for the memorisation of a subject is decided by its extent and nature and by the ability of the individual. The whole method is better than the part method when it comes to learning a short poem but the part method proves more advantageous if the poem is a long one. In this case, it would be advisable to go through the whole poem to start with, in order to relate the different parts of the poem and to follow this up by learning it in small bits. It is generally better to use whole method if the subject is difficult because it is easier to understand its different parts individually. But, at the same time, it is essential to use the part method in making sense out of the difficult portions of the subject. Thus time can be saved in using the whole method with a short subject and the part method in the perusal of a lengthy and difficult one, but in fact, the subject will have to act according to his personal capabilities besides this general law when he wants to decide on any one particular method. If we tire easily by the whole method, the part method is unquestionably better for us.

4. Active and passive method: Memorising by utterance is the active method while mental repetition is the passive method. Many experiments have been carried out to measure the economy which these methods may effect. Gates, Ebbinghaus and his followers concluded from their experiments that the active method is better than the passive method.

Actually the active method is better than the passive in following respects—

(*i*) The activity in memorising is increased.

(*ii*) The desire to leam and the effect are maintained while the relation between the various parts is established easily and naturally.

(*iii*) The subject is understood and the rythmical grouping and localisation of the various parts of the material also take place.

(*iv*) This method forms a sort of pattern of the subject in the mind of the learner and anything missing from this pattern can be recalled easily.

(*v*) This method reduces mental distraction. But this does not mean that the passive method is always less useful than the active method. Actually, in learning anything new it is always advisable to recite it mentally before memorising it by reading it aloud.

5. Rote and intelligent methods: If a person is learning or memorising something without understanding it, he is said to be using the rote or unintelligent method. There is no apperception in this. On the other hand, the use of the intelligent method involves the understanding of the subject and apperception does come about.

The experiments to measure the economy of either of these methods reveal the consistent superiority of the intelligent over the unintelligent or mechanical method. The mechanical method does not form any association between the material and the thoughts in the mind and the matter is thus not strengthened, which results in its early elimination. On the other hand, the intelligent method lends firmness to the memory which becomes more permanent.

6. Grouping and rythm: Memorisation is considerably facilitated by rythm and grouping. It is easier to memorise poetry than prose because of the rythm scheme. A couplet contains enough meaning to be spread over several pages, but the rythm makes its memorisation easier.

7. Association: Association is no less important than the other factors in memorisation. Suppose we have to remember that the first step in the solution of arithmetical problems is the solution of the bracket and the successive steps are 'of', division, multiplication, subtraction and addition. Now in order to facilitate memorisation an association between 'B' and bracket, O and of, D and division, I and into or multiplication, S and subtraction and A and addition may be formed, keeping in mind that the letters represent the first letter of each word. The letters should now be put together to form the word BODISA, which when remembered, will keep this law in mind. Other associations in different subjects may be formed similarly.

Besides the method of memorisation detailed above, all the favourable factors in retention should be used comprehensively. The desire to memorise affords considerable assistance in remembering, because of the ease in concentration which is absolutely essential. Rest and sleep also effect memorisation and due attention should be paid to them. The use of images, pertinent to the subject also helps memorisation and retention.

FORGETTING

The difficultly, or inability, of a subject in being remembered or coming to the consciousness is the mental activity due to forgetting. It contradicts remembering and it is the failure of retention. Sometimes, almost too often, the thought is retained even though it is not recalled. Its inability to come to the conscious level can be attributed to a variety of reasons. Therefore, mere failure to recall is not the same thing as forgetting. But lack of progress in relearning is definitely forgetting. Briefly, failure of recall is partial or temporary forgetting, the failure of retention is complete or permanent forgetting.

According to Ebbinghaus, forgetting is a passive mental process. The activity continues automatically with the passage of time and the mind does not interfere with it. The activity of forgetting proceeds with good speed for some four to six hours after the learning of meaningless material but by the time 5 to 7 days have passed, the enthusiasm dies out and the activity is very slow so much so that the difference between the forgetting of the 10th and 21st day is almost imperceptible.

Some psychologists have not accepted the opinion expressed by Ebbinghaus. They think that forgetting is an active mental process implying that the mind too takes a hand, the other being the passage of time, in forgetting. Forgetting is effected in no small measure by the mental processes which take place in the interval between remembering and forgetting. The least amount of forgetting takes place in sleep but if the person engages in some other activity it is comparatively more. Forgetting is also speeden up by some injury to the brain consumption of alcoholic liquids, feeling, emotion, mental tension etc. In this way forgetting is both an active and passive process.

Causes of forgetting

Many theories about causes of forgetting are current. Ebbinghaus attributes forgetting to passage of time while Freud and Bartlett are more inclined to blame the activities which take place in the interval of forgetting.

Roughly speaking, many psychologists have given the following causes for forgetting:

1. Interpolated activity: As far as the behaviourists are concerned, it is the interpolated activity after learning which causes forgetting, the extent of forgetting depending upon the divergence of these activities from the material learnt.

2. Disuse: The theory of disuse postulates that any learnt activity or accumulated knowledge will be gradually forgotten if it is not regularly practised. Psychologists who do not agree with this view assert that forgetting is due not only to disuse but also to the activities after learning.

3. Retroactive inhibition: Some learning tends to contradict some previous learning, a tendency entitled retroactive inhibition, meaning the fatal effect of interpolated activity on learning. This theory was first proved by Muller and Pilzecker. Retroactive inhibition is specially affected by the following four things:

(*i*) *Similarity between past learning and interpolated learning:* Experiments have proved that the retroactive inhibition will increase with similarity with the past learning and interpolated activities.

(*ii*) *Difference in quantities of past learning and interpolated learning:* Retroactive inhibition will be more if the quantities of past learning and interpolated learning are vastly different in favour of the latter. But if the latter is less, the hindrance will also be less.

(*iii*) *Temporal relation of the interpolated activities:* If the interpolated activities take place soon after the previous learning the hindrance will be accentuated. The most harmful interpolated activities are those which take place either immediately after learning or just before recall while the least harmful are the ones taking place in the middle of the retention period.

(*iv*) *Intelligence and age of the learner:* Retroactive inhibition is reduced with every increase in the age and intelligence of the learner.

The two factor theory expounded by Melton and Lackun singles out two factors as having extra-ordinary effect on retroactive inhibition. The learning of a new thing causes the forgetting of the old by hindering its relearning and the other factor is the competition between the old and new memory traces.

4. Repression: Psychoanalysts believe that the major cause of forgetting is repression, *i.e.*, the pushing of the experience or thoughts into the unconscious. Freud maintained that it is natural in human beings to repress sorrowful thoughts because of the pain they cause if remembered. It was the theory of repression on which Freud founded his successful analysis of everyday forgetting in writing, speaking, recognising and the forgetting by mental patients but forgetting, in cases other than these, cannot be explained by repression as the sole cause.

5. Factors affecting learning: All the factors which affect learning also affect forgetting because forgetting is the unlearning of a learnt subject. The major factors are the following:

(*i*) *Method of learning:* As a general rule it can be said that forgetting is less in the case of whole, spaced, active and intelligent learning than in the case of part, unspaced, passive and unintelligent learning.

(*ii*) *Quantity of learning:* Within a limit, the absence of overlearning may bring about forgetting, while the same effect may be produced by over-learning outside the limit. Within the limit forgetting will be less if there is over-learning.

(*iii*) *Speed of learning:* Faster learning ensures retention while slower learning is forgotten relatively quicker.

(*iv*) *Instrument of learning:* Forgetting is more in the use of a small and less extensive instrument than in the use of a bigger and more extensive instrument. Similarly, there is more forgetting in the case of sorrowful or meaningless instrument than in the use of meaningful instruments.

6. Deficiency of thinking and repetition: Mental thinking and repetition assist retention and recall and in the same manner these factors also affect forgetting *i.e.*, in the absence of these factors forgetting increases.

7. Deficiency of the mental set: Mental set is another factor of assistance in the retention and recall of a subject so that its greater concurrence will reduce forgetting.

8. Brain injury: Often when a person suffers a brain injury he forgets many incidents and experiences and the extent of the forgetting depends upon the seriousness of the injury.

9. Use of stimulants: Wine and other stimulants have a detrimental effect on the brain, because they weaken the memory traces. Thus forgetting will be increased if such intoxicants are used.

10. Altered stimulus condition: If there is an association between the stimulus and its situation, then forgetting is facilitated by any change in the situation or condition of the stimulus. People who stay abroad for long forget their native dialect.

Besides the causes mentioned above, the factors which influence retention and recall may also cause forgetting. In brief, every factor which hinders memorisation causes forgetting.

QUESTIONS FOR EXERCISE

1. What is memory? Discuss its favourable and obstructing conditions.
2. Describe economical methods of memorising.
3. What is forgetting? Discuss its causes.
4. Write short note on—Laws of Association.

26

Motivation and Frustration

WHAT IS MOTIVATION?

Motivation is essential to the operation of organizations and classroom activities. Equipment and audiovisual aids cannot be made use of unless students are motivated. From psychology we learn that normal behaviour is caused by certain causes which relate to person's needs and/or the consequences that result from acts. Motives are expressions of a person's needs. Incentives, on the other hand, are external to the person.

CLASSIFICATION OF MOTIVES

There are various ways to classify needs. A simple but significant one is: (1) Basic, physiological or primary needs, and (2) Social, psychological or secondary needs.

Conscious action arises from needs. Needs create tensions that are modified.

Diagrammed very simply, the relation of needs to action is shown in the table below:

Steps:	1	2	3	4	5
	Individual Needs (Motives) Tension	Environment	Wants (Tension Positive Negative Incentives)	Perception	Action (Tension release)

1. Physiological needs: Physiological needs include food, water, sex, sleep, breathing and satisfactory temperature. These needs arise out of the basic physiology of life and these are important to survival and preservation of the species.

2. Secondary needs: Secondary needs represent needs of the mind and spirit, rather than of the physical body. They develop a variety of motives in each person. Many of these needs are developed as one matures. Examples of secondary needs are rivalry, self-esteem, sense of duty, self-assertion, giving, belonging and receiving affection. Secondary needs complicate the motivational efforts of teachers. These have the following characteristics:

1. Strongly conditioned by experience.
2. Varying in type and intensity among people.
3. Changing within an individual.
4. Working in groups rather than alone.
5. Often hidden from conscious recognition.
6. Nebulous feelings instead of tangible physical needs.
7. They influence behaviour. It is said, "We are logical only to the extent our feelings let us be."

Although classified as primary and secondary, human needs are inseparable in a particular human being. The state of the physical body affects the mind, and the state of mind affects the physical body. Medical research shows that physical chemistry affects the emotions and feelings. According to the renowned psychiatrist, Dr. William C. Menninger, "The psychiatrist believes that the mind and body are inseparable—the holistic concept. The former tendency to regard the mind and body as separate has been discarded. Now we study the physical, the chemical, the psychological, and the social factors of every individual who comes to us for help."

THE EXPECTANCY MODEL OF MOTIVATION

In the expectancy model developed by Victor H. Vroom, Porter and Lawler and others, motivation has been defined as the valence or strength of drive toward action. The model shows that a person's motivation towards an action at a particular time is determined by the outcomes (valence) of the action, multiplied by the strength of a person's expectation that the action will lead to the outcomes. The expectancy model shows that motivation leads to increased effort, which leads to outcomes that represent desired goals. This may be expressed in the following formula:

$$\text{Valence} \times \text{Expectancy} = \text{Motivation}$$

Here valence refers to the strength of a person's preference for one's outcome in relation to others. Expectancy is the strength of belief that a particular act will be followed by particular outcomes.

A Diagram of the Expectancy Model

Valence × Expectancy

↓

Motivation

↓

Action

Outcomes (Goal Attainment)

Satisfaction

THEORIES OF MOTIVATION

Following theories of motivation explain motivation with all its distinct varieties. These theories supplement one another and point towards the same truth.

(1) Pawn Theory. (2) Energy Theory. (3) Instinct Theory. (4) Need Theory. (5) Stimulation Theory. (6) Behaviour or Learning Theory. (7) Social Theory (8) Depth Theory. (9) Physiological Theory

1. Pawn theory: Based on the transcendental approach to the problem of life, this theory maintains that we are a 'pawn', a puppet, an instrument in the hands of destiny. Both classical and Freudian Psychologists and Behaviouristic theories of learning derive their strength from this. Pawn theory passes on the responsibility of motivation to some intangible 'mysterious power'.

2. Energy theory: No energy, no motivation. According to Freud the source of physical energy is Eros and according to Jung, it is Libido. As a matter of fact this theory offers no explanation.

3. Instinct theory: According to McDougall the originator of this theory, "The human mind has certain innate or inherited tendencies which are the essential springs or motive powers of all thought and action, whether individual or collective and are the bases from which the character and will of individuals and of nations are gradually developed under the guidance of the intellectual faculties." McDougall put forward a list of 41 instincts and attached 14 emotions to them. In Britain this theory was popular with Nunn, Burt, Ross, Hughes and Valentine, etc. However, the American psychologists do not find any weight in the theory.

4. Need theory: There are two sets of needs:

(*i*) Primary or biological, and

(*ii*) Secondary or psychological. The more intense the need, the more the motivation.

5. Stimulation theory: All inner and outer stimuli that bear upon a person at one time constitute his psychological field and determine his behaviour jointly through interaction.

6. Behaviour or learning theory: This is more elaborate than the need theory. Hull and his associates are the supporters of this theory. The theory has three main tenets:

(*i*) All the motivated behaviour is based on needs and desires;

(*ii*) All learning involves reward in the sense that only those responses that reduce need or drive are stamped in; and

(*iii*) Needs may be biological or psychological, primary or secondary.

Maslow, Tolman, Hebb and Mowrer do not share this view. They argue that all learning is not like that. Learning can be 'cognitive type' also. It is not only the 'need reduction' but also 'avoidance of pain' that goads one to leant.

7. Social theory: According to social theory, causes of the social motivational behaviour are to be found in the social environment, there are two streams of this theory:

(*i*) *Cultural pattern:* According to this view, an individual is cast in the mould of the culture to which he belongs. The different cultures would, therefore, produce different types of personalities.

(*ii*) *The field theory:* According to this theory behaviour is caused by the interaction between a person and his environment. This is propounded by Kurt Lewin.

8. Depth theory: Freud is the main protagonist of this theory. According to him the spring of action is unconscious which is dark, ruthless, very powerful and illogical. Special exploratory techniques are needed to dig out the unconscious. Unconscious motives influence our conscious thought and conduct.

9. Physiological theory: This theory holds that the secrets of mind are locked within the cells of the nervous system.

10. Hierarchy theory of Maslow: Abraham Maslow has developed a theory of human motivation that integrates most of the basic motives that psychologists had discussed for a long time. Maslow's theory of motivation is based on the view that the person has an inner nature that is constantly growing and unfolding. According to Maslow this growth and unfoldment has to occur in a certain sequence, so that we may achieve the end result called self-actualization. Maslow has suggested the following six levels or hierarchy of needs:

(*i*) Basic physiological and tissue needs.

(*ii*) Stimulation needs (sex, activity, exploration, etc.)

(*iii*) Safety needs (protection from injury and security).

(*iv*) Love and belonging needs.

(*v*) Self-esteem needs (adequacy, feeling of competence).

(*vi*) Self-actualization (fulfilment of potentialities).

Maslow calls them hierarchy or levels of needs, because he believes that the needs in one lower group must be minimally satisfied before those in the next higher group dominate behaviour. For example, people who remain more or less starved will usually be more concerned with food than about love and status, they will even jeopardise their safety in order to get food. They will have no time to think of self-actualization. Similarly, those who have enough means to satisfy physiological needs but feel socially unacceptable, will give less time to strive for love and belonging needs. But they too may feel less motivated to actualize themselves or realize their potentialities.

Now, when both physiological needs and needs for love, belongingness and acceptance are satisfied, a person feels an impetus for further development, to become what one is capable of becoming.

11. Theory of achievement motivation: Achievement motivation is the desire to do better, to achieve unique accomplishment, to compete with a standard of excellence, and to involve oneself with long term achievement goals. The theory of achievement motivation has been developed by David C. McClleland at the Harvard University, and John W. Atkinson at the University of Michigan.

Some psychologists look on all human behaviour as the organism's attempt to reduce tensions and reach a state of equilibrium. But others believe that non-organic or psychogenic motives such as the drive for status or esteem can also move the individual to activity. McClleland concluded that rather than being essentially tension states which an individual tends to eliminate, motives are also driven towards action based upon expectation. He also concluded that psychogenic motives are learned by association with primary needs gratification.. For example, an infant reacts to the comforts associated with the feeding process as well as to the food itself.

Development of achievement motivation is fostered by parents who set high standards and expectations. They stress independent training at an early age and reward the child when he masters something. Compared with parents of boys with low achievement motivation, fathers and mothers of achievements motivated boys show more warmth, give less directions and higher expectation regarding the boys performance. Mothers and fathers have different influences. Studies reveal that achievement-oriented mother dominates the home.

The common measure employed to measure achievement motivation is T.A.T. type pictures showing achievements related cues for which McClleland has developed an elaborate scoring system. The individual with high achievement scores exhibits a tendency to achieve success on a particular task whereas those with low achievement scores show a tendency to avoid failure. The tendency to achieve success is greater among the former when the strength of expectancy or probability of success, and the incentive values of success at a particular task is high enough. Men who are strong in achievement motivation have been found to be more upwardly mobile in society than men who are weak in achievement motivation.

Class-room motivation techniques

The needs are the basis for motivation. Therefore techniques that the teachers employ to arouse and maintain motivation will be successful only insofar as they make them perceive that progress is being made towards need satisfaction. Since individual children differ in regard to their specific needs according to their personality patterns and socio-economic background, the teachers will have to vary their motivational techniques and employ them judiciously. Every individual pupil should be led towards the goal that he is aware of and will want to attain. Secondly, goals should be within each pupil's reach, and should seem attainable to him. Thirdly, he should be able to judge whether or not he is attaining his goals and how he is falling short.

1. Rewards: Rewards, whether material or symbolic and psychological, enhance and satisfy child's safety, belonging and esteem needs, and as such are capable of acting as incentives. Material rewards seem to work better for poor children and symbolic rewards seem to work better for children from rich homes. Thus in order to act as an incentive a reward must be preceived by the child as of some value. As extrinsic motivator, rewards may, however, become an end in themselves, and the child may not develop any intrinsic impulsion to identify himself with the learning activity.

2. Success: Experience of success motivates a child to continue an activity. Therefore the students should be helped to perceive that successful performance is more important than any extrinsic incentive like prizes, marks and certificates. The teacher should make school work, both curricular and co-curricular, sufficiently varied so that each pupil has a chance to experience success at his own level. They must ensure frequent and regular experience of success or re-inforcement throughout all phases of learning, but particularly during the earlier and more difficult phases.

Experience of success or failure, however, is highly personal and depends on what the learner originally aspired to achieve.

3. Praise or blame: Praise and blame work differently for different students. Although experiments have shown that praise is more effective than blame in motivating pupils, but it has been observed that praise given by an unpopular teacher may have a negative effect. Personality of the child is also important here. It has been found that praise is more effective with the introverts and blame with the extroverts.

4. Competition: Competition is a spur to activity. But competition on individual basis is likely to be unequal and therefore threatening to most of the students. Competition between groups makes it possible to spread the share of success or failure.

5. Co-operation: Co-operation too provides motivation since it provides social situation to learners when they find satisfaction of their acceptance and belonging needs.

6. Knowledge of progress: Pupils' knowledge of their progress, of how well they are moving towards their goal is a very effective form of motivation. It also helps them put greater efforts. Individual progress charts not only inform him of how he is doing but also keep the child involved in learning activity. Children are said to learn better through programmed learning because they get immediate information of success or failure.

7. Novelty: The striving towards self-actualization makes pupils search for the new and the different. Field trips, excursions, dramatics, sports, literary activities, etc., satisfy the pupils' needs for self-actualization by providing them opportunities. But their safety needs require that they should know beforehand when and how the new experiences will be provided.

WHY DO PEOPLE BEHAVE THE WAY THEY BEHAVE?

Learning is a change in behaviour brought about by activity. But "Why do we behave at all", "Why do we behave the way we are behaving?—are the questions which have been drawing the attention of the psychologists, almost from the beginning. Psychologists have given many answers, to these questions of "why" of behaviour.

Instincts as springs of behaviour

Probably the oldest answer is that given by psychologists like William James, William McDougall, Cyril Burt, etc., who said that the springs of human behaviour lay in "instincts". Instincts were defined as complex inherited tendencies, common to all members of a species, compelling each individual: (*i*) to perceive and pay attention to certain objects and situations, (*ii*) to experience positive or negative emotional excitement on perceiving them, and (*iii*) thereupon to act in a way which is likely in the long run to preserve the individual. According to McDougall, "The human mind has certain innate or inherited tendencies which are the essential springs or motive powers of all thought and action. " He lists the main instincts as parental, escape, pugnacity, repulsion, gregariousness, self-assertion, submission, mating, acquisitiveness and a number of minor instincts. He further says that under the working of intelligence and learning experiences, the emotional dispositions attached to each specific instinct (such as anger with pugnacity, or fear with escape, etc.) get organised around objects, persons or principles. These organizations are called sentiments of which the chief and supermost is the self-regarding sentiment. According to McDougall these sentiments determine a great deal of behaviour and make it relatively consistent and predictable. Sigmund Freud proposed two fundamental instincts, the sex instinct and the self-preservative instinct. Later on, he combined these two into one "life instinct" and proposed additional "death instinct."

Criticism of instinct theory

As explanation of the 'why' of human behaviour, instincts were soon questioned by psychologists like Burnard, Dunlop, Watson and Woodworth. They pointed out that most human behaviour, especially adult behaviour, is very much influenced by learning and is therefore not innate. A number of experiments were conducted to show that even animal behaviour depended to some extent on learning or external.

1. Social anthropologists: Social anthropologists like Linton, Mead and Benedict also asserted that far from being influenced by the innate universal instincts, human behaviour was shaped and determined by the cultural patterns like educational practices and social roles. The behaviour and personality varied widely from group to group depending upon the customs in each culture.

2. Drive theory: After the rise and decline of the instinct doctrine, a new type of explanatory theory became prominent. This was the drive theory. All organisms have physiological needs such as need for food, water elimination, etc. When such needs are not readily satisfied the organism is driven to activity. On this basis we speak of physiological drives, such as hunger drive, thirst drive, etc. Drive is the physiological deficit or tissue deficiency. The strength of a drive may be known from the speed of running towards an incentive (food, etc.), or away from an aversion stimulus (shock), the rate of pressing lever that brings the incentive, or how much shock the organism will take in order to reach a satisfying stimulus or incentive.

There are different explanations of how drives activate the organism. One explanation looks upon drives as source of energy' as energizers of behaviour in the sense that drive states are accompanied by the release of hormones and neural mechanisms. Another explanation looks upon the physiologically driven organism as in a state of physiological disequilibrium and the final act such as getting food or water is thought of as compensatory—as restoring equilibrium or homeostatis. But this explanation of drive does not hold good in the case of human beings. A well-fed person may still have a drive to eat a different variety of food. Similarly, sexual activity in the case of human beings cannot be considered as an example of homeostatic response.

Criticism of drive theory

The drive theory might explain behaviour among animals like rats, monkeys etc., but it appears inadequate to describe and explain all of human behaviour. Human beings are far more complex and show much greater plasticity of behaviour than animals. They have physiological drives, but they have other strong urges too which seem to be acquired and learned in a social environment *e.g.*, desire to acquire and hold property and other possessions.

3. Concept of motive: To explain these social strivings as well as the physiological drives found in human beings, the psychologists now use the term motives. The term motive includes influences of learning in explaining the source of human behaviour and also indicates the direction of an activity towards a goal. Thus, a motive is that which arouses, sustains and directs activity.

Types of motives: Motives are classified into three types:

(*i*) Physiological Motives.

(*ii*) Social Motives.

(*iii*) Personal Motives.

(*i*) *Physiological motives:* These include hunger, thirst, sex, sleep, elimination of body wastes, maintenance of constant body temperature, sensory stimulation, etc. Emotions too are comparable with physiological motives. The physiological correlates of emotions energize behaviour in the sense that physiological drives energize it. Like physiological motives they impel us to activity. They also engender goal-oriented activities like the lover's affectionate behaviour toward his loved one, and the angry man's aggression toward the object of his anger. Some activate the escape motive. Fear and annoyance exemplify this fact. Sometimes, emotions move us to tears or to performance of helpful and benevolent acts.

(*ii*) *Social motives:* The social motives are learned and developed differently in different cultural settings. In the daily life of an adult behaviour released by learned motive is much more in evidence than that which could merely satisfy physiological needs. Social motives are sometimes called secondary or derived in the sense that they have their origin in the gratification of primary physiological motives in infancy and childhood. For example, an individual learns to desire social approval because the experience of approval from parents and other persons has been earlier associated with the satisfaction of primary needs. The desire for approval is, therefore, said to be a derived and learned motive.

Social motives are the motives that seem to be the reasons for behaviour one sees daily among people, whose physiological needs are more than satisfied. The social motives included need for social approval, for affection, for a respected place in our group, for possessing money, gold, degrees and other status symbols. These are the motives which provide impetus to our action.

(*iii*) *Personal motives:* Many motives are much more personal than those mentioned earlier. They are sort of variations on the universal or cultural theme and are learned through one's unique life experiences. Individual interests, attitudes, self-concept and life-goals are the examples of personal motives. Since interests show an individual's feeling of like or dislike for a situation, and the attitude shows disposition to act positively or negatively in regard to something, they both function as motivators. Without an interest one may not like to act in a situation. But active interest functions as strong motive. Similarly, a person's attitudes will attract him towards certain situations and repel him from others.

One's self-concept too can act as powerful motive. Self-concept includes the cultural picture of what one is, as a teacher, as a student, as a person with particular background and level of aspiration. A person's self-image determines not only the kinds of goals he sees as suitable for him to strive for, but also his level of aspiration. One's life goals too function like strong motives.

But not all motives of personal type are manifest or known to the individual. Some of them may be unconscious and influence him strongly but he seldom knows them. Many strong dislikes, prejudices and other symptoms of maladjustment are due to unconscious motives.

ANALYTICAL PSYCHOLOGY

Jung (1879—1961), a famous Western psychoanalyst transcended both Freud and Adler and went deep into the human psyche revealing some of its mysteries. He was more of a philosopher and less of a physiologist. Starting as one of Freud's associates he started differing with him and by 1912 he developed serious ideological and personal differences and founded his own school named Analytical Psychology.

Jung considered life itself as an 'ever living fire' and self-realization as the aim of life, which is far beyond satisfaction of sex and seeking of an easy-chair high prestigious job. Of course, there are persons who are made after these two things, but this does not minimise the importance of 'self-realization'. We may brush aside such differences as individual differences.

Beyond Freud

Jung does not question the importance of sex and status but be goes beyond these. He often appears to attack Freudian Concept of Sexuality. He stresses certain clear cut aim of life before the individual. He states, "I have observed that a directed life is in general better, richer and healthier than an aimless one, and that it is better to go forward with the stream of life than backward against it."

We are living in an age of anxiety and tension and lawlessness in the outer world. Western man expects that psychology should be able to assist him in understanding the incomprehensible factors of life. Jung thinks that there cannot be law and order in this outer world so long as man does not feel at home in the inner world, in his own soul. Jung is very near the living process of the soul. He wants to lead people to responsible attitude towards life and a responsible way of living, suited to the peculiarities of each man. Jung is optimistic about human nature.

The structure of self

Jung does not deny the outer world but he gives importance to the inner world and the deep-seated unconscious. He gives a complete picture of the 'Self' with its various aspects in the outer as well as the inner world. He thinks that the term 'Self' stands for the integration of the various aspects of the personality, conscious and unconscious. Development of personality takes place when an individual chooses his way and separates himself from the crowd. His concepts about the different aspects of the self are woven into one integrated whole.

Concept of unconscious

Jung accepts conscious as well as unconscious. But his concept of unconscious is entirely different from that of Freud. He thinks that the unconscious is the matrix out of which the conscious has been evolved. Unconscious is not evolved out of the conscious but *vice-versa*. Consciousness is the product of growth, whereas unconsciousness arises from unknown depths. Jung's concept of the unconscious is that of something vaster and more comprehensive. According to Jung unconscious was just not the dumping ground of the repressed desires from the conscious as Freed thought. Jung admitted Freud's explanation of the unconscious but felt that it was only a part of the vaster unconsciousness, which is shared by an individual with all other people in all places and all times.

Types of unconscious

Jung has classified unconscious in two types:

(*i*) Primary or Racial unconscious.

(*ii*) Personal unconscious.

(*i*) *Racial unconscious:* Racial unconscious consists of primitive beliefs and modes of response handed down over centuries. We call these ancient ways of thinking as 'archetypes'.

(*ii*) *Personal unconscious:* The unnoticed, forgotten or re-pressed incidents of each person's life form personal unconscious. Here Jung agrees with Freud. The unconscious of an individual is opposite to his conscious mind and is complementary to it. The unconscious tries to correct and moderate the conscious.

We can compare the picture of the mind given by Jung with compensatory aspect of a photograph of a range of mountains mirrored in a lake below. Just as each mountain has its equal and opposite reflection, in the same way each mental attribute has its equal and opposite complement. To Jung, therefore, a man is both better and worse than he knows. The coward is a brave man and the brave is a coward in his unconscious, the romantic is realist and *vice versa*. According to Jung, different layers of unconscious are as follows:

(*i*) Animal life, (*ii*) Primitive ancestors, (*iii*) Ethnological groups (races), (*iv*) Nations, (*v*) Clans, and (*vi*) Family.

Jung further observes that conscious mind permits itself to be trained like a parrot, but the unconscious does not do so. The unconscious contains the experiences of the whole race. According to Jung, "Body is a sort of museum of its phylogenetic history so is the mind." The unconscious is more than just containing personal memories. The collective unconscious represents a sort of social memory. Certain identical customs are found in widely scattered parts of the earth. Siblings dreams are very similar even though they may be hundreds of miles apart in different milieus.

Components of racial unconscious

There is only racial unconscious at birth. It has got three things at that time:

(*i*) Individual instinctive reactions;

(*ii*) Ancestral behaviour; and

(*iii*) Ancestral interpretations, *i.e.*, belief in ghosts, fairies, etc. The unconscious forgets nothing. It is mnemic in nature.

While explaining the concept of unconsciousness Jung mentions archetypes, symbols, libido, shadow, persona and the soul images. These concepts are explained as follows:

1. Archetypes: Archetypes are ancient ways of thinking and symbols or figures which explain life. Symbols are generally based upon experience of the individual but the experience of the individual is the experience of the human race, the collective unconscious. The collective unconscious is the "all controlling deposit of ancestoral experience from untold millions of year" to which is added small amount of variation and differentiation by each century. These experiences are archetypes. Their sources are to be found in profound religious thought, in enduring literature and art which draw their universal inspiration from the depths of human psyche.

The archetypes are eternally inherited identical forms and ideas. They may appear as persons, demons, fabulous animals, natural forces, objects or geometrical forms and numbers, etc. To quote Jung, "Archetypes resemble the beds of river. An archetype is something like an old water-course along which the water of life flowed for a time, digging a deep channel for itself. The longer it flowed the deeper the channel, and the more likely it is that sooner or later the water will return."

Archetypes are psychic forces which must be taken seriously. As psychic organ archetypes are present in every one. They are complexes of experience that they affect our personal life. Archetypal foundations can never be legitimately ignored.

2. Symbols: Symbols are of greater psychological value as they are necessary openings to understand 'human experience'. They serve to reveal the depths of the soul. They are created by deep unconscious. They are found all over the world. They appear in dreams, art production, visions and fantasies. Symbols lead to the expressions of archetypal thinking.

3. Libido: While retaining the Freudian term *libido* Jung gives it a different meaning. He means by it a life energy underlying all national phenomena, including the human psyche. Sexuality is one not all manifestation of *libido*. *Libido* is essentially creative and it takes many forms. It is life itself. With the individual gaining maturity it may follow different channels. Jung suggests three stages of *libido* development: (*i*) Presexual, up to three-four years the infant has epoch of sucking, nutrition only, *i.e.*, mouth zone, (*ii*) Sharp changes take place when the child leaves the mouth zone and the individual develops and learns to turn from parents to the real world around him. (*iii*) *Libido* gets direction in two ways—Introversion and Extroversion.

4. Shadow: Shadow represents the unconscious. It is closely related to us as the dark reflection of our conscious efforts. It may become monstrous. It may actually overwhelm the ego-conscious. It is a highly personal creation. It reflects the universals of human experience. It is 'personal' only in a very limited manner.

5. Ego conscious: Jung's concept of the ego-conscious is similar to that of Freud.

6. Persona: Persona is adaptively organized image of the self which all of us form during the course of living, as we develop our goals and ideals. Extroverts can change persona as they change dress. It may differ at different times, places and persons. Idenfitication with persona is full of dangers. It represents the face we show to the world. It is necessary for social living.

7. The soul images: The soul image (Anima-Animus) lies deeper in racial unconscious. Every woman has her animus, the male component. The anima includes archetypal images of woman, the eternal mother, the virgin, the harlot, the witch, the temptress, the spiritual guide like Dante's Beatrice.

8. Psychological types: *Libido* takes two directions—Extroversion and Introversion. Both are necessary for complete living. Freud's stress on sexual relations is extroversive wliile Adler's insistence on status seeking is introversive. According to Jung attitudes complement each other. The individual has the counterpart, even within himself. The extrovert wants to adjust himself to the reality of his environment. The introvert seeks to adjust himself to the world which lies within himself. For Jung the contents of the unconscious possess a greater reality than the things of the outer world.

Each psychological type performs four functions—sensation, intuition, feeling and thinking. All the four are essential for ideal living and should work in harmony. Sensation concerns the present, intuition with the potential—what the living will be or has been, feeling gives a sense of values and thinking tells what a thing is in an abstract manner. Thinking coupled with intuition may take one away from reality and coupled with sensation, it may bring him down to reality.

Eight categories of personality

With each of these functions the same person may have one dominant general attitude in the conscious region of the mind and the other in the unconscious. Personality types fall in eight categories, according to these functions. All persons may be ranged in a continuously graded series ranging from extreme introversion to extreme extroversion.

The eight categories of personality according to the functions are the following:

(1) Thinking. (2) Empirical Thinking. (3) Sensation (Empirical). (4) Empirical Feeling. (5) Feeling. (6) Intuitive Feeling. (7) Intuitive. (8) Intuitive Thinking.

Educational implications of Jung's theory

1. Creation of proper environment: The teachers and the parents should make efforts to create proper environment for the child so that he is helped to find out his own self and motivated to contribute his best for his development. Extreme domination hinders development and *vice versa*.

2. Special assistance to extrovert and the introvert: The teacher should help both types of children in proper expression. Special help should be given to the introverted young children lest they should fall into dangers. They should be encouraged to enter into living contacts with other persons and to have their interests widened. The extrovert should be helped to lead a more balanced life.

3. Full expression: The child should get opportunities for expression. Due freedom should be given to him. No rigid discipline should be imposed.

4. Healthy pictures: Healthy pictures of different objects should be put before the child. Negative pictures with many conflicts should not be painted before the mind of the child. The teacher as well as the parents should be mentally healthy, they should not be torn between the conflicts themselves.

5. Creativity: Appropriate opportunities for creative expression should be provided in the school so that the child may express the message of unconscious through creative work which may help him in attaining integration of personality.

6. Due recognition to the child: Due recognition should be given to the child and he be treated as an individual and not considered as a 'cog in a machine'.

7. Death: According to Jung while the first half of life is spent in learning to live, the second half should be spent in learning to accept old age gracefully and in preparation for death. Proper education is required for this too.

8. Self-realization: Self-realization is the aim of life which the individuals should be taught to achieve.

9. Home: For proper emotional training to the child home should provide a pleasant environment. Children do not get proper direction in restless homes. Lack of proper freedom or licence in the home—both are injurious for the development of the child's personality the child does not get proper opportunity for communication with his unconscious in a bad home.

10. A sense of security: The school should assist the child to have a sense of security and protection.

11. Importance of religion: Religion is important in the life of man. It cannot be left out of any scheme of education for the young. The child should be taught to realize the peace and calmness that comes through religion.

12. Appropriate education at every stage: Jung observes, "To remain child too long is childish, it is just as childish to move away and then assume that childhood no longer exists because we do not see it." Thus, appropriate education at every step of life is very necessary.

13. Importance of individual differences: Jung considers individual differences very important and necessitate the provision for diversified courses.

JUNG *Vs.* FREUD

1. The unconscious: Freud thinks that the unconscious is evolved out of conscious by repression, etc. He compares the human mind with an Iceberg whose little visible part is consciousness while nine-tenth lies hidden as subconscious or unconscious. He attaches importance to ego and talks about super-ego, ego and Id. An individual wants fulfilment of his desires. The repression of these desires leads to further troubles.

Jung's approach is entirely different. He believes that conscious is evolved out of unconscious which contains experience of the whole human race. The person and ego in the conscious are referred to by Jung. He gave vaster meaning to unconscious and racial and collective unconscious. He attaches great importance to the unconscious.

2. **Religion:** Freud refers to religion as a universal neurosis, Jung regards it as a great treasure which provides source of life.

3. **Morality:** Unlike Freud, Jung regards morality to be a function of life. Morality is inborn according to Jung.

4. **Death:** Freud considers life a circuitous route to death. Jung regards death as another phase of life and states that one should be prepared for it.

5. **Creativity:** Freud does not attach importance to creativity whereas Jung thinks that unconscious expresses itself through creative work.

6. **Dreams:** Freud and Jung both think that dreams provide clue to the unconscious. Freud considers dreams wishfulfilments. According to him our repressed desires seek satisfaction in dreams and dreams preserve sleep. Jung talks of prospective and compensatory function of dreams. Dreams provide solution to the problems. Our psyche expresses human experience of the races through symbols in the dreams. Dreams are important for therapeutic purposes.

7. **Neurosis:** Freud regards neurosis as a disease. He takes it in its negative aspect. Disintegration of personality takes place in neurosis and the person moves towards abnormality. According to Jung neurosis is a positive healing factor of life. It is an attempt by the neurotic to lift himself. 'Freud's method is that of a surgeon who is concerned with removing a tumour or unhealthy growth in a patient, while Jung's is that of a physician who tries to find out the deficiencies in his vital contents or vitamins and in his general physiological system."

8. **Libido:** Freud regards *libido* as sex and emphasizes sex gratification. Even early childhood activities like thumb-sucking are termed as sex-satisfying. Jung does not agree with Freudian concept of sexuality. He retains the term 'libido' and calls it a life force which expresses itself in number of ways.

9. **Philosophy:** Freud is a determinist. He believes that childhood experiences determine one's personality. Jung also gives great importance to early childhood experiences but he remarks that one's philosophy of life can change one's attitude entirely. He believes in idealism and morality. He talks of self-realization as aim of life.

10. **Goals of life:** Freud states that there are only two goals of life—satisfaction of sex and back to the inorganic states. On the other hand, according to Jung, self-realization and self-propagation are greatest goals of life.

11. **Individual differences:** Jung seems to take more interest in individual differences but Freud is more interested in universal dynamics.

12. Basic approach: Jung is mystic philosopher; Freud, a mythological scientist; and Adler, a practical psychologist.

13. Association: Freud believes in free association. He tries to discover and depend upon the past life. As an analyst he tries to play the role of a father or mother. Jung believes in controlled association. He tries to discover and depend upon the present adaptation in life. As an analyst he tries to play the role of a God or a mythical hero besides the roles of father and mother. He recognizes 'repression' and makes use of the concept of 'regression', but in a different way.

Relative value of the three approaches

Freud's approach is best suited for a 'neurotic child' through free association and cathartic outpour of pent-up emotions. Jung's approach is best suited for a creative child through a provision of harmonious atmosphere where the racial unconscious may give expression to its archetypes through him. Adler's approach is best suited for a 'normal child' through a probe in his life style, family life and other environment providing him with an opportunity to express his best talent.

Jung seems to be more of a mystic than a realist. Some critics point out that his concepts of the 'self' and 'mind' cannot be proved scientifically. It is argued that his interpretation of dreams and dream-symbols is more subject to the whims and fancies of the interpreter which is not the case with the Freudian school. Jung unfolds new realism of 'unfathomable' collective unconscious. After giving due allowance to certain mystic elements, Jung's theory of Analytical Psychology is of immense philosophical value.

ADLER'S THEORY OF MOTIVATION

1. Fictional finalism: Shortly after Adler terminated his relations with the circle that surrounded Freud, he came under the philosophical influence of Hans Vaihinger whose book *The Psychology of "as if"* had been published in 1911. Vaihinger propounded the idea that man lives by many fictional ideas which do not have any counterpart in reality "All then are created equal", "honesty is the best policy" and "the end satisfies the means", enable man to deal more effectively with reality.

Adler took note of this philosophical doctrine of idealistic positivism while propounding his own design.

He found the idea that man is motivated more by his expectations of the future than by the experiences of the past. Neither Vaihinger nor Adler believed in predestination or fatality. Like Jung Adler identified Freud's theory with the principle of causalty and his own with the principle of finalism. He says, "Individual psychology insists absolutely on the indispensability of finalism for the understanding of all psychological phenomenon. Causes, powers, instincts, impulses and the like cannot serve to explain man's behaviour. Experiences, traumata, sexual development mechanisms cannot yield an explanation but the perspective in which these are regarded, the individual way seeing them, subordinates all life to the final goal can do so.

The final goal may be a fiction, an ideal which is nonetheless not attainable. This is a very real spur to marvellous drivings and the ultimate explanation of his conduct. A normal person could free himself from the influence of these fictions and face reality when necessity demanded. This is something that the neurotic person is not capable of doing. There were three stages in normal person's thinking:

(*i*) to be aggressive;

(*ii*) to be powerful; and

(*iii*) to be superior.

2. Striving for superiority: Adler's concept of superiority is something analogous to Jung's concept of the self or Goldstein's principle of self-actualization. It is striving for perfect completion. It is "the great upward drive." Adler writes "I began to see clearly in every psychological phenomenon the striving for superiority. It runs parallel to physical growth and is an intrinsic necessity of life itself. It strikes at the root of all solutions of life's problems and is manifested in the way in which we meet these problems. All our functions follow its direction. They strive for conquest, security, increase, either in the right or wrong direction. The impetus from minus to plus never ends. The urge from below to above never ceases. Whatever premises all our philosophers and psychologists dream of self-preservation, pleasure-principle, equalization—all these are but vague representations, attempts to express the great upward drive." Striving for superiority or perfection is innate. It is a part of life. It is life itself. It is a prepotent dynamic principle. It may manifest itself in a thousand different ways. Each person has his own concrete mode of achieving or trying to achieve perfection.

3. Inferiority feelings and compensations: According to Adler, inferiority feelings are not a signs of abnormality. They are the cause of all improvement in men's lot. They may be exaggerated by special conditions such as pampering or rejecting the child which may result in abnormal manifestations, such as the development of an inferiority complex or a compensatory superiority or a sense of incompleteness as the great driving force of mankind. Man is pushed by the need to overcome his inferiority and pulled by the desire to be superior.

4. Social interest: Adler was an advocate of social justice and supporter of social democracy. He enlarged his conception of man to include the factor of social interest. According to Adler, "Social interest is the true and inevitable compensation for all the natural weaknesses of individual human beings." Social interest is inborn. Man is a social creature by nature and not by habit. However, like any other aptitude, this innate predisposition does not appear spontaneously. It has to be brought to enjoyment by guidance and training. Adler believed in the benefits of education. He spent a great deal of his time in establishing child guidance clinics, in improving the schools and in educating the public regarding proper methods of rearing children. Social interest replaced selfish interest.

5. Style of life: Style of life is the most distinctive feature of Adler's Psychology and is the recurrent theme in all of his writings. Style of life is the principle by which the individual personality functions. It is the whole that commands the parts. It explains the uniqueness of a person. Everyone has a style of life but no two people develop the same style. One person tries to become superior through developing his intellect, while another strives to achieve muscular perfection. The intellectual has one style of life, the athlete another. The intellectual reads, studies and thinks. He lives a more solitary life than the active man does. He arranges the details of his existence, his daily routine, his relations to his family, friends and acquaintance, in accordance with his goal of intellectual superiority. Everything he does, he does with an eye to his ultimate goal. All of a person's behaviour springs from his style of life.

6. Stage of forming style of life: The style of life is formed very early in childhood, by the age of four or five. The attitudes, feelings and apperceptions become fixed and mechanized at an early age. It becomes extremely difficult to change the style of life at a later stage.

7. The creative self: The doctrine of a creative self asserts that man makes his own personality out of the raw material of heredity and experience. Adler said "Heredity only endows him with certain impressions. These abilities and impressions and the manner in which he experiences them that is to say, the interpretations he makes of these experiences—are the bricks or in other words, his attitude in life, which determines his relationship to the outside world." The creative self gives meaning to life. It creates the goal as well as the means to goal.

Concluding observations

Adler gave a humanistic theory of personality which was the antithesis of Freud's conception of man. By endowing man with altruism, humanitarianism, co-operation, creativity, uniqueness and awareness, he restored to man a sense of dignity and worth that psycho-analysis had pretty largely destroyed. His portrait of man was more satisfying and more hopeful.

FREUD, ADLER AND JUNG

Freud's system is the most intricate, Jung's most profound and Adler's most practical. Following is the comparison of the three on some fundamental issues.

1. Social Urges: In sharp contrast to Freud's major assumption that man's behaviour is motivated by inborn instinct and Jung's principal axiom that man's conduct is governed by inborn archetypes, Adler assumed that man is motivated primarily by social urges. He is inherently a social being.

Adler is just as biological in his viewpoint as Freud and Jung. All the three assume that man has an inherent nature which shapes his personality. Jung emphasized primordial thought patterns, Adler stressed social interest and Freud stressed sex. This stress upon the social determinants of behaviour which had been overlooked or minimised by Freud and Jung is Adler's greatest contribution to psychological theory. It directed the attention of psychologists to the significance of social variables. It helped to develop the field of social psychology at a time when it needed support, from the ranks of psycho-analysis.

2. Concept of creative self: Adler's self is highly personalized subjective system which interprets and makes purposeful the experiences of the organism. This concept of creative self was new to psycho-analytic theory. It helped to compensate for the extreme "Objectivism" of classical psycho-analysis which depended almost entirely upon biological needs and external stimuli to account for the dynamics of personality. It played a major role in recent theorization regarding personality.

3. Uniqueness of Personality: Adler considered each person to be a unique configuration of motives, traits, interests and values. Every act performed by a person bears the stamp of his own distinctive style of life. Adler added other significant factors to Freudian monologue on sex. Man is primarily a social and not a sexual creature. He is motivated by social and not by sexual interest. He strives to develop a unique style of life in which the sexual drive plays a minor role. Adler's dethroning of sex was a welcome relief for many people from the monotonous pansexualism of Freud.

4. Consciousness: Adler made consciousness the centre of personality. This made him pioneer in the development of ego-oriented psychology. Man is a conscious being. He is conscious of his inferiorities and the goals for which he strives. He is a self-conscious individual capable of planning and guiding his actions with full knowledge of their meaning for his own self-realization. This is in complete contrast to Freud's theory which had virtually reduced consciousness to the status of a non-entity.

Educational implications of Adlerian psychology

1. Child's style of life: Adlerian Psychology tries to discover the child's style of life to find out its goal. Education aims to lead the child to develop those abilities which are necessary for favourable character formation and to prepare it for a correct and courageous solution of the problems of life. The life style is formed during the first four or five years. Therefore the upbringing at this time is of utmost importance. The father's influence during this period is relatively small as his work hardly permits him to be as much with the child as the mother. Therefore, it is the mother who conducts the child rearing.

2. Self education: Adlerian Psychology appeals to all those having to do something with the education of the children. Self- education is prerequisite for correct education of others. The educator must renounce his striving for power so that the child is not subject to the pressures of its own inferiority and the superiority of the teacher. A teacher, a parent, a doctor and a gardener cannot afford to be pessimistic. The child is not mere wax in the hands of the educators as many think but takes an active part in the development process. The adult who is bringing up the child must observe carefully how the child comprehends this or that. In order to avoid failure the inferiority complex must be checked at its source.

3. Check on punishment: In general a teacher wants to use the quickest means to keep a class in order and they favour even whipping as punishment. However, Individual Psychology does not approve of beating in any form, the effect of whipping is quite injurious.

4. Check on rivalry and competition: The parents should avoid causing rivalry between the children. Each one must be able to develop freely without having to fear competition from the other. Children should be accustomed at an early stage to pay attention to rules and to be considerate of others. A teacher should never allow a child to lose hope. It is the sacred duty of the educationist to encourage the child.

5. Equality of sexes: Children should grow up with the firm conviction that both the sexes are equally significant but different. During the period of puberty or adolescence a period of transition which is full of difficult problems, uncertainty and doubt, the teacher has to play the part of a dependable comrade.

6. Individual Differences: Individual differences should be accepted but must not be interpreted as deficiencies.

WHAT IS FRUSTRATION?

Obstacles in the fruition of motivational activity of an individual lead to frustration, which in turn exerts considerable influence upon his conduct Frustration is the state of some desire or tendency being unfulfilled. For example, if a student desires to stand first in his class, but is foiled in his goal time and again, he is frustrated. Evidently, frustration is the outcome of obstacles in the path of an individual's goal or objective. There is no inevitable rule that obstacles must lead to frustration. Some individuals who have phenomenal will power overcome all such obstacles but sometimes the obstacles that hinder an individual's objective are so caused as to be unsurmountable. In such a situation, it is only natural for him to feel frustrated. Whenever an individual is motivated towards a particular goal whose achievement is interfered with and hindered by the presence of some object or situation, the individual is said to be frustrated.

CAUSES OF FRUSTRATION

Practically, of course, it would not be within the bounds of possibility to recount all causes of all frustrations that are experienced by individuals in different situations of life, but they can be generally divided into the following two classes:

1. External causes: Frustrations can be the result of many such external causes as physical, economic ot social situations, etc. The main external causes are the following—

(*i*) *Social factors:* Every individual acts within a specific though undefinable social context, so that he sometimes comes into conflict with society's customs and rules of conduct. In situations of this kind, social factors lead to frustration. If an individual wants to many a young lady belonging to an alien religion, he may find it difficult to obtain the sanction of his parents, in which case one can only expect him to become frustrated.

(*ii*) *Physical factors:* Man exists in a physical environment, that sometimes assists him in his endeavours, while at others it hinders his activities. He is led to frustration when such physical phenomena as floods, earthquakes, excessive rains, etc , defy his best efforts and put them to nought. Excessive rain, to take a simple example, besides interfering with an individual's food seeking activities, hinders his general movement and thus makes life difficult.

(*iii*) *Economic factors:* Most of man's activities are directly or indirectly influenced by economic factors such as economic status, demand and supply of commodities in the market, prices of essential commodities, availability of consumer goods, and others. The presence of such factors may hinder his tendencies and lead to much frustration. An individual can commonly be faced with a frustrating situation if his income is reduced, the availability of consumption goods is reduced or the prices of commodities increase beyond all reasonable limits, etc.

2. Internal factors: This classification includes all those factors that are present in the individual himself, or those for which no one else can be held accountable such as physical and mental faults, unrelated requirements, immoral aims, personality and character faults, etc. The following is a brief description of them:

(*i*) *Individual faults and limitations:* Many faults of a person are individually his own, and they hinder his aspirations These faults can relate to any form of development such as physical, mental, related to personality, character or any other aspect of his being. For example, some students fail to secure very high marks in examinations despite the most unremitting effort, for the simple reason that they are endowed with a meagre intellect. Similarly, it is natural for physically handicapped individual to experience frustration. Faults of personality can make the individual's adaptive activity difficult. Such an individual is constantly in the grip of anxiety because he cannot adapt himself to members of his family, his vocation and of society in general.

(*ii*) *Unrelated needs:* Whenever an individual feels the need for something that is completely unconcerned with his present capacity and ability he fails to satisfy it. For example, if a student belonging to the ordinary middle class family aspires to go abroad for higher education, such a wish will almost inevitably bring him considerable frustration. Similar frustration can be the result when two mutually contradictory needs are aroused since only one of them can be fulfilled and one would of necessity have to be rejected. A student may be equally keen on standing first in the class as well as on roaming around town and countryside. Normally, it would not be possible for him to combine both desires successfully, and one will have to be avoided. The rising of mutually contradictory motives and desires is a common occurrence in life, which makes choice between them unavoidable. The second or rejected motive almost invariably leads to frustration.

(*iii*) *Mental conflicts:* The greatest internal cause of frustration is mental conflict, which is caused by many factors. One of the commonest causes of mental conflict is the situation in which the individual is involved in ethical considerations of propriety and impropriety relating to some particular action or thing. A child who has been inspired to steal something is divided between the fear of being caught and disgraced on the one hand and the attraction of the object on the other. In a state of this kind, he is neither able to perpetrate the crime, and nor does the thought of stealing it leave his mind in peace. Similar though less clandestine and undesirable occasions of mental conflict occur daily in life, and even add spice to it.

MEANS OF AVOIDING FRUSTRATION

Acute frustration always has the worst effect on an individual's bodily and mental health. Normally, of course, the individual is frequently faced with frustrations, and there is no way of completely eliminating this phenomenon from life, yet it is possible to avoid extreme frustration that leads to complete debility. It is the responsibility of the parents to see that their children do not face frustrations in their development. The following ways can be adopted:

1. Fulfilment of needs: In order to protect an individual from frustration, it is essential that the individual's needs be fulfilled. For example, food, clothing, toys and other necessities should be available to the child, because he will naturally desire them when he sees other children possessing them, and if he is not provided with them, it will lead to frustration.

2. Preventing improper desires from arising: But it is not possible to satisfy all the proper and improper wishes of any individual. Once a wish has come into being, be it proper or improper, its unfulfilment will inevitably result in frustration. To avoid such consequences, it is essential that his character and personality be developed in such a manner that he is well equipped to adapt to his circumstances. Young boys and girls of today are found to develop strong desires for new and more fashionable clothes when they see others around them wearing them, forgetting completely the financial inability of their parents to satisfy such extravagant needs. In such cases, it is for the teacher to develop the right mental attitude in children.

3. Reducing unrelated objectives: Just as unrelated desires cause frustration unrelated and disjoined objectives and aims also create frustration and pain. Hence, teachers and parents should educate the children not to set themselves to contradictory goals. And for this, what can be better than to place before them such ideals as simple living and high thinking.

4. Guidance: It is difficult for any one individual to be constantly solving all his own problems, be he a child, adolescent, adult, male or female. Many of our younger generation are unaware of the subjects they should take up for study and the course that they should pursue. The obvious result is that they usually pick out subjects that do not conform to their natural talents, and have frustration and mental torture when they fail to succeed in spite of continuous intense effort. In such circumstances, it is essential that the child be given proper educational guidance. Once his education is complete, almost every young man has to decide upon a career and a particular vocation, and it is a matter of common experience that there are in fact very few fortunate young men who choose the right vocation, most others being resigned to a life of frustration and misery through having made the wrong choice at the crucial moment. Vocational guidance can usually help to avoid such serious consequences, as it can put the right man in the right job. Beside education and vocation, there may be a multitude of problems that the individual is not in a position to solve for himself. For example, many young men find it difficult to concentrate upon studies depite the most consistent application and this disturbs their mental peace and calm. Here, the only feasible thing that should be done is to give the misguided young chap some personal advice and guidance after carefully examining him and finding out the causes of his malady. Some practical solution can usually be suggested without much trouble. In this manner the individual's development is constantly riddled by such problems that require the kindly and well advised interference of his elders, parents, teachers and other well-wishers, though it is a well known dictum among some that it is the well-wishers who do the greatest harm in this world. Be that as it may, a young man can always do it with some sensible guidance and advice. But for this, it is essential that the relations between the adolescent and teachers and parents should be both cordial and intimate, as otherwise he may have some compunctions about revealing his heart to them. It should of course be kept in mind that all guidance is the province of the psychologist or the teacher with the former's kindly assistance, if it is forthcoming.

5. Atmosphere in college: It has been pointed out earlier, too, that the fundamental reason why an individual is frustrated is that he lives in an atmosphere in which his needs cannot be fulfilled, or one in which he creates and is inflicted with desires that cannot be satisfied. In this respect, the importance of atmosphere in college cannot be overestimated, since it constitutes the major portion of the atmosphere and environment for him. This in turn, is composed of such diverse elements as the personalities and conduct of teachers, the curriculum, reading rooms and library, means of games and recreation, and extra-curricular activities, etc. If all these facilities and factors are satisfactory and adequate, the child's tendencies will normally be well satisfied, while all tendencies and desires that are incapable of being satisfied will not be developed. All unsocial, immoral and destructive tendencies are rendered important.

FRUSTRATION AND EDUCATION

It is evident from the foregoing account that one part of education is the teacher's effort to prevent the development of all possible frustrations. And for this, he himself will have to guide them, put before them examples of an attractive and impressive personality, high character, high ideals of sacrifice and overall development of the child. But, on the other hand, the teacher can handle this responsibility only if he himself is free from much frustration, since it is natural for him to have frustrations in his life through social and economic exigencies that make life difficult for him. He may be completely debilitated by such factors as the absence of freedom to act in the course of his work, the absence of desirable respect in society, improperly paid job that makes it impossible for him to maintain the desirable level of economic well being; in such circumstances it is not possible to expect him to prevent frustration from overtaking his students. In this connection the responsibility lies squarely on the shoulders of society and the government. The social and economic status of a teacher should be such as to deter all frustration and for this he should be given the requisite freedom to act. He should be respected in his role of the guide of forthcoming generations. His salary should be adequate to provide him with a respectable life in society and to allow him to fulfil his modest physical requirements. His functions in the school should not be so overwhelming as to make it impossible for him to look after his own intellectual development and the progress of his students. It is only when all these circumstances have been precipitated that he can keep himself away from frustration and at the same time keep his students away from them.

QUESTIONS FOR EXERCISE

1. Explain and classify motivation and its various theories. Give class-room implications of motivation.
2. Why do people behave the way they behave? Describe various types of motives.
3. Who founded the school of Analytical Psychology? What is the structure of "Self" according to this school? How has "the unconscious" been explained by Jung? What are the educational implications of Jung's Theory?
4. How do you compare Jung with Freud? What has been the main criticism of Jung?
5. Describe the major concepts of Adler's theory of motivation.
6. How do you compare Adler with Freud and Jung? What are the educational implications of Adlerian Psychology?
7. What is frustration? What are its causes? How can it be avoided? Discuss the role of education in avoiding frustration.

27

Work and Fatigue

It is quite essential to do away with fatigue in the process of learning as fatigue becomes an obstacle in the work to be performed or at least reduces its rate of progress. The truth of the matter is that the proportion in which the student becomes fatigued, his achievement curve shows a downward trend. Achievement decreases with the increase in fatigue. Hence, educational psychology makes a detailed study of the causes of fatigue and of the methods of alleviating it.

WHAT IS FATIGUE?

What is this fatigue? Fatigue is the state of reduced interest and desire, and this constitutes psychological explanation. It is the state or condition in which the nerves do not react and mind becomes lax and inert. Evidently, fatigue is neither purely physical nor exclusively mental. It is a psychophysical state of exhaustion. Reduced efficiency or capacity of body as well as mind are implicit in this phenomenon.

Kinds of fatigue

Fatigue is of many kinds just as capacity. However, it is generally believed to be of four kinds:

1. Subjective or Mental.
2. Objective or Physical.
3. Nervous.
4. Boredom.

1. Mental fatigue: Mental work, or any kind of strain on the mind reduces the capacity of the mind for work and causes mental fatigue. Thus in mental fatigue, the mind tires or the capacity of its minute fibres for work is diminished.

2. Physical fatigue: This type of fatigue results in the reduction in the capacity of the muscles of the body and a feeling of fatigue. In this way, physical fatigue is brought about by physical exertion. Even though the body feels tired due to mental exertion which should normally result in mental fatigue, yet on account of the close relation of the two, it also produces physical fatigue. Thus mental fatigue is unavoidable and it leads to physical fatigue.

3. Nervous fatigue: The subconscious mind of man is extremely active and since in the process of its work it consumes energy, in due course of time it naturally produces a feeling of fatigue and depression. Nervous fatigue can also result if the subconscious is extremely tired due to mental conflict.

4. Boredom: Boredom and fatigue are not identical. Fatigue is the result of the use of energy but boredom is the feeling of tiredness due to an incomplete or improper expulsion of energy. If you go to a friend and he is busy in some work you become bored. Similarly, you get bored if a person persists in talking about the same thing day after day. Boredom results in restlessness, a state induced by our inability to find proper use for our capacity for work as is the case with the young lady who gets bored with her unemotional lover because she does not get a chance to express her feelings.

Means of removing fatigue

Many experiments have been carried out in psychology to discover ways and means of getting rid of fatigue, and these experiments have evolved in the following ways:

1. Sleep: Sleep is by far the best means of banishing fatigue because in sleep both the fibres in the mind and the fibres in the body are at rest while waste matter is expelled from the body. The capacity of the mind and the energy thus gained replaces fatigue.

2. Relaxation: Sitting or lying in a relaxed position also eliminates fatigue because both the body and mind are at rest in a comfortable posture and the mental as well physical capacity is thus restored.

3. Balance of work and rest: As we have mentioned earlier, too much of work, overwork and no work at all, cause fatigue. Thus, for the elimination of fatigue, work and rest are equally necessary. It is best to alternate rest and work in a manner that should bring about a proper balance.

4. Change in work: Due to the fact that different types of work cause strain on different parts of the body, fatigue is more possible if the type of work is altered every now and then. Same type of mental exertion continued for a long time also induces boredom because our other capabilities do not get a chance of expression. Thus change in work is necessary to avoid and eliminate physical and mental fatigue.

5. Recreation: Recreation creates an opportunity for the unexpressed capabilities to express themselves, at the same time it reduces mental and bodily tension. Thus it is a useful means of avoiding fatigue.

6. Change in emotions: Another factor which introduces fatigue is an unrelenting application to work and a consistent, hard and laborious way of life. Thus a change of emotions once in a while will also relieve fatigue.

Those factors which eliminate fatigue generally apply to everyone but a person may pick and choose according to his own interests. There may be other factors especially suited to persons with particular tastes, inclinations and interests.

FATIGUE AND EDUCATION

Fatigue, whatever its nature, is invariably an obstacle in education. When exhausted, the student cannot concentrate upon study and even if he forces attention upon his work he does not retain a major part of what he reads in that condition of mind and body. Hence, it is essential for the teacher to be always careful that his students are neither fatigued nor bored. Students themselves should select such time for study when they are not labouring from any strain, and if one is exhausted it is best to take rest, as working under strain is not only fruitless but is also very harmful. Learning in a state of fatigue reveals many mistakes. In an experiment on the aspect of learning, in a school, certain things were dictated to students both at the beginning of school as well as at the end of the day. Mistakes were carefully recorded and it was found that the latter dictation showed many faults. When the dictation was made in successive hours at one hour intervals it was found that mistakes progressed from 40 to 70, 120 and 190. It is only too obvious that as the mind becomes tired through exhaustion the mistakes increase.

Hence, in modern educational institution efforts are made to provide for the simultaneous removal of all fatigue from the students, as they continue in their work. Every period of study is followed by a short interval of rest, and midway between the entire period of study meals are supplied. In some cases, the hours of study are interspersed with periods of physical education or games. This also helps in reducing fatigue. Nursery schools provide arrangements for the children to go to sleep in between their study.

It can be stated on the basis of many experiments and tests that the extent of fatigue varies with the individual difficulty that each subject presents to the student in the studying of it. According to one view if the difficulty of arithmetic is evaluated at 100, that of physical exercise would be 90, of history and geography 85, natural study 80, and drawing and moral study of religion would be 70. Others have placed the curricular subjects in the following order, according to the fatigue that they cause: physical education, arithmetic, modern languages, religion, mother tongue, geography, history, music and drawing.

Having understood the significance of these remarks and facts teachers can decide upon the time for the teaching of different subjects. In informulating the time table, it should be seen that difficult subjects are put first and the easier ones later as difficult subjects cannot be grasped in a fatigued condition. But instead of teaching two difficult subjects consecutively it might be a better plan to alternate one difficult subject with an easier one to follow. This will relax the students and make it easier for them to understand the difficult subject that is to follow. Then, in addition to these measures, whatever the subject, a teacher must do his best to entertain his students and keep their attention engaged in what he is trying to impart to them. If they are given frequent opportunities to laugh they become relaxed. Learning does not fatigue or bore if the teacher follows the entertaining dramatic method.

Making the subject entertaining makes it interesting, and being interesting it does not cause any considerable fatigue. Interesting subjects can be taught continuously for much longer period without causing exhaustion or inattention. According to Thorndike, a person can work for almost twelve hours on any subject that is of interest to him. Huxley has said that an interesting work can be continued for sixteen hours. Of course, much does depend upon individual capability in this connection but there is no doubting the fact that interesting subjects can be studied for longer hours, the difference being normally beyond calculation or conjecture. Fatigue is closely related to age. Small children have less capability than their elders and consequently they tire easily. Facial expression, yawning and stretching are signs of approaching fatigue, and efforts can be made to delay it. In this manner, knowledge of how to delay fatigue can be of use both to the student as well as the teacher.

QUESTIONS FOR EXERCISE

1. What is fatigue? How can it be removed?
2. Write short note on—Fatigue and Education.

28

Attention and Interest

WHAT IS ATTENTION?

Man lives in an environment. The stimuli from the environment are always affecting him. But these stimuli do not affect him equally. It is a common place observation that some stimuli effect us more than others. This shows that man selects out of environmental stimuli. This tendency of selection shows that there is a motivational process in him which is known as attention. This attention is affected by interest, attitudes and mental set. It is a selective process which includes motivation, mental set and selection. To take an example, if a student is not motivated, he will not attend to the class lecture. While a professor is delivering a lecture in the class, there are several other sounds being made in other rooms and the surroundings. The student who hears the lecture selects professor's voice out of the noise in the surroundings. While a student is attentively hearing the lecture, one can very well note his physical set which also indicates his mental set. Receptor adjustment, bodily adjustment, postural adjustment muscular tension and central nervous adjustments are typical of bodily sets in attention. Thus, in brief, attention can be defined as a process which compels the individual to select some particular stimulus according to his interest and attitude out of the multiplicity of stimuli present in the environment.

CONDITIONS OF ATTENTION

As a selective act of the mind, attention depends upon several conditions. These conditions may be of two types—external or objective and internal or subjective. External or objective conditions are related with the environment. In the environment or surroundings of the individual there are several stimuli, but he does not attend to all of them at the same time, because some stimuli are stronger than others. The factors making these stimuli stronger, than others, are known as external determinants of attention. Besides the external conditions, the mental conditions, culture and heredity also influence attention. Owing to these internal conditions some objects attract our attention more than others. These internal factors are internal determinants of attention. The methods of drawing attention are based upon these external and internal determinants of attention.

External determinants of attention

The following are the most important external determinants of attention:

1. Nature of stimulus: Nature of stimulus means its type *i.e.*, whether it is visual, gustatory, auditory, olfactory or tactual stimulus. It has been found by experiments that comparison with other sensations, colour and sound attract more attention. Among the pictures, the pictures of human beings attract more attention than those of animals or objects. Among the pictures of human beings those of beautiful women attract more attention. Besides these, the coloured pictures attract more attention than colourless ones. All these factors are important in advertisement. In the auditory stimulus, the melodious voice attracts more attention than other voices.

2. Intensity of the stimulus: The intensity of the stimulus is a helpful condition in attention. In comparison with the weak stimuli the intense stimulus attracts more attention of the organism. High sound, excessive pressure and acute pain attract our attention. In the market there is always some buzzing sound and yet the pedestrians hear the other sounds. But, it is not always necessary that one should attend to the intensity of stimulus. Sometimes while walking on the road, calling of our name attracts so much attention that we fail to hear even the loud sound of the motor horn. As a matter of fact the attraction of the attention does not depend on any single factor, but on several factors interconnected with one another. Hence, it can be said that other things being the same, the more intense stimulus will attract more attention.

3. Size of the stimulus: In the visual stimuli, the size of the stimulus is also a determinant of attention. As a general rule the bigger size attracts more attention, but a small advertisement on a very wide background also attracts attention. Thus the attraction of an object does not depend upon its size alone, but also on its background. To illustrate, a big black spot on a black face will not attract so much attention as a very small black spot on a white face.

4. Location of the stimulus: The location of the stimulus also affects attention. In the visual stimuli, the most effective location is just in front of the eyes. The role of different pages in the newspaper or the magazine and the different places on the same page, is important in advertisement. It has been found by experiments that advertisements given on the front page or on the upper half of any page attract more attention.

5. Contrast of the stimulus: The contrast of the stimulus is also an important determinant of attention *e.g.*, the presence of a woman among men and that of a man among women definitely attracts more attention.

6. Change of the stimulus: Attention cannot be concentrated for a long time on some particular object. Hence the change of the stimulus also affects attention. Attention is sustained by change of the stimulus. The advertisers change their advertisements from time to time lest it may cease to be attractive.

7. Isolation of the stimulus: A man sitting alone in some corner of the park, hotel or club attracts more attention than others. A student sitting alone at the far corner of the class, is seen first. Thus isolation is an important external determinant of attention. This fact is based upon the reason that the isolated individual is not mixed with other individuals and hence seen separately in his own background. By experiments in advertisement it has been found that only the fact of isolation attracts 60% more attention. In the British Journal of Educational Psychology of August, 1951, D.E. Berlyne points out the following principles based upon latest experiments:

(*i*) In comparison with the unchanged stimulus the stimulus changed in the near past has more possibility of attracting attention.

(*ii*) The effect of the change goes on diminishing during passage of time.

(*iii*) Whenever stimuli are changed together and in which one is left unchanged, the effect of change is not noticeable.

(*iv*) If change goes on in the changed stimuli, the process of attention is rather permanent and strong.

The modes of change also influence the process of attention. If there is a change absolutely it attracts more attention. While studying one does not hear the sound of the clock or that of electric fan but if either of these suddenly stops, one cannot fail to attend to it. Man becomes used to regular changes and does not pay much attention to them. But if some irregular change or any sudden change occurs, it at once draws attention.

8. Duration of the stimulus: As a general rule, the stimulus having more duration attracts more attention. Thus duration of the stimulus is an important determinant of attention. But sometimes the smallest flashing of a movement attracts more attention than the bigger stimuli, *e.g.*, a sudden flash of light for several seconds will attract more attention in a dark night than the continuous burning lamp.

9. Repetition of the stimulus: Along with duration, repetition of the stimulus is also an important determinant of attention. It is a common place observation that when the teacher has to attract the attention of students towards a particular phenomena, he repeats it several times. But sometimes, man ceases to attend a phenomenon simply because it is repeated many times, *e.g.*, if a man says something about him, we take interest in it once or twice, but, if we find that he always repeats the same thing, we tend to pay attention to it.

10. Movement in the stimulus: In comparison with the static, the moving stimuli attract more attention The position of a stimulus changes due to movements. An object lying in some corner of the room will not attract our attention, but even if there is some illusion of movement in it, we cannot help attending to it. The influence of movement in stimulus is widely used by the shopkeepers and businessmen, who advertise through moving electric lights.

Internal determinants of attention

The conditions of attention as described so far are the external determinants of attention. They can also be called external laws of attention. The presence of these conditions in the environment is helpful for attention. Besides these, internal conditions are also helpful in drawing attention. These conditions are related to motives. As a matter of fact the influence of external conditions depends on these internal conditions to a very great extent. The hungry man will attend to the form and stimuli of the food. A man with full belly will not attend to food, however nice it might appear. In the advertisements those demonstrating the naked organs of the woman have the maximum power of attraction of attention. Those interested in cinema look to the advertisements of cinema at first sight. It is difficult to describe all the internal conditions helpful in attention. Hence only the most important will be enumerated here.

1. **Interests:** Innate and acquired interests draw individual's attention to a particular object. Doctors, engineers, professors, all attend to the objects of their own interest. Even among the professors an object attracting the attention of a professor of Geology, need not attract the attention of a professor of Philosophy as well. Thus the innumerable differences in interests create innumerable determinants of attention in different men. The stimuli influencing innate tendencies attract more attention than those influencing acquired interest.

2. **Basic drives:** The basic drives and impulses of the individual are important in drawing his attention. The animal attends to particular stimulus when driven by the basic drives of hunger, thirst, sex, etc., *e.g.*, a normal man motivated by sex will naturally attend to the individuals of opposite sex. We all know it by experience that when hungry we may attend to even a distasteful object, but while our belly is full, we may not attend to even the most tasteful food. Among the motives fear has got definite influence upon attention. All men who fear snake will attend to all things resembling the snake. Like fear, curiosity also influences attention. We attend to even the smallest details of the object towards which we have curiosity.

Innate need also is very important in attention. The influence of sexual need in attention is very much exploited in the advertisements. Normally, the sexual need in human beings can be easily evoked. Hunger, thirst, etc. are felt occasionally and the means to satisfy them are also readily available, but neither the sexual need is ever fully satisfied nor the means of satisfying it are available to all persons all the times. Hence, most of the advertisements draw attention by stimulating the sexual need in human beings.

3. **Mental set:** Mental set is one of the most important internal determinants of attention. Mental set means the tendency or bent of the whole mind. A man will attend to those objects towards which his mind is set. In the days of examinations, the mental set of students is generally towards the examination and hence even the smallest thing concerning the examination will attract their attention.

4. **Aim:** Aim also influences attention. Every man has some immediate and some ultimate aims, *e.g.*, the immediate aim of the student is to pass the examination while the ultimate aim may be to get a job, to earn living or anything else. The student whose aim is not to pass the examination will not

be concerned with text books or notes, etc., but one who has the aim to pass the examination will at once attend to them.

5. Meaning: In comparison with meaningless things, meaningful things and talks attract more attention. A man will not attend to a thing which has no meaning for him. Men do not like to hear meaningless talk. If some persons are talking in Tamil, a Punjabi will not like to hear it since for him it has no meaning.

6. Habit: Habit is also an important determinant of attention. If a man is habituated to rising early and winding his clock early in the morning, he must attend to the clock as soon as he gets up. It has been rightly pointed out that man learns as to which object he should attend and which he should not and thus develops habits of attending and not attending to things. Thus habit has two aspects in relation to attention. On the one side men develop a habit of attending to necessary and desirable things and on the other side they develop the habit of not attending to unnecessary and undesirable things. Both these kinds of habit help man in his daily routine.

7. Disposition and temperament: Both disposition and temperament are important internal determinants of attention *e.g.*, a man having a religious disposition and spiritual temperament will attend to religious matters, while another person having a sexual disposition and criminal temperament will attend to matters concerning sex or crimes etc. William James has rightly pointed out that it is our tendency to take interest in particular things, our innate disposition and mental development which determines that which among the crowd of sensations, should attract our attention.

8. Past experience: Past experience also affects attention. If we know it by our past experience that a particular person is sincere to us, we shall pay attention to whatever he advises us. If we know by experience that he is not sincere to us, we shall not attend even to his most serious advice.

9. Emotion: Emotion is also an important determinant of attention. It is a matter of every day experience that we attend to even the smallest fault of a person whom we hate while we do not attend even to the greatest blunder of a person whom we love. A mother seldom finds faults with her child. The lovers find the whole world singing and dancing and immersed in romance.

10. Social motives: Social motives are important determinants of attention. In advertisements the human figures attract more attention than figures of animals and things. The reason is that man is guided by his social motives. News about altruism, bravery and saving other's life by putting oneself in danger, attract our attention because we praise these qualities. Men attend to things concerning the duties for social motives.

Besides the conditions described above many other factors influence attention. Heredity, education and training have a wide influence on attention. The family, school, club, class and society of which an individual is a member, do have some influence on his attention. The physical condition, desire, purpose of the person concerned also affect his attention. Thus all the factors influencing the personality of a man affect his attention as well. As a matter of fact it is difficult to describe all direct and indirect determinants of attention. The description given here however, includes the most important of such factors.

ATTENTION AND INTEREST

Attention is a selective act of the mind. To attend to a thing is to concentrate on it by removing attention from other things. The mind can attend to one thing at a time. Hence, mind has to select. In the selection it is natural that the mind should select such objects in which it is interested. This is amply demonstrated in our daily life. The boy whose interest is in playing will not attend to study. One cannot attend to the studies by forcibly sitting for it. One can attend to the studies only when one is interested in it. Hence, the successful teacher tries to make the students interested in their studies.

Interest is affective disposition which evokes attention and maintains it. Interest is not a motor activity. It is a tendency or a mental structure which supplies sufficient motivating power to motor activity. Interest is sometimes innate and sometimes acquired. In the fulfilment of instinctive needs, the animals are naturally interested in each other. The herbivorous animals are interested in grass while the carnivorous are interested in meat. Lion is interested in goat while goat is interested in green leaves. Besides the instinctive interests there are some acquired interests as well *e.g.*, the scientist is interested in the instruments of his laboratory while they are of no interest to the ordinary lay men. Thus individuals develop different interests according to their disposition, temperament and economic, social and political status etc. Attitudes towards those things are mostly acquired. The acquired interest depends upon experience. The interest is directly related to the emotions and desires. The thing or the individual in which we are interested finds a place in our life and we develop this interest through emotions towards it. It is not necessary that the interest should be permanent. Things which do not fulfil any permanent need evoke only temporary interest. As the need is fulfilled, the individual ceases to take interest in such objects *e.g.*, if a man has to cross a river, he will be very much interested in the boat but after he crosses the river his interest in the boat will also come to an end. Permanent interests are related with emotions and sentiments. They are permanent mental conditions. According to Drever interest is a disposition in its dynamic aspect. Interest is not affective experience, but affective tendency.

According to McDougall, "Interest is latent attention, attention is interest in action." As it has already been pointed out, interest is mental structure and it is expressed through attention. When the individual does not attend to a particular object his interest in it is in a dormant form, *e.g.*, suppose a man is interested in seeing a tennis match. Whenever there is a tennis match, he always goes to see it. He reads news about tennis very attentively. But neither a tennis match is played daily nor news about it is heard every day. Hence, when this particular man is busy in the activities other than seeing the tennis match or hearing news about it, his interest in tennis remains latent. When we attend to an object, our interest in that object is manifested. If we are interested in a certain thing we must attend to it. A man interested in national progress will attend to every national issue. A man interested in women will normally pay attention to them.

Interest is a mental cause of attention. It is not necessary that all men should be acquainted with their interest. Sometimes when we attend to a thing we wonder how we came to be interested in it. Sometimes we do not know as to in which things we are interested. Sometimes we are not prepared to accept that we are interested in a particular thing.

But the intimate relation between interest and attention should not mean that one cannot attend to an object in which he is not interested or if one attends to a thing it necessarily means his interest in it. Very few persons are interested in studies. Mostly the students study with the purpose of getting a degree or finding a job by passing through the examination. But this need not cause any deficiency in their attention. Even when one is interested in his studies he can attend to it. There is no correlation between the degrees of interest and attention. As a matter of fact neither interest and attention are identical nor is there a positive correlation between them. Interest is a cause of attention, but attention is not a result of interest. By saying that there is intimate relation between the interest and attention it is meant that interest is a very helpful factor in attention.

DISTRACTION

Distraction means the dividing of attention or some interference in attention. For example, when one is studying, the sound of a song or noise breaks in upon attention. The object which causes the distraction is called the distractor. In fact, broken attention is not the absence of attention because the distractor is associated with the activity, often though not always, and it no longer interferes with the activity.

Thus, the notion that distraction invariably hinders work is misleading, it being seen, for example, that the labourers produce more when there is music. Some labourers, men and women, sing at work in view of this fact. Not a few people do their reading and writing while radio is playing. Some people work better in a noisy environment than in a peaceful one. Experiments conducted by Morgan indicated that at first distraction caused a drop in the speed of typewriting but constant pursuit of the work in the disturbed condition increased this speed, and it again dropped when the distraction was removed. But distraction, in some experiments by Weber, caused harm. Though it cannot be definitely said that distraction increases the speed of the work, it is possible to say with some degree of confidence, that a decrease in speed due to distraction is not inevitable. Actually the effect of a distraction on some work depends in no small measure upon the capacity, interest, practice, skill and mental set of the worker. If the distraction is favourable the speed will be increased but if it is unsuitable the speed will drop.

Roughly, distraction can be divided into two forms:

1. Continuous distraction: As the name suggests, it is the continuous distraction of attention. Some examples of it are the sound of radio or gramophone played continuously, the noise of the market place etc. Experiments have led to the conclusion that adjustment to continuous distraction takes place quickly.

2. Discontinuous distraction: This type is irregular, being interspersed with intervals *e.g.*, the hearing of somebody's voice every now and then. It interferes with work because of the impossibility of adjustment.

Some major means of removing distraction are the following:

1. Being active in work: Work under distraction sometimes calls for more energy, so that one way of adjusting to it, or removing distraction is to become more active in work.

2. Disregard of distraction: The presence of a distracting factor while one is working is no extra-ordinary condition, and so the best way to remove this element is to disregard it. The distraction is effective only when attention is directed to it, so that inattention, even to the most serious distraction will keep the activity from being interfered with in any way.

3. Making the distraction a part of the work: Distraction causes an obstacle only when it is distinct from or opposed to the activity since attention can be focused just on one object at one time. Therefore, another method of making a distraction ineffective is to make it a part of the work. Some people work better when listening to a song because they make it a part of their work. But it is very difficult to make an uninteresting and contradictory distraction a part of the work because in this the interests, nature and capacities of the person are involved.

QUESTIONS FOR EXERCISE

1. What is attention? Describe factors determining attention.
2. Discuss the relationship of Attention and Interest.
3. Write short note on—Distraction.

29

Sensation and Perception

WHAT IS SENSATION?

Sensation is the first response of the organism to the stimulus and is a step in the direction of perception. In practice, sensation is not separated from perception. This distinction is necessary in order to facilitate study. Ward expressed it thus "Pure sensation is a psychological myth." Sensation is received through the sense organs *e.g.*, eyes, nose, tongue, skin and ears. Apparently, there are several types of sensations, but they can be divided generally into the following three categories—

1. Organic sensations.
2. Special sensations.
3. Motor sensations.

Special sensations correspond to five sense organs, *e.g.*, visual, auditory, olfactory, tactual and sensations of taste.

WHAT IS PERCEPTION?

Perception is the interpretation of the meanings of sensations. In seeing a rose the various sensations of colour, smell, touch etc., are aroused. We are given to understand by these sensations that there is an object in front of us. We know from past experience that an object of this nature is a flower or a rose. We, therefore, conclude that we are perceiving a rose.

Perception is a mental activity which aquaints us with the situation by giving us direct knowledge of it. The sensations are viewed as a whole, in perception. In perception there is not just a prefunctory acquaintance with the object, there is a knowledge of it too. The sensation of colour alone is not a sufficient proof of the identity of the object, and it is consequently, not possible to say on the basis of the colour sensations that the pink object is a rose. The real meaning of the sensation is understood or revealed in the perception. Only then is it known that the sensation originates from the rose. Accordingly, sensation precedes perception.

Woodworth expresses it in this way: "In general, when we speak of sensation we are thinking of stimuli and investigating the relationship of the individual's experiences to various stimuli which reach his receptors, and when we speak of perception we are thinking of objects and are investigating how well the individual's experiences correspond with the objective facts."

SENSE TRAINING

Modern educational psychologists consider the training of the child in proper perception to be an important part of the educative process. As has been pointed out before, there can be many faults in perception, due to a number of causes that are also the causes of hallucination. Thus, it is necessary that the teacher should train the child to avoid all factors that interfere with and distort perception. In modern schools young children are taught the methods of correct employment of their sense organs. This is called sense training. This is an important part of the child's basic or primary education. Proper use of the sense organs also entails the automatic avoiding of conditions that cause hallucination.

According to Drever, "The sense training is the giving of the child necessary and typical perceptual experiences, the correcting, supplementing and systematizing of the unsystematic sense experience of his everyday life." Hence, proper sense education requires various kinds of apparata that are capable of providing the various sense organs with different experiences and sensations. In Madame Montessori's educational method, wooden blocks of various sizes and colours as well as coloured silk pieces are used to acquaint the child with different kinds of sensations. The child's day-to-day experiences are not systematic or organised. Sense training helps to give them just this organisation that they lack. Evidently, its objective is to train the child's mind.

The first step in sense education is the separation of normal children from those who suffer from defects in one or other of their sense organs. This is made necessary by the fact that if the malformed child is allowed to partake of training in the company of the more developed children, his education is hampered. Accordingly, blind or deaf children are put in separate schools. Such children who have some defective sense organs require more careful and specialised training than the normal child as there must be some compensation for the loss under which they suffer. Defects concerning sense organs are sometimes innate but are sometimes also caused by misuse of the organ. The sensible teacher trains his wards in the proper and healthy employment of each sense organ and the attention that it requires for its health. Psychologists have discovered means that can help cure children of their bad habits and the effect of these habits. For example, Morgan and Winter made experiments to see how a child could be cured of the habit of relieving himself in bed. The bedding was so manipulated that when it became wet because of the urine emitted by the child, completion of an electrical circuit caused a bell to ring that woke the child. Considerable repetition of this was very useful as the child woke up immediately the bell went into action, till finally he began waking up whenever he felt the need to relieve himself.

For sense training, it is essential that the child learns to distinguish between the experiences of different sense organs. Wooden blocks can be used in the distinction between weight, height, thickness, width, etc. Colour can be distinguished by the use of coloured toys. Children can learn to distinguish between sounds if they are made to hear sounds made by various animals and birds. In sense training, the child should be supplied with stimuli that are meaningful to the child and have some definite objective. And this can only be done if the child's circumstances and experiences are kept in mind while formulating the sense training.

Children normally are very curious and desirous of handling and examining all new things with which they come into contact. When given various kinds of experiences, the child's mind develops, hence, it would be desirable not to limit his education to the class-room or the college boundary but it should be extended to gardens, river banks, histone buildings, museums and zoos. Travelling widens the mental horizon and creates new interests, and is hence very beneficial.

PERCEPTION AND DEVELOPMENT OF MEANING

For the new born child, the external world is a mass of sound and fury signifying nothing but a sphere of movement. At this stage the child is in no position to distinguish between objects in his environment, and his eyes cannot focus on any one point for any length of time. Thus, he has no means of distinguishing the meaning of various stimuli and sensations. But a few months after his birth, the child begins to show some sign of reacting to these stimuli. By the time he attains to the age of three he comprehends the meaning of these sensations and can also give expression to his own experience. Perception of every object in the environment is not the same as the child can understand certain things very easily while others elude his grasp for the time being. For example, in the early stages of development, it is much easier to focus the eyes on a Stationary object than on a moving one. Similarly, to begin with it is not easy for the child to judge distances correctly because this needs both training and experience.

While it is undeniably essential for the child to be trained in a variety of experiences, it is no less important that his perception be clear and accurate. For this the factors that cause hallucination should be kept away, and the child trained in comprehending the meaning of all that he perceives. For example, he can be trained to observe that of two people who have the same height the thinner person appears to be the taller. Similarly, it is possible for a person wearing clothes with horizontal stripes to appear broader and for the one wearing vertical stripes to appear taller. In much the same manner, when two objects are moving at an equal speed the smaller appears relatively faster. Facts of this kind prove as interesting and entertaining as games when they are told to the child, and at the same time the child learns to discriminate between his perceptions and to understand their meanings and thereby to avoid mistakes.

A child's store of knowledge and meaning improves as he sees new objects, observes them and learns their names. Names are conjoined to objects in his memory. In this, the child should first be acquainted with objects that are a part of his environment. A small child cannot understand the meaning of abstract concepts. Hence concrete apparatus and objects should be used in trying to increase the child's knowledge. Whenever a language is taught to a child, the first words to be taught concern objects that the child encounters everyday. If the words taught are very difficult, the child loses his interest in the language and is likely to abandon the attempt. Meanings are easily understood and remembered if the name and the object that it connotes are presented to the child at the same time.

Along with increases in the child's vocabulary it is necessary to improve his experiences also, and for this much benefit can be derived from visiting historic places, villages, industries, new cities, etc. Maximum utilisation of concrete apparatus such as maps, charts, instruments, etc., helps the child in understanding what he is being taught. And, beside adding to the child's experience, he should also be permitted to make use of his experiences in such creative activity as making wooden objects, mud toys, painting, drawing, etc.

OBSERVATION

Perception is the basis of observation, but while in perception the child receives certain sensations from the external world, in observation he perceives some objects of his own volition. In the child's education, it is desirable to encourage him to the observation of novel objects always. By forming the habit of observation a child learns to satisfy his own curiosity and also improves his own capacity to explore new fields. The Dalton plan and the project method place the same emphasis upon development of powers of observation as Froebel and Montessori have placed on sense training. The principle of learning by doing is adopted in developing powers of observation.

QUESTION FOR EXERCISE

1. Write short note on—Sense Training.

30

Individual Differences

MEANING OF INDIVIDUAL DIFFERENCES

In education, ever since the most ancient times, students have been differentiated on the basis of age as difference in age levels entitles the children to differing levels of education. As the child's age gradually increases, the subjects of his education can be made more complex and difficult. In addition to difference in age, another factor that was partly taken into consideration is the difference in levels of intelligence. Besides this, educational attainments were also considered to be important. In this manner, during the ancient and the medieval periods individual difference was believed to be the capacity of attaining skills in a particular subject. In modern schools, other kinds of skills and abilities, and peculiarities of personality in individuals are also taken into consideration. According to Skinner, 'Today we think of individual differences as including any measurable aspect of the total personality." From this definition of individual differences it is evident that it comprehends every aspect of the human personality, albeit all aspects that are in some manner measurable. Aspects of this nature can be many such as variability, conformity, difference in the rate of learning and development of mutual relationship between the various characteristics of personality, etc. In this manner, various individual differences of physical and mental development, nature, rate of learning ability, specific abilities, interest and personality, etc.

TYPES OF INDIVIDUAL DIFFERENCES

The following brief description may serve to make individual differences a simple concept that can easily be grasped:

1. Average intelligence: Individuals are seen differing in considerable measure in respect of their general intelligence. It is not possible to send to schools children with an intelligence quotient of below 50. Children with intelligence quotients between 50 and 70 can learn only the simplest tasks. Even the small schools trouble children whose intelligence quotient varies between 70 and 80. Children between 75 and 90 I.Q. are considered morons and they have considerable difficulty in progressing along with other children in their learning. Generally, 40 to 60 per cent of the children in schools have

I.Qs. varying between 95 and 105, being the children with average intelligence who form the basis for the formulation of the syllabus and curriculum as well as the method of teaching. Children who are either above or below this level of intelligence require special educational methods and conditions. Children with intelligence quotients varying between 115 and 120 are considered brilliant or intelligent. The following facts have come to light concerning individual differences of intelligence in children:

(*i*) However good and beneficial the environment and the method of education, the moron invariably reaches his highest level of learning before the average or the intelligent child.

(*ii*) In favourable circumstances the average child generally gives a good account of himself in his academic pursuits.

(*iii*) If the circumstances are favourable, the intelligent child shows great alacrity in the process of learning.

(*iv*) Adverse circumstances have the worst effect on all children, and their learning activities are hindered.

2. Special abilities: During the junior high school as well as the college stage, the individual's differences in respect of special abilities, in addition to the general intelligence, are also important since special professions and specialised fields of vocation all need certain specific abilities. Abilities of this kind are concerned with mental, artistic, personality or motor ability.

3. Differences of background: In school the differences that the children exhibit are the outcome of their different families and their communities Attitudes towards education and authority differ in each family, culture and class. Some of these attitudes are favourable while others are unfavourable to education. In either condition, the differences of attitudes result in differences among children. Besides these attitudes, the child's emotional, social, aesthetic and moral development is influenced by his family and the neighbourhood. Hence differences of background are also manifest in individual differences.

4. Alacrity in learning: Difference in the quickness or alacrity in learning is visible not only in children of different ages but also among children in the same age group. This difference is dependent upon their maturity and educational background. Differences in the alacrity of learning result in benefits accruing from formal education.

5. Mental age: Children of differing ages as well as children of the same age show differences in their respective mental ages. Generally speaking, all students studying in the same class differ according to their mental ages. It has been observed that in the age of 6, differences in mental age range up to 5 years. Mental age and education are intimately related. The child's level of education is determined according to his mental age.

6. Motor ability: The individual's movements of the hand and feet and other physical abilities are seen to be very individual, as they do not resemble another's to any great extent. Till the individual attains adulthood, his manual dexterity, rate of muscular movement and resistance to fatigue develops continually. In this manner, the same individual in different ages and different individuals in the same age group manifest considerable differences in manual dexterity.

7. Sex differences: Makneimer and Terman discovered the following differences between men and women, on the basis of some studies:

(*i*) Women have greater skill in memory while men have greater motor ability.

(*ii*) Female handwriting is superior while men excel in mathematical logic.

(*iii*) Women show greater skill in making sensory distinctions of taste, pain, smell, etc., while men show greater reaction and consciousness of size-weight illusion.

(*iv*) Possessing greater linguistic ability, women are superior to men in languages, similitudes, word building, compositions and use of long sentences etc. On the other hand, men are superior in physics and chemistry.

(*v*) Women are better than men in mirror drawing. Faults of speech etc., in men were found to be three times of such faults in women.

(*vi*) Women are more susceptible to suggestion while there are three times as many colour-blind men as there are women.

(*vii*) Young girls take interest in stories of love, fairy tales, stories of the school and home and day-dreaming and show various levels in their play. On the other hand, boys take interest in stories of bravery, science, war and scouting, stories of games and sports, scouts stories and games of occupation and skill.

8. Racial differences: Many scientific studies have indicated the presence of various kinds of differences between individuals of different races, although differences of environment are a normal factor in causing these differences. Karl Brigham has composed the following list on the basis of differences in level of intelligence among people who have migrated to United States from other countries. These differences have been calculated by the Stanford Binet tests:

Country	Mental age	Country	Mental age
England	14.2	Belgium	12.56
Scotland	13.77	Ireland	12.2
Holland	13.75	Austria	12.16
Germany	13.41	Turkey	11.96
America	13.32	Greece	11.88
Denmark	13.26	Russia	11.45
Canada	13.25	Italy	11.42
Sweden	12.16	Poland	10.96
Norway	12.75	Negro America	10.71

On the basis of these average differences between the races, the mental age of a particular individual of a definite race cannot be calculated since this difference is based on environment.

9. Nationality: Many studies have led to the conclusion that individuals of different nations differ in respect of nature, physical and mental traits, interest and personality, etc. Such a difference is only natural since their cultural and geographic environment is distinctive.

10. Economic situation: Economic differences are seen causing differences in the children's interests, tendencies and character, etc.

11. Differences relating to learning: In respect of learning, children manifest such differences as past experience and learning, ability in the use of various kinds of apparatus, rate of learning, interest in learning, etc.

12. Difference in respect of development: Difference in development is in evidence not only in individuals of different age groups but also between individuals of the same age.

13. Difference of interests: As has been pointed out, the difference in sex leads to a difference in interests. Similarly, factors such as family background, level of development, differences of nationality and race, etc. cause difference of interests.

14. Personality: Differences in respect of personality have led psychologists to much study, and on the basis of the study, individuals have been classified into many groups. Jung, for example, has divided individuals into three groups—(*i*) Introvert, (*ii*) Extrovert, and (*iii*) Ambivert. This is the psychological classification of people. Stephenson has divided human beings into two categories—preservator and non-preservator. In this division, people of the first group are very sensitive and susceptible to experience while people of the second group are not influenced by it to quite that extent. Cattell has put people into the surgent and the surgeless or non-surgent classes. The former is similar to Jung's extrovert while the surgeless resembles his introvert individuals. Terman has put people into 9 classes according to their level of intelligence—(*i*) Genius, (*ii*) Near Genius, (*iii*) Very superior intelligence, (*iv*) Superior, (*v*) Average, (*vi*) Backward, (*vii*) Feeble minded, (*viii*) Dull, (*ix*) Idiot.

Thorndike has divided people into four categories on the basis of thinking—(*i*) Abstract thinkers, (*ii*) Ideational thinkers, (*iii*) Objective thinkers, (*iv*) Thinkers in whom sensory experience is predominant. These names indicate the peculiarities of thinking in these individuals.

From the viewpoint of nature, personality has been divided into three classes—(*i*) thought dominant, (*ii*) emotion dominant, (*iii*) action dominant.

Concerning these classifications of the human personality, it should be remembered that although one specific person may exhibit the main broad characteristics of one class of personality, he cannot be said to belong to only that class of personality as the differences between various personalities are so subtle and minute that it is not scientifically feasible to divide them into classes.

Teacher's advantage in knowing individual differences

The objective of modern education is the complete development of the child. In this connection, the teacher has the following advantage to derive from a knowledge of individual differences:

1. This can help him to form the proper attitude towards the brilliant and the dull-witted students. It is only too evident that very good results cannot be expected from dull-witted or mediocre students.
2. Any effort to bring all or a majority of the students in the class to the same level is futile since some 50 or odd percentage of them will invariably remain below this level.
3. Improvements in atmosphere, method of teaching and the apparatus of education cannot lead to the satisfactory teaching of all students since their individual ability to learn differs widely.
4. Knowing the presence of individual differences the teacher is not perturbed at the failure of some of his students since such failures are only to be expected from below-average students.
5. The teacher does not come to expect successes that are impossible. Individual difference makes it clear that all aspects of the personality are mutually related and to develop any one aspect it is essential that all the aspects be developed.

INDIVIDUAL DIFFERENCES AND EDUCATION

By the above account of benefits that a teacher can derive from a knowledge of individual differences it is evident that he can make use of it in education and teaching. The main features in this connection are the following:

1. Curriculum: In school, the curriculum should be modified to suit the needs of the dull children. Failure to achieve this, adversely affects the development of all three kinds of children. Whereas the backward students start playing truant from school the brilliant children find the studies inadequate and turn their intellect to more perverses.

2. Limited size of the class: Keeping in mind the individual differences of the students, it is advisable that if they are to be taught properly a class should not include more than 20 students. With 50 or more students it is impossible to teach them keeping in mind their specific requirements.

3. Method of education: It is never advisable or efficacious to use the same method of education in the case of all children. It should be varied to suit and conform to their individual differences and mental requirements.

4. Educational guidance: Knowing the personal differences between his students the teacher can render them signal service by guiding them in their educational career. It is the teacher who can tell them the subjects they must choose to pursue in their higher studies if they are not to do violence to their natures.

5. **Vocational guidance:** Different professions require some specific physical, mental and personality traits of the individual. Hence, knowing their peculiar mental make up and their tendencies, the teacher can guide the students in the vocation that they should adopt.

6. **Contribution of school, family and community in education:** Knowledge of differences among children determines that education in school is not sufficient since many differences are due to the family and community. Hence, according to modern educational psychologists, to attain the objective of allround development of individuals, prescribed by modern education, the co-operation of school, family, community and the religious institutions is sought.

7. **Individual training:** Having knowledge of individual differences, now many methods of individual training have been devised. In America, the Dalton plan, project method, Winnetka method, contract plan and activity programme methods have been devised for individual training. A brief resume of the various methods is given below—

(*i*) *Dalton plan:* In this, children are not taught in class rooms. They are given subjects that suit their interests and they are given a project that covers a period of 15 days to a month. Such treatment leads to the development of naturality, independence, co-operation and sociability etc.

(*ii*) *Project method:* In this the children are required to do work of every day requirements, such as cooking, stitching, furniture making, etc. And in the process of this work, they are taught novel things.

(*iii*) *Winnetka system:* In this method, the student on his own tries to attain a certain definite objective and the teacher offers very little assistance. Later on, through some tests, the extent to which the student has attained his goal, is discovered.

(*iv*) *Contract plan:* In this, similar to the Dalton method, the subjects of study are determined and similar to the Winnetka method the student's progress is measured through tests. In this manner it is a synthesis of the Dalton and Winnetka method.

(*v*) *Activity programme:* In this method, keeping in mind the interests of the students, activities are prescribed in order to define the curriculum. These activities are based on democratic principles. This helps to develop democratic notion in the children.

It is evident from the foregoing description that modern education makes proper arrangements for a child's education, keeping in view his peculiar nature and special abilities. In a democratic society every individual has the right to achieve a definite level of development. Hence, even more essential it is that individual differences be kept in mind while educating people of democratic countries.

Two facts emerge when human development is studied. One, that the development of separate individuals exhibits certain similarities. Two, that different individuals show differences from the biological and social viewpoint. Generally speaking, these differences are quantitative rather than qualitative. In other words, the same qualities are to be found in most individuals but it is the quantity or intensity of these qualities that differs in these individuals. And this difference leads to considerable difference in the education of different individuals. Hence, the teacher should keep in mind the differences between various boys and girls and he should make the necessary arrangements so that everyone be educated properly.

QUESTIONS FOR EXERCISE

1. Write short note on Individual Differences.
2. How is the knowledge of Individual Differences useful to the teacher?

31

Problems of Backward, Problematic and Gifted Children

WHAT IS A BACKWARD CHILD?

Generally speaking, no mother or father is easily prepared to accept that their child is mentally backward. But modern intelligence test techniques have indubitably established that some children are mentally backward. A backward child is more in need of assistance than one with average or above average intelligence, hence in modern schools teachers are expected to pay particular attention to the weak students in their classes. A backward child, evidently, is one who has an intelligence quotient lower than the average child. In the words of Cyril Burt, "A backward child is one who, in the middle of the school career, is unable to do the work of the class below that which is normal for his age." In this way, the backward child falls far behind other children of his age in matters of study. In school such children remain in the same class for many years, and fail to progress upward. Educational psychologists have no single opinion of the intelligence quotient below which a child can definitely be called backward. Yet generally, psychologists classify those children as backward whose intelligence quotient falls below 85.

PROBLEMS OF BACKWARD CHILDREN

Children who are backward have certain problems that are peculiarly their own. Having a very low intelligence quotient, they require to be taught many things by others. A backward child cannot lead, he is more in a position to need the help and sympathy of friends and relatives. A child who is very feeble minded, having an intelligence quotient of 70 or less, cannot obtain education in the ordinary schools, and has to be sent to special institutions Emotional adjustment of the child is completely integrated if he fails in the same class time after time. In a class, teaching approximates to the average level of students. Hence, it is only natural for the backward child to meet with failure. Failure in school leads to the assumption that he will also be a failure in life. His ambitions are destroyed and he becomes hopeless.

Backward child also faces difficulties in social adjustment. In the group he does not easily grasp even the smallest thing and rules of play have to be repeated for his benefit. His colleagues naturally heckle him. It is possible that a spark of leadership may be ignited in him if he communicates with those younger than himself but on the same intelligence level. But there he is unwelcome since other children steer clear of him because of his physical superiority. Adults pay him little or no attention, instead he is scolded from time to time. In adolescence and adulthood, too, the position of the child does not improve. He is made the butt of every joke. Activities of the group are usually on a higher level, so that he does not fit in them either.

CAUSES OF BACKWARDNESS

It is not even possible to recount all the various causes of backwardness, but the main causes are the following:

1. **Physical causes:** Due to many physical defects and abnormalities, the child lags behind other average children. Such physical conditions would be weakness of eyes, deafness or being hard of hearing, stuttering, being weak or crippled, etc. This also has an adverse effect upon his social adjustment.

2. **Mental defects:** It has teen indicated earlier that the backward child has a very low intelligence quotient, as compared with that of an average child. Having a low intelligence, his other mental characteristics and abilities also do not compare favourably with the average child.

3. **Educational immaturity:** Physical and mental shortcomings in the child result in educational immaturity. Putting it differently, he has no adequate maturity to grasp the teaching that is customary for his age level.

4. **Emotional factors:** The child's social adjustment is detected by his mental and physical abnormalities, and he meets with successive failures. He meets with criticism on every account. Hence, it is natural for him to manifest anxiety, tension, depression and other emotional factors. Sometimes, though every other defect is absent the child is backward in his class for no better reason than these psychological or emotional factors.

5. **Atmosphere in the home:** One reason of backwardness can also be the atmosphere in the home. Proper development of the child cannot occur in a virulent family atmosphere. Hence, he falls behind children of his age group. And among the factors that contribute to the defective atmosphere in the home are constant quarrelling and fighting between parents and children, unbalanced diet, strict discipline, absence of all peace and calm, poverty etc.

6. **Lack of interest:** Sometimes, even though the child is free from all the defects and shortcomings mentioned above and even those that have not been mentioned, the child falls behind the rest of the class for the simple reason that he cannot stir any interest in the various subjects being taught. This causes repealed failure.

7. **Factors concerning the schools:** The school can be a veritable storehouse factors that inhibit the child's development such as inadequate method of teaching, uneducated teachers, undesirable atmosphere, inadequate curriculum, defective time table, disgusting relations between students and teachers etc. All these causes conspire to make even the average child look backward.

Cyril Burt's opinion

Different educational psychologists have stressed different factors present in the analysis of backward children and their causes. Different factors have been considered more or less important. Cyril Burt has allocated importance to the various factors in backwardness in the following proportions:

Cause	Percentage
Poverty	20%
Home atmosphere	16%
Educational causes	11%
Health	8%
Neighbourhood	3%

Even if this kind of guesses are not relied upon, one can still say that backwardness is considerably aggravated through the contribution of physical and mental defects, atmosphere in the home, emotional causes, lack of interest in subjects of education, neighbourhood and school, etc.

SELECTION OF BACKWARD CHILDREN

Modern schools are led to believe that the backward children in a class should be specially attended to. Hence, the teacher must know how to distinguish and recognise a backward child. This can be done in four steps:

1. **Discovering the child's A.Q.:** Tests in arithmetic, language and general knowledge can be used for discovering the child's A.Q.

2. **Discovering I.Q.:** Selective children with an intelligence quotient of below 85, their exact I.Q. should then be calculated.

3. **Individual intelligence tests:** Now the results obtained from the group intelligence tests should be examined for their reliability by obtaining results through individual intelligence tests and coinciding the two conclusions.

4. **Rating by teachers:** Following this, rating by teachers should be sought concerning children who appear to be backward so that the results of tests are confirmed by educated insight.

5. **Case history:** After all the above tests have been completed, the child's detailed life history should be prepared.

Solution of the problems of backwardness

Most of the so-called backward children can be improved. In the case of children with intelligence quotients below 70, no improvement is possible through education in the ordinary schools since they need to be sent to specialised schools and institutions. In children with intelligence quotients between 70 and 85, considerable improvement is possible even in regular educational institutions. Many of these children can be raised to the level of average normality through cures so that they can find success in school and later life. If they are given some encouragement and are shown some success, they learn many simple activities. But this requires modification of the curriculum, the teacher's method of teaching, and separate educational establishments are not essential as they require only special attention and periodical expert examination. But with children of intelligence quotients below 70, separate arrangements are unavoidable.

1. Curriculum: Often many children fail repeatedly in the same class for the simpie reason that the curriculum does not suit them. Consequently, the teacher must modify his curriculum to meet the requirements of backward children so that it contains only those subjects. The entire curriculum should be so fashioned that when the backward child completes his course, he should be fitted to adopt some particular profession. Basic education should be emphasized in the curriculum. Children can also be trained for some specific professions and vocations.

2. Method of teaching: The sole quality of a teaching method is that the student should grasp what it has to teach. Hence, there should be different methods of teaching for students on different levels, it is evident that backward children will not gain much if they are taught by a method that is found suitable for average children. For them, there should be a special method of teaching with the following characteristics—

(*i*) pace of teaching should be slow;

(*ii*) lesson should be repeated more than once.

PROBLEM CHILDREN

What is a problem child?

Problem children, as is evident from the term applied to them, are children whose behaviour is not normal and it results in some or the other problem of adjustment being caused. In the words of Valentine, "Problem children is generally used to describe children whose behaviour or personality shows something seriously abnormal." In this manner the class of problem children includes all those juveniles whose character or personality shows some signs of abnormality. Some behavioural abnormalities that seem to indicate this condition are—stealing, lying, annoying children weaker and younger than themselves, not doing home assignments, running away from school, or arriving late at school. They can also be called defects or abnormalities concerning character or personality because conduct of this nature indicates shortcomings in both personality as well as character.

For an understanding of the psychology of problem children it is necessary that a detailed analysis of the behaviour be made and the problematic form of behaviour distinguished from the normal forms. It must here be recalled that the problem child is not a member of a group distinct from the normal child groups. There is no distinct line that distinguishes him from his more normal counterparts as to some extent, and at varying stages in childhood, the behaviour of every child becomes problematic. Almost every child, at some stage or the other and for one reason or another tells a lie or steals something.

Hence, it is not quite desirable to declare one completely problematic and another more or less completely normal, It has been seen that very often the child is prone to much naughtiness between the ages of two and five, and his conduct appears somewhat problematic and strange. But as he continues to grow older this naughtiness disappears and he no longer appears a problem child. It is for this reason that specialists have made very detailed studies into problem behaviour. In his book on educational psychology, Cronbach made a mention of an experiment or study by Richard Henderson which had revealed the symbols of problematic behaviour that were considered the most sure signs of problematic trouble by the test trained and particularly intelligent research workers.

Causes of problematic behaviour

Problematic behaviour can have two kinds of causes—(1) Hereditary, and (2) Environmental. Hereditary causes include physical, emotional or nervous defects, but sometimes these may also be the result of weakness. The environmental factors are the following:

1. **Atmosphere of home:** One major cause of problematic behaviour is the contaminated behaviour that exists in many homes. A large majority of problem children come from broken families of divorced persons. In a study conducted by Bannister and Rooder it became known that 66 per cent of the children come from homes that have an improper atmosphere. Certain other studies traced abnormal behaviour to such diverse causes as poverty, lack of recreation, absence of care, almost complete absence of affection and love, cruel behaviour of step mothers or other relatives, too much cinema seeing, etc. Where the entire family is compelled to live in a small house with only two rooms the child may have occasions, witnessing of which has the worst influence upon his undeveloped mind and leads him to forming bad sexual habits. Signs of problematic behaviour are also generated in children who come from homes, the atmosphere in which is either strictly disciplinarian or completely lax and uninhibited. Much of what is said regarding juvenile delinquents is also true of the problematic children.

2. **Bad company:** Besides the family, another agency that plays an important role in developing signs of abnormal behaviour in the child is his companionship. Falling into bad company the best of children learn stealing, smoking, physical outrage, cruelty or sex habits of a bad nature.

3. **Atmosphere in college:** Another important cause of problematic behaviour is the defective and contaminated atmosphere of the college. It is only natural for children to show signs of abnormal behaviour when they are compelled to study in colleges or schools in which the teachers present improper and immoral ideals before them, the method of teaching is disgusting or uninteresting, and where there is absence of wholesome recreation, etc.

Cure of problem children

Hence, the cure of problematic children demands the removal of all objectionable elements from the atmosphere at home and in college as well as from the child's company. The main facts to be noted in this connection are the following:

1. Measures concerning the family: Valentine has made the following suggestions concerning the administration of discipline in the family—

(*i*) Discipline should not take the form of pressure or fear but should aim at ultimate self-control in the child.

(*ii*) Level of conduct should not be too high.

(*iii*) The behaviour of parents should be benevolent and there should be every possible co-operation between the home and school.

(*iv*) Discipline and rules should be relative.

(*v*) The child should never be allowed to feel that he is not loved by anyone.

Following these suggestions it will be possible to improve the atmosphere in the family. Residences of families should normally be as far as possible from prostitution houses, gambling dens and factories, etc. Children should not be allowed to view very inflammatory or sexually arousing films. Parents should be affectionate and understanding in their behaviour, as the child's behaviour, character and personality depend upon these corresponding elements in themselves. Thus, they must present the best ideals to the children, and should the child develop any undesirable symptoms it should be dealt with psychologically rather than having recourse to physical punishment.

2. Good company: The company that a student keeps outside the house, in the college or in the neighbourhood should be carefully studied and kept in mind. If he has had the misfortune of falling into bad company, tactful methods should be employed to wean him of it and introduce him into better circle of friends. It is equally improper and unjustified to give the child too much pocket money or to give him none at all. There should be adequate arrangement for his recreation.

3. Methods adopted by schools: Schools can adopt the following measures for the prevention or cure of problematic behaviour in the students:

(*i*) *Presentation of high ideals by teachers:* In the school the teacher is no less than an ideal to the student or child, hence it is essential that the teacher's character, personality and conduct should be of the highest order and exemplary so that the best ideals become personified in him.

(*ii*) *Interesting method of education:* If the method of education or teaching be not interesting the children run away from school and fall into very bad habits. If they are taught by more interesting methods they will be interested and thereby prevented or protected from many ill-usages.

(*iii*) *Proper use of educational apparatus:* In schools through the medium of libraries and reading rooms children and students should get healthy literature so that their thinking may take on a healthy hue and proper form.

(*iv*) *Balanced curriculum:* The curriculum in various classes for students should be so designed as not to strain the student too much, but at the same time provide him with a variety of knowledge.

(*v*) *Arrangement of extra-curricular programmes:* Where the question of preventing problematic behaviour in children is concerned, much more can be gained by extra-curricular activities such as picnics, touring, camps, scouting, community, singing, dancing and debate, etc., than can be achieved through the formal curriculum.

(*vi*) *Means of healthy recreation:* If the child is to be persuaded to avoid any unhealthy means of entertainment it is necessary that various kinds of games and means of recreation be available to him so that he can enjoy himself without injuring his development.

(*vii*) *Self discipline:* Discipline in the college should not be foisted upon the student but should take the form of autonomous or self-discipline. This will help to increase sense of responsibility without being a burden upon them.

(*viii*) *Synthesis between family and school:* In order to prevent or to cure problematic behaviour in the child it is essential that the teacher and parents should jointly endeavour to achieve it. Hence, family and school should be synthesized.

(*ix*) *Guidance:* Children are often faced with problems the solution of which is beyond their own ability, and this resulting difficulty manifests itself in the form of symptoms of problematic behaviour. Hence, the school should provide for individual, educational as well as vocational guidance.

CHILD'S DEFECTS AND ABNORMALITIES

Children can have both defects and abnormalities. The general system of education is devised for the average and normally healthy children, as a result of which it cannot incorporate the development of abnormal children since they need special arrangements. One has to speak louder than when one is speaking to a normal person if one wants to communicate with a deaf individual. A modern teacher is concerned not only with the development of a majority of average children, but also with the development of brilliant, backward, defective and abnormal children. Hence, the system of education should also provide for such individuals. Unfortunately many circumstances conspire to make provision of such facilities impossible in all schools. Nevertheless, the teacher should definitely be aware of the defects and abnormalities that mar the development of a child, or arise during its progress. Here these defects will be divided into various categories concerning physical development, mental development and character etc.

Physical defects and abnormalities

Almost any and every organ of the body can be deformed through defects, and it is not possible to list all such defects. Secondly, all of them do not have any effect on education. Thus, the physical defects and abnormalities that are to be treated of here, are specifically those that are particularly important from the point of view of educational process.

1. Defects of the head: Of all the parts of the body, the head is most important since it houses the brain. Hence, removing defects of the head is most important. Common defects of the head are the presence of leeches, skin eruptions, pus, etc., that are mainly caused through the head being left unclean. A child cannot himself keep his head clean. Parents should keep an eye on its cleanliness. One definite measure that must be taken very regularly is that it should be cleaned with soap or other cleaning ingredient, and another is its regular massage with oil, and proper hair combing. It is always advisable for young students to keep hair short and trimmed. This both avoids putting much weight on the head and also makes for easier cleaning and maintenance. Oils that are used for lubricating the head should be those that have a good effect on the head and brain. Application of the oil itself should not involve mere smearing of it on the head but be more of the nature of massage so that the oil penetrates into the roots. There are a variety of oils available for the purpose, but only the best should invariably be preferred. If the child develops some disease of the skin or the head or acquires leeches, his head should be shaved clean following which he should be submitted to expert medical advice and care. In the classroom, the teacher himself should see the extent to which his wards keep cleanliness. If they tend to be dirty, he should invite their parents to school and point out the desirability of cleanliness and personal hygiene.

2. Defects of the eye: Another organ of the body that has considerable importance from the educational viewpoint is the eye. It, too, is another organ that is prone to many defects in the case of children. Some defects are innate, and even hereditary, but many others are the result of excessive strain on the eye.

Schools should provide facilities for regular periodical checks of the children's eyes so that it should be possible to know of a defect as soon as possible. Besides making arrangements for having any such defects cured the teacher should also advise the student as to the proper mode of eye care. Power of the eyes can be maintained and increased through such expedients as splashing cold water on the eyes, standing facing the sun early in the morning with closed eyes, palming, deep breathing, consuming almonds, white pepper, etc., and other things that increase the power of the brain. Students should never be careless on this score since it is on this that their entire future is based. Finally, as has been pointed out earlier, teachers should read books published by Dr. Bates and other nature cure specialists, so that they may acquaint their students with various exercises of eye that keep them in good health. One very useful took on this subject is Harry Benjamin's *Better Sight Without Glasses.*

3. Defects of the ear: After defects of the eye, come the defects of the ear that are no less harmful. Some children are bora deaf, with the result that they also remain dumb since language cannot be learned without hearing. Being deaf, they cannot profit by studying in the normal kinds of schools. Special schools have now been provided for the education of such handicapped children where the deaf can learn many things that the normal people know. Consequently, they are also in a position to achieve a good status in society.

Another defect that afflicts the ear is a difficulty lo hear slight sounds. Their problem resembles the problems of the deaf to some extent. But in their case this shortcoming can either to cured or made less obnoxious through the use of some mechanical devices. Social adjustment is a problem for deaf children and for those who are hard of hearing. Teachers and other well-wishers must devote some of their attention to these problems, it usually happens that in large classes, teachers have no way of knowing the various physical ailments that are affecting their students. Hence, it is for them to examine their students from time to time through tests, and advise their guardians of their condition periodically. It is as necessary to cure defects of the ear as it is to provide for their general care. Living continuously in an area that is very noisy may lead to serious auditional consequences since such conditions can cause deafness. There have been definite cases of traffic policemen in big cities going deaf through being constantly in the centre of extreme noise. When the ear accumulates dirt, most people are in the habit of cleaning it with some sharp-edged instrument a practice that is most depreciable as it endangers the ear drum. If there is dirt within the ear, then it should be removed in such a manner that it does not endanger ear drum. Itching in the ear can be cured or at least relieved by putting lukewarm castor oil or oil of neem in it. And even otherwise if some oil is put in the ear from time to time, it prevents extreme dryness of the ear. Too much dirt or any disease of the ear is a condition that only expert physician or ear specialist can treat. Considerable damage can result in such cases even from the least evidence of carelessness. Students who are hard of hearing should to given place in front of the class so that they may not miss too much of what the teacher says.

4. Defects of the teeth: Dental care is as important as the care of any other part of the tody. Usually, parents pay little attention to the care of the children's teeth. Carelessness can lead to serious diseases such as pyorrhoea, that can lead to serious general complications apart from irreparably damaging the teeth. This happens as food reaches the stomach through the teeth, It is for the teachers to arrange for periodical checking of children's teeth and for instructing them and their careless parents in the care of teeth. Cleanliness of teeth can be achieved through very regular brushing with some good dental cream or delicate branches of the neem tree. Whenever something is eaten, it should be followed by a careful gargling of the mouth so that all residue that is embeded in the teeth is eliminated. Decay of teeth often results from children drinking sweetened milk at night immediately before going to sleep since they do not then wash their mouths. Even if every meal is not succeeded by brushing of the teeth, they should be cursorily cleaned by carefully running a finger over them and removing any matter that sticks between the teeth.

5. Defects of the speech: Some children are afflicted by defects of speech, such as stumbling over words, mispronunciation, etc. Many of these defects can be got rid of through the simple expedient of regular practice. Demosthenes, a famous speaker of Greece, stuttered from birth. He made a habit of going to the seashore and speaking with pebbles in his mouth, a habit that finally cured him of the trouble after he had persisted with it for a long time. Children who falter and stutter are usually teased and laughed at by other children with the result that their social adjustment is considerably hindered. The child himself develops many undesirable attitudes. Presence of such defects makes it imperative that the advice of a good physician be sought in order to remove them. Sometimes a condition of stuttering is actually induced by parents who first initiate children because the child's faltering tongue is pleasant to listen to. And, they often try to remind children of the manner in which they used to speak. In fact, even when the child pronounces incorrectly, parents should encourage them patiently to speak correctly so that the wrong pronunciation should not become a habit. Defects of speech can be more easily corrected in childhood than at a later stage. Yet, it is not quite right to plunge the child into complexities very early, since such a method can affect his emotional development adversely. A child's pronunciation depends to a considerable extent upon the pronunciation of other family members. Hence, teachers and parents should take care to pronounce words correctly when speaking in the presence of children. If the child persists in stuttering and faltering, he should be sympathetically assisted rather than criticised or looked down upon. In this respect, family members are particularly responsible.

6. Defects of the nose: Concerning children, parents should also remember that cleaning of the nose is also important. Lack of proper care can lead to serious complications and consequences. A child himself cannot keep his nose properly clean, so that all responsibility for his hygiene is upon his parents. As soon as any disease of the difficulty in breathing is discovered, the child should be submitted to the care of an expert.

7. Extreme delicacy of the body: Another defect of the body is its extreme delicacy or weakness. A weak child finds social adjustment difficult since other children take advantage of his incapacity and bother him. General weakness of the child's body can normally be alleviated through proper food and exercise. Hence, parents should see to it that other children do not worry their weak friends, and at the same time to do their best to improve the general health and debility of the children.

8. Crippled children: Some children become crippled either through some accident or even in pregnancy. Some children experience difficulty in social adjustment and adaptation since other children are prone to make fun of the cripple. Some parents develop a habit of mentioning the child's crippled condition in front of him, and showing their disgust at it. This has the worst possible effect upon the child's mind. In fact, children of this kind should be treated with more love and care than normal children, though it should be remembered that he should not be reduced to complete helplessness and dependence where he can do nothing on his own, but needs the assistance of his parents. Sensible parents can help in the adjustment of their children. Becoming crippled, the child's education should not be reduced in any measure as adequate and proper education can lead even cripples to considerable achievement and progress.

9. Other physical defects: In order to preserve the children from normal defects, teachers should train them to walk, sit, read, write, etc. in the correct manner. Many physical defects can result if the child forms a habit of walking crookedly, siting in a doubled up position, or reading in a reclined position. Eyes can be adversely affected if the child develops a habit of reading with the book either too close or too far from the eyes. Furniture in the classroom should be comfortable and well-designed. Teachers should interrupt the students to point out defects and faults in their posture, their manner of reading, the angle of light, etc. Girls who do not know the way of carrying themselves gracefully, unwittingly deprive themselves of much of their natural charm and poise. The truth of the matter is that the right sort of carriage hides many defects while it brings into prominence all the good qualities of the individual.

Mental defects and abnormalities

Besides the physical defects and abnormalities, one also finds mental shortcomings and abnormalities in children. For example, some children have a very low intelligence quotient while those with below 20 are regarded as mentally retarded. On the other hand, some children show abnormal intelligence quotients, while those with scores of 130 and above are considered abnormal and gifted. Besides these variations within wide limits, children can also possess many kinds of mental aberrations. Mental complexes, inferiority complexes and superiority complexes are among the more normally found conditions of the mind in children, although their being found commonly does not reduce the ill effects that they have upon the personality. Some children are also subject to Epileptic and other kinds of fits. Fainting fits also are not quite unknown. Some children are over-sexed in that the sexual urge is very intense in them. Other children give evidence of neuroses and psychoses. Such mental diseases can only be cured under expert medical advice and care. Sometimes, manifestations of mental diseases are misinterpreted as extreme obstinacy in the child, for which he is severely castigated and punished by parents and even teachers. This not only does not cure the child, but rather further precipitates the conditions of illness. If the child is to be protected from emotional complexes, it is essential that he be treated with sympathy, love and understanding, with a little bit of common sense being thrown in for good measure. His problems should be understood and he should be assisted in his efforts to overcome them. Every school curriculum should make proper provision for education of backward as well as exceptionally intelligent children. Extra-curricular programmes should also be adequately modified to suit the needs of children.

Defects and abnormalities of character

Children exhibit defects and abnormalities concerning character, in addition to defects and complications in the physical and mental aspects of their being. Development of child's character is an essential part of the educative process. Character is evident in conduct, and conduct is formed of habits that are acquired in childhood. Hence, proper care and attention to the child can save him from forming harmful habits that become permanent in the form of character ailments. Faults of character usually have their origin in sex motivated activity. And in this, much of the responsibility can be placed squarely upon the shoulders of teachers and parents. Actually speaking, it is the parents and not the children who are to be blamed for these bad habits since it is for them to satisfy the child's curiosity of all forms, to explain everything to him sympathetically rather than beating him, to put an end to the string of questions he puts forward, to create such a healthy and affectionate atmosphere in the home that healthy development of the child's character is almost ensured. Once the presence of some criminal streak in the child's character is discovered, it can be eliminated through some illuminated and sensible manoeuvring. Once the sense of self-regard is developed in a child, his character then usually progresses in the right and desired direction.

STEALING

Some children start on a career of crime by stealing when they are only 5 or 6 years of age. They begin with stealing things from the house, stealing food and other domestic things. Then, gaining in confidence, they extend the sphere of their activity to the neighbourhood. Such children are often apprehended stealing books from other children when they go to school, with the result that their well-wishers and parents have sometimes to stand for much disgrace and embarrassment in front of strangers. Knowing of the child's activity, they give him a sound beating, but once the habit of stealing has set in, there is no getting rid of it, at least not so easily. Hence, what is more important is that they should not be given an opportunity to acquire any such habit in the first place. Yet, if he does form any such habit, it is essential that efforts at destroying a habit should be very tactful and imaginative. In either condition, it is essential to divine the reason why any child steals. Modern educational psychologists have discovered why children steal, and in this connection have shed some light on the psychological factors involved. Knowledge of these elements will help teachers and parents to solve the problem of stealing by children.

Causes of stealing

Main causes why children steal are the following:

1. Sense of insecurity: Children develop a sense of insecurity when the family is in turmoil, when children are indifferently treated by the parents or when they are frequently punished by them. If parents lie to their children and the children manage to find out that the parents have been misleading them, they feel insecure. And this sense of insecurity sometimes induces the child to steal. Hence, it is essential that the calm and peace of family life be maintained intact, children should be told the truth as far as is practicable and they should be treated with love.

2. Spoiling through excessive love: Love and affection are things for which the child rightly yearns, but too much of them can spoil him and make him very obstinate. A child who has his full of love and affection has far too many needs and while these needs can be satisfied in a family that is financially strong, in poor families this creates a problem. Descent from a strong financial position to an inferior level of income also creates a problem, and the child begins to steal. It is, of course, not inevitable that members of poor families steal. On the contrary, one finds habits of stealing in children who come from the richer families. Stealing or not is more positively concerned with the child being spoiled. Hence, it is essential that the child should be scolded if he does anything undesirable.

3. Strict discipline: Presence of extreme discipline in the family leads the child to complete repression of many of his tendencies. And repression leads to the formation of sentimental complexes that complicate his adjustment activity, for the fulfilment of which he turns to theft. Too much beating and punishing also instigates the child to stealing since this gives him a sense of independence. Hence, where discipline in the family is concerned, it is never desirable to wield the rod with a liberal hand.

4. Dissatisfaction of needs: The basic cause why a child steals is that his needs are not satisfied. If a child gets enough to eat, wear and play within the home he has no need for stealing. Generally, a child should also be given some pocket money when be goes to school. What actually happens is that when the child sees other children spending money on all kinds of things, it is natural for him to want the same things. When he finds no resources to do so, he steals things from school and money from his own home. It should also be remembered that if all the child's demands are promptly met with, instead of breaking off the habit of stealing, there is every possibility that it will be intensified. Lack of control spoils the child so that he has no compunctions in stealing.

5. Sex problems: Psychological studies have revealed that a child steals because of an unconscious desire to satisfy his repressed sexual desires. Scolding and punishing the child if he enquires after his curiosity on matters of sex leads to the formation of a guilt complex in the child, and he learns stealing, lying and other bad habits.

6. Sense of adventure: Some children find stealing an adventure and the excitement involved is the main consideration. Plucking flowers where it is prohibited gives them a sense of thrill.

7. Imitation: Where children observe other members of the family stealing, it is comparatively more natural for them to adopt such activities. Some women surreptitiously remove money from their husband's pockets, some other children in the family are prone to stealing. And the child imitates them.

Eliminating the Habit of Stealing

On the basis of the above mentioned causes of stealing among children, the teacher can discover the cause of stealing in the case of an individual child with the parent's help. In fact, a child's stealing is less a crime but more a bad habit and defect of character. In order to kill this habit in the child, a teacher will advise the parents to maintain an atmosphere of peace and calm within the family, to love the child, to provide him with a reasonable amount of spending money, and to look after him carefully. Children who find stealing thrilling because of the adventure involved can be broken of the habit by being busied in games that involved adventure and require courage. Children who steal because of an unconscious desire arising out of the repression of sexual impulses can be guided into the right mode of behaviour by being told the healthy things about sex and by affectionate behaviour. Actually, within the family a system should be developed whereby the children should use only what is theirs and not to pick up anything belonging to any other family member. Such a step will develop his sense of possession over what is admittedly his, and will also develop in him a habit of keeping his hands off things that do not belong to him. Scolding or punishing a child after his stealing has come to one's notice is not a very constructive measure, neither is there anything to be gained by ignoring theft. If such a condition is precipitated, the teacher can coolly discuss things with the parents and discover the causes that lead the child to crime, and will remove them before trying to break him of the habit.

LYING

Meaning and kinds of lying

Conscious and wilful saying of a thing that is known to be incorrect is called lying. If a child says something that is incorrect but is not aware of its invalidity, it is incorrect to call him a liar. He is a liar only when he has knowingly said something that is untenable. Habits of lying of this type must be removed. Lying can be of many kinds. The famous criminologist Cyril Burt has classified lying in the following manner:

1. **Playful lies:** In infancy and childhood, sometimes the child tells a lie just for the fun of it. It is no crime, it is just wantonness.

2. **Lie of confusion:** When something is in doubt, the child fails to distinguish between true and false, and says that which is false.

3. **Lie of vanity:** Some children lie for the sake of false vanity. They talk of things that they have never done. Such lying satisfies their false vanity.

4. **Lie of revenge:** Sometimes the child who has been defeated and has no means of wreaking revenge upon the winner, turns up spreading false gossip and creating all kinds of false information to manifest his superiority over his adversary.

5. **Selfish lie:** Telling a deliberate lie in order to conceal some fault of one's own doing is called a selfish lie. For example, when some children are caught being naughty, they invent all kinds of false reasons to escape the natural reckoning.

6. **Lie of loyalty:** A child is very loyal to his group and tries to cover up its objectionable activities by telling lies.

7. Pathological lie: Some lying is the result of many abnormalities and mental complexes in the individual. Such lies resulting from mental diseases can arise due to the following causes:

(*i*) Overactive imagination,

(*ii*) Facility in the use of words,

(*iii*) To hide certain bad sex habits.

Cure of lying

Once the child evinces the habit of telling lies, the teacher must endeavour to end it, since its persistence will adversely affect the development of his character and leave incomplete the function of education. Hence, teachers who catch their students telling lies, use many ways of curing them. Some of the main methods are the following:

1. Psychological treatment: In psychological treatment, the child is treated with love and affection in order to discover the causes of his lying. Having discovered them, the teacher tries to persuade the child and also causes such changes in his environments that the need for telling lies ceases to exist.

2. Indirect punishment: According to modern educational psychologists, direct punishment of the child leads to development of feelings of hatred and revolt against his teacher, hence this mode of retribution is not desirable. As an alternative, some forms of indirect punishment can be used that often prove to be more effective even than direct punishment. Some such methods are—not talking with the child, ignoring him, being indifferent towards him.

3. Avoid provocative occasions: Generally speaking, the teacher should always try to avoid all occasions that may provoke the child into lying. Testing the child by deliberate creation of such situations is not very expedient since there is no bad habit that the child is incapable of picking up. Hence, as far as is practically possible and feasible, one should avoid all occasions that provoke lying in children.

4. Confession: When a lie is detected the first time, one must try to make the child confess that he is in the wrong. This inspires him to repent, and the embarrassment involves acts as a sufficient deterrent in case of future provocation. His self-respect is injured, if he has to confess. Secondly, having confessed to his fault and having promised not to repeat it, the child himself does his best to avoid all such occasions.

5. Positive instruction: According to modern educational psychologists, a teacher should avoid negative instruction and direction as far as possible, and try to make his directive positive. It is more expedient to say, "always tell the truth", than to order the student to avoid lying. Children have an almost natural tendency of contradicting all negative orders, being more prone to accepting positively worded requests and orders.

6. Rational attitude towards the child's imagination: A child is naturally imaginative. He imagines all sorts of things by imaginatively putting himself in different situations. Sometimes he fails to do these things in the concrete, he boasts that he has done this or that, and that he has seen this or that thing. Hence, realizing child's sensitivity with regard to imagination, one should take the child to see new places, give him the independence and freedom to play all kinds of games, give him new things. When this is done, he will not tell lies among his friends for the simple reason that there will be no need to do it.

Finally, it can be said that successful elimination of the child's lying habits depends upon the teacher's psychological insight, patience and tactful behaviour. He can benefit in his efforts by the suggestions of educational psychologists.

Some children are prone to cause pain to other children junior to themselves. The teacher observes that one child is annoying others without any apparent reason. On the other hand, one student comes to him with the report that a class-fellow has beaten him up. Sometimes, reports of this kind are untrue and maliciously reported But whether the report is a lie or a fact it is for the teacher to investigate and find out, as otherwise his wards are inclined to lose faith in him, and the discipline of the school is seriously jeopardized. The child making the complaint should be sympathetically treated and made to understand that this problem will be solved and in future he will not be molested. Now, the major problem that remains is how to prevent some children from annoying others without reason. Usually, teachers punish and thrash youngsters who do these wanton things with the result that the student is awed and under the influence he is not prone to repeat his exploits. Yet, though this helps to maintain the proper discipline in the class, it defeats the purpose of education. The teacher's object is not to prevent the children from being naughty but eliminating the causes that lead him to undesirable behaviour. Hence, if he is to completely cure the child of his habit of wantonly causing pain to his juniors, it is essential that he discovers the basic causes that originated the tendency.

Causes of teasing other children

The tendency of teasing other children wantonly is one that reveals a streak of cruelty in the child. And in this the environment in the family plays a large part. Main causes in this connection can be the following:

1. Cruel behaviour on the part of family members: The child has an invariable tendency to imitate the conduct of family members. If members of the family quarrel with each other and the stronger and older beat the youngsters in the family the child will follow suit.

2. Absence of discipline in the family: Lack of discipline in the family permits the children to quarrel with each other, the seniors almost invariably triumphing over the juniors by beating them. And many parents have not the strength of will to prevent such insane behaviour. Hence, it can only be expected that children from such families will injure smaller children in school. It is sometimes seen that the parents take a hand in the punishing to stop their children behaving in this manner. This may create a state of enforced peace and acquiescence in the home, but when in school, the child will imitate his parents and injure and beat children younger and weaker than himself.

3. Relations between parents and child: If the relations between parents and children are riot loving and confident, the child becomes irritable, quarrelsome and selfish. He will manifest these qualities in fighting children younger than himself. The tendency towards cruelty is further promoted by the prejudiced and base behaviour of parents towards their children.

4. Lack of discipline in schools: In schools where senior students are seen beating and overpowering youngsters, there is little or no discipline. Teachers must adopt psychological means to create an atmosphere of discipline and rational obedience in the school.

There can be some other reasons, besides those mentioned above, why big children may injure and worry smaller children. For example, being oversexed, some children tease their juniors. Whatever the situation, the teacher must try to discover the causes involved in the situation and then try to eliminate them. Acting on two fronts, the teacher must use love and affection to persuade the student while he tries to eliminate the causes that have led to the formation of such a habit in him. Half of his battle is won if he can convince the child's parents of the need of improving the atmosphere at home. He must also try to make the student realise that it is indecent to tease smaller children. Secondly, it is for him to train the children to co-operate and work in an atmosphere of mutual confidence, love and sympathy. Once such an atmosphere has been successfully created in the school, incidents of big boys worrying small ones will be reduced. Teachers should keep an eye on such various tendencies as oversexuality, aggressiveness, false vanity and criminal tendency that arise in children from time to time, and should also resort to tactful behaviour in trying to eliminate them.

AVOIDING TASKS ALLOCATED FOR HOME WORK

In most schools, teachers allot some work to the students to complete at home. Sometimes, due to various causes that create unpredictable circumstances, the child fails to do this, but he is not to blame. But, if a child makes it a habit to avoid doing the allotted work, the teacher must do his best to break the child of such a habit. This habit can be caused by any one of the following:

1. Improper atmosphere in the home: The atmosphere in some children's houses is not at all conducive to any sort of serious effort, as a consequence of too much noise and lack of any quiet corner.

2. Lack of interest and enthusiasm: Children who are not interested in academic pursuits and have no enthusiasm for it, usually do not complete the work allotted to them.

3. Little respect and awe of teacher: If a child does not respect a particular teacher and holds him in no awe whatsoever, then that teacher's commands have no particular value for him. In fact, he does the very contrary of what is required of him. His neglecting the work allotted for completion at home is all that can be expected from the child under the circumstances.

4. Other causes: In addition to these above causes, there can be many other reasons why a student may fail to complete the work required of him. For example, if the child has failed to understand a particular lesson taught in school, how can he be expected to do any problems pertaining to it?

Solution and cure

Keeping in mind these various causes, the teacher should see to it that students do the work that he allots to them as their home work. In this effort he can, on the one hand, request the children's parents to improve the atmosphere at home, and, on the other, he can improve his own conduct in the classroom. He must be able to win the respect and admiration of his students. Having done this, it will be easy for him to have his orders obeyed. Nevertheless, if any student persists in disobeying the instructions of the teacher, then it becomes necessary to administer some indirect punishment to persuade the student to abandon his lax ways. Among them is indifference to the particular student, abstaining from holding conversations with him, and other means whereby the student himself should realise the teacher's displeasure. A teacher must invariably avoid any situation that may lead students to develop feelings of antipathy and hatred towards him, or to feel that the work allocated for home is an unnecessary burden forced upon him. Proper methods of education and desirable behaviour on the teacher's part coupled with adequate interest and inspiration in the work cause students to do their home work enthusiastically, and sometimes even go to the length of doing work on their own initiative if the teacher does not allot any, and showing it to him. Such children should be praised in front of the whole class. This will have the two-fold effect of adding to their already exuberant enthusiasm, as well as inspiring the other students to emulate them and win the teacher's admiration.

ABSCONDING FROM MATHS CLASS

Mathematics is one subject that has created aversion in more than one student and' they all do their best to avoid' it. Some of these children are enterprising enough to run away from the mathematics class. If this sort of truant behaviour is constantly noted, then the teacher is compelled to take note to solve it. He must first of all uncover the causes that induce the child to have such irresponsibility. Main causes could be from among the following:

1. Low level of maturity: Mathematics is one subject that essentially requires the presence of a certain level of maturity in its students. At different levels of maturity, the curriculum relating to mathematics should be different.

2. Defects of educational method: If the teacher takes it upon himself to teach mathematics by a method that makes the subject appear easy to the student, he will not play truant from the class. Hence, sometimes, one of the reasons why students avoid the mathematics class could be a defective and unimaginative method of teaching.

3. Student's personal difficulties: If the student has no interest in academic study, lacks enthusiasm and inspiration regarding it, a subject as notoriously dry as mathematics is the least likely to hold his attention. Repeated failure is another thing that may discourage him. There can be numerous other similar problems that may prompt the student to avoid the mathematics class. And for this, attitudes, mental abilities and qualities of the personality have a special significance.

Solution and cure

The teacher should try to discover the causes of a student's running away from the mathematics class and having done so, should try to remove it. The child should constantly practise in this difficult subject. Lessons should start with simple questions that are comparatively easy to solve Success will increase his enthusiasm, and he will be eager to delve into more difficult problems. In teaching mathematics the teacher should adopt a method that makes it easy to grasp so that students achieve a kind of auto inspiration in learning it. Besides this, if the children are found avoiding these classes through some personality defects, then the teacher should consult their parents, and through loving and affectionate behaviour, try to eliminate these shortcomings.

BEING LATE FOR SCHOOL

Causes

Being occasionally late for the class is nothing unusual. But, if a student persists in being late for the school, the teacher has of necessity to investigate and find out the cause for it, since punctuality is an important asset and a part of personality development. There can be many causes why a child is consistently late for the class, main ones among them being the following:

1. Parent's carelessness: Children can be punctual in reaching school only if their parents prepare them for school well in time. If they are careless in this respect, it is only natural that their children should be late for school.

2. Aimless wandering: Another reason why children, who are prepared for school in time by their parents, reach the school late is that they fall into bad company and play on the wayside or roam around before reaching the school. Once a child falls into a company of vagrants it is only natural for him to develop a liking for wandering. It is a kind of wander lust.

3. Tendency to avoid classes: The fundamental reason why the child is always late for school is that there is nothing in the class to interest him, and he wants to avoid it, any way. Tendency to run away from classes can be inspired by many things, among them are uninteresting methods of teaching, strict discipline, level of education being higher than the child's level of mental development, bad atmosphere in the classroom, very strict administration in school, etc.

4. Other causes: There cannot be the same reason for children being late for school. Due to different reasons and under different circumstances, children do this. It is quite possible that a child may have a special passion for some particular form of exhibition and that this exhibition may be situated on his way to school so that he may be tempted to spend a few minutes there everyday.

Cure and solution: Whatever it may be, the teacher must begin his investigation to examine the reasons why a student is delayed on his way to school. And then efforts can be made to eliminate these causes, a venture that requires the co-operation of the parents. Parents and teachers can co-operate to punish the child indirectly and thus break him of his habit. Parents must do their bit by preparing the child for school with a good bit of time to spare. If the atmosphere in school and the method of teaching is defective, it can be removed and education made more interesting. It is the duty of his seniors to save the youngster from bad company. A child naturally likes to live in the group, be it a group of good children, or one of bad children. The sole method of having the child avoid bad company is that he be put in good company. Then, he will not try to go to bad company. Parents should communicate with the teacher at regular intervals to find out whether their child is reaching the school in time. If this is not done, it is up to the teacher to immediately inform them if he thinks it fit. Such co-operation and sensible behaviour can help to rid the child of this bad habit. Secondly, this problem can also be solved by teaching the child all the virtues of punctuality. Some people fail to see the significance of doing things at the time allotted for their doing. Punctuality is a quality that is developed both in school and at home. Having become habituated to having meals, getting up, going to sleep at appointed hour and doing many things by the clock will develop into such a strong habit that he will be instinctively compelled to get to school in time. Otherwise, he is apt to reason out the little difference it makes by being late for school. But, before inculcating the wisdom of punctuality in children, it is essential that the parents and teachers themselves be very punctual. Teachers who themselves are usually late for their class can hardly expect to convince their students that punctuality is a virtue. Punctuality is a thing that is best learned by imitating one's seniors. If parents and teachers themselves are very punctual, the child will drop the habit of being late for school.

GIFTED OR SUPERNORMAL CHILDREN

Who is a gifted child?

Many studies have indicated that the intelligence quotient of children differs from one individual to another. This difference is seen not only among children of different ages but between children of the same age group also. On the basis of this, children are classified into the average, the backward and the gifted group. All psychologists do not agree about the level of intelligence required for a child to be considered gifted. Some psychologists believe that an intelligence quotient of 120 denotes exceptional gifts while others believe that the gifted child must have an I.Q. of 140. Children with an intelligence quotient even higher than 140 can be accepted as exceptionally gifted. It has been calculated that only one out of 400 children belongs to this category. Such exceptionally gifted children have an intelligence quotient ranging between 140 and 190. But an I.Q. of 170 or more is rarely seen, while an I.Q. between 140 and 150 is more common.

Characteristics of the gifted child

The gifted child differs from the average child in other respects also, in addition to his greater intelligence. Physiologically, the gifted child is frequently better built and emotionally better balanced than the average child. Leaving aside the exceptions, it is often seen that the child is gifted not only in terms of intelligence but also in terms of other individual qualities, in which he is more developed. Apparently, the gifted children enjoy the benefits of nature and environment. Most of such children are born into families with a fairly high social and economic level. They, therefore, belong to the more well-to-do group of families with the result that the care lavished on them, the food provided, the education, etc, are all considerably better than that enjoyed by the average child. Besides, they also get good training controlling their habits and emotions, which helps in developing many exceptional qualities of character and personality.

Frequently, the gifted child is one to two inches taller and a few pounds heavier than the average child. At the time of joining school, such children are seen to be 4 or 5 pounds heavier than the others. At the age of 15, such children are 10 to 15 pounds heavier. In addition to this the gifted children do not normally suffer from headaches, they have clearer skins, they are less irritable, less inclined to exhaustion and less susceptible to such common maladies as cold. In one study a group of 220 successful and 170 unsuccessful candidates were compared, and it was found that the successful candidates suffered from fewer physical defects than the unsuccessful ones. In this case there was one exception, since the gifted competitors were found to suffer from a higher incidence of visual defects. One possible explanation of this may be their excessive use of the eyes in reading and study. But physiologically they were neither weak nor dwarfed. In fact, they were taller and heavier.

It should be remembered that all gifted children are not better than the average child in their physiological characteristics, emotional stability or social adjustment. In fact, quite a few of the gifted children are below the average in this respect. In actual fact, children differ from each other very much in these respects. As a general rule, all that can be said is that defects lead to more defects while good qualities generate more good qualities, although this too cannot be accepted as a universal rule. For this reason, it is desirable that each gifted child should be studied individually.

Problems of the gifted child

As in the case of the backward child, the gifted child is also unlike the average child. As a result, certain problems arise in his case also. These problems should also be tackled with the same care and attention as is accorded to the backward child, although it is now certain that the teacher identifies a backward child much sooner than he can recognise the gifted one. It may also happen that the teacher may completely fail to observe the qualities of the gifted child, and may even consider him backward. Such a situation is extremely harmful because it hinders the gifted child's proper development, and at the same time creates administrative problems for the school and the class. The future of any nation depends upon the proper development of all the gifted children born in it. Hence, school should make special provisions for their training. But the parents also must accept responsibility for their training and education.

The education of gifted children

The following suggestions have been given for the education of gifted children:

1. Selection: The first step in their education is to find out which child is gifted. This selection can be made with the help of marks obtained at previous examinations, the advice of the class teachers, the results of psychological tests and the reports given by parents.

2. No separate classes: Some psychologists have suggested that gifted children should be taught in separate classes set apart for them, But this is not a very good psychological suggestion for this may engender a feeling of vanity and superiority in them.

3. Curriculum: Many psychologists have suggested that the gifted child should be made to study some subjects in addition to the normal syllabi intended for the average class. This is a more practical suggestion because the gifted child's abilities can be better developed by the more comprehensive syllabus. It will also help to remove inactivity, social difficulties, and also create a better atmosphere in the class. But it must be remembered that the syllabus should never be so extensive as to become a burden on the child.

4. Faster promotions to higher classes: In has also been suggested by some psychologists that the gifted child should be promoted to higher classes more rapidly than the other children. This will give them a chance to develop their minds and also save time. But from the standpoint of the child's social development, this may not prove very beneficial. He will tend to be handicapped by the fact that all the other children in his class will be older than him. It is therefore better if the gifted child is given some additional work, but without promoting him to the higher class.

5. Individual education: Now-a-days many psychologists are of the opinion that the gifted child should be educated individually with the teacher generally acting as a guide without undue interference. The child is given a particular task to perform within a fixed period. The teacher keeps an eye on his development and provides him with fresh programmes as he goes along. This method of education has proved the most useful in the case of gifted children.

6. Extra-curricular activities: Another way of developing the qualities of the gifted child is to engage him in extra-curricular activities such as games, music, dancing, other arts, practice for debates and sports competitions.

7. Facilities and apparatus: Gifted children can also be given certain kinds of special facilities such as fee concessions, opportunity to do work of exceptional responsibility or importance, etc. The school should also provide many kinds of means for learnings the arts, games and other activities. Very often the gifted child finds a good library as a very good aid.

It is clear from the above exposition that the teacher can play an important role in nation building by helping in the proper development of the gifted children tendered in his care. In actual fact, the proper development of the gifted child depends considerably more upon the intelligence, wisdom and the sense of responsibility of the teacher. He should try to make arrangements for developing special qualities in his more gifted children. But in this connection, the responsibility of the parents is not less than that of the teacher, because different means can be adopted for the child's development as effectively at home as in the school. The parents should also take special care of such children. If this is not done, their balanced development is retarded. Besides, they may even become very difficult problems for their parents. If a child shows some extra-ordinary skill at some particular work, he should be sent to a school in which he can be trained to exercise that particular skill. The Government can also facilitate the development of gifted children by providing fee concessions and other kinds of monetary aid. Thus an environment can be created in which the future leaders of the nation may develop and grow.

QUESTIONS FOR EXERCISE

1. Describe the defects and abnormalities in a child's development and point out its remedies.
2. What light has educational psychology thrown on the problem of—
   (*a*) stealing.
   (*b*) lying among children? Give examples.
3. What should the teacher do in the following circumstances:
   (*a*) A child annoys smaller children without any reason.
   (*b*) A student does not do the home work allotted to him.
   (*c*) A student always absconds in the mathematics class.
   (*d*) A student invariably comes late to the class.
4. Who is a backward child? What are the causes of backwardness and what remedies will you apply for them?
5. What do you understand by defective development? What are its causes?
6. Write short note on—Mentally deficient children.
7. How will you define a gifted child? Describe the methods by which gifted children can be identified.
8. Write short note on—Supernormal children.

32

Juvenile Delinquency and Remedial Education

In modern, civilized countries a criminal is not looked upon as a sinner or a bad person, but rather as a mentally diseased individual or one who has been victimized by circumstances. There was a time when even small children were severely punished if they committed some crime. But as psychologists proceeded to draw the attention of the civilized world to the cause of juvenile delinquency, the tradition of punishing children lost favour, to be replaced by efforts at improving and rehabilitating them. Now-a-days, in every nation efforts are made to correct the juvenile delinquent rather to punish him. To make the deviant once again a healthy and responsible citizen of society, efforts are made through reformatory schools, probation and other measures.

LEGAL DEFINITION OF JUVENILE DELINQUENCY

Legal definition of juvenile delinquency does not conform to its psychological definition as from the legal viewpoint, a juvenile delinquent is a person between the ages of 15 and 17 who indulges in anti-social activity. In U.S.A. the Ohio Code defines juvenile delinquent as one who breaks the law, is a vagrant, persists in disobeying orders, whose behaviour endangers his own moral life as well as the moral life of others, or one who tries to marry without the consent of his parents. It may as well be pointed out that the ages of the so-called juvenile delinquents have not been similarly determined in all countries. It varies from country to country but is within the usual limits of 16 and 20. Normally it is the 17 year old adolescent who qualifies for this term, but in India according to prevalent Laws, the maximum age of a juvenile delinquent is fixed at 16. Laws pertaining to this subject have been passed in U.P., M.P., Bombay, Madras, Mysore, Delhi, West Bengal, Orissa, and Punjab. In those States in which the Juvenile Acts have not been passed, the Reformatory Act of 1987 prevails. In these, the maximum age of a juvenile delinquent has been determined at 15. In Bombay and Madhya Pradesh it is 16. According to the Reformatory Act, the term Youthful Offender will be appended to any individual below 15 who has been sentenced to life imprisonment or has been convicted of some crime.

PSYCHOLOGICAL DEFINITION OF JUVENILE DELINQUENT

Differing from the legal definition of a controversial term, psychologists lay much emphasis upon the causes of juvenile delinquency in defining it.

From the legal viewpoint all those who are not apprehended are not criminals but from the psychological viewpoint all such offenders also are criminals. Consequently, the psychological definition of juvenile delinquency is more comprehensive than its legal definition. According to psychology, any and every child, of either sex, between ages of 15 and 18, who commits a crime, irrespective of the fact that he is apprehended or not is a juvenile delinquent. In this manner, juvenile delinquent is one who forcibly possesses the property of another, or causes it damage, indulges in anti-social activity, creates danger for another's life or hinders the activities of others. Hence, a child who throws stone at a car and runs away, one who sets fire without cause, creates dangers for the life of another just for the fun of it, are all juvenile delinquents, from the psychological viewpoint.

Defining juvenile delinquency, Dr. Sethna has written, "Juvenile delinquent involves wrong doing by a child or a young person who is under an age specified by the law (for the time being in force) of the place concerned." Newmeyer puts the same idea in these words, "A delinquent is a person under age who is guilty of anti-social act and whose misconduct is an infraction of law."

Difference between crime and juvenile delinquency

1. Difference of age: The above description of juvenile delinquent makes it apparent that the main difference between a juvenile delinquent and a criminal is one of age, but both indulge in anti-social activities. Working of both are subversive and hindering of social relationship. According to Dr. Haikerwal, from the social viewpoint, crime or juvenile delinquency is a form of conduct that acts as an obsolete in the system of human relationships which are believed by society to be its fundamental conditions. In this way, if a criminal is below a certain specified age, he will be designated as juvenile delinquent.

2. Difference of actions: But sometimes criminals and juvenile delinquent differ not only in respect of their ages but also in respect of the crimes that they commit. And in this connection, some actions that young men and children do lead them to be regarded as juvenile delinquents even though their activities are not actually crimes. A classification as wide as juvenile delinquent can include the vagrant, cruel, obstinate, or young boys who keep the company of thieves, dacoits, other vagrants and prostitutes, those who keep away from the house for long periods of time without the permission of their parents, those who roam the lonely streets late at night. It should be remembered here that such activities are, strictly speaking, not illegal or infringing any legal statute. Hence, the juvenile delinquent who chooses to act in these ways cannot be included in the same class as ordinary criminals. Another thing that sometimes happens is that the employed, unhoused and wandering child may be included in the category of juvenile delinquents along with the beggar, the farce being carried so far as to present the young person before a court and to try to mend his ways.

3. Difference of characteristics: Kohen has distinguished criminal from juvenile delinquents on the basis of the following distinguishing characteristics:

(*i*) A juvenile's mischief is lacking in utility as he does things that do not benefit him in the least, such as roaming about the streets without cause. On the other hand, the criminal acts with intent to gain something. A juvenile is sometimes even unaware of the objective of his own actions.

(*ii*) Sometimes a juvenile commits a crime with only an intention to enjoy himself and indulge his sense of humour. It finds expression in practical joking like breaking car glasses, putting boulders on railways tracks or pushing people into a pond of water just for the fun of it. A criminal does not find this suitable mode of manifesting his sense of humour.

(*iii*) The juvenile delinquent does not commit a crime on a preplanned and well organized basis, being more apt to do things on the spur of the moment. A hardened criminal is more inclined to plan his moves and organize crime with a certain show of skill.

Briefly, criminals and juvenile delinquents are to be distinguished by their difference of age, kinds of work, objective of activities, mode of working. Yet, normally it is the difference in age alone that is considered the sole basis of making distinction between the two classes.

METHODS OF DISCOVERING CAUSES OF JUVENILE DELINQUENCY

Before plunging into detailed study of the causes of juvenile delinquency it is essential to become acquainted with methods of discovering them as this will indicate the intrusion of psychology into the subject, as also its scientific bias. Three kinds of methods have usually been employed to devolve into causes of juvenile delinquency—(1) Statistical, (2) Case history method, and (3) Psycho-analytic method. They have also been used to discover crimes. Now these methods will be described in some detail.

1. Statistical method: The statistical method finds its best exposition in the works of Cyril Burt. He compiled a list of some specific situations or circumstances. And with the help of this inventory he attempted the discovery of circumstances that are found in criminal children, and other situations that are peculiar to the healthy ones. Some of these situations are described as follows:

(i) Circumstance of heredity: (*a*) physical, (*b*) mental, (*c*) temperamental (also sign of mental diseases).

(ii) Circumstances of environment: (*a*) Situation in the house—(*i*) poverty, (*ii*) defective family relations, (*iii*) defective discipline, (*iv*) bad characters in family.

(*b*) Situation outside the house—(*i*) neighbours, (*ii*) conditions outside the house, (*iii*) friend's circle.

(*iii*) *Physical conditions.*

(*iv*) *Mental conditions:* (*a*) Intellectual, (*b*) emotional, (*c*) interest, (*d*) emotional aberrations, (*e*) mental complexes.

On the basis of the above list of circumstances and conditions, Cyril Burt tried to discover the causes of juvenile delinquency. Some circumstances were noted through observation while others were measured through testings. The most important cause of juvenile delinquency turned to be emotional. And crime appeared to have intimate relationship with the presence of tuberculosis and other serious diseases in the physical constitution of the parents. In the environment, the status of the family was found to be the most important. Physical and mental conditions of the adolescent himself were found to be of secondary importance. Accordingly, Cyril Burt came to the conclusion that the main factors concerning juvenile delinquency were defective discipline, defective relations between the parents and emotional aberrations.

2. Case history method: Another important method of discovering the causes of juvenile delinquency is the case history method. The statistical method does not reveal the singular and actual causes as it does not include a study of the personal life of the juvenile delinquent under consideration. In the case history method, efforts are made to collect all information concerning every aspect of the subject's personality, as well as most of the circumstances of his life. The observer collects relevant information concerning the schools, home, family and any other important field of the life of the subject. Knowledge of the subject's ambitions, frustrations and problems is gained through mental tests, personality inventories and actual interviews. Detailed information is sought at the hands of the subject's parents, near relatives and intimate friends by interviewing all of them. And, on the basis of all such information that comes to hand, a complete case history is developed. An example of one such study is the book called *The Jack Roller* by Shaw. Study of the case history revealed many factors that could have led them to find crime attractive, for example, bitter criticism of all others, unceasingly blaming others, ostentatious desire to attract the attention of others, rationalisation instead of insight, inability to understand oneself and unfounded suspicion of others, etc.

3. Psychoanalytic method: The third and the most important method of discovering the cause of juvenile delinquency is the psychoanalytic method in which the external circumstances of the subject are not the only object of inquiry. What is attempted is the analysis of his subconscious mind. Psychoanalysts take recourse to many methods such as dream analysis, word association and other psychological tests with the help of which they can probe the unconscious elements in the individual's mind and uncover the hidden and submerged causes that compel him to a life of crime and disorder. In their book *Roots of Crime* Alexander and Healy have written that the criminal tendency incriminates things by the statistical method not by making inferences from the results of individual method. To understand the criminal mentality we should understand those psychological processes that are in the background of all human behaviour. It need not be specifically pointed out that psychoanalysis cannot be said to be the one method that can discover all the causes of delinquent behaviour among juveniles. In fact, none of these three methods taken alone can help in probing the causes of juvenile delinquency, and it is best to make use of all these three methods. Such an approach is the best as it throws light on the causes of delinquency by highlighting the internal and external conditions, and the peculiarities of delinquent's personality.

CAUSES OF JUVENILE DELINQUENCY

Classification

According to the novel approach and concepts of modern criminology, the causes of juvenile delinquency have been divided into two classes—personal and social causes. In delinquency, two special factors are at work—internal and external. Internal factors include physical and psychological factors while the external factors consist of social elements. Delinquents have been divided into two categories by the American criminologists—(1) Social (2) Personal. Social delinquents, in particular, are the results of social circumstances. Walter Recklace has pointed out two specific causes of delinquency—(1) Constructive and (2) Circumstantial. Some other criminologists have divided the various causes of delinquency into two parts—(1) sociogenic and (2) psychogenic. Here, the causes of juvenile delinquency will be divided into three classes for convenient study:

1. Social causes.
2. Psychological causes.
3. Economic causes.

Social causes

Of the various causes of juvenile delinquency, the most comprehensive are the social causes. Among them, the main ones are—

1. Family.
2. School.
3. Criminal area.
4. Bad company.
5. Recreation.
6. War.
7. Social disorganization
8. Displacement.

1. Defects of the family: Of the causes of juvenile delinquency, Elliott and Merrill accept distorted family influence to be the most potent. Of 4000 juvenile delinquents in Botson, Healy and Bronner found that about 50 per cent of them came from divided or broken families. The major situations in the family that cause it are:

(*i*) broken families,

(*ii*) attitude of parents,

(*iii*) character and conduct of parents,

(*iv*) affect of criminal relatives.

In order to understand the importance of family as a cause of juvenile delinquency, it is necessary to comprehend these factors:

(*i*) *Broken families:* A study of juvenile delinquency has related that the greater number of delinquents come from the broken families. A broken family, as the term indicates, is one in which family ties have been destroyed. A family is not constituted by a number of people living together but by their mutual intimate relationships. Absence of this intimacy results in the breaking up of a family, and it is in broken families that juvenile delinquents come alive. In any such family, a child is not looked after properly. In the opinion of some specialists, broken families are more apt to arouse criminal tendencies in females than in male juveniles. The Child Care Society of Bombay had 386 boys and 169 girls under its care. Of these children, the parents of two boys and two girls were serving prison sentences, two boys and five girls were under the influence of extreme discipline, six boys and nine girls were the victims of moral insecurity. In a broken family, the relationships of husband and wife, parents and children, brothers and sisters lose their healthy nature. Hence, it is only natural if the children choose the wrong paths that ruins their lives.

(*ii*) *Attitude of parents:* In the family factor in juvenile delinquency, another important condition is the relations between the two parents. According to the preface writer of *Women of the Street*, a probing and searching analysis of the prostitutes of London, the problem of the prostitute has its origin in the relationship between the parents. Often when the child is deprived of love and is scolded constantly on every opportunity, he develops feelings of revolt and hatred so that he runs away from the house at the earliest opportunity and falls into a life of crime. Disregard on the part of parents induces feelings of insecurity in the children with the result that they develop mental complexes. If the parents try to conceal many facts of their own life from children, the tendency towards crime is only aggravated. One of the most common query that children are apt to put before their parents is where did they come from. When they learn the truth from their servants insecurity is induced in them, because they feel that their parents do many things which they fear to tell their children and this injures their feelings. This sense of insecurity leads many children to sex crime.

(*iii*) *Character and conduct of parents:* The child's personality is considerably influenced by the character and conduct of its parents. One rarely comes across a child who has been able to mould his behaviour according to socially accepted values and conceptions in the face of his parent's telling lies, hypocritical behaviour, sexual immorality and thieving. In a study conducted by Miss Elliott 67 per cent parents in broken families and 44 per cent parents in united families were engaged in immoral behaviour. If the mother is already involved in prostitution, the child will have little hesitation in following suit, and with the worst conceivable consequences.

(*iv*) *Influence of brothers and sisters:* A child's personality is susceptible to the influence of his brother's and sister's personality, apart from the personality and mutual relationship of the parents. This influence is more potent in the case of girls as they are not exposed to external influences as much as boys who remain in the home for considerably less period of time. If the senior children in the family manifest criminal tendencies, the youngsters are invariably influenced by it. If the elder sister shows criminal tendencies or is engaged in immoral behaviour, the younger sister is more apt to follow her example.

It is evident from the foregoing description that the situation within the family has major part to play in turning children into criminals. But this need not lead one to the conclusion that all children in a broken family will turn out to be criminals. Healy and Bronner studied 372 broken families and in only 20 per cent of them one of every two children was delinquent. In 336 families in which each had 6 children, only 12 children were engaged in criminal activity. Such a study seems to indicate that the family being broken is not the sole cause of juvenile delinquency, but no criminologist will refute it that such a condition is undoubtedly a most potent cause.

2. Defects of school: After the family a child's personality is next influenced by the school. But one major form of juvenile delinquency is absconding from school. In 1947, Williamson found in his study that playing truant from school, theft and sex crimes were the major forms of juvenile delinquency, and even among these running away from school or roaming outside the school claimed the greatest attention and interest among children. Analyzing the causes of such behaviour, Williamson came to the conclusion that it was caused by criticism at the hands of parents, gaining membership of a gang of criminals, punishment by the teacher, weakness in some subject, and a level of education that is above the child's ability and capacity. Children who run away from the school usually spend their time in the worst sort of company and commit all kinds of crimes. This is one of the major problems confronting the teacher. It is for this reason that in most big cities, students are not allowed to view matinee shows in film exhibitions, but preventions of this nature do not help solve the problems. One of the major causes of increasing indiscipline in the present time is that education is neither recreating nor interesting, in addition to which it lays emphasis upon stuffing the brain with information rather than building up character. It can hardly be expressed that it is these factors that make the child lose interest in study and try to avoid school with the result that he fails into a life of crime.

3. Crime dominated areas: According to the results of a study by Clifford, Shaw and Mckay, some areas are not appropriate for the development of children. It is a matter of common knowledge that the neighbourhood casts important influences upon the child. Using the statistical method, Maller came to the conclusion that in New York juvenile delinquency was greatest in those quarters where the level of life was very low, child mortality was very high, there were no means of recreation, residences were not permanent. In a community that is unstable there are no social taboos or laws. Pickpockets are found in great abundance in and around hotels and other places where travellers stay since there is always some traveller or the other there. Clifford, Shaw and Mckay studied juvenile delinquency in nearly 15 towns to discover that the rate of juvenile crime was highest in the centre of the town and lowest at its furthest reaches. From this they concluded that the social traditions of backward and low economic status areas distinguished the pattern of crime from the average group. And these patterns are maintained in juvenile delinquent groups. In this way, big towns have certain areas where there is an abundance of criminals, and these areas are called criminal areas or crime dominated areas. It should be remembered here that Shaw and his assistant Henry Mckay had not accepted the place of residence as a cause of crime, but have tried to show instead that crimes are found to be the highest where conditions of poverty, mental aberrations, family disorganization, diseases, infant mortality and other forms of disorganisation are constantly maintained, or existing. Tendency to displacement is also found to prevail in crime areas. Having studied crime areas in Chicago and other cities, Shaw and Mckay came to the following conclusion:

(*i*) Rate of crime differs from one settlement to another. In some areas boys are not arrested, while in other areas a fifth of the criminals were captured every year.

(*ii*) In winter, the rate of crime increases around the factory area and decreases in the suburbs. Rate of crime decreases in proportion to the distance from the town's centre.

(*iii*) The rate of crime is also high in the areas where there is a greater tendency to abscond from school.

(*iv*) Areas where rate of crime was high in 1900, the rate was also high in 1930, despite the fact that the constitution and size of population underwent considerable change during these years.

4. Bad company: According to the famous criminologist Edwin H. Sutherland, criminal behaviour is acquired through interaction with others. He says that an individual becomes a criminal when there is excess of conditions that promote the infringement of law over conditions that prevent such infringement. And, among children, some get good company while others don't. The child who gets bad company proceeds towards crime while the child who gets into good company progresses to become an able and useful member of society. An individual's behaviour is influenced to a considerable extent by the conduct of his companions. In order to induce the children to accept and respect the values and assumptions of adult society around them, it is necessary to create such an atmosphere in which inspiration to criminal behaviour is reduced to the absolute minimum.

5. (*i*) *Absence of recreation:* Means of recreation have an important place in the child's development. It is only a good and healthy atmosphere that can provide the right sort of inspiration to the children for sensible and healthy behaviour in their spare time after school. Inability to make proper use of one's spare time is an added instigation to criminal behaviour. Play and games are essential elements in the socialization and ethical training of children. Inadequate, uncontrolled and improper recreation in a town is one of the causes of juvenile delinquency. In Thurston's study of 2507 juvenile delinquents it was found that their spare time had hung heavy on their hands.

(*ii*) *Defective recreation:* In modern times, the one means of recreation available to big and small is the cinema, which is responsible for juvenile delinquency and anti-social activity to quite an extent. New patterns of crime are presented to an individual through scenes of adventure and romance Some films have such potent influence upon the adolescents that after their screening in some towns, certain kinds of crime increased many-fold. But the reactions of children to films are determined and guided by patterns within the house or around the neighbourhood. And different children react differently to it. Scientific studies have determined that the direct influence of cinema upon the behaviour of children is very little. Actually, more important than the cinema is the child's reaction to it which keeps on functioning on the basis of his previous experience and reaction to social and cultural circumstances.

6. War and post-war conditions: Increase in the rate of juvenile delinquency have been found during war, and the post-war periods. In countries that actually participate in the war, the children's schooling is considerably hindered and effected. It often happens that in war-time the father is on the front fighting the war, while the mother goes to the factory to earn. Hence, children are not properly looked after. Lack of any control leads to much promiscuous mixing between girls and boys with the result that sexual crimes increase. In war-time, wherever there was bombing, it was the adolescents in that area who took the greatest part in looting smashed houses. Hence, the situation of war definitely encourages criminal tendencies.

7. Social disorganization: Social disorganization leads to disorganization of individuals. And disorganization of society leads to increase in criminal activity, hence it too, is one of the causes of juvenile delinquency. In modern industrial society there is lack of synthesis and equality which creates tension. This tension inspires young men and women to crime.

8. Displacement: Displacement also influences juvenile delinquency. In studying the town Berkeley, Stuart discovered that juvenile delinquents lived in an area where there was considerable displacement, but as compared with their own respective families, they themselves are much less active and dynamic.

Psychological causes

Till now, we have been discussing the social causes of juvenile delinquency, all data for which is collected on the basis of the statistical method. The application of the other two methods of discovering causes of juvenile delinquency—case history method, and psychoanalysis—have lead to some light being shed on the psychological causes of the phenomenon. Psychological causes concerning criminal activity are the following:

1. Intellectual weakness.
2. Mental diseases.

3. Characteristics of personality.
4. Emotional instability.

1. Intellectual weakness: Having rejected Lambroso's principle, Dr. Goring advanced the theory that intellectual weakness is a cause of crime. Goddard was the main exponent of the notion that mental weakness is the cause of crime. In his book *Mental Efficiency and Levels of Intelligence* he has written that the greatest single factor or cause of crime is mental weakness. After examining 4000 children for their intelligence, Healy and Bronner came to the conclusion that 13 per cent of them had an intelligent quotient below 70. This conclusion is borne out by S.S. Glueck and E.T. Glueck in their book *Unraveling Juvenile Delinquency* who studied 1000 criminal children in 1934 and came to the conclusion that 13 per cent children have an intelligent quotient of below 70.

This contention has been objected to on the ground that it is based on the study only of those juvenile delinquents who have been produced before the courts. Naturally, the intelligent and shrewed juvenile delinquents will be apprehended far less than the backward ones. In one of their studies, C.W. Mann and N.P. Mann, have confirmed this view and shown that children with an intelligent quotient of less than 90 stand a far greater chance of being apprehended than brilliant children. They calculated the median of the intelligent quotient of 1061 criminals in which the boys were discovered to have an I.Q. of 94.88 and girls 83.77. In 1947, Merrill, in his book *Problems of Child Delinquency*, calculated the average of the intelligence quotients of 500 criminals children, measured on the modified Binet scale. This average was 92.5, while examining 2904 healthy children for their intelligence quotient it was found to be 101.8. From both these inquiries Merrill concluded that a low level of intelligence cannot be accepted as a cause of crime. There can be no denying the fact that it is comparatively easier to mislead backward children, but intelligent and shrewd children are also liable to get involved in crime.

2. Mental diseases: Other criminologists have tried to establish a definite relationship between mental disease and crime. In the many studies carried out upon criminals, some mentally diseased individuals were also found. According to this view a criminal is a kind of mentally diseased individual who is in as much need of treatment as in need of punishment. Some psychiatrists and neurologists believe that the psychopathic personality is a cause of crime. Psychopathic children are born in families where there is an almost complete absence of love, affection and control. Concerning psychopathic children Tappan has written that he is very unsocialised, irritable, cruel, obstinate, suspicious, self-centred, lonely, full of feelings of revenge, backward and hyper-sexual or uncontrolled in sexual behaviour. In an extremely advanced stage, he lacks the ability to sympathize, and is completely devoid of repentance over his own cruel doings and the pain or suffering of others. A psychopathic child of this nature has the existence of an uninvited guest in his own house. He is never loved by any one but instead remains the butt of every criticism and abuse in the house. It is only natural that the child should react to such behaviour with feeling of unhindered obstinancy and homicidal tendencies. In his book Juvenile Delinquency, Tappan has described the case of a psychopathic child, Isaac. He was a very intelligent child of 14, accused of theft, truancy from school, unnatural sexual practices and general indiscipline. He was a beautiful child who almost invariably impressed all strangers. He was the only child in the family and his mother died while he was an infant. His father deserted him at the age of 2 following which he was disgustedly and disinterestedly cared for by one relative after another for short periods. Finally, he was sent to an orphanage. All these causes led to the manifestation of many complexes and aberrations in his childhood.

Isaac never paid attention to daily routine and showed no respect for authority, always giving evidence of obstinacy and bitterness in his conduct. He put forward all kinds of impossible and unrelated demands. His behaviour towards the two individuals whom he loved very much did not differ from his general behaviour. These two individuals, a farmer and a social worker, did their best to cure the child. Generally he was made aware of the folly of his ways and the nature of his behaviour. His interest in agriculture was encouraged. As a result of sympathetic behaviour over a considerable period, these two individuals came very close to Isaac, consequently becoming his ideals that went so far as to assume the form of his self-consciousness and awakening. Feeling of disgust with his previous ways was aroused in him and he then came to seek their advice in whatever he did. When Isaac manifested this tendency towards better adjustment, ideals of better behaviour were gradually put before him. Due to self-confidence and persistence of the two individuals, Isaac succeeded in reorganizing his future, to be selected in the United States Air Force in 1941 at the age of 21.

Some psychologists and criminologists have criticized the conclusions reached by the study of psychopathic criminals. Sutherland writes that a neurologist studied the prisoners in Illinois prison. After studying the symptoms he found that 98 per cent prisoners were psychopathic. When some other psychologists studied the prisoners in the same prison they found only 5 per cent of them to be psychopathic. Actually, this term has been used in so many varied senses and on the basis of so varied symptoms by different psychologists and psychiatrists that it has been left with no specific meaning that can be used to elucidate scientific facts.

3. Characteristics of personality: Tendency to crime was also found to have close relationship with characteristics of the personality. Personality is the method of an individual's adaptation to environment. Criminal children resort to illegal modes of such adaptation. Hence, Juvenile delinquents have been found to possess some characteristic features of the personality that shed light on the causes of their delinquency. In his book *Unraveling Juvenile Delinquency*, Gluek pointed out that the degree of freedom, irresponsibility, revolt, homicidal tendency, suspicion, lack of control, some forms of sadism, emotional and social maladjustment, extrovert behaviour, etc., in juvenile delinquents is much higher than in normal children. Immaturity in sentiment and lack of emotional balance were found to be some eight times more than in the normal child. A normal child is comparatively well-behaved, less explosive, peaceable, obedient and social. The juvenile delinquent, on the contrary, is found to be naughty, explosive, anything but peaceful, disobedient and unsocial. Glueck also discovered considerable difference between the general interests and forms of recreation of normal and abnormal children. Delinquent child was found to take much interest in works of an adventurous and dangerous nature. He was found to take considerable interest in seeing pictures and films. Among his interests and modes of recreation were found such practices as cigarette smoking, gambling, staying away from home, breaking things, and travelling without tickets, etc. He is often the member of one or the other group. On the contrary, normal healthy children were found engaging in games. In some study it has been proved that female juvenile delinquents exhibited considerable emotional instability and immaturity.

4. Emotional instability: In this way, emotional instability is one of the most important causes of crime. A child's personality is rendered unbalanced through lack of love and affection, emotional insecurity, very strict discipline, feeling of insufficiency and inferiority, and reaction of revolt. Such a state of mind inspires the child to criminal behaviour. In their studies, Healy and Bronner saw that 93 per cent of all juvenile delinquents manifest symptoms of emotional imbalance. A detailed analysis of these juvenile delinquents presented the following emotional patterns and influences:

(*i*) 46 prisoners or criminals showed that feeling of insecurity, lack of acceptability, extreme discrimination of an unfavourable nature, inferiority and not being properly understood existed in their minds.

(*ii*) In 28 criminals, lack of affection had led to suppression of their normal and abnormal desires.

(*iii*) 34 criminals showed that they felt inferior or inadequate in school life, family life, in the friend circle or in play.

(*iv*) 34 criminals showed signs of emotional imbalance as a result of bad behaviour of the parents, conditions of family life, mistake of parents and lack of proportion in the family.

(*v*) In 31 criminals feelings of extreme hatred and jealousy towards fellow mates were very strong.

(*vi*) In 17 criminals, illusions of an unhappy life, based possibly on past experience, were found existing.

(*vii*) 9 criminals clearly evinced the presence of self-condemnation and awareness of having committed crime due to some past criminal behaviour. These feelings were both conscious and unconscious.

Economic Causes

Crime and poverty are intimately related. Study conducted by Shaw, Mckay and Elliott revealed that among juvenile delinquents, majority belonged to families of unskilled labourers. This discovery has the support of Bonger and Fornasiri, as they too, advocate that poverty acts as an incentive to crime. Concerning these juvenile delinquents Merrill has written that a low family income compels the children to share the burden and to neglect their education. Atmosphere in the factory and mill is such that it leads the male and female child to crime. Sometimes children are entrusted with carrying messages to the homes where they often see all kinds of sexual practices. This has the worst effect on them, and they become tendencious towards crime. Statistics show that among juvenile delinquents, employed youngsters involved in crime number ten times the unemployed ones. Girls working in hotels or presentation houses are easily lured into sex crimes since their wages are low, their residences are dirty, hours of work are long, and there is no shortage of individuals who want to lure them to a life of crime. In fact, children in poor families have many desires that remain unfulfilled, and it is to satisfy them that they turn to crime. Poverty also induces sense of dissatisfaction and inferiority, another spur to criminal tendencies.

Yet, this is no reason to conclude that crime and poverty are invariably related. In fact, poverty is not the cause of crime; rather, the cause of crime is the psychological factor that arises in poverty and guides boys and girls to crime. In the treatise *Juvenile Delinquency*, Tappan has written that poverty is related to crime, but mainly because along with the subnormal economic situation other elements of the child's training and experience are also active, and these elements are more important in determining the reaction of character, value and laws. Family quarrels and dissensions, delinquent gangs and inadequate education, are factors that are more active than the preferred attraction of non-conformity to law and order. With the help of his study, Cyril Burt has exhibited that one cause of there being such a large number of poor people among all criminals that are apprehended is that being poor, they cannot escape the clutches of laws and police whereas the richer elements find it comparatively easier to avoid embarrassment. In the study conducted by Cyril Burt, only about 19 per cent juvenile delinquents were found to come from extremely poor families while another 37 per cent of them came from the average poor families. But, according to Burt, the main reason for the large proportion was not poverty but instead the ability of the children of richer families to avoid being apprehended. Whatever the cause to which the high rate of juvenile delinquency among poor families may be attributed, no criminologist can contradict the fact that poverty and juvenile delinquency are closely related. When children of poor families see individuals of very rich families using many different kinds of things, but are prevented from doing so by the lack of wealth, they develop emotions of hatred, avarice, and jealousy that ultimately lead them to crime.

The foregoing exhaustive treatment of the social, psychological and economic causes of juvenile delinquency makes it clear that the principle of specific causation does not properly apply to this phenomenon. In fact, no modern criminologist and psychologist can refute the fact that the causes of crime are many and varied. A person's activities are his modes of adjusting to his environment. And in this adjustment individuals who apply socially acceptable means are called healthy while those who use unsocial and abnormal means for this adjustment are called criminals.

METHODS TO CONTROL DELINQUENT ACTS

Generally speaking two methods are employed for the control of delinquent acts and they are: (1) Prevention, and (2) Punishment.

1. Prevention: It may be said that anti-social conduct is the outcome of a tendency of satisfying a thwarted or checked motive. So the best way of preventing such acts is to satisfy the needs of the children in respect of their social, economic and hygienic conditions. Our attention should be directed to the betterment of their environments. Ethical training should be given from the very beginning. Adaptability, altruism and harmony should be emphasized constantly. The social influence is the best way to give the child direct teaching in practical morality. Morality is not taught but caught. So, much emphasis should be laid to present examples of good moral behaviour rather than precepts. The parents should also be educated to appreciate the value of these principles.

2. Punishment: The revenge hypothesis of punishment must be rejected. The positive and correct view of punishment in a school is to reform the child by means of punishment. The child must be made to realize that he has committed a wrong act and he should not have done so. He must feel sorry for the wrong that he has done.

CHANGING CONCEPTS OF DISCIPLINE

A few words may be said on the changing conception of discipline. According to the votaries of 'Free Discipline', there should not be any interference from teacher or parents in the activities of children. They argue that since children differ widely from each other, they should be allowed to proceed with their studies and intellectual activities in their own way and with their own speed and this will help in the proper development of latent powers and capacities of children. Fredrick Burk states that in the nature of things there can be no misfit children. Educationists like Rousseau, Froebel, Montessory. Dewey, Neill and Nunn advocate the theory of *Laissez Faire*. 'All repression is dangerous', is their slogan. They contend that good habits are formed through liberty and freedom. Discipline through external measures is shortlived. It does not ensure permanent results. Repressive measures only help splitting up the personality of the child into two, *i.e.*, the outer one—orderly and obedient and the inner one—real one and rebellious.

Prevailing theory of Flogging

The prevailing theory of 'Flogging' relied on the 'rod' as the chief instrument to educate the educand. The rod and instruction were deemed inseparable. 'Fear atmosphere' prevailed in the school. The student had to abide by certain rigid rules and regulations and any breach of these meant stem penalties.

The truth lies somewhere between these two extremes. While it is admitted that resort should not be made to stern penalties, it cannot be deemed that there is some place for punishment in the school system. It is true that discipline should be self-discipline and creative but it is wrong to think that it can always be had without resorting to external discipline. Bagley rightly said, "The pupil is immature and helpless and he must not be given a long rope with which he may hang himself" Therefore, steps should be taken for the betterment of the environment so that right attitude may be developed among children. Following points may be remembered:

1. Punishment should not be given in a spirit of vindictiveness.
2. There should not be a long interval between the time of offence and punishment.
3. The child and the teacher should be very clear about the cause of punishment.
4. Punishment should be consistent.

Remedial Measures

All the three agencies, *i.e.*, the home, the teacher and the society should take up the responsibility of handling delinquents. Remedial measures are as follows:

1. Responsibilities of the parents: This implies:

(*i*) Understanding the children, their mental traits, urges and emotions.

(*ii*) Creating better conditions at home—

(*a*) providing better conditions at home;

(*b*) providing the child with all the necessary requirements;

(*c*) avoiding all those unwholesome conditions which affect child's emotional life, such as quarrels, divorce, rivalries in children, rejection, overprotection, rigidity of discipline and frequent punishments. Parents should understand the dangers of second marriage (when there are children by the former marriage), illegitimacy, orphanage, adoption, long absence from home, sexual behaviour in the presence of the child, mentioning frequently financial difficulties and cursing their children.

(*iii*) Taking preventive measures, whenever the child's behaviour tends to be abnormal. An ounce of prevention is worth a pound of cure.

(*iv*) Taking the help of specialists and disclosing to them all that is necessary for the investigation of the case.

2. Teacher's responsibilities

(*i*) Reforming all those conditions in the school life in terms of organization, curriculum, instructions, discipline, social relationship, teacher's behaviour and physical conditions, that work as the predisposing causes of delinquency.

(*ii*) Discovery of problem cases, diagnosis of the malady, prevention of the abnormalities for further increase, and adoption of remedies suggested by the specialists.

(*iii*) Giving instructions in mental hygiene.

(*iv*) Contacting parents, educating them and having intimate relations with them.

(*v*) Organizing leisure-time activities for the students and the community for the year round. Engaging the pupils in social service and community activities.

3. Responsibilities of the society

(*i*) Strengthening religious institutions, youth service agencies, educative agencies like libraries, recreative agencies like public tournaments, clubs, etc.

(*ii*) Helping the youth-service organizations like Bharat Scouts and Guides Young Men Christian Association, Y.W.C.A., N.C.C., etc.

(*iii*) Eliminating evil influences in the society like gambling, drinking, robbery, pick-pocketing, prostitution, begging, production of sexual pictures, sex-appealing advertisements, slums, unemployment and poverty.

(*iv*) Opening and strengthening reformative agencies like Juvenile Courts, Police Service, Orphanages, Mental Hospitals, Guidance Clinics, Bal Niketan, Children's Homes, District Jails, Juvenile police should be instituted to patrol areas infested with delinquents.

Methods of diagnosis

1. Medical examination of the delinquents, noting physical disabilities, if any.
2. Administering mental tests, discovering I.Q., character traits and personality traits.
3. Administering achievements tests and finding the scholastic level, educational attainments and failures.
4. Preparing case history, collecting data about the family, community life and about the school life of the child.
5. Examination by the psychiatrist, who will interview the child, engage him into playful activities, administer C.A.T. or T.A.T. tests. The psychiatrist will take him into confidence and elicit from him his problems and their sources.
6. Interpretation of the data. This will be done in a special meeting of the psychologist, psychiatrist and the social worker who gets data about the family and community.

Remedial Measures

1. The teacher's attitude must be sympathetic. He should appreciate the difficulties and help the delinquent to overcome those. He should develop wholesome human relationship.
2. The teachers should take the help of clinical services in understanding the specific problems.

3. The class-room and school atmosphere should be purged of all the evils.
4. Guided group activities must be started, like group-play, group games, scouting, social service, group therapy. This will strengthen their ego and super-ego.
5. Special classes must be started for the handicapped children.
6. Craft or skill have been found useful in engaging the less developed mind to proper action.
7. The change in the environment also helps certain cases. Children can be removed from bad homes and put in foster homes, from bad schools and admitted into reputed schools.
8. The parents should be educated and they should be appraised of the activities of the child. The parent's attitude must be changed if the father is made to understand the nature and the cause of the boy's trouble; further dangers can he averted.
9. Moral and religious teaching in the school can go a long way in strengthening the super-ego of the children. Noble sentiments should be developed.
10. Punishments, corporal or otherwise, should not be taken recourse to, as these only create reaction and revolt in the minds of delinquents.
11. Proper supervision should be done regarding the gangs and their activities in the school and community. Gang-formation leads to unsocial behaviour. On the other hand, self-government should be started in the schools so that their energies are redirected to proper course.
12. The impulses and emotions of children must he sublimated. Instead of advising them, they should be engaged in activities.

In the end it should be remembered that every case of delinquency is unique. It has at its sources a number of causes. These causes must be discovered and remedies adopted according to the causes. Although, the home, the community and the state must co-operate in dealing with the problem of delinquency, it is the school which has to play a central role.

REMEDIAL EDUCATION

What is remedial education?

In May-June 1963 the seminar organized by the N.C.E.R.T. on the 'Education of the Backward Child' described the concept of the existence of some new and magical educational formula which will enable us to remove, with a wave of the wand, all the problems that face the backward child, and speedily restore him to his rightful place in the class. Unfortunately, there is no magic formula and there is no easy way. In a sense there is no such thing as remedial education, there is only education, or perhaps, sound education. If the term remedial education actually has any meaning at all, it is only in the sense of a term of convenience used to describe a particular emphasis in educational approach. It is concerned with the individualization of education, that is, with making education need-centred in terms of the individual child. In helping the backward child with his problems, we are simply extending the approach to its logical conclusions.

Aims of the remedial programme

Once the child's errors and difficulties have been located precisely, it then becomes possible to frame a remedial programme aiming at:

1. Correcting basis errors.
2. Re-establishing the child's confidence in himself and his ability to succeed in the subject.

Principles of remedial education

Following basic principles have to be borne in mind in framing the remedial programme:

1. Rapport: Good personal relationship must be established right from the start of remedial work. If rapport between the teacher and pupil is poor, then not even the most enthusiastic effort will bring success. The teacher should seek to convey to the child his or her personal involvement, and genuine desire to help.

2. Clarity: The plan of attack on the problem should be clearly defined and set out. Where treatment is being given in a group situation, it is advisable to actually write down what you intend to try and do with each child and how you are going to do it.

3. Open Mind: An open mind must be kept on the methods and procedures used. The remedial teacher must be prepared to modify, supplement or abandon a programme at any time in the light of results and try a new approach.

4. Great Care: Great care must be exercised in the choice of materials to be used in remedial work, bearing in mind the age, ability, attainment and interest level of the child.

5. Motivation: Motivation should be optimum and all methods of enlisting interest should be used according to the child's age and attainment level. Play and story methods would, for example, be most effective with younger children, while the utility and mastery approach would probably be most effective with older groups. Where the teacher has a good relationship with the children, the child's natural desire to win praise through success will operate at all age levels.

6. Immediate Opportunities: The programme should be so designed as to furnish the pupil with immediate opportunities for success. Further, this success should be made dear and obvious to the child.

7. Involvement: The pupil himself should be involved as much as possible in the remedial programme which he is to follow. Progress should be measured not against any external standards, but in the light of his own previous levels of attainment. The keeping of progress charts and a record of timed performances, for example, are useful in this context.

8. Individuality: Treatment should be given individually or in small groups if progress is to be rapid. Each child would, of course, tend to prepare his own remedial programme.

Diagnosis in the subject areas

The first step in remedial work is to make a thorough examination of the child's difficulties in the subject or subjects in which he is failing. This is an analytical examination designed to locate:

1. the level at which break-down is occurring;
2. the seriousness of the failure;
3. the specific errors being made; and
4. the cognitive weakness, if any.

Organisation of educational provision

In order to provide for educationally retarded child it may be useful to have a look at some of the methods that have been devised in Western countries. These are as follows:

1. Provision within the School

(*i*) *Care of remedial group:* One or two interested teachers are allocated a specific number of periods a week to try and help those pupils who are educationally retarded in their specific subject areas. In all probability such teachers will have no training in remedial techniques apart from their general training as teachers. The number of such children in the remedial groups are small, not more than five or six, and some benefit, therefore, does accrue. Care has to be taken however, to ensure that no loss is incurred by the child in other subjects as a result of attendance at the remedial group.

(*ii*) *Peripatetic remedial teaching:* Special remedial teachers are appointed and trained, usually by the School Child Guidance Services, under whose general direction they work. Each teacher is allocated a number of schools which are visited, regularly once or twice a week, remedial sessions being organized for small groups of children with specific subject difficulties. Usually these teachers receive extra remuneration.

(*iii*) *Adjustment classess:* Permanent adjustment classes under a trained remedial teacher have been set up in some schools especially at the primary level. These tend to function in two main ways:

(*a*) The child is transferred temporarilly to the group until his learning difficulties have been overcome.

(*b*) The child leaves his own class at the regular time each day for remedial help in the adjustment group, *e.g.*, a child experiencing difficulty in arithmetic would leave his own class daily for extra help, but for the duration of this lesson only. The numbers in such classes are usually kept to a maximum of ten or twelve.

In some areas the adjustment class system is very well developed. It is often integrated with the school psychological service. This system may be regarded as one of the most effective, since the children requiring help can be assessed by the educational psychologist, who is usually available also to give advice and individual treatment when this is necessary.

(*iv*) *After school group:* This system utilizes the services of subject specialists to organize remedial classes outside school hours. Normally, these classes are held immediately after school and children in need of extra help attend with their parents' permission. Though untrained in remedial work, these teachers usually receive extra remuneration. Provided that the numbers in the groups are severely restricted, rewarding work can be done.

2. Provision outside the school

(*i*) *Remedial centres:* A remedial class or centre is established in one school which serves a number of schools in the district. Children with specific subject difficulties attend the remedial centres at regular times each day or week until their difficulties have been overcome.

(*ii*) *Child guidance services:* Sometimes school psychological service employs remedial teachers who work in the clinic under the direction and guidance of the educational psychologist. The children who are in need of help attend the centre or clinic at regular times each week. Normally, the Child Guidance Service only concerns itself with those children whose problems have not yielded to remedial treatment in school or are complicated by emotional factors either in the school or the home.

Suggestions for remedial education in indian context

Following suggestions may be given for remedial education in the Indian situation:

1. Ordinary teachers: Ordinary teachers who are interested in remedial work might be relieved of some of their normal duties, or have their work-load lightened to enable them to organize small remedial groups in school during school hours.

2. Remedial groups: Remedial groups could be set up immediately after school hours, two or three days per week with subject specialists in charge of the groups.

3. Educational psychologists: Educational psychologists on the staff of training institutes should aid individual schools to organize remedial groups, and give assistance in the diagnosis of learning difficulties. Small remedial groups could also be set up in the institutes themselves and utilized in training programme.

4. Training colleges: Training colleges should organize in-service programmes for teachers interested in undertaking remedial work in both Primary and Secondary schools. Departments of Extension Services could contribute here.

5. Child guidance centres: Each state should have at least one Child Guidance Centre staffed by educational psychologists under the Department of Education.

6. Educational guidance centres: Educational Guidance Centres might be established in each community to give help and guidance to parents on educational problems affecting their children. Centres might be attached to training colleges or to Departments of Education or of psychology to function as model units.

7. Parent-teachers association: Through Parent-Teacher Associations, efforts should be made to inform parents and enlist their help in instituting Guidance Centres and in helping children at home.

8. Associations of teachers and parents: Headmasters and Teachers Associations and Parent-Teacher Associations should be requested to exert some efforts in this direction.

9. Symposia and articles: Written symposia and articles on remedial education should be published regularly and widely circulated.

QUESTIONS FOR EXERCISE

1. Define juvenile delinquency and distinguish it from crime.
2. Explain methods of discovering causes of juvenile delinquency. Classify and discuss its causes.
3. Discuss methods to control delinquent acts. What remedial measures may be suggested in this direction?
4. What do you understand by remedial education? Give the aims of remedial education. What principles should be kept in view while preparing a programme for remedial education? Suggest a suitable programme of remedial education for Indian schools.

33

Mental Hygiene, Mental Health and Adjustment

Mental hygiene, literally interpreted, means the science that maintains a condition of health in connection with mental functions. Just as physical hygiene invents laws and means of maintaining healthy conditions in the body, mental hygiene discovers laws and means of maintaining the mind in a healthy condition. It not only insists on the curing of mental diseases, it also turns its attention to their prevention. Apart from the treatment of mental disease, one important function of mental hygiene is the creation of favourable conditions. According to Ryan, in its negative sense, it means the more benevolent and skilful curing of mental patients. But in its positive implication, it means the discovery of mental aberrations in their elementary stages, prevention of as many diseases of this kind as possible in society, and provision of a mentally healthy life in society for the greatest number of individuals. In this manner while in its negative sense, mental hygiene implies nothing more than the curing of mental diseases, in its positive aspect it includes all ways and means by which mental health is assured. Evidently, the functioning of mental health does not depend exclusively upon psychiatrists. Other individuals such as teachers, parents, guardians and social welfare workers as well as mendicants can make important contributions towards it. The truth of the matter is that any individual can help in maintaining mental health, and in the functioning of mental hygiene, if he has insight into and a knowledge of human psychology. The child's mental health depends to quite an extent upon the conduct of his parents. In school, it is the teacher who casts much influence upon the mental processes of children. It is now well understood that parents and teachers share the general responsibility for maintaining the child's mental health.

AIMS OF MENTAL HYGIENE

Accordingly, then, the objective of mental hygiene is not merely the prevention and curing of mental diseases, but the development of a personality in every individual in society that makes for good adjustment with the environment, that attains a proper synthesis between the intellectual, emotional and physical aspects, that is satisfied and optimistic, that experiences a minimum of tension and conflict in its conduct with other individuals in society. The aim of mental hygiene is the evolution and development of a properly adjusted and balanced personality. Briefly, the following can be its objectives:

1. **Treatment and remedying of mental defects:** Defining mental hygiene, Lawrence F. Shaffer, has written that mental hygiene, or the science of mental health is concerned with the prevention of inadequate adjustment or with those processes or methods which adjust the maladjusted individual. This definition of mental hygiene emphasizes its curative aspect. The first function of mental hygiene is the curing of mental ailments, defects and imbalances.

2. **Prevention of personality complications:** But the curative aspect of hygiene docs not exhaust its possibilities. This science prevents all kinds of personality disorders, since all mental diseases originate in them. According to Thomas V. Moore, mental hygiene is that science which studies the human personality, and its deviations, from the curative standpoint. In this manner, another objective of mental hygiene is the curing or removal of abnormalities of the personality, since it is only in the absence of such aberration that the individual can be balanced. Abnormality leads to imbalance and all kinds of mental conflicts and diseases. Prevention of such diseases takes the form both of curing them as well as prevention of further procreation from such parents since diseases are likely to be transmitted through heredity.

3. **Safeguard of mental health:** The most comprehensive function of mental hygiene is the safeguarding of mental health. According to D.B. Klein, mental hygiene prevents mental aberrations and advances mental health. Mental hygiene consistently stresses the development or creation of such qualities in the individual as optimism, confidence, co-operation, emotional adjustment and maturity, etc. It points out the means of improving the adaptability and efficiency of individuals.

Two aspects of mental hygiene

From the description of its objectives, it is apparent that mental hygiene has two prominent aspects—curative and preservative. In its curative aspect, it indicates ways and means of curing mental deviations, defects and imbalances. Ways and means of preventing them or counteracting them are suggested by it, following which any and every individual can ensure his mental health.

DEFINITION OF MENTAL HYGIENE

On the basis of the foregoing description of its meaning, its objectives and its various aspects, it is possible to design a makeshift description and definition of mental hygiene. This will further help to clarify its meaning, and promote its scientific study since the first requisite of a scientific enquiry is the precise definition of the subject matter, even if it be incomplete to some extent. Among the definitions of mental hygiene already been given, one or two definitions are more comprehensive, as for example, in the *Encyclopaedia of Modern Education*, the definition of mental hygiene has been given as that approach to human adjustment and achievement which is related to the prevention of emotional maladjustment and preparation of the individual for skilled working. According to the *Dictionary of Education,* mental hygiene is the science which studies the principles and practices of preventing mental disorders and promoting mental health. Both the above definitions, though better than others, are yet incomplete since they do not emphasize all the three aspects of mental hygiene. Finally, it can be said that mental hygiene is that science which studies laws and means of curing and preventing mental diseases, personality disorders and complications; it also discovers creative measures for the balancing, adjustment and healthy development of personality.

SCOPE OF MENTAL HYGIENE

Scope of mental hygiene is very wide

Mental hygiene comprehends the curing of mental defects, diseases and abnormalities as well as the prevention of such abnormalities, beside the active preservation of mental health, balance, pleasure and adjustment, etc., of the individual. Evidently then, the scope of mental hygiene is very vast. It comprehends the entire life of the individual. Every individual stands in need of mental health. Young children, men and women experience difficulty in adjusting to new circumstances which lead to mental complications and difficulties, that, in turn, endanger mental health. Hence, it is they who stand in greatest need of mental health and hygiene. In old age when man is past his prime, his energy is on the decrease. There are very few ways in which he can pass his time, his children are busy in the affairs of their own families while the young girls in the family have gone to their husbands. When retired from service, even the source of income is blocked. And one foot is already in the grave, as they say. Some or the other minor ailment of the body is always present, hence, it is at such times that mental health is challenged the most. If in such a state, one is to lose one's life partner, it is the last straw for the poor individual. What greater shock can there be for an individual to have his mother die at an early age, and the wife to die in old age? Hence, mental hygiene is needed very greatly by the old and senile people. Besides children and senile folk, some adults in the prime of life require mental hygiene since their mental balance is disturbed and personality disordered for some or the other reason. Such an individual can be recruited from lists of drunkards, confirmed alcoholics, gamblers, corrupt individuals and people who frequent prostitute homes, etc. They are themselves mentally diseased persons, but they are also potential threats to the mental health of society in general. Their personalities are disorganized and they improve the social disorganization of society. And the list of sufferers is completed by people who have already lost their mental balance, who are prey to mental defects, diseases and aberrations. They require mental treatment and cure.

Healthy individuals also require mental hygiene

Curative and preventive aspects of mental hygiene have been depicted clearly in the foregoing description, but its preservative aspect remain to be delineated. Hence, even healthy individuals require mental hygiene as they stand to benefit by its preservative function. In other words, people who are healthy from the mental standpoint are also in need of mental hygiene. In fact, healthy and ill are words that are relative, in practical life, there is no individual who can be declared completely healthy. Secondly, even if he is healthy at one moment there can be no guarantee that he will continue in the same state of health. Man's adjustment to the environment is not a static condition but rather a gradual dynamic process. The question of adjustment is forever present before the individual since man's condition is ever changing somewhat. Hence, there is no saying when an individual, who is at present manifesting the most perfect adjustment, may have cause to lose his mental balance. Consequently, he requires mental hygiene to see to it that he is not deprived of his mental bliss and happiness.

From the above description it is evident that the scope of mental hygiene is not contained by any considerations of age since it is required by young, old, adolescent, man, woman, the healthy and the unhealthy alike. Its sphere extends from the home to school, factory, office, shop, market, meeting, society, in fact, everywhere. It is needed in all human relationships and activities.

MENTAL HYGIENE AND EDUCATION

Mental hygiene is valued everywhere

Descriptions of the meaning and scope of mental hygiene also help to clarify its value. Its value and efficacy consists not only in the curing and preventing of mental defects, diseases and imbalances, but also in presenting a state of mental health in the individual fortunately blessed with it. It is of value for young, old, men, women, boy, girl, healthy, insane, in fact, for everyone. Just as every able bodied being requires physical hygiene for its prolonged well being, every living being with a mind needs mental Hygiene. And for him, mental hygiene has its value and significance. Hence, the requirement of mental hygiene in every sphere of human life—home, school, playground, office, profession, factory, mill, shop, etc.

Yet, this does not imply that mental hygiene possesses the same value in every sphere. Just as physical hygiene is required most by the diseased individual or one who is potentially diseased, mental hygiene is most needed by an individual whose mind is already disturbed or by one who is likely to be deprived of his reason, one who is under such strain that there is a likelihood of his collapsing under it. Mentally diseased individual as well as those who are actually insane and individuals who can be considered potential patients of mental hygiene are the senile, adolescents and the corrupt persons. Similarly, in the normal course of human life, mental hygiene is required wherever there are human relationships, yet it is most essentially needed in the home and the school since these are the two institutions which are the greatest preservatives of mental health. Hence, a complete comprehension of the value of mental hygiene can come only when one has understood its importance for the school and the home, as well as for mentally diseased persons, adolescents, senile people and corrupt persons.

Mental hygiene in the family

Most psychologists are of the opinion that the influences that mould the personality of a child during the first five or six years of his life determine his conduct throughout his future existence. It is in the family that the child learns to express, control and refine or modify his emotions, thoughts, feelings and impressions. It is in the family that he develops the traits of affection, sympathy, brotherhood, etc. His conduct towards his equals, his juniors and his seniors is moulded and formed in the family. Hence, if some situations or circumstances in the family affect him adversely his mental health is apt to suffer. Hence, it is evident that if the mental health of the future citizens of the nation is to be ensured, it is essential that mental hygiene be introduced into the family. It is not only as a child, but also as husband and father, wife and mother, that one is under family influence. Family, as an institute, is with an individual from the time he steps into the world to the time he steps out of it. Mental disease or ill-health in even one member of the family has its repercussions on the other members. Hence, it is as important to safeguard mental health in the family as it is to prevent and cure mental imbalance if it is present there. Without this, the peace and calm of family life becomes an ephemeral existent. Means of curing mental ill-health and its prevention will be described at a later stage.

Mental hygiene in school

Following the family, another institution that casts important influence upon the child's development is the school. In school, the child's personality is influenced by his teachers and colleagues. It is in school that he learns lessons of self-dependence, self-confidence and self-reliance. Now he cannot seek protection in his mother's laps from the problems that confront him, neither can he look up to his father to save him. Hence, he is compelled to conduct himself desirably towards all on his own initiative. And in his effort, it is only natural that he finds frustrations that endanger the balance of his personality with mental difficulties and complexes. Mental hygiene in school is important for preventing such unhealthy development and for preserving mental health.

Mental hygiene in adolescence

As it is, mental hygiene is of importance throughout an individual's life, but it assumes greatest importance during adolescence. Adolescence is the most volatile stage in the development of personality. Mental, physical and every other kind of development takes place at a rapid pace during this stage. Young boys and girls manifest signs of approaching adulthood. The male member develops his beard, and his voice breaks. In girls, the breasts begin to develop, and various parts of the body begin to round out. This physical development is accompanied by mental development, due to which they do not appreciate being treated as children. They prefer to be counted among the adults. And in this fresh eagerness for adulthood, many boys are seen using the blade prematurely in an effort to acquire a beard quickly. Imagination and emotionality are at their highest pitch while the adolescent is passing through this period. Interest in other sex manifests itself in many peculiar fashions, and curiosity concerning sex increases very much. The adolescent is further anxious about his future and his livelihood, regarding which he develops ambitions and dreams constantly. From this vivid description of the various problems that confront the young folk during this stage of their life, it is evident that it is now that there is greatest need for preventing mental quirks and imbalance and for ensuring mental health.

Mental hygiene in adult age

It has been pointed out earlier that in old age, maintaining a sane outlook on life becomes something of a problem, hence the old men have much to gain from mental hygiene, its ways and means. Another class of men and women who stand to gain much from this science is that of the corrupt and evil alcoholics, criminals, prostitutes and other anti-social elements. Many of their mental problems can be solved through the ways and means suggested by mental hygiene. In this manner, mental hygiene is an integral part of human welfare and life. It finds application everywhere, although reaping of the greatest possible benefit from it depends upon the skill of the person using it, and the ability with which he can control the circumstances. Mental hygiene is a science. It makes a study of the ways, means and rules that preserve mental health, prevent mental disturbance and cure mental disease. Hence mental hygiene can benefit every sphere of life such as personal, family, social, national and international relationships, inter-relations between various classes, sexes, age levels, colours, communities, races and people. This is the value of mental hygiene, and it is not influenced by the very little benefit that is derived from it in practice. Being a science, it is neutral, and in no position to bestow gifts and benefits upon people of its own accord. It is for man to reap a rich harvest from it. Its value does not deteriorate if man chooses to neglect it, since its value is proved and beyond doubt.

Importance of mental hygiene in India

It would be in keeping with the context to point out the special significance that mental hygiene has for India. In India there are many problems at the national level the solution of which depends considerably on mental hygiene. One such problem is the presence of communal tensions between Hindus and Muslims, as well as other communities. Yet another problem is the lack of discipline among students of universities and colleges. And another problem that has more recently reared its ugly head on the horizon is that of regionalism. The riots of Assam are additional proof of its existence. Language is another aspect of life in India that has led to much tension and conflict. Crime in India, and particularly the example of juvenile delinquency, is primarily a matter of mental disturbance. The greatest obstacles to democracy in the country, corruption and partyism, are the result of mental aberrations. Of course, this harangue is not meant to indicate that mental hygiene is suggested as the only solution of these problems. What is implied is that in these and other problems involving human relationship there is also a mental aspect into which only mental hygiene has access. Hence, in so far as that particular aspect is concerned, the importance of mental hygiene need not be expressly pointed out. If the situation is looked at from this standpoint, it is quite possible that people who mould the destiny of this nation may find some reasonable solutions for such problems.

DEFINITION OF MENTAL HEALTH

In a book entitled *Mental Hygiene in Public Health*, P.V. Lewkan has written that a mentally healthy individual is one who is himself satisfied, lives peacefully with his neighbours, makes healthy citizens of his children, and even after performing these fundamental duties has enough energy left to do something of benefit to society. Possessing mental health, an individual can adjust properly to his environment, and can make the best effort for his own, his family's and his society's progress and betterment. In *The Human Mind*, K.A. Menninger has written, "Let us define mental health as the adjustment of human beings to the world and to each other with a maximum of effectiveness and happiness. It is the ability to maintain an even temper, an alert intelligence, socially considerate behaviour and happy disposition." The chief characteristic of mental health, it is evident, is adjustment. The greater the degree of successful adjustment, the greater will be the mental health of the individual. Lesser mental health will lead to lesser adjustment and greater conflict. The healthy individual can interpret any new situation and adapt it to suit himself, or adapt himself to suit it. He maintains a healthy and benevolent attitude towards life. He is aware that difficulties visit everyone in life, so that running away from them is cowardice. They can be solved only by squarely facing up to them with courage.

Mental health and mental hygiene

In this manner, mental hygiene is a manner of life in which the individual's adjustment to his environment is maintained intact. N.E. Cutts and N. Moselay have also stressed the element of adjustment in mental hygiene. According to them, we can say that mental health is that ability by means of which we establish our adjustment with the difficult situations of life and mental hygiene is that means or tool which make this adjustment possible. This definition also helps to reveal the relation between mental health and mental hygiene, as well as the difference between them. Mental hygiene is the means to mental health. In other words, mental hygiene is that science which studies the laws and means of achieving mental health, of maintaining it as well as doing away with mental ill-health. Mental health is the end, and mental hygiene the means.

EDUCATION AND MENTAL HEALTH

The question that now arises is how can mental aberrations be prevented in school? It mostly happens that many students, particularly children and adolescents, cannot clarify their difficulties and problems so that they require guidance from their parents, teachers and psychologists. It is for the guide to understand the adolescent and to sympathise with him, and to offer him affectionate advice. Scolding or punishing them is not very efficacious. They should be given the opportunity of expressing their desires and mental tendencies.

Importance of family

Family has the greatest importance in maintaining a condition of mental health, and within the family the greatest burden of responsibility is on the two parents. What is mostly needed in this connection is the creation of a suitable atmosphere in which the child's personality can adequately develop. A child's delicate and sensitive personality is influenced by the character of parents, their mutual behaviour and relations, their behaviour towards the children, the child's relations with brothers, sisters and other relatives in the family. Hence, it is essential that these be healthy. There can be no hard and fast rule as to how the parents should behave towards the child under certain conditions; all that can be justifiably said is that they should consciously give the child every chance to develop his personality freely and without restraint. It is for them to prevent the child from treading the wrong path but they should not try to make him follow them in all things. The least they can do is to prevent any situation that causes repression in the child. All other things depend upon the parent's insight into child and adolescent psychology, their patience, their labour and experience.

Importance of school

Following the family, the other institution that has responsibility of promoting mental health in children is the school. It is the school that has the greatest influence, after the home in forming the child's personality. And even in school, the most important factor is the atmosphere existing there. In a healthy atmosphere the children adopt discipline and other qualities of their own. There is greater fear of some children being spoiled in school. Such children should be specially attended to and given definite and expert guidance. The greatest need is for providing each child with work adequate and proper to the needs of his personality. Hence, it is essential that the backward and the brilliant children should be given special treatment. Teachers present an ideal to the children in their charge, hence their character and conduct could be such as can be profitably imitated by the children. Pupil personnel service should be introduced to remove the difficulties with which the children are faced from time to time in school.

Factors of mental health in school

Briefly, in school the teacher should keep the following factors vividly in mind if he is to preserve mental health, prevent mental disturbance and promote mental health, among his students:

1. **Discipline:** As has been pointed out earlier, discipline in the school has an important influence upon the mental health of students. But this discipline should never be very hard since such conditions will lead to mental ill-health. Thus, discipline should be exercised not through creating fear of punishment but through arousing feeling of responsibility and the desire to be law-abiding among the students. True discipline is self-discipline. And discipline in college should be maintained by selecting its guardians from among the students themselves. It develops sense of responsibility among the students.

2. **Affectionate behaviour:** It is only too evident that affectionate behaviour towards students on the part of teachers has good effect on the former's mental health. It will inspire him to obey the teacher, respect him and to do nothing that may incur his displeasure. A teacher should maintain the same loving attitude towards all his students. Any discrimination in this treatment injures the feelings of students.

3. **Play and recreation:** Mental disturbance and unbalance is created by the repressed motives surging in a student's brain. They can be given opportunities for healthy expression through games and other forms of recreation. Play and recreation have a cathartic effect.

4. **Sex education:** In adolescence, the morale of young boys and girls shows alarming tendencies to proceed to degradation because of the sexual instinct, or alternately its repression leads to much mental distress. Teacher should make use of psychological weapons to remove any sexual deviations that may be embedded in the minds of students. And for this, the best way is to provide young boys and girls with the necessary elements of sex education This will help them, on the one hand, to develop a healthy attitude towards sex and prevent them from forming harmful complexes, as well as assist in their physical, mental and emotional development on the other; they can then later on become well developed and integrated individuals.

5. **Educational guidance:** In order to maintain a state of mental health, it is essential that they be given subjects that conform to their requirements and abilities, and their educational problems solved. Taking personal advice of a psychologist in this connection is called educational guidance.

6. **Personal guidance:** Many of the problems that arise before the student are such that they cannot be solved by the student himself, hence he needs the personal guidance of the psychologist to solve them.

7. **Vocational guidance:** Every individual is compelled to adopt some one or the other profession once his education is complete, and he begins to

worry about it even while he is still engaged in his academic pursuit. The knowledgeable teacher can help his students in their choice of a suitable career.

8. Formation of good habits: Mental health depends upon good habits. Hence, it is desirable for the teacher to help students in the formation of good habits regarding a regular life, balanced diet and exercise, good behaviour and high thinking, etc.

9. Balanced curriculum: The curriculum in school should be such as to develop all aspects of the student's personality, to increase his fund of necessary knowledge, and to avoid all unnecessary strain on the mind. The integrated development of the students can be promoted through the organizing of various kinds of extra-curricular activities in the school and college.

10. Balanced home assignment: It is improper to think that if the child is given too much homework to do, he will not have the time to indulge in destructive and naughty pranks as he wall be too busy. Loading them with too much homework only leaves them worried and anxious, with the worst influence upon their mind. Hence, the homework required of them should be carefully and sensibly formulated.

Finally, it may be stated that the prevention of mental imbalances is a problem of social and national importance. For this, efforts will have to be made to get rid of circumstances of social disorganization, exploitation, corruption, various tensions and conflicts, crimes, alcoholic effects, etc. The defects of urban life in the form of excessive crowding, unhealthy small houses, promiscuous mixing of the sexes, and noise will have to be eliminated. Suitable and interesting work for all will have to be provided, in addition to opportunities of health and recreation. It is only through efforts at the national level that proper and effective prevention of mental maladies can take place. And for this, co-operative effort on the part of government, teachers, social workers and sensible people in the public, will be necessary.

MEANING OF ADJUSTMENT

In the words of Laurence F. Shaffer, Adjustment is the process by which a living organism maintains a balance between its needs and the circumstances that influence the satisfaction of these needs." Accordingly, the process of adjustment has two primary or main elements—one, the needs of the living organism, and two, the conditions or circumstances that influence these needs. These needs can be bio-geneic, originating in society, personal or communal, or arising from any other conceivable source. On the other hand, the circumstances influencing these needs also can either be inside the individual or outside him. Factors within the individual that influence these needs are his physical and mental states, capacity, attitudes, interests, etc. For example, most weakly constituted individuals cannot fulfil their own psychological motives, and thus their needs are definitely affected by their lack of strength. Factors arising within the environment are usually geographic conditions, social conditions, political and cultural influences. And, these conditions and circumstances can help as well as deter the fulfilment of the individual's requirements. In this manner, the nature of influences upon the person's needs can be of two Kinds—favourable and unfavourable. Positive or favourable influences help in the fulfilment of needs while unfavourable influences hinder their satisfaction.

Three elements in adjustment

An analysis of the process of adjustment will reveal the presence of three main elements:

1. **Motive:** The very process of adjustment in the living being is set in motion by the presence within him of some motive or need or requirement.

2. **Thwarting condition:** When the environment does not present any features that tend to become obstacles in the fulfilment of these needs, then the adjustment is natural, facile and effortless, and no problem results. But, if circumstances create obstacles in the path of such fulfilment then the process of adjustment progresses further.

3. **Varied responses:** Once the fulfilment of a need has been obstructed, the individual indulges in various actions which are a reaction to the obstacle. Such a reaction can be normal just as much as it can be abnormal.

4. **Solution:** As a result of these reactions and responses the individual achieves a degree of adjustment with the circumstances. The problem of adjustment is thereby solved.

Example of adjustment

All these various component elements of adjustment can be well understood with the aid of a concrete example. A student is actuated by a strong desire to stand first in his class, and to do so by scoring very well. He works extremely hard but fails to achieve his objective because he has not the necessary mental equipment. Lack of the requisite intelligence forms an obstacle to the satisfaction of this motive, and hence, as a result, the student condescends to lower his aim somewhat by aiming at securing a second division. In order to accommodate this change of objective the student changes his mode of study. A change of response, a suitable modification of the objective and the objective is achieved with satisfaction. The adjustment problem is also solved. Such a process of adjustment is a universal phenomenon, and it is to be seen at every level of life, at various times and under most conditions.

Motives and adjustment

Generally speaking, the process of adjustment can be set in motion by any motive, for example, our physical needs are constantly being manifested in the form of adjustive behaviour patterns. But from our point of view these needs do not have much importance, for, on the one hand, they are easily satisfied and, on the other, in the event of their dissatisfaction, life itself ceases in the organism, thus obviating all further adjustment activity. Hence, social motives and requirements have greater importance for the adjustment process.

Social motives are developed within a cultural environment. Individuals of different cultures have different motives and different cultures do not generate identical motives. For example, our society requires the development and encouragement of such motives as self-respect, self-realization, acceptance, security, love, sympathy, etc., and these social motives naturally have definite influence upon sex and other biological needs. Just as social motives have greater importance than physiological needs, in the same manner the process of adjustment places greater emphasis upon motives that are stronger than others. Strong motives, once they have been excited, can only be satisfied. Inability to satisfy them only leads to further dissatisfaction, and this tension is not ended till the objective has been attained.

Thwarting in adjustment

It has been remarked earlier that one important element in the process of adjustment is the presence of conditions that thwart the satisfaction of motives. They are the forms that this thwarting can take, and is known to take. One form is frustration. If, for example, a person fails to catch a train and reach his destination because his wrist watch was not functioning properly, then he has to face frustration that arises out of the environment. This frustration can also be present in the individual himself. Another form of thwarting or obstacle is conflict. A state of conflict is precipitated if the individual is actuated by more than one motive arising simultaneously. And, in the throes of these various motives he cannot decide upon the direction of action that he should adopt. Among the classical examples of a state of conflict and indecision is the state of the mind of Arjuna, described in the *Gita* when he is divided between war and peace, between indecision and attraction. If, similarly, a student wants to continue his interest in games while at the same time he does not want to neglect his academic pursuit, then his mind will be a battlefield of contention between these two desires. This state of conflict and tension will continue till the individual decides upon one particular motive and rejects the other. When conflict extends over a very long period of time, the individual shows signs of mental illness and other abnormalities of behaviour and conduct.

Frustration and conflict, the two forms of thwarting mentioned earlier, are closely related. Normally, when frustration results from some obstruction, the organism involved is seen adopting aggressive and violent behaviour towards the obstacle. Such aggressive behaviour can be direct as well as indirect. In children and unintelligent people it takes a direct form while in the case of most adults and intelligent people it takes a more indirect manifestation. Now, if the child's normal expression of aggression and violence resulting from some form of frustration is curbed and restricted, then it is actually prevented, but at the same time it becomes repressed and gives rise to emotions of fear and insecurity. Thus, some people become violent on being faced with some frustrating feeling of fear and insecurity as a result of the curb on their aggressive behaviour. As to the mode of behaviour that should be adopted in dealing with obstacles that cause frustration, an individual learns through trial and error. Different situations and circumstances find him behaving differently, and the behaviour patterns of adjustment that satisfy him are repeated while the patterns that cause him displeasure are discarded and replaced. And, the various reactions concerning the adjustment to different frustrations gradually take on the form of habits. Hence, adult individuals display permanent individual differences in the patterns of adjustment.

Any state that contradicts that of adjustment is called maladjustment. In this condition contradicting that of adjustment, the individual organism fails to maintain a balance between his needs and the circumstances that influence the satisfaction of them. And, in this condition one observes reactions that are tendentious towards further imbalance. Reactions of this kind include all those behaviour patterns which can be called abnormal. For example, all kinds of mental illness will be cited as maladjusted reaction. Maladjustment will be the term to be applied to criminal, delinquent and anti-social behaviour. The maladjusted individual fails to attain to a state of adjustment with his circumstances, and, instead of trying to face up to the situation, tries to run away from it. Abnormal fears and mental formations are to be seen in the individual. Even his mistakes are construed as no mistakes, and he rationalizes upon them. Instead of working to achieve something of his own accord, he identifies himself to the achievement of others and thereby satisfies himself. He has very little capacity to co-operate with others, and he finds it difficult to live with them. He prefers solitude and loves to wander in an imaginary world. Extreme day-dreaming is a maladjusted reaction. Another example of it is the projection of one's faults upon another and holding him responsible for one's owe frustrations. Similarly, many apparently adult individuals are seen behaving in a markedly childish manner, this too is a form of maladjusted reaction. Briefly, maladjusted reactions include all such reactions which prove obstacles to adjustment.

CRITERIA OF PERSONALITY ADJUSTMENT

The implication of adjustment is the balance between an individual's needs and the circumstances that satisfy these needs. Hence, the evaluation of the adjustment achieved by a person will require the knowledge of two things. The first is the requirement of this person and second the conditions and circumstances that influence the satisfaction of his need. Once these two are known it will be necessary to find the balance that is struck between them. If the balance is good and desirable, then the individual can be said to be properly adjusted, but if the balance is disturbed, then the person will be considered maladjusted. Evidently, this adjustment will differ from individual to individual, since their needs and the conditions that satisfy them need not be common. In this manner, the criterion of personality adjustment is relative to the individual's requirements and the cultural and social complex of circumstances in which he lives. In other words, the criterion changes when these conditions change. For example, in a culture that encourages the combative and aggressive spirit men have greater need for their adjustment. On the other hand, in a culture that places very great stress upon amiability, the adjustment of personality will depend upon this motive, and it will have great influence upon the criterion of adjustment. Adjustment itself is relative to the individual and his circumstances. Thus the qualities that are required for adjustment to a particular society and culture cannot be considered efficacious in every society and culture.

Despite the fact that the above limitations are operative everywhere, certain tentative and general criteria of adjustment can be established. Main criteria would be the following:

1. Integration of personality: One criterion of adjustment is the integration of personality. Personality complex is a complex of all psycho-physical traits. In this the various mental reactions and processes of intelligence and sentiment, desire and determination, etc., do not subsist in disorder but rather in a proper organized system of functioning. Conflict is quite absent from them. Evidently, the proper integration of the personality is an ideal at which one and all should aim. It is only in such a state that personality is flexible, determined and organized. McDougall calls it the organization of character and intelligence. The higher the degree of organization in an individual's personality the better will be the degree of his adjustment, since in the absence of adjustment the personality cannot be integrated and organized. On the other hand, permanent adjustment is not possible in the absence of personality integration. The individual with an adjusted and organized personality maintains a balanced and practical outlook on life. Failures and frustrations do not disturb him unduly, and he persists on looking calm and master of the situation. His emotions, needs, thinking and other mental activities are adequately balanced and systematic. On the other hand, the personality of a maladjusted person is disintegrated. His life is disturbed, without any peace and he also tends to disturb peace of everyone else.

2. Reduction in tension: Another criterion of personality adjustment is the reduction or decrease in tension, a decrease that is consequent upon the fulfilment of his needs, irrespective of whether the fulfilment is achieved through socially acceptable or objectionable modes. It is a psychological fact that whenever some one or the other need of a person remains dissatisfied it creates a state of tension. And this tension is removed only when the object satisfying that need is obtained. Absence of adjustment results in the increase of tension while its increase helps in reducing tension. In other words, a person's adjustment can be evaluated in terms of tension existing in his mind.

3. Harmony between need and environment: As has been mentioned earlier, the adjusted personality can be recognized from a harmony between his needs and his environment. Greater the degree of such harmony, the better will be his adjustment, while on the other hand his personality will be considered less adjusted if this harmony is not of a high order. An adjusted individual has the capacity and energy to accommodate his needs and motives according to his environment, as also to mould this environment to suit his own needs and motives. In this manner, maximum satisfaction and pleasure is to be had in the mutual adjustment and harmony of both environment and requirement. Persons who fail to make an adjustment of their motives and needs to the environment in which they are placed cannot be happy even in the best of circumstances, and are always to be found complaining of the adversity of conditions. Failure of this kind also meets the individual who has not within him the power and capacity to mould conditions according to his own requirements his usual condition is one of frustration and maladjustment. Problems are a part of everyone's life, but they also add spice to its otherwise dull fare. There is hardly any, if any at all, individual who is never in his life called upon to face a situation that promises conflict, promises him frustration and anger. If such conditions are present then the enterprising individual bends himself to varying and modifying them to suit his own requirement and thus achieves adjustment or otherwise makes changes in his own requirements and needs. For example, it is commonly noticed that some people succeed in making their ends meet very facilely even on a low income, and they give every appearance of being happy and contented. Contrary to such there are people who are incessantly complaining of the paucity of their means even when they have a reasonable income. Theirs is a condition of unhappiness, since there is a wide gap between their income and expenditure, their needs are never even temporarily completely fulfilled. In such a condition the adjustment of personality is liable to be disturbed from two sides, first, in case the needs of the person do not conform to the circumstances, and in the second case when the conditions are not propitious to the fulfilment of the need. Hence, adjustment requires the balance between these two, even if modification and alteration is essential in both.

METHODS OF ADJUSTMENT

Every individual has certain definite needs, and every individual lives in certain specific conditions. It is within these conditions that his needs are fulfilled. When the conditions are favourable no particular difficulty arises in such fulfilment, but for every individual this is not always possible. A condition that is not propitious for the fulfilment of some need is not in the life of every individual, and such circumstances and conditions always prove obstacles in the satisfaction of that need thus creating problem. Difficulties refer to the conditions that prove obstacles to the satisfaction of a person's needs. As it is, one finds great individual differences in the manner of reacting to these difficulties. But even then there are certain modes of reaction that can be seen in every pattern of reaction behaviour. These methods are roughly the following:

1. Constructive adjustment: One very general form of reaction to difficulties is the mode of constructive adjustment, and examples of this mode of behaviour are to be seen everywhere in life. Students in educational institutions are constantly faced with situations that become obstacles to the achievement of their educational and vocational objectives, praise and knowledge of self needs that are basic to them. Most students have recourse to constructive adjustments in order to overcome these situations, such as putting in longer hours of study or consulting numerous books and teachers in order to overcome their academic obstacles. Similarly, when a trader is faced with some problem of his trade, he resorts to some constructive adjustment to solve that problem. If a person is in financial straits then the simplest constructive adjustment would be for him to exercise economy in his expenditure. In constructive adjustment the main feature to be remarked is that it offers a quality of facing the situation rather than running away from, and of making efforts that solve the problem instead of merely postponing it.

2. Substitute adjustment: All individuals do not have the ready wit and wisdom to achieve adjustment and thus retain their mental balance in the face of difficulties. A very large number of individuals have recourse to substitute adjustments when faced with difficult situations. This, also, is a common and usual method of reacting to difficulties. For example, in a large number of cases when students fail to pass at an examination, then, instead of urging them to work harder, they take it upon themselves to blame the teachers in particular and the entire educational system in general, and day-dream themselves into success in future. Some students start avoiding school when they fail while others more enterprising though more censured are the ones who leave home. The question that now arises is whether these reactions are activities of adjustment, since they do not tend to solve the problem inherent in the situation. A close observation will reveal that even through such reactions the individual is trying to satisfy needs that in other individuals are solved through constructive and positive adjustment activity. A student failing in an examination is usually decried and this obstructs his social ambitions and motives. Tensions that are created through this obstruction he tries to end by his activity of running away or transferring the blame on the teachers or by day-dreaming of success. Thus, for this reason are these reactions to difficulties called substitute reactions. Even though direct satisfaction is not forthcoming from such activity, yet the unsatisfied motive is indirectly and momentarily pacified, and in this manner adjustment is improved through decrease in tension. It must be noticed that adjustment is not a question of successful results but one of satisfaction of motives, irrespective of the methods that are adopted be they normal, originating in disease and mental deficiency. It is often remarked that weak, lean and thin individuals usually walk with a swagger since in lean individuals the motive of self-respect is suppressed, and in order to overcome this repression, instead of resorting to some form of constructive adjustment, they walk with a swagger, thus saving their self-respect from injury and their mental balance from collapse. Here, it must be remarked that this should not be interpreted to mean that the satisfaction afforded to a motive by constructive adjustment is equal to the satisfaction caused by a substitute adjustment. The facts of the matter are other than this. Reactions of substitute adjustment usually win scorn and ridicule for the person practising them, from other members of society, and this further causes suppression of the person's desire for social acceptance. A person running to solitude away from his life's ignoble strife can save his desire for competition from being frustrated, but then his motives of security and sociability are frustrated. Hence, it is evident that the substitute adjustment usually results only in more frustration and suppression. On the other hand, these modes of adjustment are also usually harmful for the individual. For example, certain normally ugly individuals are seen trying to attract female attention by undesirable activity since they cannot win it in the normal course, and this usually results in great inconvenience to other more reasonable members of society. One characteristic of proper and constructive adjustment is that not only the individual but the entire society benefits from it, besides improving the individual's social relationships.

3. Mental mechanisms: Another mode of reacting to difficulties is that of mental mechanisms, main among them being projection, compensation, rationalization etc. As a general rule the consequence of these mechanisms is not good either for the individual or for society. Yet, in some degree or other all or some of those mechanisms are to be found in every individual, hence no individual can be declared abnormal on their account. It is only when one of them develops out of proportion that symptoms of abnormality can be discovered. Normally, a tendency to overlook one's own fault and to blame others for one's failures is only naturally present in man, but if a person is observed doing this all the time and unduly regarding everyone else his enemy, then his conduct will undoubtedly be classed as abnormal. These mechanisms are also called the tools of adjustment, since their objective is the attainment of adjustment through various methods.

4. Adjustive reactions: Adjustive reactions, as is evident from the name, are those reactions that achieve an adjustment between the individual and his circumstances. In this manner constructive adjustment reactions are included in adjustive reactions. As a general rule the simplest method available to a person to satisfy his motives when conditions exist to frustrate them is to redouble his efforts to achieve his satisfaction and to do so with patience and persistence. When poverty besets the normal individual he does his best to overcome it by earning wealth, working hard and laboriously, and normally he meets with reasonable success. On the other hand, there are other individuals who avoid a condition of stress and conflict by controlling emotions and motives in a manner that leads to a reasonable adjustment and compromise with circumstances. Consequently, much of their existence is free from frustration. Hence, the class of adjustive reactions includes all actions and behaviour that aim at the control and delimiting of his motive or the adjustment of circumstances so that some equilibrium between motives and the conditions of their satisfaction is attained. One very important feature of adjustive reactions is that it benefits the individual organism as well as the community organisms, or at least is not harmful to such a community.

5. Partially adjustive reactions: All reactions aimed at facing obstacles so as to satisfy motive are not completely and entirely successful in achieving their objective. Some of them succeed only in attaining a partial adjustment. Simple examples of such partially successful adjustive reactions are day-dreaming as well as other forms of escape from troublesome situations. For example, a majority of poor individuals, instead of making constructive efforts to ameliorate their condition, indulge in making castles in the air, with the result that their poverty fails to pinch them as it would otherwise do. People of this kind are of a very optimistic bent of mind, and even though they never try, they are never frustrated, constantly in the hope that their days will turn, that every dog has his day, that some relative will leave them a legacy or that they will win a pool. Some partial and temporary adjustment of a kind is definitely achieved by this escapist dreaming, but no individual can get complete happiness through this kind of imaginative adjustment. Evidently, through reactions of this kind of a type is definitely achieved by this escapist dreaming, but no individual can get complete happiness through this kind of imaginative adjustment. Evidently, reactions of this kind do not achieve any considerable adjustment.

6. Non-adjustive reactions: Non-adjustive reactions as a class are activities that do not achieve any adjustment at all between the individual and his conditions. For instance, some people do not attend to some motive even when it is persistently and continually being frustrated, and they continue in activities that do not bring satisfaction for this motive. Consequently, from the standpoint of this particular motive, their activities can only be classed as non-adjustive. Poverty, to take an oft-repeated example, is painful for everyone, but many scholars ignore its demands and pass their days in scholarly and academic pursuits. And, these activities in the pursuit of knowledge and pedantry prove non-adjustive reactions for all those motives that are frustrated because of the individual's financial poverty since he makes no effort to satisfy them. Sex instinct is commonly repressed, and when this happens, some people instead of doing something to satisfy it, only choose to repress it all the more, but the efforts at repression and suppression are only non-adjustive reactions, as they achieve no real adjustment at all.

7. Maladjustive reactions: These activities, or reactions, do succeed in achieving some adjustment, by a type of adjustment that is of a wrong kind, it harms the individual organism as well as the community of organisms. This class of reactions includes all kinds of adjustive mechanisms or mental mechanisms. Frustration is to some extent avoided and postponed by the individual when he succeeds in convincing himself that someone else is to blame for his failure, but doing so only endanger his mental relationships, and ultimately he and others come to harm. Besides, a person who finds satisfaction in the achievements of other individuals by identifying himself with them gives some appearance of being adjusted, but he neither himself progresses nor does he afford assistance to others in their progress and development. Individuals who choose to satisfy their desire and overcome their frustrations through day-dreaming are not likely to succeed in practical affairs of life and waste their time to no end. Excessive repression that takes place in individuals who cannot find other means of satisfying their motives and drives usually leads to the development of common errors of daily life, abnormal behaviour and mental illness or even derangement. Consequent upon such a condition is much embarrassment for themselves as well as for others. Society glares at and vociferously criticises people who have recourse to maladjustive reactions, and, ultimately it causes them much pain and discomfort.

From the above description it is fairly evident that maladjustive reactions differ essentially from adjustive and partially adjustive reactions in this that while they do lead to some sort of adjustment they also jeopardise the person's social relationships. Secondly, reactions of this kind are origin of many forms of abnormal behaviour and mental diseases. Consequently, people with such tendencies require expert treatment and advice.

QUESTIONS FOR EXERCISE

1. What do you mean by mental hygiene? What are its aims? Trace its relation to education.
2. What is mental health? Describe its importance for education.
3. What is adjustment? How is it related to motives?
4. Discuss criteria of personality adjustment.
5. Discuss methods of adjustment in human life.

34

Guidance

WHAT IS GUIDANCE?

According to Jones "Guidance is the personal help that is given by one person to another in developing life goals, in making adjustment and in solving problems that confront him in the attainment of goals." In this manner guidance is personal assistance. Although guidance is sometimes offered at the group level, yet even in these matters every member of the group is also individually given advice. Applied psychology is based on the conception of individual difference. General experience and scientific research have both established that every single individual has certain abilities, problems and difficulties that are distinctly his own, as distinct from those of others. Evidently, if any advice or guidance is to be rendered, it must be rendered individually and personally. This personal help is forthcoming from one individual to another. One of these two individuals is a psychologist, or one who knows psychology and the other a person who is in need of psychological guidance. Guidance, then, is the help rendered to an individual by the psychologist. In its more extensive sense the term may be taken to comprehend the advice rendered by any individual who is in the know concerning psychology to another who is in need of it. For example, if a father guides his son in solving a problem, this, too, amounts to guidance, irrespective of the fact that it may or may not be based on the most correct notion of psychological principles. But this extensive meaning of the term is its general meaning and implication. In a scientific analysis it is not taken in its general meaning but reduced to more definite and precise terms whereby its meaning becomes limited. That is why it is first defined. Guidance, in psychology, means a particular advice. It is the personal advice or service rendered by a psychologist, and not by any Tom, Dick and Harry, to another person. This guidance takes the form of advice which helps the guided individual to adjust to various conditions and circumstances. If one would only look at it that way, it would become evident that adjustment is the basic problem of human life. The person who fails to adjust to his circumstances becomes a failure, suffers pain himself and inflicts it upon others, and is branded an abnormal being. In this way, educational psychology, through its helping the individual in adjusting himself, helps to spread happiness, peace and organization in society.

Problems in human life do not come to an end, because new ones keep on arising. There is no end to trouble. A child, for example, is faced by very few problems, much of his anxiety being centred around the work forced upon him by the teacher, or the means of dealing with the more recalcitrant of his friends and such minor things. He has not to worry about keeping the hearth burning. But these are problems that gradually engulf every individual as he grows older. As a general rule most people marry and have children who must go to school and with equal inevitability fall ill and be treated for it only to grow up and get married themselves and keep the almost eternal circle moving forward. Thus one trouble grows out of another, and never lets the individual being sit back contented and harried. Human psychology is much like this. One desire arises and destroys the being's peace till it is satisfied. Hence, he immediately busies himself in searching for the means to satisfy this desire and achieves this after more or less trouble. But the story does not end here, it is followed by the arising of another desire and the inevitable circle of objective, search for objective, obstacles in search for means of solving the desire, overcoming of the obstacles, possession of the satisfying object, satisfaction of the desire, and the arising of another desire. it is evident that every individual is continually faced with new objectives the achievement of which entails the facing of many other difficulties. As Jones has stated in his definition, guidance helps the overcoming of those difficulties that beset the achievement of an objective.

KINDS OF GUIDANCE

As has been pointed out, an individual has to turn to the psychologist, in the latter's role of a specialist, for personal advice when he fails to solve the problems that confront him. This personal advice is guidance. How this guidance can take effect depends on the fact that it be given in the context of some problem the solution of which is being sought. As a matter of fact it is no easy matter to recount all the possible problems that arise in various spheres of human life, but some psychologists have attempted a classification of them. For example, Jones has divided the problems of life into eight spheres on the basis of their nature:

1. Related to health and psychological development.
2. Related to house and family.
3. Related to time for recreation.
4. Concerned with personality.
5. Religious.
6. Educational.
7. Social.
8. Vocational or occupational.

Having achieved the classification of problems it becomes possible to classify the kind or forms of guidance that is to be given correspondingly. For example, vocational guidance is required in connection with profession and educational guidance in the field of education. Psychologists have professed many and various kinds of guidance. For example, Jones has mentioned the following eight kinds of guidance:

1. Vocational Guidance.
2. Educational Guidance.
3. Recreational Guidance.
4. Civic Guidance.
5. Community Service Guidance.
6. Social and Moral Guidance.
7. Health Guidance.
8. Leadership Guidance.

The present discussion, makes a study of three kinds of guidance. The Bureau of Psychology, Uttar Pradesh, has also put guidance in three categories, and much the same classification of guidance kinds have been followed in the other Indian states as well. These three kinds are: (1) Educational guidance; (2) Vocational guidance, and (3) Personal guidance.

If the matter is looked at closely, it will be seen that the above three classes in fact include all kinds of classification, if child guidance is considered, for example, and this guidance requires the opening of clinics in various places, it will be found that problems concerning the children are either concerned with education or are of a personal nature. Hence, child guidance is jointly comprehended under educational and personal guidance. Similarly, the various forms of guidance, such as health guidance, recreational guidance, civic guidance, social and moral guidance, community service guidance and leadership guidance are all comprehended in personal guidance.

Dividing of the various spheres of guidance does not imply that these spheres are completely separated and unconnected. In fact, guidance is a dynamic and progressive concept in which advice given on every aspect of human life is comprehended, but, nevertheless, with a view to convenience in discussion, its aspects and spheres have been differentiated. Educational guidance and vocational guidance are closely related, and both of them are very intimately concerned with personal guidance. The basis of this correlation between the various spheres is that all problems of human beings are connected with each other For example, when a person experiences difficulty in selecting a particular curriculum or a definite profession, his indecision may stem from certain personal difficulties. It happens quite often that young men become so engrossed in their love affairs that they are not able to devote any serious thought to their careers and future. Death of a close and loved relative may be another reason why he may be at a loss and groping in the dark. The fundamental problem here is of a personal nature, with the result that all educational or vocational guidance to such an individual will be modified by the personal guidance given to him. On the other hand, many personal problems may be the consequence of certain deficiencies of education and the lack of educational guidance. If a child runs away from school and becomes vagrant, finds no interest in study but chooses to pursue a life of crime or one of anti-social conduct, then it is evident that there is something wrong somewhere and as likely as not it may be that his choice of curriculum may have been undesirable. In much the same manner certain individual and personal problems may be the outcome of an absence of vocational guidance. A young man, for example, in his school days may have been a very fine sportsman, and by its virtue he would naturally not appreciate a job that ties him down, offers no opportunity of leadership, and does not allow the development of any of his sportsman-like qualities like motivation, patience, adventure and courage. If he is forced to take on such a job for a variety of reasons, it would be natural for him to become irritable and lose his mental balance and calm to some extent. This may lead to further complications in the form of personal problems that have been caused by lack of proper vocational guidance. Similarly, educational, vocational and personal guidance are mutually related.

Classification according to mode of guidance

The above classification that we have been viewing is made on the basis of problems for which guidance is required. If the mode of guidance is taken into consideration guidance can be classified in the following manner:

1. Individual Guidance.
2. Group Guidance.

Before going on to a detailed description of educational, vocational and personal guidance, it would be advisable to comprehend this classification of guidance made on the basis of its modes.

1. Individual guidance method: In the individual guidance method the person to be guided and his guide, the psychologist, are in direct and personal contact with each other. He visits the ill person's house and makes a study of his family conditions, and for this purpose he interviews the various members of the individual's household. Besides the family background, the individual's social, financial and cultural background is also investigated so that no possible source of information is left untapped. And for this it becomes essential to study his neighbourhood and to collect as many facts of his life as are possible so as to build up a fairly complete case history. The schools and colleges that he has attended arc contacted in order to gain information concerning his behaviour and scholastic attainments there. His teachers, too, are consulted on the matter.

Study of this type and the collection of all possible information concerning the individual is followed by testing of the individual himself. He is made to take tests of intelligence, specific mental abilities, interests, attitudes and personality. Interview is another weapon that is used to uncover much information and incidentally, to learn the patient's opinion of himself. Accordingly, then in individual guidance the following information concerning the individual is gathered:

1. Information concerning his intelligence, mental abilities, interests, aptitudes and personality.
2. Information concerning family conditions.
3. Information concerning the social, financial and cultural background.
4. Other relevant information.

Having gathered all this information it is subjected to close and intelligent scrutiny, and then curative measures are introduced to remove the problems which have made this guidance necessary. Among these efforts are logical arguments, suggestions, psycho-analysis, etc.

The individual guidance method has the following qualities:

1. It renders almost complete information concerning the individual. Hence a proper cure can be effected.
2. Cures in this method are simpler and more effective.

Despite these advantages, the method suffers from the following drawbacks:

1. It consumes much time, with the result that a very large number of psychologists are required if there is a big number of patients.
2. Accordingly, this method is extremely expensive also.
3. It needs highly trained and specialist psychologists.

2. Group guidance method: These shortcomings of the individual guidance method are not found in group method because in this a number of people are guided simultaneously. Group guidance should not be interpreted to imply that it involves guiding the group. Actually, the guidance is aimed at the individual because it consists of the personal assistance rendered by a psychologist. In the group guidance technique a complete group is guided. But this guidance is intended to help the individual members of the group to solve their own problems, the sole difference being that the group is comprised of individuals facing more or less the same problems. Evidently, then, there is no need to waste money and time in giving individual guidance to individuals who are facing similar problems and the advice given is likely to be similar. Hence there can be no questioning of the importance of the group guidance technique. It economises upon time and money.

Nevertheless, group guidance technique lacks all the advantage that accrues from an application of the individual guidance method. Due to the smaller degree of personal contact between the psychologist and his subjects, the cures are not quite so effective as in the case of individual guidance. When group guidance is administered it is also not possible to gather the same amount of authentic information concerning the subject as is feasible in the individual guidance method. Hence, it may be tentatively concluded that group guidance method can be of value only in circumstances in which the problems faced are similar to a degree without wide individual differences and are also not particularly complex.

VOCATIONAL GUIDANCE

Historical outline

Vocational guidance was defined by the 1954 Committee of the International Labour Organization in its suggestions concerning vocational guidance, as assistance rendered by an individual to another in the latter's solving of problems related to his progress and vocational selection, keeping in mind the individual's peculiarities or special abilities and their relations with his occupational opportunity. In this manner, the objective of vocational guidance is the proper and complete utilization of a nation's manpower through helping the individual to achieve his development and satisfaction in his abilities in order that both he and the nation may profit. It is not possible for any one individual to be capable of doing every job. Special kinds of jobs require particular kinds of skill and special know-how. It is possible that it may be asked why guidance thereby becomes necessary since every individual can tell the kind of skill he has and choose a profession accordingly. But if the situation is objectively viewed it will be found that it is not precisely of this nature, as only few people are able to gauge their own abilities and capabilities. A large majority of persons are wrong in their estimate while a fair number denigrating themselves. It is not possible for the proverbial human eye to see the very grit that is in it, it being implied that the human eye rarely lights upon the individual's own defects. If one were to go to any student doing post-graduate work in the university and ask him as to what he proposes to do after obtaining the degree, the most likely reply would be that he would take one of the competitive examinations, preferably the administrative service, and if not fortunate enough to be selected, carry on to do research and finally become a teacher. The audacity and overweaning self-confidence of the student is stupendous. If you were to ask him as to what he will do, neither of these contingencies come about, then it will only be a regard for your social standing that will prevent him from denouncing you on the spot. The implication is that very few of the students who fail in these and other competitive examinations realize that they do not possess the requisite qualities. When they fail, they turn their wrath upon the examiner while the more charitable abuse only their bad luck. There will hardly be one student who will acquiesce in the knowledge that it was he himself who was lacking in the qualities required in the job. Again, to prevent unnecessary meanings being read into these statements it must be pointed out that the competitive examinations held in the present era can hardly be considered sufficient to gauge an individual's inherent merit. The sole intention of introducing this example is to point out the fact that young men and women do not think rationally and scientifically when faced with the choice of profession. Vocational guidance helps in the solution of no other than this problem. Scientific testing reveals all that there is to know of the individual to the guide, who then advises the former as to the profession most suitable for him. Experiments have succeeded in pointing out individual traits. For example, efforts were made to establish the intelligence level required for various kinds of jobs. The following table states the intelligence quotient that a person should possess in order to go in for one or the other profession:

S.No.	Professional Class	I.Q.
1.	Administrative work and high level professional	150 or more work
2.	Low level professional and technical work	130 to 150
3.	Clerical or high level skilled labour	115 to 130
4.	Skilled work	100 to 115
5.	Semi-skilled work	85 to 100
6.	Work not requiring intelligence	70 to 85
7.	Labour work	50 to 70

Similarly, other tests and experiments have been conducted to establish some relation between vocation and other mental abilities. For example, engineering and other industrial work requires mechanical skill in the individual, with the result that persons who possess it in a slight degree cannot in the normal course be expected to become successful engineers or skilled technicians. Some kinds of work, for example, the repair of chronometers and surgery, require the ability to do minute accurate work skilfully. Lacking this quality no individual can become a good surgeon, watch repairer or experimenter or research worker. In much the same manner other industries and professions require different kinds of exercise and skill.

The above description makes evidence the importance inherent in vocational guidance. But this hardly means that the guide pays no attention to the person's attitude. Aptitude is one of the bases of guidance, but one thing that is beyond question is that no individual can attain much success on the sole basis of aptitude. Accordingly, the guide has to collect elaborate and detailed information concerning the individual's aptitudes and capabilities, and give guidance on the basis of such information. Vocational guidance does not involve categorical declarations that one shall be a doctor while such another shall be a clerk or an engineer. It is only a hypothesis and a suggestion that has its own limitations. What the guide says is simply that such and such a person possesses certain qualities in abundance that fit him for such a profession, and there is much greater possibility of success in that profession than in any other for that individual.

Personnel selection

It was the National Institute of Industrial Psychology that commenced research on matters concerning vocational guidance, and its results have been used much by all the big industries. Every productive unit has a large variety of functions which can best be performed by individuals having different kinds of ability and training. Now, the selection of separate individuals for each of these jobs is called personnel selection. And this personnel selection is based upon vocational guidance. Here, it is essential that the distinction between personnel selection and vocational guidance is well marked and known. In both it is essential that the qualities fit for different jobs be present in the person being considered for selection or guidance, as the case may be. But, in personnel selection, the quality required for some particular function is marked, and one person out of many applicants is selected to perform that function, of course care being taken that the best of the applicants is thereby selected. In vocational guidance, the qualities of a person are gauged and he is accordingly advised to take up some vocational training or adopt a particular profession that suits him and is likely to bring him satisfaction. Vocational guidance and personnel selection are two branches of vocational psychology. Both these branches are interdependent since the provision of the right man for the right job and right job for the right man requires, on the one hand, analysis of the individual, and an analysis of the job on the other.

Progress of vocational guidance

The Western nations have done much work concerning vocational guidance, particularly, in the United States of America personnel selection is itself a specialized job now. Considerable moderation and improvement work is being carried on there to improve the collection of information regarding the professions and the method of selection. *A Dictionary of Occupational Titles* has been prepared to search for and thereby provide information concerning vocations that are open to individuals. Then, an Occupational Code has been prepared by classifying the vocations according to the qualities that they require in the man as well as according to their different levels. Detailed information regarding every profession is collected. Job description, which is an important organ of the information concerning every profession, provides a detailed and exhaustive account of the various factors such as conditions of work, wages, responsibility, etc., that are operative in the industry or vocation. The first dictionary included details of 75 per cent of vocations and occupations, and it comprehends some 90 per cent of working population of that country. This dictionary went through additional and improved editions in 1942, 1944 and 1945 while in its 1959 revised version some 49,40,023 professions were detailed. And job analysis in 1942 had been confined to 16 professions.

Vocational guidance in India

In India, vocational guidance is not easily available, as there are few technical and specialized services. In 1945, the Training and Employment Service Organization Committee headed by Shri B. Shivarao suggested that occupational information be selected and published. As a result, during the Second Five Year Plan period a project was prepared to set up 50 vocational guidance centres to supplement the efforts of the employers in their personnel selection. There have been certain appointments in this connection but the actual achievement is not very noticeable. And the books on occupations that have been published are no scientific research material but merely constitute a description. Besides the efforts of the Government of India, the State governments have also opened some centres, while this in turn has been supplemented by certain non-governmental agencies. Among them the Y.M.C.A.. and the Rotary Club have achieved results that deserve mention.

As is apparent from the above short account, the progress in the direction of vocational guidance for a large country like India, is not worthy of praise. It need hardly be pointed out that much of this failure is to be attributed to the lack of organization.

List of abilities and traits

Much important research and modification work has been carried on in connection with finding out the qualities and traits required for different professions. The National Institute of Industrial Psychology of England has prepared a list of approximately 20 psychological abilities and traits. On the basis of this list an industrial survey was undertaken. In this survey, the specialists and senior officers working in the different occupations were requested to supply information as to the qualities and traits required for their respective functions. Specialists of different occupations effected a rating from three standpoints—average, high level, and very high level. Now the specialists of the National Institute took the average of the rating made available from, some 80 occupations. This average was categorized in the form of a table. And on the basis of this table it is possible to determine whether a particular individual is suitable for a specific profession or not. For example, this table clarifies the qualities that are requisites for the medical and the legal professions and the qualities that are quite desirable.

Tests by Dvorak and Dodge

Dvorak and Dodge conducted tests upon employees of different professions, or persons successful and unsuccessful within one profession, of people working in the same profession but in differing capacities. This testing was based upon a wide variety of authentic psychological testing techniques. These tests revealed considerable difference between the abilities of motor mechanics, successful or unsuccessful clerks, and other people. But these tests were neither extensive and comprehensive to be applied to a majority of professions nor concerted enough to have completely distinguished one profession from another. In this manner, it is essential to exercise the greatest care in applying the conclusions in these tests. Dodge himself has acknowledged this fact.

Process of vocational guidance

The preceding description of vocational guidance must have made it apparent that it requires two kinds of information or subject matter to be collected, the first concerning indispensable information about the individual, and the second pertainign to knowledge of the industrial or occupational aspect. In this manner, vocational guidance has two aspects:

1. Study of the individual.
2. Study of the occupational or professional sphere.

Study of the individual

Before any vocational guidance can be rendered to an individual, it is essential that adequate information concerning his education, level of mental abilities, aptitude, interests, physical development, health, nature, personality characteristics and economic status be gathered, because variations in any of them will necessarily require change in guidance.

1. Education: Individuals need differing levels of education for different professions, as for example, the highest education is required for advocates professors, engineers, doctors, and other such professions whereas a general and lower level of education can serve the purpose if the profession is clerks, overseer, mechanics, compounder, teacher, etc. Besides these there are certain other occupations in which the medium level of education suffices, *e.g.*, business, salesmanship etc. In such professions only the basic necessities literacy must be fulfilled, as much else depends upon practice. It is only because of this importance of various levels of education being relative ant relevant to different professions that most advertisements for call of applications for jobs contain specific instructions regarding the educational qualifications. For example, a person teaching students at the high school and intermediate level need only be a graduate while no mere graduate can teach the college or graduate level. Doctors require medical degrees while in order to qualify as an engineer it is essential that one passes an engineering examination.

2. Training: Education does not merely imply the degree obtained at the end of a session by passing a prescribed examination. Now-a-days most occupational units make it obligatory on all new entrants to be trained in addition to being educated, and this is being carried to the extent that only a trained individual is allowed to fill the post of a high school teacher. Certain occupations need training inevitably: for example, the occupation of an electrician, stenographer, chemist, compounder, etc. As it is, the tendency to have trained personnel in industry and other occupations is catching on. In certain professions, the individual after having entered it is oriented for a period of few weeks, and only then is he allowed to handle work on his own responsibility.

3. Level of intelligence: Besides differences in education, different professions require differing levels of intelligence. For example, the medical, technical, legal, teaching and administrative professions require the highest intelligence level while, on the other hand, the peon and the domestic worker can be selected from people with a much lower level of intelligence. Other professions require only the average level of intelligence, so that, evidently, before a person can be told of the profession that suits his natural endowments, it is essential to know the level of intelligence to which he belongs.

4. Special menial abilities: Individuals differ not only in respect of their intelligence but also in respect of the special mental abilities. For example, all people do not possess mechanical ability to the same degree and neither is verbal felicity shared by all in equal degree. Different professions require differing mental abilities, verbal ability being required by advocates and teachers, etc., mechanical ability by doctors and engineers, etc. Hence, prior to the selection of a profession it is essential for the individual to be aware of his mental abilities.

5. Aptitudes: Success in a particular profession seems to depend to some extent upon one's aptitude for it. If a person lacks artistic and creative aptitude, there is not much likelihood of his succeeding in the role of an artist, and one need not expect it. As a general rule, it is advisable for every person to join the profession for which he has any natural aptitude. Hence, knowledge of a person's aptitude is also essential before he can be given any vocational guidance.

6. Interests: Interest helps to increase the possibility of success in a profession. Interesting work is done enthusiastically and patiently while uninteresting work tends to fall upon most men, and requires very conscious application to be carried through. Success in work requires that serious interest be taken in the work, or that interest in that kind of work be created, and this is possible. Interests are mutable, and it is possible to create interest in work that was once repugnant. But, if the individual is originally endowed with interest for a particular occupation and is also possessed of the requisite mental abilities, then he would be best advised to adopt it. It need hardly be repeated, as a slogan is, that a knowledge of the person's interest is essential before any vocational guidance can be rendered.

7. Health and physical development: As a general rule, proper health and physical development are necessarily taken into consideration in every profession, but in certain other occupations success depends almost solely upon these factors. For success in the armed forces or in the police department, health and good physical development are quite indispensable. In the absence of these factors, the presence of no other quantities of ability will bring success to the individual. Hence, physical development, constitution and health are additional factors that must be taken into consideration when the question of vocational guidance comes up for consideration.

8. Nature: Different people show very pertinent and obvious differences in their nature, some being introverted while others more extroverted. And, different kinds of people successfully settle down only in some specific professions that suit their nature. An extroverted personality, for example, is an essential if one wants to succeed as a salesman, agent, administrator or even as a leader, while on the other hand, gifted introverts make great artists, authors scholars, scientists, etc. If choice of profession is contrary to one's natural inclination, it goes against the grain and deprives the individual's life of happiness and contentment, and the profession becomes a burden. While, if the profession conforms to one's nature then one is happy and enthusiastic in his work, and these conditions are conducive to progress and success. Hence, before vocational guidance can be ventured upon, it is necessary to know a person's nature also.

9. Personality characteristic: It is a fact generally known that different qualities of the personality are required in such widely separated professions as teaching, artistic creation, selling, labour work, etc. Hence, choice of profession should also be made with due regard for the qualities of the person's personality.

10. Other important factors: In addition to all these elements pointed out above it is necessary to keep in mind certain other factors concerning the individual before giving vocational guidance. Age of the person, for example, is another factor that must be taken account since many jobs and occupations set the maximum and minimum age limits on all applicants, so that people not qualifying for them in this respect cannot enter these services. Hence, there is hardly any point in advising them to take up such a profession. Sex of the person is another consideration in vocational guidance upon which much depends because some occupations are more suitable to the male individual while others are within the capacities of the female, and for these she is eminently suitable. Nursing and caring for the diseased in hospitals is one function that can safely and even desirably be allocated to women, while in the armed forces and the police most of the jobs, with very few exceptions, are suitable only for the male.

Study of professional world

Having collected all the necessary and desired information regarding the individual consideration, it is necessary to turn to professional world. While the psychologist must necessarily have enough information concerning the person to whom he is imparting vocational guidance, it is equally important that he be well informed on its professional and occupational aspect. Only then can he provide proper and effective assistance. It is not enough for the psychologist to be knowing the number and kinds of profession but also the kind of education, training, intelligence, mental abilities, interest, aptitudes, personality, etc., that are desired as well as the conditions of work that prevail therein.

Classification of occupations

Occupations have been classified in different ways according to the viewpoint adopted in doing so. Classification is beneficial because the individual comes to know all the professions from one point of view and can select from among them. This has the two-fold advantage of narrowing down the range from which the selection is to be made while at the same time it provides a number of alternatives. It will be advantageous now to glance at these various professions.

1. Classification according to interest: Professions have been divided into the following classes on the basis of interest:

(*i*) Occupations concerned with child life.

(*ii*) Mechanical occupations.

(*iii*) Computational occupations.

(*iv*) Scientific occupations.

(*v*) Occupations concerned with change.

(*vi*) Artistic occupations.

(*vii*) Literary occupations.

(*viii*) Musical occupations.

(*ix*) Occupations concerned with social service.

(*x*) Clerical occupations.

In each of these classes there are professions belonging to five levels, depicted in the following classification.

2. Classification on the basis of educational level, mental ability, skill, training, age and social respect: This classification of the professions is the work of Backman, as follows:

(*a*) *Executive, managerial and professional:* This class includes the following three kinds of occupations—

(*i*) Verbal, such as advocate, judge, editor, auditor, professor, etc.

(*ii*) Scientific, such as doctor, engineer, scientist, accountant, etc.

(*iii*) Executive or managerial such as the various kinds of managers and executives, etc.

(*b*) *Business and sub-professional:* This class includes the following two kinds:

(*i*) Business, such as trader, salesman, agent, etc.

(*ii*) Sub-professional, such as actor, photographer, designer, etc

(*c*) *Skilled occupation:* This class includes the following two kinds of occupations:

(*i*) Physical labour, such as electrician, dyer, machine man, and press mechanic, etc.

(*ii*) Intellectual, such as clerk, supervisor, stenographer, cashier etc.

(*d*) *Semi-skilled occupations:* Such as policeman, bus-conductor, driver, guard, etc.

(*e*) *Unskilled occupations:* Such as labourer, peon, night-watchman, etc.

3. Classification according to the form of work: Professions have been divided into the following four classes according to the nature of work done by them:

(*i*) *Social occupations:* These professions require that the person be possessed of social qualities and a high degree of sociability because he comes into contact with very many individuals. Examples of such profession are advocate, leader, trader, salesman, agent, administrator, manager, teacher, etc.

(*ii*) *Occupations of manual skill:* In these professions tools are used for work that requires a high degree of manual skill, examples being carpenter, mechanics, mason, binder, overseer, engineer, etc.

(*iii*) *Occupations concerned with offices:* This class includes all people concerned with office organization such as clerks, cashiers, peons, etc.

(*iv*) *Intellectual and scholarly occupations:* In this class come the professions that require intellectual acumen and love of academic work of the individual, examples of which are philosopher, author, inventor, poet, scientist, etc.

Job families

From the above classification of occupations it becomes evident that there are many professions that are similar in respect of their nature of work done, conditions of work, desired skill, interest, mental abilities, and personality qualities, etc. When such similar families are put together, a job family is constituted. In one job family the work can be carried on at different levels such as high, medium or low. Evidently, then, the individual will first have to select a job family, and then the level of that family on which he is capable of functioning.

Sources of information regarding occupations

The question that may justifiably intrigue the beginner is the source of all this comprehensive information regarding a profession. The following are the sources from which such information is forthcoming and can be gathered:

(*i*) Through papers and magazines.

(*ii*) Through information published by Government organizations.

(*iii*) Through radio discussions.

(*iv*) From employment exchanges.

(*v*) From information broadcast by industrial and commercial institutions.

(*vi*) Through lectures, delivered by specialists.

(*vii*) Through examination of factories and people working in them.

(*viii*) By working in any particular profession.

(*ix*) From guidance psychologist and vocational adviser.

Significant facts in vocational selection

After gathering information regarding the professions from one or more of the above mentioned sources it is possible to select one's profession but before committing oneself finally as has been pointed out before, the following things must be taken into consideration and made a note of:

1. Nature of work which includes the kind of work, charge, responsibility, duty, interest, etc.
2. Working conditions, which include both psychological and physical needs.
3. Necessary personality traits such as nature, practices in behaviour, power of leadership.
4. Level of intelligence.
5. Mental abilities.
6. Interest and aptitudes.
7. Necessary education and training.
8. Income, chances of promotion and permanence of work.
9. Procedure of entrance.
10. Necessary physical development and health.

11. Social prestige.
12. Demand of the job.

In this manner, a profession is chosen after analyzing the individual on the one hand, and the various occupations upon the other. Analysis of the individual reveals the abilities and qualities present in him while analysis of the job or profession reveals the desired qualities and abilities. Now, all that remains to be done is that the person who possesses abilities and qualities requisite for a particular profession should be prompted to join it.

EDUCATIONAL GUIDANCE

Defining educational guidance Jones has written, "Educational guidance, in so far as it can be distinguished from other aspects of guidance, is concerned with the assistance given to pupils in their choices and adjustments with relation to schools, curricula, courses and school life." This definition of guidance reveals the following facts concerning its nature:

1. Educational guidance is administered to students: Out of the many problems that the student is often faced with, there are some that he fails to solve of his own accord, and these do not even admit of any fruitful assistance from the teachers of the parents. Solution of these problems calls for the intervention of the specialist, and this specialist is none other than the psychologist.

2. Educational guidance is intended for educational selection: One part of the student's education consists in making a variety of selections, the first of them being the kind of college or school in which he would like to be educated. Then, he has to follow this in the selection of the curriculum that he imagines will be suitable for him. Another problem that confronts him is the choice of the subjects that he wishes to study. It must also be remembered in this connection that normal kind of curriculum is not suitable for either morons, brilliant children or for the backward children. The child himself has normally no way of telling whether he is a moron, a brilliant chap or a backward person. This is something that the psychologist alone can discover through his psychological examination. Hence, he needs guidance in this respect.

3. Educational guidance is rendered for adjustment in education: A student finds a peculiar atmosphere in the college, the like of which he cannot find outside, and he has to adjust himself to this atmosphere. This atmosphere is a composite of his friends, teachers, daily routine of the institution, method of teaching, curriculum, subjects taught, extra-curricular programmes, etc. This environment is the same for every individual student, whatever his personal capability or drawback. Evidently, and, as a result, problems of adjustment arise. One student finds the teaching terribly dull while his more enterprising partner runs away from school. One child might find himself tired most of the time while another is constantly bored stiff. Some of them indulge in systematically destroying discipline while others turn to crime and delinquency. Educational guidance is tendered for the solution of such problems that arise in the educative process.

Individual educational guidance method

The following information concerning the individual is required in the individual educational guidance method:

1. **Scholastic attainments:** As a general rule, if one is to discover these holistic achievements of the students all that is necessary is to secure the results obtained in the various tests or examinations taken by him. But sometimes attainment tests are also given to secure more reliable information on this point.

2. **Level of intelligence:** Different subjects require different levels of intelligence for successful study. Hence, intelligence tests are given to the student to discover his level of intelligence.

3. **Special mental abilities:** Selection of curricular subjects requires that attention be paid not only to the level of intelligence but also to special mental abilities. For example, literary subjects require verbal felicity, memory, mathematical ability, logic, flow of thought, etc., while creative subjects require speed in perception, spatial ability, etc. Different tests have been devised to discover different mental abilities.

4. **Aptitude:** Educational guidance requires that the student's aptitudes also be known.

5. **Interest:** Selection in connection with many important elements in education such as curriculum, subjects, extra-curricular programmes, etc., depends upon the individual's interests. Hence, in educational guidance interests of the individual are determined through tests and lists of interests.

6. **Personality Characteristics:** Problems of adjustment and selection concerning education are influenced in an important way by personality characteristics. Hence, the psychologist gathers facts of this through astute testing.

7. **Family background and economic condition:** Many of the problems of adjustment that appear in the college are in fact born in the family. Hence, guidance concerning them requires knowledge of the family background. Similarly, many of the educational problems that arise have an intimate relation with the student's economic condition. It is within the pale of possibility that a student may not have been able to select a desirable and suitable curriculum only because of his impecunious conditions, a scholarship should be provided, if the student be deserving.

Having gathered the above mentioned variety and quantity of information concerning the student, the next step in educational guidance is to collect useful information about the curriculum, subjects taught, the college and other allied matters. A psychologist keeps fairly extensive information concerning these things at his disposal. Now-a-days, colleges specialize in the teaching of specific subjects. Agricultural colleges impart knowledge of agricultural technique and all that there is to know on the subject while technical institutions or colleges impart technical training. Engineering and medical colleges teach their respective subjects. Besides these there are some multipurpose colleges that take up the simultaneous teaching of technical subjects along with the sciences as well as humanities. The psychologist keeps extensive information concerning all such colleges, their individual curriculum, their subjects and atmosphere, etc. In educational guidance his function is to help the student to make a choice of curriculum, subjects to be studied and a college, according to his abilities and aptitudes.

Group educational guidance method

Besides individual guidance, educational guidance is also rendered in the form of group guidance. Following are the steps in group guidance:

1. **Orientation talks:** These talks or lectures, as is apparent from the term, establish a proper orientation for guidance. Before turning to actual group guidance the psychologist first lectures the group on the importance of guidance and encourages them to collect information on the various adjuncts of educational guidance to be rendered.

2. **Psychological testing:** Following the lecture, the members of the group are then subjected to psychological testing in order to gain some data on their general and individual intelligence, mental abilities, interests, aptitudes and personality.

3. **Collection of data from the school:** A considerable fund of useful information concerning the child is normally available from his school. His scholarly achievement is usually available from marks that he obtains in the various regular tests held in the class, while interview with the teachers reveals much of the child's general behaviour, interest, personality, etc. And, in most cases, teacher is the only reliable source of such information. The small confined circle that the child has in school is a mine and treasure of information for the psychologist.

4. **Collection of data from the family:** The next step is consolidation of information by applying to the child's family. Parents and other members of the family have usually been with the child ever since his birth, and are thereby in a position to reveal many very interesting and unique facts to the psychologist, he being able to make much of them. And for them it is a personal matter as they are anxious to solve the child's difficulties. In addition to the report of the child's nature given to him by the parents and relatives, the psychologist also tries to discover the family's economic, cultural and educational status. And, in fact, many of the child's problems have their origin in his relations with his parents. Hence, it is very necessary for the psychologist to have adequate knowledge of this relation.

5. **Interview with the child:** The psychologist personally interviews the child occasionally and finds out his views on his past, present and the future that he looks forward to. Self-inventory can be of much help in this respect.

6. **Formation of profile:** Consolidating and integrating all the above information that the psychologist has compiled, a profile of the child is now constructed which supplies a good view of all aspects of the child. Educational guidance can now be rendered on the basis of this profile.

7. Follow-up studies: Educational guidance does not end with the actual giving of advice but proceeds one step further to the follow up study of the child. Having provided the guidance and advice the psychologist keeps an eye on the child to make sure that the child is in fact benefiting from his labour. If the child fails to show any appreciable progress then he is given more tests and the necessary changes in guidance are effected.

In this manner, what educational guidance amounts to is the personal advice given by the psychologist to the child for solving various problems connected with the process of education. Educational guidance forms the basis of vocational guidance, since the vocation that the child will ultimately select depends much upon the subjects that he chose in his period of education. Now, a person who has never studied science has the worst possible prospect for an engineer or overseer. But the process being one of reciprocity, educational guidance also depends upon vocational guidance since, once the matriculation level of education has been attained through a more or less general pattern, choice of subjects at the intermediate and university level is determined by the profession to be followed later by the student. Thus, educational and vocational guidance are interdependent.

Functions of educational guidance

The objective of guidance in respect of education is the solution of educational problems, helping the student select his curriculum and to impart to him the ability to adjust to school surroundings and conditions. Mainly, the following can be said to be the objectives of educational guidance:

1. Selection of curriculum according to ability and capability.
2. Improvement in the method of study.
3. Arrangement of a special method of education for the backward child.
4. Creation of special education programmes for the gifted children.
5. Consideration and solution of failures at examinations.
6. Encouraging the child's inspiration to study.
7. Removing weaknesses in particular subjects.

In order to clarify the outlines of educational guidance, it would be useful to go into a detailed description of the above mentioned problems.

1. Selection of curriculum according to ability and capability: Researches in psychology have established that success in education depends upon the student's judicious choice of a study curriculum that suits his capability and aptitude. In this, two factors are at work and have to be established. The first is that the student's abilities should be tested and evaluated and the second that the subjects conforming to those abilities determined. To take a simple example, it is essential that the qualities required for the study of mathematics should be known and found to exist in the student before any educational guidance can be rendered. Some definite and reliable knowledge of the various mental abilities required for the study of different distinct subjects has been established through psychological research. Now, the main thing that is to be done is to test the student and find the mental abilities that he happens to possess. This test of the student is designed to reveal his memory, intelligence, power of reasoning, imagination, skill in manual work, special interests and his personality. In this examination while some tests are resorted to, study of the student's living environment is also undertaken. In this manner, the psychologist tests each individual case, and then advises the young student as to the educational course he should profitably pursue. Experiments have shown that advice of this nature, concerning the selection of curriculum, has not only resulted in marked improvement in examination results but has also had the effect of appreciably improving the child's or student's chance of gaining a real ability in his sphere. Educational guidance is normally required at the 8th and 10th class level. The high school or school leaving stage is divided into four courses, one in science, the others in the arts, agriculture and commerce. The particular course that a student is to take up has to be determined by the 8th class, by reason of which this class has been called the Delta class. As a general rule the subject that a student chooses in the 10th class is also continued later, but renewed guidance is required at this stage. In India, in particular, this is all the more necessary since at this stage the student has to decide the profession. In giving educational guidance at this level, the psychologist has to keep in mind the guidance that he rendered to the same student when the latter was in the 8th class.

In rendering advice, besides paying attention to the results of various tests performed upon the student it is essential to pay attention to his progress in school as well. Much information concerning school progress takes the form of annual, bi-annual and monthly test scores, educational habits regarding general discussion and play, and the teacher's evaluation of the student's personality and ability. All this information is collected in the cumulative record, which is prepared either by the teacher or by the school psychologist.

Besides the cumulative record, another source of valuable information is the Guardian's Schedule in which the parents of the student record important facts concerning the student. Besides, the student himself is required to furnish information regarding himself and the subjects that he would prefer to study at a higher level. In this manner, the student prepares a self-inventory in which he includes mention of the subject that he prefers and other he does not and besides mentions the profession that he finds attractive and suitable. Generally, subjects are chosen from among the following classification of a general nature:

1. Literary,
2. Scientific,
3. Agricultural,
4. Commercial,
5. Technical,
6. Constructive,
7. Aeshetic.

Making use of the cumulative record, the guardian's schedule and the self-inventory, the psychologist prepares an information record, following which he interviews the student. In this interview the psychologist may also invite the parent or guardian. Following this interview the guide or psychologist offers advice to the student. Educational guidance at the delta class level is available to almost all students in the Western countries, but, unfortunately, in India at present only a few students are in a position to benefit by this scheme of things. And the paucity of such advice is evident from the fact that a state of the size and population of Uttar Pradesh has only 25 schools that provide facilities for such guidance.

One major difference between the guidance at the 8th class level and the 10th class level is that in the former case the guidance is limited solely to the concerns of curriculum selection while in the latter stage it must inevitably also be concerned with the need for future selection of profession and career. In this manner, the educational guidance after the 10th is mostly of an educational vocational nature and hence it naturally requires more information. In this, in addition to the student's educational career records such as the cumulative record, guardian's schedule and self-inventory, and teacher's rating is also solicited, and finally the student is again interviewed. What usually happens is that confound with all this information in the form of a profile the student is himself able to choose a suitable profession and curriculum, but if for some reason he is unable to sort out his way, the psychologist has to intervene and offer his assistance.

2. Improvement in the method of study: The other important aspect is the improvement in the study method of the individual. The study method is comprised of such factors as mode of taking notes, mode of reading, ability to summarize, method of memorizing, proper division of time, arrangements for rest, etc. It would be useful to go into a slightly detailed account of these factors.

(*i*) *Mode of taking notes:* Charles Bird has sagaciously observed that study improves if notes are taken, but taking notes is an art that is not given equally to all students. Taking notes does not involve taking down all that the teacher says or in noting the important points. In fact, taking notes implies taking down in brief all that is said. Signs can be used as in the case of shorthand. Notes should not be so brief as to be incomprehensible on a second reading and neither should they be so designed that all important facts mentioned should be noted and all extraneous or detailed explanatory matter excluded.

(*ii*) *Mode of reading:* Considerable research has been made in psychology concerning the mode of reading. For example, the various conditions under which and the degree to which either the whole or the part method is useful have been discovered. Reading quietly or reading aloud have their own advantages and these too have been discovered. When reading it is essential that sufficient light be available and that the least disturbance be present. Speed of reading can be improved by practice and effort.

(*iii*) *Methods of memorizing:* Considerable research on the memorizing of matter having been made, the following conclusions are available concerning the various methods of memorizing recommended:

(*a*) *Recitation:* Recitation does not mean reading a piece of matter over and over again by its repetition. This has advantages over rote learning and over numerous readings. But this does not mean that making more than one reading has no advantage. In fact, relation and repetition should go on side by side.

(*b*) *Part and whole method:* In the part method the matter to be learned is divided into suitable pieces while in the whole method it is learnt as one piece. And the method that is to be used in a particular case depends upon the quality, kind and nature of the matter as well as upon the capability of the learner. A small poem can be learnt whole but, if the poem is long, it is best to use the part method. Similarly, the whole method is advisable when the matter is difficult as this helps in the understanding of the various individual parts of the matter. But it is perhaps best to use both methods, In practical life, a student has to decide for himself but in choosing between the two methods be must he aware of his own capacity to learn and remember. Individual who tires of the whole method should use the part method while others who only warm up after a short period of study would probably benefit by using the whole method.

(*c*) *Spaced and unspaced method:* In the spaced method, as is evident from the name, memorizing is done with intervals introduced between pieces. Contrary to this, in the unspaced method, the entire subject is tackled in a single sitting. As to which method will prove more efficacious depends upon the learner's ability and the extent and nature of the subject being tackled. A small poem with no more than ten or fifteen lines can conveniently be memorized in a single sitting, but if the poem has something like 200 lines it is usually found more practicable to distribute the burden over more than one sitting. And, there is no definite rule as to the space or time period that should be provided between two successive sittings. Roughly speaking, the only thing that can definitely be said is that the second meeting should commence only when the exhaustion of the first is completely removed, and memory impression of it have had a chance to become permanent. In fact, the spaced method has many advantages. It not only provides opportunity for removing fatigue and creates chance for mental consideration of what has been memorized, it also reduces monotony and helps to concentrate attention upon the work in hand.

(*d*) *Active and passive methods:* Memorizing by reading out aloud is called the active method, whole learning quietly without any external aid is known as the passive method. Experiments have indicated that in the active method as compared with the passive method, attention is disturbed much less, a pattern of the subject is formed in the mind, and the various parts of it establish relations with each other. The learner is aware of all that he has in fact learned and the desire and effort of learning are retained. Yet it may sometimes be more convenient and profitable to precede the loud reading with a quiet reading of the subject matter.

(*e*) *Rote vs. intelligent method:* In the rote or mechanical method the learner memorizes without understanding what he is learning, whereas in the intelligent method the learner understands its meaning and comprehends it along with memorizing it. Experiments and tests have shown almost conclusively that the intelligent method of learning is almost invariably better than the rote method. In it thoughts form definite associations, the subject matter sinks into the brain, and the memorizing is more permanent and longer lasting. When the above methods of learning and memorizing are supplemented with grouping, association and rhythm is known to one and all. Association helps the newly memorized subject matter to be related to that which is already in the mind and hence improves its retention. Besides, self-confidence is another important factor in memorizing. Memory is further helped by mental set. The objective in learning a piece also helps its successful retention in the mind. Attention is quite essential as without it memorizing is impossible. Mental commentary also helps memory. In this process the subject matter learnt is repeated in the mind. Finally, appreciation, or mixing newly learnt matter with that which is present in the mind, helps the process of memorizing.

(*f*) *Method of summary:* Another aspect of learning that is very important is the method of summarizing. The main thing in this is perception of the heart of the matter and selection of terms that sufficiently sum up all that has been said in the minimum possible number of words.

(*g*) *Division of time:* As has been pointed out much benefit is to be derived by reading over divided periods of time rather than continuously. Division is also two-fold—division between periods of study and rest, and division of study period according to the subject to be studied. Division of both kinds is essential.

(*h*) *Provision of rest:* If one rests after having read for some time, the fatigue caused thereby is relieved, boredom is obviated, and all that has been read gets a chance to sink into the mind. Experiments have shown that if one sleeps after reading, all that is read in the period is retained for far greater time than any other material read under differing circumstances. This occurs because sleep provides complete rest to the brain. The extent of rest required after reading a book depends not only upon the capacity of the student himself but also upon the material read because if the subject is obstruse and difficult, rest will be needed only after a short reading, whereas in the case of a simple or light subject much reading can be done before fatigue sets in.

From the above analysis of the results of psychological investigation in study methods, students can discover the faults and advantages of their own methods and can also effect improvements in them. Students who cannot do this, stand in need of a psychologist's guidance. And in giving such guidance and advice the psychologist should find out the capacity and capability of the student, as this is intimately related to the method of study.

3. Provision of a special method of education for the backward child: One specific aspect of educational guidance is the guidance concerning backward children. This category includes children who usually fail at examinations, or show signs of indiscipline, running away from school, juvenile delinquency, or other defects of such nature. Backwardness in education can be caused by personal causes as well as by the method of teaching or external factors. The adviser must be able to gather all possible relevant information regarding the backward child whom he is called upon to guide. In this, besides getting hold of the cumulative record and guardian's schedule, or the self-inventory it is necessary to gather information from the parents and teachers. It is only on the basis of such information that any advice for the solution of educational problems can be given. In case the child is intellectually of a lower level or suffers from some mental defect, then he requires a special curriculum and a special method of teaching to suit his needs. A psychologist can advice on this matter also. If it is observed that the backward child fails to show any progress despite persistent effort then he would be advised to go into some technical profession requiring training rather than mental acumen. If the child's backwardness is due to family conditions or the school environment then the psychologist should advise his parents and teachers. Sometimes backwardness can be the result of some mental disease. In such a case the child stands in need of medical treatment rather than guidance. Briefly, the psychologist and the adviser must individually consider the case of each child and give private and separate advise to each person.

4. Provision of special educational programmes for the gifted children: While backward children require guidance and care, the unusually gifted children also require a special educational arrangement as otherwise there is fear of their falling into bad activities. A gifted child does not find the ordinary programme that satisfies and invigorates the average child, satisfying and helpful. The psychologist discovers such exceptional children, gathers all available information regarding them and guides their parents and teachers in the manner in which the children should be treated. Guidance of such cases more usually concerns suggestions for some special extra-curricular programmes that may help the child develop properly and in accordance with his special gifts. Putting it briefly, it can be said that the psychologist arranges a curriculum that suits well with the child's gifts.

5. Consideration of failures at examination: In the intermediate and high school examination held every year by the U.P. Board of High school and Intermediate examination, the results are almost invariably below 50 per cent. More than half the students that appear for the examination fail to pass them. And while one hears a few odd cases of suicide that are the result of this failure there are many more individuals who become discouraged and give up their educational career when it has just begun. Some of the more enterprising turn to anti-social activity, others lose their mental balance, while a major portion of them become morose and frustrated. Almost all educationists are of the view that as a result of this very high rate of failures, the nation's wealth and strength are being greatly undermined. On the face of it, it is a national problem or at best the fault of the state's faulty educational methods and educational organization that admits of almost no interference on the psychologist's part, but he can nevertheless resolve the factors that lead children to failure in examinations through his guidance.

6. Encouraging the child's inspiration to study: Another problem that makes itself felt to the psychologist is when a particular child evinces lack of inspiration and enthusiasm to study. Causes of this lack of motivation may be both personal as well as related to the total environment whether social, family or school. Among the personal reasons can be physical factors such as a weak constitution or mental reasons such as anxiety and irritation. Environmental factors are concerned either with the home or the school. As far as the school is concerned it may produce a variety of causes such as uninteresting curriculum and routine, the method of education or teaching being anything but psychological, absence of extra-curricular programmes, etc. The psychologist shifts all these factors and causes, and then advises the child to create motivation in him, In fact, this can be achieved more by removing causes that destroy motivation than by any guidance. For this the psychologist guides either the teacher or the parents. The parents, teachers and the psychologist can jointly exert themselves to create a condition in which the student will take an interest in his education of his own volition. Then, and only then can the child be inspired to take an interest in the study of his subjects.

7. Removing weakness in particular subjects: Yet another problem confronts the psychologist when a student shows signs of being weak in some particular subject or subjects. English, for example, is one subject in which most students in Uttar Pradesh are lamentably weak. A major portion of college students failing is of those who fail in the English language papers. Some students evade some subjects as if they were running for the safety of their very lives. Mathematics, for example, is another subject that is something of a burden for many students, equalled perhaps only by grammar for the dread it causes. Weakness in a particular subject is not due to lack of the required ability in the student, but more often because the student fails to take a keen interest in that subject. Through tests and observation the psychologist can locate the individual cause that is responsible for the weakness. If it is the study of that subject as soon as possible, or if some ability can possibly be injected into the students, efforts should be made to create it in him. If the cause of weakness is something else then in that case teachers, parents, the psychologist and the student can co-operate to put an end to the meaningless weakness threatening the student's progress.

From the above brief outline of the various aspects of educational guidance it becomes evident that it is concerned with the various problems of education. All the problems that have been mentioned in the process are only the major problems.

PERSONAL GUIDANCE

An important part of guidance is personal guidance, and it constitutes the personal and individual advice offered by a guide to an individual for the solution of latter's personal problems. This helps the person adjust to circumstances in his life. As a general rule problems are a part and parcel of human life, but not everyone is able to solve the problems that arise in his life and raffle the aim of existence. People who find no way out of the morass of problems need the guidance and opinions of a specialist and expert. And, a psychologist is the only one who can guide in the solution of these problems.

Need for personal guidance

There can be no exact prescription of the number and kind of problems that can be called essentially personal, because while the same person may be faced with a wide variety of problems at different stages of his life, the same problems may assume a different shape when they plague another individual. In this manner, personal problems are so numerous and have so many incongruous and varying forms that it is well-nigh impossible to indulge in a description of them, and yet, the main personal problems that beset the human animal can be distinguished. Roughly speaking human problems of a personal nature can be of two kinds—(1) Personal or individual, (2) Social. Individual problems include—physiological problems such as ill-health, disease and concerned problems and familial problems. Of these, the family roles are the most prominent and varied, comprehending problems of relations between the child and his parents, relations between husband and wife, conjugal problems, relations between brothers and sisters, financial status of the family, mutual adaptation of the individuals and others. And, any one of these problems is Herculean enough to destroy the peace and calm of an individual. Problems of conjugal love, for example, compel an infinity of couples to spend their life in utter misery and misunderstanding.

Very often the individual makes some slap dash trial and error efforts to solve his personal problems or turns to good friends for personal advice, or instead turns to the older family members or teachers. Though this advice may have some practical validity, yet scientifically it is difficult to find any justification for it. If we take up for consideration the problem of conjugal love and bliss, then, it will be seen that the advice rendered by the best friends and sages of the family is all based upon their personal experience, and cannot provide any real guidance for a person. The crux of the matter is that the conjugal relations between no two pairs are identical. The conjugal problem of one specific pair is a personal and particular problem. Examples from other persons and solutions can only provide some general suggestions but it is dangerous to emulate others without paying attention to the particular merits of one specific case, for which the solution is being sought. Evidently, then, the individual can tackle his own problem after making a comprehensive study and gathering considerable psychological knowledge, but if this psychological knowledge is present in him, then why should that problem arise in the first place? Naturally, it is essential for the person to turn to the psychologist for expert advice. But it must be kept in mind that guidance and advice cannot solve the problem in its entirety. This advice is more of the nature of suggestions, is scientific, and has no qualities of hit and miss about it. If the individual is to profit from such suggestions, he must be possessed of understanding, sympathy and skill.

Process of personal guidance

The first condition of personal guidance is that the person to be guided be fully and completely understood. It is desirable that the individual should himself come forward with all relevant information in the form of life history, present conditions, feelings, thoughts, activities and all main facts concerning his life, and pass it on to the psychologists. He should not try to conceal anything, irrespective of the inhibitions that may urge him to do so, for it has often been found that the root of the problems to be solved existed in things from which the person wanted to escape, that he not only did not want to reveal to others but of which he did not even want to think himself. Briefly stated, in personal guidance, the psychologist should, with the help of various tests, gather all relevant and necessary information concerning the person. Roughly, personal guidance has the following five steps:

1. Gathering the facts.
2. Diagnosis of the problem.
3. Prognosis.
4. Therapy.
5. Follow-up studies.

1. Gathering the facts: Gathering of factual information is the first and most important step in personal guidance. These facts can be of two kinds—those connected with the particular problem, and those concerned with the general life history of the person. And, the facts concerned merely with the problem also can be of two kinds—the first concerned with the individual and his characteristic qualities, the second concerned with the external circumstances of the problem. And the need for knowing these facts compels the psychologist to turn to observation, interview and various tests that yield it. The person himself is not the only one interviewed, as much valuable information is forthcoming from the interviews of people nearest to him, such as friends and relatives. In an interview it is essential that the psychologist ventures to speak as little as possible, that he asks questions that elicit the correct and desired responses by allowing the interviewed person to carry on the bulk of the talking. As in the case of educational and vocational guidance, in personal guidance too, the opportunity for interview arrives only after a profile has been formed from the other sources ransacked for information. This necessitates the use of the cumulative record, the guardians schedule, the self-inventory and the teacher's ratings, besides which a number of tests are also performed. The outline of the profile is something like what is described below:

(*i*) *Physical description:* Physical description includes the person's age, sex, and physical health.

(*ii*) *Family description:* In family description are included facts concerning the family background and hereditary relationships, parents (whether real or step, living or dead), brothers and sisters (their mutual relationships), economic status of the family, social standard of the family, mutual relations between all the members of the family, etc.

(*iii*) *History of social development:* This class includes the student's relations with other members of his class, and with other friends outside the class. If the person requiring guidance is not a student, then his relations with his neighbours and relatives outside the family will be studied.

(*iv*) *History of college life:* This classification includes the student's history in his progress through the primary, secondary and college educational stages which is constituted by results of examinations and record of the part taken in extra curricular programmes. If the person being studied and guided is not a student, then his life outside the sphere of his family should be studied to provide equivalent information. If he is engaged in some professional pursuit, it is necessary that the information regarding level of income, conditions of work, relations with other members of the profession or institution, etc., is collected.

(*v*) *Mental abilities:* By means of various tests and examinations intended for the purpose, the psy chologist gathers information concerning the individual's level of intelligence, mental abilities and aptitudes, etc.

(*vi*) *Traits of personality:* Trails of the personality have an important part in all personal problems, hence the psychologist finds it incumbent to secure information concerning the person's interests, emotional maturity, motives, ambitions, objectives and ideals, etc.

One very important part of gathering such information is the keeping of proper records so that the information be available in future. Even in an interview it is desirable for the psychologist not to depend upon his memory too much but to take adequate notes so that the information revealed is permanently available to him when it is required. But this requires an attitude of co-operation on the subject's part and a reassuring approach on the psychologist's part so that the subject should not become suspicious. If a person finds any objection to his statements being recorded, then modern tape recording machines can be used without the person being informed of them. Facts which do not qualify for this kind can be recorded after the person has been informed of their importance. For example, the psychologist should encourage and praise the subject and lead him into believing that all that he says deserves to be recorded.

2. Diagnosis of the problem: Having gathered all the facts that he wanted to collect, the psychologist is now ready to start his own work. He has to search and analyse this information in order to see some system in it as well as any pattern that will help to reveal the cause of the problem under consideration. Such a discovery of patterns is the diagnosis of the problem. And this diagnosis is the basis on which the problem is to be solved and the trouble cured. The better and more accurate the diagnosis, the better will be the cure ultimately effected. And it would be no misnomer to state that with a proper and accurate diagnosis half the psychologist's work is over.

3. Prognosis: Prognosis consists in estimating the benefit or result of the guidance. A psychologist tries to visualise the extent to which he will be able to solve the person's problem, or, in other words, to what extent is there hope of the problem being solved. For example, by seeing a person's past performance in mathematics and by measuring his mental abilities, it becomes possible to make some tentative estimate of what he will be able to achieve after the guidance is rendered.

4. Therapy: Now the time for therapy or cure has arrived, or, in other words, it is the time for the psychologist to come forward with a satisfactory solution of the problem. Seeing the profile as from the interviews with the psychologist, the counselee himself gains insight into the problem and sometimes even comes up with some sensible and practicable solution. The truth of the matter is that this, in fact, should be the aim of the psychologist, for he should try to make the counselee see his problem and its patterns, and even to think up a solution for it. If this happens, he will on the one hand gain considerable pleasure from having solved the problem of his own accord, while on the other he will have considerable enthusiasm in solving the problem, and he will exert himself to the maximum limit. Freud, who used to cure mental diseases by the psychoanalytic method, used this method very effectively. When his patients became aware of the unconscious cause of their trouble, much of the problem was solved, whereas if the psychologist insists on giving his own suggestions and motives the subject may choose to ignore it. But if the counselee fails to understand the therapeutic measures implied by the psychologist, then the latter has to take positive steps. And, in the event of such a condition being precipitated it is always best for the advice not to seem too authoritative or sermon-like, and neither should any of the person's shortcomings be mentioned. The counselee should be given some hope that his problem will be solved, and it should be so expressed that it may appear to have come from the counselee instead of the psychologist.

5. Follow-up studies: Personal guidance does not come to an end with therapeutic measures being introduced because the psychologist's job is not only to provide guidance, but also to see the actual success of his advice. Hence, even after the therapy he has to keep up contact with the subject, and to make inquiries to find out the success that he has had in solving the problem originally entrusted to his care. This not only furthers the help rendered to the counselee but also adds to the experience and knowledge of the psychologist, because much of what is learnt in guidance is through trial and error. Human psychology is so complex that it cannot be tied down by any laws. Success in guidance depends upon the psychologist's own experience and insight, and as has been said before he is assisted in acquiring these through follow-up studies. It need hardly be emphasized at this stage that personal guidance is more or less incomplete without a follow-up study.

Methods of follow-up studies

The following methods are utilized in follow-up studies:

1. Follow-up through letters: As is evident from the term applied to this method, in this method the counselee is contacted through the medium of letters. Letters reveal only a small quantity of information, but they do contribute something positively to the study. And, if need be, these letters can be used to transmit further guidance to the person or even meet him.

2. Questionnaire method: In the questionnaire method, the counselee is sent a questionnaire, and he is asked to answer it, and return it to the psychologist. Most questions selected for the purpose have the quality of requiring short, simple, concise and precise answers, most of them being in terms of positives and negatives. This questionnaire is concerned with various aspects of the progress of a problem concerning which the advice was given. Psychologist tries to find the extent to which he has succeeded in curing the person, and if not, why. The questionnaire method has the advantage of soliciting more varied and comprehensive information than mere letters, but the main disadvantage lies in the small number of questionnaires returned to the psychologists.

3. Card file method: In this method, details of an interview, in terms of the name of counselee, age, address, purpose of interview and details of the problem are inscribed. This is kept in the central office of the guidance centre, so that the counselee can contact his guide at any time that he wishes. The file method also makes use of the tickler file, in which the psychologist keeps an open file of the counselee within easy reach, which keeps details of the further contacts that have to be made. The file is so named because it tickles the guide into contacting the person guided.

The above three methods are prevalent and have beneficial results. There are some other methods also, in addition to these main ones, by means of which the contact between the psychologist and the counselee can be kept alive. Telephone, for example, is another instrument that is frequently used in U.S.A. for renewing such contact and gathering fresh information from the subject.

It would be very useful to present a realistic example of personal guidance before winding up a description of it. This will improve realisation of the actual cases that are confronted and the extent to which the State provides facilities for dealing with them.

A professor in a local college at Allahabad went to take a look at the central jail there, where he saw a young boy undergoing sentence for breaking in or affecting an entry and thieving, the term being six months. The professor had the boy released on probation and took him into his own household. The boy maltreated the professor and continued on his path of theft and crime. He was also often absent for a couple of days from home. Finally, the professor handed the boy over to the parents who were living within the college campus. The boy was sent to school where he was admitted to the sixth class, but his progress was not satisfactory by any standards. Practical skill and ability was somewhat better than the average. His other faculties were definitely weak. He naturally did not pay any attention to his study, and took no interest in social activities. At times he was filled with feeling of guilt and remorse, but at other times he showed to be very aggressive and anti-social. This boy was brought to the bureau of psychology for personal guidance, where it was advised that the boy needed a change of environment. It was opined that an understanding and sympathetic person might help to improve his adjustment to life, and that there was no benefit to be derived from further study. He should turn to acquiring training in a mechanical trade. Psychologists also felt that the boy required regular mental treatment, but as the bureau was not able to provide this assistance not much could be done in this direction. Even then, the boy did benefit somewhat from the guidance of the psychologists. He learned to understand some of his problems and this helped him in his adjustment.

QUESTIONS FOE EXERCISE

1. Explain the concept and kinds of guidance.
2. Write a short note on—Vocational Guidance.
3. "The greatest shortcoming of most vocational guidance programmes is the implicit assumption that information about the subject's aptitudes, interests and personality traits is enough for a final decision." Discuss the statement in the light of the fundamental principles of Vocational Guidance.
4. Discuss the importance of any two of the following in the technique of vocational guidance:

   (*a*) Interview, (*b*) Testing, and (*c*) Cumulative record.
5. Differentiate between vocational guidance and vocational selection.
6. What factors should be taken into consideration while giving vocational guidance?
7. Write short note on—Educational Guidance.
8. How is school guidance related to the problem of individual differences?
9. Write short note on—Personal Guidance.

35

Organization of Guidance Services in School

MEANING

Organization of guidance services in schools means supervision, planning and co-ordination on the part of the head of the institution. Moreover, it means active co-operation of the parents, the staff, the guidance experts and the pupils. Thus, organization of guidance work in schools implies the following:

1. Laying down objectives in clear terms.
2. Mustering resources and utilizing them in the possible manner.
3. Systematic planning of guidance work,
4. Co-ordination and conduct of certain activities within administrative framework.
5. Allocation of duties and responsibilities.
6. Provision of minimum essentials.
7. An able leadership to co-ordinate, supervise and direct activities.
8. Working of various guidance personnel as a team.

PRINCIPLES OF ORGANIZATION OF GUIDANCE SERVICES

1. Child-centredness: Guidance services should be organized while keeping in view the needs, interests and purposes of the students in the school.

2. Continuity: Guidance services should be continuous because individuals face problems throughout their lives. These should be meant for all and not merely for the maladjusted.

3. Wholeness: Guidance services should be concerned with the whole individual in his total environment and with specific needs and principles.

4. Prevention as well as cure: Guidance should be organized to deal not only with serious problems after they arise, but also with causes of such problems, in order to prevent them from arising or to prepare better for their solutions.

5. Specialization: Guidance is a specialized service. It should be provided by specialists like school counsellor, school psychologist, school psychiatrist, school social worker, school physician, curriculum expert, placement worker and co-ordinator of school activities. Services of these specialists should be organized and administered in such a way so that they may constantly strengthen all other members of the school personnel and help in their problems.

6. Self-knowledge and self-direction: Guidance should be directed towards improvement of self-knowledge and self-direction in the pupil.

7. Securing and recording adequate information: Guidance services should provide for securing and recording adequate information regarding educational and occupational requirements and opportunities through tests and other devices.

8. Leadership and co-ordination: Guidance service should provide for leadership and co-ordination of all the agencies of school and community for long-term guidance of youth.

9. Co-operation: Guidance service should enlist the active co-operation of parents so that better organization may be arrived at. It should also enlist the interest and efforts of every member of the school staff.

10. Simplicity: Guidance service should be as simple as possible.

11. Collection and analysis of data: Up-to-date data of the person should be obtained, properly recorded and cautiously analysed.

12. Latest ways and means: Some definite ways and means should be selected so as the latest "technical-know-how' can be imparted to the concerned worker.

13. Budgetary provision: The organization of guidance service should be according to the budgetary provisions, which should be made beforehand.

ROLE OF GUIDANCE PERSONNEL IN SCHOOL

As guidance is a specialized job in schools, it requires specialized personnel. These may include the headmaster, school counsellor, school psychologist, school social worker, child welfare worker, school physician, school psychiatrist, curriculum expert, placement worker and co-ordinator of school activities. The following is the role of various specialized personnel:

1. Headmaster: The headmaster is the leader, director and co-ordinator of guidance programme in the school. Some of his functions are the following:

(*i*) Recommending to the authorities for the employing of competent counsellor.

(*ii*) Appointing guidance committee to study the school's guidance needs.

(*iii*) Providing necessary facilities to the guidance worker and staff connected with guidance.

(*iv*) Providing assistance in planning guidance programme in the school.

(*v*) Encouraging teacher to attend special guidance courses and seminars.

(*vi*) Keeping the parents informed about the guidance activities available in schools.

(*vii*) Formulating plans and policies regarding organization of guidance programme.

(*viii*) Interpreting the programme of guidance services to the school and the community.

2. Teacher: The following is the role of the teacher in organizing guidance services in school:

(*i*) Collecting information and maintaining cumulative record.

(*ii*) Observing the pupils in various situations—in the classroom, in the library, in the playgrounds, etc.

(*iii*) Detecting maladjustment of pupils.

(*iv*) Preparing case histories of problem children.

(*v*) Helping the pupils to secure better education, personal and social adjustments.

(*vi*) Sending information about the pupils to the parents and the headmaster and taking an active part in the Parent-Teacher Associations.

(*vii*) Helping the pupils in evaluating their own growth.

(*viii*) Providing opportunities for the maximum development of the pupils.

(*ix*) Taking the help of experts.

3. Counsellor: The role of the counsellor has been explained in counselling.

4. School psychologist: The functions of the psychologist in organizing guidance services in schools may be summed up as follows:

(*i*) To know the individual, *i.e.*, his abilities, potentialities, interests and aptitudes with the help of psychological tests and other sources.

(*ii*) To help the individual in solving emotional and other problems and making maximum adjustment.

(*iii*) To conduct research.

5. Health specialist: In organizing Guidance Service in schools, the role of the health specialist is as follows:

(*i*) To make arrangement for medical examination of each child after a suitable interval.

(*ii*) To report physical handicaps of students to parents, teachers and headmaster.

(*iii*) To maintain complete record pertaining to the health of children.

(*iv*) To develop a programme of improving physical health of the pupils.

(*v*) To take up follow-up work.

VARIOUS GUIDANCE SERVICES IN SCHOOL

1. Data collection service: It collects identifying psychological data such as data regarding pupil's interests, abilities, aptitudes and personality traits, family background or social environment data, school data and data concerning educational and vocational plans. This data is collected with the help of various psychological tests such as intelligence tests, personality test and interest inventories: questionnaire, interview, observation, rating scales case history and cumulative record card. This data helps the guidance worker in understanding the pupil and also in imparting educational, vocational and psychological guidance.

2. Occupational information service: It relates to supply of information concerning occupations to pupils according to their abilities, aptitudes and interest. The information includes importance of occupation, nature of work, opportunities for advancement, remunerations, advantages and disadvantages, industrial information, training information, educational information, social, economic and cultural information. Occupational information may be supplied through: (*i*) school subjects, (*ii*) field trips and visits, (*iii*) career conferences, (*iv*) films, (*v*) radio, (*vi*) television, (*vii*) library, (*viii*) charts, (*ix*) curricular activities, and (*x*) takes on occupation by teacher-counsellor or any other specialist.

3. Self inventory service: It enables the individual to obtain information about his assets, liabilities, aptitudes, interests, limitations and personality traits without which he cannot make a wise selection of an occupation,

4. Counselling service: It enables the individual to solve educational, vocational and psychological problems through personal interviews. Counselling interviews are conducted in privacy and friendly atmosphere.

5. Vocational preparatory service: It is designed to help the individual to make preparation through pre-service training, in-service training or apprenticeship. Vocational education helps the individual in such preparation. Success in occupations mostly depends upon how this service is performed.

6. Placement service: it is concerned with assisting the pupils to get admission in suitable schools, colleges or training institutions and to get suitable jobs.

7. Follow-up service: Its purpose is to find out the progress and achievements made by the students in the educational or professional career. Counselling is incomplete without such service.

8. Research service: Research services bring about improvement in the effectiveness of the other services by conducting research regarding new techniques.

MINIMUM PROGRAMME OF GUIDANCE

1. Minimum services: The minimum services which must be started in ery school are data collection service, occupational information service and counselling service.

2. Provision in time-table: There must be a provision for guidance programme in the school time-table as well as in the school budget.

3. Co-operation: There must be active co-operation between the staff and the counsellor. A committee for guidance may be set up to enlist the co-operation of the staff. The headmaster or principal should be administrative head. The counsellor should be the advisor head of the committee.

4. Trained counsellor: There must be trained counsellor one for every 200 students in every school.

5. Facilities to teachers: Facilities to the teachers should be provided so at they may become increasingly efficient in guidance work. These include orientation courses and seminars in guidance for as many teachers as possible enable them to assess and evaluate pupils needs and the ways to meet them.

6. Guidance Bureau: In every school, there should be Guidance Bureau in the charge of an expert psychologist or under a teacher having a sound knowledge of psychology and guidance techniques like the responsibility of developing information, knowledge, skills, attitudes, interest, co-curricular activities like debates, dramas, self-government, social service programmes, sports and games and manual work of different types. He should acquaint himself with the environment and orient the pupils accordingly in educational, vocational and psychological or personal areas.

IMPORTANCE AND ADVANTAGES OF GUIDANCE SERVICES

Organization of guidance services is needed to the following advantages which prove its importance:

1. Advantages for the students

(*i*) Understanding of themselves, *i.e.*, their abilities, aptitudes, interests, personality patterns, their strengths and weaknesses.

(*ii*) Developing their potentialities in the right manner.

(*iii*) Selection of subjects, books, hobbies, co-curricular activities and preparing from the examination point of view.

(*iv*) Selection of occupation, preparing for it, entering in it and to make suitable progress in it.

(*v*) Solving personal, emotional, sexual and social problems.

(*vi*) Making educational, vocational and psychological adjustments.

2. Advantages for the teachers

(*i*) Understanding their students, *i.e.*, their abilities, aptitudes, interest, personality patterns, their strengths and weaknesses, their emotional and social characteristics, affection, self-recognition, rest, their physical condition, family history and achievements through intelligence tests, aptitude tests, personality test, interest inventories and various other data collection techniques such as questionnaire interview, rating scale, case history, cumulative record, anecdotal record, autobiography and sociometry.

(*ii*) Developing their potentialities by detecting maladjustments and solving their problems.

(*iii*) Improving classroom relationships and emotional climate through emphasis upon democratic procedures.

(*iv*) Providing educational, vocational and psychological guidance.

3. Advantages for the parents

(*i*) Understanding the abilities, aptitudes, interests, personality patterns good and weak point of their children.

(*ii*) Improving parent-child relationships.

(*iii*) Improving parent, school and community relationships.

(*iv*) Improving study habits of children

(*v*) Helping the parents in solving the problems of their children and assisting them in making adjustments.

4. Advantage for the community

(*i*) Preventing crimes and problems which may lead to mental illness.

(*ii*) Identifying and developing the talents of gifted children.

(*iii*) Producing better adjusted citizens.

(*iv*) Utilizing the staff, energy, money and other resources of the community in more efficient way.

5. Advantages for the administration

(*i*) Selecting candidates at the time of admission.

(*ii*) Selecting or recruiting staff members or employees.

(*iii*) Using appropriate techniques of evaluating the educational programme of the school.

(*iv*) Using guidance data in promotional policy and practice.

(*v*) Setting up and maintaining an effective cumulative record system.

(*vi*) Collecting, organizing and using occupational information

(*vii*) Decreasing the number of failures and increasing the achievements of the school.

(*viii*) Knowing the areas of the school where improvement is needed.

(*ix*) Planning, placement and follow up procedures.

(*x*) Increasing the overall efficiency of the school programme by providing more information through contacts between school and employer concerning the educational institutions, courses and jobs.

QUESTIONS FOR EXERCISE

1. Explain the meaning and principles of guidance services in school. What is the role of guidance personnel in school?
2. Explain various guidance services in school. Outline a minimum programme of guidance.
3. Discuss the need, importance and advantages of organizing Guidance Services.

36

Counselling

Counselling is called the crux, heart, essence, pivot or core of all guidance programme. The proper functioning and growth of the body depends upon the proper functioning of the heart. Similarly, the success or failure of the guidance programme is determined by counselling service.

WHAT IS COUNSELLING?

Some of the definitions of counselling by various experts are the following:

1. Webster's Dictionary: Consultation, mutual interchange of opinion; deliberating together.
2. Strong: Face to face relationship in which growth takes place in the counsellor as well as the counselee.
3. Robinson: The term counselling covers all types of two-person situations in which one person, the client, is helped to adjust more effectively to himself and his environment.
4. Wren: "Counselling is a personal and dynamic relationship between two individuals—an older, more experienced and wiser (counsellor) and a younger, less wise (counselee). The latter has a problem for which he seeks the help of the former. The two work together so that the problem may be more clearly defined and the counselee may be helped to a self-determined solution.

Thus counselling is a process in which the pupil is approached on an individual level. He is helped in educational, vocational or psychological field only at problem points. In counselling the subject matter is pupils needs, abilities, aims, aspirations, plans, decisions, actions and limitations. It is a sort of specialised, personalised and individualised service which makes effective use of information gathered about any individual. This information leads to self-insight, self-analysis and self-direction. This self-direction helps the individual in making maximum educational, vocational and psychological adjustment.

Characteristics of counselling

From the above discussion it is dear that the following are major characteristics of counselling:

1. Counselling is a person to person relationship.
2. It involves two individuals—one seeking help and the other, a professionally trained person who can help the first.
3. The objective is to help the counsellor to discover and solve his personal problems independently.
4. In order to help and assist properly the counsellor must establish a relationship of mutual respect, co-operation and friendliness between the two individuals.
5. The counsellor discovers the problems of the client and helps him to set up goals and guide him through difficulties and problems.
6. In the whole of counselling process the main emphasis is on the counsellor's self-direction and self-acceptance.
7. Counselling is democratic. It sets up a democratic pattern and allows the counselee to do freely whatever he likes while with the consultant and not under the consultant.

Distinction from related concepts

Counselling differs from other related terms or activities as follows:

1. Counselling and guidance: Counselling is a part of guidance, not all of it. It is a specialised or individualised part which deals with the individual at problem points. Thus all counselling is guidance but all guidance is not counselling.

2. Counselling and interview: While counselling is a part of guidance, interview is only a technique used in the process of counselling. Counselling is a wider and comprehensive term.

3. Counselling and advising: Counselling is not synonymous with giving advice. A wise counsellor never gives advice until it is absolutely essential. Counselling is a process in which the counsellor assumes the responsibility for the decisions that are made. In advising the counsellor accepts the responsibility for the quality of the decisions made. In counselling the counselee arrives at the decision as a result of process and not because of the advice of the counsellor.

4. Counselling and teaching: Counselling is not teaching. The following are some of the points of difference between counselling and teaching:

(*i*) Whereas counselling is one to one relationship, teaching is done in group.

(*ii*) Whereas counsellor is concerned with social and emotional problems, the teacher is concerned with academic and intellectual problems.

(*iii*) Counsellor uses many techniques like diagnostic tools, occupational information and several types of tests to understand the psychological make up of the counselee. Teacher uses various techniques like lecturing and audio-visual aids to make the teaching interesting and effective.

(*iv*) In counselling, the counsellor does not know the subject-matter of the counselling interview. On the other hand, in teaching the teacher knows the subject-matter of teaching.

(*v*) In counselling the most important technique is interview, but in teaching it is never used as a technique.

(*vi*) Counsellor increases information about self-occupation, training institutions, colleges, apprenticeship programmes, etc. Teacher increases information of instructional activities.

5. Counselling and psychotherapy: Counselling is not psychotherapy although it is used by psychotherapist as one of the techniques of treatment. The following are some of the points of difference between counselling and psychotherapy:

(*i*) Counselling is concerned mostly with normal individuals having normal anxieties whereas psychotherapy is concerned with individuals whose behaviours are neurotic.

(*ii*) Counsellor works in educational setting whereas psychotherapist works in medical setting.

(*iii*) Counsellor uses techniques and tools that can be used in schools whereas psychotherapist uses tools and techniques that are applicable in any situation such as play-therapy, psychodrama, sociodrama, etc

(*iv*) In counselling, psychology is not the only basis for studying the individual. In psychotherapy, psychology is the only basis for studying the individual.

(*v*) Counselling is broader in scope as it touches all the problems of the individual, but does not go deep in them. Psychotherapy is deeper rather than broader in scope. It deals with fewer problems but goes very deep in studying the personality of individuals.

BASIC PRINCIPLES OF COUNSELLING

The following are the basic principles of counselling:

1. Acceptance: All schools of counselling agree that the client must be accepted as a whole person, as a human being.

2. Respect for the individual: All schools of counselling attach importance to respect for individual.

3. Permissiveness: All schools of counselling accept relative permissiveness of counselling relationship.

4. Learning: All schools of counselling accept the learning element in counselling.

5. Thinking with client: Thinking with rather than for the client is another basic principle of counselling.

DUTIES AND FUNCTIONS OF COUNSELLOR

According to Myer, the following are the primary functions of counsellor:

1. Scheduling the interview.
2. Setting the interview.
3. Preparing the interview.
4. Conducting the interview.
5. Recording the interview.

The following are four more functions of a counsellor:

6. Group guidance.
7. Meeting the staff and getting their co-operation.
8. Meeting employment bureaus and collecting information.
9. Meeting social agencies.

According to Stewart, there are the following eight functions of counsellor:

1. Helping the pupil to evaluate his experiences.
2. Data collection about the individual.
3. Understanding the needs and problems of the individual.
4. Interview.
5. Providing liaison between school and home, school and community.
6. Co-ordinating school activity.
7. Remedial work in academic progress and social adjustment.
8. Group guidance.

On the basis of the above discussion, the following functions of a counsellor may be deduced:

1. *Programme* of guidance and its organization. It includes all the services such as vocational information service, self-inventory service, personal data collection service, counselling service, vocational preparatory service, placement or employment service, follow up or adjustment service and research service.
2. *Orientation*, a sort of preparation, including collecting the data about sources and jobs, disseminating information to pupils and planning the activities
3. *Data Collection* about the individual, administering the test and analysing the same.
4. *Interview and individual counselling.*
5. Contacting outside agencies like parents, guidance bureaus and employment exchanges.
6. Placement and follow-up work.

QUALIFICATIONS OF COUNSELLOR

Qualifications of a counsellor may be studied in the following three major headings:

(*a*) **Personality traits:** According to Walter B. Jones the counsellor should have the following five personality traits—

1. *Breadth of interest:* The counsellor should be interested in various types of people, jobs and organizations.

2. *Co-operation:* The counsellor should co-operate with all the staff in a cheerful manner.

3. *Refinement:* The counsellor should not be overconfident but on the other hand he should be modest and humble towards the pupils.

4. *Magnetism:* The counsellor should inspire confidence in others and put others at ease.

5. *Considerateness:* The counsellor should appreciate the difficulties of teachers, exhibit human understanding and possess real love for fellowmen.

(*b*) **Training and preparation:** Myer says that the counsellor must have the following mental traits:

1. Good liberal education including knowledge of humanities such as sociology, psychology, economics, history and geography etc.
2. Knowledge of objectives, curriculum and methods of secondary schools.
3. Knowledge of principles of guidance.
4. Knowledge of vocational activities.
5. Knowledge of methods of imparting occupational information.
6. Knowledge of psychological tests in guidance services.
7. Knowledge of organization of guidance services.

A seminar of headmasters held in Delhi recommended the following qualifications for counsellor:

1. M.A. in psychology or B.A. B.Ed. (with guidance) or B.A. M.Ed. (with guidance).
2. Diploma course in guidance.
3. Counsellor must have knowledge about personality problems, testing, mental hygiene and counselling techniques.

(*c*) **Experiences:** Smith requires the following six types of experiences in a counsellor:

1. Competence as a leader in guidance programme.
2. Competence as a counsellor. This includes competence in the following three directions—
   (*i*) Understanding the problem of the child.
   (*ii*) Establishing a rapport with the child.
   (*iii*) Helping the child to solve the problem.

3. Competence in interpreting and using information.
4. Competence in placement and follow up service.
5. Competence in evaluating the counselling service itself.

THEORIES OF COUNSELLING

1. Directive counselling

Directive counselling is also known as prescriptive or counsellor-centred counselling. It is problem-centred and not paido-centred. In it the counsellor prepares entire plans and sees through the process. According to the leading exponent of this school of thought E.G. Williamson, following are the assumptions of directive counselling:

(*i*) Efforts should be focused on the problem of the counselee.

(*ii*) The counsellor is more competent than the counselee. Therefore he plays a more active role than the client. He is the pivot, the centre or the leader of the situation.

(*iii*) As counselling is primarily an intellectual rather than emotional process, therefore, the intellectual aspect is given more weightage than emotional aspect.

Steps in directive counselling

According to E.G. Williamson the following steps are involved in directive counselling:

1. Analysis: Collection of data from a variety of sources by using a variety of tools and techniques. The data is needed for an adequate understanding of the client.

2. Synthesis: Summarising and organizing the data so as to reveal the client's assets, liabilities, adjustments and maladjustments.

3. Diagnosis: Finding out the root cause of the problems exhibited by the client.

4. Prognosis: Prediction of the future development of the client's problems.

5. Treatment of counselling: This may include some or all of the following procedures—

(*i*) Establishing rapport with the student.

(*ii*) Interpreting the collected data to the student.

(*iii*) Advising or planning a programme of action with the student.

(*iv*) Assisting the student in carrying out the plan of action.

(*v*) Referring to other counsellors for assistance in diagnosing or counselling.

In short, at this stage the counsellor takes steps with the student or client to bring adjustment and readjustment for him.

6. Follow up: In follow up the counsellor helps the client with new problems or with recurrences of the original problem. He determines the effectiveness of counselling provided to him.

Advantages of directive counselling: The following are the chief advantages of directive counselling:

1. Counselling is economical in time.
2. It emphasises the problem and not the individual. The counsellor can see the client more objectively than the client himself.
3. Directive counselling lays more emphasis upon the intellectual rather than the emotional aspects of the personality of the individual. The counselee is helped to solve the problem at the intellectual and not at the emotional level.
4. In directive counselling the methods used are direct, persuasive and explanatory.

Limitations of directive counselling: The following are the chief limitations of directive counselling:

1. The client or counselee does not gain any ability of self-analysis or solving new problems of adjustment by counselling.
2. Counselling serves to make the counselee over-dependent on the counsellor. He never becomes independent of the counsellor. Counselling kills his initiative.
3. Problems regarding emotional maladjustment may be better solved by non-directive counselling and not by directive counselling.
4. Sometimes counsellor lacks information regarding the counselee. This lack of information causes wrong counselling.
5. Directive counselling does not guarantee that the counselee will not make mistakes in future.

2. Non-directive counselling

Non-directive counselling is also called Permissive Counselling or Client-centred Counselling. The chief exponent of this school of thought is Carl Roger. The client, the counselee, is the pivot or the centre in this type of counselling. He plays the primary role. He actively participates in the process, gains insight into his problem with the help of the counsellor and takes decisions as to the action to be taken. The following are the assumptions underlying non-directive counselling:

1. Direction and integration of the client is more important than the client.
2. Emotional aspects are more significant than the intellectual aspects.
3. Creation of an atmosphere in which the client can work out his understanding is more important than cultivating self-understanding in the client.
4. Counselling leads to a voluntary choice of goals and a conscious selection of courses of action.

Rogers suggested the following steps in non-directive counselling:

1. The counselee recognises the need of counselling and comes for help. Thus help is sought and not given.
2. The counsellor defines the situation and creates congenial atmosphere.
3. The attitude of the counsellor is of friendship, sympathy and affection in the counselling. He feels interested in the child and encourages free expression of feelings regarding the problem of individual.
4. The counsellor tries to understand the feeling of the individual.
5. The counsellor accepts and recognises the positive as well as negative feelings.
6. The counsellor pays attention to negative self-feelings of counselee or child. He leads him from negative self-feelings to positive self-feelings, from emotional release to gradual insight.
7. The counsellor helps the counselee to translate his insight into action.
8. Positive steps are taken towards the solution of the problem situation.
9. Gradually, a decreased need for help is felt and the counselee is the one who decides to end the contact.

Advantages of non-directive counselling: The following are the advantages of Non-Directive Counselling:

1. It is a slow but sure process to make the individual capable of making adjustment.
2. No tests are used in it and thus one avoids all that is laborious and difficult.
3. It removes the emotional block and helps the individual to bring the repressed thoughts on conscious level thereby reducing the tension.

Limitations of Non-Directive Counselling: The following are the chief limitations of Non-Directive Counselling:

1. It is a slow and time consuming process. It is not possible because a counsellor has to attend many students in school.
2. As the child, the client, the student or the counselee is immature to make the decisions himself, therefore, one cannot rely upon one's resources, judgment and wisdom.
3. The counsellor's passive attitude might irritate the counselee so much that he may hesitate to express his feelings.

Directive vs. Non-Directive Counselling: The following are the distinctions between directive and non-directive counselling:

1. Different centres of interest: While in directive technique, the problem itself is the centre of interest, in non-directive technique, it is the counselee which is the centre of interest and the problem is incidental. While directive counselling is problem-centred, counsellor-centred, active, prescriptive, non-directive technique is counselee-centred, client-centred or permissive.

2. Different needs for assistance: In directive technique assistance is offered by the counsellor himself as he can see the problem and the solution better than the counselee. In non-directive technique it is assumed that the counselee has within himself the power to solve his own problem, therefore the counselee may see the problem and the solution better than the counsellor.

3. Different uses of records: In directive technique tests, records and past history are very important in finding the origin of the problem. In non-directive technique, tests, records and past history may be eliminated altogether, as they often interfere with the solution of the problem.

4. Difference in Intellectual and emotional aspects: In directive technique the intellectual aspect is given more weightage, on the other hand, in non-directive technique emotional aspect is given more weightage.

5. Difference in Type of interview: In directive technique rapport is not essential but in non-directive technique rapport is very essential.

6. Difference in Post-contact: In directive counselling post-contact is counsellor-initiated follow-up while in non-directive technique, post-contact is on conselee's initiative.

7. Difference in counsellor's role: While in directive technique counsellor's role is active, in non-directive counselling counsellor's role is one of intent listening or passive.

3. Eclectic counselling

Eclectic counselling is defined as the synthesis and combination of directive and non-directive counselling. It represents a middle status between the two extremes represented by the 'non-directive' technique on the one hand and the directive technique on the other. In eclectic counselling, the counsellor is neither too active as in directive counselling, nor too passive as in non-directive counselling. He just follows the middle path between these two extremes.

In eclectic counselling the counsellor first takes into consideration the personality and needs of the counselee. He selects the directive or non-directive technique that seems to serve the purpose best. The counsellor may start with the directive technique. When the situation demands, he may switch over to the non-directive counselling and *vice-versa*. An attempt is made to adjust the techniques to the requirements of the situation and the individual.

Steps in Eclectic Counselling: A leading exponent of eclectic counselling. Thorne suggested the following steps in the process of eclectic counselling:

1. Dignosis of the cause.
2. Analysis of the problem.
3. Preparation of a tentative plan for modifying factors.
4. Securing effective conditions for counselling.
5. Interviewing and stimulating the client to develop his own resources and to assume its responsibility for trying new modes of adjustment.

6. Proper handling of any related problems which may contribute to adjustment.

Assumptions of Eclectic Counselling: Eclectic Counselling is based on the following assumptions:

1. In general, passive methods should be used whenever possible.
2. Active methods may be used with specific indications.
3. In the early stages when the client is telling his story, passive techniques are usually the methods of choice. This permits emotional release.
4. Until simpler methods have failed, complicated method should not be attempted.
5. All counselling should be client-centred.
6. Every client should be given an opportunity to resolve his problems non-directly. Inability of the client to progress therapeutically by using passive methods alone, is an indication for utilising more directive methods.
7. Directive methods are usually indicated in situational maladjustment where a solution cannot be achieved without co-operation from other persons.
8. Even in reaching the decision to use passive methods, some degree of directiveness is inevitable in all counselling.

Limitations of Eclectic Counselling: The following are the chief limitations of eclectic counselling:

1. Eclecticism is not possible because directive and non-directive concepts cannot be merged together.
2. Eclecticism is vague, superficial and opportunistic.

To conclude one may say that in spite of the above mentioned limitations, the eclectic counselling proves to be of much practical value in the methodology of counselling.

QUESTIONS FOR EXERCISE

1. What is counselling? How does counselling differ from teaching?
2. What are the characteristics of counselling? State the difference between counselling and psychotherapy.
3. Write a detailed note on Directive and Non-Directive Counselling.
4. What is the difference between Directive and Non-Directive Counselling? Show your acquaintance with Eclectic Counselling.

37

Classroom Interaction

MEANING OF CLASSROOM INTERACTION

Classroom interaction implies interaction among persons having superior-subordinate relationship. It is the interaction between a projector entity called teacher and receptor entities which include students as individuals in a small group and as a whole class as well as inanimate objects with which the teacher interacts. The direction and dimension of classroom interaction is provided by the identification and classification of the nature of receptor entities. Its functional dimension consists of the following three tasks:

1. Communication: Communication of subject-matter or content comprising facts, names, concepts, etc., that deal with the fields of organized knowledge. It may also deal with attitudes, beliefs, ways of organizing skills and processes of instruction.

2. Inter-personal relation: Establishing and maintaining inter-personal relations among persons within the classroom so that the content task may be realized.

3. Learning: Facilitation of the learning process.

Openshaw and others have given the following classification of four dimensions of classifying teacher behaviour:

1. Source Dimension: It indicates the origin of the encounter.

(*i*) Originate: The source of the behaviour is indiscernible within the classroom setting.

(*ii*) Respond: The source of the behaviour is some discernible aspect of the classroom setting.

2. Direction Dimension: It indicates the target to which the behaviour is directed. These may be as follows:

(*i*) Individual: Focus behaviour of one person.

(*ii*) Group: Behaviour focused on more than one person but less than the total class.

(*iii*) Class: Behaviour focused on the whole class.

(*iv*) Object: Behaviour focused on inanimate elements in physical environment.

3. Sign dimension: It indicates the mode of communication of an encounter It involves the following:

(*i*) Speak: Behaviour characterized by spontaneous speech.

(*ii*) Read: Behaviour characterized by oral reading of (pointed) written matter.

(*iii*) Gesture: Behaviour characterized by purposive body movement.

(*iv*) Perform: Behaviour characterized by demonstration, non-verbal illustration, singing etc.

(*v*) Write: Behaviour characterized by chalk board presentation, writing on a chart, or overhead projector foil, etc., but excluding drawing.

(*vi*) Silence: Behaviour characterized by an absence of other signs.

(*vii*) Laugh: Behaviour characterized by inarticulate sound of mirth or decision.

4. Function dimension: It indicates the purpose of the behaviour within an encounter. It includes:

(*i*) Structure: Sets the context and focus of subsequent subject-matter and/or process:

(*a*) *Initiate:* Introduces and launches an activity, task or area for study.

(*b*) *Order:* Arranges element of subject-matter and/or process in a systemic manner.

(*c*) *Assign:* Designates required activity.

(*ii*) Develop: Elaborates and extends within an established structure.

(*a*) *Inform:* Shows relationship between ideas, objects, principles etc.

(*b*) *Check:* Requests for information concerning understanding.

(*c*) *Solicit:* Solicits a verbal response that states facts, ideas, concepts, etc.

(*d*) *Test:* Conducts a written quiz or examination, dictates questions, supplies answers without explanation.

(*e*) *Reinforce:* Confirms or sustains an idea, approach, or method through reiteration.

(*f*) *Summarize:* Restates principal prints in brief form.

(*g*) *Stimulate:* Fosters student involvement and participation.

(*iii*) Administer: Executes tasks of classroom routine and procedure:

(*a*) *Manipulate:* Arranges elements of the classroom environment personal and physical (causes others to do something.)

(*b*) *Manage Material:* Provides or co-ordinates use of media, supplies or materials.

(*c*) *Routine:* Requests for information regarding compliance with individual class or school expectations (regulations).

(*d*) *Proctor:* Monitors classroom during group activity, testing student performance, etc.

(*iv*) Regulate: Establishes and maintains inter-personal relations. It includes:

(*a*) *Set standard:* Imposes or guides development of standards of behaviour.

(*b*) *Support:* Expresses confidence, commendation or empathy.

(*c*) *Restrict:* Reprimands, threatens, punishes, etc.

(*d*) *Assist:* Provides personal help.

(*e*) *Inquire:* Ascertains student involvement.

(*d*) *Monitor-self:* Recognizes and interprets teacher's behaviour (checks own understanding).

(*v*) Evaluate: It ascertains the relevance of correctness of subject matter and its process. It includes:

(*a*) *Appraise:* Verifies by appeal to external evidence and authority.

(*b*) *Opine:* Judges on the basis of personal values and beliefs.

3. Stereotype: Reacts without stated reference to criteria or person.

MEASUREMENT OF TEACHER EFFECTIVENESS

Though it is extremely difficult to define, prepare or measure teacher's effectiveness, however, Bruce J. Biddle suggests a seven variable model for teacher's effectiveness. According to him the central problem for understanding teacher effectiveness is to establish relationships between teacher behaviours and teacher effectiveness. The seven variables stated by Biddle are as follows:

1. Formative Experiences	Main sequence variables
2. Teacher Properties	
3. Teacher Behaviours	
4. Immediate Effects	
5. Long-term Consequences	
6. Classroom Situations	Contextual variables
7. School and Community Contexts	

Variable model for teacher effectiveness

1. *School and Community Contexts:* (*i*) Physical Equipment, (*ii*) Cost of Characters, (*iii*) Laws and Customs, (*iv*) Needs and Ideas of Community Members.

2. *Classroom Situations:* (*i*) Physical Equipment, (*ii*) Social Incidents.

3. *Teacher properties:* (*i*) Skills, (*ii*) Motives, (*iii*) Habits, (*iv*) Knowledge.

4. *Teacher Behaviours:* (*i*) Traits, (*ii*) Responses to Environment.

5. *Formative Experience:* (*i*) Training, (*ii*) Socialization, (*iii*) Ascribed Positions.

6. *Immediate Effects:* (*i*) Onset Pupil Responses, (*ii*) Convert Pupil Responses.

7. *Long-term Consequences:* (*i*) Achievement or Adjustment of Pupils, (*ii*) New Ideas in Education, (*iii*) Aggrandizement of the Profession.

Manipulation of teaching

As the only education is self-education children must be left free to express themselves. Teachers must stand aside, talk less, explain less, direct less and correct less. As Adamson puts it, "The whole business is between the individual and his world and the teacher is outside it, external to it. He may facilitate it, turning his attention to one or other member of the wedded pair. He may approach the individual and his avenues of approach will be one or other of the instincts or emotional disposition which are the prime movers of mental life. He may try fear, pugnacity, curiosity, or sympathy, or a combination of them, to quicken the current which seems to him sluggish or he may approach the fact or truth, whichever of the three words it belongs to, and see whether anything can be done by lighting it up, or lining in main features and blotting to detail to facilitate adjustment. But whatever he tries, subject or object or both together, he remains outside the process, a spectator, a manipulator, perhaps a disturber; he is never in it and of it. Within that mysterious synthetic activity through which the individual is at once appropriating and contributing to his environment, forming and being formed by it... the teacher has neither place nor part." Thus, the essential activity in teaching is not the adjustment of child to teacher but the adjustment of child to world. The function of teaching is not to give information to the child but to enable him to adjust himself to the environment and also to change the environment to adjust himself. Teaching is not merely imparting knowledge to students nor is it merely giving advice. It is not hearing the students memories what they have read in the text book. It must enable the child to work independently and without the teacher at a later stage.

According to A.G. Hughes and E.H. Hughes, "It must be emphasized, however, that teachers are not as superfluous as some enthusiasts suggest, teaching is not the baneful evil, it is sometimes represented to be. It is true that children are by nature curious, assertive and creative, but they are also submissive, imitative and ready to appeal for help. It follows, therefore, that we are not necessarily working contrary to child nature when we teach. We must, however, know when to teach and when to stand aside, when to explain and when to leave children to make discoveries, when to demonstrate and when to leave children free to experiment to require children to listen and when to give them scope for free expression." Stimulation and inspiration are the two important aspects of teaching. The teachers must fire the enthusiasm of their pupils. They must encourage them in the development of their natural desires to work and to be active and guide these desires into worthwhile channels. The late president Eliot of Harvard once said, "The supreme value of a teacher lies not in the regular performance of routine duties, but in his powers to lead and inspire his students through the influence of his own mental and moral personality and examples." In the words of Burton, "Teaching is the stimulation, guidance, direction and encouragement of learning."

To sum up, the functions of teaching are:

(*i*) to provide the kind of environment which is the best suited to individual and social development;

(*ii*) to stimulate and guide healthy growth in this environment.

FLANDERS TECHNIQUE OF ANALYSIS

Teaching is an interactive process. It is mainly influence-directed. A teacher tries to influence the students. This influence is not only one way. Both the teachers and students influence each other. But the influence exerted by the teacher on the students is of greater and far reaching significance. Here a question arises, about how to describe the teacher's behaviour which is not only complex but variable as well. Flander's Interaction Analysis "is an observation procedure designed to minimize these difficulties, permit a systematic record of spontaneous act, and scrutinize the process of instruction by taking into account each small bit of interaction." It is a technique nothing less and nothing more than an observation technique. It can be used to obtain a fairly reliable record of spontaneous verbal statements. It is assumed that verbal behaviour represents to a considerable extent the total behaviour and the impact of the verbal behaviour would be nearly approximating the impact of the total behaviour.

Categories of interaction analysis

Teacher talk indirect influence:

1. Accepts feeling: The teacher accepts and clarifies the feeling tone of the students in a non-threatening manner. Feeling may be positive or negative. Predicting or recalling feelings are included.

2. Praises or encourages: The teacher praises or encourages student's action or behaviour. Jokes are included that release tension, not at the expense of another individual, nodding head or saying "Um hm" or "go on".

3. Accepts or uses idea of student: It includes clarifying, building or developing ideas suggested by a student. As teacher brings more of his own ideas into play, he shifts to category five.

4. Asks questions: It includes asking a question about content or procedure with the intent that a student answers.

5. Lecturing: It means giving facts or opinions about content or procedure; expressing his own ideas, asking rhetorical questions.

6. Giving directions: It includes directions, commands or orders to which a student is expected to comply.

7. Criticism of justifying authority: It includes statement intended to change student behaviour from non-acceptable to acceptable pattern: bowling some one out, stating why the teacher is doing what he is doing: extreme self reference.

Student talk

8. Student talk-response: It means talk by student in response to teacher. Teacher initiates the contact or solicits student statement.

9. Student talk-initiation: It includes talk by students which they initiate. If "calling on" students is only to indicate who may talk, next observer must decide whether student wanted to talk. Shift from 8 to 9 as student introduces his own ideas.

10. Silence or Confusion: It includes pauses, short periods of silence and periods of confusion in which communication cannot be understood by the observer.

Interpreting a matrix: Thus teacher talk is the sum of first 7 categories 1 to 7, *i.e.*, 1+12+32+104+105+27+13=294.

Student talk is the sum of categories 8 and 9 *i.e.*, 44+66=110.

This means that out of 421, teacher talks are 294 and student talk 110 which comes to 69.8% and 26.2% respectively.

Following conclusions may be drawn from the above:

1. The teacher is active.
2. The control of interaction rests with the teacher.
3. 50.7% of teacher's statements are indirect *i.e.*, sum of first four categories 1+12+32+104=149 out of 294.
4. The flow of communication between the teacher and the student is flexible and shifts from one category to another.
5. The class is business-like and works rapidly.

Concepts that refer to teacher behaviour

1. Indirect influence: It is defined as actions taken by the teacher which encourage and support student participation. Indirect behaviour may be operationally defined by noting the percentage of teacher statements falling into categories 1, 2, 3 and 4.

2. Direct influence: We can define direct behaviour operationally by noting the percentage of teacher statements falling into categories 5, 6 and 7. It refers to actions taken by the teacher which restrict student participation. It increases the control of the teacher and stimulates conformity and compliance. In the direct influence the net result is the decreased extent of freedom of action for the students.

Concepts that refer to student behaviour

Category 8 and 9 represent student talk. As a matter of fact these two categories are directly related to teacher talk. If the teacher does not impose restrictions there is greater student talk.

Application of interaction analysis to teacher education

Instead of emphasizing knowledge which the teachers need in order to teach effectively one will turn more and more to an analysis of teaching acts as they occur in spontaneous classroom interaction. Flanders says, "The instructor's role will shift from talking about effective teaching to the rigorous challenge of demonstrating effective teaching."

Sample Matrix (Reproduced from Flanders)

Category	1	2	3	4	5	6	7	8	9	10	Total
1	—	—	—	1	—	—	—	—	—	—	1
2	1	—	—	6	5	—	—	—	—	—	12
3	—	—	8	17	4	1	—	1	1	—	32
4	—	—	—	14	3	—	1	38	48	—	104
5	—	1	—	26	62	8	5	—	1	2	105
6	—	—	—	5	5	13	—	—	1	3	27
7	—	1	—	2	4	—	3	1	—	2	13
8	—	5	9	15	6	—	3	4	2	—	44
9	—	4	14	17	13	2	1	—	13	2	66
10	—	1	1	1	3	3	—	—	—	8	17
Total	1	12	32	104	105	27	13	44	66	17	421
% ST	0.2	2.9	7.6	24.8	25.0	6.4	3.1	10.5	15.7	4.0	100
								Teacher T = 294 (294%)			
% TT	0.3	4.1	10.9	35.4	35.7	9.2	4.4	Students T = 110 (212%)			

"It will be the responsibility of the education instructor to help prospective teachers discover what their teaching intention should be and then create training situations in which behaviour gradually matches intention with practice. Teaching will remain an art but it will be studied scientifically."

Other applications

1. Verbal Interaction: The category system can be used for research in verbal interaction for pre-service and in-service education of teachers.

2. Flexibility: The concept of "flexibility of teacher influence" can be investigated.

3. Grouping: The technique may help in the grouping of students.

Training of Observers

Flanders has listed the following principles for classroom observations:

1. No interaction analysis data should be collected unless the person is familiar with the entire process and knows its limitations.
2. Questions to be answered by inspecting the matrix should be developed before the observation takes place.
3. Value judgments about good teaching behaviour are to be avoided.
4. Emphasis is to be given to the problem being investigated so that cause-and-effect relationship can be discovered.
5. A consultation based on two observations or at least two matrices helps to eliminate value judgments or at least control them. Comparisons between the matrices are more likely or lead to principles.

The procedure of observation

1. The observer sits in a classroom in the best position to hear and see the participants.
2. At the end of each three second period he decides which category best represents the communication events just completed.
3. He writes down this category number while simultaneously assessing communication in the next period and continues at a rate of 20 to 25 observations per minute, keeping his tempo as steady as possible.
4. His notes are merely a series of numbers written in a column, top to bottom so that the original sequence of events is preserved.
5. Occasionally marginal notes are used to explain the class formation or any unusual circumstances.
6. When there is a major change in class formation the communication pattern or the subject under discussion, a double line is drawn and the time indicated.
7. As soon as the total observation is completed, the observer retires to a nearby room and completes a general description of each separate activity, the class formation and the position of the teacher.

RECIPROCAL CATEGORY SYSTEM (RCS)

The reciprocal category system (R.C.S.) was developed by Richard Ober of the University of Florida, U.S.A. in 1967. This system is an adaptation or modification of the Flander's system.

Main Features of R.C.S.

1. There are nine categories which can be applied to student or teacher talk in a reciprocal way.
2. A general category in addition to these which concerns itself with silence and confusion.
3. The observation of classroom verbal interaction with a particular street on socio-emotional climate of the classroom is possible.
4. Provision for noting the warming and cooling behaviour of students and teachers in addition to the positive and negative reinforcement factors.

Reciprocal Category System

Teacher Category Talk No.	Description of Verbal Behaviour	Student Category Talk No.
1.	*"Warms"*: (Informalizes) the climate, tends to open up, eliminates the tension, praises or encourages the action, accepts and clarifies the feeling tone of another in a friendly manner.	11
2.	*Accepts:* accepts the action, behaviour, comments on idea of others, positive reinforcement to these.	12
3.	*Amplifies:* the contribution of another, asks for clarification of, builds on and develops the action, behaviour, comments, ideas and/or contributions of another.	13
4.	*Elicits:* asks a question regarding information about the content, subject or procedure with the intent that another should answer.	14
5.	*Responds:* gives direct answers of response to questions or requests for information that are initiated by another; includes answer to one's own questions.	
6.	*Initiates:* presents facts, information and/or opinions concerning the content, subject or procedures; expresses one's own ideas.	16
7.	*Directs:* gives directions, instructions, orders, and/or assignments to which another is excepted to comply.	17
8.	*Corrects:* tells another that his answer or behaviour is inappropriate or incorrect.	18

(Contd...)

9.	*"Cools":* (formalizes) the climate makes statements intended to modify the behaviour of another from an inappropriate to appropriate pattern, may tend to create a certain amount of tension.	19
10.	*Silence or Confusion:* pauses, short period of silence and periods of confusion in which communication cannot be understood by the observer.	20

QUESTIONS FOR EXERCISE

1. What is 'Classroom Interaction'? Describe any one method in detail of analyzing 'Classroom Interaction'.
2. What are the main dimensions of classroom interaction? How can these be manipulated to make teaching more effective?
3. Describe briefly Flander's technique of analyzing teaching behaviour? How does it help the teacher in improving his classroom performance?
4. Describe briefly Flanders technique of analyzing teaching behaviour. How is an interaction matrix prepared? What are the concepts of teacher influence which can be interpreted through this matrix?
5. Explain and discuss Reciprocal Category System.

38

Creativity

The cultural, scientific and the social progress of any country depends on the extent of the development of creativity among its citizens. Creative men and women are born in different social, economic and political circumstances. Now what is this creativity? What are the characteristics found in poets like Tulsidas and Kalidas by which their activity could be inferred? In the history of the world there had been several philosophers, poets, writers and painters who were turned out of their school classes, condemned as backward students, but who created great works in their later life. Hence, in modern times the progressive nations try to develop activity in their new generations. The concept of activity, therefore, occupies a very important place in educational psychology.

MEANING OF CREATIVITY

Psychologists have presented various definitions to explain the meaning of creativity. In 1953 Morgan pointed out 25 definitions of creativity scattered in literature. One thing was common in these definition and that was the uniqueness of creativity, though all the scientists do not consider uniqueness to be the necessary characteristic of activity. These definitions also reveal that there had been not one single criterion to define creativity. This is so since the researchers have looked to creativity from different aspects. In the process, the individual, the efforts and results of creativity different definitions have laid emphasis on one or the other aspect. Every researcher has studied creative behaviour from his own particular standpoint.

In 1911 Ink Blots of Binet were used for testing creativity. Since then different experiments conducted in this field have thrown light upon the nature of creativity. The following definitions of creativity will help in the understanding of its meaning.

(1) According to **Guilford**, "Creativity sometimes refers to creativity potential sometimes to creative production, and sometimes to creative productivity." Here creative potential means the personal disposition of the individual in which there are some more or less permanent qualities which help him in creative thinking. Creative thinking leads to new ideas. Creative production does not mean production of concrete things. It means the

processes of productive thinking. Creative productivity means productivity according to socially confirmed forms of words, thoughts and phrases, etc. This definition of creativity establishes creative thinking as its primary characteristic. Emphasising this element in creativity Medniks writes, "Creative thinking consists of forming new combinations of associative elements." The most important characteristic of creative thinking is the fact that in it one finds new types of associations in place of their more common varieties.

(2) Explaining the meaning of creativity, **Torrance** writes, "I have chosen to define creative thinking as the process of sensing gaps or disturbing, missing elements, forming ideas or hypotheses, and communicating the results, possibly modifying and retesting the hypotheses." According to this definition of creativity it is clear that it involves new hypotheses, their tests and constant modification. Further clarifying the process of creative thinking, Torrance has pointed out that in it first of all a need is felt, then the problem is defined and clarified. After this there is a period of preparation which involves reading, writing, discussion and research and gathering possible solutions of the problems. After this the pros and cons of different solutions are evaluated. In the end of this process some new idea emerges in the form of insight. This new solution is now examined and new researches are conducted on its basis which leads to the creation of new principles, methods, pictures, music, poems, etc. According to **C.V. Good**," ...the factors of creativity are tentatively described as associate and ideational fluency, originality, adaptive and spontaneous flexibility that make logical evolution."

(3) The most important characteristic of creativity is its divergence or novelty. In the words of **James Drever**, "Producing an essentially new product constructive (somewhat under) use of imagination where a new combination of ideas or images is constructed strictly when it is self-initiated, rather than imitated, also of thought synthesis, where the mental product is not a mere summation." Sir Fredric has named creativity as bold thinking. Bold thinking means divergent thinking, breaking of old norms, having new experience and creating new combinations. According to Simpson, creative thinking involves new forms of thinking away from the traditional forms. Thus creativity includes curiosity, imagination, research, novelty and invention etc. A.J. Cropley has considered divergence as the most important characteristic of creativity in his small booklet on this subject. According to him this one characteristic is sufficient to identify creative children from non-creative ones.

The above definitions of creativity point out that it means original thinking, new types of associations, divergent thinking and behaviour, new solutions of old problems, flexibility and a new approach in different fields of life. The creative person is very much aware of new problems. His thinking is dynamic, flexible, original and novel. He has more than average curiosity and is always busy in finding out new solutions of the traditional problems.

NATURE OF CREATIVITY

Nature of creativity can be derived from its meaning. Different theories have explained the nature of creativity differently. According to Psychoanalytic theory the creative person satisfies frustrated ambitions and desires through creative processes. According to associative theory the creative person forms new associations or recognizes old ones. According to Campbell creativity involves change and choice. According to Gestalt theory creative thinking involves change of central point, change of meaning and a novel organization. It involves insight which is the cause of sudden emergence of new ideas. Existentialists have presented a theory similar to the Gestalt theory. According to them creativity involves perception of new objects and struggle for understanding. In the words of May, "A creative act is a process, doing specifically, a process inter-relating the person and his world." The personalists defined creativity in terms of inter-personal relationship. In the words of C.R. Roger, "Creativity is an emergence in action of novel relational product, growing out of the uniqueness of the individual on the one hand, the materials, events, people or circumstances of his life on the other." The Trait theory considers particular trait as characteristic of creativity. For example, according to Guilford the most important traits of creativity are consciousness of the problem, continuity of thinking, continuity of words, continuity of association, continuity of expression, flexibility of thinking and accommodation, originality and re-definition, etc.

The above discussion of the views of different theories concerning creativity makes it clear that each theory has laid emphasis upon a particular aspect of creativity. Each theory clarifies a particular aspect of creativity better than others. Every theory is one-sided and none defines creativity from every aspect. The following characteristics of creativity summarize its nature:

1. Commitment towards problems: In order to be creative, a person should be very well aware of the problems in his circumstances. Without this commitment towards problems he cannot have creative thinking. A creative person is aware of the problems present in his circumstances and makes every effort to find out new solutions to these problems.

2. Dynamic thinking: The creative person not only thinks creativity but his thinking constantly changes according to new circumstances. He has more capacity of adjustment, but this adjustment is sought through new combinations.

3. Divergent thinking: The most important characteristic of creatively is divergent thinking. An average person is a convergent thinker because he thinks in terms of approved social behaviour. Convergent thinking means that in it thinking is done on the basis of traditional methods leading to traditional solutions. In it the thinker depends on old learning and mechanically fits old responses in new circumstances. It has been, therefore, rightly called closed thinking. Divergent thinking, on the other hand, is open thinking. It involves continuity, flexibility and originality. These traits can be observed in the works of great scientists, philosophers and literary thinkers. In our time tests have been devised to measure creativity. These tests have established divergent thinking as the main sign of creativity. It should be remembered here that all types of anti-traditional behaviour cannot be termed creative behaviour. In order to be creative, divergence is not a sufficient trait either in thinking or in behaviour. Young men and women wearing clothes which do not confirm to social norms are hardly creative. On the other hand, many creative persons wear socially approved dress and appear to be absolutely convergent in their normal behaviour. It may be said that opposition of traditions is one of the signs of creative process, which is not a necessary element of it. Sometimes, some traits helpful in creativity have been themselves considered to be creative. For example, high I.O., developed verbal skill have been taken as creative though at best these are only traits useful in creativity.

4. Useful results: Thus besides being divergent, creativity leads to useful results. It is hence that a certain new idea gives immense pleasure to the thinker. It is hence again that creativity impresses every one. Nellar has called this trait as relevance. According to Brunor a creative product must be impressive. It is hence that the creative person is absolutely involved in his work.

5. Flexibility: An important characteristic of creativity is flexibility of thinking and behaviour. Most of the people are never prepared to re-examine their attitudes, habits, ways of behaviour, etc. They utilize old solutions to solve new problems in every situation, without caring about the novelty of the present situations. The creative person, on the other hand, is always prepared to adopt new attitude, idea or behaviour. It is hence that he succeeds in finding out new solutions to problems.

6. Originality: Originality, therefore, is a necessary trait of creativity. A creative person is not confined to ideas or experiences, read or heard. He is always prepared to conduct new experiments. He uses new ideas, new attitudes and new methods. It is natural that sometimes he falls into great difficulties, but the result of his courage is achieved in the form of originality.

7. Curiosity: In order to achieve the above mentioned traits of creativity, the creative person should have sufficient curiosity. It is due to curiosity that a person is anxious to know new things in any field. It is due to curiosity again that he seeks to utilize new methods. It is due to curiosity that the scientists, philosophers and artists find out new facts which ultimately lead to the new creations. Curiosity leads to divergence in perception, thinking and behaviour.

8. Ability to go beyond the immediate circumstances: An ordinary person is generally confined to his immediate environment and circumstance, he cannot rise above it. A creative person, on the other hand, has the ability to go beyond the immediate circumstances and show novelty in thinking and behaviour. He has the capacity to behave in a way different from the general way of behaviour in a particular situation. It is hence that these are known as creative persons.

9. Reinterpretation of the problem or its part: In order to find out new solutions it is necessary that the problem should be looked from a new point of view. Hence re-interpreation of the problem or its part is a characteristic of creativity. Allen Nevil, J.C. Shaw and Herbert Simon have considered the following as important elements in the creative solution of a problem:

(*i*) The object of thinking should be novel and valuable.

(*ii*) Thinking should be divergent.

(*iii*) Thinking should be highly motivated and constant.

(*iv*) The problem should be confused and undefined. It is only in the case of the above characteristic that problem solving can be creative.

10. Harmony of abnormal and relevant thinking: According to Guilford, creative children are those who accommodate with relevant but abnormal thinking through creative thinking, reasoning and imagination. They accept the challenge and give a creative reply to it.

11. Creative personality: In the end the nature of creativity can be understood through the traits of active personality. The most important traits in a creative personality are: capacity of original thinking, independence of judgement, curiosity, sensitivity, autonomy and humor. In his book *creativity and personality*, C.R. Parmesh has drawn the following conclusions on the basis of his research into the nature of creative personality:

(*i*) The highly creative individuals are neither significantly more nor less introverted than the low-creative individuals.

(*ii*) The highly creative individuals are not significantly different from the low creative individuals in the level of anxiety.

(*iii*) The high-creative individuals are significantly higher in ego-strength as evidenced by body-image barrier characteristics than the low-creative individuals. The high-creatives, however, are not significantly different from the low-creative individuals in body-image penetration characteristics.

(*iv*) The high-creative individuals are significantly higher on theoretical and aesthetic values as compared to the low-creative individuals.

Research on creativity

Research on creativity started in 1911 in the form of tests of creative thinking. Ink blot tests of Binet were used to find out creative ability in children. In 1915 Whipple introduced a new test for uncontrolled association. In 1916, Chassel used a number of tests for originality. In 1919, Corbett invented the factors of cleverness in the study of ratings of several personality traits. In 1927, Hargreaves found a difference in the fluency factor and originality factors. In 1898, Dearborn found that tests involving productive imagination had low correction with intelligence. This was supported by Chassel in 1916, Andrews in 1930 and Welch in 1946. In 1906, Terman recognized creativity as a cognitive variable. During the period since 1930 to 1950 not much research was conducted in the field of creativity. In 1950, Guilford drew the attention of scholars to creativity in his presidential address to American Psychological Association.

After this research in the field of creativity advanced with speed. In 1953, Guilford tried to systematise the dimensions of creative thinking. In 1963, Thorndike experimented upon the relationship of creativity and intelligence. In 1946 Ward supported the contention of Thorndike that there is a positive correlation between intelligence and creativity. These studies led to the conclusion that creativity is not absolutely free from intelligence. After this many psychologists experimented upon different factors which are considered to be the essential elements of creativity. In 1962. Torrance established the relationship of creativity and general intelligence. Among the experiments concerning the correlation of intelligence and creativity, were those of Cicirelli in 1964, Yamamoto in 1965 and Perry in 1969. All these studies were summarised by Torrance to show that there is no absolute correlation between intelligence and creativity.

Study by Getzels and Jackson

The first systematic study to distinguish between creativity and intelligence was on adolescents by Getzels and Jackson in 1952. This study attracted wide attention among scientists and the later researchers constantly remembered the results of this study. Creativity is a particular mental ability which is clear from the paper and pencil tests of the adolescents. These tests included verbal and numeral science, object space relationship, etc. According to these studies creativity depends upon the number, novelty and variety of responses to a given stimuli. They maintained that the traditional intelligence tests measure convergent and traditional mental processes involving memory. In fact these two processer are so intimately related that it is difficult to find out persons who are higher in one and not so in the other.

In the course of this study Getzels and Jackson selected two groups of subjects in which in one group the level of intelligence was high but creativity was not so much present. In the other group, the level of creativity was high but the level of intelligence was not as high as that. The study led to the conclusion that the traditional tests of intelligence are not the sufficient tests of mental processes. Low correlation was found between creativity and intelligence tests. The scientists however maintained that creativity and intelligence are different since they observed that among the creative and intelligence group there was a clear distinction of personal values, imaginative productivity, aims of career and the family background. This study has been widely criticised on the basis of method and other factors.

In 1962, Burt raised objection to the measurement of intelligence and selection of sample in this study. According to Burt creativity should be counted within general intelligence. This view was supported by Vernon in 1964. Since 1963 to 1965 Hudson in his studies of High School Children supported the conclusions arrived at by Getzels and Jackson. According to March (1964) the methods adopted in this study were not satisfactory and creativity is a factor in intelligence. In 1965, Wallach and Kogan showed that Getzels and Jackson have failed to establish a dimension of creativity independent of general intelligence. In 1966, Hasan and Butcher tested Higher Secondary students of

Scotland on a basis wider than that of Getzels and Jackson. This study aimed at finding out the relationships between creativity, intelligence and achievement. It established high correlation between creativity and I.Q. In 1965, Wallach and Kogan pointed out that creativity is different from intelligence. On the basis of their study they maintained that creativity involves some traits which are not found in the traditional concepts of intelligence. In 1967 Ward, in 1968 Cropley and in 1969 Wallach and Wing supported that contention.

Relation of creativity and personality

Besides the above studies of the relationship between creativity and intelligence, several psychologists studied the relationship between creativity and personality. In their study Getzels and Jackson have pointed out that the highly creative and highly intelligent adolescents differ not only in mental processes but also in temperament. In 1965, Wallach and Kogan clarified the interaction of personality and creativity. In 1969, Freeman concluded that creativity is not so much different from traits of intelligence as from unintelligent processes.

The first systematic idea of the relationship between creativity and personality is found in the works of Sigmund Freud. After him in 1952 Kris supported the idea of Freud that creativity is born in mental conflict. Similar ideas were presented by Klein, Beliak and Kubie in 1958. In 1965, Berlyne pointed out that more mental conflict leads to higher creativity and a more creative person is determined to solve more difficult problems. In 1937, Allport pointed out that creativity is expressed in functional autonomy in the individual. In 1939, Goldstein maintained that there is an effective tendency of self-expression through creative processes found among creative persons. In 1959, Rogers showed that the creative person has a particular tendency to struggle with the environment. In the same year May demonstrated that the creative person seeks self-expression in the world. According to Rogers creativity is openness to experience. According to Maslow in creativity one finds harmony between contradictory traits of personality. According to Barron the creative person is habitually original. All these studies established the fact that personality is intimately connected with creativity. Therefore, in 1963 Golann emphasised that personality variables can be used in the study of creativity. From Galton to present day many scientists have tried to point out traits of creativity and personality by the analysis of the biographies of creative persons. According to Galton the most important characteristic of famous and genius persons is the originality of their ideas. Ellis pointed out that among these persons one does not find mental symptoms more than the average.

In 1954, Terman showed by his studies that the more successful persons exhibit self-confidence, competition, leadership, sensitivity, social adaptation, mental stability, freedom and balanced temperament, etc. According to the study of Roe, a painter is better adjusted than other persons. Similar conclusions were arrived at concerning the scientists. Cattell pointed out in his studies that the scientific researchers are emotionally unstable and busy in their job. Other scientists have supported the ideas of Cattell. According to them, creative person is more introvert, thoughtful and having a dominant ego. Some other researchers have studied the personality traits of creative persons in other fields of occupation. Thus the personalities of artists, sculptors, painters, architects, scientific researchers, industrial inventors and creative teachers have been studied. Such studies have been conducted not only in the West but also in India. All these studies establish that the creative person is more sensitive than the average and his ego is more dominant. He is more ambitious and more thoughtful. No distinction in creativity was observed on the basis of distinction of sex. Similarly, no correlation was found in age and creativity.

Conditions of creativity

What was that in the life of Rabindra Nath which led to make him a great poet? What are the conditions which make a person a great artist like Piccasso? How does a person become a great novelist like Prem Chand? Such questions have been often raised by thoughtful persons since society has been amply benefited by poets, artists and novelists, etc. Though science could not find out the mechanism by which creative persons can be made but psychologists have pointed out conditions favourable for the growth of creativity. Of these the most important are as follows:

1. Detachment and commitment: In order to do anything effectively the individual should be capable of doing some original work with determination. Thus the capacity to be distinct from the general is a necessary condition of creativity. Trilling has referred to the detachment of poet with the society. This helps the individual to search within himself. Scientists are notorious for their unsociability. Many great authors have been cut off from society for very long periods during which they were absolutely engrossed with their work. For example, Sri Aurobindo, during his 35 years stay at Pondicherry, was visible to the outside people only 4 times a year. This detachment is only the other aspect of commitment. Without commitment it has no use. In fact the scientist or the artist who is absolutely engrossed in his work has to be detached with the society for the time being. This is as much true about a creative person as about a creative group.

2. Passion and decorum: The creative person has the desire and ability to express his emotions and tendencies through his work. It is hence said that the artist has a passion towards art. It is due to passion that he can put in so much efforts in creative direction. No one can do much in a field with the attitude of detachment to his work. Creative work not only involves interest but also passion. Helvetrus has rightly said, "...a man without passion is incapable of that degree of attention to which a superior judgment is annexed, a superiority that is perhaps less the effect of an extra-ordinary effort than an habitual attention." Thus, it is clear that the creative person has an intense passion for his particular job. But passion or ability alone are not sufficient. Creative work involves a balance, a decorum and a respect towards things and persons. In the absence of this again no high creativity is possible.

3. Autonomy of object: In the beginning a creative person starts some creative process but later on this activity itself takes him further. Therefore, the creative person should have the freedom to follow the guidance of his object. Thus, in the beginning what is a part of the mind of the creative person, later on, after expression, becomes an external object which has its own demand, its own freedom and norms. The creative person has now to follow the object which is autonomous though in the beginning it was created by the creative persons.

4. Deferral and immediacy: The creative activity sometimes involves a deferral of an activity and at other times immediate fulfilment of it. When should there be deferral and when should it be immediately fulfilled depends on the insight of the creative person but high creativity involves both. It is observed that an artist does nothing for a very long period and then in a passion he immediately fulfils the deferred work.

5. The internal drama: Creativity depends on the internal drama of the creative person. Every person has several elements in him—the ascetic elements, the child, the ego, the social elements, etc. The level of creativity is determined by the interaction of all these elements.

6. Abilities: Creativity requires several abilities such as intelligence, attention, organization, etc. Different types of creative processes require different types of abilities.

7. Conditions of creative thinking: Creativity involves creative thinking. Its characteristics are factuality, novelty, freedom and harmony. Creative thinking requires several conditions. First of all there should be the capacity to grasp new ideas. Secondly, there should be the ability of involvement with the object. Thirdly, the creative person should be able to understand the questions involved in the given problem, since only then he can arrive at the solutions. Fourthly, the creative person should learn from past failures and reform his thinking. Fifthly, he should have the capacity of detachment from the environment.

8. Traits of creative personality: One can be creative only if he has traits of creative personality. A creative person does not follow the tradition, he finds out his own path. He does not see the facts as average people do. His insight is deeper and divergent. It is hence that he arrives at new meanings of the given facts. He does not follow ordinary taboos, he has the capacity to take risk and he is not afraid of thinking on new formulae. In other words he is a bold thinker, his thinking is flexible and dynamic. Even the most hard job is like a play to him. He has a jolly and witty attitude and attends to funny aspects of life. Though his ego is dominant yet sometimes he is capable of extricating himself from the control of ego. As compared to others he expresses his tendencies much more and does not care about the social norms in this process. Thus he is a divergent person. Whereas he has a capacity to control his passions, he has an equal capacity of forceful expression of it. This expression again is revolt, lack of system and freedom of judgment but this does not mean that they are free from all repression. Many creative persons have shown much more repression than average persons and yet generally speaking, a creative person is independent, original, free and playful. He finds out new meanings of already known facts.

9. Creativity and family conditions: Some particular family conditions are more favourable for the development of creativity. As a general rule if the parents possess mental and personality traits of creativity they are likely to be inherited by the children. In families favourable to creativity, children will be given freedom of self-determination. They do not emphasize security and social control but give them sufficient opportunity to choose according to their intellects. They do not give advice about the right and wrong but respect the opinion of the children. They do not emphasize obedience but follow the policy of *Laissez Faire* in the matters concerning children. In brief they take children as respectable human beings and provide them every opportunity to grow freely.

10. Cultural conditions: It is clear from the above discussion that such cultures will be more favourable for the growth of creativity in which traits favourable to creativity are more easily available such as freedom, divergent thinking, emotionality, playfulness and originality, etc. On the contrary, cultures in which there is more rigid social control and less occasions for freedom and originality do not provide favourable conditions for the growth of the creativity.

Identification of talented and creative students

The future of any country depends on the identification of creativity in the new generation and effort for its growth. In every field of life such as mechanical, scientific, academic and artistic, creative people die and new persons are required to substitute them. If this need is not fulfilled the progress of the country in that particular field is retarded. In fact only that society can be called an ideal society in which maximum number of members get maximum opportunity for the growth of creativity. This, however, requires identification of talented and creative children. Psychologists have developed some methods for this purpose. In U.S.A. Robert F. DeHaan and Jack Rough published in 1956 a hand book entitled *Identifying Students With Special Needs.* In this teacher's guidance hand-book, characteristics for identification of talented and creative students were mentioned in details. This hand-book was utilized in collaboration with more usual tests for identification. The teacher can identify talented and creative students on the basis of his observations and tests provided in this hand-book. In this connection the teacher should not make haste in putting labels upon children. He should, however, closely observe their behaviour and secretly classify them in particular group. In this connection he should remember the following principles:[1]

1. Give each student equal consideration on each behaviour characteristic.
2. Observe each student in a variety of situations.
3. Compare each youngster with the rest of the group.

1. Robert, F. DeHann and Jack Kough, *Identifying Students With Special Needs* (1965), Science Research Associates, Inc., Chicago, pp. 12-13.

4. Be aware of your own biases.
5. Choose areas of particular concern to you.

Keeping in mind the above mentioned principles every teacher should observe one particular trait in a student at a particular time according to the principles of observation. He should remain free from all types of prejudices. He should keep a register about the students and note his observation in it. He should remember that talented children have specific problems, abilities and disabilities. He should constantly check his list. He will find that the number of talented children is much less than the average. While on an average 5% children are backward, 15 to 20% may be classified among gifted children. The sooner the process of identification of creativity among students starts the better it is. In this process besides observations, cumulative records, standardized tests, informal tests and observation in specific circumstances together with the opinion of the child guide in the school are helpful. Besides these data the teacher can find out facts about students from their friends and relatives. It should be remembered here that a talented student is not necessarily better than other students in every field of life. Talented students are generally divergent and therefore some of the teachers are against them. They may appear to be more lazy than others and yet they may be classed as talented. In an average class 15% to 20% students may be classed as talented. It is from among this group that the future artists, musicians, writers, actors and leaders are born. The students may depict different types of abilities such as Intellectual, Scientific, Leadership, Creative, Artistic, Writing, Dramatic, Musical, Mechanical and Physical skill. The following are the important points concerning identification of students with these abilities:

1. Identification of student with Intellectual ability: Intellectual ability depends both on heredity and environment. It cannot be developed purely by environment but without proper environment again, it cannot be properly developed. If both the heredity and environment are negative no one can develop intellectual ability. Robert F. DeHaan and Jack Kough have given list of identifying characteristics of intellectual ability which includes:[1]

1. Learns rapidly and easily
2. Uses a great deal of common sense and practical knowledge.
3. Reasons things out. Thinks clearly Recognizes relationships Comprehends meanings.
4. Retains what he has heard or read without much rote drill.
5. Knows about many things of which most students are unware.
6. Has a large vocabulary, which he uses easily and accurately.
7. Can read books that are one to two years in advance of the rest of the class.
8. Performs difficult mental tasks.
9. Asks many questions. Has a wide range of interests.

---

1. *Ibid.*, p. 30.

10. Does some academic work one or two years in advance of the class.
11. Is original in his thinking, uses good but unusual methods.
12. Is alert, keenly observant and responds quickly.

Besides these characteristics the teacher can supplement his observation by the study of cumulative records, uses standardized tests, etc.

2. Identifying students with scientific ability: Today every progressive country needs scientific ability in almost every field of life and therefore there is a constant effort for the identification of students with scientific ability. According to Robert F. DeHaan and Jack Kough the list of identifying characteristics for scientific ability include:[1]

1. Expressing himself clearly and accurately either through writing or speaking.
2. Reads one to two years ahead of his class.
3. Is one to two years ahead of his class in mathematical ability.
4. Has greater than average ability to grasp abstract concepts and see abstract relationships.
5. Has good motor, co-ordination, especially eye-hand co-ordination, can do fine, precise manipulations.
6. Is willing to spend time beyond ordinary assignments or schedule on things that are of interest to him.
7. Is not easily discouraged by failure of experiments or projects.
8. Wants to know the causes and reasons for things.
9. Spends much of his time on special projects of his own, such as making collections, constructing a radio, making a telescope.
10. Reads a good deal of scientific literature and finds satisfaction in thinking about and discussions of scientific affairs.

Observations of these characteristics may be supplemented by the study of cumulative records and use of standardized tests.

3. Identifying students with leadership ability: Leadership is of several kinds. Qualities of leadership are required in the fields of science, industry, government, art, sports, etc. In every class some students lead others. They have leadership ability and from among them develop future leaders of society. They have some qualities which are not found among other students. These identifying characteristics are:[2]

1. Is liked and respected by most of the members of the class.
2. Is able to influence others to work towards desirable goals.
3. Is able to influence others to work towards undesirable goals.
4. Can take charge of the group.
5. Can judge the abilities of other students and find a place for them in the group's activities.

---

1. *Ibid.*, p. 33.
2. *Ibid.*, pp. 35-36.

6. Is able to figure out what is wrong with an activity and show others how to do it better.
7. Is often asked for ideas and suggestions.
8. Is looked to by others when something must be decided.
9. Seems to sense what others want and helps them to accomplish it.
10. Is a leader in several kinds of activities.
11. Enters into activities with contagious enthusiasm.
12. Is elected to offices.

Observations of these traits may be supplemented by the study of cumulative records and sociometric tests.

4. Identifying students with creative ability: Though in a way all individuals are creative but 10% individuals show more creative ability. These can be identified on the basis of the following characteristics:[1]

1. Always seems to be full of new ideas pertaining to most subjects.
2. Invents things or creates original stories, plays, poetry, tunes, sketches, and so on.
3. Can use materials, words or ideas in new ways.
4. Sees flaws in things, including his own work and can suggest better ways to do a job or reach an objective.
5. Is willing to experiment to get answers.
6. Asks many questions. Shows a great deal of intellectual curiosity.
7. Is flexible and open-minded. Is willing to try one method after another and to change his mind if need be. Is not afraid of new ideas and will examine them before rejecting them.

Observations about these traits may be supplemented by the study of cumulative records and by giving informal tests.

5. Identifying students with artistic talent: In every class there are some students who show more artistic talent and whose artistic creations are better than others. These students with artistic talent, can be identified on the basis of following characteristics:[2]

1. Covers a variety of subjects in his drawings or paintings.
2. Takes art work seriously. Seems to find much satisfaction in it.
3. Shows originality in choice of subjects, technique and composition.
4. Is willing to try out new materials and experience.
5. Fills extra-time with drawing, painting and sculpturing activities.
6. Uses art to express his own experiences and feelings.
7. Is interested in other people's art work.
8. Likes to model with clay, carve, or work with other forms of three dimensional art.

---

1. *Ibid.*, pp. 35-36.
2. *Ibid.*, pp. 38-39.

Observations of these traits may be supplemented by the study of cumulative records and by giving special art assignments and standardized tests.

6. Identifying students with writing talent: In every class some students exhibit better writing talents. Writing talent includes writing of different types of letters, report, etc., besides original creative writing. Writing talent can be identified on the basis of the following characteristics:[1]

1. Can develop a story from its beginning, through the build up and climax, to an interesting conclusion.
2. Gives a refreshing twist, even to old ideas.
3. Uses only necessary details in telling a story, keeps the ideas organized within his story.
4. Choose descriptive words that other youngsters miss, and still gets across the central idea.
5. Enjoys writing stories and poems.
6. Makes the characters seem life-like. Captures the feelings of his characters in writing.

These observations can be supplemented by the study of cumulative records and by giving story telling and writing assignments.

7. Identifying students with dramatic talent: In every class some students express dramatic talents and derive pleasure in taking part in dramatic activities. These students have dramatic talents which can be identified on the basis of following characteristics:[2]

1. Readily shifts into the role of another character.
2. Shows interest in dramatic activities.
3. Uses voice to reflect changes of idea and mood.
4. Understands and portrays the conflict in a situation when given the opportunity to act out a dramatic event.
5. Communicates feelings by means of facial expressions, gestures, and bodily movements.
6. Enjoys evoking emotional responses from listeners.
7. Shows unusual ability to dramatize feelings and experiences.
8. Moves a dramatic situation to a climax and brings to it a well timed conclusion when telling a story.
9. Gets a good deal of satisfaction and happiness from plays acting or dramatizing.
10. Writes original plays or makes up plays from stories.
11. Can imitate others. Mimics people and animals.

These observations can be supplemented by the study of cumulative records and introduction of dramatic devices.

1. *Ibid.*, pp. 41-42.
2. *Ibid.*, p. 44-45.

8. Identifying students with musical talent: Musical talent can be identified by the following list of characteristics:[1]

1. Responds more than others to rhythm and melody.
2. Sings well.
3. Puts verve and vigour into his music.
4. Buys records. Goes out of his way to listen to music.
5. Enjoys harmonizing with others to singing in group.
6. Uses music to express his feelings and experiences.
7. Makes up original tunes.
8. Plays one or more musical instrument well.

These observations may be supplemented by the study of cumulative records, introduction of musical activities and application of standardized tests.

9. Identifying student with mechanical skills: Every progressive country needs today thousands of persons with mechanical skills. This growing need can be fulfilled only if students with mechanical skills are identified. This identification is possible on the basis of the following list:[2]

1. Does good work on craft projects.
2. Is interested in mechanical gadgets and machines.
3. Has a hobby involving mechanical devices such as radios, model trains, construction sets.
4. Can repair gadgets. Can put together mechanical things.
5. Comprehends mechanical problems, puzzles and trick questions.
6. Likes to draw plants and make sketches of mechanical objects.
7. Reads *Popular Mechanics* or other magazines or books on mechanical subjects.

These observations can be supplemented by the study of cumulative records, introduction of special projects and application of standardized tests.

10. Identifying students with physical skills: In the field of games and sports those students excel who have specific physical skills. In the modern times competition in the field of sports and games on National and International level requires the identification of students with physical skills in every country. This can be done on the basis of the following list:[3]

1. Is energetic and seems to need considerable exercise to stay happy.
2. Enjoys participating in highly competitive physical games.
3. Is consistently outstanding in many kinds of competitive games.
4. Is one of the fastest runners in the class.
5. Is one of the best co-ordinate, physically in the class.

---

1. *Ibid.*, p. 47.
2. *Ibid.*, p. 49.
3. *Ibid.*, p. 52.

6. Likes outdoor sports, hiking and camping.
7. Is willing to spend much time practising physical activities such as shooting baskets, playing tennis or base ball, or swimming.

These observations can be supplemented by the study of cumulative records and application of sociometric tests.

EDUCATIONAL PROVISIONS FOR CREATIVITY

Thus in progressive countries constant efforts are being made to identify talented and creative students. It is a matter of regret that some teachers are more attracted towards non-creative students, as they show convergent behaviour while the creative students are looked down because of their divergent behaviour. The creative students look to everything from new standpoint, raise new questions and therefore create a source of displeasure for the teacher. This, however, does not mean that creative behaviour is mischievous. Mischief is different from creativity since, while the former is harmful the latter is useful both for the person himself and for others, though it may appear as a revolt against traditions. In fact, the creative students keep the teacher standing on his feet since he is constantly inspired by them to improve his ability. They break discipline, do all sort of uncalled for things, waste valuable time and raise new question which cannot be easily answered and even sometimes indulge in divergent behaviour for pure humour or play. All these lead to their rebuke by the teacher but he does not know that it is precisely from among these students that the future leaders of the country in every path of life are born. In traditional classes teacher's behaviour is generally anti-creativity, but if the teacher is a nation builder in the true sense of the term, he should encourage creative talents even if sometimes he may have to bear difficulties and personal insults. Researches in the field of creativity in the last few years have demonstrated the important role of schools in the development of creativity. Hence, the teacher should do it with a patience and even if some time is wasted. He should not lay too much emphasis upon discipline and proper behaviour. He should remember that success in achievement in traditional examinations is not the only criterion of ability. He should realize the limitations of his evaluation. He should not only tolerate divergent behaviour but positively encourage it. He should evaluate himself and respect creative thinking. Only then will be encouraged new ideas, creative thinking, self-initiative, new experiments, constructive criticism, new knowledge and adventure in new fields.

Studies by Torrance and Myers during 1970-71 in the field of creativity have revealed important things concerning creative teacher. Some of the most effective principles facilitating creative learning are as follows:

1. Warm up: creativity by getting creativity.
2. Divergent thinking made acceptable.
3. Freedom from threat of evaluation.
4. Invitation to regress.

5. Freedom from inhibiting sets.
6. Psychologically and physically comfortable.

In 1962, Torrance advanced the following suggestions for improving creativity:

1. Value creative thinking.
2. Help children become more sensible to environmental stimuli.
3. Encourage manipulation of objects and ideas.
4. Teach how to test each idea systematically.
5. Develop tolerance of new ideas.
6. Beware of forcing a set pattern.
7. Develop a creative classroom atmosphere.
8. Teach the child to value his creative thinking.
9. Teach children skills of avoiding of copying with sanctions without sacrificing their creativity.
10. Give information about the creative process.
11. Dispel the sense of awe of masterpiece.
12. Encourage and evaluate self-initiated learning.
13. Create "thorns in the flesh", making children aware of problems and deficiencies.
14. Create necessities for creative thinking.
15. Provide for active and quiet periods.
16. Make available resources for working out ideas.
17. Encourage the habit of working out the full implications of ideas.
18. Develop skills of constructive criticism.
19. Encourage acquisition of knowledge in a variety of fields.
20. Be adventurous-spirited yourself.

Besides these, Hallman (1967) has also suggested some aids to creative teaching. These are:

1. Provide for self-initiated learning.
2. Set up no-authoritarian learning environments.
3. Encourage pupils to over-learn.
4. Encourage creative thought processes.
5. Defer judgment.
6. Promote intellectual flexibility.
7. Encourage self-evaluation.
8. Help students to become more sensitive.
9. Make use of the questions.
10. Provide opportunities for students to manipulate materials, ideas, concepts, tools and structures.
11. Assist students in coping with frustration and failure.
12. Encourage pupils to consider problems as a whole, to emphasize total structures rather than the piecemeal additive elements.

Writing in the *Journal of Creative Behaviour* Burnswick (1971) proposes his ten commandments to creative teaching. These are:

1. Thou shalt not acknowledge ANY blindly accepted answers by students but shall become a wondering, questioning echo saying, "Is it ?... Are you sure?... How can you tell... Did it?"
2. Thou shalt bite the tongue every time thou wants to settle a disagreement between two children quickly by telling them the right answer.
3. Thou shalt turn thy ears upon HIGHEST to be sure thou doesn't miss any child's comment which might lead to a self-initiated learning opportunity.
4. Thou shall not remove the strings from thy finger to always remind thou to let the learning come from the children's interests, the children's motivations, the children's wonderings.
5. Thou shalt write on the blackboard 100 times, I must not let an alarm clock run my classroom activities.
6. Thou shalt honour thy own 'crazy' ideas, curiosity and divergent thinking to cultivate a taste for those of others.
7. Thou shalt hold the breath until the feeling passes if thou ever feels like saying, "we don't have time to waste or fool around with this idea."
8. Thou shalt remember to make every day, the day to offer that encouraging word, that part of security, that sample of comfort.
9. Thou shalt not commit thyself to rigidity in contents, methods or materials.
10. Thou shalt recite these every day so that thou will come to practise what thou preaches.

Besides the above principles about the improvements of abilities among students it is felt that this presupposes helping teachers themselves to improve certain skills. In 1967, Torrance suggested the following principles needed for improving teacher's skills:

1. Recognizing and acknowledging potentialities.
2. Being respectful to questions and ideas.
3. Asking provocative questions.
4. Recognizing and valuing originality.
5. Developing elaboration ability.
6. Unevaluated practice and experimentation.
7. Developing creative readers.
8. Predicting behaviour
9. Guided planned experiences.
10. Searching for the truth with methods of research.
11. Creative problem solving skills.

In 1970, Torrance suggests several principles or strategies useful prior to a lesson, during the process of a lesson and finally following a lesson, these principles thus help the teacher in improving his performance at every stage. Many other psychologists including Williams, Davis and Scott, Taylor and Osborn have advanced methods and strategies useful for the teacher to improve his teaching. Elaborate suggestions have been given by Torrance as to how a teacher can become a creative teacher. Researches have been conducted on creative teaching in different fields of education. Besides these, Jack Kough and Robert F. DeHaan have published for teacher's guidance *Handbook For Helping Students With Special Needs*. This handbook gives elaborate instructions as to how gifted and talented students should be helped to develop their particular abilities. A brief review of the suggestions given in this book is as follows:

1. Helping students with intellectual ability: This requires class-room enrichment, acceleration, ability giving and examination of the teacher's own attitudes and goals and about gifted students. It requires physical arrangements and materials. Steps to enrich teaching courses should be based on the following principles:[1]

1. Prune your curriculum.
2. Re-examine your teaching methods.
3. Consider your gifted youngsters as your own special project for the year, whether you work with one student or more.
4. Establish goals and select techniques.
5. Discuss the plan with the individual student.
6. Plan with the gifted students as a group.
7. Use large, flexible teaching units.

It also requires an enrichment technique which includes individual research, reporting the research, learning by listening to the reports of others and evaluating any of these things. The students should be encouraged to ask questions. They may be enriched by tours to famous men, Scenes from history, Miniature government, Information please, meet the critic, Treasure chest of words. Exploring in science, Citizenship in action, The origins of words, Inventions of games, The changing world, We are there, My own theory, Our city of tomorrow, Conversion piece, Wall newspaper, Construction of magic squares, A world of different dimensions, Elementary statistic, etc.

2. Helping students with scientific ability: The first step in this process requires identification of scientifically gifted students. Then teacher's own feeling towards science should be checked. He should know the scientific method and stimulate its use in the classes of different subjects. The following suggestions are useful for enrichment of scientifically gifted students:[2]

1. Encourage library research.
2. Set high standards of achievement.
3. Encourage experimentation.

---

1. Jack Kough and Robert F. DeHaan, *Helping Students With Special Needs* (1957), Science Research Associates Inc., Chicago, pp. 15-17.

2. *Ibid.*, pp. 36-38.

4. Have students make a study of the various branches of science.
5. Get others to help stimulate the youngster's scientific interest.
6. Acquaint the student with opportunities outside the school.
7. Contact the student's family.

Special sections should be created for gifted students in science. Physical facilities should be provided and all sort of encouragement given.

3. Helping students with leadership ability: We need leaders in every field of life. Leaders are men with drive and energy, a sense of responsibility, enthusiasm, a pleasing personality, the desire to lead and several other traits. Leadership skills include ability to make a formal presentation, ability to conduct meetings by parliamentary procedure, ability to organize, ability to lead a discussion. In democratic societies leadership includes democratic attitude which means sensitivity to individual and group needs, concern for the individual and respect for the majority. Leaders can be trained both individually and in group, which require different techniques. Teachers should avoid some common mistakes such as negligence about leadership, too much advice, hindrance to leadership, lack of encouragement, etc.

4. Helping students with creative ability: The first step in this direction is of course identification of creative individual. This identification may be done by the most important marks such as intellectual curiosity, self-confidence, energy, positive attitudes towards work, sense of humour, sustained interest and motivation. The next step for the teacher is to check his own attitude towards creative students. The creative process includes four stages—Preparation, Incubation, Insight and Finding out. All these stages must be encouraged to improve creativity. In this connection the following suggestions may be helpful in fostering creativity in classroom:[1]

1. It is essential that you establish a classroom atmosphere that is conducive to creativity, where students will feel free to develop new ideas.
2. A great share of the training for creativity lies in removing any stumbling blocks.
3. Independent thought needs to be encouraged.
4. Creativity needs to have freedom from restrictive time limit.
5. Creativity is nurtured by experience.
6. Help your students to get the 'big picture'.
7. Preparation is basic to creative ability in any given field.
8. Encourage the imaginative flights of youngsters.
9. Obtain equipment necessary for certain types of creative activity.
10. Help your students get the habit of writing down their creative ideas.
11. Help your students understand the creative process.
12. The problem-solving approach to situations is the seedbed of creative activity.

---

1. *Ibid.*, pp. 57-59.

13. Motivation is extremely important in stimulating creativity. Classroom exercises and creative topics should be suggested in the classroom. Parents should be helped to encourage creativity.

5. Helping students with artistic talent: First of all, a stage for artistic expression should be set in the educational institution. Encouragement of artistic talent involves the following:[1]

1. Encourage students with talent to incorporate visual materials in their reports and to develop some from which the entire class can learn, posters, charts, murals, displays.
2. Through the techniques of full and free classroom discussions, help youngsters become aware of their feelings and impressions.
3. Be generous but judicious with your praise. It involves the following don'ts:[2]
   (*i*) Unless you are an art teacher don't "correct" students' art work, but try to see what they are trying to express in it.
   (*ii*) Don't stress competition.
   (*iii*) Don't ask students to draw objects as they appear to you. Some additional suggestions in this connection are as follows:[3]
      (*a*) Try to have basic art materials available.
      (*b*) Encourage the youngster to take part in school and community events where he can use his talent.
      (*c*) If possible, provide a place to work.

6. Helping students with writing talent: Writing may be practical or creative. Writing in different classes such as that of English, Social Studies, Science, Mathematics, Art, Music, etc., can be developed by giving suitable assignment to the students. The process of creative writing may be developed by freelance writing, editorial work and news reporting, etc. The student should be encouraged to follow his own field of creative writing. He should be provided necessary books and materials. He should be encouraged both by the teachers and parents.

7. Helping students with dramatic talent: This requires personality development and subject matter learning. The teacher's role involves setting of the stage, including students in the planning, setting the scene, call for volunteers and evaluation.

8. Helping students with musical talent: This requires creation of opportunities for music training. The relationship of the teacher and taught should be improved. Opportunities should be offered to participate in musical competitions in school, in the city and also outside. Students should be encouraged by the teachers and parents.

---

1. *Ibid.*, pp. 65-66.
2. *Ibid.*, p. 66.
3. *Ibid.*, pp. 66-67.

9. Helping students with mechanical skills: This requires provision of suitable material for the development of mechanical skills. Besides, the following steps should be taken for this purpose:[1]

1. Every community has resources outside the school which can be used by students with mechanical ability to develop their talent.
2. You can help skilled youngsters learn about the possibilities for careers in engineering, in scientific development, and in the skilled crafts.
3. Parents of youngsters with mechanical ability need to be aware of the talents of their children and what they as parents can do to foster it.
4. You can lend your support to the setting up of extra-curricular activities, clubs and groups that will provide opportunities for talented youngsters to develop their mechanical ability.
5. Look for information about contests, fairs, science fairs, and exhibits where youngsters with mechanical skills can compete and develop their abilities.

10. Helping students with physical skills: Physical abilities should be developed for development of personality, good health, socialization of the youngsters and motivation to learn. Teachers should provide specific activities for development of physical skills among all the students. Besides the natural athlete may be helped by means of the following provisions:[2]

(*i*) Encourage the youngster with physical ability to enter more than one athletic activity.

(*ii*) Help the youngster relate his physical activity to other aspects of living.

(*iii*) Use a youngster's physical skills to interest him in other valuable pursuits.

(*iv*) Try to find somebody who can give the boy or girl with physical skills a few sound pointers early in his career.

(*v*) Be sure the student knows about the facilities and programmes of the YMCA, the YWCA, the Girl Scouts, the Boy Scouts, Church, Athletic organizations and Young People's Baseball leagues.

(*vi*) Summer camps open up wonderful avenue to youngsters for developing physical skills.

(*vii*) Keep the youngsters in touch with community athletic events.

(*viii*) Let the youngsters know that you appreciate his skill and that you stand ready to help him develop his ability.

QUESTIONS FOR EXERCISE

1. Is creativity a stable trait that some people have and others do not? Or is it something that is acquired through interaction between the individual and the challenges of the environment? Explain with the help of suitable example.
2. Write an essay on Identifying Creative Talents.
3. Explain how the teacher can help students in developing various kinds of creative talents.

---

1. *Ibid.*, pp. 89-90.
2. *Ibid.*, pp. 94-95.

39

Achievements and Evaluation

IMPORTANCE OF MENTAL TESTS

Mental or psychological tests have been proved to posses great utility in many spheres. Briefly, the utility and importance of mental tests can be observed in the following spheres:

1. Guidance: As has been indicated earlier, psychological tests are indispensable in all forms of guidance.

2. Appointments: Psychological tests are now-a-days resorted to for the appointment of appropriate individuals to posts in offices, factories and Government services. It has the doubly beneficial effect of securing proper and desirable jobs for individuals according to their interests, inclinations, intelligence and abilities, as well as ensuring that the highest level of efficiency is achieved by the right man being in the right job. In this way, both the employed as well as the employer are benefited.

3. Selection for training: An individual can benefit from training for some particular job only if he is initially in possession of the requisite intelligence, abilities, besides the necessary interest in the work involved. It is evident, that the individual should be tested in respect of these qualities before any training is imparted to him. Now. all kinds of training institutes make use of psychological tests for selecting the required candidates. In India, for example, the recruitment to the Police Training Colleges, the Government Teacher's Training College, and other technical institutions is done on the basis of psychological tests. In public schools, the students who receive scholarships are selected on the basis of psychological tests in order to ensure that the scholarships are not wasted, as well they might be if they are provided to the wrong individual. Psychological tests are further used for selection of candidates for the National Defence Academy in the country. Such use of psychological tests for the selection of personnel in training schools is constantly on the increase.

4. Classification according to the level of intelligence: Now-a-days, all educationists agree that the success of education depends upon the student being provided education of a kind that accords with his level of intelligence. Hence, individual students are classified and stratified according to their level of intelligence, and different curricula and extra-curricular programmes devised for the three categories of students—the brilliant, the average and the retarded. This classification is based on intelligence tests. It is not only in the field of education but also in various vocations, armed forces and industries that intelligence tests are used to classify individuals so that they can be given the proper kind of work that is within their capacity to perform with reasonable success.

5. Prediction: The term indicates the forecasting of success in the case of an individual. When guiding the individual, a psychologist can normally make fairly accurate predictions as to the degree of success that one is likely to achieve. This prediction is based upon psychological tests; the greater the capacity of a psychological test to assist in prediction, the greater is its validity and its reliability.

6. Diagnosis: Before giving any guidance, the directing psychologist makes a diagnosis of the problem present before him. He gives suggestions for alleviating a certain condition only after he has decided upon a diagnosis, since it is only upon diagnosing some problem that he reaches the root causes. And psychological tests are essential for diagnosis. Without them, a proper diagnosis cannot be achieved.

7. Research: Psychological tests are of use in the field of psychological research. Intelligence tests, interest inventories, personality tests, tests of mental abilities and personality qualities, help in research in these specific directions.

WHAT ARE MENTAL TESTS?

Importance of psychological tests is fairly evident from the preceding exposition of the subject. Before proceeding to a study of the various kinds of tests, it is essential to know the kinds of psychological tests that are in use, and the principal elements active in them. Defining psychological tests, Mursell writes, "A psychological test, then is a pattern of stimuli selected and organised to elicit responses which will reveal certain psychological characteristics in the person who takes them." In this way, psychological tests are an organization of some stimuli. These stimuli are selected with some special objective in view. The object is to discover some psychological characteristics of the person being tested. Stimuli present in psychological tests are called test items, and they can be of all kinds—pictures, figures, wooden blocks, word groups, sentences and figures, etc. And the way in which these stimuli uncover psychological characteristics will be evident from a description of each of them.

Psychological tests differ from psychological experimentation

What should here be kept well in mind is that psychological tests differ from psychological experimentation although in both cases some stimuli are given, and it is the reactions to them that are examined. But the main difference between the two is one of purpose. As has been pointed out, the object of psychological tests is to ascertain the psychological characteristics of the subject, while in the case of psychological experimentation, the object is more purely academic as they aim at discovering a mental process concerned with the particular experiment. In this manner, it is evident that while psychological tests lead to the discovery of abilities or capabilities the psychological experiments discover and confirm various mental processes. Nevertheless, the difference between the two is very subtle, since now-a-days, psychological tests are also being used for discovering and identifying mental processes.

CLASSIFICATION OF PSYCHOLOGICAL TESTS

Mental tests are of various kinds. They have been classified from various different viewpoints and standpoints. Classifications of tests are as follows:

1. Classification according to method of testing: Tests have been divided into two classes, in this case classification based on the method involved.

(*i*) *Individual tests:* These tests are administered to one individual at one time, as is indicated by the term denoting them. They include only performance tests. In addition to these, they also include tests that require linguistic ability. Some examples of these are: Stanford Binet intelligence test, Weschler Bellevieu intelligence tests, Kohez's block design test, Rorschach's ink blot test, and T.A.T. test, etc. These tests are particularly appropriate for testing of individuals, but they are not financially suitable as they are expensive, in addition to requiring more expert training than in many other cases. Secondly, they are less objective than group tests.

(*ii*) *Group tests:* In this category the tests included are performed upon a large number of people simultaneously. Some examples are the group intelligence tests of the State Bureau of Psychology, Uttar Pradesh, interest lists, vocational lists, etc. They are more objective and less expensive requiring very little, if any, specialized training that may prove expensive. But in these tests no real rapport between the subject and the examiner is established. Hence, they are less useful for solving problems of individuals, than are the individual tests. Nevertheless, they have proved really useful in the case of educational and vocational guidance requirements.

2. Classification according to the medium of instruction: In these tests, classification is based upon the medium of teaching of the subjects. The psychological tests, from this viewpoint, are divided into the following two classes:

(*i*) *Verbal tests:* This classification comprehends tests in which questions are orally asked, linguistic and concerned abilities being essentially required. These tests are not intended for, and cannot be used inthe case of illiterates, only slightly educated persons and small children, since such people lack linguistic ability.

(*ii*) *Non-verbal tests:* This classification includes tests that do not require the use of language, but substitute figures, pictures, blocks and other implements for it. Examples of it are Pidgon's non-verbal tests and Raven's progressive matrices. Their particular felicity lies in the fact that they can be applied to the testing of illiterates, very slightly educated individuals and very young children. This category includes all non-verbal tests.

3. Classification according to the objectives of testing: Division of tests on the basis of their individual objective or aim leads them to be put into the following categories:

(*i*) *Intelligence tests:* These help to test the intelligence, in the form of both verbal and non-verbal tests. They can be administered both individually and in a large group.

(*ii*) *Tests of mental abilities:* In this is included the various tests of mental abilities such as spatial ability, artistic ability, mechanical ability, etc.

(*iii*) *Interest tests:* These tests help to discover the interests of the individual, some examples of which are Strong's Vocational Interest Blank, and Cudor's Vocational Inventory. Both of them are described in detail at a later stage. Besides these, the vocational interests list devised by the State Bureau of Psychology, Uttar Pradesh, is also an effective test.

(*iv*) *Aptitude tests:* These tests or lists are divised by combining the different tests of mental abilities.

(*v*) *Personality tests:* These help to find out the individual's personality traits or characteristics. The main method of personality testing are Rorschach's Ink Blot test and TAT.

Characteristics of good tests

Good tests of a psychological nature, bear the following features:

1. Reliability: The higher the degree of reliability that results of a test have, the greater is considered the reliability of the test itself. And the reliability of its conclusion means that if the same test is performed upon the same individual more than once, results obtained in each individual list should be the same or commensurate with the first one, if it is modified by changed circumstances.

2. Validity: The validity of test lies in the fact that it succeeds in testing the particular quality which it is designed to test. For example, intelligence tests can be said to be valid only if they, in fact, test correctly the intelligence level of the individual subject.

3. Objectivity: A test can achieve a high level of objectivity only if the answer to each of its various questions is distinct and precise, and if there is no difference of opinion, regarding it. among the various examiners. Its efficacy lies in the fact that the conclusion or result is in no way influenced by the examiner's individual thoughts or opinions, so that the same results are obtained no matter what the number of examiners who examine the same subject.

4. Comprehensiveness: Another feature of a good test is its comprehensive nature. This feature involves the inclusion of all information on all trait concerned with the one trait actually being tested. In this manner, in a comprehensive test, questions cover the trait in question as well as allied traits so that no aspect to the measured or tested ability escapes attention.

5. Discrimination power: This term applies to the ability which helps to distinguish between persons with great or less ability so that they score more or less points on marks.

6. Utility: This feature concerns the extent to which a particular test can be used with facility. And for this it is essential that the questions asked should be simple, the method easy, the time involved less and the expense negligible.

Of the above mentioned characteristics, the most important are validity and reliability. Hence, both these qualities will be described in detail here.

VALIDITY

What is validity?

It is apparent from the description of intelligence tests that all tests do not have a common degree of validity, it being completely dependent upon the extent to which any judgment based upon the test's result is objective. For example, validity in the case of intelligence tests can be attributed only to those tests that actually succeed in testing the individual's level of intelligence. A test can be accepted as valid only to that degree to which it can correctly guage the intelligence of the subject. In this way, validity of a test is that quality on the basis of which the correspondent incorrectness of judgments based upon it is evaluated. For example, the validity of interest lists is less than in the case of intelligence tests. Here there is a slight difficulty. Suppose, for the moment, that the intelligence of some students was measured by one particular method. Now the validity of that test will depend upon whether the students tested do in fact possess the intelligence that they are indicated as possessing. The problem that arises here is how can one ascertain whether the students do or do not possess the intelligence indicated by the above test. Evidently, there must be some independent criterion for deciding upon the validity of the particular test in question or tests in general. In this case, of the intelligence level of students, the examination results can be the basis for measuring the validity of the test. Generally speaking, it can be said that if there is a correlation between marks obtained at an examination and the result of the test, then the test is valid.

Kinds of validity

But, as is evident from the foregoing description, validity is a relative term, as no test can have complete validity. Hence, whenever a particular test is termed valid, or whenever the lack of validity of a test is in question, it is necessary to indicate the sense in which it is considered valid or invalid. Apparently, validity is of many kinds. Psychologists have roughly accepted the following kinds of validity:

1. Face validity: Face validity is concerned with the form of the test. Such a validity is attributed only of the test which provides an item or subject that appears valid.

2. Content validity: Another kind of validity is content validity in which the validity of the test is based on the validity of its contents. In order to obtain this kind of validity in a particular test, it is essential that the items of a test should achieve the objective for which they are originally designed. For example, content validity in the case of an intelligence test will be attributed only in the event of its succeeding in discovering all factors concerned with intelligence.

3. Factorial validity: This is inclusive of validity of the factors in the test. And in order to judge whether a test has factorial validity, it is examined by the method of factor analysis, and a correlation between this result and evident factor resultant of many tests is established.

4. Predictive validity: This is the most popular form of validity. In this, results are obtained on the basis of a particular criterion and correlation between the scores and the criterion is established. In this, the choice of a criterion requires much care and attention. The coefficient obtained by this correlation between scores and criterion is called the validity coefficient. The validity coefficient varies between 0.5 and 0.8. A lower coefficient makes the test inapplicable and lacking in utility, while a higher coefficient is not normally obtained.

5. Concurrent validity: It resembles the predictive validity since in it, too, a correlation between the test and some definite standard is established. But, despite these common features, there are also some definite variations.

From the above analysis of the various kinds of validity, it is evident that validity exists in a particular context, or in other words, every test is valid for a particular objective and for a particular age group in individuals. It can just as well be invalid for a particular age group in individuals and in a particular context. Hence, to attribute validity to test without qualification is completely unjustified and inaccurate. For the statement to have any value or meaning, it is essential to state the context and conditions in which it is applicable.

RELIABILITY

What is reliability?

In addition to validity, it is essential that in every test there be a definite element of reliability. It is only then that the conclusions of the test can be considered reliable and worthy of trust. Reliability of a test consists in any quality in the test that may inspire confidence and trust. And this quality can be attributed to only that test which provides the same score every time, it is performed on the same individual. Now, if some intelligence test yields one score for an individual at a different time, it is only too evident that such a test cannot be considered reliable. And this reliability of the test does not reside in any one part of it, but in its wholeness or completeness. Its reliability will considerably be weakened and decreased if even one part of it is inadequate in some respect. Hence, it is essential that the internal parts of a test possess internal consistency and uniformity. It is only on the basis of such a reliable test that guidance can be given.

Means of measuring reliability

Reliability can be measured in the following four ways:

1. Test retest method: One method of gauging reliability is to perform the same test on the same group of individuals on two different occasions, and to test the scores or results obtained. One group of individuals can be subjected to the Binet intelligence test. Then later on the same group of individuals can again be subjected to the Binet intelligence tests. If the results obtained in each case do not tally, then the tests cannot be considered reliable.

2. Parallel form method: Another method of judging the reliability of a particular method is to prepare a method similar to the one being judged and examined. Now the same group can be examined through the basic and then the modified or parallel methods. Finally, the results of the two can be compared to judge the reliability of the test. Gulliksen has suggested that more than one parallel method may be devised for greater accuracy.

3. Split half method: Another method of judging the reliability of a test is to divide the components of the test into even and odd items whose results can be individually obtained. Now the results can be compared to show the reliability of the test.

4. Inter item: In this method of measuring the reliability of a psychological test, only one method is applied at one time. The mutual relation between the scores obtained for each specific item in the test is observed. At the same time, the relation between the marks obtained for one specific question and the marks obtained for the whole test is also ascertained. As this method of measuring reliability involves considerable statistical skill in correlation, psychologists Cudor and Richardson, have devised some formulae for application in this method.

As has been indicated previously, the implication and meaning of reliability also change in the method of judging reliability. Hence, it is not sufficient to remark that a particular test is reliable. It is equally essential that the sense in which reliability is judged also be mentioned, or in other words mention must be made of the method by which its reliability has been established.

Of the above mentioned methods of judging reliability of psychological tests, the third is the most prevalent and useful, since it is also most easy. In this method, the necessity of collecting the same group of individuals more than once is obviated. Reliability is known from the coefficient of reliability, and this coefficient is known as the reliability coefficient.

In this manner, both reliability and validity are important qualities of tests. Validity is related to the scale or structure of the test while reliability is an attribute of its ability of testing.

PREVALENT SYSTEM OF EDUCATION

The aim and object of education is the comprehensive, overall development of the child. This development and progress is gradual. Hence, it is essential to examine the child at regular intervals to find out the extent to which he has progressed. In the school, students study a number of subjects. To test one in respect of these subjects from time to time is essential as it makes clear the success with which he is studying and understanding them. It is the examination that makes it possible for one to know the child's achievement in terms of ability in learning these subjects. Hence, in almost all schools some mode of examining the children, in respect of their attainments in learning and retaining all that is taught to them, is prevalent.

The present system of education that is prevailing in India at the moment is a legacy from the British Government which devised it to create clerks for its administrative machinery. It was never intended to achieve the complete development of the individual. As the English educational system progressed, schools based on the ancient Indian educational systems deteriorated and closed down. Christian missionaries opened many schools in India with a view to moulding children according to the Western language, religion, culture and society through education. At the time of the national movement, many schools and colleges were opened to propagate the national viewpoint. But generally the methods of education in these schools corresponded to the system inculcated by the foreign administration. From that day to the present time education has been extending and increasing, but despite the strenuous efforts of many commissions, the existing educational system has not been improved upon.

PRESENT SYSTEM OF EVALUATION

Under the present system of examinations in this country, all the students are put in a single hall, at the end of each session, and answer books are distributed to each of them. At the appointed time, the question papers are distributed to them, following which during the space of two or three hours the student is expected to answer a required number of questions. Finally, the answer books are gathered and sent to an examiner whose appointment in that capacity is previously confirmed. Sometimes, the examiner is other than the person who sets the examination paper. If the student's attempt in the answer books is considered worthy of being awarded 33 per cent marks by the examiner, he is deemed to have passed the said examination. If he fails to secure these marks, in the eyes of examiner, he is deemed to have failed to pass the examination. The individual who does not succeed is compelled to spend another session in the same class.

Defects of the present evaluation system

There is hardly any need to point out that the existing examination scheme is not conductive to the proper development of children. The following are some of its shortcomings, that have been time and again pointed out by various educationists and commissions appointed for the purpose:

1. Students do not study throughout the whole year: For the present examination system, the student is not compelled to exert himself throughout the entire session, but achieve competency for it by labouring only through the last few weeks before the examination. In this manner, the student does not attain any real ability or capability even though he passes the examination. He forgets a lesson just as rapidly as he learns it. During the first two or three months of the session, it is a rare student who is seen at his desk. In this manner from the educational viewpoint, a major portion of a student's time is completely wasted.

2. Studying from question-answer books and key books: In the present context, a student's ability is guaged from the scores he obtains in the examinations. And for obtaining good marks in the examination, there is no need to wander into a maze of extensive reading and comprehensive knowledge. In every examination paper, the student is required to do four to five questions out of nine or ten that are set. The consequence is that even without having gone through more than one-third of the course prescribed for study, the average student finds three or four questions that he is in a position to answer. And four to ten pages of writing are considered adequate in answer to each question. Thus, why should the student bother himself with reading bulky books that are likely to cause him untold fatigue and confusion? And the best books do not even include any clue as to the precise answer that would suit a particular question which is likely to be asked in the examination. Often, most of the students write out the answers to questions asked in previous years in the examinations for which they are preparing. This is considered one of the best methods of preparation for examination. And, if now the student discovers a book in the market that provides answers to all examination questions then where is the need to write out these answers himself? Hence, the student, instead of bothering to burden his brain with the actual textbooks, studies help books and succeeds in the examination. Some books in question-answer form are not sufficiently brief so that the student desirous of further economizing upon the effort to be expended in the examination can turn to a perusal of guess papers which include answers to possible examination questions in a total of approximately fifty to sixty pages. If the guess work turns out to be exact or if the student is lucky, he is sure to pass the examination. It is only too painfully evident that the student who passes his examination in this manner, possesses no knowledge whatsoever of his subject, and the object of examination is as far as possible from being fulfilled.

3. Fear of examination: In the modern examination system, the examination is taken at the end of the session with the result that the student is fearfully conscious of the examination right through the session. Teachers and students alike are normally engaged in the study of text books, there being little or no time for the student to engage in the study and perusal of any general books, not directly pertaining to his curriculum. He is also in no position to develop any real interest in other things. The natural result is that the student is not aware of anything outside the course that is prescribed. And, no curriculum or books, can ever provide complete knowledge of any subject. For such comprehensive knowledge, it is essential that many books be studied and that this study be supplemented with the necessary experience of actual practical life. Under the present examination system, the fear of examination does not conduce to any extensive study.

4. Success in examinations a matter of luck: In the way examinations are conducted at present, success is more a matter of luck than of anything else. His entire future is to be decided in two or three hours. No matter what skill a student has gained in his subject through constant labour during the entire session, his effort is completely wasted if for some reason or the other he fails to exhibit his skill in these three hours. Some students fail to attend the examination through some contingency such as illness during the examination period, or an accident or any other human involvement. On the other hand, even though they are in a position to attend the examination, they fail to give their best performance. The only consequence in such a case is that their whole year's effort is wasted.

5. Mechanical method: In this way, the existing system of education is a machine in which conclusions are reached, no importance being attached to the human elements involved. Hence, people have devised new methods of succeeding in this mechanical set-up. Some students do not bother to put in more than a few week's effort for the examinations, during which they do nothing more than make a cursory study of guess papers and question-answer forms. As a result, they are in a position to come to grips with the paper, even though there is no element of mastery involved. And in subjects in which the question paper outdoes expectation, and unexpected questions crop up, the contingency is overcome by fraternizing with the examiners and having their marks surreptitiously increased. And in the case of such a success in any examination it is only natural for the individual to be devoid of any skill whatsoever in the subject in which he has passed the examination.

6. Defects concerning evaluation of answer books: Under the present system of examination, a student's achievement in any subject is measured by the marks that he obtains during the examination. Hence, his fortune depends upon the fair evaluation of his effort m the answer book. Such a method is susceptible to numerous faults, some of them being enumerated below:

(*i*) If the teacher's mental condition is disturbed, he does not evaluate the answer books correctly. What most often occurs is that the first few copies in the bundle sent to him are examined with due care, but as he gradually tires and reaches stages of growing exhaustion, the subsequent copies are gone through as a matter of necessity and duty.

(*ii*) It is only too apparent that all copies are not examined from the given standpoint or standard. Of course, different examiners would award differing marks to the same copy, but even if the same examiner is asked to examine the same copy, it is quite likely that he will award it different marks on different occasions.

(*iii*) The maximum number of marks that any student may be awarded depends upon the examiner's mental tendency. It is a common case that the subject in which the examiner himself has never managed to score more than 60% marks in any examination that he has taken, is one in which no student will ever be awarded high marks by such an individual since he is convinced that none is equal to him, let alone anyone being superior to him. On the other hand, other examiners are very liberal and are even capable of awarding marks up to 90%. If all the answer books of a particular subject were to go to one and the same examiner, there would be some saving grace, but it usually happens that the number of students studying a subject runs into thousands so that the examiners of it are also numerous. If an individual's copy falls into the hands of a strict examiner, he is not likely to score well at all, while a less deserving candidate may score better than him if the latter's copy happens to have gone to a very liberal person. And this seems to be playing with the children's or student's abilities and capacities.

(*iv*) It often happens, that due to a very great variety of causes, the examiner has very little time at his disposal to examine the copies. One of the causes in such case is the delayed arrival of the answer books themselves, but more often it is a case of the examiner's being busy or just careless. One natural outcome of such practice is that the teachers pay half their fee to have the answer books examined by other less qualified and in some cases completely unqualified individuals. Some teachers are so lacking in ethical sense that they have their wives and students do the work of examining the copies, even though they cannot be imagined to be qualified for the work. It is easy to understand the extent to which some innocent students suffer as the result of such behaviour on the part of teachers.

(*v*) Many of the examiners are completely prejudiced or biased in their thinking, having only the most incomplete knowledge of their respective subjects. Secondly, some teachers even fail to understand the actual implications of the question asked in the question paper. It is only to be expected in such circumstances that there is no justice done to the student.

7. Long examination period: The present examination system allows the period of examination to spread over the very considerable period of at least a month. It is often seen that students get some two weeks between two individual examination dates. Such a long period of inactivity has the worst effect upon the student's attitude towards the examination as it tends to lull him towards the seriousness of the matter. Secondly, the provision of time periods between various papers is not at all proportionate. He gets no more than few hours between two papers while between another two he has a few days at his disposal. Evidently, the opportunity available for the preparation of each subject is unequal.

8. Wrong objective: The present aim of examination is to obtain marks in order to get a degree, not the desire to gain skill in any subject. Hence, the main attention in any examination is concentrated upon getting good marks so that one can have proof of one's ability or skill. There are innumerable methods of obtaining an adequate number of marks in the examination, though all of them are not formal. One of the simplest is obtaining a certificate of success in an examination without actually taking the examination, irrespective of the fact that discovery of such an incriminating fact leaves them open to criminal action in a court of law. And the objective behind obtaining a certificate or degree is no more than securing a remunerative position that offers financial security in life. Thus, students who are not particularly desirous of securing a good status in life are often careless of studying hard to obtain a degree since they require no such passport to the good things of life. And as a result of the contaminated and one-sided objectives of education existing at present, the system is riddled with defects, and an inherent and chronic corruption.

9. Defects of the essay system: Under the existing scheme of examination, the student is required to answer each question in the form of an essay, with the result that the educational system has acquired all the defects inherent in the essay system. In this method, the students pay much greater attention to learning answers to question than to understanding the subject and delving deep into it. In the examination hall, they do not more than reproduce these well learned and remembered answers on the answer books. Once the examination is over the facts learned for it are as expeditiously forgotten, since once they have been put in the answer book, they no longer possess any importance for the student. One natural outcome of this method is that even though the student may have done exceptionally well in the examination, he is more or less blank on all the subjects that he has made a pretense of studying.

Suggestions for improving the evaluation system

Many thinkers, educationists and education commissions have pointed out the above defects in the existing scheme of examinations in this country, but there are many difficulties that hinder the complete replacement of it. The main difficulty is financial besides which the extremely large number of candidates make it difficult to evolve a different examination system for them. Hence, the practicable solution is to maintain the existing scheme of things and make efforts to effect definite improvements. Main suggestions in this respect are the following:

1. Certificates should not be required for services: If the tradition of requiring certificates for various jobs and services is given up, and individuals are separately tested for qualities that the job requires, then people will give up the race for obtaining certificates and degree, and turn their attention to developing qualities required in the professions of their choice. It must, of course, be kept in mind that this method is not practicable in all professions, nevertheless, it should be used in as many as admit of its use.

2. Improvement in the evaluation of answer books: The method and system of examining and evaluating answer books should be improved. The remuneration of evaluating copies should be enough to induce the examiner to attend to them himself, and to do his work efficiently and well. The time allowed to the examiner for evaluating the answer books should be sufficient to allow him to work in peace so that no haphazard work results from hurry or strain. Every examiner should be required to send copies that he is to examine as samples so that his standard of judgment can be measured, and he should be requested to evaluate the remaining copies similarly.

3. Terminal or monthly examinations: Nevertheless, the student's knowledge of his subject cannot be property guaged once in a year in a sitting of only three hours. For this it is essential that the teacher should examine the students in the class every fifteen days or a month in the subject matter that he taught till then. The results should be announced on the basis of these monthly tests as well as the annual examination. This method will compel the students to spread their labour over the whole year.

4. Examination in other aspects of development: The aim of education is not only to impart information but to achieve the complete development of the individual. It is only information that is examined in the present examinations. Hence, it is essential that the child's physical, emotional and social development also be examined, even though the marks obtained therein may not be made the reason for detaining him if he fails. Yet, these marks will help in advising and improving him. If the children understand that it is essential for them to pass in these respects also, they themselves will try harder to improve themselves.

5. Examinees, who, for one or the other legitimate reason such as disease, accident, etc., fail to take their examination at the regular time, should be given a chance to be examined once the reason for their abstaining from the regular examination has been confirmed. Their efforts during the entire year should not be allowed to go waste.

6. Questions in the examination papers should be such as discourage the practice of rote learning but encourage the expression of the student's skill in the subject. Questions should vary radically from year to year so that the practice of basing preparation on guess papers on questions asked in previous year and then rote learning answers to them is discouraged and ultimately discarded.

7. Questions in the paper should cover every aspect of the curriculum even if more than one question are given, and the solution of one is required. Such methods will induce the students to study all that is prescribed rather than making selection from it.

8. During the period of examinations, the distribution of papers should be equitable and proportionate, the normal period of inactivity not streching over more than one or two days. Only one paper should be set for one day.

9. The number of examiners should be considerably increased so that all of them can conveniently examine a smaller number of copies in the period of one or two weeks provided to them for the purpose.

10. Strict measures should be adopted for punishing all examinees who resort to corrupt measures in passing examinations or obtaining certificate.

Finally, the fundamental fact that must be pointed out is that the improvements in the existing scheme of examinations depend upon the teachers themselves. It is for them to encourage the students in their classes to attain high degree of skill and efficiency in the subject rather than to prepare them for the examinations. In educational institutions, the principal teacher can specially attend to this aspect of the matter. Co-operation between teachers and the various examining bodies can help to improve the system of examinations.

ESSAY TYPE EXAMINATIONS

The examination system that exists at present in Indian schools and colleges is the essay type examination. In this the examinee is provided with a question paper at a definite time, the paper containing 8 or 10 questions, out of which the candidate is required to answer 4 or 5. These questions relate to the syllabus studied by the student, and normally every part of the syllabus is covered, each question requiring an answer, in essay form, that extends between 3 and 10 pages. Evidently, much depends upon the student's language, style, handwriting and mode of presentation of material, besides his knowledge of the subject. In evaluating his work, the examiner is influenced by all these factors. Every question paper is to be attempted within a definite period of two to three hours. Hence, much depends upon the student's speed in writing, since, only if he writes fast can he include much material in the answers. As the questions given in the paper do not convey their meaning very explicitly, many students fail to comprehend the actual implications of the questions, so that they fill a few pages with the most unimaginable rot. Most of their attention is focus on the necessity of filling space in order to deceive the examiner into believing that they have written something valuable and precise. It is evident that the existing system of examination is riddled with defects.

Advantages of essay type examination

Yet, it is not reasonable to conclude from the defects of the essay type examination that they are completely devoid of ail merit. It is these merits that have helped to perpetuate this system. The following are these merits:

1. **Simplicity in setting examination papers:** In the essay type examination, the paper-setter is not put to much trouble since every aspect of the syllabus is to be included, and one question to be allocated to it. He needs nothing more than a superficial knowledge of his subject.

2. **Freedom of expressing opinion:** In these examinations, the student has complete freedom to express his views, and he can arrange facts in the most original manner. His answer manifests his imagination, personality, decision and knowledge besides memory.

3. **Use of whole method:** In preparing for the essay type examination the student does not benefit by the use of the part method, since a study of the complete syllabus requires application of the whole method. And this method is superior to the part method in many respects.

4. **Expression of the student's weakness and problems:** Answers given to questions in the essay type examination have the advantage of revealing the

student's weakness and shortcoming, with the natural result that the teacher can make every effort to improve the child in the class.

Suggestions for improving the essay type examination

Once the essay type examination is improved upon, it can be made into a very useful and advantageous examination system. There can be many improvements but the main respects in which improvements are immediately needed are the construction or form of questions, the method of evaluation of answers and other academic matters. The following suggestions may help to achieve the desired improvement:

1. Improvement in forms of Questions:

(*i*) Questions should comprehend every part of the syllabus.

(*ii*) Questions should be so framed as to invite objective answers.

(*iii*) Questions should be so designed as to necessitate the expression of originality, creative power, thinking, reasoning, judgment and other traits in addition to the use of memory. Every question paper should include questions that suit individuals of varying levels of intelligence. In this connection, the setting of papers should be governed by one principle from easiest to the most difficult.

(*iv*) Questions should be designed in such a manner that answers to them fulfil the objectives of examination.

2. Improvement in evaluation: Qualities of a good evaluation are objectivity, reliability and validity. And in order to achieve these qualities the following measures can be adopted in examinations:

(*i*) The answer books should carry some code or role number rather than the candidate's name so that evaluation may not be effected by personally acquaintance.

(*ii*) In every answer book, it is the first answer that should be read first.

(*iii*) Now all the answer books should be divided into five levels according to ability and achievement. In these levels 10 per cent will be in the highest as well as the lowest levels, 20 per cent in the levels immediately below and above them, while some 40 per cent will fall in the average level.

(*iv*) Now the answer books should be read once again, and all cases that do not fall into any of these categories should be separated.

(*v*) Every student should be given a position on the answer book from among five levels such as 5, 4, 3, 2 and 1.

(*vi*) In judging every individual answer to a question, all points given above should be kept in mind. Finally, the marks obtained in individual questions can be added together to know the position secured by the candidates.

Improvements in the system of education can be made by applying the suggestions listed above. And in this connection, the novel system of objective education can be very advantageous. Better results can be obtained by supplementing the essay type examination with the objective education system since both of them have their own advantages and disadvantages.

OBJECTIVE TESTS

Characteristics of objective test

Modern educational psychologists are not in favour of examining students on the essay type of examination pattern, since it only inadequately measures the ability of the individual. Hence, the modern period has seen development of some new types of examinations. They are called objective examinations, since they objectively evaluate the worth of the individual and are not influenced by the teacher's or examiner's prejudices and questionable attitudes. Compared to the ordinary essay pattern examination, these objective tests have the following characteristics:

1. They can be modified according to specific local requirements.
2. They are better from the viewpoints of time, value and special needs.
3. The teacher himself devises these tests.
4. The results accruing from these tests form the basis for the teacher's guidance to his students personally.
5. These tests are valid and objective.
6. They lead to an objective and valuable knowledge of the student's qualities and shortcomings.

Main features of the objective tests

As has been pointed out, the objective tests are prepared by the teacher himself. Hence, in formulating them teachers keep certain facts in mind so that the tests may be made objective and valid. The main facts are the following:

1. These tests should be based upon the teacher's philosophy of education.
2. These tests should examine the main mental functioning.
3. Questions should be as straightforward and simple as possible so that the student may not be confused.
4. Questions should be chosen to conform to circumstances and time.
5. As far as possible there should not be unrelated suggestions since the student may be confused thereby.
6. Questions of the same kind should be placed in the same category.
7. Questions of the same kind should not be constantly repeated.
8. The teacher should himself gauge the difficulty of the questions.
9. Tests should aim at predetermined objectives, hence after they have been formulated they should be co-ordinated with the desired aims.
10. There should be brief points of direction for the student in order to facilitate his effort in the tests.
11. In order to examine the reliability of questions, the mean, median and mode of the marks should be discovered.

12. Questions should not be such as cannot help to distinguish between the brilliant and the mediocre students.
13. The views expressed by students should be noted so that they can be guided in the future.

Kinds of objective tests

Modern teachers have formulated many kinds of objective tests, keeping the above principles in mind. Some of the main kinds are the following:

1. The multiple choice test: In this kind of test, one question can be answered in many plausible suggested ways and the student has to select the answer that will precisely fit the questions, as

(*i*) *Ramcharitra Manas* was composed by—

Tulsidas, Surdas, Kalidas, Vyas.

(*ii*) Chanakya was a famous—

poet, philosopher, saint, politician.

Of the many alternatives in the two questions sampled above, only one alternative is precisely correct in each case. The student has to pick it out.

2. The simple recall test: In a test of this kind, the student has to answer questions by recalling the information that has been imparted to him. Answers to the questions are precise and definite, mere guess work does not help the student. Most questions can he answered either in one sentence or in one word. Two such questions are:

(*i*) Who discovered the north pole?

(*ii*) Who was the first Prime Minister of India?

3. The matching type test: In this test there are two lists of terms or names, each name in one list having some correspondence with one word on the other list, but the order of terms in the two lists is not the same. Words that correspond with each other occupy different places in the two lists. The student has to match the two lists, or, in other words, has to point out the various correspondences between the terms on either side. One such test is given below. The first list consists of the names of authors while the other consists of classics composed by them. And in the bracketed space provided in front of the second list, the student has to insert the serial number of the author in front of the classic that he has written:

(*i*) Dayanand	Sursagar	( )
(*ii*) Surdas	Mahabharat	( )
(*iii*) Vyas	Satyartha Prakash	( )

4. Completion test: In this test, certain sentences are given, but the sentences are incomplete in as much that there are blanks that have to be filled in to make sense. It is for the student to fill in these blanks so that the sentences become complete. For example:

(*i*) Jawahar Lal Nehru was born on ...

(*ii*) The Red Fort of Delhi was constructed in ... by...

5. True and false test: In a test of this kind, some sentences are given, to which are suffixed the words true and false. The student has to decide whether the statements given are true or false, so that he can mark one of the two alternatives. For example:

(*i*) Educational psychology is the scientific study of society. true/false

(*ii*) Psychology is the science of behaviour. true/false

(*iii*) The highest building in the world is in India. true/false

(*iv*) Everest is the highest mountain peak in the world. true/false

Advantages of objective tests

As compared with the essay type examination, the objective tests are better from the educational viewpoint. The following are their main advantages, as also their educational features:

1. Based on local needs: Compared with the essay type tests, these are based more on local requirements, and they can be easily converted and refashioned according to local needs.

2. Achievement of specific objectives: Through these tests, the teacher can achieve the fulfilment of definite objectives, according to which the tests are modelled.

3. Better examination in less time: The time taken in these tests is less than in the essay type tests. The examinee has to write less but to think more, hence he is better examined in a shorter period of time.

4. Guidance for the teacher: Observing the results of these tests, the teacher can himself make the required adjustments and changes in his mode of teaching, as these tests reveal the actual level, knowledge and efficiency of the students. Hence, they also provide guidance for the teacher's further teaching programme.

5. Differentiation of brilliant and mediocre students: On the basis of these tests, mediocre and brilliant students can be easily distinguished. This distinction helps the teacher in teaching these children further since he is now in a position to guide a student according to his abilities.

6. Beneficial to the students: These tests also help and benefit the students since proper evaluation of their efforts leads to much satisfaction. Success, in fact, leads to greater confidence and self-satisfaction as well as inspiration for greater effort. As there is proper evaluation, the students cannot resort to the use of unfair means, and this leads to the development of a healthy competition among them.

7. Economic structure: These tests are comparatively cheaper. Hence, they are better from the economic viewpoint also.

8. Testing of the entire syllabus: As the questions are so framed that they require only one word or sentence to be answered, the total number of questions that can be asked in one question paper is almost ten to fifteen times the number that can be asked in the essay type test. Tests of this kind have 100 to 150 questions. Hence the examiner can include questions on almost every aspect of the syllabus, and the student must of necessity study the entire prescribed course.

9. Simple answer: In these tests, giving answers is very simple. Answers to questions involve no greater physical effort than drawing a line, or writing yes and no, marking something right or wrong, or writing one or two words in all. This is doubly beneficial in that it is easy to answer questions and the student's entire range of knowledge and information can be put to test.

10. Test of knowledge and not of language: There is not much writing to be done in such examinations, hence language cannot be effectively used to couch the absence of knowledge. It is the student's actual knowledge that is revealed in these tests, not his efficiency and expertise in the use of words. And this is the real objective of any examination.

11. Valid and simple marking: In tests of this kind, the examiner's task of evaluating answer books is simplified, since the questions are answered either correctly or incorrectly. There is nothing vague about it. He has no choice but to award the actual marks deserved by the answer book. Evaluation is also more or less immune to the examiner's prejudices and attitudes, so that he has no difficulty in examining the papers.

12. No importance of chance: Examinations of this kind leave very little to chance since precise questions are to be answered in precise terms.

13. Based on knowledge rather than on rote learning: Such tests examine the real knowledge of the student because these are based more on his common sense and knowledge rather than on anything that he can learn by rote.

14. Style and handwriting do not influence: In tests of this kind the examinee has very little to write, hence his style and handwriting do not exert any influence upon the examiner's judgment and evaluation.

Disadvantages of the objective method

The above exposition of the advantages of the new method is no reason to conclude that it is completely free from defects, and that it is better than the essay type examination in every respect. While it has certain features that are better than the essay type tests, it also has some disadvantages, the following:

1. Inability in style and writing: As these tests have no use for style in language and beauty in handwriting students pay little or no attention to improving them so that they are very weak in these respects.

2. Qualitative elements of learning are not tested: In the process of education, the child learns many things that cannot be expressed in such precise terms as yes, no, right, wrong, true, untrue. Such qualitative elements of learning are not examined by this new method of testing, hence these tests have no value in descriptive subjects.

3. Does not test some important abilities: Memory is not the only important ability which also includes reasoning and imagination. Modern tests are based primarily upon memory or to some extent upon reasoning but they cannot make any examination of the imaginative aspect.

4. Misses all controversial subjects: Since all questions that are included in these tests require precise answers that admit of no doubt, the tests fail to comprehend any sphere of knowledge that is controversial. It should here be remembered that in literature and social sciences, it is the controversial and indefinite parts that are far more important than the definite and settled issues, and omitting these deprives them of all value. Actually, reasoning and imagination are required only in controversial and doubtful issues.

5. Destructive of originality and creative imagination: As each question has a very precise and definite, albeit dry, answer that is required of the examinee, his creative imagination and impulse of originality is not exercised in the least. Actually, exercise of any such faculty may lead to his losing marks rather than gaining anything. But, the development of originality and the impulse to creative imaginings is an important part of the process of education, and their being restrained makes the child's development incomplete.

6. Lack of continuity: Tests of this kind definitely examine every aspect of the syllabus but the answers to all questions are completely lacking in continuity. Hence, the child's knowledge is piecemeal, lacking in continuity and unity.

7. Effect of guess: In answering to a question in terms of yes and no and other similarly cryptic terms, the child can use his guessing power, and as it happens, guesses are correct in 5 per cent and sometimes in much greater proportion.

8. Difficulty in formulating question paper: Formulation of questions in the case of modern tests requires considerable psychological insight and ingenuity of the examiner or paper setter. Hence, the average run-of-the-mill teacher cannot easily formulate such question papers. And this leads to much complications and difficulties.

QUESTIONS FOR EXERCISE

1. Describe the nature and purpose of mental tests. In what way do they differ from the school examinations?
2. Write short note on Reliability.
3. Give a critical evaluation of the prevalent system of examination for the assessment of educational attainments. What reforms may be suggested?
4. What are essay type examinations? Point out their advantages and disadvantages and suggest remedies.
5. Point out the characteristics of objective attainment tests? How is it different from ordinary tests? Evaluate its advantages and disadvantages.

40

Personality

The word personality has been derived from the Latin word 'persona', which was the mask which Greek actors wore while acting. This, however, is not the meaning taken in the modern word personality. Thus personality is not a fixed state but a dynamic totality which is continuously changing due to interaction with the environment. Personality is known by the conduct, behaviour, activities, movements and everything else concerning the individual. It is the way of responding to the environment. The way in which an individual adjusts with the external environment is personality. In the words of Munn, "Personality may be defined as the most characteristic integration of an individual's structure, modes of behaviour, interests, attitudes, capacities, abilities and aptitudes" Behaviour requires integration. Thus integration of various traits is found differently in different persons. As a general rule every healthy individual has some sort of integration. The peculiar forms of integration in a particular individual are his personality traits. Thus personality is the most characteristic integration of an individual. It is personality which makes distinction in one man and another. In the words of Gordon Allport, "Personality is the dynamic organisation within the individual, of those psycho-physical systems that determine his unique adjustment to his environment." The personality is the organisation of the internal and external activities. It includes the external appearance, qualities, aptitudes and capacities, etc. It is the result of the interaction of the individual with the environment. It is not a collection of the traits, but a particular organisation of them. It is the total quality of the individual's behaviour. Individual affects other individuals through his personality. Thus personality is manifested in his various activities. In short, personality is the total quality of behaviour, attitudes, interests, capacities, aptitudes and behaviour patterns, which are manifested in his relation with the environment.

For some time there was a discussion among the psychologists about the relation of heredity and environment in the development of personality. In this discussion arguments were given from both sides and much matter was gathered on the basis of observation and experimentation. It was found by these data that the development of personality depends upon both the heredity and the environment. Hence, modern psychology includes both heredity and environment in the factors influencing personality.

According to Gordon Allport only the relatively stable aspects of behaviour should be recognised as personality traits. In his book, *Personality: A Psychological Interpretation*, Allport writes, "From the evidence now in hand, four important conclusions may be drawn: (1) Personality, defined as the distinctive mode of adjustment adopted by each individual in his efforts to live, is not formed at birth, but it may be said to have begun at birth. (2) The earliest distinctive adjustment in respect to which infants can be said to differ, are in the intensity and frequency of their spontaneous activity (mobility) and in their emotional expression (temperature). Both these factors are primarily products of inheritance. (3) Probably not before the fourth month is there sufficient learning and maturation to form distinctive habits of adjustment or rudimentary traits. But by the second half of the first year, adoptive responses to the physical environment and to behaviour so marked distinctiveness. (4) Distinctive qualities noted early in life tend to persist. The child seems pre-disposed to learn certain modes of adjustment and reject others. Even before these adoptive forms are clearly defined an observer can often, by the method of 'prophecy' predict later traits. Irrespective of the method used in the study of the consistency of early development, the evidence is positive, virtually in every case." Thus, heredity influences the biological features of personality. As a matter of fact, the heredity does not determine personality completely, nor it is ineffective in it.

BIOLOGICAL DETERMINANTS

The factors affecting personality can be divided into two classes (1) Biological, and (2) Social. The biological factors affecting the development of personality are of three types: (1) Ductless Glands, (2) Physique, and (3) Body Chemistry.

Endocrine glands

Ductless glands send their secretions directly to the blood without ducts. Their secretions are called hormones. These hormones are responsible for many changes in the personality. Different glands secrete one or more type of hormones. A description of the affect of some of the ductless glands will show the extent to which personality is influenced by them.

1. Pancreas: Pancreas send insulin to the blood. The amount of sugar in the blood depends upon the amount of insulin in it. When the deficiency of insulin, *i.e.*, sugar, is in the body the mental powers are weakened and the personality of the individual seems less balanced. His mood is changed, temperament becomes irritated and fear increases.

2. Thyroid gland: Thyroid gland has a very important function in the development of physical structures as well as mental development. If it is absent since the very birth the intellect of the child does not improve. Cretins, imbeciles, etc., are the result of the absence of thyroid gland. Its destruction causes a disease known as myxoedema. This disease creates laziness in man. The activities of the mind as well as those of muscles are slackened. The memory becomes weak, man is not easily concentrated and thinking becomes difficult. In the period of development the excess of the activity of thyroid gland results in rapid physical growth, specially the development of height. An excessive activity of this gland results in tensions, irritation, worry and instability in man's personality. Thus with the increase or deficiency in the activity of thyroid gland, the activity of the body as well as of the mind also increases and decreases. But this does not mean that the increase and decrease of the activity in the body is always due to the effect of thyroid gland. Occasionally it might be due to other causes as well, but thyroid gland does play an important part in them.

3. Adrenal gland: Adrenal gland secrets adrenaline. Adrenaline has an important influence upon personality. Its excess creates the sexual traits in men or women. Its excess in women is responsible for the absence of the rounded contours and feminine voice. It organises the organic capacities in the time of emergency. The excess of adrenaline causes rapid heart-beat, high blood pressure and the postponement of the activity of the intestines. The individual having more adrenaline feels relaxation in the muscles, more sweat and the pupils of the eye are extended. An entire absence of adrenaline, results in the diseases known as Addison's disease. In this disease one feels weakness and lethargy in the body, the power of resisting disease is lessened, the interest in sex activity disappears and metabolism becomes slow. The skin becomes black, the power of resisting heat and cold is lessened and behaviour becomes irritable.

4. Gonads: The secretion of the gonads *i.e.,* Sex glands, is an important factor influencing personality. Gonads secrete sex hormones. Sex hormones are very helpful in the increase of sex interest. In adolescence there is a special increment in sex hormones. Hence, changes are observed in the individuals according to their sex. In male one finds the manifestation of manual characteristics such as beard, moustaches, high pitch in voice, etc., while in the female there is development of mammary glands and other womanly traits. The processes concerning pregnancy *e.g.,* mensus, pregnancy, the bearing of the child and maternal behaviour is very much influenced by the sex hormones.

5. Pituitary glands: The hormones secreted by the pituitary glands control other glands. The hormones secreted by the front part of the pituitary gland increase the activity of other glands as well. The hormones created by the back part of pituitary glands control the blood pressure and the metabolism of water in the physical activities. These hormones also effect physical growth. In the period of physical growth the bones and muscles of the individual grow speedily due to the activity of these glands. In its excess, the height can go even upto 7 to 9 feet. But because after excessive activity this gland becomes very much inactive, these very tall persons die at an early age. If the activity of the pituitary gland is very much deficient in the period of development, individual remains a midget, though his intellect is normal and the physical structure is not unattractive. If the activity of this gland is normal during the developmental period and becomes excessive afterwards, the hands, feet, nose and lower jaw, etc. become broad. This state is known as acromegaly.

The effect of the hormones is influenced by the heredity as well as the environmental factors. Bet still the excess or deficiency in their activity create some changes quite apparent in the personality of the individual. It is not necessary that the excess of the secretion of any one of the particular gland should always show some special influence in the body *e.g.*, the excess of sex tendency should not always be supposed as due to the excess of the secretion of the sex gland, since different glands also interact upon each other due to which the activity of some is increased while that of others is decreased. The sex behaviour, for example, is very much influenced by social norms, customs, circumstances, habits and many other things. Hence, in spite of the deficiency of the sex hormones, the individual may appear to be very much interested in sex activities. On the other hand, in spite of the excess of the sex hormones, the individual may not appear to be interested in sexual activities.

Physique

Another important biological factor affecting personality is physical structure. It is seen in daily life that often the fat men are easy going and social, while the thin persons are self-controlled, irritated and unsocial. Thus the physical structure has some relation with the temperament. But even the instances contrary to this rule are also existing. As a matter of fact, the relation of physical structure and temperament has not been definitely established. More studies are required in this direction. The studies conducted so far have been mostly on college students. Before one arrives at some definite conclusion, studies must be conducted on adult person as well. But even after that, the problem of the basis of co-relation remains unanswered. Simply by co-relation the temperament cannot be taken as a result of physical structure. It should also be remembered in this context that the physical structure makes a difference in other's behaviour towards a particular person. It is observed that our behaviour towards different individuals is modified, to some extent according to their physical structure. This difference in our behaviour makes a change in their personality. Hence, a particular difference should not be supposed due to physical structure alone but also due to other's behaviour towards the particular person, though the former may be more important.

Body chemistry

Another important biological factor effecting personality is body chemistry. In ancient times the difference of temperament was supposed to be due to difference of chemical elements in different men. Thus the nervous personality was taken as the result of excess of nervous fluid. It was supposed that the sanguine persons have an excess of blood, the choleric persons an excess of bile, phlegmatic persons an excess of phlegam and the melancholic persons, an excess of spleen. This principle is not accepted in modern psychology, but still no psychologist denies the relation of personality with the proportion of chemical elements in the body. These chemical elements are of two types. Some reach the body from outside while some are created in the body itself. Thus the drugs have sufficient effect on personality. The behaviour of the drunkard is an example of such effect. Different types of intoxicating drugs have a clear influence upon the personality of the individual. The deficiency of different vitamins also causes some change in the personality. With the increase or decrease of the quantity of sugar in the body, the physical and mental state of the man is very much changed. In convalescence one finds a difference in the individual's personality. Difference is also noticed after long illness.

Besides the above mentioned biological factors many other factors influence personality, *e.g.*, sex, intelligence, intellect and nervous system, etc. The difference in the sex of male and female creates as essential difference in their personality, though it has been established that much of this difference is caused by social and cultural environment. Galton and Goddard believe that intellect is absolutely hereditary. The modern psychologists do not agree with this hereditary view though the influence of heredity is not denied. The environment effects intellect, but the development of intellect is ultimately limited. The influence of special talents, as that of music, mathematics, etc., on human personality is very well known. Like the intellect, the talents are also generally hereditary. According to Kemf, the writer of *The Autonomic Function* and *Personality* the nervous system is one of the important determinants of personality.

SOCIAL DETERMINANTS

The environments of different individuals are very much different from one another and so also their effects, but the influence of environment can roughly be divided into that of home, school and society. All these three play an important part in the development of personality.

1. Influence of Home on Personality: The environment of home has a wide influence on the development of personality. This influence, as a general rule, is according to the patterns found in a particular culture. In the family the relation of child with the parents is the most intimate. The cultural development of the child is very much influenced by the behaviour of the parents *e.g.*, a child brought up in Indian family will be very much different in his behaviour than another brought up in Western culture. But even in the same culture much difference can be observed in the parent-child relationship in different families *e.g.*, generally the child has a respectable place in Indian family, but all Indian parents do not sufficiently love and sympathize with the child. In such circumstances much repression is observed in child's behaviour. He becomes an introvert and often enjoys in his dreams, day-dreams and imaginative things which are denied to him by his parents. The influence of the presence of the parental love is again not the same in the case of all children. A child may become aggressive while another may become submissive in the same circumstances. On the other hand, if the parents show excessive affection towards the child, the child may become an extremist and excessively dependent upon the parents. A child excessively ignored shows different types of conflicts in his personality. Children brought in the psychological clinics for the cure of defects of personality showed that an important cause of their defects was the behaviour of their parents towards them. According to Sigmund Freud, the tendency to depend upon the parents in the childhood is manifested in the tendency to depend upon the leader in the adult age. If the child is allowed freedom in the matters concerning his belongings, food, clothes, books etc., he will develop a habit of free will, if all these are decided by his parents, he will not get an opportunity to utilize his judgment and so become over-dependant or submissive.

Parents are more powerful and efficient than the child. Hence, they are the ideals before him. The child wants to become like his parents. Thus he establishes his identification with either of the parent and tries to follow his manners, ways and behaviour. The child also fulfils his frustrated desires through this identification. It has been observed that the little boy wears the big shirt of the father and walks proudly like him with a stick in his hand. This identification with the parents in the childhood is later on converted into the identification of the individual with the leader. By the identification with the leader the individual is happy in leader's achievements and sorry in his failures.

In the absence of affection and sympathy, the child often turns criminal While discussing the causes of criminal tendencies, Healy and Bronner have emphasized three factors: the effort to get rid of the painful circumstances, the tendency to take revenge for the misbehaviour of the father, the efforts to satisfy the frustrating desires. Often the child has the curiosity as to from where the younger brother or sister has come. The answer to this question by the parents has an important effect on his personality. The child has a natural curiosity towards the sex tendency. Often the parents try to suppress his curiosity towards the sex or they just rebuke when he asks such questions. But the child is not silenced by this. He tries to enquire from the servants or friends in the house. But this leads to guilty conscience. The reactions in the parents about the every day matters in the family also effect the personality of the child. The relations of the mother and father among themselves also effect the personality of the child more or less.

It has been observed that the behaviour of the eldest and the youngest, the elder or the younger is not the same in the family. Similarly, it has been found that the parent's behaviour towards them is not also the same. This has led the psychologist Alfred Adler, to emphasize the importance of birth order in the development of personality. The birth order of the child fixes the status in the family which decides his roles which affect his personality. The younger child is treated with affection by every one, hence he becomes overdependant. The eldest child becomes self-sufficient and tyrant, because being the only child for some time he does not share his rights and things with others. The birth of another child in the family has an important influence on the child, since it takes away his monopoly in affection and sometimes he is neglected altogether. Hence, he feels jealous with the younger child and tries to regain his rights. On the other hand, the new child is anxious to make his place in his family. The above description of the child's problems based upon the conception of birth order has been conclusively proved.

The researchers have found similar conflicts in different birth orders. Adler has truly said that the individual develops his style of life from the pattern of his early life in the family, but there are no grounds to suppose that this style of life remains unchanged in future. It cannot be denied that the environment in the childhood is one of the most important factors determining personality, but it is difficult to believe with Freud and Adler that the personality of an individual is completely determined in childhood.

Influence of school on personality

School also has an important influence on the personality of the child. In school both the teachers and class fellows mould his personality. Just as in the family the parents are ideals before the child so are teachers in the school. The child hates the cruel and strict teacher. On the other hand, he respects good and sympathetic teachers. The personality of the teacher and his behaviour towards the child both exercise important influence on the child's personality. The child tends to identify himself with the teacher and tries to imitate his ways, manners and personality traits. This is only with the influential teachers and not with every one. Thus teachers mould the personality of the child by their example.

Besides the teacher, the classmates and playmates exercise important influence on the personality of the child. These constitute a group in which every child has his own particular status and roles corresponding to it. One can see the leader, the dare devil and the scapegoat child in the group. The leader is the mind of the group. He plans adventures and games. The dare devil executes them while the scapegoat is left to receive the blame and consequent punishment. In different types of groups of children, different traits of leadership are required according to the purpose. Thus sometimes the intelligent child leads while at other times the leader is the dare devil. This particular role in the group determines the future role of the individual in a society. This, however, is not without exceptions. The development of the personality is a complex process and serious changes are affected in new circumstances which the individual has to face.

Influence of society on personality

Society is a web of social relationships. These social relationships connect men and women with one another. These interpersonal relations influence and mould the personality of the individual. In the society each individual has some peculiar status and roles corresponding to them. For example, in Hindu community, members of different castes have different social status in society. The roles and functions of an individual are determined by his status. This mechanism controls the behaviour of the individuals. Social control is further exercised by mores, traditions, myths, legends, customs, etc. These determine the style of life of the individual. The individual cannot behave in the society as he likes. Society punishes the individual who breaks its norms. The fear of society is often more powerful than even the fear of heaven and hell or punishment by the state. Therefore, social norms influence even the ways and attitudes of the individuals. This ultimately influences his personality. The individual adopts the prevalent patterns of social behaviour. That is why one notices so much differences in the behaviour and personality of members of different societies. This, however, does not mean that there are no individual differences in the same society. In fact, in every society one can find men and women who scarcely care for the social norms. But in every case, personality is affected by the social environment. Individuality is an outcome of the process of socialisation which is impossible without society. There is constant interaction between the individual and society and this interaction moulds the personality of the individual.

STAGES OF DEVELOPMENT

The different conditions of infancy, adolescence, youth and old age are very clearly depicted in the psychological development of the man. The speed and direction of physiological development differs from one stage to another. In the different stages of the development of personality, different changes are visible in the personality of individual. In some stages these changes are faster and more comprehensive while in other stages the change is comparatively less. This change shows a change in the personality too.

1. The first six years: Freud and many other psychologists give great importance to infancy in an individual's life. Some psychologists have claimed the development of personality to start during pregnancy. In Rank's view the development of personality starts in the mother's womb. This opinion says further that the very activity of its conception effects the child's personality, the presence or absence of difficulties in it making a difference in the personality. But it has not been possible to prove this theory by experimentation. In Freud's opinion, whatever incidents take place in the first three years of a child life permanently mould his character the rest being a mere development of these peculiarities. Suckling, weaning, loving, fondling, scolding, beating, toilet training, etc., all effect the child's personality. The love and affection of the parents has a very significant effect upon the child. Excessive love and affection make a child stubborn and inconsistent. Lack of affection stunts the development of his emotions while proper love gives him emotional stability.

Besides love and affection, suckling also impresses the personality of the child. Experiments indicate that even when the child is not hungry, he does not want to release the breasts. Actually suckling is not merely a mode of satisfying hunger but also a symbol of the mother's love for the child and consequently weaning also affects the child's personality because it sometimes expresses the indifference of the mother directed at the child. If the child is suckled for a long time he becomes dependant and comfortable. Early weaning may lead to the development of the tendencies of pessimism and morbidity. An interesting experiment was carried out on college students in this context. They asked their mothers about the ages at which weaning had been carried out, and they were subsequently tested for their feelings of security or insecurity. This experiment indicated an important correlation between weaning and the feeling of security and insecurity. Those who had been weaned at an age of 6 to 9 months, but those who had not been suckled at all or only for about three months, showed no sense of insecurity whatsoever. This strange result was seen in the light of the fact that in the cultural group from among which these students had been chosen, the cause of weaning was not the desire but the inability to continue suckling. This study indicates that the weaning does not have as great an effect as indifference on the part of the mother. The effect of weaning which is felt is the effect of the mother's indifference. In the first six years, the child learns the adjustment of his needs with the environment. His relations with his mother during this adjustment leave a permanent mark on the development of his personality. The development of a feeling of insecurity at this age leads to mental conflict making a child frightened and depressed and aggressive and naughty. Even toilet training effects the child. If, in the teaching of cleanliness, of which parents and other members partake, excessive hardness and resolution are applied, the child may develop many compulsions. The birth order, and the birth of a new infant, all have an effect on the child. The relations of the parents among themselves, the social and financial status of the family, both leave an indelible mark on his personality. The outlook and reaction of the family members towards the sexual tendencies also tend to effect the child's personality. Unnecessary fear develops a criminal tendency in the child. The intelligent satisfaction of his curiosity has a good effect on his development.

Qualities of personality become apparent at a very early age of the child. The difference of will-power, friendliness, determination and impressing others, etc. between children appear at the ages of two or three. By the time a child is five he starts expressing competitiveness. It has been seen from experiments that qualities or traits like mobile adjustment, self-dependance, love for the family, humour, emotional adjustment and reaction to resistance, etc., of the personality appear at the age of one and stay permanent even after adolescence. But some traits show some change. Actually, there is a lot of truth in the fact that the foundation of the peculiarities in the personality of a person are laid in childhood.

2. Pre-Pubertal childhood: The second stage in the development of human personality continues till the on-coming of puberty and it is accordingly entitled the Pre-Pubertal childhood. At this stage, the conditions of the school start effecting the development of his personality because commonly, by now, he has started attending school and playing with other children. The child is given a particular place in the family, whereas he has to acquire for himself a position among his colleagues. He thus learns the lesson of equality and justice. His mother does not afford him security in the school, whereby he learns the traits of independence and self-dependance, and these changes are also felt in the family. The child enters his own age group and acquires a role according to his personality, and by living in a group learns the patterns of his further grown up life. It is at this stage that he learns the lesson of leadership, friendship, sympathy and social adaptation. His success or failure in group develops many good and bad traits in the child. A child extremely dependant on someone member of the family had difficulty in adjusting to the group, a state which generally results in the origination of a sense of inferiority. The practices which a child adopts are the ones which have brought him success in his attempts at the adjustment within his group. If obstinancy and self-assertion or aggression are more advantageous he will develop them and if escape is more successful the child will become an escapist.

3. Puberty and adolescence: The next stage in the development of human personality is the stage of puberty and adolescence. Puberty is a physiological condition, in which the maturation of sexual activities takes place. It is the link between childhood and adulthood. Adolescence as a psychological state is generally characterised by extensive disturbance.

Puberty does effect personality. After puberty, the interest in sexual activities becomes specified and developed. Many studies have made it known that the social behaviour of girls and boys and awareness of the physiological condition of puberty leads to a feeling of adulthood. In this stage the boys and girls want to identify themselves with adulthood, their interests becoming adult. Immediately after it the boys and girls start exhibiting the respective physical signs of their sexes. The girls start having menstrual cycles and their organs acquire rounded contours. Boys grow beards and moustaches and their voices become heavy. In this stage mental development, too, is maximum. Puberty takes place two year earlier in girls than the boys, this being the reason for their exhibition of pubertal changes.

The psychological state of adolescence effects personality in no small measure. The girls and boys start taking an interest in persons of the opposite sex. They also experience an increase in the sense of independence. The adjustment of adolescence is a problem which differs with culture. The disturbance of an adolescent in civilised societies is not found in the people of Samoa. In their society, unlike the civilised societies, there are no restrictions on sexual behaviour and the individual becomes self-dependent at an early age. The disturbance of the adolescent stage is due to those mental conflicts through which a civilised person has to pass. These conflicts arise from many social problems like independence from the parents, sexual adjustment, self-dependence, choice of profession, etc. In this age, if the parents still look on the youth as a child, he will either make a strong revolt against it or submit to it, the latter course leading to a stop in the development of his personality. The indifference to sex education makes these adolescent problems even more intricate. In India, there is more sex education and less sex restrictions in primitive tribes than there is in the Hindu society. Thus the transition from adolescence to adulthood is easier for the tribal youths than the Hindu youths. Absence of the means of satisfying sexual curiosities and social feeling of evil related to them increase the guilt conscience and anxiety of the adolescent, and this does not allow the proper development of his personality. It is a baseless idea that the person becomes entirely new during adolescence or that there is a complete reorganization of his entire personality. Adolescence is a stage in the development of personality and development is a continuous process in which infancy effects adolescence and adolescence effects adulthood.

4. Adulthood and after: The fourth stage, following adolescence in the development of personality is adulthood. Many studies and researches have revealed that equilibrium is at a low ebb in the beginning of adulthood and just before old age, between them there being comparatively better adjustment. After adolescence upon entering adulthood a person adopts some permanent occupation, gets married and develops a family. All these three tasks demand extensive adjustment and a lot of change is brought in the personality. After this, till old age, not much change is needed. This static stage develops a dogmatic forbearing and social outlook. This outline of general development is not found essentially in all. Actually, it depends on the adjustments of the adult age, one of the problems being economic adjustment. Getting a lower post than anticipated, long periods of unemployment, getting an uninteresting occupation, freedom from dependence on employment, all have profound effect upon the individual. Many serious problems arise in the adjustment towards the marriage partner in adulthood and all the adult life is bereft of calm and peace. Similarly, incidents like absence of children, death of the offspring, too many children and in India, too many daughters, tend to keep a man in worry and misery till old age. In brief, as we have said above, occupation, marriage and offspring are essential for an adult. If their condition is satisfactory the person's personality remains balanced but if there is any disturbance it becomes difficult for the person to retain his balance and complacence.

5. Old age and before it: After adult life, in old age and just before it, many troubles surround the person, major ones concerning the diminution in his physical energies, economic power and social prestige. In old age people who find themselves dependent on others do not retain their mental balance. People who retire with a pension or a provident fund of some thousand rupees are not in a very satisfactory state unless they have developed some occupation from their adult life. The problem of adjustment arises before the mother who has nothing to do after her children have been married off. If now she does not take to some work, religion, or activity the only thing left for her is to criticise the neighbouring daughters-in-law or to create unnecessary troubles and obstacles in the lives of the younger generation.

It must have become obvious, from this rough outline of the stages in the development of personality, that it means the adjustment with new needs, conflicts and frustrations. New problems of adjustment keep on arising in the different stages in the physiological and psychological development of personality and from the changing environment. It is often seen that the deficiencies of one stage in the development are fulfilled in the next stage. But besides this, in every stage new problems arise whose solution is essential. The development of personality is a continuous process passing through these stages, devoid of any interval.

PERSONALITY INTEGRATION

Personality is the dynamic organisation of the psycho-physical traits exhibited in the adjustment with the environment. If the organisation of psycho-physical traits in personality is not in tune to the environment, such a personality will be called disintegrated.

What is integration of personality?

The integration of personality is necessary in order to effect complete adjustment with the environment. Adjustment will be natural and easy if this integration is strong. The integration of personality is the integration of all the psycho-physical traits of personality. There is an absence of conflicts in it. In it, mind and emotion, desire and determination, and all mental activities are in no way disorganised but all of them work in an organised way. An integrated personality is flexible, strong and organised, as well as balanced. In it there is a compromise of mind and emotions. McDougall has called it the organisation of character and intellect.

The integration of personality is found in every one to a lesser or greater degree. If this integration is less than is essential, then problems of adjusting to the environment arise. Freud believes in three elements in personality—Id, Ego and Super Ego. Id includes the person's desires, instincts, suppressed desires, etc., Super Ego is the representative of social control, the result of the person's socialisation. It exercises social control over the person while the Id demands the fulfilment of animal desires. Ego includes the tendencies, which work for the existence of life. Thus, often the Super Ego conflicts with the Id or Ego. The problems of personality are the problems of the mental adjustment of these three.

How is the personality to be integrated?

The weakness of the ego is the fundamental in personality problems in the person. Either the person's ego cannot control his desires and instincts or it cannot adjust with the super ego. For the integration of personality, it is necessary that the person maintains a balanced and realistic outlook. Some failures and frustrations cross everyone's path, and the person should pursue his life task without being extra-ordinarily disturbed by happiness or sorrow. Balance is the golden path of life. It is only the balance of emotions, demands, needs and imagination and thinking which can keep the personality integrated.

Importance of emotionality and sociability

The definition of the integration of personality must have made it clear that it needs socialisation essentially without which the person finds it difficult to adjust to the environment. The social environment is not the total environment of the person and neither is sociability by itself the adequate trait for the adaptation to society, but in spite of this it can be said that sociability is an essential trait in the adaptation to society. Sociability, as the name suggests, is that tendency by which a person mixes with the other people of the society and lives with them. An unsocial person is introspective and likes to live alone.

He experiences difficulty in meeting other people and having relations with them or behaving towards them. In daily life, the problems which arise in his meeting with other people assume alarming proportions while the social man solves them with ease. For example, the unsocial person feels lonely when he is alone, and bored and restless upon the advent of new people while the social person mixes with them easily and occupies his correct position.

Effects of the deficiency of integration

The most glaring example of a deficiency of integration is seen in the absence of adjustment with the environment, which also exhibits the effects of deficiency. The reason is that in the absence of integration the personality is unbalanced, there being no proper blending of psycho-physcial traits. It is not essential that deficiency of integration will render him incapable of work. Many of the greatest persons suffered from grave deficiencies in the integration of their personalities, but though this did not hinder or restrict their greatness, their personalities were incomplete and one-sided. With people of average capabilities any such deficiency will effect even their skill in behaviour. It can be generally said that in case of deficiency in integration of personality, the person can neither be skilled in his behaviour nor gets success in his life's works. He not only makes his own life disturbed but also disturbs the peace in the lives of others. Thus psychologists help people in the integration of their personalities by giving suggestions.

TYPES OF PERSONALITY

In psychology, people have been classified on the basis of physiological and mental traits and temperaments.

Physiological types

Physiological types in personality are exemplified in the classification of personalities by E. Kretchmer in his book *Physique* and *Character*. Kretchmer has classified people into two classes according to their physical structure:

1. **Cycloid:** These people are fat. Their temperament is objective, sociable and happy.

2. **Schizoid:** These people are thin and tall. They are temperamentally self-centred, emotional, reticent, peaceful and lovers of solitude.

Besides these two types, Kretchmer has mentioned many sub-classes on the basis of physical structure, some of the main ones being:

1. **Asthenic:** People of this group are short and thin. They are of a self-centred, emotional, dreamy, intellectual, peaceful and solitude loving temperament.

2. **Athletic:** As the name suggests, their built is very good having broad shoulders and slim waist. In temperament they are sociable, adept in behaviour and active.

3. **Picnic:** These people are fat. Their stomachs protrude and they have round faces. They are naturally happy and sociable.

Classification has been made on the basis of temperaments, besides the physical structure. One example of such classification can be found in W.H. Sheldon's book, *The Varieties of Temperament*. Before this, the bases of classification were the anthropological measurements, by which the shape and structure of the body of people were classified.

On the basis of shape and size, Sheldon classified people into these groups:

1. **Endomorphic:** Their stomach is big and the large intestines are developed.
2. **Mesomorphic:** In this case, the bones and muscles are developed.
3. **Ectomorphic:** Their bones are long and soft while the physical structure is weak.

Types based on temperament

On the same basis, temperament too is classified into three classes

1. **Viscerotonic:** In this tvpe activities of easing predominate. They love comfort and food and seek the love of others. They also sleep deeply. They like others to help them when in trouble. People with endomorphic physical structure fall into this category.

2. **Somatotonic:** The mesomorphic people constitute this group. They are of brittle, clear and competitive nature, and are generally powerful, daring, authoritative and loud talkers. In trouble they are more active.

3. **Cerebrotonic:** This class includes the ectomorphic type of people. They are controlled, withdrawing and sensing. They are habituated to suppressing their emotions. They love solitude and instead of seeking assistance in trouble, they like to stay within their own limits. They speak slowly and their sleep is disturbed.

Morgan and Gilliland have mentioned four types of personality on the basis of temperament—

1. *Elated:* They are optimistic, elated and happy.
2. *Depressed:* These people are pessimistic, depressed and emotional.
3. *Irritable:* They are the interfering, irritable and of hot tempered type.
4. *Unstable:* Their mood is unbalanced, unstable and emotional.

Psychological type

The most important classification of personality is done by Jung. On the basis of sociability he has accepted two types of people—Extroverts and Introverts.

1. **Extroverts:** These people take more interest in others and like to mix with people of similar temperaments. They are realistic and face the problems of life objectively and are always ready to partake of any social activity around them. They take part freely in any social give and take. They are dominated by emotions whereby they take decisions quickly and act on them with delay. They are skilled in ettiquette. The extrovert group is made up of traders, players, actors, social and political leaders, etc.

2. Introvert: As the name suggests, the mental tendencies of these people are directed, not outwards to people around them, but rather inwards to themselves. They are thus self-centred and lovers of solitude. With them, thinking predominates and they are engaged in thinking and contemplation. They are busy in their thoughts and they try to impress others only by their thoughts. They are idealists who think very much about the future. Usually, they take more interest in the physical environment composed of trees, plants, machines, etc., than they do in their social environment. Neither do they come to any decision in haste and nor do they act on it promptly. They are not experts in behaviour, but they pay more attention to thought than work. People like scientists, philosophers and poets make up this group.

The following table is intended to make clearer the differences between introverts and extroverts:

Extroverts	Introverts
1. Turned to other people.	1. Turned to themselves.
2. Emotion predominates.	2. Thought predominates.
3. Quick determination.	3. Determination takes some time.
4. Prompt action on decision.	4. Delayed action on decision.
5. Skilled in behaviour.	5. Unskilled in behaviour.
6. Pay attention to the present.	6. Pay attention to the future.
7. Prefer work to thought.	7. Prefer thought to work.
8. Realists.	8. Idealists.
9. Like society.	9. Like solitude.
10. Objective outlook.	10. Subjective outlook.

3. Ambiverts: The above table about the extroverts and the introverts makes it very obvious that these two types are exactly opposed to each other. But in the real world these two types are rarely found pure. Mostly, some peculiarities of both the extroverts and the introverts are found in people. These intermediate people are called "ambiverts". Later still, Jung divided these people into sensing, thinking, feeling and instinctive types.

Criticism

The above mentioned theories of classifying personalities are not accepted in modern psychology. On this subject the following criticisms are important:

1. Experience and observation make it obvious that most people cannot be fitted into any one type.
2. The 'type' raises doubts on the subject of cause and effect. It would be incorrect to assert that a certain person is solitude loving because he is an introvert.
3. Types cannot be established by measurements. Only the different traits of personality can be measured. It is not essential that these qualities will remain the same in a person.

Thus, the attempt of dividing people into groups is not only without advantage and impractical but also useless.

METHODS OF PERSONALITY ASSESSMENT

Psychology employs a number of methods by which it measures personality, *e.g.*, situation test, psycho-analystic test and projective method, etc. Besides these, the case history method, interview, questionnaire and rating methods have their own importance. Briefly, the methods of measuring personality are:

1. Case History Method
2. Interview Method
3. Questionnaire Method
4. Performance Method
5. Rating Method
6. Situation Test
7. Psycho-Analytic Test
8. Projection Method.

Among the above mentioned methods, the projection method is the most popular. A brief description of the other methods, before we make a detailed description of this specific method, would be quite in keeping with the context.

1. Case history method: In the case history method, as the name obviously indicates, the facts concerning the life of the subject are collected.

This case history supplies all the large and small facts related to his environment and heredity. This method can study both normal and abnormal people's personalities but it needs very experienced examiners.

2. Interview method: The interview method is the most normal of all the methods for the study of personality. It is the method widely used in the selection of personnel in government services. In this, the subject and the examiner sit facing each other while the former answers questions asked by the latter. Besides the answers which the subject offers, his personality is indicated by his expressions, methods and various other things. This method, like the case history method, needs very experienced examiners who ask questions which can probe correct thing and which enable the subject to express himself without apprehension. To tell the truth, the interview method depends as much on the examiner as it does on the subject.

3. Questionnaire method: Questionnaires have been used extensively in the investigation of personality. The name suggests that it is the list of selected questions the answers to which throw light upon the peculiarities of personality. 'Yes' and 'No' are written m front of these questions. The student either strikes out the wrong answer or indicates the correct one. Questionnaires are used to gain knowledge of traits like self-confidence, sociability, introversion or extroversion, tendency to dominate or be dominated, etc.

There are some difficulties in the questionnaire methods. It has the following limitations:

1. Often the subjects conceal the true facts and give wrong answers.
2. Sometimes the framing of the questions is such that the examiner takes them to mean one thing and subject another.

3. Usually the subjects write the answer without an adequate amount of thinking thus leaving possibility of mistakes.

In spite of these difficulties, the questionnaire method has proved to be of tremendous value. Allport and Minnesota, etc., have formed questionnaires which enable the study of some subtle traits of the personality. It affords a lot of assistance to comparative study because of the various answers of the subjects to the same questions. The conclusions based on these questionnaires are comparative as well as numerical. They also facilitate study because a number of people can be studied simultaneously.

4. Performance method: The performance method was conceived by May and Hartshorne. In this method the subject is given a variety of specific jobs to be performed and the subtle quality of his personality examined. For example, in order to test the honesty of children, 8 or 10 weights, with little difference between them, were located at some place. The exact weight of each was written under it and the children were told to place them in the correct order. The honest children experienced great difficulty while the dishonest read the weights under them and placed them in the order promptly.

A very simple method of judging the honesty of the students in the class could be something like this. Some piece should be dictated and the copies collected. The mistakes of each should be secretdly noted without any markings on the copy, following which the copies should be returned with the direction that the mistakes are to be noted and marks allocated. The dictation should be written on the black board. The honest will cancel their mistakes while the dishonest will quietly correct them. The honesty of the students can be judged by comparing these with the mistakes previously noted.

5. Rating method: Another method of measuring personality is the rating method, in which roughly the work is done in two ways. One, the subject is asked to answer questions related to traits of personality. The answer which the subject offers to the answers which he selects indicate his personality. Another way of applying the rating method is to place the subject in real situations and then study his behaviour and reactions. For example, in order to judge traits like skill, honesty, sincerity, labour, etc., in a person, he may be given a variety of jobs to perform.

As it is, the rating method is deceptively simple. But it needs very skilful examiners. Roughly speaking, it presents the following difficulties:

1. Skill and capability are essential in the examiner.
2. The possibility of prejudice is very great because it is a general truth that no person observes the delects of his near and dear ones.
3. Another grave difficulty of this method is the fact that upon observing a particular good or bad quality we class his personality as good or bad and then see good or bad in the other apsects of his personality.
4. It is very difficult to enumerate or evaluate the quantity of one subtle trait. Mistakes are often made in this.

In spite of the above difficulties both social and industrial psychologists too, make adequate use of this method. As has been pointed out previously too, it can be made realistic to a large extent only if the examiner has all the essential qualities.

6. Situation test: As usual, the name suggests, the nature of the method. In it, the subject is placed in some specific situations and the traits of his personality are ascertained. Actually, it resembles the performance method, the difference lying in the fact that in this case the person is placed in a situation while in the performance method he is given some work to do. Most psychologists have identified the two together, rendering a separate discussion indispensable.

7. Psycho-analytic method: Two types of tests, in the psycho-analytic method of investigation of personality, are more popular—Free Association and Dream Analysts. Both these tests show the peculiarities of the psycho-analytic personality, in its unconscious aspect. In dream analysis, the subject describes his dream and without using the mind, meaning thereby the unrestricted state of the mind, associates freely the dream objects and activities. Because of the absence of the mental element, the truth of the unconscious mind is expressed by this association, by which the psycho-analyst discovers many peculiarities of his character. The psycho-analytic method is mostly used in discovering the personality peculiarities, mental complexes and mental ailments of abnormal people. Its main difficulty lies in the need for a skilled and experienced psycho-analyst. Often the psycho-analyst analyses his own mind in order to remove the possibility of any prejudice.

8. Project method: The most famous and popular of all the methods for the investigation of personality is the project method. Its name suggests the fact that it is founded upon the element of projection. Projection means the observation of some specific thing in some thing or action, according to one's personality and mental state. The Taj Mahal, to take an example, is a marble building many people go to see. Different people find in it different things, in keeping with the peculiarities of their personalities. An emotional person sees it in the form of a formal symbol of emotions while, to the person who gives importance to political and economic questions, it may be a symbol of exploitation. This is an example of a material object but it does make clear the fact that human being does not see an object as it is but also projects this specialities of his own personality upon it. Many peculiarities of the personality are investigated by an analysis of this projection and comparison of it with the projections effected by others.

Two tests in the project method are more famous:

1. Rorschach ink blot test.
2. Murray's Thematic Apperception Test, known in brief as T.A.T. They are extensively used in the investigation of personality in general. These will, therefore, be described briefly here.

Tests in the project method

1. Rorschach ink blot test: This test was conceived by the Swiss scientist Harman Rorschach. He used 10 original ink blot cards which are still in use today. There is no picture made in these blots. Five of these are black, two black and red and the other three multicoloured. To investigate personality, they are exhibited before the subject one after the other and he is asked to describe everything he sees in the blot. These are shown for a determined interval of time. These cards are shown to the subject for a second time and he is asked to point out the location, of whatever he had seen, on the blot. In order to establish the meaning of the subject's reaction to the blots, the psychologist analyses the location, deciding factors and the object. The analysis of the location serves to indicate whether the subject reacted to some particular spot on the blot or towards the blot as a whole. As a general rule, it is believed that the person who reacts more completely is more principled. The analysis of the deciding factor is an attempt to find out whether the reaction of the subject is towards the shape of the blot or colour in the blot or the motion of the blot. As to the object, the analysis shows whether the subject sees in it, the figure of a man or an animal or anything else.

Besides the above analysis, facts like the time taken by the subject to react to the whole blot, the number of activities which he did and whether he did them normally or not, are also noted and observed. All these things tend to help in the analysis and investigation of the conceived and unconscious peculiarities of the subject.

The biggest difficulty in the ink blot test is that the description of the subject's reactions becomes quite subjective, which conceals to some extent the correct personality traits of the subject. But maximum efforts are being made to make this test scientific.

2. Murray's thematic apperception test: The founder of this test, Murray investigated the traits of personality with the help of some pictures. These pictures are still considered to be conclusive. Observing these pictures, the subject, by projection, identifies himself with the characters in the picture. The pictures are presented one by one to the subject who has to compose a story on them in some fixed time period, say five minutes. Unknowingly, the subject expresses many of the peculiarities of his personality, in this story by projection. He does not get time to think. Therefore, the story expresses his natural desires, emotions, sentiments, etc. On the basis of these stories, the psychologist analyses the personality of the subject and uncovers traits.

As in the Rorschach ink blot test, there is a lot of difficulties in Murray's thematic apperception test, and the personality investigation done by it is not numerical but qualitative with grave possibility of mistakes. But, still there is no doubt that an experienced and skilful psychologist can use this method to uncover the traits of the personality of the subject. This test helps in the discovery of many mental distortions, enabling subsequently their curing.

QUESTIONS FOR EXERCISE

1. Give a definition of personality. Explain any two methods of measuring personality.
2. "Personality is the whole man." Comment on the above and make out a case for the view that personality cannot be measured.
3. Discuss the determinants of personality.
4. Discuss biological and cultural determinants of personality.
5. Discuss different stages in the development of personality.
6. What do you understand by the integration of personality? Discuss the factors of emotionality and sociality in this integration. Describe some results of the lack of this integration.
7. Write short note on Personality Types.
8. Explain briefly the various methods by which the personality can be studied.

41

Theories of Personality

PSYCHO-ANALYTIC THEORY

In his books Freud has emphasized the role of unconscious processes in human behaviour. According to Freud almost the entire mental life is directed from the unconscious forces. The conscious level is a very small part of the unconscious mind. The unconscious is the reservoir of the unfulfilled motives. It stores repressed unfulfilled infantile sexual desires. According to Freud the repressed desires do not disappear but go to the unconscious of the man, and there await suitable changes for manifestation. Of these almost all the desires are sexual. It is the sexual desire which is the cause of much of these sexual desires with the name *libido* as the motivation force in human life.

The Id

Thus, according to Freud, man's unconscious is the store house of instinctive impulses, frustrated desires and repressed feelings. It is not in the contact of the environment. Freud calls it Id. In the Id there are the directing forces of the man. Earlier, Freud conceived if to be directed by the pleasure principle alone, but later on he accepted the existence of death instinct as well. Thus, in the Id there are impulses connected both with life and death. These impulses assume the form of particular desires which are directed towards the environment. Thus they very much influence the conscious life of a man. In the Id most of these desires are sexual.

The Ego

In the beginning Freud conceived Id as unconscious and the ego as conscious, and explained their conflict in terms of the conflict of the unconscious and conscious. Later on, he modified his concept of the polarity of the conscious and the unconscious. Earlier he thought that the conscious level is the level of the ego and on this level the unwanted desires are repressed and sent to the unconscious. But later on Freud found that many of his patients who were analyzed, themselves did not know these resistances consciously. They were presenting some sort of resistances, while remembering their past experiences. This showed that the resistance and repression is unconscious. According to this modified view ego is partly conscious and partly unconscious. In the unconscious aspect it is in the contact of the environment. This contact with the environment is through the muscles. The ego is also concerned with the inner mind of the man. This is the internal unconscious. The concept of this unconscious is proved through conscious pleasure and pain. According to Freud there is a constant conflict between this conscious or the ego with this unconscious level. The ego mediates between both these worlds because it is partly conscious and partly unconscious. In his famous book *The Ego* and *Id*, Freud writes, "The ego tries to mediate demands of the world and the Id, to make the Id comply with the world's demand and, by means of it, always in search of pleasure." Id searches for pleasure blindly according to pleasure principle. But the Id must work through the Ego and the Ego follows the reality principle. In the beginning Ego is weak and undeveloped. Hence it has to face many difficulties to fulfil Id's desires. It runs after the objects which are not found in the environment. When the ego has to achieve his favourite object, it keeps its image in it and identifies itself with the object. Thus, by adopting the characteristic of the coveted object, the Ego gradually develops. When successfully developed, the Ego is systematic and well organized and adjusted to the environment. The Id is always primitive and unorganized.

The Super Ego

Super Ego is called conscience to the ordinary sense. It is also known as Ego ideal. In the analysis of the behaviour of his patients, Freud sometimes found much sense of guilt. Hence, he had to postulate a Super Ego besides the Id and Ego.

Like the conscience this Super Ego tries to oppress Ego by several rules and taboos. It tries to direct Ego regarding what it has to do and what it has not to do. These directions are not based on particular needs. They are categorical imperatives.

There is another significant difference between the Super Ego and the Ego. The Super Ego develops only in the human beings, while the Ego is found in some form in all the developed animals. This is because man has to pass through a very long period of infancy and his sexual urge takes much time to arrive at its object in the adult sexual life. According to Freud, the Ego develops in the life of the individual whereas the sources of the Super Ego can be traced from the primitive man. Thus man gets the Super Ego not only in his own life, but through traditions as well. Yet most of the part of the Super Ego develops anew in every child. Freud has traced its origin to the frustrated sexual desires in the child. According to Freud in the child there is a real sex impulse which searches a person of different sex. According to this view the boy loves the mother and the girl loves the father. Not only this but the boy finds rival in the father while the girl finds a rival in the mother. Thus, the mind of the child is a field of terrible conflict which creates mental complexes. It is through these conflicts that the Super Ego develops.

Regarding the nature of Ego Adler and Jung differ from Freud in certain aspects. For example, whereas for Freud the Ego follows the reality principle, according to Adler it does not do so. Jung has taken the *libido* of Freud in a very wide sense and identified it with physical energy. Of these, Freud's hypothesis has proved to be most helpful in the explanation of human behaviour, specially those of the abnormal persons.

Theory of psycho-sexual genesis

In the opinion of Freud the sexual instinct in man has biological as well as psychological influence, and he believes that most tendencies that result in mental illness have psycho-sexual aggressivity genesis. According to Freud, the sexual instinct becomes evident in man in infancy, and for this reason frustrations of human life have their origin in infant life. Freud also put forward the contention that in the psychological viewpoint there is no distinction between normal and abnormal individuals and that their behaviour should be elaborated on similar principles and theories. The development of mentally ill people does not differ from those of normal people in kind, and this conception of Freud has been borne out by the observation of abnormal and ill children. A fact that is generally recognized by abnormal psychology today is that every mental disease has its psychological as well as physiological aspect.

Sexual tendency in children

Freudian theory of the presence of sexual instinct in children was intensely opposed, and severely chastised, but modern sexologists and psychologists as well as physicians recognized this fact. For attaining adulthood in sex it is essential that infantile sexuality be repressed. The sexual instinct passes through a latent period from about 7 to 14 years of age, after the infantile stage has been passed and before adolescence is attained. During this period the sexual instinct is latent, but later on in youth it is again revived. Freud has always seen the human personality as a psyche that is involved in interaction with the environmental forces. Through the process of this interaction the individual has to suffer many frustrations and repressions that create considerable change in the personality.

Stages in sex development

Freud has described the following stages in the development of the sex instinct:

1. **Oral stage:** In this much of the sexual activity is confined to oral biting and oral sucking.

2. **Anal stage:** In this two tendencies are prominent—the anal expulsive tendency and the anal retentive tendency. At this stage the child is imparted toilet training, and this has considerable influence upon his personality. If too much frustration is effected his personality develops all kinds of abnormalities.

3. **Phallic stage:** In this condition most of the frustrations are concerned with infantile masturbation.

4. **Period of latency:** In this the experiences of sexuality are latent, not apparent.

5. Genital stage: In this sexuality is again apparent, and following this stage sexuality is manifested in normal adult relationships.

TRAIT THEORY

Definition of personality

The American psychologist Gorden W. Allport (1887-1967) presented his theory of personality in his famous books: *Personality: A Psychological Interpretation* (1937), *Basic Consideration for a Psychology of Personality* (1955) and *Pattern and Growth in Personality* (1961). G.W. Allport defined personality as, "Dynamic organization within the individual of those psycho-physical systems that determine his unique adjustments to his environment." According to Allport human personality is a developing and changing organization of habits, attitudes and traits. The term psycho-physical, used by Allport, points out that personality systems are both mental and physical processes. Allport maintained that motivational systems are functionally autonomous. They are not dependent upon the antecedent conditions from which they arise. For example, a good craftsman may continue to make fine objects of furniture even though his income no longer depends upon it. Similarly, a businessman may amass wealth not because he needs it, but because he has become habitual and his motivation is independent of the needs that originally stimulated it.

Importance of personality traits

According to Allport personality trait is the best and most valid concept for the study of personality. According to him, personality traits are the systems that have the capacity to make a variety of stimuli functionally equivalent and to initiate and guide behaviour. For example, a prejudiced individual will react to all the members of a minority group (stimuli) as though they were identical (functionally equivalent) when in fact they are not so. Moreover one can expect such an individual to react consistently in approximately the same manner. The traits are similar to habits. Some traits are primarily individual traits. These are the personality traits that are more or less specific to a given individual. On the other hand, common traits are those that are found in most individuals to some degree and which therefore make measurement possible. Examples of such traits are sociability, dominance, etc. However, Allport does not wish to say that personality is mere collection of traits. The concept of proprium is central in Allport's system of personality. This concept includes what traditional psychology has called self, ego and study of life. According to Allport the related concept of propriate striving is of self or proprium. According to Allport propriate striving includes all those forms of behaviour which attempt to realize the self's potentialities, the goals of life, the struggle to realize ideals.

Role of motivation

Allport's theory of personality emphasizes abundancy motivation as opposed to deficiency motivation. It lays emphasis upon man's seeking of new horizons, going forward and always becoming something new. This is opposed to the view of the systems which emphasize man as seeking equilibrium of homeostasis. Allport's system may be characterized as relying on social against the biological factors, although biological factors are not excluded. In the end, Allport's system emphasizes the individual as a whole or self rather than as a congregation of parts of mechanisms.

In the field of personality psychology Gordon Allport has emphasized personality traits. At some places he appears to be traditional while on the other he appears to be very much original and contemporary. In fact, Allport has synthesized traditional ideas with contemporary researches to arrive at his theory of personality.

Influence of gestalt psychology

One finds the influence of Gestalt psychology, William Stern, William James and William McDougall on his theory of personality. Since he has laid emphasis upon individual differences in personality, therefore, his theory of personality is known as psychology of the individual. Again, since he has considered traits as the most important element in personality, therefore, his theory is known as Trait theory. According to Allport the unity of the individual is maintained in the complexity of human life. Individual factors are the most important determinants of the behaviour of the individual. Due to importance of motivation in the individual behaviour, self and ego are most important in personality. According to Allport personality is not the result of the past but of the present. Not unconscious but conscious motivation have been considered to be important in his theory. He does not admit continuity between normal and abnormal, child and the adult, animal and the human. He is not prepared to accept psycho-analytic theory in this connection. On the other hand, he is also not prepared to seek the help of physical science in the interpretation of human behaviour, since according to him methods of natural sciences cannot explain the complex human behaviour but only create difficulties in its study. Mechanical model, animal model or child model is insufficient to understand human behaviour.

Therefore, Allport has sought the help of various social sciences in the interpretation of social behaviour. He has used the concept of conditioned response, habit, attitude, self and ego to explain human personality. Among these also levels of personality have been decided by traits, attitudes and intentions. What Murray has called need Freud has called instinct and McDougall sentiment, it has been called traits by Allport.

Personality and character

Allport has distinguished between personality and character. Character, according to him, refers to conduct for which the terms good and bad are applied. Thus character is a moral concept while personality is psychological or rather psycho-physical. Distinguishing between character and personality Allport has written "Character is personality evaluated and personality is character devaluated."

Personality and temperament

Similarly, personality is also different from temperament. Temperament means dispositions connected with biological and physical determinants and therefore it is slow changing. Personality, on the other hand, is more changing. It includes temperament. Temperament is more influenced by heredity than personality.

Meaning of personality traits

Defining personality trait, Allport has called it, "A generalized and focalised neuropsychic system with the capacity to render many stimuli functionally equivalent and to initiate and guide consistent forms of adaptive and expressive behaviour" Personality trait is the ultimate reality in the psychological organization. It is free from the observer, since it is given in the mental structure. Traits are different from habits though both are determinant propensities. As compared to habit, a personality trait is more general. In fact, it is a result of synthesis of at least two or more habits. Trait is also different from attitude. Both are dispositions to react, both are unique, both initiate and guide behaviour and both are factors and result of learning. However, while attitude is connected with particular objects or class of objects, personality trait is more general. As the number of objects of attitude increases, it progresses in the direction of becoming a personality trait. An attitude may be general or particular but a trait is always general. Attitude evaluates an object but this is not done by traits.

Types of personality traits

However, attitude and trait are different concepts. Again, traits are not types. Man has a trait but he is not a type. Types have been invented by observers as models in which individuals are fitted without any consideration of their peculiarities. Traits, on the other hand, show uniqueness of the individual. Thus, while traits are actual, types are artificial. In order to understand Allport's theory of personality, it is necessary to examine various types of traits. These are as follows:

1. **Individual traits:** In a sense all traits are individual since they are unique and applicable to one individual. However, individual traits are peculiar traits.

2. **Common traits:** Common traits are those which are found similarly in so many individuals. For example, members of the same culture exhibit common modes of adjustments. These are general traits. However, strictly speaking, there are no general trails, since traits are found not in communities and groups but in the individuals.

General traits are not actual traits but an aspect of the individual traits which can be measured. Individuals can be compared with the help of common traits. However, the researchers should always remember that common traits do not always express the personality of the individual.

3. **Cardinal traits:** Cardinal traits are those which influence all the activities. An individual is known by cardinal traits. This is also known as the ruling or the master sentiment. It is not found similarly in all the individuals.

4. Central traits: These are the tendencies peculiar to an individual and can be easily observed. Their number is limited to 5 or 10.

5. Secondary traits: These are comparatively less important in the description of personality since their influences are limited.

6. Expressive traits: These dispositions undoubtedly influence types of behaviour but do not motivate them. Some of its examples are dogmatism and the trait of spending too much. These traits express the individual making effort to realize an aim.

7. Attitudinal traits: As is clear by the adjective, these traits influence some particular areas of life.

Identification of traits

The above discussion of the type of traits shows that as compared to other, some traits are motivating and changing. Most of the traits do not receive the external stimuli similarly. In fact, the individual himself searches for stimuli, for the expression of personality trait of sociability, he does not wait for the occasion but creates circumstances in which he may interact with other individuals and express his personality trait.

Pointing out the independence of traits, Allport has maintained that the peculiar characteristic of a trait is not its independence but local quality. It has a centre, around which lies the area of influence. Thus no sharp line can be drawn between one trait and another. In fact, traits are interconnected and should not be admitted as separate. Therefore, Allport is against a rigid classification of traits.

The character identifying a trait is its consistency. In other words, a trait can be recognised by identifying some consistency in the conduct and behaviour of a person. Since an individual is motivated by different traits, consistency is a rare virtue. Again, the organization of traits in an individual is unique and therefore leads to inconsistency in behaviour. It is wrong to assume that personality is generally integrated. Both integration and disintegration are different activities of an individual. Allport has tried to classify thousands of words expressing personality traits. This has been attempted to see what the traits show as evaluative terms in present conditions.

Functional autonomy

Personality traits, according to Allport, are different from other motivations in having functional autonomy. This is the most central and the most controversial concept in Allport's theory of personality. According to it any activity or form of behaviour, starting due to some particular causes in the beginning gradually becomes end in itself. Several reactions start due to biological causes and gradually become necessary part of behaviour. For example, a hunter hunts for food in the beginning but gradually, hunting becomes his vocation. Here Allport's views are similar to those of other psychologists. He has given examples from so many areas to prove his concepts. He has pointed out that several individuals express child-like activities which started due to some particular reasons in the beginning but later on continued even without reasons. Thus they become independent activities. Anderson calls it externalization of motive. Proofs have been gathered in this connection by experiments upon animals. According to Allport, functional autonomy is due to the reason that a particular act is repressed so many times that in the end it becomes goal or motivation. On this concept of Allport, Bertocci has raised several objections, some of which have been replied by Allport in his ego psychology. According to him two types of functions are autonomous-preservative and propriate. Preservative behaviour is equally found among animal and human beings and in it several biological functions are maintained even after their goal is achieved. Propriate motives are concerned with acquired interests, values, sentiments and style of life.

These propriate organize the personality. This organization is not due to an ego but a result of integration in different patterns. Thus, personality is an organization of traits, intentions, self-images and patterns, etc., as functional units. This organization is the result of gradual evolution. According to Allport the adult individual does not have necessary connection between behaviour and basic tendencies. On the other hand, adult behaviour is not functionally independent since it also expresses child-like activities. However, so far as autonomy is found in individual motive, his personality may be called matured and so far his present motives are directed by past motives, his personality is immature.

The most important question concerning a theory of personality is the advantages of believing it. The concept of functional identity helps in distinguishing the past, it may be studied separately. Secondly, on the basis of this concept can be established the uniqueness of personality. According to Allport, his theory shows that motives are contemporary, their form changes according to motives and learning besides individuals' motivations. Thus, a developed personality is the result of changes in instinctive behaviour.

Development of personality

Personality development continues from infancy to adulthood. In the explanation of infant behaviour Allport is a traditionalist, he does not say anything new in the interpretation of first two or three years of man's life. According to him the neonate is an organism behaving due to heredity, primitive drives and reflexes. It has no unique characteristics. It has no personality. It only seeks to satisfy physical needs. Besides, it also acts due to certain reflexes. Gradually, it evolves from combined activities to individual actions. This evolution is due to interaction with the environment. Even in the first year of his life the infant shows some peculiar characteristics which gradually become patterns of his personality. In the process of becoming an adult the infant personality extends through differentiation, integration, maturity, limitation, learning, functional autonomy and the field of the ego. Mental traumas also contribute to this process but nothing new has been said by Allport about it. In brief, the human infant is a biological organism which gradually becomes a person after passing through the stages of evoking ego, maturing traits and realizing ends. Functional autonomy has special significance in his evolution.

Studies of overt behaviour

Allport and his associates started studies of overt behaviour since 1930. Allport has distinguished between two types of human activities, adoptive component concerned with functional value and leading to a goal, and expressive component expressing the style of action. Most of the people use similar adoptive component in the distinction of a personality and it is the proper subject of study by the psychologists. In the study of an individual his peculiarities show his personality. Expressed behaviour is connected with unconscious and deeper motivation. The style of actions is determined by these deeper factors. Therefore, by its study we can know the deeper motivating sources. The style of life is not only determined by the individual factors but it is also influenced by socio-cultural determinants, temporary moods, physical conditions and other such factors. This does not lessen the validity of expressed behaviour which can be classified according to the type of activity, such as facial expressions, voice and handwriting, etc.

According to Allport the psychologist should not pay attention to a particular type of expressed behaviour but to all its kinds. In this direction he inducted important studies in collaboration with P.E. Vernon. On the basis of these studies he concluded that the expressions and hand-writing of the individual are stable constituents of his individual style. His expressions are mutually inter-related and his attitudes, traits and values are intimately related. On the basis of other studies, Allport and his disciple Stanely Eates concluded that personality can be estimated by the expressed behaviour. In several studies of voice, according to him, physical tendencies are not free but express the feeling. Allport and his disciple C.W. Huntley studied self-assertion on the basis of expressed behaviour and arrived at several conclusions. According to them one finds differences in physical tendencies and not complete coherence. Personality can be known by any symptom. For example, it may be known by handwriting or the expressions through eyes, hands or other physical organs. Just as the personality organisation is partial, similarly, the organization of expression is also partial. Personality and attitudes both are complex.

Evaluation of present position

Allport did not organize any school against other psychologies. However, his influence upon his disciples is evident. Of these the most well-known are A.L. Brunner, H. Cantrill, J.S. Brunner and M.B. Smith. Allport presented his views after continued research for more than two decades. His recent theory is more systematic. Though many psychologists do not agree with him yet every one is impressed. In this connection it has been admitted in a recent survey that Allport has made maximum contribution in the field of personality theory after Sigmund Freud. Contemporary psycho-analysts have also taken interest in it. Undoubtedly, some of Allport's ideas are quite original. His ideas concerning ego have impressed most of the psychologists. It was he who first of all established the value of conscious determinants on personality. In the methods of personality assessment he showed a new direction by emphasizing individual methods. He is one of the few psychologists who have synthesized tradition and behaviour in psychology. He studied the value of present and future, in place of past in personality. Looking from the point of view of the influence of psychoanalysis in this field, this showed a new direction.

Criticism of the Theory

Several remarks have been made against Allport's theory of personality. Many psychologists have condemned it. Allport has not replied to all his criticisms. Most of the persons admit that apart from the field of expressed behaviour there is no data for experimental studies on the basis of Allport's theory. Therefore, his theory is not a suitable basis for research. According to many psychologists the concept of functional autonomy could not advance any interpretation but merely described what actually happens. Another remark has been made that Allport has wrongly established gaps between the infant and the adult, the normal and the abnormal personality. The psychologists seek to know common traits in personality assessment though nobody denies individual peculiarities. By laying emphasis upon individual peculiarities, the power of prediction is diminished. Allport's theory does not explain as to which dimensions should be used in personality study. Finally, sufficient attention has not been paid to socio-cultural determinants of behaviour. However, it should be remembered that Allport never thought himself to be beyond criticism.

REGNANCY THEORY

The American Psychologist Murray presented his theory of personality in his book *Explorations in Personality* (1938). He elaborated it in his work *Assessment of Men* (1948). He defines personality as "a continuity of functional forms and forces manifested through sequences of organized regnant processes and overt behaviour from birth to death." In this definition, by regnant processes Murray means brain processes. According to his view human behaviour is functionally dependent upon the central nervous system. Murray's definition of personality also emphasizes the longitudinal continuity of personality and its endurance patterns of behaviour. According to him, personality is an organization and functioning. The most important needs pointed out by Murray are: needs for affiliation, deference, nurturance, succorance, harm avoidance, needs for avoiding inferiority feelings, blame, basement; needs for passivity, seclusion and inviolacy. In addition, there are such needs as aggression, autonomy, dominance, rejection, achievement, recognition, exhibition, sex, acquisition, cognisance, construction and order. Murray's list of human needs leans heavily on Freudian concepts. This shows his life-long interest in psychoanalysis Personality needs are closely related to what Murray calls presses (singular and plural). This reflects what significance an object or person has for the individual. According to Murray, some of the more important presses are: absence or death of parent, danger or misfortune, birth of a sibling, dominance by another, exposure to sex, illness, and awareness of inferiority feeling. Needs and press are interrelated in Murray's theory of personality. Presses depend upon needs. If there is no existing need, an environment object or person has no significance for the individual and therefore cannot be a press.

According to Murray personality is revealed in the proceedings or concrete activities of the individual over a period of time. The proceedings may be external or internal. Internal proceedings include thoughts, memories and fantasies. External proceedings comprise the individual's attempt to fight with environmental evils. Thus the development of personality in its interaction with the environment and significant individuals in the environment follows the same line of development as pointed out by Freud in his theory of personality. Thus, Murray has accepted Freud's concept of personality from Freudian literature with modifications and additions. The methods of personality study supported by Murray include the use of interview, psychoanalysis and projective techniques such as Thematic Apperception Test.

Murray has defined psychology as the science of behaviour including both external behaviour and the inner consciousness. According to him psychology should commence with the study of objective behaviour. In studying behaviour the psychologists should attempt to construct and explain it. He lays emphasis upon the necessity for the formulation of central processes in personality. This approach agrees with studying man as an organism. Murray has synthesized the opposite positions of introspectionists and the behaviourists. According to him, "A psychology which on principle neglects the problems of happiness can never be more than an eccentric collection of dogmas."

The Regnancy

The system which allows the organism to act as a unit, a hierarchy of controlling process on the summits of which is a dominant and intricate element, Murray calls "Regnancy". He admits that we do not know where the regnancy is located beyond the fact that it is within the brain. He defines it, "As the organized aggregate of mutually dependent processes which momentarily determine the functioning of the organism as unit." Thus regnancy dominates the activity of the organism when it has a total character. Murray examines conjunctivity of regnancy not overlooking conflicts and dissociation. According to him regnancy includes integrative and emotive processes. Personality is not the constitution of the entire body. It means the individual as a whole. In the words of Menninger, "It means that any one is an all that he is try ing to become."

The Regnancy and the consciousness

According to Murray, regnancy and consciousness are the two aspects of personality. He points out that this is the best and most widely accepted solution of the mind-body dilemma. This double aspect hypothesis maintains that every conscious process is the subjective aspect of some regnant process. Thus, to explain a conscious event or to explain a behaviour event, all the major variables of the regnancy must be known.

Variables of the regnancy

According to Murray, "In formulating regnant phenomena, constructs derived from subjective experience are at present more useful than derived from physiological investigation." Therefore, he uses the terms perception, image and cognition to explain regnancy. Each of the selected variables must be conscious to have an objective aspect. The functional organization may be explained in theorems of primary and secondary needs. The special task of the psychologists is to discover all the supportable variables, components, attributes and dimensions which may combine to determine the trend of behaviour. He has to analyse the classified trends as well as internal events.

Murray has himself summarized his theory of personality in these words, "This conviction has led to the proposal of the following tentative hypothesis:

1. The processes which are of final interest to the psychologist are those which organize experience and control the behaviour of living organisms.
2. In higher forms these processes occur in brain region at the top of hierarchical system of dominant nerve centres.
3. It is these organizing and controlling cephalic processes which the psychologist must attempt to conceptualize.
4. The apparently continuous stream of processes is made up of discontinuous, rapidly succeeding occurrences. If this is not strictly correct, it is at least permissible for theoretical purposes to divide the ceaseless flow into very small temporal units each to be called a regnancy.
5. Each regnancy may be regarded as a sensorimotor propagation—a complex integrate of mutually dependent processes which ensures for a fraction of a second.
6. According to the double aspect theory—the most convenient working hypothesis for a psychologist—the constituents of the regnancy are capable of achieving consciousness.
7. To explain a conscious event as well as to explain a behaviour event, however, one must take account of more variables than are, at the moment, present in consciousness. Therefore, it is necessary to conceptualize unconscious regnant processes.
8. In formulating regnant phenomena, constructs derived from subjective experience are at present more useful than those derived from physiological investigations. It should be understood, however, that every psychological term employed refers to some hypothetical physical variables.

9. A man's life is a long history of successive regnancies, each regnancy being at once a culmination, an assimilation, and a prophecy .
10. A regnancy is an utterly hypothetical or metaphysical unit, since it is impossible to catch and inspect a single one of them.
11. A single regnancy is organized and successive regnancies are linked together by the endurance of a particular directional tension, to be called a need.
12. A need is a force which (if uninhibited) promotes activity which (if competent) bring about a situation that is opposite (as regards its relevant dynamical properties) to the one which aroused it.
13. Successive stimuli may be bound together by a similarity of signification into a single stimuli Gestalt, to be called a press.
14. The endurance of a certain kind of press-perception in combination with a certain kind of need organizes regnancies into a convenient temporal unit, to be called an event.
15. A need may be internally evoked in a persistence environment. When this happens, the persistence of the tension alone determines the duration of the event.
16. For a psychologist an event is the most actual "thing" there is, and is the proper matter for analysis.
17. The dynamical structure of an event is given by the particular press-need combination which is exemplified. This is called its theme.
18. Endopsychic events and pure phantasies of exopsychic events should be recognized. These also have their themes.
19. Describing an event.
20. An abstract biography, or psychography, may be written in terms of the characteristic themes and thematic relations occurring during each stage of a subject's development.
21. A single meeting, of a series of recurrent associations between a subject and particular object (a thing, an animal, a human, or an institution), is to be called a relational. An enduring relational may be taken as the basis for a psychograph."

FACTORIAL THEORY

Raymond B. Cattel, the American psychologist, presented his famous theory of personality in a number of books including: *A Guide to Mental Testing* (1936), *General Psychology* (1941), *Description and Measurement of Personality* (1946), *Personality: A Systematic, Theoretical and Factual Study* (1952), *The Meaning and Measurement of Neuroticism and Anxiety* (1961), *Motivation and Dynamic Structure* (1975), *Personality and Learning Theory* (1980) and *The Inheritance of Personality and Ability* (1981). Cattell's theory of personality is called factorial theory of personality. In this theory, personality is a system based on the identification of personality traits and their measurement through factor analysis.

Cattel defined personality in terms of, "That which permits a prediction of what a person will do in a given situation." He believes that prediction concerning personality is possible by the identification and measurement through objective tests and rating scales, or those traits which lie at the source of the behaviour patterns that make a personality. According to Cattel, ordinary tests, questionnaires, rating scales and other such devices measure surface traits. The surface traits are subjected to factor analysis after gathering them in large scale sampling. It is only with results of this factor analysis that the psychologists arrive at the source traits of personality. In such studies the surface traits of personality are revealed in correlation clusters. Groups of tests that show high correlations with each other and relatively low correlations with other clusters reveal surface traits. The source traits are relatively independent factor loadings that have been identified in a number of studies as fundamental modes of behaviour. Among those traits that have been repeatedly verified are the following:

1. Sizothymia *versus* Affectothymia.
2. General Mental Ability *versus* Mental defect.
3. Emotional stability *versus* Emotional instability.
4. Dominance *versus* Submissiveness.

Of these traits some such as Sizothymia-Affectothymia have been called constitutional traits by Cattell. These are due to heredity influence. Other personality traits are determined by the environment. These include traits such as conservatism-radicalism. Again, some traits are dynamic and others are ability or capacity traits.

According to Cattell, personality is further characterized by the operation of ergs or innate dispositions to certain objects and to continue to react until a goal is reached. According to Cattell, meta-ergs are similar to ergs except that they are environmentally determined rather than innate. The most important of the meta-ergs are sentiments or dynamic attitudes.

Cattell has borrowed heavily from psychoanalysis in the development of his theory of personality growth and development. The individual must learn to satisfy ergs and in doing so he successfully develops characteristic modes of behaviour. Deprivation, blockage and frustration are important cross-roads that the individual must meet and cope with. Adolescence is the period during which the greater demands are put upon the individual in learning how to cope with problems. Maturity is the learning of social interests in place of family and individual interests. The prediction of the individual's personality must take into account the institutions and social context in which he develops.

Cattell has recently extended his theory of personality into area of neurotic patterns of personality in an attempt to bring together his factor-analysis findings and those from the clinic to make possible more exact descriptions of the latter. These studies have resulted in the identification of new traits and measuring techniques, which should prove useful in the measurement of anxiety of neurotic reactions.

SOCIAL LEARNING THEORY

Social learning theory grew out of the work of Johan Dollard (1900—1980) and Neel Miller (1909) at Yale University in the decade of 1940. It has been further studied by Albert Bandura who is contemporary exponent of this point of view.

Social learning theory is modified form of learning which stresses the importance of congnitive processes as casual agents in behaviour. Dollard and Miller emphasized the theoretical importance of imitation in the development of behaviour. This hypothesis was confirmed by Bandura, the American psychologist in his works *Personality* (1963), *Principles of Behaviour Modifications* (1966), *Aggression* (1973), *Social Learning Theory* (1977). The last work is the foundation of Bandura's Social Learning Theory. In this theory it has been demonstrated that children can learn aggression by watching adult's model aggressive behaviour. This is an important finding. It maintains that aggression in human beings is not necessarily in-born. Mostly, it may be the result of therapeutic techniques. It was used in the case of subjects who fear object and situations, These subjects were taught skills useful in coping with their fears by observing other and then behave towards the situation without fear. According to Bandura belief, exception, choice and self-reinforcement are important determinants of behaviour. This is in contrast to the radical behaviourists who assert that reinforcements act on behaviour without regard to conscious or cognitive processes. Bandura has emphasized cognitive processes in the causation of behaviour. In contrast to the use of animals by traditional behaviourists, Bandura utilized human subject in his study of behaviour. His work received wide critical acclaim. It influenced recent trends in cognitive psychology and behaviour therapy.

FIELD THEORY

Field theory of personality was particularly presented by Kurt Lewin. It is a systematic point of view in personality theory. It is closely related to Gestalt psychology. However, in it motivation and social factors are emphasized. According to this theory personality works in the psychological field which includes the individual life space of the space containing his actions. From the psychological viewpoint, the environment is that which is perceived by the individual in relation to his needs, goals and purposes. Therefore, environment is very much selective. While some objects and persons are ignored, some considered of little importance, others are given much importance. The important object will have positive valance, it will be attractive. Other objectives may be repulsive and having the negative valance. The individual personality is shown in the life space as directed towards or away from objects by a bearer. This is particularly in conflict situation. Vector analysis, as developed by Lewin, was brought into the system in order to represent needs and motives. Lewin brought valance into the system. Tensions are general in motivation stage. Lewin used the rudiments of topology for making the life space and showing the individual, his goal and routs. His work was particularly appreciated so far as the level of aspiration, regressive behaviour, democratic *versus* authoritarian conflicts are concerned.

Current status of personality theories

Psychologists have generally accepted the following propositions about personality:

1. Man is a purposive animal.
2. Human personality is sufficiently determined by unconscious determinants.
3. Reward and punishment play important role in the development of human personality.
4. Association in social institutions is the most important determinant of different aspects of the personality.
5. Learning process is an important factor in the growth and development of different aspects of the personality.
6. Most of the personality theories explain personality structure. This explanation generally involves learning as well as acquisition.
7. Generally speaking, hereditary factors have not been considered to be very important but also not unimportant.
8. Events taking place early in development, play an important role in the future development of personality.
9. Personality development is a continuous process through several stages.
10. Most of the personality psychologists believe in organicism. Generally speaking, their approaches are holistic. They consider the field important in the development of personality.
11. Most of the psychologists suggest a complex model of behaviour to explain human personality.
12. Psychologists present different concepts of self which has been considered as the centre of personality.
13. The value of psychological environment in personality development has been accepted.
14. Group membership is an important determinant of personality.
15. Most of the psychologists have adopted interdisciplinary attitude in their personality theories.
16. While some psychologists have given long lists of motives, others have limited it to a few. However all have equally accepted the value of motivation in the development of personality.

Summing up the present position of research in personality and its future direction, C.S. Hall and G. Lindzey remark, "Personality theory and research are in need of an increase of both radicalism and conservatism." As a general rule any theory which explains more aspects of personality is better than other theories. Without sufficient data available in favour of theory, it cannot pass as a sound theory of personality. Therefore, personality theories must be examined on the basis of data gathered from actual study of personality. From this point of view no single theory of personality can be said to be absolutely satisfactory theory of personality, it is necessary to gather sufficient and multi-sided data. In the last 25 years valuable data have been gathered about personality. It may be hoped that this may help in the formulation of a better theory of personality in future.

QUESTIONS FOR EXERCISE

1. Critically examine the psycho-analytic theory of personality as given by Freud.
2. Explain Allport's Trait Theory of personality. Evaluate its present position.
3. Explain Regnancy theory of personality as advanced by Murray.
4. Write short notes on the following theories of personality:

   (*a*) Factorial Theory (*b*) Social Learning Theory.
5. Explain field theory of personality. Point out the current status of personality theories.

42

Contemporary Schools of Psychology and Education

STRUCTURALISM

There are two different ways in which the behaviour of a living organism can be described, either according to its structure or in terms of its functioning. And both points of view have been adopted in the history of psychology. Those studying behaviour from the point of view of structure are called structuralists and the other called functionalists.

Fundamental tenets

One of the fundamental tenets of the school is that the human consciousness is the sum of various mental abilities and the analysis of consciousness requires the analysis of its constituent mental abilities. Mental elements have a special place within the structure of consciousness. Such mental elements are sensation, direct knowledge, attention, imagination and the rest. Their sum total goes to make up consciousness. In order to understand structuralism completely it would be best to understand the respect in which it differs from the other schools.

1. Structuralism and faculty psychology: Structuralism is not the same as faculty psychology because the various faculties of mind which direct knowledge, sensation, imagination, etc., are accepted as ingredients of the mind, in the latter discipline, but as distinct ingredients. On the other hand, structuralism accepts them as indivisible mental element and consciousness is the name given to the unity thus created.

2. Structuralism and associationism: Structuralism differs also from associationism. Associationism accepts sensations through which mental activities such as perception, imagination, attention, thought, etc., take place. In other words, it is the association of sensations that forms the basis for every kind of mental activity. Structuralism, on the other hand, does not accept this explanation, for this school holds sensation to be separate mental element, on the same plane as perception, attention and the rest. The sum total of all these mental elements is called consciousness. Besides, the basis of structuralism is primarily experimental. And its progress depends upon the experiments carried on in the field of psychology. On the other hand, it is not possible to have scientific study of the acts of associationism because they are not basically scientific.

Two other names for structuralist psychology are existentialist and introspective psychology. Titchener adopted the introspective method, and on that account it came to be known as introspective psychology.

Structuralism is one of the important schools of psychology and its contribution to psychology is also considerable. And in a brief evaluation of it, it is possible to assert that it has emphasized the use of a scientific methodology in psychology. With their use of the introspective method, the structural psychologists started a new trend and throughout it succeeded in providing extensive studies of sensation, affection and imagination, the three mental elements.

It was structuralism which provided knowledge about the kind of mental elements that form part of human experience. It also emphasized the need to analyse mind and consciousness and examine their nature by studying the mental elements.

But the structuralist school also underwent considerable criticism, the main trouble being that it did not pay any attention to the synthetic and functional unity of the mind. Besides, its explanation of different kinds of mental experiences on the whole has been lifeless and mechanical. And the root of the trouble is that introspection cannot help the complete study of an individual's conflicts. Besides, the school does not provide a convincing body of knowledge on such subjects as motivation, personality and adjustment.

Contribution to education

Structuralism has made some positive contribution to the science of psychology. Its most important contribution was to free psychology from metaphysics. It gave an experimental method of data collection though it had been severely criticized by psychologists on account of its method of data collection: experimental introspection. It developed scientific psychology. It emerged out of laboratory experiments in Germany. It made its impact on contemporary educational theory through its spirit of science and emphasis on systematic observations of the activities of mind.

FUNCTIONALISM

Chicago school

The functional school of psychology had its beginning and early development in America. It believed to have begun about the year 1898 at the Chicago University and for that reason it is also sometimes referred to as the Chicago School. Its innovators were James Rowland Angell and James Dewey, Angell being the director of the psychology department at the Chicago University. He was a prominent psychologist of recognized ability. He came into contact with John Dewey who was professor of philosophy at the same University and was ten years his senior in age. Both studied psychology together and in the process of their work gave birth to the school of functionalism.

One notable fact about functionalism is that it developed as a system of philosophy in reaction to Titchener's structural psychology. Structuralism accepted mental elements and processes as objects while functionalism puts a different Interpretation on them. It believes that the mental elements and processes are active, continuously occurring and aimed at some particular objective. Success is one of the results of studying them. In other words, the philosophical background of their study under this system is provided by pragmatism.

Columbia School

Besides the work done at Chicago University, the psychologists of Columbia University also evinced some interest in functionalism. Functionalism is devoted to the study of mental functions. And it believes that the aim of psychology is to find out how and why mental activities take place and what is their utility? Functionalism does not pay much attention to the structure of the mind, if believes that the mind and body are bound in an adjustment that causes all mental activity. Putting it differently, one can say that the aim of functional psychology is to find out how an individual establishes some kind of adjustments with his environment. Mind and body are not treated as two distinct elements, but rather elements which are intrinsically one though apparently they appear distinct. All mental activity is the outcome of adjustment between the two. And it is the object of functional psychology to study them.

The extent to which functional psychology has succeeded in contributing to psychology will be calculated on the basis of facts and theories propagated by the various functional theorists. These psychologists are John Dewey, Angell and Harvey Carr, for it is to them that the credit for developing this system of psychology must go.

Contribution to psychology

Much importance is attached to all that functionalism has contributed to modern psychology, and a systematic though short analysis of it is given below:

1. Study of personality: Functionalism stressed the need for a study of the complete personality and highlighted the fact that both personality and its environment should be subjected to detailed investigation so that the psychology of the personality can be clearly understood.

2. Relation between mind and the body: Functionalism accepts the mind and body duality with scepticism choosing to believe both of them to be identical. Mind and body are inseparable so that mind is incomplete without body and body without the mind. A study of the complete personality makes it necessary that both psychological and physiological aspects be studied. As a result the popularity of psychology increased and other scientists like doctors, anthropologists and biologists began to take an interest in it.

3. Emphasis upon adjustment: Functionalism placed much stress on adjustment, and in modern psychology the branch of adjustment psychology is an important one. Functionalism accepted the fact that individual achieves satisfactory adjustment between his life and environment. In this matter the functionalist psychologists stressed the fact of adjustment and therapy helped in the development of dynamic psychology.

4. Progress in different branches of psychology: The fourth contribution to psychology is that through its good offices other branches like child psychology, animal psychology, educational psychology and others developed, along with development in the tests employed for learning, intelligence and individual differences.

Keeping in mind all that has been said about it is possible to assert that the entire field of applied psychology is the creation of functional psychology. It was functionalism which paved the way for the advent of behaviourism.

Contribution to education

The following are the important contributions of functionalism to education:

1. Emphasis on adjustment: Functionalism emphasized that behaviour is adaptive to new situations of life. School should teach for proper adjustment of children in society. Functionalism gives importance to the environment in the process of learning. Therefore, the principal and the teachers should try their best to provide conducive environment to the learners so that their motivation in learning may be sustained.

2. Revolutionized curriculum: Functionalism revolutionized the curriculum which was previously overloaded by theoretical concepts. It replaced theory by practical approach. Learning by doing was given central importance in school curriculum.

3. Study of problems: Study of various problems of the individual and their solution is emphasized by functionalism in education.

4. Educational psychology: Functionalism contributed a lot to educational psychology, mental testing and child psychology.

5. Needs of Children: Functionalism gives more importance to the needs of children at different age levels.

6. Utilitarian Theory: Functionalism gave birth to the utilitarian theory of education. It emphasized the importance of the child in the process of learning. Only those subjects should be included in the curriculum which are important from the point of their utility in society.

7. New Methods: Functionalism developed new methods of teaching and learning.

BEHAVIOURISM

Revolt against subjectivism

According to the behaviourist school, psychology is a purely experimental branch of the natural sciences the object of which is to elaborate, control and predict behaviour. The behaviourists wanted to improve the psychological methodology till it became scientific. Hence, they were opposed to the use of the existence of such a thing as consciousness from the domain of psychology.

Later behaviourists objected to the use of such concepts as mental states, mind, volition, images and others. They wished to analyse and understand all behaviour and conduct in terms of the stimulus and the consequent response to the stimulus. Under the leadership of Watson the behaviourist school rose as a protest against functionalism and structuralism, and the younger generation of psychology accepted the leadership of Watson because they believed that he intended to rid psychology of its prejudices, mysteries and philosophical traditions. Watson placed much reliance on the elements of environment in personality development. It was his confident belief that by making appropriate changes in the environment it is possible to make possible to visualize a society, in which there were no ills because the frailty of the human element could be eliminated through psychology. One consequence of this was that Watson, in addition to being the leader of a new psychological group, also became a popular leader. In one other field, that of animal psychology, Watson has contributed as much by his own research and had been confined to the field of animals psychology for he believed that by carrying on experiments upon the animals it was possible to learn many important facts concerning human beings. Hence, he stressed the need for increased research in animal psychology.

Objective methods

From the account of Watson and other psychologists belonging to the earlier or the later bahaviourists and the psychological theories that they propounded, it is evident that the behaviourist psychologists stressed objective concepts as well as methods. Besides, there can be no doubt that as psychology is a science it is incumbent upon psychologists to be austerely objective in the choice of their concepts and methods, but there is a limit to it. Experience also possesses subjective aspect and by ignoring it the behaviourist finds it impossible to give an adequate explanation of behaviour. Sometimes the behaviourist has to resort to verbal reports, even if it is only to find out whether his audience has grasped all that he is trying to put across. And he must of necessity rely on the verbal report. Objective methods have their own importance in psychology but they do not in any way detract from the value of such methods as introspection. At present the majority of psychologists are convinced that there are certain aspects of experience the understanding of which makes it necessary to use the introspective method. Watson placed much emphasis upon the importance attached to environment in the development of personality. He claimed that given an average child and the right to determine its environment in all its aspects he could make the child precisely anything he desired. But this was a claim he did not make good. Besides, it was an impractical idea because personality is the outcome of interaction between heredity and environment. In much the same way Watson's ideas on thinking, emotion, learning and other subjects were becoming obsolete and were being successively disproved so much so that even the modern behaviourists do not agree with them. Hence the chief contribution of Watson and his faithful followers to the field of psychology is the regulated emphasis upon objective methods and concepts, and there can be no two opinions about the importance of this achievement.

Reaction against structuralism

Watsonian behaviourism arose as a reaction against the structural and functional psychologies in vogue. Watson defined psychology as the science of behaviour and objectively elaborated upon the nature of behaviour. He effected a complete refutation of the concepts of consciousness and the introspective methods. He emphasized the importance of animal psychology and analyzed behaviour, sensation, perception, memory, images, feelings and emotions, learning and thinking from the behaviourist standpoint. According to him the development of personality depends upon the environment. Behaviour is guided by the senses and it can be explained in terms of stimulus and response. Watson's importance is not owing to his ideas on psychology but to his hopeful, realistic and progressive attitude. After Watson the work done by the early behaviourists and the later behaviourists deserves mention in the history of behaviourism. Max Meyer and A.P. Weiss are among the more important early behaviourists while the chief among the later behaviourists are Hunter, Tolman, Hull, Skinner and Karl S. Lashley. Among them many not only modified the ideas originally propagated by Watson but even went to the length of contradicting them.

Contribution to education

(*i*) *Learning and motivation:* Behaviourism greatly contributed to the psychology of learning and motivation.

(*ii*) *Against mentalism:* Behaviourism brought psychology out from the controversy of mentalistic approach to human behaviour.

(*iii*) *Child Behaviour:* Behaviourism impressed all areas of psychology and child behaviour.

(*iv*) *Methodology:* Behaviourism gave a new methodology of teaching known as programmed learning which has been successfully used in many countries.

(*v*) *Environment:* Behaviourism laid emphasis on the importance of environment and its impact on human growth.

(*vi*) *Interaction:* Behaviourism believed that all behaviour is learned in the constant process of interaction with environment.

(*vii*) *Maladjustment:* Behaviourism developed new methods and techniques of dealing with maladjustment in children.

Pointing out the implication of behaviourism for teaching and learning Percival Symonds wrote, "The most potent reward (reinforcement) for class room learning is the teacher's acceptance what the pupil does and the way he does it because this acceptance becomes a guide in his future activities. This acceptance on the part of the teacher can take the form of the tangible tokens, such as gold stars, honour's rolls and the like. But there is a tendency to short-circuit rewards so that a "correct or right" will do equally well..."

GESTALT SCHOOL

Historical background

Gestalt school of psychology developed as a movement against the theory of behaviourism and conditioning. In its present form it developed by the continuous contribution of psychologists from time to time. Its beginning may be traced back to the initiative at Wurzburg school of imageless thought. Kulpe studied higher mental processes and redefined psychology as the science of facts of experience, an inductive science whose peculiar property is the dependency of facts of experience upon experiencing individuals. Max Wertheimer, the founder of Gestalt Psychology, worked with Kulpe for his Ph. D. degree. At the Wurzburg school (1901—1909) psychologists conducted a number of experiments on thought process which had direct relevance to Gestalt school of psychology. Edgar Rubin (1886—1951) conducted experiments on visual perception of figure-ground phenomena. Franz-Brentano (1838—1917) developed phenomenology and act psychology. He defined psychology as the science of physical phenomena, regarding phenomena as active rather than static acts of a person. He introduced act psychology at the University of Graz in Austria.

The birth of Gestalt psychology is traced from 1912 when Wertheimer published his classic papers on 'phi-phenomena' (apparent movement). Explaining the process of phi-phenomena he wrote: "Two objects were successively given as stimuli. They were perceived first 'a' was seen, then 'b', between, 'a' to 'b' was seen, without the corresponding motion or the spatially and temporally continuous position between a and b actually being exposed as stimulated. When the time interval flashes between a and b are over 200 milliseconds the phenomenal appearance is one of succession. In 'phi-phenomenon' no trace of an object is left, only pure motion is perceived." The experiments on phi-phenomena were the result of the co-operation of Kurt Koffka and Wolfgang Kohler at the University of Frankfurt.

Tenets of Gestalt School

Gestalt is a German word which means form, shape or configuration and Gestalt psychologists have added the meaning of organic whole and organization to it. Following are the chief tenets of Gestalt school:

1. Whole dominance: The first principle of Gestalt psychology is that it is the whole which determines the behaviour of its parts. We perceive whole not parts. It was a revolutionary finding against the atomistic psychology that emphasized the importance of parts. For atomists parts make the whole. Atomistic concept of behaviour was challenged by Gestaltists. Wertheimer wrote, "There are contexts in which, what is happening in the whole, cannot be deduced from the characteristics of the separate pieces, but conversely;

what happens to a part of the whole is, in clear cut cases, determined by the laws of inner structure of its whole."

2. Phenomenological approach: The Gestalt approach is phenomenologically-oriented, antipositivistic and molar.

3. Opposed to quantification: This school of psychology is against the quantification of human behaviour. It emphasized the importance of qualitative assessment of behaviour.

4. Measuring tools are unreliable: Gestaltists had no faith in the reliability and validity of measuring tools. They were against the behaviourist's explanation of human behaviour on the basis of stimulus-response (S-R) connections. They introduced the concept of organization in between stimulus-response (S-R) connections.

5. Laws of perception: Gestalt psychology was born out of experimental findings on perception. The following principles of perceptions have been developed by them:

(*i*) *Laws of whole:* The principle of wholes means that our perceptual organization will always be a whole in the prevailing conditions. The principle plays an important role in motivation.

(*ii*) *Laws of organization:* Closure, proximity and similarity, Gestalt laws also follow these three principles. Closure means that mind has a tendency to complete imperfect wholes into perfect and close forms. A dynamic variation of the laws of pregnanz is the principle of closure which operates in perception, thought, action and memories.

According to the principle of proximity, objects are perceived as a unity when they are observed in close proximity. The principle of similarity states that objects observed in like forms or colour will be perceived as assuming a grouped formation.

6. Psychophysical isomorphism: The concept of psychophysical isomorphism was borrowed by Kohler from his professor Max Planck who developed quantum theory. Psychophysical isomorphism means that Gestalt is both physical and mental. The brain functions tend to take the form of specific molar events corresponding to those structures that are found in experience. Kohler defined isomorphism, "As the thesis that our experiences and the processes which underlie these experiences have the same structure."

7. Insight: Gestalt psychologists developed the theory of learning by insight. They invented the theory of productive thinking which emphasized the importance of perceiving meaningful wholes, grasping relations and finally acquisition of insight.

Kurt Lewin worked with Kohler and Wertheimer as an assistant in the psychological institute and the University of Berlin, He was very much impressed by holistic psychology propounded by them. Though he never became a Gestaltist but he was convinced of the basic approach of Gestalt psychology. He developed his own approach popularly known as the Field Theory.

Contribution to Education

1. **Wholes:** Gestaltists emphasized the importance of perception of relation, organization and wholes in learning. Teacher should try to present his subject matter as a whole in the class.

2. **Molar:** Gestalt school gave importance to molar behaviour approach. Experience cannot be broken into stimulus-response (S-R.) connections.

3. **Inter-disciplinary:** Gestalt psychology emphasized Interdisciplinary approach in education.

4. **Environment:** According to the Gestaltists the present environment plays an important role in the development of personality. School environment should be conducive to learning.

5. **Learning:** This school threw new light on the problems of social learning in classroom. Group behaviour and its influence has been recognized as an important factor in learning.

6. **Problem solving:** Gestalt psychologists provided new approaches to problem solving and learning.

7. **Value of Goals:** According to Gestalt psychologists goals and purposes have an important place in learning. The teacher must set individual goals. Goal creates tension which is reduced by action on the part of the learners. Goals activate the Learners.

8. **Organization:** According to Gestaltists, teachers, principal and students work as an organized whole to improve the teaching process in school.

9. **Paido-centric:** According to this school the teacher should try to know the students from their own point of views. He should start where the student's perceptions are and not where his own happens to be.

PSYCHO-ANALYSIS

Psycho-analysis, as is evident from the name, is a branch of psychology in which mental processes are discovered through analysis of verbal speech. It is sometimes known by the name of Emotion Psychology or even Depth Psychology. It is rather closely concerned with psychiatry: Indeed, it has its origin in that science. Psychologists with psychoanalytic leanings, established a belief in psychic tendency in opposition to that in somatic tendency that had been prevalent. Most of its psychologists were successful mental doctors, and its innovator is said to be Sigmund Freud. The contributions of this Viennese doctor are hardly likely to be equalled by any other individual in the field of psychology. It was Freud who formulated the psychoanalytic method of treating mental diseases. This method of his still claims an important place among the methods of psychotherapy. Many of the psychologists are inclined to question the tenets of Freudian psychology but there can be no doubting that with the exception of Aristotle, Freud is the greatest contributor to knowledge concerning human psychology.

Freud's contribution in psychology

In its chronological order the published contribution of Freud to psychology can be arranged in the following manner:

1893 — *Psychic Mechanism of Hysterical Phenomena*, published in collaboration with Brewer.

1895 — *Studies in Hysteria*, published in collaboration with Brewer.

1900 — Publication of *The Interpretation of Dreams* in which an analysis of dreams was presented.

1904 — Publication of *Psychopathology of Everyday Life*. In this a psychoanalytic theory of common errors of speech and memory was presented.

1905 — *Three Contributions to the Theory of Sex*, in which the theory of sex was presented.

1905 — Propagation of psycho-analysis at Clark University, America. These Lectures of Freud helped to acquaint the general public with psychoanalysis.

1910 — First International Psychoanalytic Congress at Nuremberg.

1915 — Publication of *The Unconscious* in which the unconscious was elaborated upon.

1918 — Publication of *Introduction to Psycho-Analysis* in German Language.

1920 — Publication of *Beyond the Pleasure Principle* in which the notion of a death instinct was put forward.

1923 — Publication of *The Ego and The Id* in which psycho-analytic concept of personality was published. In the same year *The Problem of Anxiety* was published in which Freud put forward his own theory.

1925-1939 — Main texts published in this period are: *The Future of an Illusion, Civilization and its Discontents, Moses and Monotheism, Totem and Taboo.*

Contribution of Psycho-analysis

Psycho-analysis can be seen in three forms. One, that it is a method of searching and examining the dynamics of the conscious and unconscious aspects of human life. Two, that it is a kind of mental pathology or cure. It helps to restore to normalcy persons who are abnormal as well as to improve the life of those who are already normal. Three, that it is a particular school of thought in the domain of psychology. It has put forward an organized and systematic psychology from a special point of view. It also affects an analysis of human consciousness, but more particularly unconscious, mental activity. It provides much useful data on the subject of the psychology of primitive man, psychology of aesthetics, psychology of religion, child psychology as well as social psychology.

At the root of psycho-analysis is the Freudian theory of innate instincts of man that analyses the dynamics of the entire range of human behaviour. In every man there are mutually contradictory instincts and tendencies, and due to these tendencies many kinds of conflicts are caused. The mode of solving or facing these conflicts has much psychological importance. In Psycho-analysis Freud's concept of the human personality is of great importance. Similarly, the Freudian theory of psycho-sexual genesis is fundamental to psycho-analysis. Apart from the aspects of psycho-analysis that have so far been reviewed there are other fields in which this method is employed for research and discovery. Organic medicine is one field in which psycho-analysis has been used with profit. The psycho-analytic method was used by Ferenczi in 1925 in his mental cure. In this method the dualism of mental and physical diseases is abolished as modern psychiatry does not accept this duality. Psycho-analysis has achieved much even in the field of aesthetics. Freud himself has written on Michelangelo. Leonardo Da Vinci, Keller and Jensen, while Bonaparte has written about Edgar Allan Poe. Goethe was the subject of Reik's study. Many problems of aesthetics were reviewed and studied by Sachs and Rank. All these texts are of much value for the student of literature and art. Besides the field of aesthetics, other fields in which psycho-analysts have dabbled are the spheres of sociology, anthropology, etc. Freud's own work in these fields has been mentioned earlier. But besides Freud, other important psychoanalysts have made analytical studies of material derived from the fields of sociology and anthropology—Erich Fromm, Horney, Glover, Hopkins, Dollard and Brown. Their texts are of great importance and valued for the students of both these subjects. Religion and philosophy are two spheres that have attracted the eyes of followers of this School. Freud's '*The Future of An Illusion*' is a vivid criticism of religion and its different aspects. His '*Civilization and its Discontents*' is another book that makes a minute study of present day civilization, reveals its basic psychological problems and suggests changes and improvements.

Contribution of education

1. *Revolution:* Psycho-analysis revolutionized the theory and practice of education. Freud discovered unconscious motivation which plays an important role in the process of learning.

2. *Importance of Childhood:* Psycho-analysis laid stress on the importance of the child and his early experiences in the process of education. Early experiences of home up to the age of five years lay down the foundation of personality of the child. Love, affection and sympathy in early childhood develop positive attitudes in the child towards life. On the other hand, punishment and other negative reinforcements create problems.

3. *Catharsis:* Psycho-analysis attached great importance to the process of catharis. Children should get opportunities to express their emotions and motives freely in the class and outside the class.

4. *Child Education:* The findings of psycho-analysis gave impetus to the movements of early childhood education.

5. *Diagnosis of Maladjustment:* The greatest contribution of psycho-analysis is that it has thrown light on the causes of maladjustment in children.

6. *Value of emotions:* Psycho-analysis shows the importance of emotions in the process of education.

7. *Emphasis on freedom:* Psycho-analysis laid emphasis on freedom in education and advocated the importance of the development of whole personality

8. *Extra-curricular activities:* Psycho-analysis gave due importance to extra-curricular activities in schools so that pent up feelings may be realized.

9. *Role of teacher:* Psycho-analysis maintained that the teacher plays a significant role in the life of students. He can influence the behaviour of his students in interpersonal relationship, and can form positive attitudes towards life. The teacher should be positive and concentrate on what students can do.

QUESTIONS FOE EXERCISE

1. Discuss the contribution of structuralism and functionalism to psychology and education.
2. Describe the contribution of Behaviourism to education.
3. Explain the fundamental tenets of Gestalt School and summarize its contribution to education.
4. Discuss psycho-analysis as a school of psychology. Explain its contribution to education.

Question Bank for Educational Psychology

1. Your class has to memorise a prose passage. How will you instruct the pupils to set about their task so that they achieve the best results? Will your instruction be different if they have to memorise a poem?
2. On the basis of your experience and study of the materials what conditions do you regard as most effective in facilitating learning process?
3. State the principles that should be used in teaching to enable pupils to remember what they learn.
4. Explain the perceptual process. Illustrate with examples the factors which influence visual perception.
5. What is meant by the term conditioning? Distinguish clearly between classical conditioning and instrumental operant conditioning. Assess the educational significance of each.
6. Why do different scholars of Psychology interpret motivation in different ways? What are some of these different views on motivation? What are the consequent implications to teaching?
7. What is the role of motivation in learning? Suggest concrete methods for studying the achievement motive of a group of adolescent pupils.
8. Distinguish between retention and retroaction. Suggest ways of improving retention in pupils.
9. Discuss the extent to which reward and punishment can be used to motivate learning in schools.
10. Describe in detail the various types of learning.
11. Explain how insight assists learning.
12. Explain in detail the laws of learning according to Thorndike and point out their educational implications.
13. What features determine readiness of learning? Discuss with reference to difference among individuals you may encounter in the classroom.
14. What are the important conditions and methods that facilitate effective learning, retention and transfer? How will you seek to secure these in your teaching?
15. In which subject area of transfer through generalization most likely to occur? Justify your answer.
16. From your own experience give examples of transfer of training. Indicate whether the transfer was by way of identical components or generalization.

17. What is transfer of training? What are the conditions that aid positive transfer from one field of studies to another? How will the training increase the transfer effects of school learning in the pupils?
18. Enumerate the merits and demerits of rewards and punishment in motivation of school learning. What are the precautions you will take in the use of reward and punishment in the class?
19. Suggest three positive causes that often lead to inattention of pupils in classes. How can these be eliminated?
20. Enumerate the important objective factors affecting attention and illustrate how do you use each of these in the classroom.
21. Bring out the relation between attention and interest. As a teacher how would you use the principles underlying attention to improve your teaching?
22. Efficiency in learning depends to a large extent on factors of attention. Discuss.
23. What is counselling? Compare directive and non-directive counselling.
24. Define mental health. What are the various conditions which will help you to remain mentally healthy?
25. What can schools do to promote sound mental health among pupils?
26. What do you mean by defence mechanism? Enumerate the various defence mechanisms and show how they are helpful in maintaining one's sound mental health.
27. Discuss the role of counselling in a schools system?
28. What do you mean by educational guidance? How would you develop a guidance programme in your school?
29. Define Educational Psychology and bring out its importance to a teacher.
30. Discuss the nature and scope of Educational Psychology.
31. What are the various methods used by educational psychologists? Discuss in detail any one of the methods.
32. Name only three methods used by Educational Psychology in the investigation of educational problems and explain their merits and demerits.
33. Explain the nature of the experimental method in Psychology and state whether Psychology could be completely experimental in the approach to problems.
34. Discuss the extent to which Educational Psychology has attained the status of a science.
35. Discuss the part played by Heredity and Environment in the development of an individual.

36. Explain with suitable examples the influence of environmental factors on the development of an individual. If acquired traits cannot be automatically transmitted to succeeding generations, what purpose does education serve? What should be the attitude of teachers to the problem of heredity *versus* environment?
37. To what extent do the factors of heredity and environment contribute to learning?
38. An interplay to heredity and environment is responsible for individual difference. Comment.
39. Describe some experiments that were performed to prove the importance of heredity.
40. Distinguish between social heredity and biological heredity and discuss how both are important for learning.
41. Distinguish between growth and development and discuss their relation to maturation.
42. Describe the different stages of physical growth.
43. Describe the essential features of physical development during adolescence.
44. It is said that adolescence is a period of stress and strain. Do you agree with the statement? If so, justify your answer with an illustration.
45. Discuss the physical and phychological characteristics of children between 8 and 12 years. What provisions would you make in schools for these children?
46. Look up several recent definitions of intelligence. What similarities do you note in the definitions? What differences?
47. A child is bright in Tamil but only average in Arithmetic. How do you account for it in theories of intelligence? Why is it important for teachers to know them?
48. Is intelligence innate or acquired? How is it measured? What do we know about its growth and how is it distributed in the total population? How is intelligence related to the classrooms work?
49. Discuss the emotional problems of adolescence and state how, as a teacher you would deal with them.
50. What is meant by socialization of an individual? Discuss the role of institutional physical factors in the process.
51. What are the various factors contributing toward social development of an individual? Illustrate your answer.
52. What are the problems of social adjustment that an adolescent faces? Determine the causes of the same and state how, as a teacher, you would deal with them.
53. Describe projective techniques and show how they are used in personality assessment.

SHORT ANSWER QUESTIONS

1. Compare insight learning with trial and error learning.
2. Describe an experiment on insight learning.
3. Describe the nature of transfer in learning.
4. What are the causes of forgetting? State any three ways of improving retention.
5. What are the differences between classical and operant conditioning?
6. Describe an experiment illustratory of classical conditioning.
7. Draw a learning curve and explain its characteristics.
8. What are the causes for the occurrence of plateau in learning curves? How can they be overcome?
9. Define transfer of training and give an example.
10. Describe the conditions aiding positive transfer.
11. What are the educational implications of the 'law of disuse'?
12. How has the law of the effect influenced our educational thinking and practice?
13. What methods would you adopt in removing fear in a small child?
14. Briefly describe Pavlov's experiment on conditioning.
15. What are the factors that determine perception?
16. Describe how conditioned response may be induced and later eliminated in an animal.
17. Distinguish between primary and secondary motives.
18. Of the possible motives for learning are co-operation and competition, which of the two would you prefer?
    Give at least three reasons for your choice.
19. How does Maslow classify the various needs?
20. Explain briefly the relationship between interest and attention.
21. Write a brief note on (*a*) fluctuation of attention and (*b*) division of attention.
22. State how you will overcome distraction in the classroom.
23. What is attention? How can you as a teacher gain and maintain attention?
24. What are the various factors affecting perception of things as a whole?
25. Enumerate some devices your teachers have used to stimulate your interest.
26. Distinguish between perception and conception.
27. Explain briefly the role of the unconscious in maladjusted behaviour.
28. What are some adjustment problems adolescents face at home and at school?
29. Bring out the importance of counselling in schools.

30. Distinguish between educational and vocational guidance with examples.
31. How does a teacher make use of a cumulative record of a child?
32. What is cumulative folder? How does a teacher maintain it?
33. What are the characteristics of directive counselling?
34. Distinguish between directive and non-directive counselling.
35. What are the qualities of a counsellor?
36. What are the various steps involved in counselling?
37. What are the functions of a school counsellor?
38. Define 'Primary and Secondary' social groups giving two examples of each.
39. What is a test? What are the general principles underlying testing?
40. Discuss the nature and range of individual differences.
41. Differentiate between standardised tests and teacher made tests.
42. What are standardised tests? What are the major steps of standardisation?
43. Compare oral and written tests with reference to their construction and use.
44. Differentiate between achievement, diagnostic and prognostic tests.
45. What are the most important general suggestions for the construction of objective test items?
46. How can the teacher make an effective use of evaluative tests, tools and techniques in a classroom?
47. What is a normal probability curve?
48. What individual differences significant for education did you notice among the pupils of your class?
49. What is evaluation? How is it different from measurement? List four values of evaluation to the teacher.
50. What are norms? What are the different kinds of norms usually found in evaluation programmes? What purpose do they serve?
51. Enumerate any five significant values of knowledge of Educational Psychology to teachers and illustrate with two concrete examples.
52. Mention the various steps involved in the experimental method using an illustrative example.
53. Briefly state the scope of Educational Psychology.
54. Discuss the ways in which individuals differ.
55. State the laws of heredity.
56. Mention any three uses of group tests of intelligence.
57. Define I.Q.
58. What do you understand by distribution of intelligence according to normal probability curve?
59. What are aptitudes?

60. Mention the stages of concept formation.
61. What are the different types of intelligence tests?
62. What are the Performance tests?
63. Give two definitions of intelligence.
64. What are culture-free tests of intelligence?
65. Give 6 items from an intelligence test.
66. Mention the three dimensions of Guilford's structure of the intellect.
67. What are 'G & S' factors of intelligence?
68. What do you mean by DAT?
69. What do you mean by a battery of tests?
70. What is the formula for calculating I.Q.?
71. Distinguish between *verbal, non-verbal* and performance tests.
72. List the important characteristics of an emotionally mature person.
73. What are some of the emotions predominant in adolescence?
74. How do you remove fear in a three year old child?
75. Define social development.
76. What is meant by socialization of an individual?
77. What are social norms?
78. What is meant by cultural heritage?
79. Define personality.
80. What do you mean by projective technique?
81. Mention the use of a personality test.
82. What do you mean by T.A.T?
83. Define adjustment.
84. Define intelligence.
85. What is evaluation?

Bibliography

Beaumont, H., and Macomber, F.G., *Psychological Factors in Education*, New York: McGraw Hill Book Company, 1949.

Bruce, W.F., and S.F. Freeman, *Development and Learning*, Boston: Houghton Miffin Company, 1942.

Cole, Lawrence E. and Bruce, W.F., *Educational Psychology*. Yonkers, New York: World Book Company, 1950.

Commins, W.D., *Principles of Educational Psychology*. New York: The Ronald Press Company. 1937.

Crow, L.D., and Crow A., *Educational Psychology*, New York: American Book Company, 1948.

Cruze, W.W., *Educational Psychology*, New York: The Ronald Press Company, 1942.

Davis, R.A., *Educational Psychology*, New York: McGraw-Hill Book Company, 1948.

Douglas, O.B., and Holland, B.F., *Educational Psychology*, New York, The MacMillan Company, 1938.

Eurich, A.C., and Carroll., H.A., *Educational Psychology*, Boston: D.C. Heath and Company, 1935.

Flecher, J.M., *Psychology in Education*, New York: Odyssey Press, 1934.

Gates, A.I., Jersild, A.T., McConnell T.R., and Challman, R.C., *Educational Psychology*, New York: The MacMillan Company, 1948.

Griffith, C.R., *An Introduction to Educational Psychology*, New York: The Rinehart and Company, 1935.

Grifith, *Psychology Applied to Teaching and Learning*, New York: The Rinehart and Company, 1939.

Guthrie, Edwin R. and Powers, Francis, F., *Educational Psychology*, New York: The Ronald Press Company, 1950.

Hartman, G.W. *Educational Psychology*, New York: American Book Company, 1941.

Hollingworth, H.L., *Educational Psychology*, New York: Appleton Century-Crofts, Inc., 1933.

Jordan, A.M., *Educational Psychology*, Revised Edition, New York: Henry Holt and Company, 1942.

Judd, C.H., *Educational Psychology*, Boston: Houghton Miffin Company, 1939.

Kelly, W., *Educational Psychology*, Revised Ed. Milwaukee: Bruce Publishing Company, 1946.

Kingsley, H.L., *Nature and Conditions of Learning*, New York: Prentice Hall, Inc., 1946.

La Rue, D.W., *Educational Psychology*, New York: Thomas Nelson and Sons, 1939.

Leary, B.D., *Educational Psychology*, New York: W.W. Norton and Company, 1939.

Mursell, J.L., *Development Teaching*, New York: McGraw-Hill Book Company, 1949.

Mursell, J.L., *Successful Teaching*, New York: McGraw-Hill Book Company, 1946.

Peterson, H., MarZolf, S. and Bayley, N., *Educational Psychology*, New York: The MacMillan Company, 1948.

Pressey, S.L. and Robinson, F.P., *Psychology and the New Education*, New York: Harper and Bros., 1941.

Sandiford, P., *Foundations of Educational Psychology*, New York: Longmans, Green and Company, 1938.

Sharma, R.N., *Educational Psychology*. Rastogi Publications, Meerut, Second Edition, 1974.

Skinner C.E., (Ed.), *Elementary Educational Psychology*, Revised Ed. New York: Prentice-Hall, Inc., 1950.

Sorenson, H., *Psychology in Education*, Revised Ed., New York: McGraw-Hill Book Company, 1948.

Starch, D., Stanton H.M., and Koerth, W., *Psychology in Education*, New York: The MacMillan Company, 1951.

Stephens, J.M., *Educational Psychology*, New York: Henry Holt and Company, 1951.

Stroud, J.B., *Educational Psychology*. New York: The MacMillan Company, 1935.

